Readings on the Ultimate Questions

Readings on the Ultimate Questions

An Introduction to Philosophy

SECOND EDITION

Edited by

Nils Ch. Rauhut
Coastal Carolina University

PENGUIN ACADEMICS

New York   Boston   San Francisco
London   Toronto   Sydney   Tokyo   Singapore   Madrid
Mexico City   Munich   Paris   Cape Town   Hong Kong   Montreal

Meiner Schwester Ute Sabine Rauhut gewidmet

Editor-in-Chief: Eric Stano
Executive Marketing Manager: Ann Stypuloski
Project Coordination, Text Design, and Electronic Page Makeup:
  Integra Software Services Private Limited
Senior Cover Designer/Manager: Nancy Danahy
Cover Illustration/Photo: Burstein Collection/CORBIS
Senior Manufacturing Buyer: Dennis J. Para
Printer and Binder: Courier Corporation
Cover Printer: Phoenix Color Corporation

For permission to use copyrighted material, grateful acknowledgment is made
to the copyright holders on pp. 623–625, which are hereby made part of this
copyright page.

Library of Congress Cataloging-in-Publication Data
Readings on the ultimate questions : an introduction to philosophy/
[compiled by] Nils Ch. Rauhut, Renée Smith.—2nd ed.
    p.   cm.
  ISBN 0-321-41300-8
  1. Philosophy.   I. Rauhut, Nils Ch.   II. Smith, Renée.
B74.R39 2006
100—dc22
                                            2006014766

Please visit us at www.ablongman.com

ISBN 0-321-41300-8

1 2 3 4 5 6 7 8 9 10—ptr code—09 08 07 06

Contents

SECTION 7   What Ought We To Do?   503

Preface

In this second edition of the anthology *Readings on the Ultimate Questions: An Introduction to Philosophy*, I have followed the same principles as in the first edition. I have selected philosophical essays that complement the topics and approach of *Ultimate Questions: Thinking About Philosophy,* and I have selected readings that are accessible to beginning students and that will encourage philosophical thought and lively discussion in class.

The main changes in this second edition can be grouped under three headings. First, I have included more classical materials that are frequently used in introductory classes. For example, the second edition contains John Locke's "An Essay Concerning Human Understanding," Arthur Schopenhauer's "Essay on the Freedom of the Will," St. Thomas Aquinas's "Five Ways," and Jeremy Bentham's "The Principle of Utility." Second, I have added further examples of excellent, and accessible, contemporary philosophy. I have included essays by Thomas Nagel, Richard Swinburne, Derek Parfit, Mark Siderits, and Rae Langton. These articles introduce beginning students to the ways in which contemporary philosophers approach philosophical problems. Finally, I have eliminated some articles from the first edition that turned out to be less accessible to students than I had hoped. It is my hope that *Ultimate Questions: A Reader*, together with *Ultimate Questions: Thinking About Philosophy,* will awaken students' philosophical curiosity by providing them with both contemporary and classical work in philosophy that is accessible, engaging, and thought-provoking.

Acknowledgments

I would like to thank those readers who have provided me with helpful feedback: Andrew Cathcart, University of North Florida; Ellen Cox, Transylvania University; John Elia, University of Georgia; Theodore

Faulders, College of the Canyons; Sister Judith K. Parsons, Immaculata University; Edward Schoen, Western Kentucky University; Eric Sotnak, University of Akron; and Michael Strawser, University of Central Florida. Special thanks are also due to Adam Christensen, Donna Garnier, Priscilla McGeehon, and Eric Stano from Longman Publishers. Without their help and excellent advice this second edition would not exist. Finally, I would like to thank my wife Karin for her love and support.

Nils Ch. Rauhut
Myrtle Beach

WHY STUDY PHILOSOPHY?

Philosophy—the love of wisdom—seeks to find plausible answers to the most fundamental of all questions. Philosophers want to know, for instance, whether or not God exists or whether or not humans have souls. These questions have provoked many conflicting responses, and final resolutions of these questions are not in sight. Why then should we bother to study philosophy at all? Would it not be better to spend our time on those disciplines that promise firm answers and solid recommendations? In this first section of our introductory anthology, we explore various ways in which philosophers have responded to this challenge.

In his essay "What Is Enlightenment?" Immanuel Kant argues that each and every human being has the duty to answer philosophical questions without the guidance of another person. If we avoid this duty, we live in a self-imposed immaturity that is incompatible with the dignity and freedom of humankind.

The seventeenth-century philosopher Baruch Spinoza came to philosophy in a different way. In his *Treatise on the Emendation of the Intellect,* he writes that it was his desire to find a *true good* that would bring him continuous and supreme joy to all eternity that turned him toward philosophy. Spinoza discovered that those goods which are normally considered to be of extreme importance—namely money, fame, and sensual pleasure—are intrinsically uncertain and stand in the way of true happiness. He thus followed a new path of thinking and living that made him understand that the human mind forms a union with the whole of Nature.

The Ancient Greek philosopher Epicurus agrees that philosophical reflection is an essential part of the good life. In his "Letter to Menoeceus" he argues that no one should delay the study of philosophy. Philosophical reflection alone helps us to overcome the fear of death and the fear of divine punishment. If we follow the path of philosophy further and subscribe to the intelligent pursuit of pleasure that values friendship and self-sufficiency, we have the possibility of living "like a god among men."

A contemporary perspective on the value of the philosophical life is offered by Alfred Mele. In the essay "Philosophy, a Bus Ride, and Dumb Luck," Mele describes his first foray into philosophical thinking when, as a child, he wondered whether or not it is possible to love God more than one's own parents. Although he eventually decided to major in philosophy, he did not set out to become a philosopher himself. It was a chance meeting with his teacher Robert Baker on a bus that prompted him to think seriously about attending graduate school in philosophy. While writing his dissertation on Aristotle, he realized that he had fallen in love with philosophy and that he could not imagine a better way to spend his life.

These four selections show that philosophers are often convinced that the philosophical life is very rewarding. The general public, on the other hand, is often afraid that philosophy has a negative influence on young people. Socrates, for example, was accused by his fellow citizens of introducing new religious beliefs and of corrupting the young men of Athens who enjoyed listening to him. We include Socrates' famous defense against these charges. In Plato's *Apology*, Socrates argues that he is not ashamed to have followed a philosophical way of life and that his questioning of prominent Athenian men has provided a great service to all Athenians. According to Socrates, one should not let any day pass without discussing goodness and virtue. A life that avoids such examinations is not worth living.

Bertrand Russell too provides a defense of the philosophical life against common objections. In "The Value of Philosophy," Russell writes that it is often held that philosophy is nothing but useless trifling about matters concerning which knowledge is impossible. In response, Russell argues that philosophy is not to be studied for the sake of any definite answers to its questions, but rather "for the sake of the questions themselves." Philosophical questions "enlarge our conception of what is possible . . . and prepare our mind for the union with the universe which constitutes its highest good."

What Is Enlightenment?[1]

Immanuel Kant   (*Translated by Ted Humphrey*)

Enlightenment is man's emergence from his self-imposed immaturity.[2]
Immaturity is the inability to use one's understanding without guidance
from another. This immaturity is *self-imposed* when its cause lies not in
lack of understanding, but in lack of resolve and courage to use it without guidance from another. *Sapere Aude!*[3] "Have courage to use your
own understanding!"—that is the motto of enlightenment.

Laziness and cowardice are the reasons why so great a proportion
of men, long after nature has released them from alien guidance
(*naturaliter maiorennes*),[4] nonetheless gladly remain in lifelong
immaturity, and why it is so easy for others to establish themselves as
their guardians. It is so easy to be immature. If I have a book to serve
as my understanding, a pastor to serve as my conscience, a physician
to determine my diet for me, and so on, I need not exert myself at all.
I need not think, if only I can pay: others will readily undertake the
irksome work for me. The guardians who have so benevolently taken
over the supervision of men have carefully seen to it that the far
greatest part of them (including the entire fair sex) regard taking the
step to maturity as very dangerous, not to mention difficult. Having
first made their domestic livestock dumb, and having carefully made
sure that these docile creatures will not take a single step without the
go-cart to which they are harnessed, these guardians then show them
the danger that threatens them, should they attempt to walk alone.
Now this danger is not actually so great, for after falling a few times
they would in the end certainly learn to walk; but an example of this
kind makes men timid and usually frightens them out of all further
attempts.

Thus, it is difficult for any individual man to work himself out of the
immaturity that has all but become his nature. He has even become fond
of this state and for the time being is actually incapable of using his own
understanding, for no one has ever allowed him to attempt it. Rules and
formulas, those mechanical aids to the rational use, or rather misuse, of
his natural gifts, are the shackles of a permanent immaturity. Whoever
threw them off would still make only an uncertain leap over the smallest
ditch, since he is unaccustomed to this kind of free movement.
Consequently, only a few have succeeded, by cultivating their own minds,
in freeing themselves from immaturity and pursuing a secure course.

But that the public should enlighten itself is more likely; indeed, if it is only allowed freedom, enlightenment is almost inevitable. For even among the entrenched guardians of the great masses a few will always think for themselves, a few who, after having themselves thrown off the yoke of immaturity, will spread the spirit of a rational appreciation for both their own worth and for each person's calling to think for himself. But it should be particularly noted that if a public that was first placed in this yoke by the guardians is suitably aroused by some of those who are altogether incapable of enlightenment, it may force the guardians themselves to remain under the yoke—so pernicious is it to instill prejudices, for they finally take revenge upon their originators, or on their descendants. Thus a public can only attain enlightenment slowly. Perhaps a revolution can overthrow autocratic despotism and profiteering or power-grabbing oppression, but it can never truly reform a manner of thinking;[5] instead, new prejudices, just like the old ones they replace, will serve as a leash for the great unthinking mass.

Nothing is required for this enlightenment, however, except *freedom;* and the freedom in question is the least harmful of all, namely, the freedom to use reason *publicly* in all matters. But on all sides I hear: "*Do not argue!*" The officer says, "Do not argue, drill!" The taxman says, "Do not argue, pay!" The pastor says, "Do not argue, believe!" (Only one ruler in the world[6] says, "*Argue* as much as you want and about what you want, *but obey!*") In this we have [examples of] pervasive restrictions on freedom. But which restriction hinders enlightenment and which does not, but instead actually advances it? I reply: The *public* use of one's reason must always be free, and it alone can bring about enlightenment among mankind; the *private use* of reason may, however, often be very narrowly restricted, without otherwise hindering the progress of enlightenment. By the public use of one's own reason I understand the use that anyone as a *scholar* makes of reason before the entire *literate world.* I call the private use of reason that which a person may make in a *civic post* or office that has been entrusted to him.[7] Now in many affairs conducted in the interests of a community, a certain mechanism is required by means of which some of its members must conduct themselves in an entirely passive manner so that through an artificial unanimity the government may guide them toward public ends, or at least prevent them from destroying such ends. Here one certainly must not argue, instead one must obey. However, insofar as this part of the machine also regards himself as a member of the community as a whole, or even of the world community, and as a consequence addresses the public in the role of a scholar, in the proper sense of that term, he can most certainly argue, without thereby harming the affairs for which as a passive member he is partly responsible. Thus it would be disastrous if an officer on duty who was given a command by his superior were to question the appropriateness or utility of the order. He must obey. But as a scholar he cannot be justly constrained from making comments about errors in military service, or from placing them before the public for its judgment. The citizen cannot refuse to pay the taxes imposed on him; indeed, impertinent criticism of such levies, when they should be paid by him, can be punished as a scandal (since it can lead to widespread insubordination). But the same person does not act contrary to civic duty when, as a scholar, he publicly expresses his thoughts regarding the impropriety or even injustice of such taxes. Likewise a pastor is bound to instruct his catechumens and congregation in accordance with the symbol of the church he serves, for he was appointed on that condition. But as a scholar he has complete freedom, indeed even the calling, to impart to the public all of his carefully considered and well-intentioned thoughts concerning mistaken aspects of that symbol,[8] as well as his suggestions for the better arrangement of religious and church matters. Nothing in this can weigh on his conscience. What he teaches in consequence of his office as a servant of the church he sets out as something with regard to which he has no discretion to teach in accord with his own lights; rather, he offers it under the direction and in the name of another. He will say, "Our church teaches this or that and these are the demonstrations it uses." He thereby extracts for his congregation all practical uses from precepts to which he would not himself subscribe with complete conviction, but whose presentation he can nonetheless undertake, since it is not entirely impossible that truth lies hidden in them, and, in any case, nothing contrary to the very nature of religion is to be found in them. If he believed he could find anything of the latter sort in them, he could not in good conscience serve in his position; he would have to resign. Thus an appointed teacher's use of his reason for the sake of his congregation is merely *private,* because, however large the congregation is, this use is always only domestic; in this regard, as a priest, he is not free and cannot be such because he is acting under instructions from someone else. By contrast, the cleric—as a scholar who speaks through his writings to the public as such, i.e., the world—enjoys in this *public use* of reason an unrestricted freedom to use his own rational capacities and to speak his own mind. For that the (spiritual) guardians of a people should themselves be immature is an absurdity that would insure the perpetuation of absurdities.

But would a society of pastors, perhaps a church assembly or venerable presbytery (as those among the Dutch call themselves), not be justified in binding itself by oath to a certain unalterable symbol in order to secure a constant guardianship over each of its members and through them over the people, and this for all time: I say that this is wholly impossible. Such a contract, whose intention is to preclude forever all further enlightenment of the human race, is absolutely null and void, even if it should be ratified by the supreme power, by parliaments, and by the most solemn peace treaties. One age cannot bind itself, and thus conspire, to place a succeeding one in a condition whereby it would be impossible for the later age to expand its knowledge (particularly where it is so very important), to rid itself of errors, and generally to increase its enlightenment. That would be a crime against human nature, whose essential destiny lies precisely in such progress; subsequent generations are thus completely justified in dismissing such agreements as unauthorized and criminal. The criterion of everything that can be agreed upon as a law by a people lies in this question: Can a people impose such a law on itself?[9] Now it might be possible, in anticipation of a better state of affairs, to introduce a provisional order for a specific, short time, all the while giving all citizens, especially clergy, in their role as scholars, the freedom to comment publicly, i.e., in writing, on the present institution's shortcomings. The provisional order might last until insight into the nature of these matters had become so widespread and obvious that the combined (if not unanimous) voices of the populace could propose to the crown that it take under its protection those congregations that, in accord with their newly gained insight, had organized themselves under altered religious institutions, but without interfering with those wishing to allow matters to remain as before. However, it is absolutely forbidden that they unite into a religious organization that nobody may for the duration of a man's lifetime publicly question, for so doing would deny, render fruitless, and make detrimental to succeeding generations an era in man's progress toward improvement. A man may put off enlightenment with regard to what he ought to know, though only for a short time and for his own person; but to renounce it for himself, or, even more, for subsequent generations, is to violate and trample man's divine rights underfoot. And what a people may not decree for itself may still less be imposed on it by a monarch, for his lawgiving authority rests on his unification of the people's collective will in his own. If he only sees to it that all genuine or purported improvement is consonant with civil order, he can allow his subjects to do what they find necessary to their spiritual well-being, which is not his affair. However, he must prevent anyone from forcibly interfering with another's working as best he can to determine and promote his well-being. It detracts from his own majesty when he interferes in these matters, since the writings in which his subjects attempt to clarify their insights lend value to his conception of governance. This holds whether he acts from his own highest insight—whereby he calls upon himself the reproach, "*Caesar non est supra grammaticos.*"[10]—as well as, indeed even more, when he despoils his highest authority by supporting the spiritual despotism of some tyrants in his state over his other subjects.

If it is now asked, "Do we presently live in an *enlightened* age?" the answer is, "No, but we do live in an age of *enlightenment.*" As matters now stand, a great deal is still lacking in order for men as a whole to be, or even to put themselves into a position to be able without external guidance to apply understanding confidently to religious issues. But we do have clear indications that the way is now being opened for men to proceed freely in this direction and that the obstacles to general enlightenment—to their release from their self-imposed immaturity—are gradually diminishing. In this regard, this age is the age of enlightenment, the century of Frederick.[11]

A prince who does not find it beneath him to say that he takes it to be his *duty* to prescribe nothing, but rather to allow men complete freedom in religious matters—who thereby renounces the arrogant title of *tolerance*—is himself enlightened and deserves to be praised by a grateful present and by posterity as the first, at least where the government is concerned, to release the human race from immaturity and to leave everyone free to use his own reason in all matters of conscience. Under his rule, venerable pastors, in their role as scholars and without prejudice to their official duties, may freely and openly set out for the world's scrutiny their judgments and views, even where these occasionally differ from the accepted symbol. Still greater freedom is afforded to those who are not restricted by an official post. This spirit of freedom is expanding even where it must struggle against the external obstacles of governments that misunderstand their own function. Such governments are illuminated by the example that the existence of freedom need not give cause for the least concern regarding public order and harmony in the commonwealth. If only they refrain from inventing artifices to keep themselves in it, men will gradually raise themselves from barbarism.

I have focused on religious matters in setting out my main point concerning enlightenment, i.e., man's emergence from self-imposed immaturity, first because our rulers have no interest in assuming the role of their subjects' guardians with respect to the arts and sciences, and secondly because that form of immaturity is both the most pernicious and disgraceful of all. But the manner of thinking of a head of state who favors religious enlightenment goes even further, for he realizes that there is no danger to his *legislation* in allowing his subjects to use reason *publicly* and to set before the world their thoughts concerning better formulations of his laws, even if this involves frank criticism of legislation currently in effect. We have before us a shining example, with respect to which no monarch surpasses the one whom we honor.

But only a ruler who is himself enlightened and has no dread of shadows, yet who likewise has a well-disciplined, numerous army to guarantee public peace, can say what no republic[12] may dare, namely: *"Argue as much as you want and about what you want, but obey!"* Here as elsewhere, when things are considered in broad perspective, a strange, unexpected pattern in human affairs reveals itself, one in which almost everything is paradoxical. A greater degree of civil freedom seems advantageous to a people's *spiritual* freedom; yet the former established impassable boundaries for the latter; conversely, a lesser degree of civil freedom provides enough room for all fully to expand their abilities. Thus, once nature has removed the hard shell from this kernel for which she has most fondly cared, namely, the inclination to and vocation for free *thinking*, the kernel gradually reacts on a people's mentality (whereby they become increasingly able to *act freely*), and it finally even influences the principles of *government*, which finds that it can profit by treating men, *who are now more than machines*, in accord with their dignity.*

Königsberg in Prussia, 30 September 1784
I. Kant

Notes

1. A. A., VIII, 33–42. This essay first appeared in the *Berlinische Monatsschrift*, December, 1784.
2. The German is *Unmündigkeit*, which quite literally means "minority," where one is referring to the inability to make decisions for oneself. Kant's point in the essay is that by virtue of understanding and reason men have the inherent right and ability to make all intellectual, political and religious decisions for themselves. That they do not is a function of certain, perhaps implicit, choices they make in regard to exercising rights and developing capacities.

*Today I read in Büsching's *Wöchentliche Nachrichten* for September 13th a notice concerning this month's *Berlinischen Monatsschift* that mentions *Mendelssohn's* answer to this same question. I have not yet seen this journal, otherwise I would have withheld the foregoing reflections, which I now set out in order to see to what extent two person's thoughts may coincidentally agree.·

3. "Dare to know!" (Horace, *Epodes*, 1, 2, 40.) This motto was adopted by the Society of the Friends of Truth, an important circle of the German Enlightenment.
4. "Those who have come of age by virtue of nature."
5. The term Kant uses here and later, on p. 41, is *Denkungsart;* it occurs in the second edition preface to the *Critique of Pure Reason*, where he works out his famous analogy of the Copernican Revolution in philosophy, which he refers to as a revolution in the method of thought. (B vii–xxiv) The term refers to one's characteristic pattern of thought, whether it is marked by systematic, rational procedures or by prejudice and superstition, criticism or dogmatism.
6. Frederick II (the Great) of Prussia.
7. See *Theory and Practice*, 304.
8. Kant distinguishes between two classes of concepts, those that we can schematize, i.e., directly represent in experience (intuition), and those that we must symbolize, i.e., indirectly represent in experience (intuition). Symbolized concepts, such as the one we have of God, are those for which no experience can provide adequate content; consequently, experience can only be used to indicate the content we intend. All religious concepts have this character. By symbol in this context, then, Kant means those beliefs and practices in which a group expresses the content of its concept of the divine. (*Crit. Judgment*, 351–54)
9. This would seem a peculiarly political expression of the Categorical Imperative, particularly as it is expressed in *Groundings*, 428–29.
10. "Caesar is not above the grammarians." See *Perpetual Peace*, 368 f.
11. Frederick II (the Great), King of Prussia.
12. The term Kant uses here is *Freistaat,* which is idiomatically translated "republic." However, Kant never again uses this Germanic rooted word in the essays included in this volume. In all the other essays he uses the Latin loan word *Republic.* I point this out because what Kant says here about a *Freistaat* is inconsistent with what he says elsewhere about a *Republic.*

Treatise on the Emendation of the Intellect

Baruch Spinoza   *(Translated by Samuel Shirley)*

After experience had taught me the hollowness and futility of everything that is ordinarily encountered in daily life, and I realized that all the things which were the source and object of my anxiety held nothing of good or evil in themselves save in so far as the mind was influenced by them, I resolved at length to enquire whether there existed a true good, one which was capable of communicating itself and could alone affect the mind to the exclusion of all else, whether, in fact, there was something whose discovery and acquisition would afford me a continuous and supreme joy to all eternity.

I say 'I resolved at length,' for at first sight it seemed ill-advised to risk the loss of what was certain in the hope of something at that time uncertain. I could well see the advantages that derive from honor and wealth, and that I would be forced to abandon their quest if I were to devote myself to some new and different objective. And if in fact supreme happiness were to be found in the former, I must inevitably fail to attain it, whereas if it did not lie in these objectives and I devoted myself entirely to them, then once again I would lose that highest happiness.

I therefore debated whether it might be possible to arrive at a new guiding principle—or at least the sure hope of its attainment—without changing the manner and normal routine of my life. This I frequently attempted, but in vain. For the things which for the most part offer themselves in life, and which, to judge from their actions, men regard as the highest good, can be reduced to these three headings: riches, honor, and sensual pleasure. With these three the mind is so distracted that it is quite incapable of thinking of any other good. With regard to sensual pleasure, the mind is so utterly obsessed by it that it seems as if it were absorbed in some good, and so is quite prevented from thinking of anything else. But after the enjoyment of this pleasure there ensues a profound depression which, if it does not completely inhibit the mind, leads to its confusion and enervation. The pursuit of honor and wealth, too, engrosses the mind to no small degree, especially when the latter is sought exclusively for its own sake,[1] for it is then regarded as the highest good. Even more so is the mind obsessed with honor, for this is always regarded as a good in itself and the ultimate end to which everything is directed. Then again, in both these cases, there is no repentance as in the case of sensual pleasure. The more each of them is possessed, the more our joy is enhanced, and we are therefore more and more induced to increase them both. But if it should come about that our hopes are disappointed, there ensues a profound depression. And finally, honor has this great drawback, that to attain it we must conduct

---

[1]This could be explained more fully and clearly by making a distinction between wealth that is sought for its own sake, for the sake of honor, for sensual pleasure, for health, or for the advancement of the sciences and the arts. But this is reserved for its proper place, such a detailed investigation being inappropriate here.

our lives to suit other men, avoiding what the masses avoid and seeking what the masses seek.

So when I saw that all these things stood in the way of my embarking on a new course, and were indeed so opposed to it that I must necessarily choose between the one alternative and the other, I was forced to ask what was to my greater advantage; for, as I have said, I seemed set on losing a certain good for the sake of an uncertain good. But after a little reflection, I first of all realized that if I abandoned the old ways and embarked on a new way of life, I should be abandoning a good that was by its very nature uncertain—as we can clearly gather from what has been said—in favour of one that was uncertain not of its own nature (for I was seeking a permanent good) but only in respect of its attainment. Then persistent meditation enabled me to see that, if only I could be thoroughly resolute, I should be abandoning certain evils for the sake of a certain good. For I saw that my situation was one of great peril and that I was obliged to seek a remedy with all my might, however uncertain it might be, like a sick man suffering from a fatal malady who, foreseeing certain death unless a remedy is forthcoming, is forced to seek it, however uncertain it be, with all his might, for therein lies all his hope. Now all those objectives that are commonly pursued not only contribute nothing to the preservation of our being but even hinder it, being frequently the cause of the destruction of those who gain possession of them, and invariably the cause of the destruction of those who are possessed by them.[2] For there are numerous examples of men who have suffered persecution unto death because of their wealth, and also of men who have exposed themselves to so many dangers to acquire riches that they have finally paid for their folly with their lives. Nor are there less numerous examples of men who, to gain or preserve honor, have suffered a most wretched fate. Finally, there are innumerable examples of men who have hastened their death by reason of excessive sensual pleasure.

These evils, moreover, seemed to arise from this, that all happiness or unhappiness depends solely on the quality of the object to which we are bound by love. For strife will never arise on account of that which is not loved; there will be no sorrow if it is lost, no envy if it is possessed by another, no fear, no hatred—in a word, no emotional agitation, all of which, however, occur in the case of the love of perishable things, such as all those of which we have been speaking. But love towards a thing eternal and infinite feeds the mind with joy alone, unmixed with

---

[2]This is to be demonstrated at greater length.

any sadness. This is greatly to be desired, and to be sought with all our might. However, it was not without reason that I used these words, 'If only I could be earnestly resolute,' for although I perceived these things quite clearly in my mind, I could not on that account put aside all greed, sensual pleasure, and desire for esteem.

This one thing I could see, that as long as my mind was occupied with these thoughts, it turned away from those other objectives and earnestly applied itself to the quest for a new guiding principle. This was a great comfort to me, for I saw that those evils were not so persistent as to refuse to yield to remedies. And although at first these intermissions were rare and of very brief duration, nevertheless, as the true good became more and more discernible to me, these intermissions became more frequent and longer, especially when I realised that the acquisition of money, sensual pleasure, and esteem is a hindrance only as long as they are sought on their own account, and not as a means to other things. If they are sought as means, they will then be under some restriction, and far from being hindrances, they will do much to further the end for which they are sought, as I shall demonstrate in its proper place.

At this point I shall only state briefly what I understand by the true good, and at the same time what is the supreme good. In order that this may be rightly understood, it must be borne in mind that good and bad are only relative terms, so that one and the same thing may be said to be good or bad in different respects, just like the terms perfect and imperfect. Nothing, when regarded in its own nature, can be called perfect or imperfect, especially when we realize that all things that come into being do so in accordance with an eternal order and Nature's fixed laws.

But human weakness fails to comprehend that order in its thought, and meanwhile man conceives a human nature much stronger than his own, and sees no reason why he cannot acquire such a nature. Thus he is urged to seek the means that will bring him to such a perfection, and all that can be the means of his attaining this objective is called a true good, while the supreme good is to arrive at the enjoyment of such a nature, together with other individuals, if possible. What that nature is we shall show in its proper place; namely, the knowledge of the union which the mind has with the whole of Nature.[3]

This, then, is the end for which I strive, to acquire the nature I have described and to endeavour that many should acquire it along with me. That is to say, my own happiness involves my making an effort to

[3]This is explained more fully in its proper place.

persuade many others to think as I do, so that their understanding and their desire should entirely accord with my understanding and my desire. To bring this about, it is necessary[4] (1) to understand as much about Nature as suffices for acquiring such a nature, and (2) to establish such a social order as will enable as many as possible to reach this goal with the greatest possible ease and assurance. Furthermore, (3) attention must be paid to moral philosophy and likewise the theory of the education of children; and since health is of no little importance in attaining this end, (4) the whole science of medicine must be elaborated. And since many difficult tasks are rendered easy by contrivance, and we can thereby gain much time and convenience in our daily lives, (5) the science of mechanics is in no way to be despised. [. . .]

Letter to Menoeceus

Epicurus   (*Translated by Brad Inwood and L. P. Gerson*)

Let no one delay the study of philosophy while young nor weary of it when old. For no one is either too young or too old for the health of the soul. He who says either that the time for philosophy has not yet come or that it has passed is like someone who says that the time for happiness has not yet come or that it has passed. Therefore, both young and old must philosophize, the latter so that although old he may stay young in good things owing to gratitude for what has occurred, the former so that although young he too may be like an old man owing to his lack of fear of what is to come. Therefore, one must practise the things which produce happiness, since if that is present we have everything and if it is absent we do everything in order to have it. [. . .]

Get used to believing that death is nothing to us. For all good and bad consists in sense-experience, and death is the privation of sense-experience. Hence, a correct knowledge of the fact that death is nothing to us makes the mortality of life a matter for contentment, not by adding a limitless time [to life] but by removing the longing for immortality. For there is nothing fearful in life for one who has grasped that there is nothing fearful in the absence of life. Thus, he is a fool who says that he fears death not because it will be painful when present but because it is painful when it is still to come. For that which while present causes no

[4]Note that here I am only concerned to enumerate the sciences necessary to our purpose, without regard to their order.

distress causes unnecessary pain when merely anticipated. So death, the most frightening of bad things, is nothing to us; since when we exist, death is not yet present, and when death is present, then we do not exist. Therefore, it is relevant neither to the living nor to the dead, since it does not affect the former, and the latter do not exist. But the many sometimes flee death as the greatest of bad things and sometimes choose it as a relief from the bad things in life. But the wise man neither rejects life nor fears death. For living does not offend him, nor does he believe not living to be something bad. And just as he does not unconditionally choose the largest amount of food but the most pleasant food, so he savours not the longest time but the most pleasant. He who advises the young man to live well and the old man to die well is simple-minded, not just because of the pleasing aspects of life but because the same kind of practice produces a good life and a good death. Much worse is he who says that it is good not to be born, "but when born to pass through the gates of Hades as quickly as possible."[1] For if he really believes what he says, why doesn't he leave life? For it is easy for him to do, if he has firmly decided on it. But if he is joking, he is wasting his time among men who don't welcome it. We must remember that what will happen is neither unconditionally within our power nor unconditionally outside our power, so that we will not unconditionally expect that it will occur nor despair of it as unconditionally not going to occur. [. . .]

And this is why we say that pleasure is the starting-point and goal of living blessedly. For we recognized this as our first innate good, and this is our starting point for every choice and avoidance and we come to this by judging every good by the criterion of feeling. And it is just because this is the first innate good that we do not choose every pleasure; but sometimes we pass up many pleasures when we get a larger amount of what is uncongenial from them. And we believe many pains to be better than pleasures when a greater pleasure follows for a long while if we endure the pains. So every pleasure is a good thing, since it has a nature congenial [to us], but not every one is to be chosen. Just as every pain too is a bad thing, but not every one is such as to be always avoided.

So when we say that pleasure is the goal we do not mean the pleasures of the profligate or the pleasures of consumption, as some believe, either from ignorance and disagreement or from deliberate misinterpretation, but rather the lack of pain in the body and disturbance in the soul. For it is not drinking bouts and continuous partying and enjoying boys and women, or consuming fish and the other dainties of an extravagant

---

[1]Theognis 425, 427.

table, which produce the pleasant life, but sober calculation which searches out the reasons for every choice and avoidance and drives out the opinions which are the source of the greatest turmoil for men's souls. [. . .]

Practise these and the related precepts day and night, by yourself and with a like-minded friend, and you will never be disturbed either when awake or in sleep, and you will live as a god among men. For a man who lives among immortal goods is in no respect like a mere mortal animal.

Philosophy, a Bus Ride, and Dumb Luck
Alfred Mele

It is easy enough for philosophers to find signs of a philosophical disposition in their childhood. However, if, as I suspect, most children entertain philosophical questions and thoughts, these signs probably count for little. Children strike me as being by nature small athletes, scientists, and artists as well. Perhaps some of us, for some reason or other, never shed our childlike curiosity about things philosophical and our associated appetite for explanation.

I remember pondering as a child questions that I now know to be philosophical: when I was eight or nine, for example, my catechism teacher told the class that we must love God more than we love our parents. I worried about that all day. I knew that I loved my parents most, and I didn't see any way to change that. Furthermore, I did not understand how children *could* love God more than their parents, since we knew our parents but didn't know God. I decided that the catechism teacher had to be wrong, that God could not make impossible demands on people; and I felt OK. The next day, after church, I asked my brother Ron whom he loved more. He said "God," and I started to worry again. But I suspect that many of the kids in my catechism class had similar worries—or worse ones: the venial/mortal sin distinction was a real puzzler, for example; and if one couldn't get straight on that, how was one to avoid hell? In any case, I (and they) thought just as hard about issues that we later learned fell under the heading "physics," or "biology." Once, at about the same time, after learning that the earth rotates, I tried to figure out how anything on the earth could move in the direction of the earth's rotation unless it moved faster than the earth rotates. I spun my globe and raced one of my toy cars along its surface, over and over again, but I don't recall coming to a conclusion.

So much for my childhood. It was intellectually uninspiring, as you can see. Besides, I spent most of my free time playing baseball and football.

I first heard of philosophy, I think, in high school—a Catholic high school in Detroit. I was doing some research for an essay on religion when I came across Tolstoy's *My Religion*. That was my first encounter with what I regarded as rational reflection on religion. It struck me as brilliant, and when I finished it I wanted to read more. A search of the card catalogue, however, turned up only Tolstoy's fiction; so, I decided that I would just wait for college and take a philosophy course there. (We did read Paul Tillich in high school, but I recall thinking that Tillich sounded a lot like the nuns, and I was already fed up with them. Understandably, the feeling was mutual. I was expelled a month or so before graduation in 1969 for radical behavior—refusing to cut my collar-length hair, as I recall. My mother tried to persuade the good sisters to let me back in, using a dozen homemade pizzas to soften them up. That failed, and so did I.)

Eventually, I got to college by being recruited by the football coach of the Kalamazoo College Fighting Hornets: The conjunction of my SAT scores and All-State football honors outweighed all those Fs in my final term of high school. I took a class in philosophy of religion in my first term. The reading material (which undoubtedly was first-rate) seemed to me to pale by comparison with Tolstoy. So I turned to mathematics for a time before transferring, at the end of my freshman year, to Wayne State University—back in Detroit. In the meantime, I married Connie, who transformed me into a serious student.

At Wayne State, I gave philosophy another try. At the same time, however, I re-discovered literature. After a year or so, I had to make a choice between English and philosophy. Surprisingly, in retrospect, it wasn't an easy choice to make. I stayed up all night—first trying to decide on a decision procedure, and then, after I settled that issue, making the actual decision. What it came down to, as I recall, was this: Both philosophy and literature were enormously enjoyable (this was in the pre-deconstruction days, of course), but philosophy, in addition, was challenging; and, I thought, enjoyment plus challenge defeats mere enjoyment.

I had no thought at the time of actually becoming a philosopher myself, which wasn't surprising, since I rarely thought more than a month ahead back then. In fact, I'm not sure that I would even have gone to graduate school if I hadn't run into Robert Baker (another teacher of mine) on the bus one day on my way home from school. He asked what I was planning to do after graduation. I replied that I hadn't given it much thought. He mentioned graduate school as a possibility, which struck me as interesting, so I asked him where I might apply. He recommended the University of Michigan, which was pretty much in the neighborhood, and after a thoroughly enjoyable year laying bricks and painting HUD houses, I went there.

That is where I fell in love with philosophy, though it took several years. It was twelve to fifteen hours a day in the company of absolute brilliance that did it—Aristotle, that is, whose theory of motivation was my dissertation topic. Prior to that time, my main philosophical interest was in solving philosophical puzzles. That is how I approached interpreting Aristotle as well. How can virtuous actions uniformly be products of choice, and therefore of deliberation, if, as Aristotle also said, there are instances of "sudden" virtuous action, as on the battlefield? How can it be true that virtuous agents uniformly perform virtuous actions for the sake of the actions themselves, or as ends, if virtuous actions issue from deliberation, and the function of deliberation is to identify means to ends? And so on. To feel confident that one understands Aristotle well enough to see how textual tensions are to be resolved, one needs to read a lot of Aristotle, which I did. That was my first real exposure to systematic philosophy. Everything in Aristotle, I came to believe, was importantly related to everything else—metaphysics, ethics, philosophy of mind, physics, logic, political theory, epistemology, philosophy of biology, and so on. I finally had a glimpse of philosophy writ large, and I was hooked.

Only when my dissertation was nearly complete—by then I was thinking about two months ahead—did it become clear to me that I wanted to stay in this line of work. Fortunately, I found a teaching job that year—at Davidson College. I enjoyed teaching and had ample time to continue exploring Aristotle and some of the philosophical issues that he addressed. I could think of no better way to spend my remaining years.

Like most philosophers, I now find it hard to imagine myself doing anything else for a living. If catechism and high school religion classes made a contribution to my now being a philosopher, I am grateful for them. It is a good thing, too, that I ran into Robert Baker on the bus.

Apology

Plato   *(Translated by G. M. A. Grube)*

I do not know, men of Athens,[1] how my accusers affected you; as for me, I was almost carried away in spite of myself, so persuasively did they speak. And yet, hardly anything of what they said is true. Of the many lies they told, one in particular surprised me, namely that you should be careful not to be deceived by an accomplished speaker like me. That they were not ashamed to be immediately proved wrong by the facts, when I show myself not to be an accomplished speaker at all, that I thought was most shameless on their part—unless indeed they call an accomplished speaker the man who speaks the truth. [. . .]

Very well then, men of Athens. I must surely defend myself and attempt to uproot from your minds in so short a time the slander that has resided there so long. I wish this may happen, if it is in any way better for you and me, and that my defense may be successful, but I think this is very difficult and I am fully aware of how difficult it is. Even so, let the matter proceed as the god may wish, but I must obey the law and make my defense.

Let us then take up the case from its beginning. What is the accusation from which arose the slander in which Meletus trusted when he wrote out the charge against me? What did they say when they slandered me? I must, as if they were my actual prosecutors, read the affidavit they would have sworn. It goes something like this: Socrates is guilty of wrongdoing in that he busies himself studying things in the sky and below the earth; he makes the worse into the stronger argument, and he teaches these same things to others. You have seen this yourself in the comedy of Aristophanes, a Socrates swinging about there, saying he was walking on air and talking a lot of other nonsense about things of which I know nothing at all. I do not speak in contempt of such knowledge, if someone is wise in these things—lest Meletus bring more cases against me—but, gentlemen, I have no part

---

[1] Jurors were selected by lot from all the male citizens thirty years of age or older who offered themselves on the given day for service. They thus functioned as representatives of the Athenian people and the Athenian democracy. In cases like Socrates', they judged on behalf of the whole citizen body whether or not their interests had been undermined by the accused's behavior. Hence Socrates can address them as if he were addressing the people of Athens at large, and in particular the partisans of the democracy against its oligarchic opponents. Socrates addresses the jury as "men of Athens" rather than employing the usual mode of address, "gentlemen of the jury." He explains that only those who voted to acquit him deserved that honor.

in it, and on this point I call upon the majority of you as witnesses. I think it right that all those of you who have heard me conversing, and many of you have, should tell each other if any one of you has ever heard me discussing such subjects to any extent at all. From this you will learn that the other things said about me by the majority are of the same kind. [. . .]

One of you might perhaps interrupt me and say: "But Socrates, what is your occupation? From where have these slanders come? For surely if you did not busy yourself with something out of the common, all these rumors and talk would not have arisen unless you did something other than most people. Tell us what it is, that we may not speak inadvisedly about you." Anyone who says that seems to be right, and I will try to show you what has caused this reputation and slander. Listen then. Perhaps some of you will think I am jesting, but be sure that all that I shall say is true. What has caused my reputation is none other than a certain kind of wisdom. What kind of wisdom? Human wisdom, perhaps. It may be that I really possess this, while those whom I mentioned just now are wise with a wisdom more than human; else I cannot explain it, for I certainly do not possess it, and whoever says I do is lying and speaks to slander me. Do not create a disturbance, gentlemen, even if you think I am boasting, for the story I shall tell does not originate with me, but I will refer you to a trustworthy source. I shall call upon the god at Delphi as witness to the existence and nature of my wisdom, if it be such.[2] You know Chaerephon. He was my friend from youth, and the friend of most of you, as he shared your exile and your return. You surely know the kind of man he was, how impulsive in any course of action. He went to Delphi at one time and ventured to ask the oracle—as I say, gentlemen, do not create a disturbance—he asked if any man was wiser than I, and the Pythian replied that no one was wiser. Chaerephon is dead, but his brother will testify to you about this.

Consider that I tell you this because I would inform you about the origin of the slander. When I heard of this reply I asked myself: "Whatever does the god mean? What is his riddle? I am very conscious that I am not wise at all; what then does he mean by saying that I am the wisest? For surely he does not lie; it is not legitimate for him to do so." For a long time I was at a loss as to his meaning; then I very reluctantly

---

[2]The god Apollo had a very famous shrine at Delphi, where his oracles were delivered through the mouth of a priestess, the "Pythian."

turned to some such investigation as this; I went to one of those reputed wise, thinking that there, if anywhere, I could refute the oracle and say to it: "This man is wiser than I, but you said I was." Then, when I examined this man—there is no need for me to tell you his name, he was one of our public men—my experience was something like this: I thought that he appeared wise to many people and especially to himself, but he was not. I then tried to show him that he thought himself wise, but that he was not. As a result he came to dislike me, and so did many of the bystanders. So I withdrew and thought to myself: "I am wiser than this man; it is likely that neither of us knows anything worthwhile, but he thinks he knows something when he does not, whereas when I do not know, neither do I think I know; so I am likely to be wiser than he to this small extent, that I do not think I know what I do not know." After this I approached another man, one of those thought to be wiser than he, and I thought the same thing, and so I came to be disliked both by him and by many others.

After that I proceeded systematically. I realized, to my sorrow and alarm, that I was getting unpopular, but I thought that I must attach the greatest importance to the god's oracle, so I must go to all those who had any reputation for knowledge to examine its meaning. And by the dog,[3] men of Athens—for I must tell you the truth—I experienced something like this: In my investigation in the service of the god I found that those who had the highest reputation were nearly the most deficient, while those who were thought to be inferior were more knowledgeable. I must give you an account of my journeyings as if they were labors I had undertaken to prove the oracle irrefutable. After the politicians, I went to the poets, the writers of tragedies and dithyrambs and the others, intending in their case to catch myself being more ignorant than they. So I took up those poems with which they seemed to have taken most trouble and asked them what they meant, in order that I might at the same time learn something from them. I am ashamed to tell you the truth, gentlemen, but I must. Almost all the bystanders might have explained the poems better than their authors could. I soon realized that poets do not compose their poems with knowledge, but by some inborn talent and by inspiration, like seers and prophets who also say many fine things without any understanding of what they say. The poets seemed to me to have had a similar experience. At the same time I saw that, because of their poetry, they thought themselves very wise

---

[3]A curious oath, occasionally used by Socrates, it appears in a longer form in *Gorgias* (482b) as "by the dog, the god of the Egyptians."

men in other respects, which they were not. So there again I withdrew, thinking that I had the same advantage over them as I had over the politicians.

Finally I went to the craftsmen, for I was conscious of knowing practically nothing, and I knew that I would find that they had knowledge of many fine things. In this I was not mistaken; they knew things I did not know, and to that extent they were wiser than I. But, men of Athens, the good craftsmen seemed to me to have the same fault as the poets: each of them, because of his success at his craft, thought himself very wise in other most important pursuits, and this error of theirs overshadowed the wisdom they had, so that I asked myself, on behalf of the oracle, whether I should prefer to be as I am, with neither their wisdom nor their ignorance, or to have both. The answer I gave myself and the oracle was that it was to my advantage to be as I am.

As a result of this investigation, men of Athens, I acquired much unpopularity, of a kind that is hard to deal with and is a heavy burden; many slanders came from these people and a reputation for wisdom, for in each case the bystanders thought that I myself possessed the wisdom that I proved that my interlocutor did not have. What is probable, gentlemen, is that in fact the god is wise and that his oracular response meant that human wisdom is worth little or nothing, and that when he says this man, Socrates, he is using my name as an example, as if he said: "This man among you, mortals, is wisest who, like Socrates, understands that his wisdom is worthless." So even now I continue this investigation as the god bade me—and I go around seeking out anyone, citizen or stranger, whom I think wise. Then if I do not think he is, I come to the assistance of the god and show him that he is not wise. Because of this occupation, I do not have the leisure to engage in public affairs to any extent, nor indeed to look after my own, but I live in great poverty because of my service to the god.

Furthermore, the young men who follow me around of their own free will, those who have most leisure, the sons of the very rich, take pleasure in hearing people questioned; they themselves often imitate me and try to question others. I think they find an abundance of men who believe they have some knowledge but know little or nothing. The result is that those whom they question are angry, not with themselves but with me. They say: "That man Socrates is a pestilential fellow who corrupts the young." If one asks them what he does and what he teaches to corrupt them, they are silent, as they do not know, but, so as not to appear at a loss, they mention those accusations that are available against all philosophers, about "things in the sky and things below the earth," about "not believing in the gods" and "making the worse the stronger argument;" they would not want to tell the truth, I'm sure, that they have been proved to lay claim to knowledge when they know nothing. These people are ambitious, violent, and numerous; they are continually and convincingly talking about me; they have been filling your ears for a long time with vehement slanders against me. [. . .]

I do not think, men of Athens, that it requires a prolonged defense to prove that I am not guilty of the charges in Meletus' deposition, but this is sufficient. On the other hand, you know that what I said earlier is true, that I am very unpopular with many people. This will be my undoing, if I am undone, not Meletus or Anytus but the slanders and envy of many people. This has destroyed many other good men and will, I think, continue to do so. There is no danger that it will stop at me.

Someone might say: "Are you not ashamed, Socrates, to have followed the kind of occupation that has led to your being now in danger of death?" However, I should be right to reply to him: "You are wrong, sir, if you think that a man who is any good at all should take into account the risk of life or death; he should look to this only in his actions, whether what he does is right or wrong, whether he is acting like a good or a bad man." According to your view, all the heroes who died at Troy were inferior people, especially the son of Thetis who was so contemptuous of danger compared with disgrace.[4] When he was eager to kill Hector, his goddess mother warned him, as I believe, in some such words as these: "My child, if you avenge the death of your comrade, Patroclus, and you kill Hector, you will die yourself, for your death is to follow immediately after Hector's." Hearing this, he despised death and danger and was much more afraid to live a coward who did not avenge his friends. "Let me die at once," he said, "when once I have given the wrongdoer his deserts, rather than remain here, a laughingstock by the curved ships, a burden upon the earth." Do you think he gave thought to death and danger?

This is the truth of the matter, men of Athens: wherever a man has taken a position that he believes to be best, or has been placed by his commander, there he must I think remain and face danger, without a thought for death or anything else, rather than disgrace. It would have been a dreadful way to behave, men of Athens, if, at Potidaea, Amphipolis, and Delium, I had, at the risk of death, like anyone else, remained at my post where those you had elected to command had

---

[4]The scene between Thetis and Achilles is from the *Iliad* xviii.94 ff.

ordered me, and then, when the god ordered me, as I thought and believed, to live the life of a philosopher, to examine myself and others, I had abandoned my post for fear of death or anything else. That would have been a dreadful thing, and then I might truly have justly been brought here for not believing that there are gods, disobeying the oracle, fearing death, and thinking I was wise when I was not. To fear death, gentlemen, is no other than to think oneself wise when one is not, to think one knows what one does not know. No one knows whether death may not be the greatest of all blessings for a man, yet men fear it as if they knew that it is the greatest of evils. And surely it is the most blameworthy ignorance to believe that one knows what one does not know. It is perhaps on this point and in this respect, gentlemen, that I differ from the majority of men, and if I were to claim that I am wiser than anyone in anything, it would be in this, that, as I have no adequate knowledge of things in the underworld, so I do not think I have. I do know, however, that it is wicked and shameful to do wrong, to disobey one's superior, be he god or man. I shall never fear or avoid things of which I do not know, whether they may not be good rather than things that I know to be bad. Even if you acquitted me now and did not believe Anytus, who said to you that either I should not have been brought here in the first place, or that now I am here, you cannot avoid executing me, for if I should be acquitted, your sons would practice the teachings of Socrates and all be thoroughly corrupted; if you said to me in this regard: "Socrates, we do not believe Anytus now; we acquit you, but only on condition that you spend no more time on this investigation and do not practice philosophy, and if you are caught doing so you will die;" if, as I say, you were to acquit me on those terms, I would say to you: "Men of Athens, I am grateful and I am your friend, but I will obey the god rather than you, and as long as I draw breath and am able, I shall not cease to practice philosophy, to exhort you and in my usual way to point out to any one of you whom I happen to meet: Good Sir, you are an Athenian, a citizen of the greatest city with the greatest reputation for both wisdom and power; are you not ashamed of your eagerness to possess as much wealth, reputation, and honors as possible, while you do not care for nor give thought to wisdom or truth, or the best possible state of your soul?" Then, if one of you disputes this and says he does care, I shall not let him go at once or leave him, but I shall question him, examine him, and test him, and if I do not think he has attained the goodness that he says he has, I shall reproach him because he attaches little importance to the most important things and greater importance to inferior things. I shall treat in this way anyone I happen to meet, young and old, citizen and stranger, and more so the citizens because you are more kindred to me. Be sure that this is what the god orders me to do, and I think there is no greater blessing for the city than my service to the god. For I go around doing nothing but persuading both young and old among you not to care for your body or your wealth in preference to or as strongly as for the best possible state of your soul, as I say to you: "Wealth does not bring about excellence, but excellence makes wealth and everything else good for men, both individually and collectively."[5]

Now if by saying this I corrupt the young, this advice must be harmful, but if anyone says that I give different advice, he is talking nonsense. On this point I would say to you, men of Athens: "Whether you believe Anytus or not, whether you acquit me or not, do so on the understanding that this is my course of action, even if I am to face death many times." Do not create a disturbance, gentlemen, but abide by my request not to cry out at what I say but to listen, for I think it will be to your advantage to listen, and I am about to say other things at which you will perhaps cry out. By no means do this. Be sure that if you kill the sort of man I say I am, you will not harm me more than yourselves. Neither Meletus nor Anytus can harm me in any way; he could not harm me, for I do not think it is permitted that a better man be harmed by a worse; certainly he might kill me, or perhaps banish or disfranchise me, which he and maybe others think to be great harm, but I do not think so. I think he is doing himself much greater harm doing what he is doing now, attempting to have a man executed unjustly. Indeed, men of Athens, I am far from making a defense now on my own behalf, as might be thought, but on yours, to prevent you from wrongdoing by mistreating the god's gift to you by condemning me; for if you kill me you will not easily find another like me. I was attached to this city by the god—though it seems a ridiculous thing to say—as upon a great and noble horse which was somewhat sluggish because of its size and needed to be stirred up by a kind of gadfly. It is to fulfill some such function that I believe the god has placed me in the city. I never cease to rouse each and every one of you, to persuade and reproach you all day long and everywhere I find myself in your company.

[5]Alternatively, this sentence could be translated: "Wealth does not bring about excellence, but excellence brings about wealth and all other public and private blessings for men."

Another such man will not easily come to be among you, gentlemen, and if you believe me you will spare me. You might easily be annoyed with me as people are when they are aroused from a doze, and strike out at me; if convinced by Anytus you could easily kill me, and then you could sleep on for the rest of your days, unless the god, in his care for you, sent you someone else. That I am the kind of person to be a gift of the god to the city you might realize from the fact that it does not seem like human nature for me to have neglected all my own affairs and to have tolerated this neglect now for so many years while I was always concerned with you, approaching each one of you like a father or an elder brother to persuade you to care for virtue. Now if I profited from this by charging a fee for my advice, there would be some sense to it, but you can see for yourselves that, for all their shameless accusations, my accusers have not been able in their impudence to bring forward a witness to say that I have ever received a fee or ever asked for one. I, on the other hand, have a convincing witness that I speak the truth, my poverty.

It may seem strange that while I go around and give this advice privately and interfere in private affairs, I do not venture to go to the assembly and there advise the city. You have heard me give the reason for this in many places. I have a divine or spiritual sign which Meletus has ridiculed in his deposition. This began when I was a child. It is a voice, and whenever it speaks it turns me away from something I am about to do, but it never encourages me to do anything. This is what has prevented me from taking part in public affairs, and I think it was quite right to prevent me. Be sure, men of Athens, that if I had long ago attempted to take part in politics, I should have died long ago, and benefited neither you nor myself. Do not be angry with me for speaking the truth; no man will survive who genuinely opposes you or any other crowd and prevents the occurrence of many unjust and illegal happenings in the city. A man who really fights for justice must lead a private, not a public, life if he is to survive for even a short time.

I shall give you great proofs of this, not words but what you esteem, deeds. Listen to what happened to me, that you may know that I will not yield to any man contrary to what is right, for fear of death, even if I should die at once for not yielding. The things I shall tell you are commonplace and smack of the lawcourts, but they are true. I have never held any other office in the city, but I served as a member of the Council, and our tribe Antiochis was presiding at the time when you wanted to try as a body the ten generals who had failed to pick up the survivors of the naval battle.[6] This was illegal, as you all recognized later. I was the only member of the presiding committee to oppose your doing something contrary to the laws, and I voted against it. The orators were ready to prosecute me and take me away, and your shouts were egging them on, but I thought I should run any risk on the side of law and justice rather than join you, for fear of prison or death, when you were engaged in an unjust course.

This happened when the city was still a democracy. When the oligarchy was established, the Thirty[7] summoned me to the Hall, along with four others, and ordered us to bring Leon from Salamis, that he might be executed. They gave many such orders to many people, in order to implicate as many as possible in their guilt. Then I showed again, not in words but in action, that, if it were not rather vulgar to say so, death is something I couldn't care less about, but that my whole concern is not to do anything unjust or impious. That government, powerful as it was, did not frighten me into any wrongdoing. When we left the Hall, the other four went to Salamis and brought in Leon, but I went home. I might have been put to death for this, had not the government fallen shortly afterwards. There are many who will witness to these events.

Do you think I would have survived all these years if I were engaged in public affairs and, acting as a good man must, came to the help of justice and considered this the most important thing? Far from it, men of Athens, nor would any other man. Throughout my life, in any public activity I may have engaged in, I am the same man as I am in private life. I have never come to an agreement with anyone to act unjustly, neither with anyone else nor with any one of those who they slanderously say are my pupils. I have never been anyone's teacher. If anyone, young or old, desires to listen to me when I am talking and dealing with my own concerns, I have never begrudged this to anyone, but I do not converse when I receive a fee and not when I do not. I am equally ready to question the rich and the poor if anyone is willing to answer my

[6]This was the battle of Arginusae (south of Lesbos) in 406 B.C., the last Athenian victory of the war. A violent storm prevented the Athenian generals from rescuing their survivors. For this they were tried in Athens and sentenced to death by the assembly. They were tried in a body, and it is this to which Socrates objected in the Council's presiding committee which prepared the business of the assembly. He obstinately persisted in his opposition, in which he stood alone, and was overruled by the majority. Six generals who were in Athens were executed.

[7]This was the harsh oligarchy that was set up after the final defeat of Athens by Sparta in the Peloponnesian War in 404 B.C. and that ruled Athens for some nine months in 404–3 before the democracy was restored.

questions and listen to what I say. And I cannot justly be held responsible for the good or bad conduct of these people, as I never promised to teach them anything and have not done so. If anyone says that he has learned anything from me, or that he heard anything privately that the others did not hear, be assured that he is not telling the truth.

Why then do some people enjoy spending considerable time in my company? You have heard why, men of Athens; I have told you the whole truth. They enjoy hearing those being questioned who think they are wise, but are not. And this is not unpleasant. To do this has, as I say, been enjoined upon me by the god, by means of oracles and dreams, and in every other way that a divine manifestation has ever ordered a man to do anything. This is true, gentlemen, and can easily be established.

If I corrupt some young men and have corrupted others, then surely some of them who have grown older and realized that I gave them bad advice when they were young should now themselves come up here to accuse me and avenge themselves. If they were unwilling to do so themselves, then some of their kindred, their fathers or brothers or other relations should recall it now if their family had been harmed by me. I see many of these present here, first Crito, my contemporary and fellow demesman, the father of Critobulus here; next Lysanias of Sphettus, the father of Aeschines here; also Antiphon the Cephisian, the father of Epigenes; and others whose brothers spent their time in this way; Nicostratus, the son of Theozotides, brother of Theodotus, and Theodotus has died so he could not influence him; Paralius here, son of Demodocus, whose brother was Theages; there is Adeimantus, son of Ariston, brother of Plato here; Aeantodorus, brother of Apollodorus here.

I could mention many others, some one of whom surely Meletus should have brought in as witness in his own speech. If he forgot to do so, then let him do it now; I will yield time if he has anything of the kind to say. You will find quite the contrary, gentlemen. These men are all ready to come to the help of the corruptor, the man who has harmed their kindred, as Meletus and Anytus say. Now those who were corrupted might well have reason to help me, but the uncorrupted, their kindred who are older men, have no reason to help me except the right and proper one, that they know that Meletus is lying and that I am telling the truth. [. . .]

Quite apart from the question of reputation, gentlemen, I do not think it right to supplicate the jury and to be acquitted because of this, but to teach and persuade them. It is not the purpose of a juryman's office to give justice as a favor to whoever seems good to him, but to judge according to law, and this he has sworn to do. We should not accustom you to perjure yourselves, nor should you make a habit of it. This is irreverent conduct for either of us.

Do not deem it right for me, men of Athens, that I should act towards you in a way that I do not consider to be good or just or pious, especially, by Zeus, as I am being prosecuted by Meletus here for impiety; clearly, if I convinced you by my supplication to do violence to your oath of office, I would be teaching you not to believe that there are gods, and my defense would convict me of not believing in them. This is far from being the case, gentlemen, for I do believe in them as none of my accusers do. I leave it to you and the god to judge me in the way that will be best for me and for you.

[The jury now gives its verdict of guilty, and Meletus asks for the penalty of death.]

There are many other reasons for my not being angry with you for convicting me, men of Athens, and what happened was not unexpected. I am much more surprised at the number of votes cast on each side, for I did not think the decision would be by so few votes but by a great many. As it is, a switch of only thirty votes would have acquitted me. I think myself that I have been cleared on Meletus' charges, and not only this, but it is clear to all that, if Anytus and Lycon had not joined him in accusing me, he would have been fined a thousand drachmas for not receiving a fifth of the votes.

He assesses the penalty at death. So be it. What counter-assessment should I propose to you, men of Athens? Clearly it should be a penalty I deserve, and what do I deserve to suffer or to pay because I have deliberately not led a quiet life but have neglected what occupies most people: wealth, household affairs, the position of general or public orator or the other offices, the political clubs and factions that exist in the city? I thought myself too honest to survive if I occupied myself with those things. I did not follow that path that would have made me of no use either to you or to myself, but I went to each of you privately and conferred upon him what I say is the greatest benefit, by trying to persuade him not to care for any of his belongings before caring that he himself should be as good and as wise as possible, not to care for the city's possessions more than for the city itself, and to care for other things in the same way. What do I deserve for being such a man? Some good, men of Athens, if I must truly make an assessment according to my deserts, and something suitable. What is suitable for a poor benefactor who needs leisure to exhort you? Nothing is more suitable, gentlemen, than for such a man to be fed in the Prytaneum[8]—much more suitable for him than for any one of you who has won a victory at Olympia with a pair or a team of horses. The Olympian victor makes you think yourself happy; I make you be happy. Besides, he does not need food, but I do. So if I must make a just assessment of what I deserve, I assess it as this: free meals in the Prytaneum.

When I say this you may think, as when I spoke of appeals to pity and entreaties, that I speak arrogantly, but that is not the case, men of Athens; rather it is like this: I am convinced that I never willingly wrong anyone, but I am not convincing you of this, for we have talked together but a short time. If it were the law with us, as it is elsewhere, that a trial for life should not last one but many days, you would be convinced, but now it is not easy to dispel great slanders in a short time. Since I am convinced that I wrong no one, I am not likely to wrong myself, to say that I deserve some evil and to make some such assessment against myself. What should I fear? That I should suffer the penalty Meletus has assessed against me, of which I say I do not know whether it is good or bad? Am I then to choose in preference to this something that I know very well to be an evil and assess the penalty at that? Imprisonment? Why should I live in prison, always subjected to the ruling magistrates, the Eleven? A fine, and imprisonment until I pay it? That would be the same thing for me, as I have no money. Exile? For perhaps you might accept that assessment.

I should have to be inordinately fond of life, men of Athens, to be so unreasonable as to suppose that other men will easily tolerate my company and conversation when you, my fellow citizens, have been unable to endure them, but found them a burden and resented them so that you are now seeking to get rid of them. Far from it, gentlemen. It would be a fine life at my age to be driven out of one city after another, for I know very well that wherever I go the young men will listen to my talk as they do here. If I drive them away, they will themselves persuade their elders to drive me out; if I do not drive them away, their fathers and relations will drive me out on their behalf.

Perhaps someone might say: But Socrates, if you leave us will you not be able to live quietly, without talking? Now this is the most difficult point on which to convince some of you. If I say that it is impossible for me to keep quiet because that means disobeying the god, you will not

---

[8]The Prytaneum was the magistrates' hall or town hall of Athens in which public entertainments were given, particularly to Olympian victors on their return home.

believe me and will think I am being ironical. On the other hand, if I say that it is the greatest good for a man to discuss virtue every day and those other things about which you hear me conversing and testing myself and others, for the unexamined life is not worth living for men, you will believe me even less.

What I say is true, gentlemen, but it is not easy to convince you. At the same time, I am not accustomed to think that I deserve any penalty. If I had money, I would assess the penalty at the amount I could pay, for that would not hurt me, but I have none, unless you are willing to set the penalty at the amount I can pay, and perhaps I could pay you one mina of silver. So that is my assessment.

Plato here, men of Athens, and Crito and Critobulus and Apollodorus bid me put the penalty at thirty minas, and they will stand surety for the money. Well then, that is my assessment, and they will be sufficient guarantee of payment.

[The jury now votes again and sentences Socrates to death.]

It is for the sake of a short time, men of Athens, that you will acquire the reputation and the guilt, in the eyes of those who want to denigrate the city, of having killed Socrates, a wise man, for they who want to revile you will say that I am wise even if I am not. If you had waited but a little while, this would have happened of its own accord. You see my age, that I am already advanced in years and close to death. I am saying this not to all of you but to those who condemned me to death, and to these same ones I say: Perhaps you think that I was convicted for lack of such words as might have convinced you, if I thought I should say or do all I could to avoid my sentence. Far from it. I was convicted because I lacked not words but boldness and shamelessness and the willingness to say to you what you would most gladly have heard from me, lamentations and tears and my saying and doing many things that I say are unworthy of me but that you are accustomed to hear from others. I did not think then that the danger I ran should make me do anything mean, nor do I now regret the nature of my defense. I would much rather die after this kind of defense than live after making the other kind. Neither I nor any other man should, on trial or in war, contrive to avoid death at any cost. Indeed it is often obvious in battle that one could escape death by throwing away one's weapons and by turning to supplicate one's pursuers, and there are many ways to avoid death in every kind of danger if one will venture to do or say anything to avoid it. It is not difficult to avoid death, gentlemen; it is much more difficult to avoid wickedness, for it runs faster than death. Slow and elderly as I am, I have been caught by the slower pursuer, whereas my accusers, being clever and sharp, have been caught by the quicker, wickedness. I leave you now, condemned to death by you, but they are condemned by truth to wickedness and injustice. So I maintain my assessment, and they maintain theirs. This perhaps had to happen, and I think it is as it should be.

Now I want to prophesy to those who convicted me, for I am at the point when men prophesy most, when they are about to die. I say, gentlemen, to those who voted to kill me, that vengeance will come upon you immediately after my death, a vengeance much harder to bear than that which you took in killing me. You did this in the belief that you would avoid giving an account of your life, but I maintain that quite the opposite will happen to you. There will be more people to test you, whom I now held back, but you did not notice it. They will be more difficult to deal with as they will be younger and you will resent them more. You are wrong if you believe that by killing people you will prevent anyone from reproaching you for not living in the right way. To escape such tests is neither possible nor good, but it is best and easiest not to discredit others but to prepare oneself to be as good as possible. With this prophecy to you who convicted me, I part from you.

I should be glad to discuss what has happened with those who voted for my acquittal during the time that the officers of the court are busy and I do not yet have to depart to my death. So, gentlemen, stay with me awhile, for nothing prevents us from talking to each other while it is allowed. To you, as being my friends, I want to show the meaning of what has occurred. A surprising thing has happened to me, jurymen— you I would rightly call jurymen. At all previous times my familiar prophetic power, my spiritual manifestation, frequently opposed me, even in small matters, when I was about to do something wrong, but now that, as you can see for yourselves, I was faced with what one might think, and what is generally thought to be, the worst of evils, my divine sign has not opposed me, either when I left home at dawn, or when I came into court, or at any time that I was about to say something during my speech. Yet in other talks it often held me back in the middle of my speaking, but now it has opposed no word or deed of mine. What do I think is the reason for this? I will tell you. What has happened to me may well be a good thing, and those of us who believe death to be an evil are certainly mistaken. I have convincing proof of this, for it is impossible that my familiar sign did not oppose me if I was not about to do what was right.

Let us reflect in this way, too, that there is good hope that death is a blessing, for it is one of two things: either the dead are nothing and have no perception of anything, or it is, as we are told, a change and a relocating for the soul from here to another place. If it is complete lack of perception, like a dreamless sleep, then death would be a great advantage. For I think that if one had to pick out that night during which a man slept soundly and did not dream, put beside it the other nights and days of his life, and then see how many days and nights had been better and more pleasant than that night, not only a private person but the great king would find them easy to count compared with the other days and nights. If death is like this I say it is an advantage, for all eternity would then seem to be no more than a single night. If, on the other hand, death is a change from here to another place, and what we are told is true and all who have died are there, what greater blessing could there be, gentlemen of the jury? If anyone arriving in Hades will have escaped from those who call themselves jurymen here, and will find those true jurymen who are said to sit in judgment there, Minos and Rhadamanthus and Aeacus and Triptolemus and the other demigods who have been upright in their own life, would that be a poor kind of change? Again, what would one of you give to keep company with Orpheus and Musaeus, Hesiod and Homer? I am willing to die many times if that is true. It would be a wonderful way for me to spend my time whenever I met Palamedes and Ajax, the son of Telamon, and any other of the men of old who died through an unjust conviction, to compare my experience with theirs. I think it would be pleasant. Most important, I could spend my time testing and examining people there, as I do here, as to who among them is wise, and who thinks he is, but is not.

What would one not give, gentlemen of the jury, for the opportunity to examine the man who led the great expedition against Troy, or Odysseus, or Sisyphus, and innumerable other men and women one could mention? It would be an extraordinary happiness to talk with them, to keep company with them and examine them. In any case, they would certainly not put one to death for doing so. They are happier there than we are here in other respects, and for the rest of time they are deathless, if indeed what we are told is true.

You too must be of good hope as regards death, gentlemen of the jury, and keep this one truth in mind, that a good man cannot be harmed either in life or in death, and that his affairs are not neglected by the gods. What has happened to me now has not happened of itself, but it is clear to me that it was better for me to die now and to escape from trouble. That is why my divine sign did not oppose me at any point. So I am certainly not angry with those who convicted me, or with my accusers. Of course that was not their purpose when they accused and convicted me, but they thought they were hurting me, and for this they deserve blame. This much I ask from them: When my sons grow up, avenge yourselves by causing them the same kind of grief that I caused you, if you think they care for money or anything else more than they care for virtue, or if they think they are somebody when they are nobody. Reproach them as I reproach you, that they do not care for the right things and think they are worthy when they are not worthy of anything. If you do this, I shall have been justly treated by you, and my sons also.

Now the hour to part has come. I go to die, you go to live. Which of us goes to the better lot is known to no one, except the god.

The Value of Philosophy

Bertrand Russell

Having now come to the end of our brief and very incomplete review of the problems of philosophy, it will be well to consider, in conclusion, what is the value of philosophy and why it ought to be studied. It is the more necessary to consider this question, in view of the fact that many men, under the influence of science or of practical affairs, are inclined to doubt whether philosophy is anything better than innocent but useless trifling, hair-splitting distinctions, and controversies on matters concerning which knowledge is impossible.

This view of philosophy appears to result, partly from a wrong conception of the ends of life, partly from a wrong conception of the kind of goods which philosophy strives to achieve. Physical science, through the medium of inventions, is useful to innumerable people who are wholly ignorant of it; thus the study of physical science is to be recommended, not only, or primarily, because of the effect on the student, but rather because of the effect on mankind in general. This utility does not belong to philosophy. If the study of philosophy has any value at all for others than students of philosophy, it must be only indirectly, through

Source: From Bertrand Russell, *The Problems of Philosophy* (Oxford University Press, 1969). Reprinted by permission of Oxford University Press.

its effects upon the lives of those who study it. It is in these effects, therefore, if anywhere, that the value of philosophy must be primarily sought.

But further, if we are not to fail in our endeavour to determine the value of philosophy, we must first free our minds from the prejudices of what are wrongly called 'practical' men. The 'practical' man, as this word is often used, is one who recognizes only material needs, who realizes that men must have food for the body, but is oblivious of the necessity of providing food for the mind. If all men were well off, if poverty and disease had been reduced to their lowest possible point, there would still remain much to be done to produce a valuable society; and even in the existing world the goods of the mind are at least as important as the goods of the body. It is exclusively among the goods of the mind that the value of philosophy is to be found; and only those who are not indifferent to these goods can be persuaded that the study of philosophy is not a waste of time.

Philosophy, like all other studies, aims primarily at knowledge. The knowledge it aims at is the kind of knowledge which gives unity and system to the body of the sciences, and the kind which results from a critical examination of the grounds of our convictions, prejudices, and beliefs. But it cannot be maintained that philosophy has had any very great measure of success in its attempts to provide definite answers to its questions. If you ask a mathematician, a mineralogist, a historian, or any other man of learning, what definite body of truths has been ascertained by his science, his answer will last as long as you are willing to listen. But if you put the same question to a philosopher, he will, if he is candid, have to confess that his study has not achieved positive results such as have been achieved by other sciences. It is true that this is partly accounted for by the fact that, as soon as definite knowledge concerning any subject becomes possible, this subject ceases to be called philosophy, and becomes a separate science. The whole study of the heavens, which now belongs to astronomy, was once included in philosophy; Newton's great work was called 'the mathematical principles of natural philosophy'. Similarly, the study of the human mind, which was a part of philosophy, has now been separated from philosophy and has become the science of psychology. Thus, to a great extent, the uncertainty of philosophy is more apparent than real: those questions which are already capable of definite answers are placed in the sciences, while those only to which, at present, no definite answer can be given, remain to form the residue which is called philosophy.

This is, however, only a part of the truth concerning the uncertainty of philosophy. There are many questions—and among them those that are of the profoundest interest to our spiritual life—which, so far as we can see, must remain insoluble to the human intellect unless its powers become of quite a different order from what they are now. Has the universe any unity of plan or purpose, or is it a fortuitous concourse of atoms? Is consciousness a permanent part of the universe, giving hope of indefinite growth in wisdom, or is it a transitory accident on a small planet on which life must ultimately become impossible? Are good and evil of importance to the universe or only to man? Such questions are asked by philosophy, and variously answered by various philosophers. But it would seem that, whether answers be otherwise discoverable or not, the answers suggested by philosophy are none of them demonstrably true. Yet, however slight may be the hope of discovering an answer, it is part of the business of philosophy to continue the consideration of such questions, to make us aware of their importance, to examine all the approaches to them, and to keep alive that speculative interest in the universe which is apt to be killed by confining ourselves to definitely ascertainable knowledge.

Many philosophers, it is true, have held that philosophy could establish the truth of certain answers to such fundamental questions. They have supposed that what is of most importance in religious beliefs could be proved by strict demonstration to be true. In order to judge of such attempts, it is necessary to take a survey of human knowledge, and to form an opinion as to its methods and its limitations. On such a subject it would be unwise to pronounce dogmatically; but if the investigations of our previous chapters have not led us astray, we shall be compelled to renounce the hope of finding philosophical proofs of religious beliefs. We cannot, therefore, include as part of the value of philosophy any definite set of answers to such questions. Hence, once more, the value of philosophy must not depend upon any supposed body of definitely ascertainable knowledge to be acquired by those who study it.

The value of philosophy is, in fact, to be sought largely in its very uncertainty. The man who has no tincture of philosophy goes through life imprisoned in the prejudices derived from common sense, from the habitual beliefs of his age or his nation, and from convictions which have grown up in his mind without the co-operation or consent of his deliberate reason. To such a man the world tends to become definite, finite, obvious; common objects rouse no questions, and unfamiliar possibilities are contemptuously rejected. As soon as we begin to philosophize, on the contrary, we find, as we saw in our opening chapters, that even the most everyday things lead to problems to which only very incomplete answers can be given. Philosophy, though unable to tell us with certainty what is the true answer to the doubts which it raises, is able to suggest many possibilities which enlarge our thoughts and free them from the tyranny of custom. Thus, while diminishing our feeling of certainty as to what things are, it greatly increases our knowledge as to what they may be; it removes the somewhat arrogant dogmatism of those who have never travelled into the region of liberating doubt, and it keeps alive our sense of wonder by showing familiar things in an unfamiliar aspect.

Apart from its utility in showing unsuspected possibilities, philosophy has a value—perhaps its chief value—through the greatness of the objects which it contemplates, and the freedom from narrow and personal aims resulting from this contemplation. The life of the instinctive man is shut up within the circle of his private interests: family and friends may be included, but the outer world is not regarded except as it may help or hinder what comes within the circle of instinctive wishes. In such a life there is something feverish and confined, in comparison with which the philosophic life is calm and free. The private world of instinctive interests is a small one, set in the midst of a great and powerful world which must, sooner or later, lay our private world in ruins. Unless we can so enlarge our interests as to include the whole outer world, we remain like a garrison in a beleagured fortress, knowing that the enemy prevents escape and that ultimate surrender is inevitable. In such a life there is no peace, but a constant strife between the insistence of desire and the powerlessness of will. In one way or another, if our life is to be great and free, we must escape this prison and this strife.

One way of escape is by philosophic contemplation. Philosophic contemplation does not, in its widest survey, divide the universe into two hostile camps—friends and foes, helpful and hostile, good and bad—it views the whole impartially. Philosophic contemplation, when it is unalloyed, does not aim at proving that the rest of the universe is akin to man. All acquisition of knowledge is an enlargement of the Self, but this enlargement is best attained when it is not directly sought. It is obtained when the desire for knowledge is alone operative, by a study which does not wish in advance that its objects should have this or that character, but adapts the Self to the characters which it finds in its objects. This enlargement of Self is not obtained when, taking the Self as it is, we try to show that the world is so similar to this Self that knowledge of it is possible without any admission of what seems alien. The desire to prove this is a form of self-assertion and, like all self-assertion, it is an obstacle to the growth of Self which it desires, and of which the Self knows that it is capable. Self-assertion, in philosophic speculation as elsewhere, views the world as a means to its own ends; thus it makes the world of less account than Self, and the Self sets bounds to the greatness of its goods. In contemplation, on the contrary, we start from the not-Self, and through its greatness the boundaries of Self are enlarged; through the infinity of the universe the mind which contemplates it achieves some share in infinity.

For this reason greatness of soul is not fostered by those philosophies which assimilate the universe to Man. Knowledge is a form of union of Self and not-Self; like all union, it is impaired by dominion, and therefore by any attempt to force the universe into conformity with what we find in ourselves. There is a widespread philosophical tendency towards the view which tells us that Man is the measure of all things, that truth is man-made, that space and time and the world of universals are properties of the mind, and that, if there be anything not created by the mind, it is unknowable and of no account for us. This view, if our previous discussions were correct, is untrue; but in addition to being untrue, it has the effect of robbing philosophic contemplation of all that gives it value, since it fetters contemplation to Self. What it calls knowledge is not a union with the not-Self, but a set of prejudices, habits, and desires, making an impenetrable veil between us and the world beyond. The man who finds pleasure in such a theory of knowledge is like the man who never leaves the domestic circle for fear his word might not be law.

The true philosophic contemplation, on the contrary, finds its satisfaction in every enlargement of the not-Self, in everything that magnifies the objects contemplated, and thereby the subject contemplating. Everything, in contemplation, that is personal or private, everything that depends upon habit, self-interest, or desire, distorts the object, and hence impairs the union which the intellect seeks. By thus making a barrier between subject and object, such personal and private things become a prison to the intellect. The free intellect will see as God might see, without a *here* and *now*, without hopes and fears, without the trammels of customary beliefs and traditional prejudices, calmly, dispassionately, in the sole and exclusive desire of knowledge—knowledge as impersonal, as purely contemplative, as it is possible for man to attain. Hence also the free intellect will value more the abstract and universal knowledge into which the accidents of private history do not enter, than the knowledge brought by the senses, and dependent, as such knowledge must be, upon an exclusive and personal point of view and a body whose sense-organs distort as much as they reveal.

The mind which has become accustomed to the freedom and impartiality of philosophic contemplation will preserve something of the same freedom and impartiality in the world of action and emotion. It will view its purposes and desires as parts of the whole, with the absence of insistence that results from seeing them as infinitesimal fragments in a world of which all the rest is unaffected by any one man's deeds. The impartiality which, in contemplation, is the unalloyed desire for truth, is the very same quality of mind which, in action, is justice, and in emotion is that universal love which can be given to all, and not only to those who are judged useful or admirable. Thus contemplation enlarges not only the objects of our thoughts, but also the objects of our actions and our affections: it makes us citizens of the universe, not only of one walled city at war with all the rest. In this citizenship of the universe consists man's true freedom, and his liberation from the thraldom of narrow hopes and fears.

Thus, to sum up our discussion of the value of philosophy; Philosophy is to be studied, not for the sake of any definite answers to its questions, since no definite answers can, as a rule, be known to be true, but rather for the sake of the questions themselves; because these questions enlarge our conception of what is possible, enrich our intellectual imagination and diminish the dogmatic assurance which closes the mind against speculation; but above all because, through the greatness of the universe which philosophy contemplates, the mind also is rendered great, and becomes capable of that union with the universe which constitutes its highest good.

SECTION TWO

WHAT DO WE KNOW?

The readings in this section address the nature and scope of human knowledge—that area of philosophy called *epistemology*. This area of philosophical inquiry dates back at least as far as to Plato's time (circa 400 BCE) when, in the *Meno*, he describes Socrates' inquiry into the difference between mere *belief* (*doxa*) and *knowledge* (*episteme*). There is, it seems, something real knowledge has that mere belief lacks. One goal of philosophy is to discover what this difference is. The classical analysis of knowledge, which is usually attributed to Plato, is that knowledge is justified true belief. This definition of knowledge can be seen as giving rise to the central questions of epistemology: Is knowledge even possible? That is, can we ever satisfy these criteria? What does it take for a belief to be justified? Are these criteria sufficient for knowledge? What are the limits of knowledge? And, how do we acquire knowledge?

In the first reading, sections I and II of the *Meditations*, René Descartes states that what distinguishes real knowledge from mere belief is the added feature of *indubitability*. That is, while one may have many beliefs, only those whose truth cannot be doubted, those of which one is certain, will count as knowledge. Thus Descartes introduces a *criterion of certainty*. In the two meditations included here, Descartes subjects his formerly held opinions—his beliefs—to doubt in an attempt to discover which, if any, meet the criterion of certainty. If Descartes is working with the correct criteria for knowledge, and if nothing can satisfy that criteria, then the result would be an extreme form of skepticism—the view that knowledge is not possible. However, even though Descartes employs a skeptical approach to knowledge, in the end, Descartes rejects skepticism. Ultimately, he defends a rationalist epistemology—he argues that beliefs justified *a priori*, or on the basis of reason, satisfy the criterion of certainty.

In "Bad Dreams, Evil Demons, and the Experience Machine: Philosophy and *The Matrix*" Christopher Grau reminds us that Descartes' worries are not so foreign or outdated; instead, they are *the* stuff of contemporary science fiction. Like the character Neo in *The Matrix*, we might wonder if this so-called life is only a very convincing dream. Grau expresses this familiar Cartesian skeptical worry by asking, "How can any of us be sure that we have ever *genuinely* woken up? Perhaps . . . our dreams thus far have in fact been dreams *within* dreams." Still, to most of us, it seems rather far-fetched to think that we, like Neo, are being deceived on such a grand scale; however, we need a sound argument to justify our belief that things are as they seem. In the second part of Grau's essay, he explores a contemporary version of Cartesian skepticism called "brain-in-a-vat skepticism." Like Descartes' character who wonders whether or not he is dreaming, and Neo who wonders whether he is or is not in the Matrix, we might ask ourselves how we know that we are not disembodied brains "plugged-in" to a super-computer that stimulates our brains in such a way that it seems to us that we are "normal" people with "normal" lives.

Skepticism might strike many of us as a "mere theoretical position" that has nothing to do with common sense and the real world. However, Bertrand Russell argues in "On the Value of Skepticism" that a certain moderate skepticism would revolutionize and improve human life as we know it. He points out that most opinions about politics and religion are held with great passion, but on the basis of scant evidence. If one were to adopt a moderate form of skepticism, one would realize that many beliefs that are the cause of war, political unrest, or persecutions are nothing but wild speculations about doubtful matters.

Although some forms of skepticism are attractive, G. E. Moore thinks that it is a "scandal of philosophy" that skepticism about the external world has not been eliminated. In his "Proof of an External World," Moore argues that the experience of seeing one's own hands provides an excellent starting point to prove the existence of things that are external to our minds. Moore is convinced that his proof is "perfectly rigorous . . . and that it is perhaps impossible to give a better proof of anything whatever."

Edmund Gettier's short but influential paper, "Is Justified True Belief Knowledge?" challenges the sufficiency of the classical "justified true belief" analysis of knowledge. Gettier offers a counterexample to this analysis; that is, he describes a case in which a person has a *justified true belief* that P and yet does not *know* that P. If having a justified true belief were sufficient for knowledge, then person would know that P. So, having a justified true belief is not sufficient for knowledge.

One obvious response to Gettier's objection is to question whether or not his subjects' beliefs are really justified given that they are based on a false intermediate belief. Richard Feldman, in his essay "An Alleged Defect in Gettier Counter-Examples," responds to the charge that Gettier has relied on a false principle in challenging the sufficiency of the classical analysis of knowledge. He offers a revised "Gettier-style" counterexample to the justified true belief analysis that, unlike Gettier's, does not depend on the subject having a false intermediate belief. Thus, proponents of the classical analysis of knowledge are left with the burden of providing a satisfactory response to Gettier-style counterexamples that do not depend on a false intermediary belief.

John Locke's *An Essay Concerning Human Understanding* provides a good introduction to an empiricist position in epistemology. According to Locke, our minds are at birth nothing but "blank slates." It is experience and experience alone that provides us with ideas. Locke therefore rejects any appeal to inborn ideas, and argues that we can know the world only insofar as we can deduce our complex ideas from simpler ones that are ultimately derived from sensory experience.

Empiricism is an attractive position in epistemology only if we have good reasons for thinking that the future resembles the past. For suppose that this is not the case, that is, suppose that the future had nothing to do with the past. In that case, past experiences would be of little use in predicting what the future holds, and skepticism would be triumphant. This means that any convinced empiricist should be concerned to show that past experiences are a good guide for knowing the future. But can this be done? The project of providing reasons for why the past allows us to know the future is called the problem of induction. It is one of the thorniest problems in epistemology. John Hospers offers what is called a pragmatic solution to the problem of induction. In short, he argues that we are justified in justifying our beliefs inductively because, practically speaking, induction works.

In the final selection in this section, "The Problem of Induction—Old and New," Howard Kahane and Paul Tidman offer a concise statement of the problem of induction and explain why several standard sorts of responses to the problem, including a pragmatic solution like Hospers', are unsatisfactory. In the second section of this reading, Kahane and Tidman explain what has been coined "the new riddle of induction." This problem concerns the nature of confirming evidence itself. In science, certain observations count as *evidence* in support of certain hypotheses. The "old" riddle of induction (the problem of induction) is the problem of justifying the *inductive inference* from some bit of evidence to some conclusion or hypothesis. The new riddle of induction, however, focuses on the *nature of the confirming evidence* itself. What exactly should count as confirming evidence?

Meditations 1 and 2
René Descartes   *(Translated by F. E. Sutcliffe)*

First Meditation

About the Things We May Doubt

It is some time ago now since I perceived that, from my earliest years, I had accepted many false opinions as being true, and that what I had since based on such insecure principles could only be most doubtful and uncertain; so that I had to undertake seriously once in my life to rid myself of all the opinions I had adopted up to then, and to begin afresh from the foundations, if I wished to establish something firm and constant in the sciences. But as this undertaking seemed to me very great, I waited until I had attained an age sufficiently mature that I could not hope, at a later stage in life, to be more fit to execute my plan; and this has made me delay so long that I should henceforth consider that I was committing a fault if I were still to use in deliberation the time which remains to me for action.

Now therefore, that my mind is free from all cares, and that I have obtained for myself assured leisure in peaceful solitude, I shall apply myself seriously and freely to the general destruction of all my former opinions. Now it will not be necessary, in order to accomplish this aim, to prove that they are all false, a point which perhaps I would never reach; but inasmuch as reason persuades me already that I must avoid believing things which are not entirely certain and indubitable, no less carefully than those things which seem manifestly false, the slightest ground for doubt that I find in any, will suffice for me to reject all of them. And to this end there will be no need for me to examine each one individually, which would be an endless task; but because the destruction of the foundations necessarily brings down with it the rest of the edifice, I shall make an assault first on the principles on which all my former opinions were based.

Everything I have accepted up to now as being absolutely true and assured, I have learned from or through the senses. But I have sometimes found that these senses played me false, and it is prudent never to trust entirely those who have once deceived us.

But, although the senses sometimes deceive us, concerning things which are barely perceptible or at a great distance, there are perhaps many other things about which one cannot reasonably doubt, although we know them through the medium of the senses, for example, that I am here, sitting by the fire, wearing a dressing-gown, with this paper in my hands, and other things of this nature. And how could I deny that these hands and this body belong to me, unless perhaps I were to assimilate myself to those insane persons whose minds are so troubled and clouded by the black vapours of the bile that they constantly assert that they are kings, when they are very poor; that they are wearing gold and purple, when they are quite naked; or who imagine that they are pitchers or that they have a body of glass. But these are madmen, and I would not be less extravagant if I were to follow their example.

However, I must here consider that I am a man, and consequently that I am in the habit of sleeping and of representing to myself in my dreams those same things, or sometimes even less likely things, which insane people do when they are awake. How many times have I dreamt at night that I was in this place, dressed, by the fire, although I was quite naked in my bed? It certainly seems to me at the moment that I am not looking at this paper with my eyes closed; that this head that I shake is not asleep; that I hold out this hand intentionally and deliberately, and that I am aware of it. What happens in sleep does not seem as clear and distinct as all this. But in thinking about it carefully, I recall having often been deceived in sleep by similar illusions, and, reflecting on this circumstance more closely, I see so clearly that there are no conclusive signs by means of which one can distinguish clearly between being awake and being asleep, that I am quite astonished by it; and my astonishment is such that it is almost capable of persuading me that I am asleep now.

Let us suppose, then, that we are now asleep, and that all these particulars, namely, that we open our eyes, move our heads, hold out our hands, and such like actions, are only false illusions; and let us think that perhaps our hands and all our body are not as we see them. Nevertheless, we must at least admit that the things which appear to us in sleep are, as it were, pictures and paintings which can only be formed in the likeness of something real and true; and that therefore these general things at least, namely, eyes, head, hands and all the rest of the body are not imaginary things but are real and existent. For indeed painters, even when they study with the utmost skill to represent Sirens and Satyrs by strange and extraordinary shapes, cannot attribute to them entirely new forms and natures, but only make a certain mixture and compound of the limbs of various animals; or if perhaps their imagination is extravagant enough to invent something so new that we have never seen the like of it, and that, in this way, their work presents us with something purely fictitious and absolutely false, at least the colours of which they have composed it are real. And by the same reasoning, although these general things, viz. eyes, head, hands and the like, may be imaginary, we have to admit that there are even simpler and more universal things which are true and exist, from the mixture of which, no more or less than from the mixture of certain real colours, all the images of things, whether true and real or fictitious and fantastic, which dwell in our thoughts, are formed. Corporeal nature in general, and its extension, are of this class of things: together with the figure of extended things, their quantity or size, and their number, as also the place where they are, the time during which they exist, and such like.

This is why perhaps that, from this, we shall not be wrong in concluding that physics, astronomy, medicine, and all the other sciences which depend on the consideration of composite things, are most doubtful and uncertain, but that arithmetic, geometry and the other sciences of this nature, which deal only with very simple and general things, without bothering about their existence or non-existence, contain something certain and indubitable. For whether I am awake or sleeping, two and three added together always make five, and a square never has more than four sides; and it does not seem possible that truths so apparent can be suspected of any falsity or uncertainty.

Nevertheless, I have for a long time had in my mind the belief that there is a God who is all-powerful and by whom I was created and made as I am. And who can give me the assurance that this God has not arranged that there should be no earth, no heaven, no extended body, no figure, no magnitude, or place, and that nevertheless I should have the perception of all these things, and the persuasion that they do not exist other than as I see them? And, further, as I sometimes think that others are mistaken, even in the things they think they know most certainly, it is possible that God has wished that I should be deceived every time I add two and three or count the sides of a square, or form some judgement even simpler, if anything simpler than that can be imagined. But perhaps God has not wished me to be deceived in this way, for he is said to be supremely good. However, if it were in contradiction to his goodness to have made me in such a way that I always deceived myself, it would seem also to be contrary to his goodness to allow me to be wrong sometimes, and nevertheless it is beyond doubt that he permits it.

There will be some perhaps who would prefer to deny the existence of a God so powerful than to believe that all other things are uncertain. But let us not oppose them for the moment, and let us suppose in their favour that everything said here about a God is a fable. Nevertheless, however they suppose that I reached the state and being which I possess, whether they attribute it to some destiny or fate, or to chance or to a continuous sequence and conjunction of events, it is certain that, because fallibility and error are a kind of imperfection, the less powerful the author to whom they attribute my origin, the more probable it will be that I am so imperfect as to be deceived all the time. I have certainly nothing to say in reply to such reasonings, but am constrained to avow that, of all the opinions that I once accepted as true, there is not one which is not now legitimately open to doubt, not through any lack of reflection or lightness of judgement, but for very strong and deeply considered reasons; so that if I wish to find anything certain and assured in the sciences, I must from now on check and suspend judgement on these opinions and refrain from giving them more credence than I would do to things which appeared to me manifestly false.

But it is not enough to have made these observations; I must also take care to remember them; for those old and customary opinions still recur often in my mind, long and familiar usage giving them the right to occupy my mind against my will and, as it were, to dominate my mind. And I shall never rid myself of the habit of acquiescing in them and of having confidence in them so long as I look upon them as what in fact they are, that is to say, in some degree doubtful, as I have just shown, and yet highly probable, so that it is more reasonable to believe than to deny them. This is why I think I shall proceed more prudently if, taking an opposite course, I endeavour to deceive myself, pretending that all these opinions are false and imaginary, until, having so balanced my prejudices that they may not make my judgement incline more to one side than to another, my judgement may no longer be overpowered as hitherto by bad usage and turned from the right path which can lead it to the knowledge of truth. For I am assured that, meanwhile, there can be no danger or error in this course, and that, for the present, it would be impossible to press my distrust too far, for it is not now action I seek as my end but simply meditation and knowledge.

I shall suppose, therefore, that there is, not a true God, who is the sovereign source of truth, but some evil demon, no less cunning and deceiving than powerful, who has used all his artifice to deceive me. I will suppose that the heavens, the air, the earth, colours, shapes, sounds and all external things that we see, are only illusions and deceptions which he uses to take me in. I will consider myself as having no hands, eyes, flesh, blood or senses, but as believing wrongly that I have all these things. I shall cling obstinately to this notion; and if, by this means, it is not in my power to arrive at the knowledge of any truth, at the very least it is in my power to suspend my judgement. This is why I shall take great care not to accept into my belief anything false, and shall so well prepare my mind against all the tricks of this great deceiver that, however powerful and cunning he may be, he will never be able to impose on me.

But this undertaking is arduous, and a certain indolence leads me back imperceptibly into the ordinary course of life. And just as a slave who was enjoying in his sleep an imaginary freedom, fears to be awakened when he begins to suspect that his liberty is only a dream, and conspires with these pleasant illusions to be deceived by them longer, so I fall back of my own accord into my former opinions, and fear to awake from this slumber lest the laborious wakeful hours which would follow this peaceful rest, instead of bringing me any light of day into the knowledge of truth, would not be sufficient to disperse the shadows caused by the difficulties which have just been raised.

Second Meditation

Of the Nature of the Human Mind; and That It Is Easier to Know Than the Body

The Meditation of yesterday has filled my mind with so many doubts that it is no longer in my power to forget them. And yet I do not see how I shall be able to resolve them; and, as though I had suddenly fallen into very deep water, I am so taken unawares that I can neither put my feet firmly down on the bottom nor swim to keep myself on the surface. I make an effort, nevertheless, and follow afresh the same path upon which I entered yesterday, in keeping away from everything of which I can conceive the slightest doubt, just as if I knew that it was absolutely false; and I shall continue always in this path until I have encountered something which is certain, or at least, if I can do nothing else, until I have learned with certainty that there is nothing certain in the world.

Archimedes, in order to take the terrestrial globe from its place and move it to another, asked only for a point which was fixed and assured.

So also, I shall have the right to entertain high hopes, if I am fortunate enough to find only one thing which is certain and indubitable.

I suppose therefore that all the things I see are false; I persuade myself that none of those things ever existed that my deceptive memory represents to me; I suppose I have no senses; I believe that body, figure, extension, movement and place are only fictions of my mind. What, then, shall be considered true? Perhaps only this, that there is nothing certain in the world.

But how do I know there is not some other thing, different from those I have just judged to be uncertain, about which one could not have the slightest doubt? Is there not a God, or some other power, which puts these thoughts into my mind? But that is unnecessary, for perhaps I am capable of producing them myself. Myself, then, at least am I not something? But I have already denied that I have any senses or any body. I hesitate, however, for what follows from that? Am I so dependent on body and senses that I cannot exist without them? But I had persuaded myself that there was nothing at all in the world: no sky, no earth, no minds or bodies; was I not, therefore, also persuaded that I did not exist? No indeed; I existed without doubt, by the fact that I was persuaded, or indeed by the mere fact that I thought at all. But there is some deceiver both very powerful and very cunning, who constantly uses all his wiles to deceive me. There is therefore no doubt that I exist, if he deceives me; and let him deceive me as much as he likes, he can never cause me to be nothing, so long as I think I am something. So that, after having thought carefully about it, and having scrupulously examined everything, one must then, in conclusion, take as assured that the proposition: *I am, I exist,* is necessarily true, every time I express it or conceive of it in my mind.

But I, who am certain that I am, do not yet know clearly enough what I am; so that henceforth I must take great care not imprudently to take some other object for myself, and thus avoid going astray in this knowledge which I maintain to be more certain and evident than all I have had hitherto.

For this reason, I shall now consider afresh what I thought I was before I entered into these last thoughts; and I shall retrench from my former opinions everything that can be invalidated by the reasons I have already put forward, so that absolutely nothing remains except that which is entirely indubitable. What, then, did I formerly think I was? I thought I was a man. But what is a man? Shall I say rational animal? No indeed: for it would be necessary next to inquire what is meant by animal, and what by rational, and, in this way, from one single question, we would fall unwittingly into an infinite number of others, more difficult and awkward than the first, and I would not wish to waste the little time and leisure remaining to me by using it to unravel subtleties of this kind. But I shall rather stop to consider here the thoughts which sprang up hitherto spontaneously in my mind, and which were inspired by my own nature alone, when I applied myself to the consideration of my being. I considered myself, firstly, as having a face, hands, arms, and the whole machine made up of flesh and bones, such as it appears in a corpse and which I designated by the name of body. I thought, further-more, that I ate, walked, had feelings and thought, and I referred all these actions to the soul; but I did not stop to consider what this soul was, or at least, if I did, I imagined it was something extremely rare and subtle, like a wind, flame or vapour, which permeated and spread through my most substantial parts. As far as the body was concerned, I was in no doubt as to its nature, for I thought I knew it quite distinctly, and, if I had wished to explain it according to the notions I had of it, I would have described it in this way: by body, I understand all that can be terminated by some figure; that can be contained in some place and fill a space in such a way that any other body is excluded from it; that can be perceived, either by touch, sight, hearing, taste or smell; that can be moved in many ways, not of itself, but by something foreign to it by which it is touched and from which it receives the impulse. For, as to having in itself the power to move, to feel and to think, I did not believe in any way that these advantages might be attributed to corporeal nature; on the contrary, I was somewhat astonished to see that such faculties were to be found in certain bodies.

But as to myself, who am I, now that I suppose there is someone who is extremely powerful and, if I may so say, malicious and cun-ning, who employs all his efforts and industry to deceive me? Can I be sure of having the least of all the characteristics that I have attributed above to the nature of bodies? I pause to think about it carefully, I turn over all these things in my mind, and I cannot find one of which I can say that it is in me. There is no need for me to stop and enumer-ate them. Let us pass, then, to the attributes of the soul, and see if there are any of these in me. The first are eating and walking; but if it is true that I have no body, it is true also that I cannot walk or eat. Sensing is another attribute, but again this is impossible without the body; besides, I have frequently believed that I perceived in my sleep many things which I observed, on awakening, I had not in reality perceived. Another attribute is thinking, and I here discover an attribute which does belong to me; this alone cannot be detached from me. *I am, I exist*: this is certain; but for how long? For as long as I think, for it might perhaps happen, if I ceased to think, that I would at the same time cease to be or to exist. I now admit nothing which is not necessarily true: I am therefore, precisely speaking, only a thing which thinks, that is to say, a mind, understanding, or reason, terms whose significance was hitherto unknown to me. I am, however, a real thing, and really existing; but what thing? I have already said it: a thing which thinks. And what else? I will stir up my imagination in order to discover if I am not something more. I am not this assemblage of limbs called the human body; I am not a thin and penetrating air spread through all these members; I am not a wind, a breath of air, a vapour, or anything at all that I can invent or imagine, since I have supposed that all those things were nothing, and yet, without changing this supposition, I find I am nevertheless certain that I am something.

But also, it may be that these same things that I suppose do not exist, because they are unknown to me, are not in truth different from me whom I know. I do not know; I am not debating this point now. I can judge only of things which are known to me: I have recognized that I exist, and I, who recognize I exist, seek to discover what I am. It is most certain, however, that this notion and knowledge of myself, thus precisely taken, do not depend on things the existence of which is not yet known to me; neither, consequently, and *a fortiori,* do they depend on any of those which are feigned and invented by the imagination. And even these terms feigning and imagining, warn me of my error; for I should be feigning, in truth, if I were to imagine that I am anything, since imagining is nothing other than contemplating the figure or image of a corporeal object. Now I know already for certain that I exist, and at the same time that it is possible that all those images, and, in general, all the things one relates to the nature of body, are nothing but dreams or chimera. From this I see clearly that it is as unreasonable for me to say: I shall stir up my imagination in order to know more distinctly what I am, as to say: I am now awake, and I perceive something real and true; but, because I do not perceive it clearly enough, I shall go to sleep expressly so that my dreams may show this object to me with greater truth and clearness. And in this way, I recognize certainly that nothing of all that I can understand by means of imagination belongs to this knowledge that I have of myself, and that it is necessary to call one's mind back and turn it away from this mode of thinking, so that it can itself recognize its own nature very distinctly.

But what, then, am I? A thing that thinks. What is a thing that thinks? That is to say, a thing that doubts, perceives, affirms, denies, wills, does not will, that imagines also, and which feels. Indeed this is not a little, if all these properties belong to my nature. But why should they not so belong? Am I not still this same being who doubts of almost everything; who nevertheless understands and conceives certain things; who affirms those alone to be true; who denies all the rest; who wishes and desires to know more of them and does not wish to be deceived; who imagines many things, even sometimes in spite of himself; and who also perceives many, as if through the intermediary of the organs of the body? Is there nothing in all this which is as true as it is certain that I am, and that I exist, even though I were always to be sleeping, and though he who has given me my being should use all his power to deceive me? Is there also any one of these attributes which may be distinguished from my thought, or that one could say was separate from me? For it is so self evident that it is I who doubt, who understand and who wish, that there is no need here to add anything to explain it. And I have equally certainly the power to imagine, for even though it may be (as I have supposed above) that the things I imagine are not true, nevertheless, this capacity for imagining does not cease to be really in me, and forms part of my thinking. Finally, I am the same being who senses, that is to say who apprehends and knows things, as by the sense-organs, since, in truth, I see light, hear noise and feel heat. But it will be said that these appearances are false and that I am dreaming. Let it be so; all the same, at least, it is very certain that it seems to me that I see light, hear a noise and feel heat; and this is properly what in me is called perceiving and this, taken in this precise sense, is nothing other than thinking. From this I begin to know what I am, a little more clearly and distinctly than hitherto.

But I cannot help believing that corporeal objects, whose images are formed by my thoughts, and which come under the senses, are more distinctly known to me than that, I know not what, part of me which does not fall within the grasp of the imagination; although in truth it may seem very strange that things I find doubtful and distant, are more clearly and easily known to me than those which are true and certain, and which belong to my own nature. But I see very well how it is: my mind likes to wander, and cannot yet contain itself within the precise limits of truth. Let us therefore give it its head once more, so that, later on, tightening the reins gently and opportunely, we shall the more easily be able to govern and control it.

Let us begin by considering the most common things, those which we believe we understand the most distinctly, namely, the bodies we touch and see. I am not speaking of bodies in general, for these general notions are usually more confused, but of one body in particular. Let us take, for example, this piece of wax which has just been taken from the hive; it has not yet lost the sweetness of the honey it contained; it still retains something of the smell of the flowers from which it was gathered; its colour, shape and size, are apparent; it is hard, cold, it is tangible; and if you tap it, it will emit a sound. So, all the things by which a body can be known distinctly are to be found together in this one.

But, as I am speaking, it is placed near a flame: what remained of its taste is dispelled, the smell disappears, its colour changes, it loses its shape, it grows bigger, becomes liquid, warms up, one can hardly touch it, and although one taps it, it will no longer make any sound. Does the same wax remain after this change? One must admit that it does remain, and no one can deny it. What, then, was it that I knew in this piece of wax with such distinctness? Certainly it could be nothing of all the things which I perceived by means of the senses, for everything which fell under taste, smell, sight, touch or hearing, is changed, and yet the same wax remains. Perhaps it was what I now think, namely, that the wax was not the sweetness of honey, or the pleasant smell of flowers, the whiteness, or the shape, nor the sound, but only a body which a little earlier appeared to me in these forms, and which is now to be perceived in other forms. But to speak precisely, what is it that I imagine when I conceive it in this way? Let us consider it attentively, and setting aside everything that does not belong to the wax, let us see what remains. Indeed nothing remains, except something extended, flexible and malleable. Now, what does that mean: flexible and malleable? Is it not that I imagine that this wax, being round, is capable of becoming square, and of passing from a square to a triangular figure? No indeed, it is not that, for I conceive of it as capable of undergoing an infinity of similar changes, and as I could not embrace this infinity by my imagination, consequently this conception I have of the wax is not the product of the faculty of imagination.

What, now, is this extension? Is it not also unknown, since it increases as the wax melts, is greater when the wax is completely melted, and very much greater still when the heat is intensified; and I should not conceive clearly and according to truth what the wax is, if I did not remember that it is capable of taking on more variations in extension that I have ever imagined. I must therefore agree that I could not even conceive by means of the imagination what this wax is, and that it is my understanding alone which conceives it. I say this piece of wax in particular, for, as to wax in general, this is still more evident. Now, what is this wax, which cannot be conceived except by the understanding or mind? Indeed it is the same which I see, touch, imagine, and which I knew from the start. But, and this is to be noted, the perception of it, or the action by which one perceives it, is not an act of sight, or touch, or of imagination, and has never been, although it seemed so hitherto, but only an intuition of the mind, which may be imperfect and confused, as it was formerly, or else clear and distinct, as it is at present according as my attention directs itself more or less to the elements which it contains and of which it is composed.

However, I am greatly astonished when I consider the weakness of my mind, and its proneness to error. For although, without speaking, I consider all this in my own mind, yet words stop me, and I am almost led into error by the terms of ordinary language. For we say we see the same wax if it is put before us, and not that we judge it to be the same, because it has the same colour and shape: whence I would almost conclude that one knows the wax by the eyesight, and not by the intuition of the mind alone. If I chance to look out of a window on to men passing in the street, I do not fail to say, on seeing them, that I see men, just as I say that I see the wax; and yet, what do I see from this window, other than hats and cloaks, which can cover ghosts or dummies who move only by means of springs? But I judge them to be really men, and thus I understand, by the sole power of judgement which resides in my mind, what I believed I saw with my eyes.

A man who wishes to lift his knowledge above the common, must feel ashamed to seek occasions for doubting from the forms and terms of common speech. I prefer to avoid this and to go on to consider whether I conceived more evidently and perfectly what the wax is when I first saw it, and believed I knew it by means of my external senses, or at the very least by the common sense, as it is called, that is to say by the imaginative faculty, than I conceive it at present, after having more carefully examined what it is and by what means it can be known. Indeed, it would be ridiculous to have any doubt on this point. For what was there in that first perception that was distinct and evident, and which could not be perceived in the same way by the senses of the least of animals? But when I distinguish the wax from its external forms, and, just as if I had removed its garments, I consider it quite naked, it is certain that, although some error in my judgement may still be encountered, I cannot conceive of it in this way without possessing a human mind.

But finally, what shall I say of this mind, that is to say of myself? For so far I admit in myself nothing other than a mind. What shall I say of myself, I ask, I who seem to conceive so clearly and distinctly this piece of wax? Do I not know myself, not only with much more truth and certainty, but also more distinctly and clearly? For if I judge that the wax is, or exists, because I see it, certainly it follows much more evidently from the same fact that I myself am, or exist. For it may well be that what I see is not in effect wax; it may also be that I do not even have eyes with which to see anything; but it cannot be that, when I see or (which I no longer distinguish) think I see, I, who think, am nothing. Similarly, if I judge that the wax exists because I touch it, the same conclusion follows, namely, that I am. And if I judge thus because my imagination persuades me that it is so, or on account of any other cause whatever, I shall still draw the same conclusion. And what I have said here about the wax can apply to all the other things external to me.

Now, if my notion and knowledge of the wax seems to be more precise and distinct after it has become known to me not only by sight or touch, but also in many other ways, with how much greater distinctness, clarity and precision must I know myself, since all the means which help me to know and perceive the nature of wax, or of any other body, prove much more easily and evidently the nature of my mind? And so many other things besides are to be found in the mind itself, which can contribute to the clarification of its nature, that those which depend on the body, such as these mentioned here, scarcely deserve to be taken into account.

But now I have come back imperceptibly to the point I sought; for, since it is now known to me that, properly speaking, we perceive bodies only by the understanding which is in us, and not by the imagination, or the senses, and that we do not perceive them through seeing them or touching them, but only because we conceive them in thought, I know clearly that there is nothing more easy for me to know than my own mind. But, because it is almost impossible to rid oneself so quickly of a long-held opinion, I should do well to pause at this point, so that, by long meditation, I may imprint this new knowledge more deeply in my memory.

Bad Dreams, Evil Demons, and the Experience Machine: Philosophy and *The Matrix*

Christopher Grau

I. Dream Skepticism

MORPHEUS: Have you ever had a dream, Neo, that you were so sure was real?

MORPHEUS: What if you were unable to wake from that dream, Neo? How would you know the difference between the dreamworld and the real world?

Neo has woken up from a hell of a dream—the dream that was his life. How was he to know? The cliché is that if you are dreaming and you pinch yourself, you will wake up. Unfortunately, things aren't quite that simple. It is the nature of most dreams that we take them for reality—while dreaming, we are unaware that we are in dream world. Of course, we eventually wake up, and when we do, we realize that our experience was all in our mind. Neo's predicament makes us wonder, though how can any of us be sure that we have ever genuinely woken up? Perhaps, like Neo prior to his downing the red pill, our dreams thus far have in fact been dreams *within* a dream.

The idea that what we take to be the real world could all be just a dream is familiar to many students of philosophy, poetry, and literature. Most of us, at onetime or another, have been struck with the thought that we might mistake a dream for reality, or reality for a dream. Arguably the most famous exponent of this worry in the western philosophical tradition is the seventeenth-century French philosopher René Descartes. In an attempt to provide a firm foundation for knowledge, he began his *Meditations* by clearing the philosophical ground through doubting all that could be doubted. This was done, in part, in order to determine if anything that could count as certain knowledge could survive such rigorous and systematic skepticism. Descartes takes the first step toward this goal by raising (through his fictional narrator) the possibility that we might be dreaming:

> How often, asleep at night am I convinced of just such familiar events—that I am here in my dressing-gown, sitting by the fire—when in fact I am lying undressed in bed! Yet at the moment my eyes are certainly wide awake when I look at this piece of paper; I shake my head and it is not asleep; as I stretch out and feel my hand I do so deliberately, and I know what I am doing. All this would not happen with such distinctness to someone asleep. Indeed! As if I did not remember other occasions when I have been tricked by exactly similar thoughts while asleep! As I think about this more carefully, I see plainly that there are never any sure signs by means of which being awake can be distinguished from being asleep. The result is that I begin to feel dazed, and this very feeling only reinforces the notion that I may be sleep.[1]

When we dream, we are often blissfully ignorant that we are dreaming. Given this, and the fact that dreams often seem as vivid and "realistic" as real life, how can you rule out the possibility that you might be dreaming even now, as you sit and read this? This is the kind of perplexing thought that Descartes forces us to confront. It seems we have no justification for the belief that we are not dreaming. If so, then it seems we similarly have no justification in thinking that the world we experience is the *real* world. Indeed, it becomes questionable whether we are justified in thinking that any of our beliefs are true.

The narrator of Descartes's *Meditations* worries about this, but he ultimately maintains that the possibility that one might be dreaming cannot by itself cast doubt on all we think we know; he points out that even if all our sensory experience is but a dream, we can still conclude that we have *some* knowledge of the nature of reality. Just as a painter cannot create ex nibilo but must rely on pigments with which to create her image, certain elements of our thought must exit prior to our imaginings. Among the items of knowledge that Descartes thought survived dream skepticism are truths arrived at through the use of reason, such as the truths of mathematics: "For whether I am awake or asleep, two and three added together are five, and a square has no more than four sides" (296–297).

While such an insight offers little comfort to someone wondering whether the people and objects she confronts are genuine, it served

---

[1] René Descartes, *Mediations on First Philosophy*, ed. and trans. J. Cottingham (Cambridge University Press 1985); see appendix, pp. 295–296. Further citations will be in the text.

Descartes's larger philosophical project: he sought, among other things, to provide a foundation for knowledge in which truths arrived at through reason are given priority over knowledge gained from experience. (This bias shouldn't surprise those who remember that Descartes was a brilliant mathematician in addition to being a philosopher.) Descartes was not himself a skeptic—he employs this skeptical argument so as to help remind the reader that the truths of mathematics (and other truths of reason) are on firmer ground than the data provided to us by our senses.

Despite the fact that Descartes's ultimate goal was to demonstrate how genuine knowledge is possible, he proceeds in *The Meditations* to utilize a much more radical skeptical argument, one that casts doubt on even his beloved mathematical truths. In the next section we will see that, many years before the Wachowskis dreamed up *The Matrix*, Descartes had imagined an equally terrifying Possibility.

II. Brains in Vats and the Evil Demon

MORPHEUS: What is the Matrix? Control.
MORPHEUS: The Matrix is a computer-generated dreamworld built to keep us under control in order to change a human being into this. [holds up a battery]
NEO: No! I don't believe it! It's not Possible!

Before breaking out of Matrix, Neo's life was not what he thought it was. It was a lie, Morpheus describes it as a "dreamworld," but unlike a dream, this world is not the creation of Neo's mind. The truth is more sinister: the world is a creation of the artificially intelligent computers that have taken over the Earth and have subjugated humanity in the process. These creatures have fed Neo a simulation that he couldn't possibly help but take as the real thing. What's worse, it isn't clear how any of us can know with certainty that we are not in a position similar to Neo before his "rebirth." Our ordinary confidence in our ability to reason and our natural tendency to trust the deliverances of our senses can both course to seem rather naive once confront this possibility of deception.

A viewer of *The Matrix* is naturally led to wonder: how do I know I am not in the Matrix? How do I know for sure that my world is not also a sophisticated charade, put forward by some superhuman intelligence in such a way that I cannot possibly detect the ruse? Descartes suggested a similar worry: the frightening possibility that all of one's experiences might be the result of a powerful outside force, a "malicious demon":

> And yet firmly rooted in my mind is the long opinion that there is an omnipotent God who made me the kind of creature that I am. How do I know that he has not brought it about that there is no earth, no sky, no extend thing, no shape, no size, no place, while at the same time ensuring that all these things appear to me to exit just as they do now? What is more, just as I consider that others sometimes go astray in cases where they think they have the most perfect knowledge, how do I know that God has not brought it about that too go wrong every time I add two and three or count the sides of a square, or in some even simpler matter, if that is imaginable? But perhaps God would not have allowed me to be deceived in this way, since he is said to be supremely good:. . . I will suppose therefore that not God, Who is supremely good and the source of truth, but rather some malicious demon of the utmost power and cunning has employed all his energies in order to deceive me. I shall think that the sky, the air, the earth, colours, shapes, sounds and all external things are merely the delusions of dreams which he has devised to ensure my judgement (297–298).

The narrator of Descartes's *Meditations* concludes that none of his former opinion are safe. Such a demon could not only deceive him about his perceptions, it could conceivably cause him to go wrong when performing even the simplest acts of reasoning.

This radical worry seems inescapable. How could you possibly prove to yourself that you are not in the kind of nightmarish situation Descartes describes? It would seem that any argument, evidence, or proof you might put forward could easily be yet another trick played by the demon. As ludirous as the idea of the evil demon may sound at first, it is hard, upon reflection, not to share Decartes's worry: for all you know, you may well be a mere plaything of such a malevolent intelligence. More to the point of our general discussion: for all you know, you may well be trapped in the Matrix.

Many contemporary philosophers have discussed a similar skeptical dilemna that is a bit closer to the scenario described in *The Matrix*. It has come to be known as the "brain in a vat" hypothesis, and one powerful formulation of the idea is presented by philosopher Jonathan Dancy:

> You do not know that you are not a brain, suspended in a vat full of liquid in a laboratory, and wired to a computer which is feeding you your current experiences under the control of some ingenious technician

scientist the nevoleat of malevolent according to tasle). For if you ware such a brain, then, provided that the scientist is successful, nothing in your experience could possibly reveal that you were; for your experience is *ex hypothesis* identical with that of something which is not a brain in a vat. Since you have only your own experience to appeal to, and that experience is the same in either situation, nothing can reveal to you which situation is the acloualone.[2]

If you cannot know whether you are in the real world or in the world of a computer simulation, you cannot be sure that your beliefs about the world are true. And, what was even more frightening to Descartes, in this kind of scenario it seems that your ability to reason is no safer than the deliverances of the senses: the evil demon or malicions scientist could be ensuring that your reasoning is just as flawed as your perceptions.

As you have probably already guessed, there is no easy way out of this philosophical problem (or at least there is no easy *Philosophical* way out). Philosophers have proposed a dizzying variety of "solutions" to this kind of skepticism but, as with many philosophical problems, there is nothing close to unanimous agreement regarding how the puzzle should be solved.

Descartes's own way out of his evil-demon skepticism was to first argue that one cannot genuinely doubt the existence of oneself. He pointed out that all thinking presupposes a thinker: even in doubting, you realize that there must at least be a self which is doing the doubting. (Thus Descartes's most famous line: "I think, therefore I am.") He then went on to claim that, in addition to our innate idea of self, each of us has an idea of God as an all-powerful, all-good, and infinite being implanted in our minds and that this idea could only have come *from* God. Since this shows us that an all-good God does exist, we can have confidence that he would not allow us to be so drastically deceived about the nature of our perceptions and their relationship to reality. While Descartes's argument for the existence of the self has been tremendously influential and is still actively debated, few philosophers have followed him in accepting his particular theistic solution to skepticism about the external world.

One of the more interesting contemporary challenges to the kind of radical skepticism suggested by Descartes has come from philosopher Hilary Putman. His point is not so much to defend our ordinary claims to knowledge as to question whether the brain-in-a-vat hypothesis is

---

[2]Jonathan Dancy, *Introduction to Contemporary Epistanology* (Blackwell 1965), p. 10.

coherent, given certain plausible assumptions about how our language refers to objects in the world. He asks us to consider a variation on the standard brain-in-a-vat story that is uncannify similar to the situation described in *The Matrix:*

> Instead of having just one brain in a vat, we could imagine that all human beings (perhaps all sentient beings) are brains in a vat for nervous systems in a vat in case some beings with just nervous systems count as "sentient"). Of course, the evil scientist would have to be outside? or would he? Perhaps there is no evil scientist, perhaps (though this is absurd) the universe just happens to consist of automatic machinery tending a vat full of brains and nervous systems. This time let us suppose that the automatic machinery is programmed to give us all a *collective* hallucination, rather than a number of separate unrelated hallucinations. Thus, when I seem to myself to be talking to you, you seem to yourself to be hearing my words. . . . I want now to ask a question which will seem very silly and obvious (at least to some people, including some very sophisticated Philosophers), but which will take us to real Philosophical depiles rather quickly. Suppose this whole story were actually true. Could we, if we were brains in a vat in this way, *say* or *think* that we were![3]

Putnam's surprising answer is that we cannot coherently think that we are brains in vats, and so skepticism of that kind can never really get off the ground. While it is difficult to do justice to Putnam's ingenious argument in a short summary, his point is roughly as follows: not everything that goes through our heads is a genuine thought, and far from everything we say is a meaningful utterance. Sometimes we get confused or think in an incoherent manner; Sometimes we say things that are simply nonsense. of course, we don't always realize at the time that we aren't making sense: sometimes we earnestly believe we are saying (or thinking) something meaningful. High on nitrous oxide, the philosopher William James was convinced he was having profound insights into the nature of reality; he was convinced that his thoughts were both sensical and important. Upon subering up and looking at the notebook in which he had written his drug-addled thoughts, he saw only gibberish.

Just as I might say a sentence that is nonsense, I might also use a name or a general term that is meaningless in the sense that it fails to look up to the world. Philosophers talk of such a term as "failing to

---

[3]Hilary Putnam, *Reason, Truth, and History* (Cambridge University Press 1981); set appendix, pp. 317–318.

refer" to an object. In order to successfully refer when we use language, there must be an appropriate relationship between the speaker and the object refered to. If a dog playing on the beach manages to scrawl the world "Ed" in the sand with a stick, few would want to claim that the dog actually meant to refer to someone named Ed. Presumably the dog doesn't know anyone named Ed, and even if he did, he wouldn't be capable of intending to write Ed's name in the sand. The point of such an example is that words do not refer to objects "magically" or intrinsically: certain conditions must be met in the world in order for us to accept that a given written or spoken word has any meaning and whether it actually refers to anything at all.

Putnam claims that one condition which is crucial for successful reference is that there be an appropriate casual connection between the object referred to and the speaker referring. Specifying exactly what should count as "appropriate" here is a notoriously difficult task, but we can get some idea of the kind of thing required by considering cases in which reference fails through an inappropriate connection: if someone unfamiliar with the film *The Matrix* manages to blurt out the word "Neo" while sneezing, few would be inclined to think that this person has actually *referred* to the character Neo. The kind of casual connection between the speaker and the object referred to (Neo) is just not in place. For reference to succeed, it can't be simply accidental that the name was uttered. (Another way to think about it: the sneezer would have uttered "Neo" even if the film *The Matrix* had never been made.)

The difficulty, according to Putnam, in coherently supposing the brain-in-a-vat story to be true is that brains raised in such an environment could not successfully refer to genuine brains, or vats, or anything else in the real world. Consider the example of some people who lived their entire lives in the Matrix: when they talk of "chickens," they don't actually refer to real *chickens* at best they refer to the computer representations of chickens that have been sent to their brains. Similarly, when they talk of human bodies being trapped in pods and fed data by the Matrix, they don't successfully refer to real bodies or pods. They can't refer to physical bodies in the real world because they cannot have the appropriate casual connection to such objects. Thus, if someone were to utter the sentence "I am simply a body stuck in a pod somewhere being fed sensory information by a computer," that sentence would itself be necessarily false. If the person is in fact not trapped in the Matrix, then the sentence is straightforwardly false. If the person is trapped in the Matrix, then he can't successfully refer to real human bodies when he utters the term "human body," and so it appears that under this circumstance, his statement must *also* be false.

Such as a person seems thus doubly trapped: incapable of knowing that he is in the Matrix and even incapable of successfully expressing the thought that he might be in the Matrix (Could this he why at one point Morpheas tells Neo that "no one can be told what the Matrix is"?).

Putnam's argument is controversial, but it is noteworthy because it shows that the kind of situation described in *The Matrix* raises not just the expected philosophical issues about knowledge and skepticism, but more general issues regarding meaning, language, and the relationship between the mind and the world. . . .

On the Value of Skepticism

Bertrand Russell

I wish to propose a doctrine which may, I fear, appear wildly paradoxical and subversive. The doctrine in question is this: that it is undesirable to believe a proposition when there is no ground whatever for supposing it true. I must, of course, admit that if such an opinion became common it would completely transform our social life and our political system; since both are at present faultless, this must weigh against it. I am also aware (what is more serious) that it would tend to diminish the incomes of clairvoyants, bookmakers, bishops, and others who live on the irrational hopes of those who have done nothing to deserve good fortune here or hereafter. In spite of these grave arguments, I maintain that a case can be made out of my paradox, and I shall try to set it forth.

First of all, I wish to guard myself against being thought to take up an extreme position. [. . .] I am prepared to admit the ordinary beliefs of common sense, in practice if not in theory. I am prepared to admit any well-established result of science, not as certainly true, but as sufficiently probable to afford a basis for rational action.

There are matters about which those who have investigated them are agreed; the dates of eclipses may serve as an illustration. There are other matters about which experts are not agreed. Even when the experts all agree, they may well be mistaken. Einstein's view as to the magnitude of the deflection of light by gravitation would have been rejected by all experts not many years ago, yet it proved to be right. Nevertheless the opinion of experts, when it is unanimous, must be accepted by non-experts as more likely to be right than the opposite opinion. The skepticism that I advocate amounts only to this: (1) that when the experts are agreed, the opposite opinion cannot be held to be certain; (2) that when they are not agreed, no opinion can be regarded as certain by a non-expert; and (3) that when they all hold that no sufficient grounds for a positive opinion exist, the ordinary man would do well to suspend his judgment.

These propositions may seem mild, yet, if accepted, they would absolutely revolutionize human life.

The opinions for which people are willing to fight and persecute all belong to one of the three classes which this skepticism condemns. When there are rational grounds for an opinion, people are content to set them forth and wait for them to operate. In such cases, people do not hold their opinions with passion; they hold them calmly, and set forth their reasons quietly. The opinions that are held with passion are always those for which no good ground exists; indeed the passion is the measure of the holder's lack of rational conviction. Opinions in politics and religion are almost always held passionately. Except in China, a man is thought a poor creature unless he has strong opinions on such matters; people hate skeptics far more than they hate the passionate advocates of opinions hostile to their own. It is thought that the claims of practical life demand opinions on such questions, and that, if we became more rational, social existence would be impossible. I believe the opposite of this, and will try to make it clear why I have this belief.

Take the question of unemployment in the years after 1920. One party held that it was due to the wickedness of trade unions, another that it was due to the confusion on the Continent. A third party, while admitting that these causes played a part, attributed most of the trouble to the policy of the Bank of England in trying to increase the value of the pound sterling. This third party, I am given to understand, contained most of the experts, but no one else. Politicians do not find any attractions in a view which does not lend itself to party declamation, and ordinary mortals prefer views which attribute misfortune to the machinations of their enemies. Consequently people fight for and against quite irrelevant measures, while the few who have a rational opinion are not listened to because they do not minister to any one's passions. To produce converts, it would have been necessary to persuade people that the Bank of England is wicked. To convert Labour, it would have been necessary to show that directors of the Bank of England are hostile to trade unionism; to convert the Bishop of London, it would have been necessary to show that they are "immoral." It would be thought to follow that their views on currency are mistaken. [. . .]

I will now venture on a topic which people find even more difficulty in treating dispassionately, namely marriage customs. The bulk of the population of every country is persuaded that all marriage customs other than its own are immoral, and that those who combat this view do so only in order to justify their own loose lives. In India, the remarriage of widows is traditionally regarded as a thing too horrible to contemplate. In Catholic countries divorce is thought very wicked, but some failure of conjugal fidelity is tolerated, at least in men. In America divorce is easy, but extra-conjugal relations are condemned with the utmost severity. Mohammedans believe in polygamy, which we think degrading. All these differing opinions are held with extreme vehemence, and very cruel persecutions are inflicted upon those who contravene them. Yet no one in any of the various countries makes the slightest attempt to show that the custom of his own country contributes more to human happiness than the custom of others.

When we open any scientific treatise on the subject, such as (for example) Westermarck's *History of Human Marriage,* we find an atmosphere extraordinarily different from that of popular prejudice. We find that every kind of custom has existed, many of them such as we should have supposed repugnant to human nature. We think we can understand polygamy, as a custom forced upon women by male oppressors. But what are we to say of the Tibetan custom, according to which one woman has several husbands? Yet travellers in Tibet assure us that family life there is at least as harmonious as in Europe. A little of such reading must soon reduce any candid person to complete skepticism, since there seem to be no data enabling us to say that one marriage custom is better or worse than another. Almost all involve cruelty and intolerance towards offenders against the local code, but otherwise they have nothing in common. It seems that sin is geographical. From this conclusion, it is only a small step to the further conclusion that the notion of "sin" is illusory, and that the cruelty habitually practiced in punishing it is unnecessary. It is just this conclusion which is so unwelcome to many minds, since the infliction of cruelty with a good conscience is a delight to moralists. That is why they invented Hell.

Nationalism is of course an extreme example of fervent belief concerning doubtful matters. I think it may be safely said that any scientific historian, writing now a history of the Great War, is bound to make statements which, if made during the war, would have exposed him to imprisonment in every one of the belligerent countries on both sides. Again, with the exception of China, there is no country where people tolerate the truth about themselves; at ordinary times the truth is only thought ill-mannered, but in war-time it is thought criminal. Opposing systems of violent belief are built up, the falsehood of which is evident from the fact that they are believed only by those who share the same national bias. But the application of reason to these systems of belief is thought as wicked as the application of reason to religious dogmas was formerly thought. When people are challenged as to why skepticism in such matters should be wicked, the only answer is that myths help to win wars, so that a rational nation would be killed rather than kill. The view that there is something shameful in saving one's skin by wholesale slander of foreigners is one which, so far as I know, has hitherto found no supporters among professional moralists outside the ranks of Quakers. If it is suggested that a rational nation would find ways of keeping out of wars altogether, the answer is usually more abuse.

What would be the effect of a spread of rational skepticism? Human events spring from passions, which generate systems of attendant myths. Psychoanalysts have studied the individual manifestations of this process in lunatics, certified and uncertified. A man who has suffered some humiliation invents a theory that he is King of England, and develops all kinds of ingenious explanations of the fact that he is not treated with that respect which his exalted position demands. In this case, his delusion is one with which his neighbours do not sympathize, so they lock him up. But if, instead of asserting only his own greatness, he asserts the greatness of his nation or his class or his creed, he wins hosts of adherents, and becomes a political or religious leader, even if, to the impartial outsider, his views seem just as absurd as those found in asylums. In this way a collective insanity grows up, which follows laws very similar to those of individual insanity. Every one knows that it is dangerous to dispute with a lunatic who thinks he is King of England; but as he is isolated, he can be overpowered. When a whole nation shares a delusion, its anger is of the same kind as that of an individual lunatic if its pretensions are disputed, but nothing short of war can compel it to submit to reason.

The part played by intellectual factors in human behaviour is a matter as to which there is much disagreement among psychologists. There are two quite distinct questions: (1) how far are beliefs operative as causes of actions? (2) how far are beliefs derived from logically adequate evidence, or capable of being so derived? On both questions, psychologists are agreed in giving a much smaller place to the intellectual factors than the plain man would give, but within this general agreement there is room for considerable differences of degree. Let us take the two questions in succession.

(1) How far are beliefs operative as causes of action? Let us not discuss the question theoretically, but let us take an ordinary day of an ordinary man's life. He begins by getting up in the morning, probably from force of habit, without the intervention of any belief. He eats his breakfast, catches his train, reads his newspaper, and goes to his office, all from force of habit. There was a time in the past when he formed these habits, and in the choice of the office, at least, belief played a part. He probably believed, at the time, that the job offered him there was as good as he was likely to get. In most men, belief plays a part in the original choice of a career, and therefore, derivatively, in all that is entailed by this choice.

At the office, if he is an underling, he may continue to act merely from habit, without active volition, and without the explicit intervention of belief. It might be thought that, if he adds up the columns of figures, he believes the arithmetical rules which he employs. But that would be an error; these rules are mere habits of his body, like those of a tennis player. They were acquired in youth, not from an intellectual belief that they corresponded to the truth, but to please the schoolmaster, just as a dog learns to sit on its hind legs and beg for food. I do not say that all education is of this sort, but certainly most learning of the three R's is.

If, however, our friend is a partner or director, he may be called upon during his day to make difficult decisions of policy. In these decisions it is probable that belief will play a part. He believes that some things will go up and others will go down, that so-and-so is a sound man, and such-and-such on the verge of bankruptcy. On these beliefs he acts. It is just because he is called upon to act on beliefs rather than mere habits that he is considered such a much greater man than a mere clerk, and is able to get so much more money—provided his beliefs are true.

In his home-life there will be much the same proportion of occasions when belief is a cause of action. At ordinary times, his behaviour to his wife and children will be governed by habit, or by instinct modified by habit. On great occasions—when he proposes marriage, when he decides what school to send his son to, or when he finds reason to suspect his wife of unfaithfulness—he cannot be guided wholly by habit. In proposing marriage, he may be guided more by instinct, or he may be influenced by the belief that the lady is rich. If he is guided by instinct, he no doubt believes that the lady possesses every virtue, and this may seem to him to be a cause of his action, but in fact it is merely another effect of the instinct which alone suffices to account for his action. In choosing a school for his son, he probably proceeds in much the same way as in making difficult business decisions; here belief usually plays an important part. If evidence comes into his possession showing that his wife has been unfaithful, his behaviour is likely to be purely instinctive, but the instinct is set in operation by a belief, which is the first cause of everything that follows.

Thus, although beliefs are not directly responsible for more than a small part of our actions, the actions for which they are responsible are among the most important, and largely determine the general structure of our lives. In particular, our religious and political actions are associated with beliefs.

(2) I come now to our second question, which is itself twofold: (*a*) how far are beliefs in fact based upon evidence? (*b*) how far is it possible or desirable that they should be?

(*a*) The extent to which beliefs are based upon evidence is very much less than believers suppose. Take the kind of action which is most nearly rational: the investment of money by a rich City man. You will often find that his view (say) on the question whether the French franc will go up or down depends upon his political sympathies, and yet is so strongly held that he is prepared to risk money on it. In bankruptcies it often appears that some sentimental factor was the original cause of ruin. Political opinions are hardly ever based upon evidence, except in the case of civil servants, who are forbidden to give utterance to them. There are of course exceptions. In the tariff reform controversy which began several years ago, most manufacturers supported the side that would increase their own incomes, showing that their opinions were really based on evidence, however little their utterances would have led one to suppose so. We have here a complication. Freudians have accustomed us to "rationalizing," i.e. the process of inventing what seem to ourselves rational grounds for a decision or opinion that is in fact quite irrational. But there is, especially in English-speaking countries, a converse process which may be called "irrationalizing." A shrewd man will sum up, more or less subconsciously, the pros and cons of a question from a selfish point of view. (Unselfish considerations seldom weigh subconsciously except where one's children are concerned.) Having come to a sound egoistic decision by the help of the unconscious, a man proceeds to invent, or adopt from others, a set of high-sounding phrases showing how he is pursuing the public good at immense personal sacrifice. Anybody who believes that these phrases give his real reasons must suppose him quite incapable of judging evidence, since the supposed public good is not going to result from his action. In this case a man appears less rational than he is; what is still more curious, the irrational part of him is conscious and the rational part unconscious. It is this trait in our characters that has made the English and Americans so successful.

Shrewdness, when it is genuine, belongs more to the unconscious than to the conscious part of our nature. It is, I suppose, the main quality required for success in business. From a moral point of view, it is a humble quality, since it is always selfish; yet it suffices to keep men from the worst crimes. If the Germans had had it, they would not have adopted the unlimited submarine campaign. If the French had had it, they would not have behaved as they did in the Ruhr. If Napoleon had had it, he would not have gone to war again after the Treaty of Amiens. It may be laid down as a general rule to which there are few exceptions that, when people are mistaken as to what is to their own interest, the course that they believe to be wise is more harmful to others than the course that really is wise. Therefore anything that makes people better judges of their own interest does good. There are innumerable examples of men making fortunes because, on moral grounds, they did something which they believed to be contrary to their own interests. For instance, among early Quakers there were a number of shopkeepers who adopted the practice of asking no more for their goods than they were willing to accept, instead of bargaining with each customer, as everybody else did. They adopted this practice because they held it to be a lie to ask more than they would take. But the convenience to customers was so great that everybody came to their shops, and they grew rich. (I forget where I read this, but if my memory serves me right it was in some reliable source.) The same policy *might* have been adopted from shrewdness, but in fact no one was sufficiently shrewd. Our unconscious is more malevolent than it pays us to be; therefore the people who do most completely what is in fact to their interest are those who deliberately, on moral grounds, do what they believe to be against their interest. Next to them come the people who try to think out rationally and consciously what is to their own interest, eliminating as far as possible the influence of passion. Third come the people who have instinctive shrewdness. Last of all come the people whose malevolence overbalances their shrewdness, making them pursue the ruin of others in ways that lead to their own ruin. This last class embraces 90% of the population of Europe.

I may seem to have digressed somewhat from my topic, but it was necessary to disentangle unconscious reason, which is called shrewdness, from the conscious variety. The ordinary methods of education have practically no effect upon the unconscious, so that shrewdness cannot be taught by our present technique. Morality, also, except where it consists of mere habit, seems incapable of being taught by present methods; at any rate I have never noticed any beneficent effect upon those who are exposed to frequent exhortations. Therefore on our present lines any deliberate improvement must be brought about by intellectual means. We do not know how to teach people to be shrewd or virtuous, but we do know, within limits, how to teach them to be rational: it is only necessary to reverse the practice of education authorities in every particular. We may hereafter learn to create virtue by manipulating the ductless glands and stimulating or restraining their secretions. But for the present it is easier to create rationality than virtue—meaning by "rationality" a scientific habit of mind in forecasting the effects of our actions.

(*b*) This brings me to the question: How far could or should men's actions be rational? Let us take "should" first. There are very definite limits, to my mind, within which rationality should be confined; some of the most important departments of life are ruined by the invasion of reason. Leibniz in his old age told a correspondent that he had only once asked a lady to marry him, and that was when he was fifty. "Fortunately," he added, "the lady asked time to consider. This gave me also time to consider, and I withdrew the offer." Doubtless his conduct was very rational, but I cannot say that I admire it.

Shakespeare puts "the lunatic, the lover, and the poet" together, as being "of imagination all compact." The problem is to keep the lover and the poet, without the lunatic. I will give an illustration. In 1919 I saw *The Trojan Women* acted at the Old Vic. There is an unbearably pathetic scene where Astyanax is put to death by the Greeks for fear he should grow up into a second Hector. There was hardly a dry eye in the theatre, and the audience found the cruelty of the Greeks in the play hardly credible. Yet those very people who wept were, at that very moment, practicing that very cruelty on a scale which the imagination of Euripides could have never contemplated. They had lately voted (most of them) for a Government which prolonged the blockade of Germany after the armistice, and imposed the blockade of Russia. It was known that these blockades caused the death of immense numbers of children, but it was felt desirable to diminish the population of enemy countries: the children, like Astyanax, might grow up to emulate their fathers. Euripides the poet awakened the lover in the imagination of the audience; but lover and poet were forgotten at the door of the theatre, and the lunatic (in the shape of the homicidal maniac) controlled the political actions of these men and women who thought themselves kind and virtuous.

Is it possible to preserve the lover and the poet without preserving the lunatic? In each of us, all three exist in varying degrees. Are they so bound up together that when the one is brought under control the others perish? I do not believe it. I believe there is in each of us a certain energy which must find vent in art, in passionate love, or in passionate hate, according to circumstances. Respectability, regularity, and routine—the whole cast-iron discipline of a modern industrial society—have atrophied the artistic impulse, and imprisoned love so that it can no longer be generous and free and creative, but must be either stuffy or furtive. Control has been applied to the very things which should be free, while envy, cruelty, and hate sprawl at large with the blessing of nearly the whole bench of Bishops. Our instinctive apparatus consists of two parts—the one tending to further our own life and that of our descendants, the other tending to thwart the lives of supposed rivals. The first includes the joy of life, and love, and art, which is psychologically an offshoot of love. The second includes competition, patriotism, and war. Conventional morality does everything to suppress the first and encourage the second. True morality would do the exact opposite. Our dealings with those whom we love may be safely left to instinct; it is our dealings with those whom we hate that ought to be brought under the dominion of reason. In the modern world, those whom we effectively hate are distant groups, especially foreign nations. We conceive them abstractly, and deceive ourselves into the belief that acts which are really embodiments of hatred are done from love of justice or some such lofty motive. Only a large measure of skepticism can tear away the veils which hide this truth from us. Having achieved that, we could begin to build a new morality, not based on envy and restriction, but on the wish for a full life and the realization that other human beings are a help and not a hindrance when once the madness of envy has been cured. This is not a Utopian hope; it was partially realized in Elizabethan England. It could be realized tomorrow if men would learn to pursue their own happiness rather than the misery of others. This is no impossibly austere morality, yet its adoption would turn our earth into a paradise.

Is Justified True Belief Knowledge?

Edmund L. Gettier

Various attempts have been made in recent years to state necessary and sufficient conditions for someone's knowing a given proposition. The attempts have often been such that they can be stated in a form similar to the following:[1]

> (a) S knows that P   *IFF*   (i) P is true,
>   (ii) S believes that P, and
>   (iii) S is justified in believing that P.

For example, Chisholm has held that the following gives the necessary and sufficient conditions for knowledge:[2]

> (b) S knows that P   IFF   (i) S accepts P,
>   (ii) S has adequate evidence for P, and
>   (iii) P is true.

Ayer has stated the necessary and sufficient conditions for knowledge as follows:[3]

> (c) S knows that P   IFF   (i) P is true,
>   (ii) S is sure that P is true, and
>   (iii) S has the right to be sure that P is true.

I shall argue that (a) is false in that the conditions stated therein do not constitute a *sufficient* condition for the truth of the proposition that S knows that P. The same argument will show that (b) and (c) fail if 'has adequate evidence for' or 'has the right to be sure that' is substituted for 'is justified in believing that' throughout.

I shall begin by noting two points. First, in that sense of 'justified' in which S's being justified in believing P is a necessary condition of S's knowing that P, it is possible for a person to be justified in believing a proposition that is in fact false. Secondly, for any proposition P, if S is

---

[1]Plato seems to be considering some such definition at *Theaetetus* 201, and perhaps accepting one at *Meno* 98.

[2]Roderick M. Chisholm, *Perceiving: a Philosophical Study,* Cornell University Press (Ithaca, New York, 1957), p. 16.

[3]A. J. Ayer, *The Problem of Knowledge,* Macmillan (London, 1956), p. 34.

justified in believing P, and P entails Q, and S deduces Q from P and accepts Q as a result of this deduction, then S is justified in believing Q. Keeping these two points in mind, I shall now present two cases in which the conditions stated in (a) are true for some proposition, though it is at the same time false that the person in question knows that proposition.

Case I:

Suppose that Smith and Jones have applied for a certain job. And suppose that Smith has strong evidence for the following conjunctive proposition:

> (d) Jones is the man who will get the job, and Jones has ten coins in his pocket.

Smith's evidence for (d) might be that the president of the company assured him that Jones would in the end be selected, and that he, Smith, had counted the coins in Jones's pocket ten minutes ago. Proposition (d) entails:

> (e) The man who will get the job has ten coins in his pocket.

Let us suppose that Smith sees the entailment from (d) to (e), and accepts (e) on the grounds of (d), for which he has strong evidence. In this case, Smith is clearly justified in believing that (e) is true.

But imagine, further, that unknown to Smith, he himself, not Jones, will get the job. And, also, unknown to Smith, he himself has ten coins in his pocket. Proposition (e) is then true, though proposition (d), from which Smith inferred (e), is false. In our example, then, all of the following are true: (*i*) (e) is true, (*ii*) Smith believes that (e) is true, and (*iii*) Smith is justified in believing that (e) is true. But it is equally clear that Smith does not *know* that (e) is true; for (e) is true in virtue of the number of coins in Smith's pocket, while Smith does not know how many coins are in Smith's pocket, and bases his belief in (e) on a count of the coins in Jones's pocket, whom he falsely believes to be the man who will get the job.

Case II:

Let us suppose that Smith has strong evidence for the following proposition:

> (f) Jones owns a Ford.

Smith's evidence might be that Jones has at all times in the past within Smith's memory owned a car, and always a Ford, and that Jones has just offered Smith a ride while driving a Ford. Let us imagine, now, that Smith has another friend, Brown, of whose whereabouts he is totally ignorant. Smith selects three place-names quite at random, and constructs the following three propositions:

(g) Either Jones owns a Ford, or Brown is in Boston;

(h) Either Jones owns a Ford, or Brown is in Barcelona;

(i) Either Jones owns a Ford, or Brown is in Brest-Litovsk.

Each of these propositions is entailed by (f). Imagine that Smith realizes the entailment of each of these propositions he has constructed by (f), and proceeds to accept (g), (h), and (i) on the basis of (f). Smith has correctly inferred (g), (h), and (i) from a proposition for which he has strong evidence. Smith is therefore completely justified in believing each of these three propositions. Smith, of course, has no idea where Brown is.

But imagine now that two further conditions hold. First, Jones does *not* own a Ford, but is at present driving a rented car. And secondly, by the sheerest coincidence, and entirely unknown to Smith, the place mentioned in proposition (h) happens really to be the place where Brown is. If these two conditions hold then Smith does *not* know that (h) is true, even though (*i*) (h) *is* true, (*ii*) Smith does believe that (h) is true, and (*iii*) Smith is justified in believing that (h) is true.

These two examples show that definition (a) does not state a *sufficient* condition for someone's knowing a given proposition. The same cases, with appropriate changes, will suffice to show that neither definition (b) nor definition (c) do so either.

An Alleged Defect in Gettier Counter-Examples

Richard Feldman

A number of philosophers have contended that Gettier counter-examples to the justified true belief analysis of knowledge all rely on a certain false principle. For example, in their recent paper, 'Knowledge

Source: From Richard Feldman, *The Australasian Journal of Philosophy*, vol. 52 (Oxford University Press, 1974): 68–69. Reprinted by permission of Oxford University Press.

Without Paradox',[1] Robert G. Meyers and Kenneth Stern argue that 'counter-examples of the Gettier sort all turn on the principle that someone can be justified in accepting a certain proposition *h* on evidence *p* even though *p* is false'.[2] They contend that this principle is false, and hence that the counter-examples fail. Their view is that one proposition, *p*, can justify another, *h*, only if *p* is true. With this in mind, they accept the justified true belief analysis.

D. M. Armstrong defends a similar view in *Belief, Truth and Knowledge*.[3] He writes:

> This simple consideration seems to make redundant the ingenious argument of . . . Gettier's . . . article . . . Gettier produces counter-examples to the thesis that justified true belief is knowledge by producing true beliefs based on justifiably believed grounds, . . . but where these grounds are in fact *false*. But because possession of such grounds could not constitute possession of *knowledge*, I should have thought it obvious that they are too weak to serve as suitable grounds.[4]

Thus he concludes that Gettier's examples are defective because they rely on the false principle that false propositions can justify one's belief in other propositions. Armstrong's view seems to be that one proposition, *p*, can justify another, *h*, only if *p* is known to be true (unlike Meyers and Stern who demand only that *p* in fact be true).[5]

I think, though, that there are examples very much like Gettier's that do not rely on this allegedly false principle. To see this, let us first consider one example in the form in which Meyers and Stern discuss it, and then consider a slight modification of it.

> Suppose Mr. Nogot tells Smith that he owns a Ford and even shows him a certificate to that effect. Suppose, further, that up till now Nogot has always been reliable and honest in his dealings with Smith. Let us call the conjunction of all this evidence *m*. Smith is thus justified in believing that Mr. Nogot who is in his office owns a Ford (*r*) and, consequently, is justified in believing that someone in his office owns a Ford (*h*).[6]

As it turns out, though, *m* and *h* are true but *r* is false. So, the Gettier example runs, Smith has a justified true belief in *h*, but he clearly does not know *h*.

---

[1]*The Journal of Philosophy*, 6 (March 22, 1973), pp. 147–60.
[2]*Ibid.*, p. 147.
[3](1973).
[4]*Ibid.*, p. 152.
[5]Armstrong ultimately goes on to defend a rather different analysis.
[6]Meyers and Stern, *op. cit.*, p. 151.

What is supposed to justify *h* in this example is *r*. But since *r* is false, the example runs afoul of the disputed principle. Since *r* is false, it justifies nothing. Hence, if the principle is false, the counter-example fails.

We can alter the example slightly, however, so that what justifies *h* for Smith is true and he knows that it is. Suppose he deduces from *m* its existential generalization:

> (*n*) There is someone in the office who told Smith that he owns a Ford and even showed him a certificate to that effect, and who up till now has always been reliable and honest in his dealings with Smith.

(*n*), we should note, is true and Smith knows that it is, since he has correctly deduced it from *m*, which he knows to be true. On the basis of *n* Smith believes *h*—someone in the office owns a Ford. Just as the Nogot evidence, *m*, justified *r*—Nogot owns a Ford—in the original example, *n* justifies *h* in this example. Thus Smith has a justified true belief in *h*, knows his evidence to be true, but still does not know *h*.

I conclude that even if a proposition can be justified for a person only if his evidence is true, or only if he knows it to be true, there are still counter-examples to the justified true belief analysis of knowledge of the Gettier sort. In the above example, Smith reasoned from the proposition *m*, which he knew to be true, to the proposition *n*, which he also knew, to the truth *h*; yet he still did not know *h*. So some examples, similar to Gettier's, do not 'turn on the principle that someone can be justified in accepting a certain proposition . . . even though (his evidence) . . . is false'.[7]

Proof of an External World
G. E. Moore

In the preface to the second edition of Kant's *Critique of Pure Reason* some words occur, which, in Professor Kemp Smith's translation, are rendered as follows:

> It still remains a scandal to philosophy . . . that the existence of things outside of us . . . must be accepted merely on *faith*, and that, if anyone

[7]*Ibid.*, p. 147.

thinks good to doubt their existence, we are unable to counter his doubts by any satisfactory proof.[1]

It seems clear from these words that Kant thought it a matter of some importance to give a proof of 'the existence of things outside of us' or perhaps rather (for it seems to me possible that the force of the German words is better rendered in this way) of 'the existence of *the* things outside of us'; for had he not thought it important that a proof should be given, he would scarcely have called it a 'scandal' that no proof had been given. And it seems clear also that he thought that the giving of such a proof was a task which fell properly within the province of philosophy; for, if it did not, the fact that no proof had been given could not possibly be a scandal to *philosophy*.

Now, even if Kant was mistaken in both of these two opinions, there seems to me to be no doubt whatever that it is a matter of some importance and also a matter which falls properly within the province of philosophy, to discuss the question what sort of proof, if any, can be given of 'the existence of things outside of us'. And to discuss this question was my object when I began to write the present lecture. But I may say at once that, as you will find, I have only, at most, succeeded in saying a very small part of what ought to be said about it.

[. . .] There is a passage (*K.d.r.V.*, A 373) in which Kant himself says that the expression 'outside of us' 'carries with it an unavoidable ambiguity'. He says that 'sometimes it means something which exists *as a thing in itself* distinct from us, and sometimes something which merely belongs to external *appearance*'; he calls things which are 'outside of us' in the first of these two senses 'objects which might be called external in the transcendental sense', and things which are so in the second '*empirically external* objects'; and he says finally that, in order to remove all uncertainty as to the latter conception, he will distinguish empirically external objects from objects which might be called 'external' in the transcendental sense, 'by calling them outright things which are *to be met with in space*'.

I think that this last phrase of Kant's 'things which are to be met with in space', does indicate fairly clearly what sort of things it is with regard to which I wish to inquire what sort of proof, if any, can be given that there are any things of that sort. My body, the bodies of other men, the bodies of animals, plants of all sorts, stones, mountains,

---

[1]B xxxix, note: Kemp Smith, p. 34. The German words are 'so bleibt es immer ein Skandal der Philosophie . . . , das Dasein der Dinge ausser uns . . . bloss auf *Glauben* annehmen zu müssen, und wenn es jemand einfällt es zu bezweifeln, ihm keinen genugtuenden Beweis entgegenstellen zu können'.

the sun, the moon, stars, and planets, houses and other buildings, manufactured articles of all sorts—chairs, tables, pieces of paper, etc., are all of them 'things which are to be met with in space'. In short, all things of the sort that philosophers have been used to call 'physical objects', 'material things', or 'bodies' obviously come under this head. But the phrase 'things that are to be met with in space' can be naturally understood as applying also in cases where the names 'physical object', 'material thing', or 'body' can hardly be applied. For instance, shadows are sometimes to be met with in space, although they could hardly be properly called 'physical objects', 'material things', or 'bodies'; and although in one usage of the term 'thing' it would not be proper to call a shadow a 'thing', yet the phrase 'things which are to be met with in space' can be naturally understood as synonymous with 'whatever can be met with in space', and this is an expression which can quite properly be understood to include shadows. I wish the phrase 'things which are to be met with in space' to be understood in this wide sense; so that if a proof can be found that there ever have been as many as two different shadows it will follow at once that there have been at least two 'things which were to be met with in space', and this proof will be as good a proof of the point in question as would be a proof that there have been at least two 'physical objects' of no matter what sort.

The phrase 'things which are to be met with in space' can, therefore, be naturally understood as having a very wide meaning—a meaning even wider than that of 'physical object' or 'body', wide as is the meaning of these latter expressions. But wide as is its meaning, it is not, in one respect, so wide as that of another phrase which Kant uses as if it were equivalent to this one; and a comparison between the two will, I think, serve to make still clearer what sort of things it is with regard to which I wish to ask what proof, if any, can be given that there are such things.

The other phrase which Kant uses as if it were equivalent to 'things which are to be met with in space' is used by him in the sentence immediately preceding that previously quoted in which he declares that the expression 'things outside of us' 'carries with it an unavoidable ambiguity' (A 373). In this preceding sentence he says that an 'empirical object' 'is called *external,* if it is presented (*vorgestellt*) in *space*'. He treats, therefore, the phrase 'presented in space' as if it were equivalent to 'to be met with in space'. But it is easy to find examples of 'things', of which it can hardly be denied that they are 'presented in space', but of which it could, quite naturally, be emphatically denied that they are 'to be met with in space'. [. . .] I took the trouble to cut out of a piece of white paper a four-pointed star, to place it on a black ground, to 'look steadfastly' at it, and then to turn my eyes to a white sheet of paper: and I did find that I saw a grey patch for some little time—I not only saw a grey patch, but I saw it *on* the white ground, and also this grey patch was of roughly the same shape as the white four-pointed star at which I had 'looked steadfastly' just before—it also was a four-pointed star. I repeated this simple experiment successfully several times. Now each of those grey four-pointed stars, one of which I saw in each experiment, was what is called an 'after-image' or 'after-sensation'; and can anybody deny that each of these after-images can be quite properly said to have been 'presented in space'? I saw each of them on a real white background, and, if so, each of them was 'presented' on a real white background. [. . .]

Negative after-images of the kind described are, therefore, one example of 'things' which, though they must be allowed to be 'presented in space', are nevertheless *not* 'to be met with in space', and are *not* 'external to our minds' in the sense with which we shall be concerned. [. . .]

It is clear, then, I think, that by no means everything which can naturally be said to be 'presented in space' can also be naturally said to be 'a thing which is to be met with in space'. Some of the 'things', which are presented in space, are very emphatically *not* to be met with in space: or, to use another phrase, which may be used to convey the same notion, they are emphatically *not* 'physical realities' at all. The conception 'presented in space' is therefore, in one respect, much wider than the conception 'to be met with in space': many 'things' fall under the first conception which do not fall under the second—many after-images, one at least of the pair of 'images' seen whenever anyone sees double, and most bodily pains, are 'presented in space', though none of them are to be met with in space. From the fact that a 'thing' is presented in space, it by no means follows that it is to be met with in space. But just as the first conception is, in one respect, wider than the second, so, in another, the second is wider than the first. For there are many 'things' to be met with in space, of which it is not true that they are presented in space. From the fact that a 'thing' is to be met with in space, it by no means follows that it is presented in space. I have taken 'to be met with in space' to imply, as I think it naturally may, that a 'thing' *might be* perceived; but from the fact that a thing *might be* perceived, it does not follow that it is perceived; and if it is not actually perceived, then it will not be presented in space. It is characteristic of the sorts of 'things', including shadows, which I have described as 'to be met with in space', that there is no absurdity in supposing with regard to any one of them which *is,* at a given time, perceived, both (1) that it might have existed at that very time, without being perceived; (2) that it might have existed at another time, without being perceived at that other time; and (3) that during the whole period of its existence, it need not have been perceived at any time at all. There is, therefore, no absurdity in supposing that many things, which were at one time to be met with in space, never were 'presented' at any time at all, and that many things which *are* to be met with in space now, are not now 'presented' and also never were and never will be. To use a Kantian phrase, the conception of 'things which are to be met with in space' embraces not only objects of actual experience, but also objects of *possible* experience; and from the fact that a thing is or was an object of *possible* experience, it by no means follows that it either was or is or will be 'presented' at all.

I hope that what I have now said may have served to make clear enough what sorts of 'things' I was originally referring to as 'things outside us' or 'things external to our minds'. I said that I thought that Kant's phrase 'things that are to be met with in space' indicated fairly clearly the sorts of 'things' in question; and I have tried to make the range clearer still, by pointing out that this phrase only serves the purpose, if (a) you understand it in a sense, in which many 'things', e.g., after-images, double images, bodily pains, which might be said to be 'presented in space', are nevertheless *not* to be reckoned as 'things that are to be met with in space', and *(b)* you realize clearly that there is no contradiction in supposing that there have been and are 'to be met with in space' things which never have been, are not now, and never will be perceived, nor in supposing that among those of them which have at some time been perceived many existed at times at which they were not being perceived. I think it will now be clear to everyone that, since I do not reckon as 'external things' after-images, double images, and bodily pains, I also should not reckon as 'external things', any of the 'images' which we often 'see with the mind's eye' when we are awake, nor any of those which we see when we are asleep and dreaming; and also that I was so using the expression 'external' that from the fact that a man was at a given time having a visual hallucination, it will follow that he was seeing at that time something which was *not* 'external' to his mind, and from the fact that he was at a given time having an auditory hallucination, it will follow that he was at the time hearing a sound which was *not* 'external' to his mind. But I certainly have not made my use of these phrases, 'external to our minds' and 'to be met with in space', so clear that in the case of every kind of 'thing' which might be suggested, you would be able to tell at once whether I should or should not reckon it as 'external to our minds' and 'to be met with in space'. For instance, I have said nothing which makes it quite clear whether a reflection which I see in a looking-glass is or is not to be regarded as 'a thing that is to be met with in space' and 'external to our minds', nor have I said anything which makes it quite clear whether the sky is or is not to be so regarded. In the case of the sky, everyone, I think, would feel that it was quite inappropriate to talk of it as 'a thing that is to be met with in space'; and most people, I think, would feel a strong reluctance to affirm, without qualification, that reflections which people see in looking-glasses are 'to be met with in space'. And yet neither the sky nor reflections seen in mirrors are in the same position as bodily pains or after-images in the respect which I have emphasized as a reason for saying of these latter that they are *not* to be met with in space—namely that there is an absurdity in supposing that *the very same* pain which I feel could be felt by someone else or that *the very same* after-image which I see could be seen by someone else. In the case of reflections in mirrors we should quite naturally, in certain circumstances, use language which implies that another person may see the same reflection which we see. We might quite naturally say to a friend: 'Do you see that reddish reflection in the water there? I can't make out what it's a reflection of', just as we might say, pointing to a distant hill-side: 'Do you see that white speck on the hill over there? I can't make out what it is.' And in the case of the sky, it is quite obviously *not* absurd to say that other people see it as well as I.

It must, therefore, be admitted that I have not made my use of the phrase 'things to be met with in space', nor therefore that of 'external to our minds', which the former was used to explain, so clear that in the case of every kind of 'thing' which may be mentioned, there will be no doubt whatever as to whether things of that kind are or are not 'to be met with in space' or 'external to our minds'. But this lack of a clear-cut definition of the expression 'things that are to be met with in space', does not, so far as I can see, matter for my present purpose. For my present purpose it is, I think, sufficient if I make clear, in the case of many kinds of things, that I am so using the phrase 'things that are to be met with in space', that, in the case of each of these kinds, from the proposition that there are things of that kind it *follows* that there are things to be met with in space. And I have, in fact, given a list (though by no means an exhaustive one) of kinds of things which are related to my use of the expression 'things that are to be met with in space' in this way. I mentioned among others the bodies of men and of animals, plants, stars, houses, chairs, and shadows; and I want now to emphasize that I am so using 'things to be met with in space' that, in the case of each of these kinds of 'things', from the proposition that there are 'things' of that kind it *follows* that there are things to be met with in space: e.g., from the proposition that there are plants or that plants exist it *follows* that there are things to be met with in space, from the proposition that shadows exist, it *follows* that there are things to be met with in space, and so on, in the case of all the kinds of 'things' which I mentioned in my first list. That this should be clear is sufficient for my purpose, because, if it is clear, then it will also be clear that, as I implied before, if you have proved that two plants exist, or that a plant and a dog exist, or that a dog and a shadow exist, etc. etc., you will *ipso facto* have proved that there are things to be met with in space: you will not require *also* to give a separate proof that from the proposition that there are plants it *does* follow that there are things to be met with in space.

Now with regard to the expression 'things that are to be met with in space' I think it will readily be believed that I may be using it in a sense such that no proof is required that from 'plants exist' there follows 'there are things to be met with in space'; but with regard to the phrase 'things external to our minds' I think the case is different. People may be inclined to say: 'I can see quite clearly that from the proposition "At least two dogs exist at the present moment" there *follows* the proposition "At least two things are to be met with in space at the present moment", so that if you can prove that there are two dogs in existence at the present moment you will *ipso facto* have proved that two things at least are to be met with in space at the present moment. I can see that you do not also require a separate proof that from "Two dogs exist" "Two things are to be met with in space" *does* follow; it is quite obvious that there couldn't be a dog which wasn't to be met with in space. But it is not by any means so clear to me that if you can prove that there are two dogs or two shadows, you will *ipso facto* have proved that there are two things *external to our minds*. Isn't it possible that a dog, though it certainly must be "to be met with in space", might *not* be an external object—an object external to our minds? Isn't a separate proof required that anything that is to be met with in space must be external to our minds? Of course, if you are using "external" as a mere synonym for "to be met with in space", no proof will be required that dogs are external objects: in that case, if you can prove that two dogs exist, you will *ipso facto* have proved that there are some external things. But I find it difficult to believe that you, or anybody else, do really use "external" as a mere synonym for "to be met with in space"; and if you don't, isn't some proof required that whatever is to be met with in space must be external to our minds?'

Now Kant, as we saw, asserts that the phrases 'outside of us' or 'external' are in fact used in two very different senses; and with regard to one of these two senses, that which he calls the 'transcendental' sense, and which he tries to explain by saying that it is a sense in which 'external' means 'existing *as a thing in itself* distinct from us', it is notorious that he himself held that things which are to be met with in space are *not* 'external' in that sense. There is, therefore, according to him, *a* sense of 'external', a sense in which the word has been commonly used by philosophers—such that, if 'external' be used in that sense, then from the proposition 'Two dogs exist' it will *not* follow that there are some external things. What this supposed sense is I do not think that Kant himself ever succeeded in explaining clearly; nor do I know of any reason for supposing that philosophers ever have used 'external' in a sense, such that in *that* sense things that are to be met with in space are *not* external. But how about the other sense, in which, according to Kant, the word 'external' has been commonly used—that which he calls 'empirically external'? How is this conception related to the conception 'to met with in space'? It may be noticed that, in the passages which I quoted Kant himself does not tell us at all clearly what he takes to be the proper answer to this question. He only makes the rather odd statement that, in order to remove all uncertainty as to the conception 'empirically external', he will distinguish objects to which it applies from those which might be called 'external' in the transcendental sense, by 'calling them outright things which are *to be met with in space*'. These odd words certainly suggest, as one possible interpretation of them, that in Kant's opinion the conception 'empirically external' is *identical* with the conception 'to be met with in space'—that he does think that 'external', when used in this second sense, is a mere synonym for 'to be met with in space'. But, if this is his meaning, I do find it very difficult to believe that he is right. Have philosophers, in fact, ever used 'external' as a mere synonym for 'to be met with in space'? Does he himself do so?

I do not think they have, nor that he does himself; and, in order to explain how they have used it, and how the two conceptions 'external to our minds' and 'to be met with in space' are related to one another, I think it is important expressly to call attention to a fact which hitherto I have only referred to incidentally: namely the fact that those who talk of certain things as 'external to' our minds, do, in general, as we should naturally expect, talk of other 'things', with which they wish to contrast the first, as 'in' our minds. It has, of course, been often pointed out that when 'in' is thus used, followed by 'my mind', 'your mind', 'his mind', etc., 'in' is being used metaphorically. And there are some metaphorical uses of 'in', followed by such expressions, which occur in common speech, and which we all understand quite well. For instance, we all understand such expressions as 'I had you in mind, when I made that arrangement' or 'I had you in mind, when I said that there are some people who can't bear to touch a spider'. In these cases 'I was thinking of you' can be used to mean the same as 'I had you in mind'. But it is quite certain that this particular metaphorical use of 'in' is not the one in which philosophers are using it when they contrast what is 'in' my mind with what is 'external' to it. On the contrary, in their use of 'external', you will be external to my mind even at a moment when I have you in mind. If we want to discover what this peculiar metaphorical use of *in* my mind' is, which is such that nothing, which is, in the sense we are now concerned with, 'external' to my mind, can ever be 'in' it, we need, I think, to consider instances of the sort of 'things' which they would say are 'in' my mind in this special sense. I have already mentioned three such instances, which are, I think, sufficient for my present purpose: any bodily pain which I feel, any after-image which I see with my eyes shut, and any image which I 'see' when I am asleep and dreaming, are typical examples of the sort of 'thing' of which philosophers have spoken as 'in my mind'. And there is no doubt, I think, that when they have spoken of such things as my body, a sheet of paper, a star—in short 'physical objects' generally—as 'external', they have meant to emphasize some important difference which they feel to exist between such things as these and such 'things' as a pain, an after-image seen with closed eyes, and a dream-image. But *what* difference? What difference do they feel to exist between a bodily pain which I feel or an after-image which I see with closed eyes, on the one hand, and my body itself, on the other—what difference which leads them to say that whereas the bodily pain and the after-image are 'in' my mind, my body itself is *not* 'in' my mind—not even when I am feeling it and seeing it or thinking of it? I have already said that one difference which there is between the two, is that my body is to be met with in space, whereas the bodily pain and the after-image are not. But I think it would be quite wrong to say that this is *the* difference which has led philosophers to speak of the two latter as 'in' my mind, and of my body as *not* 'in' my mind.

The question what the difference is which has led them to speak in this way, is not, I think, at all an easy question to answer; but I am going to try to give, in brief outline, what I *think* is a right answer.

It should, I think, be noted, first of all, that the use of the word 'mind', which is being adopted when it is said that any bodily pains which I feel are 'in my mind', is one which is not quite in accordance with any usage common in ordinary speech, although we are very familiar with it in philosophy. Nobody, I think, would say that bodily pains which I feel are 'in my mind', unless he was also prepared to say that it is *with* my mind that I feel bodily pains; and to say this latter is, I think, not quite in accordance with common non-philosophic usage. It is natural enough to say that it is with my mind that I remember, and think, and imagine, and feel *mental* pains—e.g., disappointment, but not, I think, quite so natural to say that it is with my mind that I feel *bodily* pains, e.g., a severe headache; and perhaps even less natural to say that it is with my mind that I see and hear and smell and taste. There is, however, a well-established philosophical usage according to which seeing, hearing, smelling, tasting, and having a bodily pain are just as much *mental* occurrences or processes as are remembering, or thinking, or imagining. This usage was, I think, adopted by philosophers, because they saw a real resemblance between such statements as 'I saw a cat', 'I heard a clap of thunder', 'I smelt a strong smell of onions', 'My finger smarted horribly', on the one hand, and such statements as 'I remembered having seen him', 'I was thinking out a plan of action', 'I pictured the scene to myself', 'I felt bitterly disappointed', on the other—a resemblance which puts all these statements in one class together, as contrasted with other statements in which 'I' or 'my' is used, such as, e.g., 'I was less than four feet high', 'I was lying on my back', 'My hair was very long'. What is the resemblance in question? It is a resemblance which might be expressed by saying that all the first eight statements are the sort of statements which furnish data for psychology, while the three latter are not. It is also a resemblance which may be expressed, in a way now common among philosophers, by saying that in the case of all the first eight statements, if we make the statement more specific by adding a date, we get a statement such that, if it is true, then it *follows* that I was 'having an experience' at the date in question, whereas this does not hold for the three last statements. For instance, if it is true that I saw a cat between 12 noon and 5 minutes past, today, it *follows* that I was 'having some experience' between 12 noon and 5 minutes past, today; whereas from the proposition that I was less than four feet high in December 1877, it does not *follow* that I had any experiences in December 1877. But this philosophic use of 'having an experience' is one which itself needs explanation, since it is not identical with any use of the expression that is established in common speech. An explanation, however, which is, I think, adequate for the purpose, can be given by saying that a philosopher, who was following this usage, would say that I was at a given

time 'having an experience' if and only if either (1) I was conscious at
the time or (2) I was dreaming at the time or (3) something else was true
of me at the time, which resembled what is true of me when I am conscious and when I am dreaming, in a certain very obvious respect in
which what is true of me when I am dreaming resembles what is true of
me when I am conscious, and in which what would be true of me, if at
any time, for instance, I had a vision, would resemble both. This explanation is, of course, in some degree vague; but I think it is clear enough
for our purpose. It amounts to saying that, in this philosophic usage of
'having an experience', it would be said of me that I was, at a given
time, having *no* experience, if I was at the time neither conscious nor
dreaming nor having a vision nor *anything else of the sort*; and, of
course, this is vague in so far as it has not been specified what else
would be *of the sort*: this is left to be gathered from the instances given.
But I think this is sufficient: often at night when I am asleep, I am
neither conscious nor dreaming nor having a vision nor *anything else of
the sort*—that is to say, I am having no experiences. If this explanation
of this philosophic usage of 'having an experience' is clear enough, then
I think that what has been meant by saying that any pain which I feel or
any after-image which I see with my eyes closed is '*in* my mind', can be
explained by saying that what is meant is neither more nor less than
that there would be a contradiction in supposing *that very same pain* or
that very same after-image to have existed at a time at which I was
having no experience; or, in other words, that from the proposition,
with regard to any time, that *that* pain or *that* after-image existed at
that time, it *follows* that I was having some experience at the time in
question. And if so, then we can say that the felt difference between
bodily pains which I feel and after-images which I see, on the one hand,
and my body on the other, which has led philosophers to say that any
such pain or after-image is '*in* my mind', whereas my body *never* is but
is always 'outside of' or 'external to' my mind, is just this, that whereas
there is a contradiction in supposing a pain which I feel or an after-
image which I see to exist at a time when I am having no experience,
there is no contradiction in supposing my body to exist at a time when
I am having no experience; and we can even say, I think, that just this
and nothing more is what they have meant by these puzzling and
misleading phrases 'in my mind' and 'external to my mind'.

But now, if to say of anything, e.g., my body, that it is external to *my*
mind, means merely that from a proposition to the effect that it existed at
a specified time, there in no case follows the further proposition that
I was having an experience at the time in question, then to say of

anything that it is external to *our* minds, will mean similarly that from a proposition to the effect that it existed at a specified time, it in no case follows that any of *us* were having experiences at the time in question. And if by *our* minds be meant, as is, I think, usually meant, the minds of human beings living on the earth, then it will follow that any pains which animals may feel, any after-images they may see, any experiences they may have, though not external to *their* minds, yet are external to *ours*. And this at once makes plain how different is the conception 'external to our minds' from the conception 'to be met with in space'; for, of course, pains which animals feel or after-images which they see are no more to be met with in space than are pains which *we* feel or after-images which *we* see. From the proposition that there are external objects—objects that are not in any of *our* minds, it does *not* follow that there are things to be met with in space; and hence 'external to our minds' is not a mere synonym for 'to be met with in space': that is to say, 'external to our minds' and 'to be met with in space' are two different conceptions. And the true relation between these conceptions seems to me to be this. We have already seen that there are ever so many kinds of 'things', such that, in the case of each of these kinds, from the proposition that there is at least one thing of that kind there *follows* the proposition that there is at least one thing to be met with in space: e.g., this follows from 'There is at least one star', from 'There is at least one human body', from 'There is at least one shadow', etc. And I think we can say that of every kind of thing of which this is true, it is also true that from the proposition that there is at least one 'thing' of that kind there *follows* the proposition that there is at least one thing external to our minds: e.g., from 'There is at least one star' there follows not only 'There is at least one thing to be met with in space' but also 'There is at least one external thing', and similarly in all other cases. My reason for saying this is as follows. Consider any kind of thing, such that anything of that kind, if there is anything of it, must be 'to be met with in space': e.g., consider the kind 'soap-bubble'. If I say of anything which I am perceiving, 'That is a soap-bubble', I am, it seems to me, certainly implying that there would be no contradiction in asserting that it existed before I perceived it and that it will continue to exist, even if I cease to perceive it. This seems to me to be part of what is meant by saying that it is a real soap-bubble, as distinguished, for instance, from a hallucination of a soap-bubble. Of course, it by no means follows, that if it really is a soap-bubble, it did in fact exist before I perceived it or will continue to exist after I cease to perceive it: soap-bubbles are an example of a kind of 'physical object' and 'thing to be met with in space', in the case of which it is notorious that particular specimens of the kind often do exist only so long as they are perceived by a particular person. But a thing which I perceive would not be a soap-bubble unless its existence at any given time were *logically independent* of my perception of it at that time; unless that is to say, from the proposition, with regard to a particular time, that it existed at that time, it *never* follows that I perceived it at that time. But, if it is true that it would not be a soap-bubble, unless it *could* have existed at any given time without being perceived by me at that time, it is certainly also true that it would not be a soap-bubble, unless it *could* have existed at any given time, without its being true that I was having any experience of any kind at the time in question: it would not be a soap-bubble, unless, whatever time you take, from the proposition that it existed at that time it does *not* follow that I was having any experience at that time. That is to say, from the proposition with regard to anything which I am perceiving that it is a soap-bubble, there *follows* the proposition that it is external to *my* mind. But if, when I say that anything which I perceive is a soap-bubble, I am implying that it is external to *my* mind, I am, I think, certainly also implying that it is also external to all other minds: I am implying that it is not a thing of a sort such that things of that sort *can* only exist at a time when somebody is having an experience. I think, therefore, that from any proposition of the form 'There's a soap-bubble!' there does really *follow* the proposition 'There's an external object!' 'There's an object external to *all* our minds!' And, if this is true of the kind 'soap-bubble', it is certainly also true of any other kind (including the kind 'unicorn') which is such that, if there are any things of that kind, it follows that there are *some* things to be met with in space.

I think, therefore, that in the case of all kinds of 'things', which are such that if there is a pair of things, both of which are of one of these kinds, or a pair of things one of which is of one of them and one of them of another, then it will follow at once that there are some things to be met with in space, it is true also that if I can prove that there are a pair of things, one of which is of one of these kinds and another of another, or a pair both of which are of one of them, then I shall have proved *ipso facto* that there are at least two 'things outside of us'. That is to say, if I can prove that there exist now both a sheet of paper and a human hand, I shall have proved that there are now 'things outside of us'; if I can prove that there exist now both a shoe and sock, I shall have proved that there are now 'things outside of us'; etc.; and similarly I shall have proved it, if I can prove that there exist now two sheets of paper, or two human hands, or two shoes, or two socks, etc. Obviously, then, there are thousands of different things such that, if, at any time,

I can prove any one of them, I shall have proved the existence of things outside of us. Cannot I prove any of these things?

It seems to me that, so far from its being true, as Kant declares to be his opinion, that there is only one possible proof of the existence of things outside of us, namely the one which he has given, I can now give a large number of different proofs, each of which is a perfectly rigorous proof; and that at many other times I have been in a position to give many others. I can prove now, for instance, that two human hands exist. How? By holding up my two hands, and saying, as I make a certain gesture with the right hand, 'Here is one hand', and adding, as I make a certain gesture with the left, 'and here is another'. And if, by doing this, I have proved *ipso facto* the existence of external things, you will all see that I can also do it now in numbers of other ways: there is no need to multiply examples.

But did I prove just now that two human hands were then in existence? I do want to insist that I did; that the proof which I gave was a perfectly rigorous one; and that it is perhaps impossible to give a better or more rigorous proof of anything whatever. Of course, it would not have been a proof unless three conditions were satisfied; namely (1) unless the premiss which I adduced as proof of the conclusion was different from the conclusion I adduced it to prove; (2) unless the premiss which I adduced was something which I *knew* to be the case, and not merely something which I believed but which was by no means certain, or something which, though in fact true, I did not know to be so; and (3) unless the conclusion did really follow from the premiss. But all these three conditions were in fact satisfied by my proof. (1) The premiss which I adduced in proof was quite certainly different from the conclusion, for the conclusion was merely 'Two human hands exist at this moment'; but the premiss was something far more specific than this—something which I expressed by showing you my hands, making certain gestures, and saying the words 'Here is one hand, and here is another'. It is quite obvious that the two were different, because it is quite obvious that the conclusion might have been true, even if the premiss had been false. In asserting the premiss I was asserting much more than I was asserting in asserting the conclusion. (2) I certainly did at the moment *know* that which I expressed by the combination of certain gestures with saying the words 'There is one hand and here is another'. I *knew* that there was one hand in the place indicated by combining a certain gesture with my first utterance of 'here' and that there was another in the different place indicated by combining a certain gesture with my second utterance of 'here'. How absurd it would be to suggest that I did not know it, but only believed it, and that perhaps it was not the case! You might as well suggest that I do not know that I am now standing up and talking—that perhaps after all I'm not, and that it's not quite certain that I am! And finally (3) it is quite certain that the conclusion did follow from the premiss. This is as certain as it is that if there is one hand here and another here *now*, then it follows that there are two hands in existence *now*.

My proof, then, of the existence of things outside of us did satisfy three of the conditions necessary for a rigorous proof. Are there any other conditions necessary for a rigorous proof, such that perhaps it did not satisfy one of them? Perhaps there may be; I do not know; but I do want to emphasize that, so far as I can see, we all of us do constantly take proofs of this sort as absolutely conclusive proofs of certain conclusions—as finally settling certain questions, as to which we were previously in doubt. Suppose, for instance, it were a question whether there were as many as three misprints on a certain page in a certain book. A says there are, B is inclined to doubt it. How could A prove that he is right? Surely he *could* prove it by taking the book, turning to the page, and pointing to three separate places on it, saying 'There's one misprint here, another here, and another here': surely that is a method by which it *might* be proved! Of course, A would not have proved, by doing this, that there were at least three misprints on the page in question, unless it was certain that there was a misprint in each of the places to which he pointed. But to say that he *might* prove it in this way, is to say that it *might* be certain that there was. And if such a thing as that could ever be certain, then assuredly it was certain just now that there was one hand in one of the two places I indicated and another in the other.

I did, then, just now, give a proof that there were *then* external objects; and obviously, if I did, I could *then* have given many other proofs of the same sort that there were external objects *then*, and could now give many proofs of the same sort that there are external objects *now*.

But, if what I am asked to do is to prove that external objects have existed *in the past*, then I can give many different proofs of this also, but proofs which are in important respects of a different *sort* from those just given. And I want to emphasize that, when Kant says it is a scandal not to be able to give a proof of the existence of external objects, a proof of their existence in the past would certainly *help* to remove the scandal of which he is speaking. He says that, if it occurs to anyone to question their existence, we ought to be able to confront him with a satisfactory proof. But by a person who questions their existence, he certainly means not merely a person who questions whether any exist at the moment of speaking, but a person who question whether any have *ever* existed; and a proof that some have existed in the past would certainly therefore be relevant to *part* of what such a person is questioning. How then can I prove that there have been external objects in the past? Here is one proof. I can say: 'I held up two hands above this desk not very long ago; therefore two hands existed not very long ago; therefore at least two external objects have existed at some time in the past, Q.E.D.' This is a perfectly good proof, provided I *know* what is asserted in the premiss. But I *do* know that I held up two hands above this desk not very long ago. As a matter of fact, in this case you all know it too. There's no doubt whatever that I did. Therefore I have given a perfectly conclusive proof that external objects have existed in the past; and you will all see at once that, if this is a conclusive proof, I could have given many others of the same sort, and could now give many others. But it is also quite obvious that this sort of proof differs in important respects from the sort of proof I gave just now that there were two hands existing *then*.

I have, then, given two conclusive proofs of the existence of external objects. The first was a proof that two human hands existed at the time when I gave the proof; the second was a proof that two human hands had existed at a time previous to that at which I gave the proof. These proofs were of a different sort in important respects. And I pointed out that I could have given, then, many other conclusive proofs of both sorts. It is also obvious that I could give many others of both sorts now. So that, if these are the sort of proof that is wanted, nothing is easier than to prove the existence of external objects.

But now I am perfectly well aware that, in spite of all that I have said, many philosophers will still feel that I have not given any satisfactory proof of the point in question. And I want briefly, in conclusion, to say something as to why this dissatisfaction with my proofs should be felt.

One reason why, is, I think, this. Some people understand 'proof of an external world' as including a proof of things which I haven't attempted to prove and haven't proved. It is not quite easy to say *what* it is that they want proved—*what* it is that is such that unless they got a proof of it, they would not say that they had a proof of the existence of external things; but I can make an approach to explaining what they want by saying that if I had proved the propositions which I used as *premisses* in my two proofs, then they would perhaps admit that I had proved the existence of external things, but, in the absence of such a proof (which, of course, I have neither given nor attempted to give), they will say that I have not given what they mean by a proof of the existence of external things. In other words, they want a proof of what I assert *now* when I hold up my hands and say 'Here's one hand and here's another'; and, in the other case, they want a proof of what I assert *now* when I say 'I did hold up two hands above this desk just now'. Of course, what they really want is not merely a proof of these two propositions, but something like a general statement as to how *any* propositions of this sort may be proved. This, of course, I haven't given; and I do not believe it can be given: if this is what is meant by proof of the existence of external things, I do not believe that any proof of the existence of external things is possible. Of course, in some cases what might be called a proof of propositions which seem like these can be got. If one of you suspected that one of my hands was artificial he might be said to get a proof of my proposition 'Here's one hand, and here's another', by coming up and examining the suspected hand close up, perhaps touching and pressing it, and so establishing that it really was a human hand. But I do not believe that any proof is possible in nearly all cases. How am I to prove now that 'Here's one hand, and here's another'? I do not believe I can do it. In order to do it, I should need to prove for one thing, as Descartes pointed out, that I am not now dreaming. But how can I prove that I am not? I have, no doubt, conclusive reasons for asserting that I am not now dreaming; I have conclusive evidence that I am awake: but that is a very different thing from being able to prove it. I could not tell you what all my evidence is; and I should require to do this at least, in order to give you a proof.

But another reason why some people would feel dissatisfied with my proofs is, I think, not merely that they want a proof of something which I haven't proved, but that they think that, if I cannot give such extra proofs, then the proofs that I have given are not conclusive proofs at all. And this, I think, is a definite mistake. They would say: 'If you cannot prove your premiss that here is one hand and here is another, then you do not know it. But you yourself have admitted that, if you did not know it, then your proof was not conclusive. Therefore your proof was not, as you say it was, a conclusive proof.' This view that, if I cannot prove such things as these, I do not know them, is, I think, the view that Kant was expressing in the sentence which I quoted at the beginning of this lecture, when he implies that so long as we have no proof of the existence of external things, their existence must be accepted merely on *faith*. He means to say, I think, that if I cannot prove that there is a hand here, I must accept it merely as a matter of faith—I cannot know it. Such a view, though it has been very common among philosophers, can, I think, be shown to be wrong—though shown only by the use of premises which are not known to be true, unless we do know of the existence of external things. I can know things, which I cannot prove; and among things which I certainly did know, even if (as I think) I could not prove them, were the premises of my two proofs. I should say, therefore, that those, if any, who are dissatisfied with these proofs merely on the ground that I did not know their premises, have no good reason for their dissatisfaction.

An Essay Concerning Human Understanding

John Locke

Since it is the understanding that sets man above the rest of sensible beings, and gives him all the advantage and dominion which he has over them, it is certainly a subject, even for its nobleness, worth our labour to enquire into. [. . .]

It is therefore worth while to search out the bounds between opinion and knowledge, and examine by what measures, in things whereof we have no certain knowledge, we ought to regulate our assent, and moderate our persuasions. In order whereunto, I shall pursue this following method.

First, I shall enquire into the original of those ideas, notions, or whatever else you please to call them, which a man observes, and is conscious to himself he has in his mind; and the ways whereby the understanding comes to be furnished with them.

Secondly, I shall endeavour to show what knowledge the understanding hath by those ideas, and the certainty, evidence, and extent of it.

Thirdly, I shall make some enquiry into the nature and grounds of faith, or opinion; whereby I mean that assent which we give to any proposition as true, of whose truth yet we have no certain knowledge; and here we shall have occasion to examine the reasons and degrees of assent. [. . .]

But, before I proceed on to what I have thought on this subject, I must here in the entrance beg pardon of my reader for the frequent use of the word *idea* which he will find in the following treatise. It being that term which, I think, serves best to stand for whatsoever is the object of the understanding when a man thinks, I have used it to express whatever is meant by *phantasm, notion, species,* or whatever it is which the mind can be employed about in thinking; and I could not avoid frequently using it.

I presume it will be easily granted me that there are such ideas in men's minds; everyone is conscious of them in himself, and men's words and actions will satisfy him that they are in others.

Our first enquiry then shall be how they come into the mind. [. . .]

Let us then suppose the mind to be, as we say, white paper, void of all characters, without any ideas; how comes it to be furnished? Whence comes it by that vast store which the busy and boundless fancy of man has painted on it with an almost endless variety? Whence has it all the materials of reason and knowledge? To this I answer, in one word, from *experience;* in that all our knowledge is founded, and from that it ultimately derives itself. Our observation, employed either about external sensible objects, or about the internal operations of our minds, perceived and reflected on by ourselves, is that which supplies our understandings with all the materials of thinking. These two are the fountains of knowledge, from whence all the ideas we have, or can naturally have, do spring.

First, our senses, conversant about particular sensible objects, do convey into the mind several distinct perceptions of things, according to those various ways wherein those objects do affect them: And thus we come by those ideas we have of yellow, white, heat, cold, soft, hard, bitter, sweet, and all those which we call sensible qualities; which when I say the senses convey into the mind, I mean they from external objects convey into the mind what produces there those perceptions. This great source of most of the ideas we have, depending wholly upon our senses, and derived by them to the understanding, I call *sensation.*

Secondly, the other fountain from which experience furnisheth the understanding with ideas is the perception of the operations of our own mind within us, as it is employed about the ideas it has got; which operations, when the soul comes to reflect on and consider, do furnish the understanding with another set of ideas, which could not be had from things without. And such are perception, thinking, doubting, believing, reasoning, knowing, willing, and all the different actings of our own minds; which we being conscious of and observing in ourselves, do from these receive into our understandings as distinct ideas, as we do from bodies affecting our senses. This source of ideas every man has wholly in himself; and though it be not sense, as having nothing to do with external objects, yet it is very like it, and might properly enough be called internal sense. But as I call the other *sensation,* so I call this *reflection,* the ideas it affords being such only as the mind gets by reflecting on its own operations within itself. By reflection, then, in the following part of this discourse, I would be understood to mean that notice which the mind takes of its own operations, and the manner of them; by reason whereof there come to be ideas of these operations in the understanding. These two, I say, viz. external material things as the objects of sensation, and the operations of our own minds within as the objects of reflection, are to me the only originals from whence all our ideas take their beginnings. The term *operations* here I use in a large sense, as comprehending not barely the actions of the mind about its ideas, but some sort of passions arising sometimes from them, such as is the satisfaction or uneasiness arising from any thought.

The understanding seems to me not to have the least glimmering of any ideas which it doth not receive from one of these two. External objects furnish the mind with the ideas of sensible qualities, which are all those different perceptions they produce in us: And the mind furnishes the understanding with ideas of its own operations.

These, when we have taken a full survey of them, and their several modes, combinations, and relations, we shall find to contain all our whole stock of ideas; and that we have nothing in our minds which did not come in one of these two ways. Let anyone examine his own thoughts, and thoroughly search into his understanding; and then let him tell me whether all the original ideas he has there are any other than of the objects of his senses, or of the operations of his mind, considered as objects of his reflection; and how great a mass of knowledge soever he imagines to be lodged there, he will, upon taking a strict view, see that he has not any idea in his mind but what one of these two have imprinted; though perhaps with infinite variety compounded and enlarged by the understanding, as we shall see hereafter. [. . .]

The better to understand the nature, manner, and extent of our knowledge, one thing is carefully to be observed concerning the ideas we have; and that is, that some of them are simple, and some complex.

Though the qualities that affect our senses are, in the things themselves, so united and blended that there is no separation, no distance between them; yet it is plain the ideas they produce in the mind enter by the senses simple and unmixed. For though the sight and touch often take in from the same object, at the same time, different ideas; as a man sees at once motion and colour; the hand feels softness and warmth in the same piece of wax; yet the simple ideas thus united in the same subject are as perfectly distinct as those that come in by different senses: The coldness and hardness which a man feels in a piece of ice being as distinct ideas in the mind as the smell and whiteness of a lily; or as the taste of sugar, and smell of a rose. And there is nothing can be plainer to a man than the clear and distinct perception he has of those simple ideas; which, being each in itself uncompounded, contains in it nothing but one uniform appearance or conception in the mind, and is not distinguishable into different ideas.

These simple ideas, the materials of all our knowledge, are suggested and furnished to the mind only by those two ways above-mentioned, viz. sensation and reflection. When the understanding is once stored with these simple ideas, it has the power to repeat, compare, and unite them, even to an almost infinite variety, and so can make at pleasure new complex ideas. But it is not in the power of the most exalted wit, or enlarged understanding, by any quickness or variety of thought, to invent or frame one new simple idea in the mind not taken in by the ways before mentioned: Nor can any force of the understanding destroy those that are there. The dominion of man, in this little world of his own understanding, being much-what the same as it in the great world of visible things, wherein his power, however managed by art and skill, reaches no farther than to compound and divide the materials that are made to his hand, but can do nothing towards the making the least particle of new matter, or destroying one atom of what is already in being. The same inability will everyone find in himself who shall go about to fashion in his understanding any simple idea not received in by his senses from external objects, or by reflection from the operations of his own mind about them. I would have anyone try to fancy any taste which had never affected his palate; or frame the idea of a scent he had never smelt: Any when he can do this, I will also conclude that a blind man hath ideas of colours, and a deaf man true distinct notions of sounds. [. . .]

To discover the nature of our ideas the better, and to discourse of them intelligibly, it will be convenient to distinguish them as they are ideas or perceptions in our minds, and as they are modifications of matter in the bodies that cause such perceptions in us: that so we may not think (as perhaps usually is done) that they are exactly the images and resemblances of something inherent in the subject; most of those of sensation being in the mind no more the likeness of something existing without us than the names that stand for them are the likeness of our ideas, which yet upon hearing they are apt to excite in us.

Whatsoever the mind perceives in itself, or is the immediate object of perception, thought, or understanding, that I call *idea;* and the power to produce any idea in our mind I call a *quality* of the subject wherein that power is. Thus a snow-ball having the power to produce in us the ideas of white, cold, and round, the power to produce those ideas in us, as they are in the snow-ball, I call qualities; and as they are sensations or perceptions in our understandings, I call them ideas; which ideas, if I speak of sometimes as in the things themselves, I would be understood to mean those qualities in the objects which produce them in us.

Qualities thus considered in bodies are, first, such as are utterly inseparable from the body, in what state soever it be; such as in all the alterations and changes it suffers, all the force can be used upon it, it constantly keeps; and such as sense constantly finds in every particle of matter which has bulk enough to be perceived, and the mind finds inseparable from every particle of matter, though less than to make itself singly be perceived by our senses, v.g. Take a grain of wheat, divide it into two parts, each part has still solidity, extension, figure, and mobility; divide it again, and it retains still the same qualities; and so divide it on till the parts become insensible, they must retain still each of them all those qualities. For division (which is all that a mill, or pestle, or any other body does upon another, in reducing it to insensible parts) can never take away either solidity, extension, figure, or mobility from any body, but only makes two or more distinct separate masses of matter, of that which was but one before: all which distinct masses, reckoned as so many distinct bodies, after division make a certain number. These I call *original* or *primary qualities* of body, which I think we may observe to produce simple ideas in us, viz. solidity, extension, figure, motion or rest, and number.

Secondly, such qualities which in truth are nothing in the objects themselves but powers to produce various sensations in us by their primary qualities, i.e. by the bulk, figure, texture, and motion of their insensible parts, as colours, sounds, tastes, &c., these I call *secondary qualities*. To these might be added a third sort, which are allowed to be barely powers, though they are as much real qualities in the subject as those which I, to comply with the common way of speaking, call qualities, but, for distinction, secondary qualities. For the power in fire to produce a new colour or consistency in wax or clay by its primary qualities is as much a quality in fire as the power it has to produce in me a new idea or sensation of warmth or burning, which I felt not before, by the same primary qualities, viz. the bulk, texture, and motion of its insensible parts.

The next thing to be considered is how bodies produce ideas in us; and that is manifestly by impulse, the only way which we can conceive bodies to operate in.

If, then, external objects be not united to our minds when they produce ideas therein, and yet we perceive these original qualities in such of them as singly fall under our senses, it is evident that some motion must be thence continued by our nerves, or animal spirits, by some parts of our bodies, to the brains or the seat of sensation, there to produce in our minds the particular ideas we have of them. And since the extension, figure, number, and motion of bodies of an observable bigness may be perceived at a distance by the sight, it is evident some singly imperceptible bodies must come from them to the eyes, and thereby convey to the brain some motion which produces these ideas which we have of them in us.

After the same manner that the ideas of these original qualities are produced in us, we may conceive that the ideas of secondary qualities are also produced, viz., by the operation of insensible particles on our senses. For it being manifest that there are bodies and good store of bodies, each whereof are so small that we cannot, by any of our senses, discover either their bulk, figure, or motion as is evident in the particles of the air and water, and others extremely smaller than those, perhaps as much smaller than the particles of air and water as the particles of air and water are smaller than peas or hail-stones: Let us suppose at present that the different motions and figures, bulk and number of such particles, affecting the several organs of our senses, produce in us those different sensations which we have from the colours and smells of bodies; v.g. that a violet, by the impulse of such insensible particles of matter of peculiar figures and bulks, and in different degrees and modifications of their motions, causes the ideas of the blue colour and sweet scent of that flower to be produced in our minds; it being no more impossible to conceive that God should annex such ideas to such motions with which they have no similitude than that he should annex the idea of pain to the motion of a piece of steel dividing our flesh, with which that idea hath no resemblance.

What I have said concerning colours and smells may be understood also of tastes and sounds, and other the like sensible qualities; which, whatever reality we by mistake attribute to them, are in truth nothing in the objects themselves but powers to produce various sensations in us, and depend on those primary qualities, viz. bulk, figure, texture, and motion of parts, as I have said.

From whence I think it easy to draw this observation, that the ideas of primary qualities of bodies are resemblances of them, and their patterns do really exist in the bodies themselves; but the ideas produced in us by these secondary qualities have no resemblance of them at all. There is nothing like our ideas existing in the bodies themselves. They are, in the bodies we denominate from them, only a power to produce those sensations in us: And what is sweet, blue, or warm in idea is but the certain bulk, figure, and motion of the insensible parts in the bodies themselves, which we call so.

Flame is denominated hot and light; snow, white and cold; and manna, white and sweet, from the ideas they produce in us: Which qualities are commonly thought to be the same in those bodies that those ideas are in us, the one the perfect resemblance of the other, as they are in a mirror; and it would by most men be judged very extravagant if one should say otherwise. And yet he that will consider that the same fire that at one distance produces in us the sensation of warmth, does at a nearer approach produce in us the far different sensation of pain, ought to bethink himself what reason he has to say that his idea of warmth, which was produced in him by the fire, is actually in the fire; and his idea of pain, which the same fire produced in him the same way, is not in the fire. Why are whiteness and coldness in snow, and pain not, when it produces the one and the other idea in us, and can do neither, but by the bulk, figure, number, and motion of its solid parts?

The particular bulk, number, figure, and motion of the parts of fire or snow are really in them, whether anyone's senses perceive them or no: And therefore they may be called *real qualities,* because they really exist in those bodies: But light, heat, whiteness, or coldness are no more really in them than sickness or pain is in manna. Take away the sensation of them; let not the eyes see light, or colours, nor the ears hear sounds; let the palate not taste, nor the nose smell; and all colours, tastes, odours, and sounds, as they are such particular ideas, vanish and cease, and are reduced to their causes, i.e. bulk, figure, and motion of parts. [. . .]

Ideas being thus distinguished and understood, we may be able to give an account how the same water, at the same time, may produce the idea of cold by one hand and of heat by the other; whereas it is impossible that the same water, if those ideas were really in it, should at the same time be both hot and cold: For if we imagine warmth, as it is in our hands, to be nothing but a certain sort and degree of motion in the minute particles of our nerves, or animal spirits, we may understand how it is possible that the same water may, at the same time, produce the sensations of heat in one hand, and cold in the other; which yet figure never does, that never producing the idea of a square by one hand, which has produced the idea of a globe by another. But if the sensation of heat and cold be nothing but the increase or diminution of the motion of the minute parts of our bodies, caused by the corpuscles of any other body, it is easy to be understood that if that motion be greater in one hand than in the other; if a body be applied to the two hands, which has in its minute particles a greater motion than in those of one of the hands, and a less than in those of the other, it will increase the motion of the one hand, and lessen it in the other, and so cause the different sensations of heat and cold that depend thereon. [. . .]

A Pragmatic Solution to the Problem of Induction

John Hospers

Thus far we have been content to say that, while we cannot *know* that tomorrow water will boil, the sun will rise, and so forth, we have considerable *evidence* that these things will happen, and that the statements asserting that they will happen are, although not certain, at least extremely *probable*. At this point, however, a much more radical kind of question is sometimes raised: how does the fact that something has happened in the past constitute *any evidence whatever* that it will continue so in the future? What if someone said, "Very well—it's always happened that way in the past; so what? What has that to do with the future?"

Here is one comment we should consider first, lest it confuse the issue later: "You can't be so general about it—the occurrence of some regularities, or uniformities, in the past *is* evidence for their continuance in the future, but not so for others." Bertrand Russell uses the example of the chicken that has gone to its roost every night for several months in the belief that it will be secure there, perhaps because it has been secure there on past nights. But finally one night its owner comes into the henhouse and wrings its neck. If the chicken assumed that because it had been

Source: *Introduction to Philosophical Analysis*, Third Edition by Hospers. Reprinted by permission of Pearson Education, Inc., Upper Saddle River, NJ.

undisturbed in the past it would continue to be undisturbed in the future, it was mistaken. Some beliefs of this kind become *less* probable rather than more so with repetition: when you are eighty years old it's less probable that you will live till morning than it was when you were twenty, although the number of instances backing up the generalization is far greater at eighty. Whether the generalization is made more probable or less probable by the addition of repeated instances depends on the evidence we have for *other* generalizations relevant to the situation. We believe that the sun will rise tomorrow more confidently than we believe the eighty-year-old will live till morning because we know some statistics about the incidence of deaths and also some physiological laws about the human body, and we also know some things about the solar system, the earth's rotation on its axis, laws of planetary motion, principles of acceleration and momentum, and some of the other things that would have to be different if the sun were *not* to rise tomorrow. We have arrived at other generalizations about the behavior of nature besides the repeated rising of the sun; and these others all contribute, and add probability, to the statement about the continued rising of the sun. It is different with the case of the chicken, for our other generalizations—rather vague ones about the habits of chickens and farmers and the chicken market—do *not* lead to the belief that the past security of the chicken in any way guarantees its subsequent security. And the same with the example about the octogenarian: if the mere fact that he had lived so many days made it probable that he would live to see every next day that dawned, you would arrive at the conclusion that he would live forever! The mere repetition of days of life is subordinate to wider generalizations about the human constitution, which make it, every day that he lives, *less* probable that he will live to see the next day.

Both common sense and science would accept this view of the reasons for believing in continued uniformity in the case of the sun rising but not in the other cases. The same logical problem remains, however. It does not help to fortify the generalization about the sun's continued rising by appealing to *other* generalizations which are in precisely the same predicament that it is. How do we know that these other laws which are invoked to support the generalization about the sun will continue to hold? Being laws, they too involve the future, and therefore are as fallible as the generalization they are invoked to support. If the past affords us no evidence that the sun will rise in the future, how can it afford us evidence that the Law of Gravitation will continue to hold true, and that all the other laws that are used to support it will do the same? How, then, has our situation improved? It seems not to have improved at all.

One might suggest the easy way out, that of proving a law deductively. Thus:

> What has always occurred regularly in the past will continue to occur regularly in the future.
>
> The sun's rising has occurred regularly in the past.
>
> ---
>
> Therefore, The sun's rising will continue to occur regularly in the future.

Here we have proved our conclusion deductively. The trouble is, of course, . . . that you cannot prove the *truth* of a conclusion by valid deduction from premises; the premises must themselves be true. And if we do not know that our present conclusion is true, because it involves the future, how can we know that the major premise (the first line) is true, since it too involves the future? It is, in fact, a bigger generalization than is the conclusion. This is clearly no way out: if you want to deduce a conclusion which makes some reference to the future, there must be some reference to the future in one or more of the premises from which that conclusion is deduced. In that case the same skeptical questionings that can be made about the conclusion can be equally made about the premise (or those premises). The question has merely shifted; it has not been resolved.

The general principle, the one that covers all cases, that is usually invoked as a major premise in arguments of this type is the *Principle of Uniformity of Nature*. It is not always formulated in the same way, but it comes to this: "If Nature has always been uniform in the past (generalizations have held good), then Nature will continue to be uniform in the future." Some particular uniformity in the past will then be stated in the minor premise, and the continuance of that uniformity in the future will be deduced in the conclusion. From the Principle of Uniformity of Nature, then, we can deduce the desired conclusion. But how does one establish the Principle of Uniformity of Nature? From what true premises can *it* be deduced? "Well, the Principle of Uniformity of Nature has been true of the past; therefore the Principle of Uniformity of Nature will continue to be true of the future." But this conclusion does not logically follow. It does not follow unless we add another premise:

> What has held true of the past will hold true of the future.
>
> The Principle of Uniformity of Nature has held true of the past.
>
> ---
>
> Therefore, The Principle of Uniformity of Nature will hold true of the future.

And thus we are back in the same situation: how are we going to prove *this* major premise?

Or we could put the problem this way. "In the past, our predictions about the continued uniformity of nature have turned out to be true; in other words, our past predictions of the future have been verified. Thus we have considerable evidence that nature will continue to be uniform. After all, it's not as if we had never observed our predictions turning out right." "But that's not the question. I grant that our past predictions have been verified by the facts. In other words, our past predictions about the then-future were verified when that future was no longer future but became past. Now I'm not asking about past futures; I'm asking about future futures! What have the past futures to do with it? The fact that past futures turned out to be so-and-so doesn't prove that future futures will turn out to be so-and-so. If you assume that because past futures were so-and-so therefore the future futures will be so-and-so also, you are again assuming the very point to be proved!"

In other words, every time we try to prove the Principle of Uniformity of Nature we assume the principle in the very process of the proof. We cannot prove the principle by means of itself; and yet without doing this we cannot prove it at all. . . . No statement about nature being uniform in the past will prove that nature will be uniform in the future unless we assume that the fact of uniformity in the past proves future uniformity. Yet clearly it does not; from "The uniformity of nature has held in the past" we cannot deduce "The uniformity of nature will hold in the future."

If deduction fails us, how about induction? Induction, as we have seen, is not a method of proof, but only a method of estimating the probability of a conclusion; and it is the very basis of induction itself that is being questioned here. What we are examining is our very right to use inductive procedure in making generalizations. We cannot, therefore, justify this inductive procedure on the basis of inductive reasoning.

Our question, then, still remains: Can the uniformities of the past and the present render uniformities in the future any more probable? Does the fact that the past has turned out a certain way render even probable the statement that the future will turn out that way too?

There is much more agreement on the nature of the problem than on the solution of it. Unfortunately most attempted solutions become too technical to be discussed here. Nevertheless, two comments can be given which may alleviate the pressure of the problem:

1. If someone seriously says that the way things have occurred in the past affords *no* evidence whatever about the future, we can ask him what he means when he uses the word "evidence." A million times in the past when I have let go of a book or a stone it has fallen; never once has it risen into the air. This, and all the other things I know about the behavior of material objects, lead me to believe that it will fall when I let go of it this time. Is there really *no* evidence either way as to what the stone will do next time? To say this is to abandon all prediction and all science, and, more important here, *all meaning for the word "evidence."* For if the fact that it has fallen a million times is *not* evidence, what *would* be? If you so use the word "evidence" that *nothing* that ever happened could be evidence, what would you mean by the word "evidence"? Would it not just be a meaningless noise? (You could not even say, "There is *no* evidence that X will happen," for that sentence contains the word "evidence," which must be given a meaning before it can meaningfully be used.)

The same point could be made regarding the word "probable." If the fact that the stone has always fallen and never risen, together with all the other things we have observed about stones and other material objects, does not even render more *probable* the statement that the stone will fall the next time, what in the world *could* make it so? And if nothing could, then what meaning can be attached by the speaker to the word "probable," or for that matter the word "improbable"? Remember that it would be just as meaningless to say "It is *im*probable that X will occur" as it would be to say "It is probable that X will occur"—for if the word "probable" has been deprived of all possible application to the universe, its opposite, which acquires meaning only by contrast with it, suffers precisely the same fate.

2. If the question is still asked, "How are we going to prove the Principle of Uniformity of Nature which is required to establish our inductions?" the answer is of course that we cannot. It cannot be proved by means of itself, and it cannot be proved without itself. As we have already seen, to prove (deductively) a conclusion involving the future we must have a proposition involving the future in the premises. In other words—as in the case of the principles of logic—we cannot give a *logical* justification for the Principle of Uniformity of Nature; we cannot give a logical basis for the very principle which is itself the logical basis for the deduction of laws.

It would seem, then, that to demand a logical basis for the principle is as unreasonable as to demand it in the case of the principles of logic themselves. Yet the principle is needed if our inductive conclusions (laws) are to be proved, since they involve the future. Laws are the basis of our predictions. "Why do you think that stone will fall?" "All unsupported bodies fall." If this last statement did not involve the future, it could not be employed to predict anything about the future, which it clearly *is* being employed to do.

What, then, can we do under the circumstances? As in the case of the principles of logic, . . . we can give a pragmatic justification for our *adoption* of these principles. In the case of the principles of logic it was the impossibility of any coherent discourse without the use of them; in the present case the situation is not quite so radical: it is the fruitlessness of any scientific procedure without the adoption of the Principle of Uniformity of Nature, which alone enables us to make inferences from past and present to future. We cannot prove that the principle which enables us to do this is true, but *if* we want to attempt any predictions at all—and as human beings we must all do this if we want to stay alive (do we not refrain from going to the street via the fifth-floor window because we are convinced that the uniformity of behavior of freely falling bodies will continue?)—then the laws of nature are the only sound basis for such prediction. It is these or nothing. We cannot prove deductively that these laws are true, for we cannot prove that the uniformities will hold in the future, and this is what every law implicitly asserts; but *if* nature is uniform, and *if* there is an order of nature which extends into the future, then the inductive method is the way in which to gain knowledge of this order. We want successful prediction; we cannot prove that our predictions, however well they may have worked out in the past, will be successful in the next instance; but if successful prediction is to be possible at all, it will be so only by means of these laws. This is our pragmatic basis, our practical justification, for asserting these laws, in spite of the fact that we cannot prove that the laws are true, or can prove them only by using an unprovable principle as a premise.

There is, to be sure, another way out of the situation: we can assert that the Principle of Uniformity of Nature is a synthetic necessary statement, something which *necessarily* holds of the universe. But here again, of course, there are difficulties: what entitles us to say that the principle is necessary? How do we know this, if we know it? To many it would seem that this way of resolving the Gordian knot is not by unraveling it but by cutting it with a knife.

The Problem of Induction— Old and New

Howard Kahane and Paul Tidman

Induction Is Unjustified—The Old Riddle of Induction

Recall that the characteristic mark of all inductive (nondeductive) reasoning is a "gap" between premises and conclusion. As soon as this gap was realized,[1] the question of *how any inductive argument can be justified* was raised; that is, the question was raised about the *rationality* of the acceptance of hypotheses on inductive grounds.

Unfortunately, a good answer to this question has been hard to come by. A great many solutions to the problem of induction have been proposed, most of which can be classified into four categories.

(1) The most obvious thought is that we are justified in using induction because it "works." All of science is based on inductive conclusions of some sort or other, and everyone knows how successful science is. Everyone knows that the scientific method, which uses induction, *works*.

Unfortunately, this obvious solution to the problem is not satisfactory. It simply isn't true that we know that induction works, or is successful. At best, what we know is that it *has worked, or has been successful*. But will it be successful in the future? We don't know. Indeed, the problem seems to be that we haven't the slightest reason to think induction will be successful in the future.

It often is claimed that in fact we do have a very good reason for thinking that induction will be successful in the future, namely its success in the past. But only a little thought is needed to see that this reason will not do. For to argue that induction will be successful because it *has* been successful is to argue *inductively*. (The premise of such an argument is "Induction has been successful [on the whole] up to now," and its conclusion is "Induction always will be successful

---

[1]The philosopher David Hume was the first person to perceive it clearly and to try to bridge it. See *A Treatise of Human Nature*, Book I., Part IV., Section I: and *An Enquiry Concerning Human Understanding*, Section V.

[on the whole]." Clearly, this argument itself is an inductive argument.) So when we argue this way, we use induction to justify itself, which means that we argue circularly, and hence fallaciously.

(2) Perhaps the most popular solutions to the problem of induction are those that use some principle concerning the *uniformity of nature,* such as the principle that *every event has a cause.*

For instance, if we assume that nature is uniform, then we can reason inductively from the fact that all examined pieces of copper are uniform with respect to conductivity to the conclusion that all pieces of copper (examined or as yet unexamined) are uniform with respect to the conducting of electricity.

But solutions of this kind are unsatisfactory. First, even if nature is uniform, there is no guarantee that the particular uniformities we have observed up to a given time will hold in the future; the true uniformities of nature may be more complex or subtle. And second, the assumption itself that every event has a cause, or that nature is uniform, can be challenged. Why assume that nature is uniform? Again, there seems to be no answer. (Remember that we cannot argue that the assumption that nature is uniform has been fruitful in the past, and hence is likely to be fruitful in the future, for such an argument would be an inductive argument, and we cannot use induction to justify a principle of uniformity and then use that principle to justify the use of induction.)

(3)   Some philosophers have proposed justifications based on the so-called self-corrective nature of induction.[2] For example, suppose we conclude that half of 10,000 tosses of a coin will land heads up, on the basis of the evidence that half of the first 100 tosses of this coin landed heads up. Suppose this conclusion is false. Then we can "correct" it simply by observing larger and larger coin tossing samples, basing our conclusion about the relative frequency of heads in the total series of 10,000 tosses on the relative frequency of heads in the largest sample we have at any given time. If we continue the process long enough, at some point we must reach the correct value. Hence, it is claimed, we are justified in using inductive reasoning in such cases because the process is self-correcting: repeated applications must get us closer and closer to the truth.

---

[2]See, for instance, Charles Peirce, "Induction as Experimental and Self-Correcting." *Collected Papers of Charles Sanders Peirce,* vol. VI. Charles Hartshome and Paul Weiss, eds. (Cambridge, MA: Harvard University Press, 1935). Reprinted in Edward H. Madden. *The Structure of Scientific Thought* (Boston: Houghton Mifflin, 1960), pp. 296–298.

Suppose, for instance, that one half of 10,000 tosses of a coin in fact will land heads up. If we get heads on exactly half of the first 5,000 tosses, then we know with deductive certainty that the relative frequency of heads compared to total tosses in the entire series of 10,000 tosses must be somewhere between 1/4 and 3/4.[3] Hence our prediction that half of the 10,000 tosses will be heads cannot be off by more than ±1/4.

Now, suppose that after 8,000 tosses the observed relative frequency of heads is still 1/2. Then we know at this point that the relative frequency of heads in the total series of 10,000 tosses must be somewhere between 2/5 and 3/5.[4] Hence, at this point our prediction that half of the 10,000 tosses will be heads cannot be off by more than ±1/10. So we are getting closer and closer to the correct value (no matter what that value happens to be), because the *largest possible error* in our predictions keeps getting smaller and smaller.

The trouble is that our predictions get closer and closer to the correct value because larger and larger portions of the series concern *past tosses* and are incorporated into our *evidence*, while smaller and smaller portions of the series concern *future tosses*. At no point do we have any guarantee that we are getting any closer to the actual relative frequency of heads among future (unexamined) tosses of the coin. But if the self-corrective claim is to have any force, it must apply to predictions about the future (or the as yet unexamined past).

The situation is even worse for infinitely long series, because the relative frequency of any given finite portion of an infinite series is compatible with any relative frequency whatever in the infinite series. For instance, even if every one of millions of tosses of a coin lands heads up, the *limit* of such an infinite series of tosses (assuming an infinite series of tosses is possible) still might equal zero. Hence, for an infinite series, inductive practices embody no self-corrective feature whatever.

We must conclude, then, that we cannot justify the use of induction on the grounds that it is self-correcting.

(4) Finally, there are the so-called dissolutions of the problem of induction, according to which the very problem itself is a pseudoproblem.[5]

---

[3]If the 5,000 remaining tosses all are tails, then the relative frequency will be 1/4, and if they all are heads, then the relative frequency will be 3/4.

[4]If the 2,000 remaining tosses all are tails, then the relative frequency will be 2/5, and if they all are heads, then the relative frequency will be 3/5.

[5]See for instance, A. J. Ayer, *Language, Truth and Logic* (New York: Dover Publications), pp. 49–50.

We shall consider two of the many solutions of this kind. In the first, it is claimed that it is not rational to doubt the principles of inductive reasoning because these principles themselves *determine* (in part) what it means to be rational. In other words, if we doubt the rationality (the reasonableness) of the use of induction, then we simply don't know what it means to be rational.

Unfortunately, this argument is defective. Were we to find ourselves in a community in which it is considered rational to believe everything said by the oldest member of the community, it would be reasonable to inquire if it *really* is rational to do so. And if the reply were that what it *means* to be rational is to believe the oldest member of the community, then it would be perfectly proper to ask *why* we should be rational. Put into this context, the problem of induction is that we seem to have no answer to the question "Why be rational?" either for the peculiar concept of rationality in the imaginary community just described or for the concept of rationality in the real community.

According to the second kind of "dissolution" of the problem, there is no problem of justifying the use of inductive principles because *no justification is possible*, and if none is possible, then none can be required. Two kinds of arguments have been presented in support of this claim.

First, it has been argued that such a justification would have to be either *inductive* or *deductive*. An inductive justification would be circular because it would use the very principles of reasoning we are trying to justify. And we could never construct a valid deductive justification, because it is impossible to prove deductively that nature is uniform, or that every event has a cause, or that the future will resemble the past.[6]

But this argument is defective. It is true that metaphysical assumptions, such as the uniformity of nature, cannot be proved deductively. But a deductive justification does not necessarily require that any such principle be proved. Perhaps other kinds of assumptions can be proved that will justify the use of induction.[7]

---

[6]What is often meant by such an argument is that metaphysical principles of this kind are not *theorems of logics, or deductively obtainable from the null set of premises, or knowable prior to any particular empirical observations.*

[7]For instance, the pragmatic justification presented by Hans Reichenbach in *The Theory of Probability* (Berkeley: University of California Press, 1949), pp. 469–482, is based on an attempt to prove deductively that if any method of predicting the future is successful, then the use of induction will be successful.

Second, it has been argued that just as the theorems in an axiom system cannot all be proved (without circularity or infinite regress), so also all principles of *reasoning* or *inferring* cannot be justified (without circularity or infinite regress). Hence, we should not be surprised that no justification of induction is possible.

Clearly, there is something to this last argument. It is true that we cannot justify every principle of reasoning any more than we can prove every theorem. And it may well be that the basic inductive principle will be among those that remain forever unjustified and hence remain forever as a kind of primitive inference rule. But the argument in question does not prove this. All that it proves is that some principle or other will remain unjustified. It does not prove induction is that principle.

On the other hand, recognition of the important fact that some principle or other must remain unjustified may make it more tolerable that as yet no one seems to have been able to justify the basic principle of induction.

Not All Instances of Theories Confirm Them—The New Riddle of Induction

Perhaps the most curious of the objections raised against our account of scientific method is the one posed by Nelson Goodman's so-called *new riddle of induction.*

The old riddle, you will recall, has to do with justifying induction and inductive inferences in general, and in particular with justifying the belief that generalizations are confirmed by their instances (as, say, the generalization "All dogs have tails" is confirmed by finding an instance of it—namely a dog with a tail). The new riddle, according to Goodmanites, has to do with distinguishing those generalizations that *are* confirmed by their instances from those that are not.

To see the difference between these two kinds of cases, consider the following example. Suppose 100 emeralds, all of them green, are observed for color. This would usually be considered good evidence for the hypothesis or generalization (H-1) "All emeralds are green." But now let's introduce a new color term, "grue," referring to all things examined for color *before* a particular time t, say January 1, 2001, that are green, and to other things just in case they are blue. Then emeralds, for instance, will be "grue" just in case they either are green and the time in question is before time t or are blue and the time in question is at t or after. An emerald examined now and found to be green would thus be "grue," but one examined in the twenty-first century and found to be green would not be "grue" (it would, however, be *bleen*, that is, it would be either examined before time t and blue, or not so examined and green).

All of the 100 green emeralds observed in our hypothetical example are "grue," as well as green, because they're green and the time is prior to time t. So according to what has been said so far about confirmation, it would seem that the 100 observed "grue" emeralds constitute confirming instances of the hypothesis (H-2): "All emeralds are grue," just as these same emeralds, being green, confirm (H-1): "All emeralds are green." But (H-1) and (H-2) *conflict* with each other, because according to (H-1) emeralds observed after time t will be green while according to (H-2) they will be blue. In fact, of course, no one would accept (H-2) no matter how many confirming cases we find in its favor. Goodman's problem is to find some way to distinguish "grue-like" illegitimate predicates and hypotheses from legitimate green-like ones, so that hypotheses like (H-1) will be confirmed by their instances while those like (H-2) will not.

Most of the proposed solutions to this problem are seriously defective. Rudolf Carnap, for example, argued that terms like "grue" are what he called "positional," meaning that they are terms whose definitions in part refer to individual objects, or to individual places or times. But Carnap's solution is unsatisfactory, in particular because lots of "good" predicates are positional and in fact are used in acceptable generalizations all the time. Some examples given by Goodman are "Ming," "Arctic," and "Pleistocene." Generalizations like "All Ming vases are expensive" would usually be held to be confirmed by their instances (in this case, by particular Ming vases that are expensive).

The interesting thing about Goodman's riddle is that an obvious answer lies right at hand, and was proposed soon after Goodman formulated the problem; indeed it must have occurred independently to countless readers of the literature since then. Take our two competing hypotheses (H-1) "All emeralds are green," and (H-2) "All emeralds are grue." The first contains the "good" term "green," the second the "bad" term "grue." What is good about the former but bad about the latter? The first thought many of us have is that all green things *resemble* each other in a certain way, namely by being green in color, while there is no such color resemblance uniting all grue things, because items that are grue prior to time t are green, while those that are grue after time t are blue. What the term "green" *means* requires all items referred to by that predicate to resemble each other in color—share a common color—namely green. But what the term "grue" means does not require this; prior to time *t* grue things are green, after time *t* they are blue. By simply saying that only those generalizations containing terms like "green" are confirmed by their instances, the problem would seem to be solved. That is, it seems as though we can quite easily solve the problem by rejecting all generalizations containing terms, like "grue," which select classes of items that do not necessarily all resemble each other in some relevant way. One idea behind inductive reasoning is, after all, to find items that resemble each other in some specified way that also share some other common property. In the case of (H-1): "All emeralds are green," we find stones that resemble each other in being beryl silicates (and thus emeralds)[8] and discover that they also share the common property of being green. In the case of (H-2) "All emeralds are grue," there also is a shared common property, namely that of being grue, but that is not a *resembling* property—all grue things do not resemble each other in the appropriate way.

Perhaps, the main reason why this obvious solution to the grue problem has not settled the matter is that Goodman provided what most writers on the subject have accepted as a conclusive objection to it. Goodman argued that given any two things, however different they may seem, we can always invent a property they both share, as we did in fact in inventing the property of being grue. That is, he argued that all grue things do in fact share a common property, namely that of being grue, and thus do in fact resemble each other (because they all are grue). We've noticed that all emeralds have resembled each other by being green, perhaps, because "green" is a term we've become familiar with through long use—it has become well *entrenched* in our language. But we've failed to notice that all emeralds so far encountered have resembled each other by being grue, perhaps because we're not familiar with and haven't used the term "grue"—it hasn't become entrenched in our language.

Underlying Goodman's view on the grue question is an extreme version of a very old philosophical position, called *nominalism* (something some of the nonnominalistic writers on the subject seem to have overlooked). In its extreme form, nominalism says that "there is nothing common to a class of particulars called by the same name other

---

[8]Goodman's choice of example was unfortunate in that according to one common definition of *emerald* a non-green beryl silicate would not be an emerald.

than that they *are* called by the same name."[9] That is why Goodman says that just as green things resemble each other in being green so also grue things *equally* resemble each other in being grue.[10]

But suppose we reject the nominalist's view and accept the common-sense, everyday idea of resemblance that makes it wrong to speak of "grue" things as resembling each other just as much as do green things. (This is in fact what the vast majority of philosophers have done over the ages.) Then the Goodman problem fails to get off the ground,[11] and our account of the philosophy of science remains intact.

---

[9]A. D. Woozley in his article "Universals," in the *Encyclopedia of Philosophy*, Paul Edwards, ed. (New York: Collier Macmillan 1967). Woozley's article also contains an excellent rebuttal of this extreme form of nominalism (in the opinion of this writer).1

[10]Goodman's basic nominalistic principle is that there are individual things in the world, and sums of individual things, but no general properties. See his article "A World of Individuals" in *The Problem of Universals* (Notre Dame, IN: Notre Dame, University Press, 1956). But he is quickly led to the version of nominalism Woozley discussed, and without doubt believes that any two things (for example, any two grue emeralds) may resemble each other just as much as any other two things (for example, any two green emeralds).

[11]There are, of course, some wrinkles to take care of. For example, Goodman argues that lots of acceptable terms, such as "electrical conductor," are not resembling terms in the everyday sense; we therefore have to show what the resemblances might be like in these cases. See my "Pathological Predicates and Projections" (*American Philosophical Quarterly*, vol. 8 (1971), pp. 171–178), for more on this, and also for some other thoughts on the grue problem and how to solve it, as well as for a bibliography on the subject.

SECTION THREE

DO WE HAVE FREE WILL?

We often find ourselves deliberating between alternative courses of action. Doing so leaves us with a strong sense of freedom, and we may conclude that our present and future choices are up to us. Unfortunately, there is reason for doubting this. Is it possible that our choices are determined by factors beyond our control? If our choices are caused by events in our past, and if the past cannot be changed, then it seems that our present and future choices are beyond our control as well. Reconciling human freedom with the fact that actions are caused is the philosophical problem of free will.

We start our readings with a selection from Arthur Schopenhauer's *Essay on the Freedom of the Will*. According to Schopenhauer, the problem of free will is a "touchstone by which one can distinguish the deeply thinking minds from the superficial ones." It only appears to us as if we are free. If we think a bit deeper about the true nature of the world, it becomes obvious that we must act in the way we act. Schopenhauer argues that there are excellent reasons for believing that our character and personality are fixed from birth. However, it is our character and our personality that determine how we act in given situations. Schopenhauer therefore defends a position that is known as hard determinism.

W. T. Stace comes to a different conclusion about free will. In his article "Compatibilism," Stace argues that those thinkers like Schopenhauer who see a conflict between causality and freedom overlook that there is a great difference between a caused action and a forced action. Stace gives the example of a man who leaves his office because he wants to eat lunch and a man who leaves his office because he is forcibly removed by the police. Both of these actions are caused, but only one of the actions is not free.

Stace concludes that "acts freely done are those whose immediate causes are psychological states in the agent and acts not freely done are those whose immediate causes are states of affairs external to the agent." This position is known as compatibilism or soft determinism.

It is exactly this form of compatibilism that Peter van Inwagen attacks in his article "The Incompatibility of Free Will and Determinism." One of van Inwagen's starting points is the common belief that an agent *P* deserves to be called free with respect to an act only if the agent has the ability to either perform or refrain from performing the act. Van Inwagen considers the case of a judge, who after a period of calm and rational deliberation, decides to refrain from raising his hand and thus condemns a criminal to being put to death. Van Inwagen argues that, if we assume that the judge's act is causally determined, it follows that the judge could not have raised his hands to save the criminal. The judge, and any other agent who acts in a causally determined world, is therefore not free.

Mark Siderits, on the other hand, thinks that Van Inwagen's incompatibilism is ultimately an illusion. In the essay "Beyond Compatibilism: A Buddhist Approach to Freedom and Determinism," Siderits argues that standard Buddhist ideas about personal identity offer us new ways to "defeat the claim that freedom is incompatible with determinism."

In the debate about free will, the principle of alternate possibilities plays a central role. The principle says that an agent can be free and responsible only if the agent could have acted other than she in fact did act. In his essay "Alternate Possibilities and Moral Responsibility," Harry Frankfurt argues that it is very well possible that a person who is coerced into doing an act, and has no alternative to performing it, is nevertheless morally responsible for performing it. According to Frankfurt, we should reject the principle of alternate possibilities because it is logically possible to separate the concepts of being morally responsible from the concept of being able to act otherwise.

We finish our discussion of free will with a classic essay by Roderick Chisholm. In "Human Freedom and the Self," Chisholm argues that anyone who holds that human beings are fully responsible agents must reject the idea that our actions are either causally determined or simply happen by chance. Chisholm suggests that there is a third option: free actions are caused "not by other events or states of affairs, but by the agent." He thereby introduces the idea of "agent causation" and develops a libertarian solution to the problem of free will. According to this position, "each of us, when we act, is a prime mover unmoved."

Essay on the Freedom of the Will

Arthur Schopenhauer   *(Translated by Konstantin Kolenda)*

[. . .] The individual character is *inborn;* it is not a work of art or of accidental circumstances, but the work of nature itself. It manifests itself already in the child and shows there on a small scale what it will be in the future on a large one. Hence two children who have exactly the same upbringing and surroundings will most clearly exhibit fundamentally different characters, characters which they will still have as old men. In its basic features character is even hereditary.

From this presentation of the nature of individual character it follows of course that virtues and vices are inborn. This truth may be inconvenient to some prejudices and some old wives' philosophy, with its so-called practical interests, that is, its petty, narrow concepts and limited school-children views, but it was already the conviction of the father of morality, Socrates, who according to Aristotle maintained: "Being virtuous or vicious is not a matter of our choice."[1] What Aristotle maintains to the contrary here is evidently bad: for he also shares this opinion of Socrates and expresses it most clearly in the *Nicomachean Ethics:* "For all men think that each type of character belongs to its possessors in some sense by nature; for from the very moment of birth we are just or fitted for self-control or have the other moral qualities."[2]

If we survey all the virtues and vices in Aristotle's book *On Virtues and Vices,* where they are reviewed briefly, we shall find that in actual people all of them can be thought of only as inborn traits, and only as such can they be authentic. If on the other hand they came from reflection and were arbitrarily assumed, they would really amount to a sort of dissimulation; they would be unauthentic. Also for this reason we could not count at all on their permanence and reliability under pressure of circumstances.

When we consider in addition the Christian virtue of love, *caritas*—which is absent in Aristotle and in all ancients—the matter is no different. How could the untiring goodness of one man and the incorrigible, deeply rooted wickedness of another—say the character of the

[1][Aristotle, *Magna Moralia* (tr. W. D. Ross), I, 9, 1187a, 7.–Tr.]
[2][Aristotle, *Nicomachean Ethics* (tr. W. D. Ross), VI, 13, 1144b, 4.–Tr.]

Antonines, Hadrian, or Titus on the one hand, and that of Caligula, Nero, or Domitian on the other—alight upon them from the outside, be the work of accidental circumstances, or of mere knowledge and teaching? Didn't Nero have Seneca for a tutor? It is rather the case that the germ of all virtues and vices lies in the inborn character, in that real core of the whole man. This conviction, so natural to an unsophisticated man, guided also the hand of Valleius Paterculus as he wrote the following about Cato: "He resembled virtue herself, and in all his acts he revealed a character nearer to that of gods than of men. He never did a right action solely for the sake of seeming to do the right, but because he could not do otherwise."[3] [. . .]

On the other hand, if one assumes the freedom of the will, it is absolutely impossible to say what is the source both of virtue and of vice, or of the fact that two men who were brought up in the same way act quite differently, indeed in an opposite way, under entirely equal circumstances and occasions. The actual, original, basic difference of the characters is incompatible with the assumption of a freedom of the will which means that for any man, in any situation, two contrary actions are equally possible. For then his character must be by nature a *tabula rasa*, like Locke's intellect, and can have no inborn tendency in one direction or another, since this would indeed eliminate that complete equilibrium which one thinks of in the *liberum arbitrium indifferentiae*. Hence, when this is assumed, the basis of the difference in the manner in which different people act cannot be found in the subjective aspect. But even less can it be found in the objective aspect, for then the *objects* would determine action, and the required freedom would be completely lost. Then at best only this way out would be left, namely to locate the origin of that truly great difference in behavior in a middle ground between subject and object, that is, to regard it as arising from the different ways in which the objective is grasped by the subjective, or as it was cognized by different people. But then everything would revert to a correct or incorrect knowledge of the given circumstances, whereby the moral difference in behavior would be transformed into a mere difference of the correctness of judgment, and morality would be transformed into logic.

---

[3][Velleius Paterculus, *Res Gestae Divi Augusti* (London, New York: 1924), p. 125, trans. Shipley.–Tr.] This pasage is gradually becoming a standard weapon in the arsenal of the determinists, an honor of which the good old historian, 1800 years ago, certainly never dreamed. First it was praised by Hobbes, and after him by Priestley. Then it was quoted by Schelling in his treatise on freedom [F. W. J. v. Schelling, "Ueber das Wesen der menschlichen Freiheit," *Schellings Werke* (Leipzig: 1907), III, 489.–Tr.], in a translation somewhat falsified for his purposes; for which reason he does not name Valleius Paterculus directly, but, with equal shrewdness and elegance, says, "an ancient." Finally, I also did not want to miss the opportunity to quote it, since it really is relevant here.

If now the adherents of the freedom of the will should try to get out of that difficult dilemma by saying that there is indeed no inborn difference of characters but that such a difference arises from external circumstances, impressions, experiences, examples, teachings, etc.—and if a character had come into being for once in this way, the difference of behavior could be subsequently explained from that—then we must reply, first, that according to this view the character would put in an appearance very late (whereas actually it can already be recognized in children) and that most people would die before having attained a character; and second, that all those external circumstances whose effect the character was supposed to be lie completely outside of our power and would be brought about in one or the other way by chance (or, if one prefers, by Providence). Now, if it is from these that the character and from this in turn the difference of behavior arises, then all moral responsibility for the latter would completely disappear, since obviously this difference would ultimately be the work of chance or of Providence. [. . .]

The question of the freedom of the will is really a touchstone by which one can distinguish the deeply thinking minds from the superficial ones, or it is a milestone at which their ways part, all the former maintaining the necessary occurrence of an action when the character and the motive are given, and the latter, together with the great masses, clinging to the freedom of the will. There is also a type of a middle-of-the-roader who, feeling embarrassed, tacks back and forth, shifts the target for himself and others, hides behind words and phrases, or turns and twists the question so long that one no longer knows what it amounted to. This was what Leibniz did, who was much more of a mathematician and a learned man than a philosopher.[4] But in order to make such vacillating talkers face the question, one must put it to them in the following way and insist that they answer it.

1) To a given man under given circumstances, are two actions possible, or only one?—The answer of all who think deeply: only one.

2) Let us consider that a man's character remains unchanged and also that the circumstances whose influence he had to experience were necessarily determined throughout and down to the least detail by external causes, which always take place with strict necessity and whose chain, entirely consisting of likewise necessary links, continues

---

[4]Leibniz' want of principle in this matter shows itself most clearly in his letter to Coste, *Opera phil.,* ed. Erdmann, p. 447, and later also in *Theodicy,* pp. 45–53.

into infinity. Could the completed life course of such a man turn out in any respect, even the smallest, in any happening, any scene, differently from the way it did?—No! is the consistent and correct answer.

The conclusion from both propositions is: Everything that happens, from the largest to the smallest, happens necessarily. *Quidquid fit necessario fit.*

Anyone who is frightened by these propositions has still to learn some things and unlearn others. But then he will realize that they are the most abundant source of comfort and tranquility. Our acts are indeed not a first beginning; therefore nothing really new comes through them into being. But this is true: *through that which we do we only find out what we are.*

On the conviction of the strict necessity of all that happens, a conviction not clearly recognized and yet felt, rests also the concept of fate or destiny which was so firmly held by the ancients. So does the fatalism of the Mohammedans, and even the ineradicable belief in omens. This is so because even the smallest accident happens necessarily and all occurrences, so to speak, keep time with one another, so that everything reverberates in everything else. Finally, connected with this is even the fact that a man who has crippled or killed another without the slightest intention, or quite accidentally, regrets this misfortune throughout the rest of his life with a feeling which seems akin to that of guilt. Moreover, as a *persona piacularis* (unfortunate person) he finds in the eyes of others a peculiar kind of discredit. Indeed, the felt conviction of the unchangeability of character and the necessity of its manifestation was probably not without an influence even on the Christian doctrine of election by grace.

Finally, I do not want to suppress still another incidental observation, which anyone may either accept or reject, according to the way he thinks about some matters. If we do not accept the strict necessity of all that happens by means of a causal chain which connects all events without exception, but allow this chain to be broken in countless places by an absolute freedom, then all foreseeing of the future, in dreams, in clairvoyant somnambulism, second sight, becomes objective and hence absolutely impossible, and so inconceivable. Because then there is no objectively real future which could possibly be foreseen, but instead of saying this we merely doubt the subjective conditions, hence the subjective possibility of this foresight. Even this doubt can no longer be entertained today by the well-informed, after innumerable testimonies of the most trustworthy kind have established those anticipations of the future.

Let me add just a few more considerations as corollaries to the established doctrine of the necessity of all that happens.

What would become of this world if necessity did not permeate all things and hold them together, but especially govern the procreation of individuals? A monster, a rubbish heap, a caricature without sense and meaning—namely, the work of a true and real chaos.

To wish that some event had not taken place is a silly self-torture, for this means to wish something absolutely impossible, and is as irrational as is the wish that the sun should rise in the West. Precisely because everything that happens, great or small, happens with strict necessity, it is altogether useless to reflect on how insignificant and accidental were the causes which brought that event about, and how easily they could have been different. For this is illusory. All of them have happened with just as strict necessity and have done this work with just as full a power as that in virtue of which the sun rises in the East. We should rather consider the events, as they happen, with the same eye as we consider the printed word which we read, knowing full well that it was there before we read it. [. . .]

Compatibilism
W. T. Stace

. . . I shall first discuss the problem of free will, for it is certain that if there is no free will there can be no morality. Morality is concerned with what men ought and ought not to do. But if a man has no freedom to choose what he will do, if whatever he does is done under compulsion, then it does not make sense to tell him that he ought not to have done what he did and that he ought to do something different. All moral precepts would in such case be meaningless. Also if he acts always under compulsion, how can he be held morally responsible for his actions? How can he, for example, be punished for what he could not help doing?

It is to be observed that those learned professors of philosophy or psychology who deny the existence of free will do so only in their professional moments and in their studies and lecture rooms. For when it comes to doing anything practical, even of the most trivial kind, they invariably behave as if they and others were free. They inquire from you at dinner whether you will choose this dish or that dish. They will ask

From Religion and the Modern Mind *(Philadephia: Lippincott, 1952).*

a child why he told a lie, and will punish him for not having chosen the way of truthfulness. All of which is inconsistent with a disbelief in free will. This should cause us to suspect that the problem is not a real one; and this, I believe, is the case. The dispute is merely verbal, and is due to nothing but a confusion about the meanings of words. It is what is now fashionably called a semantic problem.

How does a verbal dispute arise? Let us consider a case which, although it is absurd in the sense that no one would ever make the mistake which is involved in it, yet illustrates the principle which we shall have to use in the solution of the problem. Suppose that someone believed that the word "man" means a certain sort of five-legged animal; in short that "five-legged animal" is the correct *definition* of man. He might then look around the world, and rightly observing that there are no five-legged animals in it, he might proceed to deny the existence of men. This preposterous conclusion would have been reached because he was using an incorrect definition of "man." All you would have to do to show him his mistake would be to give him the correct definition; or at least to show him that his definition was wrong. Both the problem and its solution would, of course, be entirely verbal. The problem of free will, and its solution, I shall maintain, is verbal in exactly the same way. The problem has been created by the fact that learned men, especially philosophers, have assumed an incorrect definition of free will, and then finding that there is nothing in the world which answers to their definition, have denied its existence. As far as logic is concerned, their conclusion is just as absurd as that of the man who denies the existence of men. The only difference is that the mistake in the latter case is obvious and crude, while the mistake which the deniers of free will have made is rather subtle and difficult to detect.

Throughout the modern period, until quite recently, it was assumed, both by the philosophers who denied free will and by those who defended it, that *determinism is inconsistent with free will*. If a man's actions were wholly determined by chains of causes stretching back into the remote past, so that they could be predicted beforehand by a mind which knew all the causes, it was assumed that they could not in that case be free. This implies that a certain definition of actions done from free will was assumed, namely that they are actions *not* wholly determined by causes or predictable beforehand. Let us shorten this by saying that free will was defined as meaning indeterminism. This is the incorrect definition which has led to the denial of free will. As soon as we see what the true definition is we shall find that the question whether the world is deterministic, as Newtonian science implied, or in a measure indeterministic, as current physics teaches, is wholly irrelevant to the problem.

Of course there is a sense in which one can define a word arbitrarily in any way one pleases. But a definition may nevertheless be called correct or incorrect. It is correct if it accords with a *common usage* of the word defined. It is incorrect if it does not. And if you give an incorrect definition, absurd and untrue results are likely to follow. For instance, there is nothing to prevent you from arbitrarily defining a man as a five-legged animal, but this is incorrect in the sense that it does not accord with the ordinary meaning of the word. Also it has the absurd result of leading to a denial of the existence of men. This shows that *common usage is the criterion for deciding whether a definition is correct or not.* And this is the principle which I shall apply to free will. I shall show that indeterminism is not what is meant by the phrase "free will" *as it is commonly used.* And I shall attempt to discover the correct definition by inquiring how the phrase is used in ordinary conversation.

Here are a few samples of how the phrase might be used in ordinary conversation. It will be noticed that they include cases in which the question whether a man acted with free will is asked in order to determine whether he was morally and legally responsible for his acts.

JONES: I once went without food for a week.
SMITH: Did you do that of your own free will?
JONES: No. I did it because I was lost in a desert and could find no food.

But suppose that the man who had fasted was Mahatma Gandhi. The conversation might then have gone:

GANDHI: I once fasted for a week.
SMITH: Did you do that of your own free will?
GANDHI: Yes. I did it because I wanted to compel the British Government to give India its independence.

Take another case. Suppose that I had stolen some bread, but that I was as truthful as George Washington. Then, if I were charged with the crime in court, some exchange of the following sort might take place:

JUDGE: Did you steal the bread of your own free will?
STACE: Yes. I stole it because I was hungry.

Or in different circumstances the conversation might run:

JUDGE: Did you steal of your own free will?
STACE: No. I stole because my employer threatened to beat me if I did not.

At a recent murder trial in Trenton some of the accused had signed confessions, but afterwards asserted that they had done so under police duress. The following exchange might have occurred:

JUDGE: Did you sign this confession of your own free will?
PRISONER: No. I signed it because the police beat me up.

Now suppose that a philosopher had been a member of the jury. We could imagine this conversation taking place in the jury room.

FOREMAN OF THE JURY: The prisoner says he signed the confession because he was beaten, and not of his own free will.
PHILOSOPHER: This is quite irrelevant to the case. There is no such thing as free will.
FOREMAN: Do you mean to say that it makes no difference whether he signed because his conscience made him want to tell the truth or because he was beaten?
PHILOSOPHER: None at all. Whether he was caused to sign by a beating or by some desire of his own—the desire to tell the truth, for example—in either case his signing was causally determined, and therefore in neither case did he act of his own free will. Since there is no such thing as free will, the question whether he signed of his own free will ought not to be discussed by us.

The foreman and the rest of the jury would rightly conclude that the philosopher must be making some mistake. What sort of a mistake could it be? There is only one possible answer. The philosopher must be using the phrase "free will" in some peculiar way of his own which is not the way in which men usually use it when they wish to determine a question of moral responsibility. That is, he must be using an incorrect definition of it as implying action not determined by causes.

Suppose a man left his office at noon, and were questioned about it. Then we might hear this:

JONES: Did you go out of your own free will?
SMITH: Yes. I went out to get my lunch.

But we might hear:

JONES: Did you leave your office of your own free will?
SMITH: No. I was forcibly removed by the police.

We have now collected a number of cases of actions which, in the ordinary usage of the English language, would be called cases in which people have acted of their own free will. We should also say in all these cases that they *chose* to act as they did. We should also say that they could have acted otherwise, if they had chosen. For instance, Mahatma Gandhi was not compelled to fast; he chose to do so. He could have eaten if he had wanted to. When Smith went out to get his lunch, he chose to do so. He could have stayed and done some more work, if he had wanted to. We have also collected a number of cases of the opposite kind. They are cases in which men were not able to exercise their free will. They had no choice. They were compelled to do as they did. The man in the desert did not fast of his own free will. He had no choice in the matter. He was compelled to fast because there was nothing for him to eat. And so with the other cases. It ought to be quite easy, by an inspection of these cases, to tell what we ordinarily mean when we say that a man did or did not exercise free will. We ought therefore to be able to extract from them the proper definition of the term. Let us put the cases in a table:

Free Acts	Unfree Acts
Gandhi fasting because he wanted to free India.	The man fasting in the desert because there was no food.
Stealing bread because one is hungry.	Stealing because one's employer threatened to beat one.
Signing a confession because one wanted to tell the truth.	Signing because the police beat one.
Leaving the office because one wanted one's lunch.	Leaving because forcibly removed.

It is obvious that to find the correct definition of free acts we must discover what characteristic is common to all the acts in the left-hand column, and is, at the same time, absent from all the acts in the right-hand column. This characteristic which all free acts have, and which no unfree acts have, will be the defining characteristic of free will.

Is being uncaused or not being determined by causes, the characteristic of which we are in search? It cannot be, because although it is true that all the acts in the right-hand column have causes, such as the beating by the police or the absence of food in the desert, so also do the acts in the left-hand column. Mr. Gandhi's fasting was caused by his desire to free India, the man leaving his office by his hunger, and so on. Moreover there is no reason to doubt that these causes of the free acts were in turn caused by prior conditions, and that these were again the results of causes, and so on back indefinitely into the past. Any physiologist can tell us the causes of hunger. What caused Mr. Gandhi's tremendously powerful desire to free India is no doubt more difficult to discover. But it must have had causes. Some of them may have lain in peculiarities of his glands or brain, others in his past experiences, others in his heredity, others in his education. Defenders of free will have usually tended to deny such facts. But to do so is plainly a case of special pleading, which is unsupported by any scrap of evidence. The only reasonable view is that all human actions, both those which are freely done and those which are not, are either wholly determined by causes, or at least as much determined as other events in nature. It may be true, as the physicists tell us, that nature is not as deterministic as was once thought. But whatever degree of determinism prevails in the world, human actions appear to be as much determined as anything else. And if this is so, it cannot be the case that what distinguishes actions freely chosen from those which are not free is that the latter are determined by causes while the former are not. Therefore, being uncaused or being undetermined by causes, must be an incorrect definition of free will.

What, then, is the difference between acts which are freely done and those which are not? What is the characteristic which is present to all the acts in the both sets of actions have causes, the causes of those in the left-hand column are *of a different kind* from the causes of those in the right-hand column? The free acts are all caused by desires, or motives, or by some sort of internal psychological states of the agent's mind. The unfree acts, on the other hand, are all caused by physical forces or physical conditions, outside the agent. Police arrest means physical force exerted from the outside; the absence of food in the desert is a physical condition of the outside world. We may therefore frame the following rough definitions. *Acts freely done are those whose immediate causes are psychological states in the agent. Acts not freely done are those whose immediate causes are states of affairs external to the agent.*

It is plain that if we define free will in this way, then free will certainly exists, and the philosopher's denial of its existence is seen to be what it is—nonsense. For it is obvious that all those actions of men which we should ordinarily attribute to the exercise of their free will, or of which we should say that they freely chose to do them, are in fact actions which have been caused by their own desires, wishes, thoughts, emotions, impulses, or other psychological states.

In applying our definition we shall find that it usually works well, but that there are some puzzling cases which it does not seem exactly to fit. These puzzles can always be solved by paying careful attention to the ways in which words are used, and remembering that they are not always used consistently. I have space for only one example. Suppose that a thug threatens to shoot you unless you give him your wallet, and suppose that you do so. Do you, in giving him your wallet, do so of your own free will or not? If we apply our definition, we find that you acted freely, since the immediate cause of the action was not an actual outside force but the fear of death, which is a psychological cause. Most people, however, would say that you did not act of your own free will but under compulsion. Does this show that our definition is wrong? I do not think so. Aristotle, who gave a solution of the problem of free will substantially the same as ours (though he did not use the term "free will") admitted that there are what he called "mixed" or borderline cases in which it is difficult to know whether we ought to call the acts free or compelled. In the case under discussion, though no actual force was used, the gun at your forehead so nearly approximated to actual force that we tend to say the case was one of compulsion. It is a borderline case.

Here is what may seem like another kind of puzzle. According to our view an action may be free though it could have been predicted beforehand with certainty. But suppose you told a lie, and it was certain beforehand that you would tell it. How could one then say, "You could have told the truth"? The answer is that it is perfectly true that you could have told the truth *if* you had wanted to. In fact you would have done so, for in that case the causes producing your action, namely your desires, would have been different, and would therefore have produced different effects. It is a delusion that predictability and free will are incompatible. This agrees with common sense. For if, knowing your character, I predict that you will act honorably, no one would say when you do act honorably, that this shows you did not do so of your own free will.

Since free will is a condition of moral responsibility, we must be sure that our theory of free will gives a sufficient basis for it. To be held morally responsible for one's actions means that one may be justly punished or rewarded, blamed or praised, for them. But it is not just to punish a man for what he cannot help doing. How can it be just to punish him for an action which it was certain beforehand that he would do? We have not attempted to decide whether, as a matter of fact, all events, including human actions, are completely determined. For that question is irrelevant to the problem of free will. But if we assume for the purposes of argument that complete determinism is true, but that we are nevertheless free, it may then be asked whether such a deterministic free will is compatible with moral responsibility. For it may seem unjust to punish a man for an action which it could have been predicted with certainty beforehand that he would do.

But that determinism is incompatible with moral responsibility is as much a delusion as that it is incompatible with free will. You do not excuse a man for doing a wrong act because, knowing his character, you felt certain beforehand that he would do it. Nor do you deprive a man of a reward or prize because, knowing his goodness or his capabilities, you felt certain beforehand that he would win it.

Volumes have been written on the justification of punishment. But so far as it affects the question of free will, the essential principles involved are quite simple. The punishment of a man for doing a wrong act is justified, either on the ground that it will correct his own character, or that it will deter other people from doing similar acts. The instrument of punishment has been in the past, and no doubt still is, often unwisely used; so that it may often have done more harm than good. But that is not relevant to our present problem. Punishment, if and when it is justified, is justified only on one or both of the grounds just mentioned, The question then is how, if we assume determinism, punishment can correct character or deter people from evil actions.

Suppose that your child develops a habit of telling lies. You give him a mild beating. Why? Because you believe that his personality is such that the usual motives for telling the truth do not cause him to do so. You therefore supply the missing cause, or motive, in the shape of pain and the fear of future pain if he repeats his untruthful behavior. And you hope that a few treatments of this kind will condition him to the habit of truthtelling, so that he will come to tell the truth without the infliction of pain. You assume that his actions are determined by causes, but that the usual causes of truth-telling do not produce in him their usual effects. You therefore supply him with an artificially injected motive, pain and fear, which you think will in the future cause him to speak truthfully.

The principle is exactly the same where you hope, by punishing one man, to deter others from wrong actions. You believe that the fear of punishment will cause those who might otherwise do evil to do well.

We act on the same principle with non-human, and even with inanimate, things, if they do not behave in the way we think they ought to behave. The rose bushes in the garden produce only small and poor blooms, whereas we want large and rich ones. We supply a cause which will produce large blooms, namely fertilizer. Our automobile does not go properly. We supply a cause which will make it go better, namely oil in the works. The punishment for the man, the fertilizer for the plant, and the oil for the car, are all justified by the same principle and in the same way. The only difference is that different kinds of things require different kinds of causes to make them do what they should. Pain may be the appropriate remedy to apply, in certain cases, to human beings, and oil to the machine. It is, of course, of no use to inject motor oil into the boy or to beat the machine.

Thus we see that moral responsibility is not only consistent with determinism, but requires it. The assumption on which punishment is based is that human behavior is causally determined. If pain could not be a cause of truth-telling there would be no justification at all for punishing lies. If human actions and volitions were uncaused, it would be useless either to punish or reward, or indeed to do anything else to correct people's bad behavior. For nothing that you could do would in any way influence them. Thus moral responsibility would entirely disappear. If there were no determinism of human beings at all, their actions would be completely unpredictable and capricious, and therefore irresponsible. And this is in itself a strong argument against the common view of philosophers that free will means being undetermined by causes. [. . .]

Beyond Compatibilism: A Buddhist Approach to Freedom and Determinism

Mark Siderits

RECENT work by Derek Parfit[1] suggests that a reductionist view of persons has important consequences for our concepts of rationality and morality. I shall argue that such a view has yet another significant consequence: it enables us to see that freedom is compatible with determinism. As Parfit points out (*op. cit.*, p. 273), the Buddha held a reductionist view of persons; and while early Buddhism (the Buddhist tradition prior to the development of Buddhist scholastic philosophy) has no explicit position on free will and determinism, it is implicitly committed to compatibilism. I shall seek to turn implicit acceptance into explicit defense. I will do this by first presenting the Buddhist account of personal identity and showing how the early Buddhists make use of this account to answer an objection concerning desert. I will then try to show how the strategy of this reply can be used to defeat the claim that freedom is incompatible with determinism. The reader should be warned, however, that the sort of compatibilism that will emerge differs markedly from traditional so-called soft determinism—hence my title.

It is a fundamental tenet of early Buddhism that there is no such thing as the 'I'. Early Buddhists attempted to prove this through a two-fold strategy. On the one hand, they sought to show that there is no single entity the self that serves as bearer of personal identity through all the stages of a life. On the other hand they argued that since there is no such thing as a whole that is either identical with or distinct from its constituent part, there is likewise no such entity as a person. The first part of this strategy involves an examination of the physical and mental constituents of persons. It is argued that if there were such a thing as the self, it should be some one thing that exists continuously at least from birth until death, and that performs the executive function in the person (evaluating and initiating changes in the states of the person). Since no constituent of a person meets these conditions, it is concluded that there is no self. In order to defeat the remaining alternative, that the bearer of personal identity is not some one part of a person but rather the complex of bodily and mental constituents, early Buddhists argue that wholes are unreal and only parts are real.[2] Thus the person, as a complex series of physical and mental entities and states, is likewise unreal. There is, then, no 'I', no owner of one's bodily and mental states.

The obvious difficulty with this program is that we all have a strong sense of personal continuity at least over stretches of our lives. I am distressed at the thought of the suffering I will undergo tomorrow because of the foolish deed I committed today. I take pride in my accomplishments of a year ago, and am profoundly embarrassed to recall certain things I did seven years ago. I identify with my past and future stages, that is, view them as past and future stages of *me,* the being now considering them. How, if there is no self and if persons are unreal, is this sense of personal continuity to be explained?

The early Buddhist response to this objection makes use of a distinction between two levels of truth, ultimate and conventional. A statement is true in the ultimate sense if and only if it corresponds to the facts and neither asserts nor entails that wholes exist. For instance, supposing that pains and moments of consciousness are simples and that someone feels a pain at place p at time t, the sentence, "A pain sensation is apprehended by a moment of consciousness at place p at time t," would be true in the ultimate sense. A statement is true conventionally if and only if it is acceptable to common sense. While some statements are true both ultimately and conventionally, the vast majority of statements we accept are conventionally true but ultimately false. This situation occurs just in case a statement that would be accepted as corresponding to the facts contains a use of what the Buddhists call a convenient designation, a term that purports to refer to wholes. For instance the statement, "The desk in the Philosophy Department office is brown," is conventionally true but ultimately false, for while that which is conveniently designated "the desk in the Department office" is brown, a desk is a whole made up of parts, and thus there is strictly speaking no such thing as the desk in the Department office.

This distinction between two levels of truth might seem pointless, in that a statement that is conventionally true but ultimately false could be seen as no more than a shorthand device for expressing a statement that is ultimately true. Since the Buddhists maintain that each convenient designation of a whole may be replaced by some specification of the real parts and the relations constituting that whole, it follows that for every statement that is conventionally true but ultimately false there is an ultimately true statement that more completely specifies the state of affairs that the original statement purports to describe. Could we not then view statements that are true only conventionally as mere devices for avoiding hopeless prolixity? If so, then it would seem misleading to call such statements ultimately false.

The Buddhist response is that, given the widespread acceptance of naive semantic realism, our use of convenient designations invariably leads to the acceptance of mere conceptual fictions into our ontology. That is, since we tend to think of meaning as reference, the use of a convenient designation in meaningful sentences quite naturally leads us to suppose that there is some one entity or kind of entity that is the term's referent. Acceptance of "The desk is brown," leads to belief in the existence of something unreal, the desk. It is for this reason that such statements are said to be ultimately false. While such statements *could* be used as mere abbreviatory devices, their use more commonly leads us to accept the existence of such fictions as trees, forests, cities, armies, and, more significantly, persons.

Our use of convenient designations is governed to some extent by our pragmatic interests: we are, for instance, more likely to apply a single term to a set of reals in relation when those entities so related have some function that serves human needs. But there are other factors as well that influence our choices as to how to group the ultimate constituents of the world. Two of these factors are illustrated by the stock Buddhist example of "the one light that shines all night." Having lit a candle that burns all night, we would tend to say that it was one light that illuminates the room throughout the night. Now what illuminates the room at any moment is a candle flame; but our knowledge of the physics of candle flames tells us that the collection of incandescent gas molecules that constitutes the flame at one moment is numerically distinct from the collection of molecules making up a flame at any earlier or later moment. The "one light" is in fact a series of flames, but there are two features that make the application of a convenient designation particularly compelling. First, each flame in the series tends to resemble its predecessor. And since there are no temporal gaps between flames, this resemblance makes it easy to overlook the fact that these are distinct flames. Second, this a causal series—each flame serves as a causal factor in the production of its successor. It is this fact which explains the spatio-temporal contiguity of the members of the series.

What we call a person is, on the Buddhist view, a complex causal series of physical and mental constituents. At any moment a person consists of a set of bodily parts, plus such psychological states as pains, visual images, desires, and consciousness. Each such constituent goes out of existence in time, but in going out of existence it gives rise to some successor bodily or mental constituent. Thus the physical event of a sense's functioning may cause pleasure, pleasure in turn may cause desire, and desire cause some new bodily event or state. Moreover, many members of this series strongly resemble certain of their predecessors and successors. This is clearest in the case of body parts, which when they go out of existence are typically replaced by qualitatively identical successors. But it is also true of such things as images (of which we may form copies through memory-traces), habitual desires, and moments of consciousness.

Given these facts about person-series—that they are causal series with strong resemblance relations among many of the successive elements—plus the obvious fact that there are great practical advantages to be gained from learning to predict and control many of the functions of such series, it is hardly surprising that "person" should be among the most firmly entrenched of our convenient designations. This entrenchment in turn explains our tendency to think of persons as distinct entities that exist over and above their bodily and mental constituents and that own those constituents. And herein lies the origin of our sense of continuous personal identity: having learned to apply the term "person" to the causal series that I am, I go on to view the bodily and mental constituents that make up this series as the parts and states *of me*. Thus as each of my bodily parts and my thoughts, sensations, and desires goes out of existence and is replaced by some successor, there is the sense that there is some one entity to which these alterations are occurring.

Now all of this is an illusion, according to the Buddhists, and moreover an illusion that must be overcome if we are to escape suffering. Nonetheless they grant that there is great practical utility in using such convenient designations as "persons." Given the immense number of bodily and mental constituents that make up a person at any one moment, and the overwhelming complexity of the causal relations that obtain between those constituents and their predecessors and successors, it would prove quite impossible for me ever to succeed in referring to a person-series if I were forbidden the use of a convenient designation. The trick, then, is to learn to speak with the vulgar while thinking with the enlightened.[3] But this strategy has its potential pitfalls. One such pitfall that the early Buddhists discuss is what they might call the illusion of no desert: having discovered that there is no such thing as a person that endures over time, we may be tempted to conclude that no one ever deserves to be rewarded or punished for deeds that were performed earlier. The Buddhists seek to show that this is an illusion that results from conflating the two levels of truth. I shall discuss their attempt to prove this. I will then suggest that they could also claim that the illusion of incompatibilism is another such pitfall that can likewise be avoided if we exercise proper caution in distinguishing between the two levels of truth.

The illusion of no desert arises as follows. The Buddhist reductionist position appears to have the following consequence: since most if not all of the constituents of a person at one moment in that person's life are numerically distinct from the constituents that make up that person at an earlier or later moment, distinct stages in what we think of as one person's existence in fact constitute distinct persons. But it is not justifiable to reward or punish one person for deeds that were performed by some other person. It then follows that on the Buddhist position it is never justifiable to reward or punish a person for deeds performed earlier.

This strategy is often used as an objection to the Buddhist position on karma and rebirth. The early Buddhists accept the widespread Indian belief that the moral character of one's desires in this life determines the nature of one's next life. The Buddhists insist, however, that rebirth is not transmigration: there is no entity or set of entities that passes over from this life to the next. Instead, at death one's karmic accumulation from this life merely serves as cause of the beginning of life in some human or animal womb. The objection is that since there is no entity that is common to my life of wretched misdeeds and the life of the malnourished infant born to impoverished, illiterate peasants that immediately succeeds this life of mine, that infant cannot be said to be me. But the doctrines of karma and rebirth are meant to explain inequality of birth in a way that is compatible with moral justice: those of my misdeeds that go unpunished in this life bring about hardships for me in my next life. The malnourished infant should thus deserve its fate, but on the Buddhist account it does not since it is not me, the author of the misdeeds that caused its plight.

The Buddhists begin their reply to this objection by rejecting the claim that different constituents make for distinct persons. The Buddhist position is that "person" designates a series of sets of physical and mental entities with the right sorts of causal connections. For instance the infant M.S. and the adult M.S. are the same person, since the physical and psychological states of the infant are among the relevant causal ancestors of the physical and psychological states of the adult. While it is true that what makes me and my qualitatively identical Twin Earth counterpart two persons and not one is the fact that we are made up of different constituents, successive sets of distinct constituents may make up stages of one person provided they bear the right sorts of causal relations to one another. And this, the Buddhist claims, is as true of successive lives as it is of different stages of one life.

But such claims as, "Infant and adult are the same person," and "Unless I mend my ways, I will be reborn as a starving peasant," are true only at the conventional level. At the ultimate level we can only describe the constituents of person-series and their causal interrelations. And herein lie the seeds of the illusion of no desert. Because it is ultimately true that there are no persons that endure through distinct life stages, we are tempted to conclude that ultimately nothing deserves to be rewarded or punished for deeds performed earlier. But in fact it is ultimately false that nothing deserves to be rewarded or punished. It is ultimately false because the concept of desert as we are using it here applies only to persons, and persons are conceptual fictions.[4] Such a claim could be true only at the conventional level of truth. But in fact it is false at that level as well: at least some persons do deserve to be rewarded or punished for their earlier deeds.

Care should be taken in understanding the two claims I have just stated. The Buddhists maintain that at the ultimate level of truth there are no persons and thus the question of desert does not arise. They also claim that at the conventional level of truth at least some judgments of desert are true, since there are persons at least some of whom are responsible for their earlier deeds. This is not to say that we live our lives at two distinct levels of reality—a level of impersonal entities and events devoid of moral significance and a level of enduring persons rich with moral meaning. There is just one set of facts here, which we can describe in either of two ways. That we can discuss Franco-German relations in either of two ways—as relations of enmity and mutual distrust between two nations, or more laboriously in terms of many discrete interactions between various French and German officials and private citizens— would not be taken to show that the nations of France and Germany exist at one but not another level of reality. To say that I deserve to be punished for my earlier misdeeds is just to say that those constituents that now make up what is conveniently designated "M.S." bear the right sorts of causal relations to prior entities that brought about certain events, and that it is not unjust that suffering be among those present constituents. It is just easier (though also more easily misunderstood) to say, "I did it and I deserve to be punished."

Nor should we be surprised that the concept of desert should be applicable only at that level at which we employ the term "person." In making judgments of desert we are interested in affecting the future behavior of person-series. This aim is frustrated if we are unable to treat relatively long stretches of such series as enduring wholes. Again, the concept of desert is intimately connected with the concepts of agency and responsibility, and these too require us to think of certain causal series as persons. Desert seems to disappear when we speak the ultimate truth only because the illusion of a person disappears, to be replaced by a causal series. Without this illusion, our familiar concept of desert has no application. But the facts remain the same—only our way of describing them has changed.

The theory of phlogiston was not without some degree of explanatory and predictive power. Thus we would not say that those who accepted this theory were talking about nothing whatever, as we might in the case of certain mythical accounts of the origin of the world. Instead we could say that what they were *really* talking about was the process of oxidation as currently understood in chemical theory. The claim that persons sometimes deserve reward and punishment likewise has its uses. And the utility of this belief must have some explanation. But since there are ultimately no persons, this explanation can only appeal to impersonal fact. We can thus say that what the belief in desert is *really* about is just those impersonal facts. What we mean by this is that the facts remain the same but our manner of conceptualizing them has undergone significant revision. And we can say this because we retain at the ultimate level the ability to carve up the facts in the way as did the concept of desert.

But another point needs to be made as well in order to completely dispel the illusion of no desert. When it is claimed that the doer of the evil deed and the one who is later punished for the deed are different persons, it is mistakenly assumed that there are persons, just no enduring persons. The claim that these are different persons purports to be made at the ultimate level of truth, for it reaches this conclusion through the use of the Buddhist point that no person-part endures through all the stages of a life. But it is equally wrong, at the ultimate level of truth, to say that these are the same person *and* to say that these are different persons. A momentary person is just as much a fiction as an enduring person. The parts of the latter are temporally extended, the parts of the former are not, but both are wholes and thus unreal. Once we see this we lose all temptation to say that the situation as described at the ultimate level of truth is one in which the wrong person is punished. At this level there are only impersonal facts, and of impersonal facts we can say neither that they deserve nor that they fail to deserve reward or punishment.

I turn now to the issue of free will and determinism. While everything I have said up to this point has been based on my understanding of the early Buddhist texts, I shall now be striking out on my own, for on this issue the Buddhist texts are silent. It is clear that the early Buddhists are implicitly committed to some form of compatibilism. For they explicitly accept psychological determinism—they hold that each psychological state in a person-series is caused by some prior physical or psychological state. And they also claim, against the fatalists, that humans are free in that they are able to act on those choices reached through deliberation. They were not, however, confronted with the question, how these two views are compatible. Thus in my discussion I shall seek to extend their approach to the illusion of no desert to what I tendentiously call the illusion of incompatibilism. It is possible that in doing so I shall be doing violence to the early Buddhist position. But my chief aim here is not historical; it is rather to show how the Buddhist account of personal identity may be used to support a compatibilist view of freedom.

Given the Buddhist strategy for dispelling the illusion of no desert, it is relatively easy to anticipate the general approach I shall take to the illusion of incompatibilism. Many people would agree that we deserve to be rewarded or punished for our earlier acts only if we are responsible for those acts, and that we are responsible for our acts only if we acted freely in performing them. Thus if the concept of desert has application only at the conventional level of truth, it would seem that this will be true of the concept of free agency as well. Thus the question of whether an action is free simply does not arise at the level of ultimate truth. Psychological determinism, on the other hand, is a claim not about persons but about the ultimate psychological constituents of person-series. It is thus properly expressed only at the level of ultimate truth. Psychological determinism and the claim that persons are capable of acting freely are thus two ships passing each other in the night—and one of the two is a submarine. This is the general approach I shall follow, but the details need to be worked out with much greater care.

In what follows it will be important to bear in mind that the Buddhists are eliminative reductionists about persons. Our common-sense talk of persons is not one of two equally justifiable ways of describing the impersonal facts that make up person-series. For, say the Buddhists, our ordinary conception of a person leads to such false beliefs as that persons endure over time, perform an executive function, and are capable of attaining happiness. But while the concept of a person is part of a false theory, the vast majority of claims we make using that concept have real explanatory and predictive value. There must, then, be impersonal facts which account for the success we meet with in making such claims. When we eliminate conventional truth in favor of ultimate truth, we lose our concept of personal identity; but the relations among physical and mental constituents of person-series that ground our use of the concept "same person" remain. I shall argue that we must likewise lose our concept of freedom. But the impersonal events and relations that constitute the underlying grounds of application of that concept and explain its utility remain.

It should now become clear why my approach is not that of the traditional compatibilist. Indeed much of what follows should help explain such *incompatibilist* intuitions as the idea that freedom must be contra-causal. I explicitly deny that freedom and determinism can both be true of the same things in the same way. Mine is nonetheless the reconciling project of traditional compatibilism. As ordinarily conceived of, person-series have freedom. Properly understood, the members of such series are causally determined. Our ordinary concept of persons is false, and our concept of freedom must be abandoned. But while "release of phlogiston" is now seen as a discredited concept, the facts it was meant to explain—what we now describe as release of radiant energy through oxidation—remain. While psychological determinism is incompatible with our concept of freedom, it is compatible with those facts which underlie that concept.

I begin with the claim that if psychological determinism is true, it can only be true at the ultimate level of truth. I shall defend this claim by arguing that psychological determinism is incompatible with the folkpsychological concept of a person. This will mean that it cannot be held to be true at that level of truth within which we think of ourselves as persons. I claim that a key ingredient of folk psychology is the concept of a person as practical reasoner. We think of ourselves as beings that seek out evidence concerning our external and internal environments in order to arrive at correct representations of them. And we do this, we suppose, so that we might engage in deliberation and choice concerning which of our desires it would be appropriate to satisfy and how such desires can best be satisfied. Psychological determinism is the claim that every psychological state of a person is causally determined by some antecedent physical or mental state. Consider what becomes of our concept of ourselves as rational agents when considered in the light of psychological determinism. There is, of course, nothing odd in supposing that certain of our beliefs and choices are causally induced. To say, for instance, that my physical environment and the nature of my sensory apparatus together cause me to believe that there is water before me, is not by itself to impugn that belief. Certainly it might be the product of a deviant causal chain, but I know this and so can, if need be, evaluate the belief in light of this knowledge. Difficulties only begin to emerge when we go on to suppose that the principles we use to evaluate beliefs, and the second-order volitions and preference-rankings we use in deliberating, are also causally induced. For if this is true then belief-formation, deliberation, and choice can never measure up to the standards of full rationality. This is so because our behavior now comes to seem thoroughly tropistic. If, for instance, the evaluative criteria we use in testing causally induced beliefs are themselves causally induced, then there remains the possibility that these have been induced in us by causally deviant chains. To say this is not to say that a sophisticated causal system could never form adequate representations of its environment. The point is rather that the notions of evaluation and endorsement of beliefs lose all purchase. If my environment and my nature are thought of as together causing me to endorse a belief by inducing certain evaluative procedures in me, then I cannot see myself as having engaged in the processes of seeking out evidence bearing on this belief, determining how much evidence is enough, deciding on the weights to be assigned different pieces of evidence, and thereby coming to rationally accept the belief. Rational acceptance requires, for instance, that I know how much evidence I must gather to assess a belief. If I take the procedure I employ to have been causally induced, then no matter how adequate this procedure may in fact be, I can never see myself as having good reason to accept it. The point, once again, is not that a tropistic system can always be deceived by an ingeniously contrived or outrageously alien environment. For it is conceivable that a sufficiently sophisticated and flexible causal system could prove the match of any environment, at least in the long run. The point is rather that if I am to see myself as rationally endorsing a belief, then I must also see myself as free to choose the criteria whereby I evaluate the belief. And this I cannot do if I view those criteria as causally induced in me.

This is, I think, the truth that lies at the core of the incompatibilist's position. The incompatibilist has seized upon a key ingredient in the folk-psychological notion of a person—the notion of an executor who engages in and controls the processes of rational belief formation, deliberation, and choice. I agree that this notion is incompatible with the truth of psychological determinism. I deny, however, that this is the whole truth about free will and determinism. What has been shown is that psychological determinism cannot be true at that level of truth—the conventional level—in which we think of ourselves as persons. But we have good reason to think psychological determinism is true, and so it must be true at the ultimate level of truth. Does it follow that persons are not free at the ultimate level of truth? No more than it follows that persons do not, ultimately, deserve to be rewarded or punished for earlier deeds. It does not follows because there are no persons at the ultimate level of truth. And concerning what, if not persons, could the question of freedom be raised?

The last point requires elaboration and defense. It should be noted that my task here shall be to characterize our ordinary conception of freedom as derived from folk psychology. Locke said that it is persons and not the will that can be said to be free. This is partly right and partly wrong. The wrong part concerns his reasons for saying that only persons could be free. He thought that we act freely when we have the power to do as we will. But this is not the sort of freedom we are interested in. He also thought that asking whether the will, rather than the person, is free is an evasion. Yet it might very well not be an evasion of responsibility for me to claim that I willed to perform an act, and had it in my power to act according to my will, and so acted, yet still claim that I did not act freely. For my will may have been tampered with, for instance through hypnosis or brainwashing. It would be natural in such a case to say that my will was not free.

But Locke is still, I think, right to be suspicious of this way of talking. He gives a more compelling argument when he alleges that it involves viewing the will as a homunculus. His second account of freedom shows why this is so. In this second account he characterizes not the freedom to do as one chooses, the uninteresting kind of freedom, but rather the freedom that is involved in an act that is freely chosen. He characterizes this as involving the suspension of the natural transition from inclination to action, so that one may rationally deliberate, choose on the basis of one's deliberations, and then act on the basis of one's choice or will. While not all the actions we would say are freely performed involve deliberation, Locke has surely given us the paradigm that helps explain those other cases. And in this paradigm case, I see myself as the person who deliberates, chooses, and acts. To view the will as something that can itself be free is to view it as something that engages in deliberation and rational choice—as a rational homunculus. And this is surely wrong. It is *persons* who engage in deliberation and rational choice; willing is something that persons do. This should give us an insight into an important source of the illusion of incompatibilism.

To see myself as capable of acting freely, I must view myself as the sort of entity that can endorse the actions it performs. This requires that I take deliberating and willing as abilities or faculties that I possess. This possibility is denied us at the ultimate level of truth. At that level there are events that correspond to what we ordinarily call deliberating and willing; but there are no persons who are the authors of those events, for a person is a mere conceptual fiction that is constructed out of those and other events. It is only at the conventional level, where we employ the convenient designation "person," that we are able to think of deliberating and willing as activities of persons. Thus it is only at the conventional level that an action may be said to be freely performed.

It follows that freedom may be reconciled with psychological determinism. Since psychological determinism is not true of persons, its truth poses no threat to the freedom of persons. Now many will no doubt be highly suspicious of this sort of levels approach to the problem. In particular it will be suspected that I have established not that incompatibilism is an illusion but that freedom is an illusion. In what follows I shall do what I can to disarm such suspicions.

The illusion of incompatibilism may arise in either or two ways—either by smuggling the concept of a person into the ultimate level of truth, or by importing psychological determinism into our conventional talk of persons. We are particularly likely to commit the first mistake when we think of the events that constitute deliberation and choice as performances of homunculi. When we then consider that those entities are, ultimately, causally determined, we conclude that the homunculi that perform the actions of deliberation and choice are not free. Just as the illusion of no desert may arise when we think of a set of physical and mental constituents co-existing at a moment as a person, so the illusion of incompatibilism may arise when we think of deliberation and choice as performances of homunculi. Both are equally illusions. A time-slice of a person-series is not a person-series but a slice of a person-series. And a person-series is not made up of many distinct but co-enduring person-series; it is rather made up of many distinct and momentary physical and mental events in causal interaction, all of which may collectively be referred to as a person.

Moreover, the fact that each of the events making up what we call evaluation, deliberation and choice is caused, does not show that this sequence of events is not one to which the conventional predicate "freely performed action" would apply. Just as a sufficiently sophisticated causal system may live up to the standards of rational belief-formation, so such a system may behave in such a way as to warrant application of this predicate. The ultimate truth precludes my thinking of myself in accordance with the folk-psychological concept of a rational agent, but this does not show that none of my beliefs is rationally justified. For all that is lost in the ascent to the ultimate truth is the notion of the executor whose hands are on the steering wheel. To lose this is to lose a key part of the way folk psychology teaches us to think of rational agency; but it is not to lose rational justification itself. By the same token, when we lose this notion we can no longer view human actions as free in the way folk psychology has taught us. But this, the Buddhist claims, is only because the executor is an illusion, not because freedom is unreal.

Perhaps the more interesting case of the illusion of incompatibilism arises when we illicitly smuggle psychological determinism into our talk of persons. This happens in the following way. First, much of the point of our concept of freedom lies in its connections with the concepts of agency and responsibility. And the point of a judgment of responsibility is that it gives us some ability to control the future behavior of persons. We praise and blame persons only for those acts for which they are responsible, and we hold them responsible only for those acts which they performed freely. And by "freely" here we mean proceeding from the agents themselves. The reason for this should be obvious. Praising someone for an action will not lead that person to act similarly in the future if the origins of the act do not lie in the domain of control of the person. Thus our most clear-cut example of an action not done freely is the case where another person or a natural force directly causes the agent's bodily movements. Here praise or blame are not likely to have their intended effects because it is unlikely that the agent will be able to bring about or prevent similar occurrences in the future. The opposite is true in the case of an action that approximates to our paradigm of free performance, where we have the sense of having endorsed the action in the light of complete information and rational deliberation. Here it is much more likely that the agent will have the ability to bring about similar occurrences in the future, and so praise and blame may have their intended effects.

Now between the poles of these two paradigm cases lies a continuum of actions that are more or less freely performed. Toward the "free" end of this continuum lie habitual actions that involve little if any deliberation. Toward the "unfree" end lie those actions in which the agent was threatened or coerced. Toward the middle of the continuum lie actions in which the agent's rationality has been impaired or has been tampered with—through drugs, hypnosis, mental disorder, addiction, being provided misinformation, and the like.

I suggest that for many of these cases in the middle of the spectrum there is no non-arbitrary answer to the question, whether such actions are freely performed. The reason for this indeterminacy is simple. Our paradigm of an action not freely performed is the case in which the person as a whole is caused to behave in a certain way. We say that the source of the action is "outside" the person. Our paradigm of an action freely performed is the case in which the person as a whole *engages* in the action—that which behaves in a certain way is the same thing as that which endorses the action. Here we say that the source of the action is the person herself. The problematic cases in the middle are problematic precisely because we have no clear criteria for determining just what is to count as "outside" the person and "inside" the person. But this is just what we should expect, given that a person is a conceptual fiction, and given the pragmatic interests that govern our use of this concept and the related concepts of freedom and responsibility. For instance, one sort of case from the middle of the spectrum might involve the actions of a person who was subjected to a program of "brainwashing"—a program whereby others implanted a large set of beliefs in the person through such means as environmental deprivation. When we are unsure what to say about such a case, it is because we are not sure whether this is more nearly like the case in which the person as a whole is caused to behave in a certain way, or more nearly like the case in which the person as a whole engages in an action. Arguments can be given for either view. But the question arises only because we are interested in affecting future behavior. And there may simply not be sufficient data for us to determine how best to accomplish this—by assimilating the case to the "unfree" pole or to the "free" pole.

The key point that emerges from this is that the criteria we actually employ in deciding whether an act was freely performed or not involve judgments concerning persons as wholes. And herein lie the seeds of the notion that freedom is contra-causal. Our paradigm of an action not freely performed is the case in which the person as a whole is caused by some distinct entity to behave in a certain way. A freely performed action lacks this feature. Thus when we understand psychological determinism as involving the claim that all of a person's actions are caused, we take this to mean that a person's actions are never freely performed.

Perhaps the best way of seeing why this route to incompatibilism is a mistake is this. An action that is caused is thereby, we say, not freely performed. What must be borne in mind here is that at least one of the relata of this "caused" must be a *person*: an action that is not freely performed is one in which the person is caused to behave in a certain way. But the causal relations that psychological determinism asserts to obtain among certain physical and mental events do not have persons as relata. Hence it does not follow from the truth of psychological determinism that a person's actions are not freely performed.

The incompatibilist might object that if all the psychological events that constitute deliberation, evaluation, choice, and initiation of action are caused, then the person is indeed caused to behave in a certain way. To this it may be replied that our sense of freedom derives not from the abrogation of causal laws but rather from the sense that it is I who engage in deliberation, evaluation, choice and action. As countless traditional compatibilists have pointed out, we are never aware of behaving in a contra-causal fashion. We are tempted to embrace such a view of freedom only because folk-psychology requires us to think of deliberation, evaluation and choice as faculties of the person, and psychological determinism properly understood undermines this faculty psychology. For psychological determinism, as part of the ultimate truth, undermines our belief in the executor, the 'I' who engages in the activities of deliberation, evaluation, choice and action. But while the 'I' who has deliberation, etc., as faculties may be an illusion, this does not show that I am never justified in believing that I have acted freely. I have argued that while we cannot both think of ourselves as causal systems and apply to ourselves the folk-psychological concept of a rational deliberator, still a sophisticated causal system may be a rational deliberator and so be justified in applying this concept to itself. The same holds true of our folk-psychological concept of freedom. True,

I cannot consistently apply this concept so long as I think of myself as a complex causal series. But I may nonetheless act in a way that warrants application of this concept even though I am in fact just such a series.

I have argued that imcompatibilism is an illusion at both the conventional and the ultimate levels of truth. Do persons ever in fact act freely? This is an empirical question. I believe the answer is, yes. Persons do sometimes engage in inquiry, deliberation, and choice, and act upon their choices. But there will no doubt be those who believe I must answer, no. Perhaps they will think this because I claim that ultimately persons do not exist. If ultimately there are no persons but only physical and mental events in a complex causal series, then the ultimate truth about "us" must be that "we" are not free.

To this there are two answers. The first is that while those entities and events that are ultimately constitutive of what we conveniently designate "persons" are not free, neither are they unfree. They are neither free nor unfree because, once again, the question of freedom cannot arise unless we are permitted the use of the concept of a person.

Many will no doubt find this answer unsatisfying, and so I provide a second answer. Most people would agree that persons do sometimes engage in inquiry, deliberation, and choice, and act upon their choices. They would also agree that when persons do these things they act freely. I claim in addition that persons do not ultimately exist, that "person" is a useful fiction. Strictly speaking what we call a person is nothing but a set of physical and mental constituents in complex causal interrelations. Am I thereby committed to the claim that freedom is unreal or illusory, something we believe to exist only because we falsely believe that there is such a thing as a person?

Consider a more mundane example. A modern Buddhist would no doubt accept micro-reductionism in physics: the ultimate truth about macro-physical objects is just what micro-physics tells us. And micro-physics has no use for the concept of a table. What we call a table is just a swarm of interacting particles. Would it then follow that tables are illusions? Yes and no. Insofar as a table is a whole made up of parts—one among infinitely many possible ways of grouping swarms of particles—a table is unreal. But there is a reason for our having come to choose this particular grouping; we have a term for this kind of swarm because it serves certain human needs. Now micro-physics will explain why such swarms have those properties we care about—e.g., rigidity, stability, and transportability. And the ultimate truth will also include the fact that humans have sensory organs with only relatively coarse-grained resolution, as well as the fact that humans have needs which are in fact best met by those swarms that we call tables. Thus at the ultimate level of truth we retain the ability to distinguish between what we ordinarily call tables and what we do not. The same cannot be said of the concept of demons as causes of disease; having overcome our belief in demons we do not retain the ability to distinguish between, e.g., evil and benign demons. While we can no longer think of a table as an entity when we come to see that wholes are unreal, tables are not thereby shown to be illusory in the way that demons are illusory.

Is freedom illusory? Yes and no. Yes, our concept of freedom involves the illusion of persons as agents, and so the concept is to that extent infected with illusoriness. But recall the pragmatic grounding of the concept—our concern to affect the future behavior of person-series. Praise and blame have their intended effects in those cases we would characterize as freely performed actions, and they fail in the opposite sort of cases. At the ultimate level of truth we cannot say that some actions are free, others unfree. But we can fully capture the difference between the two sorts of cases, for instance in terms of the presence or absence of certain sorts of deliberation-events, and the causal relations between deliberation-events and choice-events. We ordinarily believe there to be a difference between those actions that we say are freely performed and those that we say are not. The ultimate truth must agree—otherwise there would be no explaining the utility of the concept of freedom. But presumably what we care about is not the concept but that there be a difference between the two sorts of cases. Since the ultimate truth succeeds in capturing this difference, what we care about is preserved at the ultimate level of truth. Only the names have been changed to protect the ignorant. Freedom is not an illusion.[5]

Notes

1. Derek Parfit, *Reasons and Persons* (Oxford: Oxford University Press, 1984).
2. This obviously involves commitment to "partless parts"; much of the subsequent history of Buddhist philosophy can be seen as an exploration of the consequences of this commitment.
3. Here it is crucial to bear in mind the Buddhist claim that wholes are unreal: there is no such thing as a person, whether it be construed as identical with or distinct from the parts in relation. In this regard it might be useful to distinguish between what could be called identity reductionism and eliminative reductionism. A reductionist about persons holds that the fact of a person's

continued existence over time consists in the holding of certain more particular facts, facts that can be described in a completely *impersonal* way (Parfit 210). An identity reductionist makes the further claim that we are equally justified in describing these facts in either of two ways: by using our familiar concept of a person; or by completely specifying the particular facts and their relations. An eliminative reductionist denies this. According to this form of reductionism, our concept of a person is like the concept of phlogiston, a part of a false theory about the world. While those who used the term "phlogiston" were not speaking of *nothing*—radiant energy *is* produced by combustion—the facts they sought to describe are not arranged as the concept and its theory maintained. Likewise, while there are certain facts that explain the utility of our use of "person," this concept brings with it certain false beliefs about those facts: that there is some non-arbitrary principle whereby they unite to form a whole; that this whole is the bearer of its physical and mental states; and the like. Thus the concept of a person should be eliminated; to get around the problem of prolixity we might replace it with "complex causal series." While Parfit prefers the identity form of reductionism, the Buddhists maintain the eliminative variety. Thus the enlightened person when speaking with the vulgar is not in fact employing *their* concept of a person.

4. Some further remarks are in order at this point concerning the semantics of ultimate truth. Any statement that either asserts or entails that wholes exist is ultimately false. The simplest case is when we assert that there are instances of a kind of whole, e.g.,

> There are persons

This statement is ultimately false, and its negation,

> There are no persons

is ultimately true. Statements containing no convenient designations but containing predicates that apply only to wholes are trickier. The statement,

> Something deserves punishment

is ultimately false, for given that the concept of desert applies only to persons, this statement entails that persons exist. We would then expect its negation,

> Nothing deserves punishment

to be ultimately true. But in fact the Buddhists claim that this statement is ultimately false as well. One way to understand this would take them to be saying that the negation is internal ("nominally bound" is how Indian logicians would put it), with the negative predicate being such that it applies only to persons; the statement would then entail that persons exist. An alternative interpretation would be that any statement containing such a predicate occasions a truth-value gap. But however this is interpreted, the basic intuition is that such terms are inappropriate at the ultimate level in that they give rise to the implication that conceptual fictions exist.

5. I received helpful comments on an earlier draft of this paper from Robert Steinman and Mark Timmons. I especially wish to thank Kevin Possin for the many helpful comments, criticism and suggestions he provided at all stages of development of this project. Of course none of these causal series is responsible for any defects that remain.

The Incompatibility of Free Will and Determinism

Peter van Inwagen

In this paper I shall define a thesis I shall call "determinism," and argue that it is incompatible with the thesis that we are able to act otherwise than we do (i.e., is incompatible with "free will"). Other theses, some of them very different from what *I* shall call "determinism," have at least an equal right to this name, and, therefore, I do not claim to show that *every* thesis that could be called "determinism" without historical impropriety is incompatible with free will. I shall, however, assume without argument that what I call 'determinism' is legitimately so called.

In Part I, I shall explain what I mean by "determinism." In Part II, I shall make some remarks about "can." In Part III, I shall argue that free will and determinism are incompatible. In Part IV, I shall examine some possible objections to the argument of Part III. I shall not attempt to establish the truth or falsity of determinism, or the existence or non-existence of free will.

I

In defining "determinism," I shall take for granted the notion of a proposition (that is, of a non-linguistic bearer of truth-value), together with certain allied notions such as denial, conjunction, and entailment. Nothing in this paper will depend on the special features of any particular account of propositions. The reader may think of them as functions from possible worlds to truth-values or in any other way he likes, provided they have their usual features (e.g., they are either true or false; the conjunction of a true and a false proposition is a false proposition; they obey the law of contraposition with respect to entailment).

Our definition of "determinism" will also involve the notion of "the state of the entire physical world" (hereinafter, "the state of the world") at an instant. I shall leave this notion largely unexplained, since the argument of this paper is very nearly independent of its content. Provided the following two conditions are met, the reader may flesh out "the state of the world" in any way he likes:

(i) Our concept of "state" must be such that, given that the world is in a certain state at a certain time, nothing follows *logically* about its states at other times. For example, we must not choose a concept of "state" that would allow as part of a description of the momentary state of the world, the clause, " . . . and, at t, the world is such that Jones's left hand will be raised 10 seconds later than t."

(ii) If there is some observable change in the way things are (e.g., if a white cloth becomes blue, a warm liquid cold, or if a man raises his hand), this change must entail some change in the state of the world. That is, our concept of "state" must not be so theoretical, so divorced from what is observably true, that it be possible for the world to be in the *same* state at t_1 and t_2, although (for example) Jones's hand is raised at t_1 and not at t_2.

We may now define "determinism." We shall apply this term to the conjunction of these two theses:

(a) For every instant of time, there is a proposition that expresses the state of the world at that instant.
(b) If A and B are any propositions that express the state of the world at some instants, then the conjunction of A with the laws of physics entails B.

By a proposition that expresses the state of the world at time t, I mean a true proposition that asserts of some state that, at t, the world is in that state. The reason for our first restriction on the content of "state" should now be evident: if it were not for this restriction, "the state of the world" could be defined in such a way that determinism was trivially true. We could, without this restriction, build sufficient information about the past and future into each proposition that expresses the state of the world at an instant, that, for every pair of such propositions, each *by itself* entails the other. And in that case, determinism would be a mere tautology, a thesis applicable to every conceivable state of affairs.

This amounts to saying that the "laws of physics" clause on our definition does some work: whether determinism is true depends on the character of the laws of physics. For example, if all physical laws were vague propositions like "In every nuclear reaction, momentum is *pretty nearly* conserved," or "Force is *approximately* equal to mass times acceleration," then determinism would be false.

This raises the question, What is a law of physics? First, a terminological point. I do not mean the application of this term to be restricted to those laws that belong to physics in the narrowest sense of the word. I am using "law of physics" in the way some philosophers use "law of nature." Thus, a law about chemical valences is a law of physics in my sense, even if chemistry is not ultimately "reducible" to physics. I will not use the term "law of nature," because, conceivably, *psychological* laws, including laws (if such there be) about the voluntary behaviour of rational agents, might be included under this term.[1] Rational agents are, after all, in some sense part of "Nature." Since I do not think that everything I shall say about laws of physics is true of such "voluntaristic laws," I should not want to use, instead of "laws of physics," some term like "laws of nature" that might legitimately be applied to voluntaristic laws. Thus, for all that is said in this paper, it may be that some version of determinism based on voluntaristic laws is compatible with free will.[2] Let us, then, understand by "law of physics" a law of nature that is not about the voluntary behaviour of rational agents.

But this does not tell us what "laws of nature" are. There would probably be fairly general agreement that a proposition cannot be a law of nature unless it is true and contingent, and that no proposition is a law of nature if it entails the existence of some concrete individual, such as Caesar or the earth. But the proposition that there is no solid gold sphere 20 feet in diameter (probably) satisfies these conditions, though it is certainly not a law of nature.

It is also claimed sometimes that a law of nature must "support its counter-factuals." There is no doubt something to this. Consider, however, the proposition, "Dogs die if exposed to virus V." The claim that this proposition supports its counter-factuals is, I think, equivalent to the claim that "Every dog is such that if it were exposed to virus V, it would die" is *true*. Let us suppose that this latter proposition *is* true, the quantification being understood as being over all dogs, past, present, and future. Its truth, it seems to me, is quite consistent with its being the case that dog-breeders *could* (but will not) institute a programme of selective breeding that *would* produce a sort of dog that is immune to virus V. But if dog-breeders *could* do this, then clearly "Dogs die if exposed to virus V" is not a law of nature, since in that case the truth of the corresponding universally quantified counter-factual depends upon an accidental circumstance: if dog-breeders were to institute a certain programme of selective breeding they are quite capable of instituting, then "Every dog is such that if it were exposed to virus V, it would die" would be false. Thus a proposition may "support its counter-factuals" and yet not be a law of nature.

I do not think that any philosopher has succeeded in giving a (non-trivial) set of individually necessary and jointly sufficient conditions for a proposition's being a law of nature or of physics. *I* certainly do not know of any such set. Fortunately, for the purposes of this paper we need not know how to analyse the concept "law of physics." I shall, in Part III, argue that certain statements containing "law of physics" are analytic. But this can be done in the absence of a satisfactory analysis of "law of physics." In fact, it would hardly be possible for one to *provide* an analysis of some concept if one had no pre-analytic convictions about what statements involving that concept are analytic.

For example, we do not have to have a satisfactory analysis of memory to know that "No one can remember future events" is analytic. And if someone devised an analysis of memory according to which it was possible to remember future events, then, however attractive the analysis was in other respects, it would have to be rejected. The analyticity of "No one can remember future events" is one of the *data* that anyone who investigates the concept of memory must take account of. Similarly, the claims I shall make on behalf of the concept of physical law seem to me to be basic and evident enough to be data that an analysis of this concept must take account of: any analysis on which these claims did not 'come out true' would be for that very reason defective.

II

It seems to be generally agreed that the concept of free will should be understood in terms of the *power* or *ability* of agents to act otherwise than they in fact do. To deny that men have free will is to assert that what a man *does* do and what he *can* do coincide. And almost all philosophers[3] agree that a necessary condition for holding an agent responsible for an act is believing that that agent *could have* refrained from performing that act.[4]

There is, however, considerably less agreement as to how "can" (in the relevant sense) should be analysed. This is one of the most difficult questions in philosophy. It is certainly a question to which I do not know any non-trivial answer. But, as I said I should do in the case of "law of physics," I shall make certain conceptual claims about "can" (in the "power" or "ability" sense) in the absence of any analysis. Any suggested analysis of "can" that does not support these claims will either be neutral with respect to them, in which case it will be incomplete, since it will not settle *all* conceptual questions about "can," or it will be inconsistent with them, in which case the arguments I shall present in support of these claims will, in effect, be arguments that the analysis fails. In Part IV, I shall expand on this point as it applies to one particular analysis of "can," the well-known "conditional" analysis.

I shall say no more than this about the meaning of "can." I shall, however, introduce an idiom that will be useful in talking about ability and inability in complicated cases. Without this idiom, the statement of our argument would be rather unwieldy. We shall sometimes make claims about an agent's abilities by using sentences of the form:

S can render |could have rendered| . . . false.

where " . . . " may be replaced by names of propositions.[5] Our ordinary claims about ability can easily be translated into this idiom. For example, we translate:

He could have reached Chicago by midnight.

as

He could have rendered the proposition that he did not reach Chicago by midnight false.

and, of course, the translation from the special idiom to the ordinary idiom is easy enough in such simple cases. If we were interested only in everyday ascriptions of ability, the new idiom would be useless. Using it, however, we may make ascriptions of ability that it would be very difficult to make in the ordinary idiom. Consider, for example, the last true proposition asserted by Plato. (Let us assume that this description is, as logicians say, "proper.") One claim that we might make about Aristotle is that he could have rendered this proposition false. Now, presumably, we have no way of discovering *what* proposition the last true proposition asserted by Plato was. Still, the claim about Aristotle would seem to be either true or false. To discover its truth-value, we should have to discover under what conditions the last true proposition asserted by Plato (i.e., that proposition having as one of its accidental properties, the property of being the last true proposition asserted by

Plato) would be false, and then discover whether it was within Aristotle's power to produce these conditions. For example, suppose that if Aristotle had lived in Athens from the time of Plato's death till the time of his own death, then the last true proposition asserted by Plato (whatever it was) would be false. Then, if Aristotle could have lived (i.e. if he had it within his power to live) in Athens throughout this period, he could have rendered the last true proposition asserted by Plato false. On the other hand, if the last true proposition asserted by Plato is the proposition that the planets do not move in perfect circles, then Aristotle could not have rendered the last true proposition asserted by Plato false, since it was not within his power to produce any set of conditions sufficient for the falsity of this proposition.[6]

It is obvious that the proposition expressed by "Aristotle could have rendered the last true proposition asserted by Plato false," is a proposition that we should be hard put to express without using the idiom of rendering propositions false, or at least, without using some very similar idiom. We shall find this new idiom very useful in discussing the relation between free will (a thesis about abilities) and determinism (a thesis about certain propositions).

III

I shall now imagine a case in which a certain man, after due deliberation, refrained from performing a certain contemplated act. I shall then argue that, if determinism is true, then that man *could not have* performed that act. Because this argument will not depend on any features peculiar to our imagined case, the incompatibility of free will and determinism *in general* will be established, since, as will be evident, a parallel argument could easily be constructed for the case of any agent and any unperformed act.

Here is the case. Let us suppose there was once a judge who had only to raise his right hand at a certain time, T, to prevent the execution of a sentence of death upon a certain criminal, such a hand-raising being the sign, according to the conventions of the judge's country, of a granting of special clemency. Let us further suppose that the judge—call him "J"—refrained from raising his hand at that time, and that this inaction resulted in the criminal's being put to death. We may also suppose that the judge was unbound, uninjured, and free from paralysis; that he decided not to raise his hand at T only after a period of calm, rational, and relevant deliberation; that he had not been subjected to any "pressure" to decide one way or the other about the criminal's death; that he was not under the influence of drugs, hypnosis, or anything of that sort; and finally, that there was no element in his deliberations that would have been of any special interest to a student of abnormal psychology.

Now the argument. In this argument, which I shall refer to as the "main argument," I shall use "T_0" to denote some instant of time earlier than J's birth, "P_0" to denote the proposition that expresses the state of the world at T_0. "P" to denote the proposition that expresses the state of the world at T, and "L" to denote the conjunction into a single proposition of all laws of physics. (I shall regard L itself as a law of physics, on the reasonable assumption that if A and B are laws of physics, then the conjunction of A and B is a law of physics.) The argument consists of seven statements, the seventh of which follows from the first six:

1. If determinism is true, then the conjunction of P_0 and L entails P.
2. If J had raised his hand at T, then P would be false.
3. If (2) is true, then if J could have raised his hand at T, J could have rendered P false.[7]
4. If J could have rendered P false, and if the conjunction of P_0 and L entails P, then J could have rendered the conjunction of P_0 and L false.
5. If J could have rendered the conjunction of P_0 and L false, then J could have rendered L false.
6. J could not have rendered L false.
∴7. If determinism is true, J could not have raised his hand at T.

That (7) follows from (1) through (6) can easily be established by truth-functional logic. Note that all conditionals in the argument except for (2) are truthfunctional. For purposes of establishing the *validity* of this argument, (2) may be regarded as a simple sentence. Let us examine the premises individually.

(1) This premiss follows from the definition of determinism.

(2) If J had raised his hand at T, then the world would have been in a different state at T from the state it was in fact in. (See our second condition on the content of "the state of the world.") And, therefore, if J had raised his hand at T, some contrary of P would express the state of the world at T. It should be emphasized that "P" does not *mean* "the proposition that expresses the state of the world at T." Rather, "P" *denotes* the proposition that expresses the state of the world at T. In Kripke's terminology, "P" is being used as a *rigid designator,* while "the proposition that expresses the state of the world at T" is perforce nonrigid.[8]

(3) Since *J*'s hand being raised at *T* would have been sufficient for the falsity of *P*, there is, if *J* could have raised his hand, at least one condition sufficient for the falsity of *P* and *J* could have produced.

(4) This premiss may be defended as an instance of the following general principle:

If *S* can render *R* false, and if *Q* entails *R*, then *S* can render *Q* false.

This principle seems to be analytic. For if *Q* entails *R*, then the denial of *R* entails the denial of *Q*. Thus, any condition sufficient for the falsity of *R* is also sufficient for the falsity of *Q*. Therefore, if there is some condition that *S* can produce that is sufficient for the falsity of *R*, there is some condition (that same condition) that *S* can produce that is sufficient for the falsity of *Q*.

(5) This premiss may be defended as an instance of the following general principle, which I take to be analytic:

If *Q* is a true proposition that concerns only states of affairs that obtained before *S*'s birth, and if *S* can render the conjunction of *Q* and *R* false, then *S* can render *R* false.

Consider, for example, the propositions expressed by

The Spanish Armada was defeated in 1588.

and

Peter van Inwagen never visits Alaska.

The conjunction of these two propositions is quite possibly true. At any rate, let us assume it is true. Given that it is true, it seems quite clear that I can render it false if and only if I can visit Alaska. If, for some reason, it is not within my power ever to visit Alaska, then I *cannot* render it false. This is a quite trivial assertion, and the general principle (above) of which it is an instance is hardly less trivial. And it seems incontestable that premiss (5) is also an instance of this principle.

(6) I shall argue that if anyone *can* (i.e., has it within his power to) render some proposition false, then that proposition is not a law of physics. This I regard as a conceptual truth, one of the data that must be taken account of by anyone who wishes to give an analysis of "can"

or "law." It is this connection between these two concepts, I think, that is at the root of the incompatibility of free will and determinism.

In order to see this connection, let us suppose that both of the following are true:

1. Nothing ever travels faster than light.
2. Jones, a physicist, can construct a particle accelerator that would cause protons to travel at twice the speed of light.

It follows from (A) that Jones will never exercise the power that (B) ascribes to him. But whatever the reason for Jones's failure to act on his ability to render (A) false, it is clear that (A) and (B) are consistent, and that (B) entails that (A) is not a law of physics. For given that (B) is true, then Jones is able to conduct an experiment that would falsify (A); and surely it is a feature of any proposition that is a physical law that no one *can* conduct an experiment that would show it to be false.

Of course, most propositions that look initially as if they might be physical laws, but which are later decided to be non-laws, are rejected because of experiments that are actually performed. But this is not essential. In order to see this, let us elaborate the example we have been considering. Let us suppose that Jones's ability to render (A) false derives from the fact that he has discovered a mathematically rigorous proof that under certain conditions C, realizable in the laboratory, protons would travel faster than light. And let us suppose that this proof proceeds from premises so obviously true that all competent physicists accept his conclusion without reservation. But suppose that conditions C never obtain in nature, and that actually to produce them in the laboratory would require such an expenditure of resources that Jones and his colleagues decide not to carry out the experiment. And suppose that, as a result, conditions C are never realized and nothing ever travels faster than light. It is evident that if all this were true, we should have to say that (A), while *true,* is not a law of physics. (Though, of course, "Nothing ever travels faster than light except under conditions C" might be a law.)

The laboratories and resources that figure in this example are not essential to its point. If Jones *could* render some proposition false by performing *any* act he does not in fact perform, even such a simple act as raising his hand at a certain time, this would be sufficient to show that that proposition is not a law of physics.

This completes my defence of the premises of the main argument. In the final part of this paper, I shall examine objections to this argument suggested by the attempts of various philosophers to establish the compatibility of free will and determinism.

IV

The most useful thing a philosopher who thinks that the main argument does not prove its point could do would be to try to show that some premiss of the argument is false or incoherent, or that the argument begs some important question, or contains a term that is used equivocally, or something of that sort. In short, he should get down to cases. Some philosophers, however, might continue to hold that free will and determinism, in the sense of Part I, are compatible, but decline to try to point out a mistake in the argument. For (such a philosopher might argue) we have, in everyday life, *criteria* for determining whether an agent could have acted otherwise than he did, and these criteria determine the *meaning* of "could have acted otherwise"; to know the meaning of this phrase is simply to know how to apply these criteria. And since these criteria make no mention of determinism, anyone who thinks that free will and determinism are incompatible is simply confused.[9]

As regards the argument of Part III (this philosopher might continue), this argument is very complex, and this complexity must simply serve to hide some error, since its conclusion is absurd. We must treat this argument like the infamous "proof" that zero equals one: It may be amusing and even instructive to find the hidden error (if one has nothing better to do), but it would be a waste of time to take seriously any suggestion that it is sound.

Now I suppose we do have "criteria," in some sense of this overused word, for the application of "could have done otherwise," and I will grant that knowing the criteria for the application of a term can plausibly be identified with knowing its meaning. Whether the criteria for applying 'could have done otherwise' can (as at least one philosopher has supposed[10]) be taught by simple ostension is another question. However this may be, the "criteria" argument is simply invalid. To see this, let us examine a simpler argument that makes the same mistake.

Consider the doctrine of "predestinarianism." Predestinarians hold (i) that if an act is foreseen it is not free, and (ii) that all acts are foreseen by God. (I do not claim that anyone has ever held this doctrine in precisely this form.) Now suppose we were to argue that predestinarianism must be compatible with free will, since our criteria for applying "could have done otherwise" make no reference to predestinarianism. Obviously this argument would be invalid, since predestinarianism is incompatible with free will. And the only difference I can see between this argument and the "criteria" argument for the compatibility of free will and determinism is that predestinarianism, unlike determinism, is *obviously* incompatible with free will. But, of course, theses may be incompatible with one another even if this incompatibility is not obvious. Even if determinism cannot, like predestinarianism, be seen to be incompatible with free will on the basis of a simple formal inference, there is, nonetheless, a conceptual connection between the two theses (as we showed in our defence of premiss [6]). The argument of Part III is intended to draw out the implications of this connection. There may well be a mistake in the argument, but I do not see why anyone should think that the very idea of such an argument is misconceived.

It has also been argued that free will *entails* determinism, and, being itself a consistent thesis, is *a fortiori* compatible with determinism. The argument, put briefly, is this. To say of some person on some particular occasion that he acted freely is obviously to say at least that *he* acted on that occasion. Suppose, however, that we see someone's arm rise and it later turns out that there was *no cause whatsoever* for his arm's rising. Surely we should have to say that *he* did not really raise his arm at all. Rather, his arm's rising was a mere chance happening, that, like a muscular twitch, had nothing to do with *him*, beyond the fact that it happened to involve a part of his body. A necessary condition for this person's really having raised his hand is that *he* caused his hand to rise. And surely "*he* caused" means "*his* character, desires, and beliefs caused."[11]

I think that there is a great deal of confusion in this argument, but to expose this confusion would require a lengthy discussion of many fine points in the theory of agency. I shall only point out that if this argument is supposed to refute the conclusion of Part III, it is an *ignoratio elenchi*. For I did not conclude that free will is incompatible with the thesis that every event has a cause, but rather with determinism as defined in Part I. And the denial of this thesis does not entail that there are uncaused events.

Of course, one might try to construct a similar but relevant argument for the falsity of the conclusion of Part III. But, so far as I can see, the plausibility of such an argument would depend on the plausibility of supposing that if the present movements of one's body are not completely determined by physical law and the state of the world before one's birth, then these present movements are not one's own doing, but, rather, mere random happenings. And I do not see the least shred of plausibility in this supposition.

I shall finally consider the popular "conditional analysis" argument for the compatibility of free will and determinism. According to the advocates of this argument—let us call them 'conditionalists'—what statements of the form:

(8) *S* could have done *X*

mean is:

(9) If *S* had chosen to do *X*, *S* would have done *X*.[12]

For example, "Smith could have saved the drowning child" means, "If Smith had chosen to save the drowning child, Smith would have saved the drowning child." Thus, even if determinism is true (the conditionalists argue), it is possible that Smith did not save but *could have* saved the drowning child, since the conjunction of determinism with "Smith did not save the child" does not entail the falsity of "If Smith had chosen to save the child, Smith would have saved the child."

Most of the controversy about this argument centres around the question whether (9) is a correct analysis of (8). I shall not enter into the debate about whether this analysis is correct. I shall instead question the relevance of this debate to the argument of Part III. For it is not clear that the main argument would be unsound if the conditional analysis *were* correct. Clearly the argument is *valid* whether or not (8) and (9) mean the same. But suppose the premises of the main argument were rewritten so that every clause they contain that is of form (8) is replaced by the corresponding clause of form (9)—should we then see that any of these premisses is false? Let us try this with premiss (6), which seems, prima facie, to be the crucial premiss of the argument. We have:

(6a) It is not the case that if *J* had chosen to render *L* false, *J* would have rendered *L* false.

Now (6a) certainly seems true: If someone chooses to render false some proposition *R*, and if *R* is a law of physics, then surely he will fail. This little argument for (6a) *seems* obviously sound. But we cannot overlook the possibility that someone might discover a mistake in it and, perhaps, even construct a convincing argument that (6a) is false. Let us, therefore, assume for the sake of argument that (6a) is demonstrably false. What would this show? I submit that it would show that (6a) does not mean the same as (6), since (6) is, as I have argued, *true*.

The same dilemma confronts the conditionalist if he attempts to show, on the basis of the conditional analysis, that any of the other premises of the argument is false. Consider the argument got by replacing every clause of form (8) in the main argument with the corresponding clause of form (9). If all the premises of this new argument are true, the main argument is, according to the conditionalist's own theory, sound. If, on the other hand, any of the premises of the new argument is false, then (*I* would maintain) this premiss is a counter-example to the conditional analysis. I should not be begging the question against the conditionalist in maintaining this, since I have given arguments for the truth of each of the premises of the main argument, and nowhere in these arguments do I assume that the conditional analysis is wrong.

Of course, any or all of my arguments in defence of the premises of the main argument may contain some mistake. But unless the conditionalist could point to some such mistake, he would not accomplish much by showing that some statement he *claimed* was equivalent to one of its premises was false.[13]

Notes

1. For example, "If a human being is not made to feel ashamed of lying before his twelfth birthday, then he will lie whenever he believes it to be to his advantage."

2. In "The Compatibility of Free Will and Determinism," *Philosophical Review*, 1962, J. V. Canfield argues convincingly for a position that we might represent in this terminology as the thesis that a determinism based on voluntaristic laws could be compatible with free will.

3. See, however, Harry Frankfurt, "Alternate Possibilities and Moral Responsibility," *Journal of Philosophy*, 1969.

4. Actually, the matter is rather more complicated than this, since we may hold a man responsible for an act we believe he could not have refrained from, provided we are prepared to hold him responsible for his being unable to refrain.

5. In all the cases we shall consider, " . . . " will be replaced by names of *true* propositions. For the sake of logical completeness, we may stipulate that any sentence formed by replacing " . . . " with the name of a *false*

proposition is trivially true. Thus, "Kant could have rendered the proposition that $7 + 5 = 13$ false" is trivially true.

6. Steven M. Cahn and Richard Taylor have argued (most explicitly in
   "Time, Truth and Ability" by "Diodorus Cronus," *Analysis*, 1965 that
   every true proposition is such that, necessarily, no one is able to render it
   false. On my view, this thesis is mistaken, and their arguments for it can be
   shown to be unsound. I shall not, however, argue for this here. I shall
   argue in Part III that we are unable to render *certain sorts of* true proposition false, but my arguments will depend on special features of these sorts
   of proposition. I shall, for example, argue that no one can render false a
   law of physics; but I shall not argue that this is the case because laws of
   physics are *true,* but because of other features that they possess.

7. "*J* could have raised his hand at *T*" is ambiguous. It might mean either
   (roughly) "*J* possessed, at *T,* the ability to raise his hand," or "*J* possessed
   the ability to bring it about that his hand rose at *T.*" If *J* was unparalysed
   at *T* but paralysed at all earlier instants, then the latter of these would be
   false, though the former might be true. I mean "*J* could have raised his
   hand at *T*" in the latter sense.

8. See Saul Kripke, "Identity and Necessity," in *Identity and Individuation,*
   ed. Milton K. Munitz (New York, 1971).

9. Cf. Antony Flew, "Divine Omniscience and Human Freedom," *New
   Essays in Philosophical Theology,* ed. Antony Flew and Alasdair
   MacIntyre (London: SCM Press, 1955), 149–51 in particular.

10. Flew, loc cit.

11. Cf. R. E. Hobart, "Free Will as Involving Determination and
    Inconceivable Without It," *Mind*, 1934; A. J. Ayer, "Freedom and
    Necessity," in his collected *Philosophical Essays* (New York, 1954)
    P. H. Nowell-Smith, "Freewill and Moral Responsibility," *Mind*, 1948,
    J. J. C. Smart, "Free Will, Praise, and Blame," *Mind*, 1961.

12. Many other verbs besides "choose" figure in various philosophers' condi-
    tional analyses of ability: e.g., "wish," "want," "will," "try," "set one-
    self." Much of the important contemporary work on this analysis, by
    G. E. Moore, P. H. Nowell-Smith, J. L. Austin, Keith Lehrer, Roderick
    Chisholm, and others is collected in *The Nature of Human Action,* ed.
    Myles Brand (Glenview, Ill., 1970). See also "Fatalism and Determinism,"
    by Wilfrid Sellars, in *Freedom and Determinism,* ed. Keith Lehrer (New
    York, 1966), 141–74.

13. For an argument in some respects similar to what I have called the "main
    argument," see Carl Ginet's admirable article, "Might We Have No
    Choice?" in Lehrer, 87–104. Another argument similar to the main argu-
    ment, which is (formally) much simpler than the main argument, but
    which is stated in language very different from that of traditional state-
    ments of the free-will problem, can be found in my "A Formal Approach
    to the Problem of Free Will and Determinism," *Theoria*, 1974.

Alternative Possibilities and Moral Responsibility

Harry G. Frankfurt

A dominant role in nearly all recent inquiries into the free-will problem has been played by a principle which I shall call "the principle of alternate possibilities." This principle states that a person is morally responsible for what he has done only if he could have done otherwise. Its exact meaning is a subject of controversy, particularly concerning whether someone who accepts it is thereby committed to believing that moral responsibility and determinism are incompatible. Practically no one, however, seems inclined to deny or even to question that the principle of alternate possibilities (construed in some way or other) is true. It has generally seemed so overwhelmingly plausible that some philosophers have even characterized it as an *a priori* truth. People whose accounts of free will or of moral responsibility are radically at odds evidently find in it a firm and convenient common ground upon which they can profitably take their opposing stands.

But the principle of alternate possibilities is false. A person may well be morally responsible for what he has done even though he could not have done otherwise. The principle's plausibility is an illusion, which can be made to vanish by bringing the relevant moral phenomena into sharper focus.

I

In seeking illustrations of the principle of alternate possibilities, it is most natural to think of situations in which the same circumstances both bring it about that a person does something and make it impossible for him to avoid doing it. These include, for example, situations in which a person is coerced into doing something, or in which he is impelled to act by a hypnotic suggestion, or in which some inner compulsion drives him to do what he does. In situations of these kinds there are circumstances that make it impossible for the person to do otherwise, and these very circumstances also serve to bring it about that he does whatever it is that he does.

However, there may be circumstances that constitute sufficient conditions for a certain action to be performed by someone and that therefore make it impossible for the person to do otherwise, but that do not actually impel the person to act or in any way produce his action. A person may do something in circumstances that leave him no alternative to doing it, without these circumstances actually moving him or leading him to do it—without them playing any role, indeed, in bringing it about that he does what he does.

An examination of situations characterized by circumstances of this sort casts doubt, I believe, on the relevance to questions of moral responsibility of the fact that a person who has done something could not have done otherwise. I propose to develop some examples of this kind in the context of a discussion of coercion and to suggest that our moral intuitions concerning these examples tend to disconfirm the principle of alternate possibilities. Then I will discuss the principle in more general terms, explain what I think is wrong with it, and describe briefly and without argument how it might appropriately be revised.

II

It is generally agreed that a person who has been coerced to do something did not do it freely and is not morally responsible for having done it. Now the doctrine that coercion and moral responsibility are mutually exclusive may appear to be no more than a somewhat particularized version of the principle of alternate possibilities. It is natural enough to say of a person who has been coerced to do something that he could not have done otherwise. And it may easily seem that being coerced deprives a person of freedom and of moral responsibility simply because it is a special case of being unable to do otherwise. The principle of alternate possibilities may in this way derive some credibility from its association with the very plausible proposition that moral responsibility is excluded by coercion.

It is not right, however, that it should do so. The fact that a person was coerced to act as he did may entail both that he could not have done otherwise and that he bears no moral responsibility for his action. But his lack of moral responsibility is not entailed by his having been unable to do otherwise. The doctrine that coercion excludes moral responsibility is not correctly understood, in other words, as a particularized version of the principle of alternate possibilities.

Let us suppose that someone is threatened convincingly with a penalty he finds unacceptable and that he then does what is required of him by the issuer of the threat. We can imagine details that would make it reasonable for us to think that the person was coerced to perform the action in question, that he could not have done otherwise, and that he bears no moral responsibility for having done what he did. But just what is it about situations of this kind that warrants the judgment that the threatened person is not morally responsible for his act?

This question may be approached by considering situations of the following kind. Jones decides for reasons of his own to do something, then someone threatens him with a very harsh penalty (so harsh that any reasonable person would submit to the threat) unless he does precisely that, and Jones does it. Will we hold Jones morally responsible for what he has done? I think this will depend on the roles we think were played, in leading him to act, by his original decision and by the threat.

One possibility is that Jones$_1$ is not a reasonable man: he is, rather, a man who does what he has once decided to do no matter what happens next and no matter what the cost. In that case, the threat actually exerted no effective force upon him. He acted without any regard to it, very much as if he were not aware that it had been made. If this is indeed the way it was, the situation did not involve coercion at all. The threat did not lead Jones$_1$ to do what he did. Nor was it in fact sufficient to have prevented him from doing otherwise: if his earlier decision had been to do something else, the threat would not have deterred him in the slightest. It seems evident that in these circumstances the fact that Jones$_1$ was threatened in no way reduces the moral responsibility he would otherwise bear for his act. This example, however, is not a counterexample either to the doctrine that coercion excuses or to the principle of alternate possibilities. For we have supposed that Jones$_1$ is a man upon whom the threat had no coercive effect and, hence, that it did not actually deprive him of alternatives to doing what he did.

Another possibility is that Jones$_2$ was stampeded by the threat. Given that threat, he would have performed that action regardless of what decision he had already made. The threat upset him so profoundly, moreover, that he completely forgot his own earlier decision and did what was demanded of him entirely because he was terrified of the penalty with which he was threatened. In this case, it is not relevant to his having performed the action that he had already decided on his own to perform it. When the chips were down he thought of nothing but the threat, and fear alone led him to act. The fact that at an earlier time Jones$_2$ had decided for his own reasons to act in just that way may be relevant to an evaluation of his character; he may bear full moral responsibility for having made *that* decision. But he can hardly be said to be morally responsible for his action. For he performed the action simply as a result of the coercion to which he was subjected. His earlier decision played no role in bringing it about that he did what he did, and it would therefore be gratuitous to assign it a role in the moral evaluation of his action.

Now consider a third possibility. Jones$_3$ was neither stampeded by the threat nor indifferent to it. The threat impressed him, as it would impress any reasonable man, and he would have submitted to it wholeheartedly if he had not already made a decision that coincided with the one demanded of him. In fact, however, he performed the action in question on the basis of the decision he had made before the threat was issued. When he acted, he was not actually motivated by the threat but solely by the considerations that had originally commended the action to him. It was not the threat that led him to act, though it would have done so if he had not already provided himself with a sufficient motive for performing the action in question.

No doubt it will be very difficult for anyone to know, in a case like this one, exactly what happened. Did Jones$_3$ perform the action because of the threat, or were his reasons for acting simply those which had already persuaded him to do so? Or did he act on the basis of two motives, each of which was sufficient for his action? It is not impossible, however, that the situation should be clearer than situations of this kind usually are. And suppose it is apparent to us that Jones$_3$ acted on the basis of his own decision and not because of the threat. Then I think we would be justified in regarding his moral responsibility for what he did as unaffected by the threat even though, since he would in any case have submitted to the threat, he could not have avoided doing what he did. It would be entirely reasonable for us to make the same judgment concerning his moral responsibility that we would have made if we had not known of the threat. For the threat did not in fact influence his performance of the action. He did what he did just as if the threat had not been made at all.

III

The case of Jones$_3$ may appear at first glance to combine coercion and moral responsibility, and thus to provide a counterexample to the doctrine that coercion excuses. It is not really so certain that it does so, however, because it is unclear whether the example constitutes a genuine instance of coercion. Can we say of Jones$_3$ that he was coerced to do something, when he had already decided on his own to do it and when he did it entirely on the basis of that decision? Or would it be more correct to say that Jones₃ was not coerced to do what he did, even though he himself recognized that there was an irresistible force at work in virtue of which he had to do it? My own linguistic intuitions lead me toward the second alternative, but they are somewhat equivocal. Perhaps we can say either of these things, or perhaps we must add a qualifying explanation to whichever of them we say.

This murkiness, however, does not interfere with our drawing an important moral from an examination of the example. Suppose we decide to say that Jones₃ was *not* coerced. Our basis for saying this will clearly be that it is incorrect to regard a man as being coerced to do something unless he does it *because* of the coercive force exerted against him. The fact that an irresistible threat is made will not, then, entail that the person who receives it is coerced to do what he does. It will also be necessary that the threat is what actually accounts for his doing it. On the other hand, suppose we decide to say that Jones₃ *was* coerced. Then we will be bound to admit that being coerced does not exclude being morally responsible. And we will also surely be led to the view that coercion affects the judgment of a person's moral responsibility only when the person acts as he does because he is coerced to do so—i.e., when the fact that he is coerced is what accounts for his action.

Whichever we decide to say, then, we will recognize that the doctrine that coercion excludes moral responsibility is not a particularized version of the principle of alternate possibilities. Situations in which a person who does something cannot do otherwise because he is subject to coercive power are either not instances of coercion at all, or they are situations in which the person may still be morally responsible for what he does if it is not because of the coercion that he does it. When we excuse a person who has been coerced, we do not excuse him because he was unable to do otherwise. Even though a person is subject to a coercive force that precludes his performing any action but one, he may nonetheless bear full moral responsibility for performing that action.

IV

To the extent that the principle of alternate possibilities derives its plausibility from association with the doctrine that coercion excludes moral responsibility, a clear understanding of the latter diminishes the appeal of the former. Indeed the case of Jones₃ may appear to do more than illuminate the relationship between the two doctrines. It may well seem to provide a decisive counterexample to the principle of alternate possibilities and thus to show that this principle is false. For the irresistibility of the threat to which Jones$_3$ is subjected might well be taken to mean that he cannot but perform the action he performs. And yet the threat, since Jones$_3$ performs the action without regard to it, does not reduce his moral responsibility for what he does.

The following objection will doubtless be raised against the suggestion that the case of Jones$_3$ is a counterexample to the principle of alternate possibilities. There is perhaps a sense in which Jones$_3$ cannot do otherwise than perform the action he performs, since he is a reasonable man and the threat he encounters is sufficient to move any reasonable man. But it is not this sense that is germane to the principle of alternate possibilities. His knowledge that he stands to suffer an intolerably harsh penalty does not mean that Jones$_3$, strictly speaking, *cannot* perform any action but the one he does perform. After all it is still open to him, and this is crucial, to defy the threat if he wishes to do so and to accept the penalty his action would bring down upon him. In the sense in which the principle of alternate possibilities employs the concept of "could have done otherwise." Jones$_3$'s inability to resist the threat does not mean that he cannot do otherwise than perform the action he performs. Hence the case of Jones$_3$ does not constitute an instance contrary to the principle.

I do not propose to consider in what sense the concept of "could have done otherwise" figures in the principle of alternate possibilities, nor will I attempt to measure the force of the objection I have just described. For I believe that whatever force this objection may be thought to have can be deflected by altering the example in the following way. Suppose someone—Black, let us say—wants Jones$_4$ to perform a certain action. Black is prepared to go to considerable lengths to get his way, but he prefers to avoid showing his hand unnecessarily. So he waits until Jones$_4$ is about to make up his mind what to do, and he does nothing unless it is clear to him (Black is an excellent judge of such things) that Jones$_4$ is going to decide to do something *other* than what he wants him to do. If it does become clear that Jones$_4$ is going to decide to do something else, Black takes effective steps to ensure that Jones$_4$ decides to do, and that he does do, what he wants him to do. Whatever Jones$_4$'s initial preferences and inclinations, then, Black will have his way.

What steps will Black take, if he believes he must take steps, in order to ensure that Jones$_4$ decides and acts as he wishes? Anyone with a theory concerning what "could have done otherwise" means may answer this question for himself by describing whatever measures he would regard as sufficient to guarantee that, in the relevant sense, Jones$_4$ cannot do otherwise. Let Black pronounce a terrible threat, and in this way both force Jones$_4$ to perform the desired action and prevent him from performing a forbidden one. Let Black give Jones$_4$ a potion, or put him under hypnosis, and in some such way as these generate in Jones$_4$ an irresistible inner compulsion to perform the act Black wants performed and to avoid others. Or let Black manipulate the minute processes of Jones$_4$'s brain and nervous system in some more direct way, so that causal forces running in and out of his synapses and along the poor man's nerves determine that he chooses to act and that he does act in the one way and not in any other. Given any conditions under which it will be maintained that Jones$_4$ cannot do otherwise, in other words, let Black bring it about that those conditions prevail. The structure of the example is flexible enough, I think, to find a way around any charge of irrelevance by accommodating the doctrine on which the charge is based.

Now suppose that Black never has to show his hand because Jones$_4$, for reasons of his own, decides to perform and does perform the very action Black wants him to perform. In that case, it seems clear, Jones$_4$ will bear precisely the same moral responsibility for what he does as he would have borne if Black had not been ready to take steps to ensure that he do it. It would be quite unreasonable to excuse Jones$_4$ for his action, or to withhold the praise to which it would normally entitle him, on the basis of the fact that he could not have done otherwise. This fact played no role at all in leading him to act as he did. He would have acted the same even if it had not been a fact, Indeed, everything happened just as it would have happened without Black's presence in the situation and without his readiness to intrude into it.

In this example there are sufficient conditions for Jones$_4$'s performing the action in question. What action he performs is not up to him. Of course it is in a way up to him whether he acts on his own or as a result of Black's intervention. That depends upon what action he himself is inclined to perform. But whether he finally acts on his own or as a result of Black's intervention, he performs the same action. He has no alternative but to do what Black wants him to do. If he does it on his own, however, his moral responsibility for doing it is not affected by the fact that Black was lurking in the background with sinister intent, since this intent never comes into play.

V

The fact that a person could not have avoided doing something is a sufficient condition of his having done it. But, as some of my examples show, this fact may play no role whatever in the explanation of why he did it. It may not figure at all among the circumstances that actually brought it about that he did what he did, so that his action is to be accounted for on another basis entirely. Even though the person was unable to do otherwise, that is to say, it may not be the case that he acted as he did *because* he could not have done otherwise. Now if someone had no alternative to performing a certain action but did not perform it because he was unable to do otherwise, then he would have performed exactly the same action even if he *could* have done otherwise. The circumstances that made it impossible for him to do otherwise could have been subtracted from the situation without affecting what happened or why it happened in any way. Whatever it was that actually led the person to do what he did, or that made him do it, would have led him to do it or made him do it even if it had been possible for him to do something else instead.

Thus it would have made no difference, so far as concerns his action or how he came to perform it, if the circumstances that made it impossible for him to avoid performing it had not prevailed. The fact that he could not have done otherwise clearly provides no basis for supposing that he *might* have done otherwise if he had been able to do so. When a fact is in this way irrelevant to the problem of accounting for a person's action it seems quite gratuitous to assign it any weight in the assessment of his moral responsibility. Why should the fact be considered in reaching a moral judgment concerning the person when it does not help in any way to understand either what made him act as he did or what, in other circumstances, he might have done?

This, then, is why the principle of alternate possibilities is mistaken. It asserts that a person bears no moral responsibility—that is, he is to be excused—for having performed an action if there were circumstances that made it impossible for him to avoid performing it. But there may be circumstances that make it impossible for a person to avoid performing some action without those circumstances in any way bringing it about that he performs that action. It would surely be no good for the person to refer to circumstances of this sort in an effort to absolve himself of moral responsibility for performing the action in question. For those circumstances, by hypothesis, actually had nothing to do with his having done what he did. He would have done precisely the same thing, and he would have been led or made in precisely the same way to do it, even if they had not prevailed.

We often do, to be sure, excuse people for what they have done when they tell us (and we believe them) that they could not have done otherwise. But this is because we assume that what they tell us serves to explain why they did what they did. We take it for granted that they are not being disingenuous, as a person would be who cited as an excuse the fact that he could not have avoided doing what he did but who knew full well that it was not at all because of this that he did it.

What I have said may suggest that the principle of alternate possibilities should be revised so as to assert that a person is not morally responsible for what he has done if he did it because he could not have done otherwise. It may be noted that this revision of the principle does not seriously affect the arguments of those who have relied on the original principle in their efforts to maintain that moral responsibility and determinism are incompatible. For if it was causally determined that a person perform a certain action, then it will be true that the person performed it because of those causal determinants. And if the fact that it was causally determined that a person perform a certain action means that the person could not have done otherwise, as philosophers who argue for the incompatibility thesis characteristically suppose, then the fact that it was causally determined that a person perform a certain action will mean that the person performed it because he could not have done otherwise. The revised principle of alternate possibilities will entail, on this assumption concerning the meaning of "could have done otherwise," that a person is not morally responsible for what he has done if it was causally determined that he do it. I do not believe, however, that this revision of the principle is acceptable.

Suppose a person tells us that he did what he did because he was unable to do otherwise; or suppose he makes the similar statement that he did what he did because he had to do it. We do often accept statements like these (if we believe them) as valid excuses, and such statements may well seem at first glance to invoke the revised principle of alternate possibilities. But I think that when we accept such statements as valid excuses it is because we assume that we are being told more than the statements strictly and literally convey. We understand the person who offers the excuse to mean that he did what he did *only because* he was unable to do otherwise, or *only because* he had to do it. And we understand him to mean, more particularly, that when he did what he did it was not because that was what he really wanted to do. The principle of alternate possibilities should thus be replaced, in my opinion, by the following principle: a person is not morally responsible for what he has done if he did it only because he could not have done otherwise. This principle does not appear to conflict with the view that moral responsibility is compatible with determinism.

The following may all be true: there were circumstances that made it impossible for a person to avoid doing something; these circumstances actually played a role in bringing it about that he did it, so that it is correct to say that he did it because he could not have done otherwise; the person really wanted to do what he did; he did it because it was what he really wanted to do, so that it is not correct to say that he did what he did only because he could not have done otherwise. Under these conditions, the person may well be morally responsible for what he has done. On the other hand, he will not be morally responsible for what he has done if he did it only because he could not have done otherwise, even if what he did was something he really wanted to do.

Human Freedom and the Self

Roderick Chisholm

A staff moves a stone, and is moved by a hand, which is moved by a man.
ARISTOTLE, *PHYSICS*, 256A

1. The metaphysical problem of human freedom might be summarized in the following way: Human beings are responsible agents; but this fact appears to conflict with a deterministic view of human action (the view that every event that is involved in an act is caused by some other event); and it *also* appears to conflict with an indeterministic view of human action (the view that the act, or some event that is essential to the act, is not caused at all). To solve the problem, I believe, we must make somewhat far-reaching assumptions about the self or the agent— about the man who performs the act.

Perhaps it is needless to remark that, in all likelihood, it is impossible to say anything significant about this ancient problem that has not been said before.[1]

2. Let us consider some deed, or misdeed, that may be attributed to a responsible agent: one man, say, shot another. If the man *was* responsible for what he did, then, I would urge, what was to happen at the time of the shooting was something that was entirely up to the man himself. There was a moment at which it was true, both that

he could have fired the shot and also that he could have refrained from firing it. And if this is so, then, even though he did fire it, he could have done something else instead. (He didn't find himself firing the shot "against his will," as we say.) I think we can say, more generally, then, that if a man is responsible for a certain event or a certain state of affairs (in our example, the shooting of another man), then that event or state of affairs was brought about by some act of his, and the act was something that was in his power either to perform or not to perform.

But now if the act which he *did* perform was an act that was also in his power *not* to perform, then it could not have been caused or determined by any event that was not itself within his power either to bring about or not to bring about. For example, if what we say he did was really something that was brought about by a second man, one who forced his hand upon the trigger, say, or who, by means of hypnosis, compelled him to perform the act, then since the act was caused by the *second* man it was nothing that was within the power of the *first* man to prevent. And precisely the same thing is true, I think, if instead of referring to a second man who compelled the first one, we speak instead of the *desires* and *beliefs* which the first man happens to have had. For if what we say he did was really something that was brought about by his own beliefs and desires, if these beliefs and desires in the particular situation in which he happened to have found himself caused him to do just what it was that we say he did do, then, since *they* caused it, he was unable to do anything other than just what it was that he did do. It makes no difference whether the cause of the deed was internal or external; if the cause was some state or event for which the man himself was not responsible, then he was not responsible for what we have been mistakenly calling his act. If a flood caused the poorly constructed dam to break, then, given the flood and the constitution of the dam, the break, we may say, *had* to occur and nothing could have happened in its place. And if the flood of desire caused the weak-willed man to give in then he, too, had to do just what it was that he did do and he was no more responsible than was the dam for the results that followed. (It is true, of course, that if the man is responsible for the beliefs and desires that he happens to have, then he may also be responsible for the things they lead him to do. But the question now becomes: *is* he responsible for the beliefs and desires he happens to have? If he is, then there was a time when they were within his power either to acquire or not to acquire, and we are left, therefore, with our general point.)

One may object: But surely if there were such a thing as a man who is really *good,* then he would be responsible for things that he would do; yet, he would be unable to do anything other than just what it is that he does do, since, being good, he will always choose to do what is best. The answer, I think, is suggested by a comment that Thomas Reid makes upon an ancient author. The author had said of Cato, "He was good because he could not be otherwise," and Reid observes: "This saying, if understood literally and strictly, is not the praise of Cato, but of his constitution, which was no more the work of Cato than his existence."[2] If Cato was himself responsible for the good things that he did, then Cato, as Reid suggests, was such that, although he had the power to do what was not good, he exercised his power only for that which was good.

All of this, if it is true, may give a certain amount of comfort to those who are tender-minded. But we should remind them that it also conflicts with a familiar view about the nature of God—with the view that St. Thomas Aquinas expresses saying that "every movement both of the will and of nature proceeds from God as the Prime Mover."[3] If the act of the sinner *did* proceed from God as the Prime Mover, then God was in the position of the second agent we just discussed—the man who forced the trigger finger, or the hypnotist—and the sinner, so-called, was *not* responsible for what he did. (This may be a bold assertion, in view of the history of western theology, but I must say that I have never encountered a single good reason for denying it.)

There is one standard objection to all of this and we should consider it briefly.

3. The objection takes the form of a stratagem—one designed to show that determinism (and divine providence) is consistent with human responsibility. The stratagem is one that was used by Jonathan Edwards and by many philosophers in the present century, most notably, G. E. Moore.[4]

One proceeds as follows: The expression

(a) He could have done otherwise,

it is argued, means no more nor less than

(b) If he had chosen to do otherwise, then he would have done otherwise.

(In place of "chosen," one might say "tried," "set out," "decided," "undertaken," or "willed.") The truth of statement (b), it is then pointed out, is consistent with determinism (and with divine providence); for even if all of the man's actions were causally determined, the man could still be such that, *if* he had chosen otherwise, then he would have done otherwise. What the murderer saw, let us suppose, along with his beliefs and desires, *caused* him to fire the shot; yet he was such that *if,* just then, he had chosen or decided *not* to fire the shot, then he would not have fired it. All of this is certainly possible. Similarly, we could say, of the dam, that the flood caused it to break and also that the dam was such that, *if* there had been no flood or any similar pressure, then the dam would have remained intact. And therefore, the argument proceeds, if (b) is consistent with determinism, and if (a) and (b) say the same thing, then (a) is also consistent with determinism; hence we can say that the agent *could* have done otherwise even though he was caused to do what he did do; and therefore determinism and moral responsibility are compatible.

Is the argument sound? The conclusion follows from the premises, but the catch, I think, lies in the first premise—the one saying that statement (a) tells us no more nor less than what statement (b) tells us. For (b), it would seem, could be true while (a) is false. That is to say, our man might be such that, if he had chosen to do otherwise, then he would have done otherwise, and yet *also* such that he could not have done otherwise. Suppose, after all, that our murderer could not have *chosen,* or could not have *decided,* to do otherwise. Then the fact that he happens also to be a man such that, if he had chosen not to shoot he would not have shot, then he could not have done anything other than just what it was that he did do. In a word: from our statement (b) above ("If he had chosen to do otherwise, then he would have done otherwise"), we cannot make an inference to (a) above ("He could have done otherwise") unless we can *also* assert:

(c) He could have chosen to do otherwise.

And therefore, if we must reject this third statement (c), then, even though we may be justified in asserting (b), we are not justified in asserting (a). If the man could not have chosen to do otherwise, then he would not have done otherwise—*even if* he was such that, if he *had* chosen to do otherwise, then he would have done otherwise.

The stratagem in question, then, seems to me not to work, and I would say, therefore, that the ascription of responsibility conflicts with a deterministic view of action.

4. Perhaps there is less need to argue that the ascription of responsibility also conflicts with an indeterministic view of action—with the view that the act, or some event that is essential to the act, is not caused

at all. If the act—the firing of the shot—was not caused at all, if it was fortuitous or capricious, happening so to speak out of the blue, then, presumably, no one—and nothing—was responsible for the act. Our conception of action, therefore, should be neither deterministic nor indeterministic. Is there any other possibility?

5. We must not say that every event involved in the act is caused by some other event; and we must not say that the act is something that is not caused at all. The possibility that remains, therefore, is this: We should say that at least one of the events that are involved in the act is caused, not by any other events, but by something else instead. And this something else can only be the agent—the man. If there is an event that is caused, not by other events, but by the man, then there are some events involved in the act that are not caused by other events. But if the event in question is caused by the man then it *is* caused and we are not committed to saying that there is something involved in the act that is not caused at all.

But this, of course, is a large consequence, implying something of considerable importance about the nature of the agent or the man.

6. If we consider only inanimate natural objects, we may say that causation, if it occurs, is a relation between *events* or *states of affairs*. The dam's breaking was an event that was caused by a set of other events—the dam being weak, the flood being strong, and so on. But if a man is responsible for a particular deed, then, if what I have said is true, there is some event, or set of events, that is caused, *not* by other events or states of affairs, but by the agent, whatever he may be.

I shall borrow a pair of medieval terms, using them, perhaps, in a way that is slightly different from that for which they were originally intended. I shall say that when one event or state of affairs (or set of events or states of affairs) causes some other event or state of affairs, then we have an instance of *transeunt* causation. And I shall say that when an *agent*, as distinguished from an event, causes an event or state of affairs, then we have an instance of *immanent* causation.

The nature of what is intended by the expression "immanent causation" may be illustrated by this sentence from Aristotle's *Physics.* "Thus, a staff moves a stone, and is moved by a hand, which is moved by a man" (Book VII, Chap. 5, 256a, 6–8). If the man was responsible, then we have in this illustration a number of instances of causation—most of them transeunt but at least one of them immanent. What the staff did to the stone was an instance of transeunt causation, and thus we may describe it as a relation between events: "the motion of the staff caused the motion of the stone." And similarly for what the hand did to the staff: "the motion of the hand caused the motion of the staff." And, as we know from physiology, there are still other events which caused the motion of the hand. Hence we need not introduce the agent at this particular point, as Aristotle does—we *need* not, though we *may*. We *may* say that the hand was moved by the man, but we may *also* say that the motion of the hand was caused by the motion of certain muscles; and we may say that the motion of the muscles was caused by certain events that took place within the brain. But some event, and presumably one of those that took place within the brain, was caused by the agent and not by any other events.

There are, of course, objections to this way of putting the matter; I shall consider the two that seem to me to be most important.

7. One may object, firstly: "If the *man* does anything, then, as Aristotle's remark suggests, what he does is to move the *hand*. But he certainly does not do anything to his brain—he may not even know that he *has* a brain. And if he doesn't do anything to the brain, and if the motion of the hand was caused by something that happened within the brain, then there is no point in appealing to 'immanent causation' as being something incompatible with 'transeunt causation'—for the whole thing, after all, is a matter of causal relations among events or states of affairs."

The answer to this objection, I think, is this: It is true that the agent does not *do* anything with his brain, or to his brain, in the sense in which he *does* something with his hand and does something to the staff. But from this it does not follow that the agent was not the immanent cause of something that happened within his brain.

We should note a useful distinction that has been proposed by Professor A. I. Melden—namely, the distinction between "making something A happen" and "doing A."[5] If I reach for the staff and pick it up, then one of the things that I *do* is just that—reach for the staff and pick it up. And if it is something that I *do*, then there is a very clear sense in which it may be said to be something that I know that I do. If you ask me, "Are you doing something, or trying to do something, with the staff?," I will have no difficulty in finding an answer. But in doing something with the staff, I also make various things happen which are not in this same sense things that I do: I will make various air-particles move; I will free a number of blades of grass from the pressure that had been upon them; and I may cause a shadow to move from one place to another. If these are merely things that I make happen, as distinguished from things that I do, then I may know nothing whatever about them; I may not have the slightest idea that, in moving the staff, I am bringing about any such thing as the motion of air-particles, shadows, and blades of grass.

We may say, in answer to the first objection, therefore, that it is true that our agent does nothing to his brain; but from this it does not follow that the agent is not the immanent cause of some event within his brain; for the brain event may be something which, like the motion of the air-particles, he made happen in picking up the staff. The only difference between the two cases is this: in each case, he made something happen when he picked up the staff; but in the one case—the motion of the air-particles or of the shadows—it was the motion of the staff that caused the event to happen; and in the other case—the event that took place in the brain—it was this event that caused the motion of the staff.

The point is, in a word, that whenever a man does something A, then (by "immanent causation") he makes a certain cerebral event happen, and this cerebral event (by "transeunt causation") makes A happen.

8. The second objection is more difficult and concerns the very concept of "immanent causation," or causation by an agent, as this concept is to be interpreted here. The concept is subject to a difficulty which has long been associated with that of the prime mover unmoved. We have said that there must be some event A, presumably some cerebral event, which is caused not by any other event, but by the agent. Since A was not caused by any other event, then the agent himself cannot be said to have undergone any change or produced any other event (such as "an act of will" or the like) which brought A about. But if, when the agent made A happen, there was no event involved other than A itself, no event which could be described as *making* A happen, what did the agent's causation consist of? What, for example, is the difference between A's just happening, and the agent's *causing* A to happen? We cannot attribute the difference to any event that took place within the agent. And so far as the event A itself is concerned, there would seem to be no discernible difference. Thus Aristotle said that the activity of the prime mover is nothing in addition to the motion that it produces, and Suarez said that "the action is in reality nothing but the effect as it flows from the agent."[6] Must we conclude, then, that there is no more to the man's action in causing event A than there is to the event A's happening by itself? Here we would seem to have a distinction without a difference—in which case we have failed to find a *via media* between a deterministic and an indeterministic view of action.

The only answer, I think, can be this: that the difference between the man's causing A, on the one hand, and the event A just happening, on the other, lies in the fact that, in the first case but not the second, the event A *was* caused and was caused by the man. There was a brain event A; the agent did, in fact, cause the brain event; but there was nothing that he did to cause it.

This answer may not entirely satisfy and it will be likely to provoke the following question: "But what are you really *adding* to the assertion that A happened when you utter the words 'The agent *caused* A to happen'?" As soon as we have put the question this way, we see, I think, that whatever difficulty we may have encountered is one that may be traced to the concept of causation generally—whether "immanent" or "transeunt." The problem, in other words, is not a problem that is peculiar to our conception of human action. It is a problem that must be faced by anyone who makes use of the concept of causation at all; and therefore, I would say, it is a problem for everyone but the complete indeterminist.

For the problem, as we put it, referring just to "immanent causation," or causation by an agent, was this: "What is the difference between saying, of an event A, that A just happened and saying that someone caused A to happen?" The analogous problem, which holds for "transeunt causation," or causation by an event, is this: "What is the difference between saying, of two events A and B, that B happened and then A happened, and saying that B's happening was the *cause* of A's happening?" And the only answer that one can give is this—that in the one case the agent was the cause of A's happening and in the other case event B was the cause of A's happening. The nature of transeunt causation is no more clear than is that of immanent causation.

9. But we may plausibly say—and there is a respectable philosophical tradition to which we may appeal—that the notion of immanent causation, or causation by an agent, is in fact more clear than that of transeunt causation, or causation by an event; and that it is only by understanding our own causal efficacy, as agents, that we can grasp the concept of *cause* at all. Hume may be said to have shown that we do not derive the concept of *cause* from what we perceive of external things. How, then, do we derive it? The most plausible suggestion, it seems to me, is that of Reid, once again: namely that "the conception of an efficient cause may very probably be derived from the experience we have had . . . of our own power to produce certain effects."[7] If we did not understand the concept of immanent causation, we would not understand that of transeunt causation.

10. It may have been noted that I have avoided the term "free will" in all of this. For even if there is such a faculty as "the will," which somehow sets our acts agoing, the question of freedom, as John Locke said, is not the question *"whether the will be free"*; it is the question *"whether a man be free."*[8] For if there is a "will," as a moving faculty, the question is whether the man is free to will to do these things that he does will to do—and also whether the man is free *not* to will any of those things that he does will to do, and, again, whether he is free to will any of those things that he does not will to do. Jonathan Edwards tried to restrict himself to the question—"Is the man free to do what it is that he wills?"—but the answer to the question will not tell us whether the man is responsible for what it is that he *does* will to do. Using still another pair of medieval terms, we may say that the metaphysical problem of freedom does not concern the *actus imperatus*, it does not concern the question whether we are free to accomplish whatever it is that we will or set out to do; it concerns the *actus elicitus*, the question whether we are free to will or to set out to do those things that we do will or set out to do.

11. If we are responsible, and if what I have been trying to say is true, then we have a prerogative which some would attribute only to God: each of us, when we act, is a prime mover unmoved. In doing what we do, we cause certain events to happen, and nothing—or no one—causes us to cause those events to happen.

12. If we are thus prime movers unmoved and if our actions, or those for which we are responsible, are not causally determined, then they are not causally determined by our *desires*. And this means that the relation between what we want or what we desire, on the one hand, and what it is that we do, on the other, is not as simple as most philosophers would have it.

We may distinguish between what we might call the "Hobbist approach" and what we might call the "Kantian approach" to this question. The Hobbist approach is the one that is generally accepted at the present time, but the Kantian approach, I believe, is the one that is true. According to Hobbism, if we *know,* of some man, what his belief and desires happen to be and how strong they are, if we know what he feels certain of, what he desires more than anything else, and if we know the state of his body and what stimuli he is being subjected to, then we may *deduce*, logically, just what it is that he will do—or, more accurately, just what it is that he will try, set out, or undertake to do. Thus Professor Melden has said that "the connection between wanting and doing is logical."[9] But according to the Kantian approach to our problem, and this is the one that I would take, there is no such logical connection between wanting and doing, nor need there even be a causal connection. No set of statements about a man's desires, beliefs, and stimulus situation at any time implies any statement telling us what the man will try, set out, or undertake to do at that time. As Reid put it, though we may "reason from men's motives to their actions and, in many cases, with great probability," we can never do so "with absolute certainty."[10]

This means that, in one very strict sense of the terms, there can be no science of man. If we think of science as a matter of finding out what laws happen to hold, and if the statement of a law tells us what kinds of events are caused by what other kinds of events, then there will be human actions which we cannot explain by subsuming them under any laws. We cannot say, "It is causally necessary that, given such and such desires and beliefs, and being subject to such and such stimuli, the agent will do so and so." For at times the agent, if he chooses, may rise above his desires and do something else instead.

But all of this is consistent with saying that, perhaps more often than not, our desires do exist under conditions such that those conditions necessitate us to act. And we may also say, with Leibniz, that at other times our desires may "incline without necessitating."

Notes

1. The general position to be presented here is suggested in the following writings among others: Aristotle, *Eudemian Ethics,* book II, ch. 6; *Nicomachean Ethics*, book III, chs 1–5; Thomas Reid, *Essays on the Active Powers of Man.* C.A. Campbell, "Is 'Free Will' a Pseudo-Problem?" *Mind*, n.s. 60 (1951), pp. 441–65; Roderick M. Chisholm, "Responsibility and Avoidability," and Richard Taylor, "Determination and the Theory of Agency," in Sidney Hook, ed., *Determinism and Freedom in the Age of Modern Science* (New York: New York University Press, 1958).

2. Thomas Reid, *Essays on the Active Powers of the Human Mind* (Cambridge MA: MIT Press, 1969; first published 1788), p. 261.

3. *Summa Theologia,* First Part of the Second Part, Question VI: "On the Voluntary and Involuntary."

4. Jonathan Edwards, *Freedom of the Will* (New Haven, Conn.: Yale University Press, 1957); G. E. Moore, *Ethics* (Home University Library, 1912), ch. 6.

5. A. I. Melden, *Free Action* (Oxford: Blackwell, 1961), especially ch. 3. Mr. Melden's own views, however, are quite the contrary of those proposed here.

6. Aristotle, *Physics*, book III, ch. 3; Suarez, *Disputations Metaphysicae*, Disputation 18, Section 10.

7. Reid, *Essays on the Active Powers*, p. 39.

8. John Locke, *Essay Concerning Human Understanding*, book II, ch. 21.

9. Melden, *Free Action*, p. 166.

10. Reid, *Essays on the Active Powers*, p. 291.

IS THERE AN ENDURING SELF?

We cannot deny that we change a good deal during our lifetime. As time goes by, we change from being a baby into an adult and then an older person. This leads to an obvious question: Does the same self persist through all these changes? This question becomes especially relevant when we approach death. Can we be sure that the death of our physical bodies ends all? Is it not at least logically possible that we might survive the destruction of our bodies?

John Perry addresses these issues in "A Dialogue on Personal Identity and Immortality." The dialogue introduces us to three characters: Gretchen Weirob, a philosopher who is seriously injured in a motorcycle accident and who awaits her death in a hospital bed; Sam Miller, a chaplain and Gretchen's longtime friend; and Dave Cohen, Gretchen's former student. Sam tries to convince a skeptical Gretchen that it is quite possible that she might survive her looming death. His initial arguments are based on a "soul theory" of personal identity. But Gretchen raises serious objections to Sam's comforting words, and an entertaining and thoughtful conversation about personal identity and life after death develops.

Our second reading introduces us to an Eastern way of thinking about the self. In his essay "The Buddhist Theory of 'No-Self'" Serge-Christopher Kolm describes a Buddhist way of dissolving the Western conception of a permanent self that persists through time. Kolm agrees that all of us are tempted to believe that there is such a permanent self. However, once we begin to see that this self really exists as a manifold of distinct elements, we understand that a *permanent self* is a creation of reason and imagination. It is a way of seeing and composing the world, but not an entity that really exists.

In "Personal Identity: The Dualist Theory," Richard Swinburne starts off with a lucid survey of various empiricist and physicalist theories of personal identity. He concludes, however, that these standard theories are not entirely satisfactory. In light of this result, Swinburne defends a dualist theory of personal identity, which holds that a person consists of two parts: soul and body.

Brain transplants are, theoretically, operations in which one person's brain is put into the body of another person, and the transplanted brain continues to function in the new body just as well as it did before. Special versions of brain transplants are cases in which one person's brain is split in half, and each half is transplanted into a different healthy body. Although these kinds of operations are not yet physically possible, philosophers have treated these splitting cases as important thought experiments. In "Brain Transplants and Personal Identity" Derek Parfit and Godfrey Vesey discuss the effect that splitting cases have on our understanding of personal identity. Parfit suggests that these splitting cases can be handled much more easily if we accept that what matters for the survival of the self is not the relationship of strict identity but rather relationships of degree.

In "Where Am I?" Daniel Dennett explores what would happen to him and his sense of self if his brain were to be separated from his body. Dennett imagines that he is asked by the Pentagon to undergo such a brain-body separation operation so that his body can safely retrieve a nuclear warhead under Tulsa, Oklahoma, while his brain is safely located in a life support system in the Spacecraft Center in Houston, Texas. After undergoing a successful operation, Dennett is initially confused and wants to know whether he is identical to his brain, which he calls "Yorek," or whether he is identical to his body, which he calls "Hamlet." After some hard reflecting, he gets used to the idea that he is in two places at the same time and that he has become a "scattered individual."

In the final reading, "Feminist Perspectives on the Self," Diana Meyers gives an overview of recent feminist work on the self. According to many feminist writers, the standard conception of the self that emerges in Western philosophy is predominately derived from the perspective of white, heterosexual, mostly economically advantaged men who have wielded social, economic, and political power. Such a self sees itself as a rational chooser and economic planner who is free of obligations and difficulties that arise in interpersonal relationships and unforeseen economic circumstances. Meyers explains why such a view of self is, in the eyes of many feminist writers, incomplete at best and seriously misleading at worst.

A Dialogue on Personal Identity and Immortality
John Perry

This is a record of conversations of Gretchen Weirob, a teacher of philosophy at a small midwestern college, and two of her friends. The conversations took place in her hospital room on the three nights before she died from injuries sustained in a motorcycle accident. Sam Miller is a chaplain and a long-time friend of Weirob's; Dave Cohen is a former student of hers.

The First Night

COHEN: I can hardly believe what you say, Gretchen. You are lucid and do not appear to be in great pain. And yet you say things are hopeless?

WEIROB: These devices can keep me alive for another day or two at most. Some of my vital organs have been injured beyond anything the doctors know how to repair, apart from certain rather radical measures I have rejected. I am not in much pain. But as I understand it that is not a particularly good sign. My brain was uninjured and I guess that's why I am as lucid as I ever am. The whole situation is a bit depressing, I fear. But here's Sam Miller, perhaps he will know how to cheer me up.

MILLER: Good evening, Gretchen. Hello, Dave. I guess there's not much point in beating around the bush, Gretchen; the medics tell me you're a goner. Is there anything I can do to help?

WEIROB: Crimenetley, Sam! You deal with the dying every day. Don't you have anything more comforting to say than "Sorry to hear you're a goner"?

MILLER: Well, to tell you the truth, I'm a little at a loss for what to say to you. Most people I deal with are believers like I am. We talk of the prospects for survival. I give assurance that God, who is just and merciful, would not permit such a travesty as that our short life on this earth should be the end of things. But you and I have talked about religious and philosophical issues for years.

I have never been able to find in you the least inclination to believe in God; indeed, it's a rare day when you are sure that your friends have minds, or that you can see your own hand in front of your face, or that there is any reason to believe that the sun will rise tomorrow. How can I hope to comfort you with the prospect of life after death, when I know you will regard it as having no probability whatsoever?

WEIROB: I would not require so much to be comforted, Sam. Even the possibility of something quite improbable can be comforting, in certain situations. When we used to play tennis, I beat you no more than one time in twenty. But this was enough to establish the possibility of beating you on any given occasion, and by focusing merely on the possibility I remained eager to play. Entombed in a secure prison, thinking our situation quite hopeless, we may find unutterable joy in the information that there is, after all, the slimmest possibility of escape. Hope provides comfort, and hope does not always require probability. But we must believe that what we hope for is at least possible. So I will set an easier task for you. Simply persuade me that my survival after the death of this body, is *possible,* and I promise to be comforted. Whether you succeed or not, your attempts will be a diversion, for you know I like to talk philosophy more than anything else.

MILLER: But what is possibility, if not reasonable probability?

WEIROB: I do not mean possible in the sense of likely, or even in the sense of conforming to the known laws of physics or biology. I mean possible only in the weakest sense—of being conceivable, given the unavoidable facts. Within the next couple of days, this body will die. It will be buried and it will rot away. I ask that, given these facts, you explain to me how it even makes *sense* to talk of me continuing to exist. Just explain to me what it is I am to *imagine,* when I imagine surviving, that is consistent with these facts, and I shall be comforted.

MILLER: But then what is there to do? There are many conceptions of immortality, of survival past the grave, which all seem to make good sense. Surely not the possibility, but only the probability, can be doubted. Take your choice! Christians believe in life, with a body, in some Hereafter—the details vary, of course, from sect to sect. There is the Greek idea of the body as a prison, from which we escape at death—so that we have continued life without a body. Then there are conceptions in which, so to speak, we merge with the flow of being—

WEIROB: I must cut short your lesson in comparative religion. Survival means surviving, no more, no less. I have no doubts that I shall merge with being; plants will take root in my remains, and the chemicals that I am will continue to make their contribution to life. I am enough of an ecologist to be comforted. But survival, if it is anything, must offer comforts of a different sort, the comforts of *anticipation*. Survival means that tomorrow, or sometime in the future, there will be someone who will experience, who will see and touch and smell—or at the very least, think and reason and remember. And this person will be *me*. This person will be related to me in such a way that it is correct for me to anticipate, to look forward to, those future experiences. And I am related to her in such a way that it will be right for her to remember what I have thought and done, to feel remorse for what I have done wrong, and pride in what I have done right. And the only relation that supports anticipation and memory in this way, is simply *identity*. For it is never correct to anticipate, as happening to oneself, what will happen to someone else, is it? Or to remember, as one's own thoughts and deeds, what someone else did? So don't give me merger with being, or some such nonsense. Give me identity, or let's talk about baseball or fishing—but I'm sorry to get so emotional. I react strongly when words which mean one thing are used for another—when one talks about survival, but does not mean to say that the same person will continue to exist. It's such a sham!

MILLER: I'm sorry. I was just trying to stay in touch with the times, if you want to know the truth, for when I read modern theology or talk to my students who have studied Eastern religions, the notion of survival simply as continued existence of the same person seems out of date. Merger with Being! Merger with Being! That's all I hear. My own beliefs are quite simple, if somewhat vague. I think you will live again—with or without a body, I don't know—I draw comfort from my belief that you and I will be together again, after I also die. We will communicate, somehow. We will continue to grow spiritually. That's what I believe, as surely as I believe that I am sitting here. For I don't know how God could be excused, if this small sample of life is all that we are allotted; I don't know why He should have created us, if these few years of toil and torment are the end of it—

WEIROB: Remember our deal, Sam. You don't have to convince me that survival is probable, for we both agree you would not get to first base. You have only to convince me that it is possible. The only condition is that it be real survival we are talking about, not some up-to-date ersatz survival, which simply amounts to what any ordinary person would call totally ceasing to exist.

MILLER: I guess I just miss the problem, then. Of course, it's possible. You just continue to exist, after your body dies. What's to be defended or explained? You want details? Okay. Two people meet a thousand years from now, in a place that may or may not be part of this physical universe. I am one and you are the other. So you must have survived. Surely you can imagine that. What else is there to say?

WEIROB: But in a few days *I* will quit breathing, *I* will be put into a coffin, *I* will be buried. And in a few months or a few years *I* will be reduced to so much humus. That, I take it, is obvious, is given. How then can you say that I am one of these persons a thousand years from now?

Suppose I took this box of Kleenex and lit fire to it. It is reduced to ashes and I smash the ashes and flush them down the john. Then I say to you, go home and on the shelf will be *that very box of Kleenex*. It has survived! Wouldn't that be absurd? What sense could you make of it? And yet that is just what you say to me. I will rot away. And then, a thousand years later, there I will be. What sense does that make?

MILLER: There could be an *identical* box of Kleenex at your home, one just like it in every respect. And, in this sense, there is no difficulty in there being someone identical to you in the Hereafter, though your body has rotted away.

WEIROB: You are playing with words again. There could be an *exactly similar* box of Kleenex on my shelf. We sometimes use "identical" to mean "exactly similar," as when we speak of "identical twins." But I am using "identical" in a way in which *identity* is the condition of memory and correct anticipation. If I am told that tomorrow, though I will be dead, someone else that looks and sounds and thinks just like me will be alive—would that be comforting? Could I correctly *anticipate* having her experiences? Would it make sense for me to fear her pains and look forward to her pleasures? Would it be right for her to feel remorse at the harsh way I am treating you? Of course not. Similarity, however exact, is not identity. I use identity to mean there is but one thing. If I am to survive, there must be one person who lies in this bed now, and who talks to someone in your Hereafter ten or a thousand years from now. After all, what comfort could there be in the notion of a heavenly imposter, walking around getting credit for the few good things I have done?

MILLER: I'm sorry. I see that I was simply confused. Here is what I should have said. If you were merely a live human body—as the Kleenex body is merely cardboard and glue in a certain arrangement—then the death of your body would be the end of you. But surely you are more than that, fundamentally more than that. What is fundamentally you is not your body, but your soul or self or mind.

WEIROB: Do you mean these words, "soul," "self," or "mind" to come to the same thing?

MILLER: Perhaps distinctions could be made, but I shall not pursue them now. I mean the nonphysical and nonmaterial aspects of you, your consciousness. It is this that I get at with these words, and I don't think any further distinction is relevant.

WEIROB: Consciousness? I am conscious, for a while yet. I see, I hear, I think, I remember. But "to be conscious"—that is a verb. What is the subject of the verb, the thing which is conscious? Isn't it just this body, the same object that is overweight, injured, and lying in bed?—and which will be buried and not be conscious in a day or a week at the most?

MILLER: As you are a philosopher, I would expect you to be less muddled about these issues. Did Descartes not draw a clear distinction between the body and the mind, between that which is overweight, and that which is conscious? Your mind or soul is immaterial, lodged in your body while you are on earth. The two are intimately related but not identical. Now clearly, what concerns us in survival is your mind or soul. It is this which must be identical to the person before me now, and to the one I expect to see in a thousand years in heaven.

WEIROB: So I am not really this body, but a soul or mind or spirit? And this soul cannot be seen or felt or touched or smelt? That is implied, I take it, by the fact that it is immaterial?

MILLER: That's right. Your soul sees and smells, but cannot be seen or smelt.

WEIROB: Let me see if I understand you. You would admit that I am the very same person with whom you had lunch last week at Dorsey's?

MILLER: Of course you are.

WEIROB: Now when you say I am the same person, if I understand you, that is not a remark about this body you see and could touch and I fear can smell. Rather it is a remark about a soul, which you cannot see or touch or smell. The fact that the same body that now lies in front of you on the bed was across the table from you at Dorsey's— that would not mean that the same *person* was present on both occasions, if the same soul were not. And if, through some strange turn of events, the same soul were present on both occasions, but lodged in different bodies, then it *would* be the same person. Is that right?

MILLER: You have understood me perfectly. But surely, you understood all of this before!

WEIROB: But wait. I can repeat it, but I'm not sure I understand it. If you cannot see or touch or in any way perceive my soul, what makes you think the one you are confronted with now *is* the very same soul you were confronted with at Dorsey's?

MILLER: But I just explained. To say it is the same soul and to say it is the same person, are the same. And, of course, you are the same person you were before. Who else would you be if not yourself? You *were* Gretchen Weirob, and you *are* Gretchen Weirob.

WEIROB: But how do you know you are talking to Gretchen Weirob at all, and not someone else, say Barbara Walters or even Mark Spitz!

MILLER: Well, it's just obvious. I can see who I am talking to.

WEIROB: But all you can see is my body. You can see, perhaps, that the same body is before you now that was before you last week at Dorsey's. But you have just said that Gretchen Weirob is not a body but a soul. In judging that the same person is before you now as was before you then, you must be making a judgment about souls—which, you said, cannot be seen or touched or smelt or tasted. And so, I repeat, how do you know?

MILLER: Well, I *can* see that it is the same body before me now that was across the table at Dorsey's. And I know that the same soul is connected with the body now that was connected with it before. That's how I know it's you. I see no difficulty in the matter.

WEIROB: You reason on the principle, "Same body, same self."

MILLER: Yes.

WEIROB: And would you reason conversely also? If there were in this bed Barbara Walters' body—that is, the body you see every night on the news—would you infer that it was not me, Gretchen Weirob, in the bed?

MILLER: Of course I would. How would you have come by Barbara Walters' body?

WEIROB: But then merely extend this principle to Heaven, and you will see that your conception of survival is without sense. Surely this very body, which will be buried and as I must so often repeat, *rot away,* will not be in your Hereafter. Different body, different person. Or do you claim that a body can rot away on earth, and then still wind up somewhere else? Must I bring up the Kleenex box again?

MILLER: No, I do not claim that. But I also do not extend a principle, found reliable on earth, to such a different situation as is represented by the Hereafter. That a correlation between bodies and souls has been found on earth does not make it inconceivable or impossible that they should separate. Principles found to work in one circumstance may not be assumed to work in vastly altered circumstances. January and snow go together here, and one would be a fool to expect otherwise. But the principle does not apply in southern California.

WEIROB: So the principle, "same body, same soul," is a well-confirmed regularity, not something you know "*a priori.*"

MILLER: By "*a priori*" you philosophers mean something which can be known without observing what actually goes on in the world—as I can know that two plus two equals four just by thinking about numbers, and that no bachelors are married, just by thinking about the meaning of "bachelor"?

WEIROB: Yes.

MILLER: Then you are right. If it was part of the meaning of "same body" that wherever we have the same body we have the same soul, it would have to obtain universally, in Heaven as well as on earth. But I just claim it is a generalization we know by observation on earth, and it need not automatically extend to Heaven.

WEIROB: But where do you get this principle? It simply amounts to a correlation between being confronted with the same body and being confronted with the same soul. To establish such a correlation in the first place, surely one must have some *other* means of judging sameness of soul. You do not have such a means; your principle is without foundation; either you really do not know the person before you now is Gretchen Weirob, the very same person you lunched with at Dorsey's, or what you do know has nothing to do with sameness of some immaterial soul.

MILLER: Hold on, hold on. You know I can't follow you when you start spitting out arguments like that. Now what is this terrible fallacy I'm supposed to have committed?

WEIROB: I'm sorry. I get carried away. Here—by way of a peace offering—have one of the chocolates Dave brought.

MILLER: Very tasty. Thank you.

WEIROB: Now why did you choose that one?

MILLER: Because it had a certain swirl on the top which shows that it is a caramel.

WEIROB: That is, a certain sort of swirl is correlated with a certain type of filling—the swirls with caramel, the rosettes with orange, and so forth.

MILLER: Yes. When you put it that way, I see an analogy. Just as I judged that the filling would be the same in this piece as in the last piece that I ate with such a swirl, so I judge that the soul with which I am conversing is the same as the last soul with which I conversed when sitting across from that body. We *see* the outer wrapping and infer what is inside.

WEIROB: But how did you come to realize that swirls of that sort and caramel insides were so associated?

MILLER: Why, from eating a great many of them over the years. Whenever I bit into a candy with that sort of swirl, it was filled with caramel.

WEIROB: Could you have established the correlation had you never been allowed to bite into a candy and never seen what happened when someone else bit into one? You could have formed the hypothesis, "same swirl, same filling." But could you have ever established it?

MILLER: It seems not.

WEIROB: So your inference, in a particular case, to the identity of filling from the identity of swirl would be groundless?

MILLER: Yes, it would. I think I see what is coming.

WEIROB: I'm sure you do. Since you can never, so to speak, bite into my soul, can never see or touch it, you have no way of testing your hypothesis that sameness of body means sameness of self.

MILLER: I daresay you are right. But now I'm a bit lost. What is supposed to follow from all of this?

WEIROB: If, as you claim, identity of persons consisted in identity of immaterial unobservable souls, then judgments of personal identity of the sort we make every day whenever we greet a friend or avoid a pest are really judgments about such souls.

MILLER: Right.

WEIROB: But if such judgments were really about souls, they would all be groundless and without foundation. For we have no direct method of observing sameness of soul, and so—and this is the point made by the candy example—we can have no indirect method either.

MILLER: That seems fair.

WEIROB: But our judgments about persons are not all simply groundless and silly, so we must not be judging of immaterial souls after all.

MILLER: Your reasoning has some force. But I suspect the problem lies in my defense of my position, and not the position itself. Look here—there *is* a way to test the hypothesis of a correlation after all. When I entered the room, I expected you to react just as you did—argumentatively and skeptically. Had the person with this body reacted completely differently perhaps I would have been forced to conclude it was not you. For example, had she complained about not being able to appear on the six o'clock news, and missing Harry Reasoner, and so forth, I might eventually have been persuaded it *was* Barbara Walters and not you. Similarity of psychological characteristics—a person's attitudes, beliefs, memories, prejudices, and the like—is observable. These are correlated with identity of body on the one side, and of course with sameness of soul on the other. So the correlation between body and soul can be established after all by this intermediate link.

WEIROB: And how do you know that?

MILLER: Know what?

WEIROB: That where we have sameness of psychological characteristics, we have sameness of soul.

MILLER: Well, now you are really being just silly. The soul or mind is just that which is responsible for one's character, memory, belief. These are aspects of the mind, just as one's height, weight, and appearance are aspects of the body.

WEIROB: Let me grant for the sake of argument that belief, character, memory, and so forth are states of mind. That is, I suppose, I grant that what one thinks and feels is due to the states one's mind is in at that time. And I shall even grant that a mind is an immaterial thing— though I harbor the gravest doubts that this is so. I do not see how it follows that similarity of such traits requires, or is evidence to the slightest degree, for identity of the mind or soul.

Let me explain my point with an analogy. If we were to walk out of this room, down past the mill and out towards Wilbur, what would we see?

MILLER: We would come to the Blue River, among other things.

WEIROB: And how would you recognize the Blue River? I mean, of course if you left from here, you would scarcely expect to hit the Platte or Niobrara. But suppose you were actually lost, and came across the Blue River in your wandering, just at that point where an old dam partly blocks the flow. Couldn't you recognize it?

MILLER: Yes, I'm sure as soon as I saw that part of the river I would again know where I was.

WEIROB: And how would you recognize it?

MILLER: Well, the turgid brownness of the water, the sluggish flow, the filth washed up on the banks, and such.

WEIROB: In a word, the states of the water which makes up the river at the time you see it.

MILLER: Right.

WEIROB: If you saw the blue clean water, with bass jumping, you would know it wasn't the Blue River.

MILLER: Of course.

WEIROB: So you expect, each time you see the Blue, to see the water, which makes it up, in similar states—not always exactly the same, for sometimes it's a little dirtier, but by and large similar.

MILLER: Yes, but what do you intend to make of this?

WEIROB: Each time you see the Blue, it consists of *different* water. The water that was in it a month ago may be in Tuttle Creek Reservoir or in the Mississippi or in the Gulf of Mexico by now. So the *similarity* of states of water, by which you judge the sameness of river, does not require *identity* of the water which is in those states at these various times.

MILLER: And?

WEIROB: And so just because you judge as to personal identity by reference to similarity of states of mind, it does not follow that the mind, or soul, is the same in each case. My point is this. For all you know, the immaterial soul which you think is lodged in my body might change from day to day, from hour to hour, from minute to minute, replaced each time by another soul psychologically similar. You cannot see it or touch it, so how would you know?

MILLER: Are you saying I don't really know who you are?

WEIROB: Not at all. *You* are the one who says personal identity consists in sameness of this immaterial, unobservable, invisible, untouchable soul. I merely point out that *if* it did consist in that, you *would* have no idea who I am. Sameness of body would not necessarily mean sameness of person. Sameness of psychological characteristics would not necessarily mean sameness of person. I am saying that if you do know who I am then you are wrong that personal identity consists in sameness of immaterial soul.

MILLER: I see. But wait. I believe my problem is that I simply forgot a main tenet of my theory. The correlation can be established in my own case. I know that *my* soul and my body are intimately and consistently found together. From this one case I can generalize, at least as concerns life in this world, that sameness of body is a reliable sign of sameness of soul. This leaves me free to regard it as intelligible, in the case of death, that the link between the particular soul and the particular body it has been joined with is broken.

WEIROB: This would be quite an extrapolation, wouldn't it, from one case directly observed, to a couple of billion in which only the body is observed? For I take it that we are in the habit of assuming, for every person now on earth, as well as those who have already come and gone, that the principle "one body, one soul" is in effect.

MILLER: This does not seem an insurmountable obstacle. Since there is nothing special about my case, I assume the arrangement I find in it applies universally until given some reason to believe otherwise. And I never have been.

WEIROB: Let's let that pass. I have another problem that is more serious. How is it that you know in your own case that there is a single soul which has been so consistently connected with your body?

MILLER: Now you really cannot be serious, Gretchen. How can I doubt that I am the same person I was? Is there anything more clear and distinct, less susceptible to doubt? How do you expect me to prove anything to you, when you are capable of denying my own continued existence from second to second? Without knowledge of our own identity, everything we think and do would be senseless. How could I think if I did not suppose that the person who begins my thought is the one who completes it? When I act, do I not assume that the person who forms the intention is the very one who performs the action?

WEIROB: But I grant you that a single *person* has been associated with your body since you were born. The question is whether one immaterial soul has been so associated—or more precisely, whether you are in a position to know it. You believe that a judgment that one and the same person has had your body all these many years is a judgment that one and the same immaterial soul has been lodged in it. I say that such judgments concerning the soul are totally mysterious, and that if our knowledge of sameness of persons consisted in knowledge of sameness of immaterial soul, it too would be totally mysterious. To point out, as you do, that it is not mysterious, but perhaps the most secure knowledge we have, the foundation of all reason and action, is simply to make the point that it cannot consist of knowledge of identity of an immaterial soul.

MILLER: You have simply asserted, and not established, that my judgment that a single soul has been lodged in my body these many years is mysterious.

WEIROB: Well, consider these possibilities. One is that a single soul, one and the same, has been with this body I call mine since it was born. The other is that one soul was associated with it until five years ago and then another, psychologically similar, inheriting all the old memories and beliefs, took over. A third hypothesis is that every five years a new soul takes over. A fourth is that every five minutes a new soul takes over. The most radical is that there is a constant flow of souls through this body, each psychologically similar to the preceding, as there is a constant flow of water molecules down the Blue. What evidence do I have that the first hypothesis, the "single soul hypothesis" is true, and not one of the others? Because I am the same person I was five minutes or five years ago? But the issue in question is simply whether from sameness of person, which isn't in doubt, we can infer sameness of soul. Sameness of body? But how do I establish a stable relationship between soul and body? Sameness of thoughts and sensations? But they are in constant flux. By the nature of the case, if the soul cannot be observed, it cannot be observed to be the same. Indeed, no sense has ever been assigned to the phrase "same soul." Nor could any sense be attached to it! One would have to say what a single soul looked like or felt like, how an encounter with a single soul at different times differed from encounters with different souls. But this can hardly be done, since a soul according to your conception doesn't look or feel like *anything* at all. And so of course "souls" can afford no principle of identity. And so they cannot be used to bridge the gulf between my existence now and my existence in the hereafter.

MILLER: Do you doubt the existence of your own soul?

WEIROB: I haven't based my argument on there being no immaterial souls of the sort you describe, but merely on their total irrelevance to questions of personal identity, and so to questions of personal survival. I do indeed harbor grave doubts whether there are any immaterial souls of the sort to which you appeal. Can we have a notion of a soul unless we have a notion of the *same* soul? But I hope you do not think that means I doubt my own existence. I think I lie here, overweight and conscious. I think you can see me, not just some outer wrapping, for I think I am just a live human body. But that is not the basis of my argument. I give you these souls. I merely observe that they can by their nature provide no principle of personal identity.

MILLER: I admit I have no answer.

I'm afraid I do not comfort you, though I have perhaps provided you with some entertainment. Emerson said that a little philosophy turns one away from religion, but that deeper understanding brings one back. I know no one who has thought so long and hard about philosophy as you have. Will it never lead you back to a religious frame of mind?

WEIROB: My former husband used to say that a little philosophy turns one away from religion, and more philosophy makes one a pain in the neck. Perhaps he was closer to the truth than Emerson.

MILLER: Perhaps he was. But perhaps by tomorrow night I will have come up with a better argument.

WEIROB: I hope I live to hear it.

Note

1. THE FIRST NIGHT: The arguments against the position that personal identity consists in identity of an immaterial soul are similar to those found in John Locke. "Of Identity and Diversity," chapter 27 of Book II of the *Essay Concerning Human Understanding*. This chapter first appeared in the second edition of 1694.

The Buddhist Theory of 'No-Self'

Serge-Christophe Kolm   (*Translated by Martin Thom*)

. . . For Buddhism it is clear, therefore, that *badness is unhappiness*. The true unhappiness, however, is not poverty but attachment, which is virtually its opposite, and the bad that there is in attaching oneself consists not in the attachment but in the self that is attached. Fortunately, however, this 'self' does not really exist, it is merely an illusion. One simply has to become aware of this for one's attachments, and therefore one's miseries, to cease.

In order to prove that the 'self' does not exist, Buddhism employs a fairly impressive argument. It consists in considering the person as a set of simple elements which has no reality in itself but only in the mind of the observer. And one is advised to apply this perspective to oneself, whilst taking great care to ensure that the corresponding knowledge is itself a set of elements belonging to those that it uncovers. If one genuinely succeeds in bringing off this ploy, all discomfort would seem to disappear. One would also seem to require more than one life to understand it, and several to apply it, declares the *tathagata* Guatama (the Tibetan Milarepa, a long time after him, is the only one to have effected this in a single life). All the more reason, then, to start straightaway.

One begins by acknowledging that a person is composed of several elements. The profane person would see this as a 'decomposition' of the still perceptible person into several elements. One would then make him see that what he believed to be a person *is only* this set of elements that he stubbornly persisted in regarding as a whole: there is nothing else, the world is empty of 'self'.

The West has long been habituated to such analytic dismantling of being. From Plato, through Descartes to Freud, we find a division between appetite, reason and mind, or we hear of the ghost in the machine, or of id, ego and superego, or of conscious and subconscious, or of conscious, unconscious and preconscious, or of the cognitive, the conative and the affective, etc. But the dismantling that the Buddha (a century before Plato) proposes is infinitely more refined than the crude divisions into two or three elements imagined by Westerners. Even when Hume says, much as a Buddhist would, that 'the mind is only a bundle or collection of different perceptions linked by causalities, he only grasps one out of the six *skandhas* (it may be that he employs the word 'perception' in a slightly wider sense, but he is hardly explicit about this).

Buddhism is concerned with elementary or simple, indecomposable elements, ontological 'atoms', as it were, which are said by it to be the only things enjoying any reality, and which are called *dharmas* in Sanskrit (*dhammas* in Pali). This word also refers to the Buddha's doctrine, a double reference which is frequent in Buddhist language (*dharma* has many other meanings also, and although most Buddhist terms have several meanings it is probably the richest of them all). As a consequence, the first two words of the Buddhist *credo, ye dhamma,* mean both 'I follow the doctrine' and 'I am only [composed of] simple elements.' If these two apparently very different meanings coexist, it is because the deepest meaning of *dharma* is 'ultimate reality' (or 'ultimate truth'). These *dharma* elements occur in many different forms. The elementary manuals in the monasteries describe several dozen of them, but several hundred are said to exist. These types of *dharma* are classed in different ways, according to different criteria. Before being ordained as *bhikkhus,* the novices must learn three of these classifications: in terms of *skandhas,* in terms of *ayatanas,* and in terms of *dhatus.* The most famous is the classification in terms of *skandhas* or 'aggregates' (of *dharmas*), which are five in number. To begin with, there are the ten properties of matter, of material things which, where a person is concerned, means his body and the things which he owns, with the body referring also to his ideas, thoughts and mental images. Then there are the sensations of the six senses (the sixth sense involves perception and sensation of ideas, thoughts and mental images by the mental and cerebral organ—an expression that John Locke was later to reinvent). Then there are the fifty-eight volitions, impulses or 'mental formations'. Finally, the consciousnesses of all the above crown the whole series. The classification into *ayatanas* obeys a cognitive criterion; its twelve categories are the six senses and the things that they know, the latter being the sixty-four types of mental *dharma*. The division into *dhatus* serves to describe the 'current' (*santana*) of causal relations between *dharmas* which seem to constitute an 'individual' (*pudgala*). It consists of eighteen classes, adding the consciousnesses of the corresponding properties–perceptions–sensations to the twelve of the preceding classification. But Buddhism sometimes puts itself at the level of modern scholarship by distinguishing three categories, matter, spirit and forces, a classification which it teaches to small children and to them only. The dual division between spirit and matter is also present.

The important point to note is that, once the person is dissolved in this way, Buddhism sees no reason to reassemble these elements into so-called individuals. It dismantles the human machine conceptually, and with great finesse, but then it disdains to put it together again. Man remains in detached and scattered pieces. A Buddhist observing you will see a pile of elements, a bag containing several hundred types of things, an aggregate of aggregates, a flux of events, a current of causal relations, but not *you*. The Buddhist gaze is a ray which disintegrates being. It is fortunate, then, that it is himself that a Buddhist will spend his time thus scrutinizing.

What thus is this thing which so interests people, which activates their passions, which they care for so intensely, about which they talk so much, their 'self'? It is a concept, a construction of the reason and of the imagination, a way of seeing and of composing the world, but not an entity which really exists. In other words, it is an *illusion*. But does not man excel most at transforming his ideas into suffering? The idea of the 'self', Buddhism says, is the heart of all pain. The worst possible thing to do would therefore be to reassemble the robot, and to believe that this montage on the part of the mind has a real existence.

The idea of the 'self' is not the only thing, Buddhism generously adds, to which this argument applies. The same is true of every mental construction. For instance, a cart consists of wheels, shafts, frame, etc. It *is* these elements; the entity 'cart' is a creature of the mind, an illusion. Or, to put it another way, one must not say that this fruit *has* this form, this colour, this smell, but rather that this fruit *is* this form and this colour and this smell and so on. Likewise, the mind doesn't *have* sensations, sentiments, ideas, volitions, etc., but what one calls 'mind' is these things. And the 'self' is that plus material elements. But to believe in a cart or in a pear does not have the same consequences as believing in oneself.

The main conclusion we can draw from this is that the 'self' is a mental construction, and by realizing this one may suppress pain.

Precise analysis of the causes of suffering, of the perceptions which bring it, of its sensation of the consciousness of these facts, enables one either to remove this conscious sensation or to take a detached and objective view of it, and thereby to remove the pain. It is worth noting that Buddhism claims that this latter method is its own peculiar achievement, arrived at thanks to the no-self (the cutting off of sensation, reputed to have been the means employed by the Buddha's last *guru,* did not satisfy the Buddha, inducing him to search for his own answer by embarking upon a long meditation, from which he was to emerge 'awakened' to the solution.) At any rate, more or less training is required to produce these results. This is particularly the case with physical sufferings, where one has to overcome the danger and the fear that its absence would deprive us of the warning that the body is incurring some serious destruction. And things are much easier in the case of self-love, jealousy, hatred, pride, and of shame, honour or love! When one understands the causes and mechanisms of suffering, when one becomes aware of their basic sequences, suffering ceases. In the West, Spinoza (in his *Ethics,* in particular) had certain intuitions about this phenomenon, but he provided no account of the precise mode of functioning, or even of the structure of the psyche such as would enable one to understand it, and such as Buddhism provides. One is tempted, however, to improve the latter doctrine by saying: only strive to dismantle mentally those things which do you harm; attach yourself when it is possible and painless or agreeable, disengage yourself when it ceases to be so; opt for the agreeable side of things, and only analyse the rest in a Buddhist manner! This should be all the more possible that Buddhist psychology provides all the warning and knowledge which are required in order to prevent that a voluntary attachment turns into a sadistic master.

In this diagnosis of the cause of human unhappiness, and therefore in the therapeutic practice which derives from it, Buddhism proves to be the exact opposite of the Western tradition (which includes both Marx and Freud). The latter sees unhappiness, despair, neurosis, alienation, etc. in human beings who are divided, in fragments and internally dismembered, and equilibrium, the necessary condition for happiness (and a concept reminiscent of that of *nirvana*), in the integrated personality. Buddhism, by contrast, regards the latter as the cause of all ills. In order to remedy it, it shatters man (the illusion of man in man's eyes) and is only too glad to leave him in pieces. Is there then a fundamental contradiction between these two theories, each of which is firmly anchored in a tradition? The important thing to note is that the divisions of the personality identified by these two traditions are by no means the same. In Buddhism, the elements are psychological categories which, although connected, belong to different planes, whilst for Freud, for example, the superego and id may collide head-on over particular choices.

To be more precise, however large the number of 'things' (or, more exactly, of 'facts') Buddhism sees in an 'individual', there is one which he will not find there, namely, the 'I', the heart of being, which would be at once the subject of volitions and the object of suffering, and therefore a link between desire and *dukkha*. Chapter 19 in Kolm (1982)[1] analyses precisely and in detail this question of the 'I', and it explains that Buddhist advanced philosophy considers in fact many kinds of 'I', some of which are real by definition or by nature and some of which are illusory. It is the illusion of the 'I in itself', both based upon and providing the basis for desires and attachments, which Buddhists hold to be the specific cause common to all sufferings. Critical examination of the 'self' enables one to show that an individual contains no entity of this sort. When, therefore, one has succeeded in realizing this and in convincing oneself of it, both desires and pains fade away.

Having thus presented a more detailed account of the Buddhist conception of the self, we are now in a better position to gauge whether it can be reconciled with the theory of choices. If the 'self' is simply an illusion, what reality can the 'order of preferences' have? If it is composed of various 'aggregates' and specified elements, can the whole of behaviour be explained in terms of this ultra-simple entity? If everything is provisional, 'impermanent' and in a perpetual flux of change, as Buddhism declares it to be, what can the stability of these preferences be worth? If 'everything has a cause' and 'everything is determined', which is another base of this philosophy, it applies to individual's actions, and can one then speak of a person's free choice, or even of choice at all? And if 'I' does not exist, who is it that does the choosing?

An illusion is something quite real for the person observing someone who is in a state of illusion (his theoretician, as it were), and if this illusion guides or influences its victim's acts, one can perhaps describe this effect in terms of the theory of choices. But, for a Buddhist, the illusion of the *self* has a crucial effect on the decisions of a non-Buddhist or, more exactly, on non-Buddhist decisions. Only an *arahant*, because he has understood, is an exception to this, but he is a rare phenomenon and undoubtedly acts very little. On the other

[1]S. C. Kolm (1982). *Le Bonheur-liberté*.

hand, the action entailed by the theory of choices is indeed caused by constraints and preferences, which are themselves caused by something else. The instability of preferences, for its part, does not obstruct the pure theory of choices which dates them; it may, however, hinder certain of its practical applications. Buddhism states that everything changes, everything disappears, without specifying the speed of this process or the delays that occur. It may take a lifetime, or an aeon. Finally, the fact that out of five 'aggregates' one may only derive one 'self' does not necessarily imply that one cannot derive an order of preferences from them. For the *perceptions* of the available alternatives produce more or less agreeable sensations, and this gives rise to an order which is a *mental and volitional formation,* all of this being liable to be more or less *conscious* (with certainly a higher degree of rationality in the sense of transitivity the more conscious it is). . . .

Personal Identity: The Dualist Theory
Richard Swinburne

1 Empiricist Theories

There are two philosophical questions about personal identity. The first is: what are the logically necessary and sufficient conditions for a person P_2 at a time t_2 being the same person as a person P_1 at an earlier time t_1,[1] or, loosely, what does it mean to say that P_2 is the same person as P_1? The second is: what evidence of observation and experience can we have that a person P_2 at t_2 is the same person as a person P_1 at t_1 (and how are different pieces of evidence to be weighed against each other)? Many writers about personal identity have, however, needed to give only one account of personal identity, because their account of the logically necessary and sufficient conditions of personal identity was in terms of

---

[1]The logically necessary and sufficient conditions for something being so are those conditions such that if they are present, that thing must be so; and if they are absent, that thing cannot be so—all this because of considerations of logic.

the evidence of observation and experience which would establish or oppose claims of personal identity. They have made no sharp distinction between the meaning of such claims and the evidence which supported them. Theories of this kind we may call empiricist theories.

In this section I shall briefly survey the empiricist theories which have been offered and argue that they are ultimately unsatisfactory, and so go on to argue that my two questions have very different answers. What we mean when we say that two persons are the same is one thing; the evidence which we may have to support our claim is something very different.

The most natural theory of personal identity which readily occurs to people, is that personal identity is constituted by bodily identity. P_2 is the same person as P_1 if P_2's body is the same body as P_1's body. The person to whom you are talking now and call 'John' is the same person as the person to whom you were talking last week and then called 'John' if and only if he has the same body. To say that the two bodies—call them B_1 and B_2—are the same is not to say that they contain exactly the same bits of matter. Bodies are continually taking in new matter (by people eating and drinking and breathing in) and getting rid of matter. But what makes the bodies the same is that the replacement of matter is only gradual. The matter which forms my body is organized in a certain way, into parts—legs, arms, heart, liver, etc., which are interconnected and exchange matter and energy in regular ways. What makes my body today the same body as my body yesterday is that most of the matter is the same (although I may have lost some and gained some) and its organization has remained roughly the same.[2]

---

[2]Some writers have attempted to analyse the notion of 'most of the matter' of yesterday's body being the same as 'most of the matter' of today's body in terms of today's body being composed largely of chunks of matter which are 'spatiotemporally continuous' with chunks of matter of yesterday's body, i.e., as linked to such chunks by a spatiotemporal chain. Two chunks of matter M_1 at time t_1 and M_2 at time t_2 are spatiotemporally continuous if and only if there is a material object M' identical in quantity and intrinsic properties to both M_1 and M_2 at every temporal instant t' between t_1 and t_2, such that each M' at each t' occupies a place contiguous with the place occupied by the M' at prior and succeeding instants of time if you take instants close enough in time to t'. (More precisely 'such that the place occupied by each M' at each t' is contiguous to places occupied by an M' at some instant t'' later than t' and all instants between t'' and t' and to places occupied by an M' at some instant t''' earlier than t' and all instants between t''' and t'.) It is very plausible to suppose that spatiotemporal continuity is a necessary condition for the identity of chunks of matter—chunks of matter cannot go from one place to another without moving along a path joining the places. But it is not so plausible to suppose that spatiotemporal continuity is a sufficient condition of the identity of chunks of matter, i.e., is enough to ensure that two chunks of matter are the same. It does not seem logically impossible that two qualitatively identical chunks should emerge from a given chunk. Something else than spatiotemporal continuity is needed to ensure that two chunks of matter are the same. On this, see Hirsch 1982, especially ch. 4.

This bodily theory of personal identity gives a somewhat similar account of personal identity to the account which it is natural to give of the identity of any material object or plant, and which is due ultimately to Aristotle (*Metaphysics*, Bk 7). Aristotle distinguished between substances and properties. Substances are the individual things, like tables and chairs, cars and plants, which have properties (such as being square or round or red). Properties are 'universals', that is they can be possessed by many different substances; many different substances can be square or red. Substances are the individual substances which they are because of the matter out of which they are made and the form which is given to that matter. By 'the form' is meant those properties (normally of shape and organization), the possession of which is essential if a substance is to be the substance in question, the properties which it cannot lose without ceasing to exist. We thus distinguish between the essential properties of a substance—those which constitute its form—and the accidental properties of a substance. It is among the essential properties of a certain oak tree that it has under normal conditions, a certain general shape and appearance, a certain life cycle (of producing leaves in spring and acorns in autumn); but its exact height, its position, and the distribution of leaves on its tallest branch are accidental properties. If the matter of the oak tree is reduced to a heap of planks, the oak tree, lacking its essential properties, has ceased to exist. We think of substances as belonging to different kinds, natural—e.g., oak trees or ferns; or artificial—e.g., cars or desks; and the defining properties of a kind constitute the form of a substance which belongs to it. Normally there is one and only one obvious kind to which we ascribe some given chunk of matter—a particular chunk of matter which we classify as an oak tree we would find it very unnatural to classify as belonging to any other kind . . .

What makes a substance the same substance as an earlier substance is that its matter is the same, or obtained from the matter of the former substance by gradual replacement, while continuing to possess the essential properties which constitute its form. The table at which I am writing today is the same table at which I was writing yesterday because it consists of the same matter (or at any rate, most of the same matter), organized in the same way—into the form of a table. For inanimate things, however, too much replacement of matter, however gradual, will destroy identity. If I replace the drawer of my desk by another drawer, the desk remains the same desk. But if, albeit gradually, I replace first the drawers and then the sides and then the top, so that there is none of the original matter left, we would say that the resulting desk was no longer the same desk as the original desk. For living things, such as plants, total replacement of matter—so long as it is gradual, and so long as physiology and anatomy also change only gradually if at all—will not destroy identity. The oak tree is the same as the sapling out of which it has grown, because replacement of matter has been gradual, and form (i.e., shape, physiology, and behavior) has been largely preserved while any changes in it have been gradual.[3] [. . .]

Persons too are substances. (Men, or human beings, are persons of a certain kind—viz., those with similar anatomy, physiology, and evolutionary origin to ourselves. There may be persons, e.g., on another planet, who are not human beings.) If we apply Aristotle's general account of the identity of substances to persons, it follows that for a person to be the same person as an earlier person, he has to have the same matter (or matter obtained from that earlier person by gradual replacement) organized into the form of person. The essential properties which make the form of a person would include, for Aristotle, not merely shape and physiological properties, but a kind of way of behaving and a capacity for a mental life of thought and feeling. For P_2 at t_2 to be the same person as P_1 at t_1, both have to be persons (to have a certain kind of body and mental life) and to be made of the same matter (i.e., to be such that P_2's body is obtained from P_1's by gradual replacement of parts). Such is the bodily theory of personal identity. It does not deny that persons have a mental life, but insists that what makes a person the same person as an earlier person is sameness of body.[4]

The difficulty which has been felt by those modern philosophers basically sympathetic to a bodily theory of personal identity is this. One part of the body—viz., the brain—seems to be of crucial importance for determining the characteristic behaviour of the rest. The brain controls not merely the physiology of the body but the way people behave and

---

[3]Aristotle did not himself go into the problem of how much matter has to continue the same if the substance is to be the same.

[4]Aristotle himself seemed to have some hesitation about the applicability of his theory of the identity of substances to the identity of persons. See, *De Anima* at 413a. He writes, first, 'that, therefore, the soul or certain parts of it, if it is divisible, cannot be separated from the body is quite clear'. But then he qualifies this by writing 'Not that anything prevents at any rate some parts from being separable'. He seems to be supposing that there are some capacities, e.g., for thought, which need no bodily material for their exercise. (For similar remarks see his 403a, 408b, 413b.) Aquinas develops these points into his doctrine that the Aristotle-type soul (the form of the body) is separable from the body. See below, pp. 31f for this doctrine and criticism of it.

talk and think. If a man loses an arm or a leg, we do not think that the subsequent person is in any way different from the original person. If a man has a heart transplant or a liver transplant, again we do not think that the replacement makes a different person. On the other hand, if the brain of a person P_1 were removed from his body B_1 and transplanted into the skull of a body B_2 of a person P_2, from which the brain was removed and then transplanted into the empty skull of B_1 (i.e., if brains were interchanged), we would have serious doubt whether P_1 had any more the same body. We would be inclined to say that the person went where his brain went—viz., that P_1 at first had body B_1, and then, after the transplant, body B_2. The reason why we would say this is that (we have very good scientific reason to believe), the person with B_2's body would claim to be P_1, to have done and experienced the things which we know P_1 to have done, and would have the character, beliefs, and attitudes of P_1. What determines my attitude towards a person is not so much the matter out of which his body is made, but who he claims to be, whether he has knowledge of my past life purportedly on the basis of previous acquaintance with me, and more generally what his beliefs about the world are and what are his attitudes towards it. Hence a philosopher seeking a materialist criterion of personal identity, will come to regard the brain, the core of the body, rather than the rest of the body as what matters for personal identity. So this modified bodily theory states: that P_2 is the same person as P_1 if and only if P_2 has the same central organ controlling memory and character, viz., same brain, as P_1. Let us call it the brain theory of personal identity. A theory along these lines (with a crucial qualification, to be discussed shortly) was tentatively suggested by David Wiggins in *Identity and Spatiotemporal Continuity.*[5]

The traditional alternative to a bodily theory of personal identity is the memory-and-character theory. This claims that, given the importance for our attitude towards persons of their memory claims and character, continuity in respect of these would constitute personal identity—whether or not this continuity is caused by continuity of some bodily organ, such as the brain; and the absence of continuity of memory and character in some particular case involves the absence of personal identity, even if there is continuity in respect of that bodily organ which produces such continuity between other persons on other occasions.

The simplest version of this theory was that given by John Locke. According to Locke, memory alone, (or 'consciousness', as he often

---

[5]Wiggins is even more tentative in the amended version of the book, *Sameness and Substance.*

calls it) constitutes personal identity. Loosely—P_2 at t_2 is the same person as P_1 at an earlier time t_1, if and only if P_2 remembers having done and experienced various things, where these things were in fact done and experienced by P_1.[6]

Before expounding Locke's theory further we need to be clear about the kind of memory which is involved. First, it is what is sometimes called personal memory, i.e., memory of one's own past experiences. It is thus to be distinguished from factual memory, which is memory of some fact known previously; as when I remember that the battle of Hastings was fought in 1066. This is not a memory of a past experience. Personal memory is also to be distinguished from remembering-how (e.g., to swim or to ride a bicycle), which is remembering how to perform some task. Secondly, it is personal memory in the weak sense. In the normal or strong sense of 'remember', one can only remember doing something if one really did it. I may say that I 'remember' going up the Eiffel Tower, but if I didn't do it, it seems natural to say that I cannot really remember having done it. In this sense, just as you can only know what is true, so you can only remember what you really did. However, there is also a weak sense of 'remember' in which a man remembers whatever he believes that he remembers in the strong sense. One's weak memories are not necessarily true ones. Now if the memory criterion defined personal identity in terms of memory in the strong sense, it would not be very useful; for to say that P_2 remembers having done what P_1 did would already entail their being the same person, and anyone in doubt as to whether P_2 was the same person as P_1, would have equal doubt whether P_2 really did remember doing what P_1 did. What the criterion as stated is concerned with is memory in the weak sense, which (because the strong sense is the more natural one) I shall henceforward call apparent memory.

So Locke's theory can now be rephrased as follows: P_2 at t_2 is the same person as P_1 at an earlier time t_1, if and only if P_2 apparently remembers having done and experienced various things when those things were in fact done and experienced by P_1. A person is who he thinks that he is. Note that what a person believes about his identity

---

[6]Although Locke's account of what it is for two persons to be the 'same person' is the simple memory account given above, he complicates it by providing a different account of what it is for two persons to be the 'same man'. This account is basically the bodily account which I have just outlined. P_1 is the same man as whoever has the same body as P_1, but the same person as whoever has the same memories as P_1. But Locke regards personal identity (which person, rather than which man, one is) as what is of importance for the way in which we should treat people, e.g., whom we are to reward or punish.

may be different from what he claims publicly. We only take public memory claims to be evidence of personal identity when we believe them to be honest, to express genuine memory beliefs, i.e., in my stated sense apparent memories. No doubt it is normally right to suppose that memory claims express apparent memories. But there may be circumstances in which it is reasonable to doubt this; e.g., if the subject has a source other than memory of the information which he claims to remember, if it is to his interest to pretend to remember, and if he is known to be deceitful.

Locke is very clear about the nature and consequences of his theory. If I do not apparently remember having done something, then I am not the same person as the person who did it. And if I do apparently remember having done the deeds of some person long since dead, then it follows that I am that person.

> If Socrates and the present mayor of Queenborough agree in [identity of consciousness], they are the same person: if the same Socrates waking and sleeping does not partake of the same consciousness, Socrates waking and sleeping is not the same person. And to punish Socrates waking for what sleeping Socrates thought, and waking Socrates was never conscious of, would be no more right, than to punish one twin for what his brother twin did, whereof he knew nothing. (Locke, *Essay*, sec. 19)

Locke's theory needs tidying up if we are to avoid absurdity. Consider, first, the following objection made by Thomas Reid:

> Suppose a brave officer to have been flogged when a boy at school for robbing an orchard, to have taken a standard from the enemy in his first campaign, and to have been made a general in advanced life; suppose also, which must be admitted to be possible, that, when he took the standard, he was conscious of his having been flogged at school, and that, when made a general, he was conscious of his taking the standard, but had absolutely lost the consciousness of his flogging. These things being supposed, it follows, from Mr Locke's doctrine, that he who was flogged at school is the same person who took the standard, and that he who took the standard is the same person who was made a general. Whence it follows if there be any truth in logic, that the general is the same person with him who was flogged at school. But the general's consciousness does not reach so far back as his flogging; therefore according to Mr Locke's doctrine, he is not the same person who was flogged. Therefore the general is, and at the same time is not, the same person with him who was flogged at school. (Reid, *Essays* III, ch. 6)

The objection illustrates the important point that identity is a transitive relation; if *a* is identical with *b* and *b* is identical with *c*, then necessarily *a* is identical with *c*. We can meet the objection by reformulating Locke's theory as follows: P_2 at t_2 is the same person as P_1 at an earlier time t_1 if and only if *either* P_2 apparently remembers what P_1 did and experienced, or he apparently remembers what some person P' at an intermediate time t' did and experienced, when P' apparently remembers what P_1 did and experienced, *or* they are linked by some longer intermediate chain. (That is, P_2 apparently remembers what P' did and experienced, P' apparently remembers what P'' did and experienced, and so on until we reach a person who apparently remembers what P_1 did and experienced.) If P_1 and P_2 are linked by such a chain, they are, we may say, linked by continuity of memory. Clearly, the apparent memories of the deeds and experiences of the previous person at each stage in the chain need not be completely accurate memories of what was done and experienced. But they do need to be fairly accurate memories of what was done and experienced, if the later person is to be the person who did and experienced those things.

Secondly, Locke ought to allow that while in general apparent memory guarantees personal identity and so amounts to genuine memory, there are cases where it does not. One kind of case is one to which in effect I have just referred. If a person apparently remembers being the person who did or experienced a certain thing, that apparent memory is not genuine if no one did or experienced that thing. My apparent memory of having led a victorious army against the Russians in battle in 1976 is not genuine if no one did this deed. Also, an apparent memory is not genuine if it is caused by a chain of causes which runs outside the person (e.g., it is caused by some informant). If my apparent memory of having met my great-grandfather at the age of three months was caused by my mother telling me much later in life that I had done this thing, and my having forgotten that she was the sole source of my belief that I had met my great-grandfather, then my apparent memory is not genuine. Finally, if apparent memories are inconsistent (e.g., I apparently remember being in Australia at a certain time and I also apparently remember being in England at exactly that same time), then at least one of them cannot be genuine. Locke can allow that there are these exceptions, and that if any of them are found to hold we cannot regard an apparent memory as genuine, while insisting that, but for them, apparent memory guarantees personal identity.

Locke's memory theory was a simple theory, and a more compli-cated version of the theory which takes in other connected points was developed by Hume.[7] It is not only his apparent memory which determines the attitude which others have towards a person. How others treat a person depends also on his beliefs about the world and his attitudes towards it, whether they are changeable or constant, and what leads them to change—that is, on the person's character. Hume brings these in. He is also aware that if memory is not mistaken (and he assumes it normally to be correct), it is a causal relation. If in the strong sense I remember some past experience, this involves my past experience being in part the cause of my having the apparent memory which I do.

Hume regards a person as basically a mental state with a body attached; but the mental state is just a 'bundle or collection of different perceptions', i.e., of thoughts, sensations, and images. Some of these are caused by past 'perceptions' and among these are memories, which for Hume are faint copies of past 'perceptions'. The bundle of 'perceptions' C_2, which is my mental state now, is linked to the bundle of perceptions C_1, which we call my mental state yesterday, by the fact that some members of C_2 are caused by and resemble (e.g., include memories of and similar thoughts to) members of C_1, or are linked by a causal chain which passes through similar bundles. (Hume does not say what links 'perceptions' into one bundle—i.e., what makes all the 'perceptions' which I have at one time all mine.) Hume calls that kind of identity 'fictitious', because the 'perceptions' which belong to some bundle are really distinct entities from the 'perceptions' which belong to some other bundle, although linked causally to them; he contrasts it with the real identity which would be possessed by a substance which continued to exist in a perfectly unchanged state.

A number of more recent writers have developed more careful ver-sions of a memory theory of personal identity, including Grice (1941) and Quinton (1962).

Many advocates of a memory theory have not always been very clear in their exposition about whether the apparent memories which form the links in the chain of memory need to be actual memories, or whether they need only to be hypothetical memories. By 'actual memories' I mean actual recallings of past experiences. The trouble with the suggestion that actual memories are required is that we do

---

[7]Hume subsequently found this view outlined above and expanded in the main text of the *Treatise* unsatisfactory, as he wrote in his Appendix. But the grounds of his dissatisfaction are not clear. See Stroud 1977, ch. 6.

not very often recall our past, and it seems natural to suppose that the deeds and experiences of some moments of a person's life never get recalled. Yet the memory theory, as stated so far, rules out that possibility. If I am not connected by a chain of memories with the deeds and experiences done by a person at a certain time, then I am not identical with that person. It is perhaps better if the theory claims that the apparent memories which form the links need only be hypothetical memories—i.e., what a person would apparently remember if he were to try to remember the deeds and experiences in question, e.g., in consequence of being prompted.[8]

There is however a major objection to any memory theory of personal identity, arising from the possibility of duplication. The objection was made briefly by Reid and at greater length in an influential article by Bernard Williams (1956–57). Williams imagines the case of a man whom he calls Charles who turns up in the twentieth century claiming to be Guy Fawkes:

> All the events he claims to have witnessed and all the actions he claims to have done point unanimously to the life-history of some one person in the past—for instance Guy Fawkes. Not only do all Charles' memory-claims that can be checked fit the pattern of Fawkes' life as known to historians, but others that cannot be checked are plausible, provide explanations of unexplained facts, and so on. (Williams, 1956–57, p. 332)

The fact that memory claims which 'cannot be checked are plausible, provide explanations of unexplained facts, and so on' is evidence that Charles is not merely claiming to remember what he has in fact read in a book about Guy Fawkes, and so leaves us back with the supposition, natural to make in normal cases, that he is reporting honestly his apparent memories. So, by a memory theory Charles would be Guy Fawkes. But then suppose, Williams imagines, that another man Robert turns up, who satisfies the memory criteria for being Guy Fawkes equally well. We cannot say that they are both identical with Guy Fawkes, for if they were, they would be identical with each other—which they are not since they currently live different lives and have different thoughts and feelings from

---

[8]We would need some well-justified theory by means of which we could infer what some person would apparently remember if he were to try, if we were ever to apply our theory to answering particular questions of the form 'Is P_2 identical with P_1?' The theory would need to be established without presupposing which past person, some person who is not now currently recalling anything, was. For although it is reasonable to suppose that such a person would remember many of his recent deeds and experiences, if he were to try, we cannot know which recent deeds and experiences were his until we know what he would apparently remember, according to the memory theory.

each other. So apparent memory cannot constitute personal identity, although it may be fallible evidence of it.

The objection from the possibility of duplication, together with other difficulties which will be mentioned in later chapters, have inclined the majority of contemporary writers to favour a theory which makes some sort of bodily continuity central to personal identity. As we have seen, the brain theory takes into account the insight of memory-and-character theory into the importance of these factors for personal identity, by selecting the brain, as the organ causally responsible for the continuity of memory and character, as that part of the body, the continuity of which constitutes the continuity of the person.

The trouble is that any brain theory is also open to the duplication objection. The human brain has two very similar hemispheres—a left and a right hemisphere. The left hemisphere plays a major role in the control of limbs of and processing of sensory information from the right side of the body (and from the right sides of the two eyes); and the right hemisphere plays a major role in the control of limbs of and processing of sensory information from the left side of the body (and from the left sides of the two eyes). The left hemisphere plays a major role in the control of speech. Although the hemispheres have different roles in the adult, they interact with each other; and if parts of a hemisphere are removed, at any rate early in life, the roles of those parts are often taken over by parts of the other hemisphere. Brain operations which remove substantial parts of the brain are not infrequent. It might be possible one day to remove a whole hemisphere, without killing the person. There are no logical difficulties in supposing that we could transplant one of P_1's hemispheres into one skull from which a brain had been removed, and the other hemisphere into another such skull, and that both transplants should take, and it may well be practically possible to do so. It is certainly more likely to occur than the Guy Fawkes story told by Williams! If these transplants took, clearly each of the resulting persons would behave to some extent like P_1, and indeed both would probably have some of the apparent memories of P_1. Each of the resulting persons would then be good candidates for being P_1.

After all, if one of P_1's hemispheres had been destroyed and the other remained intact and untransplanted, and the resulting person continued to behave and make memory claims somewhat like those of P_1, we would have had little hesitation in declaring that person to be P_1. The same applies, whichever hemisphere was preserved—although it may well be that the resulting person would have greater capacities (e.g., speech) if one hemisphere was preserved than if the other one was preserved. We have seen earlier good reason for supposing that the person goes where his brain goes, and if his brain consists only of one hemisphere, that should make no difference. So if the one remaining hemisphere is then transplanted, we ought to say that the person whose body it now controls is P_1. Whether that person is P_1 can hardly be affected by the fact that instead of being destroyed, the other hemisphere is also transplanted so as to constitute the brain of a person. But if it is, that other person will be just as good a candidate for being P_1. So a Wiggins-type account might lead us to say that both resulting persons are P_1. But, for the reason given earlier in connection with the Guy Fawkes examples, that cannot be—since the two later persons are not identical with each other. Hence, Wiggins adds to his tentative definition a clause stating that P_2 who satisfies his criterion stated earlier is the same person as P_1, only if there is no other later person who also satisfies the criterion.[9]

But the introduction into any theory, whether a memory theory, a brain theory, or whatever, of a clause stating that a person who satisfies the criterion in question for being the same as an earlier person is the same, only so long as there is no other person who satisfies the criterion also or equally well, does have an absurd consequence. Let us illustrate this for the brain theory. Suppose P_1's left hemisphere is transplanted into some skull and the transplant takes. Then, according to the theory, whether the resulting person is P_1, i.e., whether P_1 survives, will depend on whether the other transplant takes. If it does, since both resulting persons will satisfy the memory and brain continuity criteria equally well, neither will be P_1. But if the other transplant does not take, then since there is only one person who satisfies the criterion, that person is P_1. So whether I survive an operation will depend on what happens in a body entirely different from the body which will be mine, if I do survive. But how can who I am depend on what happens to you? A similar absurd consequence follows when a similar clause forbidding duplication is added to a memory theory.

Yet if we abandon the duplication clause, we are back with the original difficulty—that there may be more than one later person who satisfies any memory criterion or brain criterion, or combination thereof, for being the same person as an earlier person. Our discussion brings to our attention also the fact that both these criteria are criteria

[9]He suggests analysing 'person' in such a way that 'coincidence under the concept person logically required the continuance in one organized parcel of all that was causally sufficient and causally necessary to the continuance of essential and characteristic functioning, no autonomously sufficient part achieving autonomous and functionally separate existence' (Wiggins 1967, p. 55).

which may be satisfied to varying degrees. P_2 can have 90 per cent, or 80 per cent, or less than 50 per cent of the brain of P_1; and likewise the similarity of apparent memory and character may vary along a spectrum. Just how well do criteria have to be satisfied for the later person to be the same person as the earlier person? Any line one might draw seems totally artificial. One might think that it was non-arbitrary to insist on more than 50 per cent of the original brain matter—for only one later person could have more than 50 per cent of the original brain matter (whereas if our criterion demands only a smaller proportion, more than one later person could satisfy it). But would we really want to say that P_6 was the same person as P_1 if P_2 was obtained from P_1 by a transplant of 60 per cent (and so more than half) of P_1's brain matter, P_3 was obtained from P_2 by a transplant of 60 per cent of P_2's brain matter, and so on until we came to P_6. By the criterion of 'more than half of the brain matter', P_6 would be the same person as P_5, P_5 as P_4 and so on, and so by the transitivity of identity P_6 would be the same person as P_1—although he would have very little of P_1's brain matter. Any criterion of the proportion of brain matter transferred, to be plausible, would have to take account of whether there had been similar transplants in the past, and the length of the interval between them. And then the arbitrariness of the criterion would stare us in the face.

This problem pushes the thinker towards one of two solutions. The first solution is to say that personal identity is a matter of degree. P_2 is the same person as P_1 to the extent to which there is sameness of brain matter and continuity of memory. After all, survival for inanimate things is a matter of degree. As we gradually replace bits of a desk with new bits, the resulting desk is only more or less the same as the original desk. And if my car is taken to pieces and some of the bits are used to make one new car, and some of the bits used to make another new car, both cars are partly the same as and partly different from the old car. Why cannot we say the same of people? Normally we are not inclined to talk thus, because brain operations are rare and brain hemisphere transplants never happen. Hence there is normally at most only one candidate for being the same person as an earlier person, and he is normally a very strong candidate indeed—having a more or less identical brain and very great similarities of apparent memory and character. So we tend to think of personal identity as all or nothing. But it is not thus in its logic, the argument goes. There is the logical possibility, which could become an empirical possibility, of intermediate cases—of persons who are to some extent the same as and to some extent different from original persons.

This view has been advocated by Derek Parfit (1971b). When a person divides, as a result of a split brain transplant, he 'survives' in part, Parfit holds, as each of two persons. They constitute his later 'selves', neither of whom, to speak strictly, are identical with the original person.

This theory which Parfit calls the complex view,[10] does however, run up against a fundamental difficulty that it commits him to substantial empirical claims which to all appearance could very easily be false. I can bring this out by adopting Bernard Williams's famous mad surgeon story (in Williams 1970). Suppose that a mad surgeon captures you and announces that he is going to transplant your left cerebral hemisphere into one body, and your right one into another. He is going to torture one of the resulting persons and free the other with a gift of a million pounds. You can choose which person is going to be tortured and which to be rewarded, and the surgeon promises to do as you choose. You believe his promise. But how are you to choose? You wish to choose that you are rewarded, but you do not know which resultant person will be you. Now on the complex theory each person will be you to the extent to which he has your brain and resembles you in his apparent memories and character. It would be in principle empirically ascertainable whether and to what extent persons with right hemisphere transplants resemble their originals in apparent memories and character more or less than persons with left hemisphere transplants. But clearly the difference is not going to be great. So Parfit must say that your choice does not greatly matter. Both subsequent persons will be in part you—although perhaps to slightly different degrees. And so you will—although perhaps to slightly different degrees—in part suffer and in part enjoy what each suffers and enjoys. So you have reason both for joyous expectation and for terrified anticipation. But one problem is: how could you have reason for part joyous expectation and part terrified anticipation, when no one future person is going to suffer a mixed fate?

But even if this notion of partial survival does make sense, the more serious difficulty remains, which is this. We can make sense of the supposition that the victim makes the wrong choice, and has the experience of being tortured and not the experience of being rewarded; or the right choice, and has the experience of being rewarded and not the experience of being tortured. A mere philosophical analysis of the concept of personal identity cannot tell you which experiences will be yours tomorrow. To use Bernard Williams's telling word, any choice

---

[10]He introduces this terminology in his paper, Parfit 1971a.

would be a 'risk'. But on Parfit's view no risk would be involved—for knowing the extent of continuity of brain, apparent memory, and character, you would know the extent to which a future person would be you and so the extent to which his experiences would be yours. Although it *may* be the case that if my cerebral hemispheres are transplanted into different bodies, I survive partly as the person whose body is controlled by one and partly as the person whose body is controlled by the other, it may not be like that at all. Maybe I go where the left hemisphere goes; and when my right hemisphere is separated from the left hemisphere and comes to control a body by itself, either a new person is formed, or the resulting organism, although behaving to some extent like a person is really a very complicated non-conscious machine. As we have noted, the fate of some parts of my body, such as my arms and legs, is quite irrelevant to the fate of me. And plausibly the fate of some parts of my brain is irrelevant—can I not survive completely a minor brain operation which removes a very small tumor? But then maybe it is the same with some larger parts of the brain too. We just don't know. If the mad surgeon's victim took the attitude that it didn't matter which way he chose, we must, I suggest, regard him as taking an unjustifiably dogmatic attitude.

The alternative way out of the duplication problem is to say that although apparent memory and brain continuity are, as they obviously are, evidence of personal identity, they are fallible evidence and personal identity is something distinct from them. Just as the presence of blood stains and fingerprints matching those of a given man are evidence of his earlier presence at the scene of the crime, and the discovery of Roman-looking coins and buildings is evidence that the Romans lived in some region, so the similarity of P_2's apparent memory to that of P_1 and his having much the same brain matter, is evidence that P_2 is the same person as P_1. Yet blood stains and fingerprints are one thing and a man's earlier presence at the scene of the crime another. His presence at the scene of the crime is not analysable in terms of the later presence of blood stains and fingerprints. The latter is evidence of the former, because you seldom get blood stains and fingerprints at a place matching those of a given man, unless he has been there leaving them around. But it might happen. So, the suggestion is, personal identity is distinct from, although evidenced by, similarity of memory and continuity of brain.

This account, which for the moment I will follow Parfit in calling the simple view, can meet all the difficulties which have beset the other theories which we have discussed. The difficulty for the complex view was that it seemed very peculiar to suppose that mere logic could determine which of the experiences had by various persons, each of which was to some extent continuous with me in apparent memory and brain matter, would be mine. There seemed to be a further truth—that I would or would not have those experiences—beyond any truths about the extent of similarity in apparent memory and matter of future persons to myself. The simple view claims explicitly that personal identity is one thing, and the extent of similarity in matter and apparent memory another. There is no contradiction in supposing that the one should occur without the other. Strong similarity of matter and apparent memory is powerful evidence of personal identity. I and the person who had my body and brain last week have virtually the same brain matter and such similar apparent memory, that it is well-nigh certain that we are the same person. But where the brain matter is only in part the same and the memory connection less strong, it is only fairly probable that the persons are the same. Where there are two later persons P_2 and P_2^*, each of whom had some continuity with the earlier person P_1, the evidence supports to some extent each of the two hypotheses—that P_2 is the same person as P_1, and that P_2^* is the same person as P_1. It may give more support to one hypothesis than to the other, but the less well supported hypothesis might be the true one, or maybe neither hypothesis is true. Perhaps P_1 has ceased to exist, and two different persons have come into existence. So the simple view fully accepts that mere logic cannot determine which experiences will be mine, but it allows that continuity of apparent memory and brain provides fallible evidence about this. And of course the duplication objection that they allow for the two subsequent persons being the same person, which we brought against the brain and the memory theories, has no force against the simple theory. For although there can be equally good evidence that each of two later persons is the same person as an earlier person, that evidence is fallible; and since clearly only one person at one time can be strictly the same person as some person at an earlier time, it follows that in one case the evidence is misleading—although we may not know in which case.

[. . .] In the next section I will expound and develop the simple view, and show that it amounts to the same as Cartesian dualism—the view that a person consists of two parts, soul, and body. [. . .]

2 The Dualist Theory

The brain transplant considerations of the first section leading to the simple view of personal identity showed that significant continuity of brain and memory was not enough to ensure personal identity. They did not show that continuity of brain or memory were totally dispensable; that P_2 at time t_2 could be the same person as P_1 at an earlier time t_1, even though P_2 had none of the brain matter (or other bodily matter) of P_1 and had no apparent memory of P_1's actions and experiences. A number of more extravagant thought-experiments do, however, show that there is no contradiction in this latter supposition.

There seems no contradiction in the supposition that a person might acquire a totally new body (including a completely new brain)—as many religious accounts of life after death claim that men do. To say that this body, sitting at the desk in my room is my body is to say two things. First it is to say that I can move parts of this body (arms, legs, etc.), just like that, without having to do any other intentional action and that I can make a difference to other physical objects only by moving parts of this body. By holding the door handle and turning my hand, I open the door. By bending my leg and stretching it I kick the ball and make it move into the goal. But I do not turn my hand or bend my leg by doing some other intentional action; I just do these things.[11] Secondly, it is to say that my knowledge of states of the world outside this body is derived from their effects on this body—I learn about the positions of physical objects by seeing them, and seeing them involves light rays reflected by them impinging on my eyes and setting up nervous impulses in my optic nerve. My body is the vehicle of my agency in the world and my knowledge of the world. But then is it not coherent to suppose that I might suddenly find that my present body no longer served this function, that I could no longer acquire information through these eyes or move these limbs, but might discover that another body served the same function? I might find myself moving other limbs and acquiring information through other eyes. Then I would have a totally new body. If that body, like my last body, was an occupant of the Earth, then we would have a case of reincarnation, as Eastern religions have understood that. If that body was an occupant of some distant planet, or an environment which did not belong to the same space[12] as our world, then we

---

[11]Following A. C. Danto (1965), philosophers call those intentional actions which we just do, not by doing some other intentional action, basic actions, and those which we do by doing some other intentional action, mediated actions. An intentional action is one which an agent does, meaning to do. No doubt certain events have to happen in our nerves and muscles if we are to move our arms and legs, but we do not move our arms and legs by intentionally making these events occur.

[12]Two objects belong to the same space if they are at some distance from each other, if you can get from one to the other by going along a path in space which joins them. For a fuller account of the meaning of the claim that an object occupies a different space from our space, see Swinburne 1981b, chs 1 and 2.

would have a case of resurrection as on the whole Western religions (Christianity, Judaism and Islam) have understood that.

This suggestion of a man acquiring a new body (with brain) may be more plausible, to someone who has difficulty in grasping it, by supposing the event to occur gradually. Suppose that one morning a man wakes up to find himself unable to control the right side of his body, including his right arm and leg. When he tries to move the right-side parts of his body, he finds that the corresponding left-side parts of his body move; and when he tries to move the left-side parts, the corresponding right-side parts of his wife's body move. His knowledge of the world comes to depend on stimuli to his left side and to his wife's right side (e.g., light rays stimulating his left eye and his wife's right eye). The bodies fuse to some extent physiologically as with Siamese twins, while the man's wife loses control of her right side. The focus of the man's control of and knowledge of the world is shifting. One may suppose the process completed as the man's control is shifted to the wife's body, while the wife loses control of it.

Equally coherent, I suggest, is the supposition that a person might become disembodied. A person has a body if there is one particular chunk of matter through which he has to operate on and learn about the world. But suppose that he finds himself able to operate on and learn about the world within some small finite region, without having to use one particular chunk of matter for this purpose. He might find himself with knowledge of the position of objects in a room (perhaps by having visual sensations, perhaps not), and able to move such objects just like that, in the ways in which we know about the positions of our limbs and can move them. But the room would not be, as it were, the person's body; for we may suppose that simply by choosing to do so he can gradually shift the focus of his knowledge and control, e.g., to the next room. The person would be in no way limited to operating and learning through one particular chunk of matter. Hence we may term him disembodied. The supposition that a person might become disembodied also seems coherent.

I have been arguing so far that it is coherent to suppose that a person could continue to exist with an entirely new body or with no body at all. [. . .] Could a person continue to exist without any apparent memory of his previous doings? Quite clearly, we do allow not merely the logical possibility, but the frequent actuality of amnesia—a person forgetting all or certain stretches of his past life. Despite Locke, many a person does forget much of what he has done.

But, of course, we normally only suppose this to happen in cases where there is the normal bodily and brain continuity. Our grounds for supposing that a person forgets what he has done are that the evidence of bodily and brain continuity suggests that he was the previous person who did certain things, which he now cannot remember having done. And in the absence of both of the main kinds of evidence for personal identity, we would not be justified in supposing that personal identity held. For that reason I cannot describe a case where we would have good reason to suppose that P_2 was identical with P_1, even though there was neither brain continuity nor memory continuity between them. However, only given verificationist dogma, is there any reason to suppose that the only things which are true are those of whose truth we can have evidence, and I shall suggest in section 3 [not included here] that there is no good reason for believing verificationism to be true. We can make sense of states of affairs being true, of which we can have no evidence that they are true. And among them surely is the supposition that the person who acquires another body loses not merely control of the old one, but memories of what he did with its aid. Again, many religions have taken seriously stories of persons passing through the waters of Lethe (a river whose waters made a person forget all his previous life) and then acquiring a new body. Others who have heard these stories may not have believed them true; but they have usually claimed to understand them, and (unless influenced by philosophical dogma) have not suspected them of involving contradiction.

Those who hope to survive their death, despite the destruction of their body, will not necessarily be disturbed if they come to believe that they will then have no memory of their past life on Earth; they may just want to survive and have no interest in continuing to recall life on Earth. Again, apparently, there seems to be no contradiction involved in their belief. It seems to be a coherent belief (whether or not true or justified). Admittedly, there may be stories or beliefs which involve a hidden contradiction when initially they do not seem to do so. But the fact that there seems (and to so many people) to be no contradiction hidden in these stories is good reason for supposing that there is no contradiction hidden in them—until a contradiction is revealed. If this were not a good reason for believing there to be no contradiction, we would have no good reason for believing any sentence at all to be free of hidden contradiction. [. . .]

In section 1, I set out Aristotle's account of the identity of substances: that a substance at one time is the same substance as a substance at an earlier time if and only if the later substance has the same form as, and continuity of matter with, the earlier substance. On this view a person is the same person as an earlier person if he has the same form as the earlier person (i.e., both are persons) and has continuity of matter with him (i.e., has the same body).

Certainly, to be the same person as an earlier person, a later person has to have the same form—i.e., has to be a person. If my arguments for the logical possibility of there being disembodied persons are correct, then the essential characteristics of a person constitute a narrower set than those which Aristotle would have included. My arguments suggest that all that a person needs to be a person are certain mental capacities—for having conscious experiences (e.g., thoughts or sensations) and performing intentional actions. Thought-experiments of the kind described earlier allow that a person might lose his body, but they describe his continuing to have conscious experiences and his performing or being able to perform intentional actions, i.e., to do actions which he means to do, bring about effects for some purpose.

Yet if my arguments are correct, showing that two persons can be the same, even if there is no continuity between their bodily matter, we must say that in the form stated the Aristotelian account of identity applies only to inanimate objects and plants and has no application to personal identity.[13] We are then faced with a choice either of saying that the criteria of personal identity are different from those for other substances, or of trying to give a more general account than Aristotle's of the identity of substances which would cover both persons and other substances. It is possible to widen the Aristotelian account so that we can do the latter. We have only to say that two substances are the same if and only if they have the same form and there is continuity of the stuff of which they are made, and allow that there may be kinds of stuff other than matter. I will call this account of substance identity the wider Aristotelian account. We may say that there is a stuff of another kind, immaterial stuff, and that persons are made of both normal bodily matter and of this immaterial stuff but that it is the continuity of the latter which provides that continuity of stuff which is necessary for the identity of the person over time.

---

[13] I do not discuss the difficult issue of whether the Aristotelian account applies to animals other than man, e.g., whether continuity of matter and form is necessary and sufficient for the identity of a dog at a later time with a dog at an earlier time.

This is in essence the way of expressing the simple theory which is adopted by those who say that a person living on Earth consists of two parts—a material part, the body; and an immaterial part, the soul. The soul is the essential part of a person, and it is its continuing which constitutes the continuing of the person. While on Earth, the soul is linked to a body (by the body being the vehicle of the person's knowledge of and action upon the physical world). But, it is logically possible, the soul can be separated from the body and exist in a disembodied state (in the way described earlier) or linked to a new body. This way of expressing things has been used in many religious traditions down the centuries, for it is a very natural way of expressing what is involved in being a person once you allow that a person can survive the death of his body. Classical philosophical statements of it are to be found in Plato and, above all, in Descartes. I shall call this view classical dualism.

I wrote that 'in essence' classical dualism is the view that there is more stuff to the person than bodily matter, and that it is the continuing of this stuff which is necessary for the continuing of the person, because a writer such as Descartes did not distinguish between the immaterial stuff, let us call it soul-stuff, and that stuff being organized (with or without a body) as one soul. Descartes and other classical dualists however did not make this distinction, because they assumed (implicitly) that it was not logically possible that persons divide—i.e., that an earlier person could be in part the same person as each of two later persons. Hence they implicitly assumed that soul-stuff comes in essentially indivisible units. That is indeed what one has to say about soul-stuff, if one makes the supposition (as I was inclined to do, in section 1), that it is not logically possible that persons divide. There is nothing odd about supposing that soul-stuff comes in essentially indivisible units. Of any chunk of matter, however small, it is always logically, if not physically, possible that it be divided into two. Yet it is because matter is extended, that one can always make sense of it being divided. For a chunk of matter necessarily takes up a finite volume of space. A finite volume of space necessarily is composed of two half-volumes. So it always makes sense to suppose that part of the chunk which occupies the left half-volume of space to be separated from that part of the chunk which occupies the right half-volume. But that kind of consideration has no application to immaterial stuff. There is no reason why there should not be a kind of immaterial stuff which necessarily is indivisible; and if the supposition of section 1 is correct, the soul-stuff will have that property.

So then—once we modify the Aristotelian understanding of the criteria for the identity of substances, the simple view of personal identity finds a natural expression in classical dualism. The arguments which Descartes gave in support of his account of persons are among the arguments which I have given in favour of the simple theory and since they take for granted the wider Aristotelian framework, they yield classical dualism as a consequence. Thus Descartes argues:

> Just because I know certainly that I exist, and that meanwhile I do not remark that any other thing necessarily pertains to my nature or essence, excepting that I am a thinking thing, I rightly conclude that my essence consists solely in the fact that I am a thinking thing. And although possibly . . . I possess a body with which I am very intimately conjoined, yet because, on the one side, I have a clear and distinct idea of myself inasmuch as I am only a thinking and unextended thing, and as, on the other, I possess a distinct idea of body, inasmuch as it is only an extended and unthinking thing, it is certain that this I [that is to say, my soul by which I am what I am], is entirely and absolutely distinct from my body, and can exist without it.[14]

Descartes is here saying that he can describe a thought-experiment in which he continues to exist although his body does not. I have also described such a thought-experiment and have argued, as Descartes in effect does, that it follows that his body is not logically necessary for his existence, that it is not an essential part of himself. Descartes can go on 'thinking' (i.e., being conscious) and so existing without it. Now if we take the wider Aristotelian framework for granted that the continuing of a substance involves the continuing of some of the stuff of which it is made, and since the continuing existence of Descartes does not involve the continuing of bodily matter, it follows that there must now be as part of Descartes some other stuff, which he calls his soul, which forms the essential part of Descartes.

Given that for any present person who is currently conscious, there is no logical impossibility, whatever else may be true now of that person, that that person continue to exist without his body, it follows that that person must now actually have a part other than a bodily part which can continue, and which we may call his soul— and so that his possession of it is entailed by his being a conscious

---

[14]Descartes, *Meditations*, p. 190. The clause in square brackets occurs only in the French translation, approved by Descartes.

thing. For there is not even a logical possibility that if I now consist of nothing but matter and the matter is destroyed, that I should nevertheless continue to exist. From the mere logical possibility of my continued existence there follows the actual fact that there is now more to me than my body; and that more is the essential part of myself. A person's being conscious is thus to be analysed as an immaterial core of himself, his soul being conscious.[15]

So Descartes argues, and his argument seems to me correct—given the wider Aristotelian framework. If we are prepared to say that substances can be the same, even though none of the stuff (in a wide sense) of which they are made is the same, the conclusion does not follow. The wider Aristotelian framework provides a partial definition of 'stuff' rather than a factual truth. To say that a person has an immaterial soul is not to say that if you examine him closely enough under an acute enough microscope you will find some very rarefied constituent which has eluded the power of ordinary microscopes. It is just a way of expressing the point within a traditional framework of thought that persons can—it is logically possible—continue, when their bodies do not. It does, however, seem a very natural way of expressing the point— especially once we allow that persons can become disembodied. Unless we adopt a wider Aristotelian framework, we shall have to say that there can be substances which are not made of anything, and which are the same substances as other substances which are made of matter.

It does not follow from all this that a person's body is no part of him. Given that what we are trying to do is to elucidate the nature of those entities which we normally call 'persons', we must say that arms and legs and all other parts of the living body are parts of the person. My arms and legs are parts of me. The crucial point that Descartes was making is that the body is only, contingently and possibly temporarily, part of the person; it is not an essential part. However, Descartes does seem in a muddle about this. In the passage from the *Meditations* just cited, as elsewhere in his works,[16] he claims sometimes (wrongly) that my body is no part of me, and at other times (correctly) that my body is not an essential part of me.

The other arguments which I have given for the 'simple theory', e.g., that two embodied persons can be the same despite their being no bodily continuity between them, can also, like the argument of

---

[15][In the original text Surinburne states in this footnote a formal modal version of this argument. This has been omitted.]
[16]For examples and commentary, see pp. 63–6 of Smart 1977.

Descartes just discussed, if we assume the wider Aristotelian framework, be cast into the form of arguments for classical dualism.

As we have seen, classical dualism is the way of expressing the simple view of personal identity within what I called the wider Aristotelian framework. However, this framework is a wider one than Aristotle himself would have been happy with, allowing a kind of stuff other than Aristotle would have countenanced. There has been in the history of thought a different and very influential way of modifying Aristotle, to take account of the kind of point made by the simple view. This way was due to St Thomas Aquinas (see, e.g., *Summa contra Gentiles*). Aquinas accepted Aristotle's general doctrine that substances are made of matter, organized by a form; the desk is the desk which it is because of the matter of which it is made and the shape which is imposed upon it. The form was normally a system of properties, universals which had no existence except in the particular substances in which they were instantiated. However, Aquinas claimed that for man the form of the body, which he called the soul, was separable from the body and capable of independent existence. The soul of man, unlike the souls of animals or plants, was in Aquinas's terminology, an 'intellectual substance'.

However, if we are going to modify Aristotle to make his views compatible with the simple theory of personal identity, this seems definitely the less satisfactory way of doing so. Properties seem by their very nature to be universals and so it is hard to give any sense to their existing except when conjoined to some stuff. Above all, it is hard to give sense to their being individual—a universal can be instantiated in many different substances. What makes the substances differ is the different stuff of which they are composed. The form of man can be instantiated in many different men. But Aquinas wants a form which is a particular, and so could only be combined with one body. All of this seems to involve a greater distortion of Aristotle's system than does classical dualism. Aquinas's system does have some advantages over classical dualism—for example, it enables him to bring out the naturalness of a person being embodied and the temporary and transitory character of any disembodiment—but the disadvantages of taking Aristotle's approach and then distorting it to this unrecognizable extent are in my view very great. Hence my preference for what I have called classical dualism. I shall in future express the simple view in the form of classical dualism, in order to locate this view within the philosophical tradition which seems naturally to express it. [. . .]

Brain Transplants and Personal Identity

Derek Parfit and Godfrey Vesey

In 1973 in the *Sunday Times* there was a report of how a team from the Metropolitan Hospital in Cleveland under Dr. R. J. White had successfully transplanted a monkey's head on to another monkey's body.[1] Dr. White was reported as having said, 'Technically a human head transplant is possible', and as hoping that 'it may be possible eventually to transplant *parts* of the brain or other organs inside the head.'

The possibility of brain transplants gives rise to a fascinating philosophical problem. Imagine the following situation:

> Two men, a Mr Brown and a Mr Robinson, had been operated on for brain tumours and brain extractions had been performed on both of them. At the end of the operations, however, the assistant inadvertently put Brown's brain in Robinson's head, and Robinson's brain in Brown's head. One of these men immediately dies, but the other, the one with Robinson's body and Brown's brain, eventually regains consciousness. Let us call the latter 'Brownson'. Upon regaining consciousness Brownson exhibits great shock and surprise at the appearance of his body. Then, upon seeing Brown's body, he exclaims incredulously 'That's me lying there!' Pointing to himself he says 'This isn't my body; the one over there is!' When asked his name he automatically replies 'Brown'. He recognizes Brown's wife and family (whom Robinson had never met), and is able to describe in detail events in Brown's life, always describing them as events in his own life. Of Robinson's past life he evinces no knowledge at all. Over a period of time he is observed to display all of the personality traits, mannerisms, interests, likes and dislikes, and so on, that had previously characterized Brown, and to act and talk in ways completely alien to the old Robinson.[2]

The next step is to suppose that Brown's brain is not simply transplanted whole into someone else's brainless head, but is divided in two and half put into each of *two* other people's brainless heads. The same memory having been coded in many parts of the cortex, they *both* then say they are Brown, are able to describe events in Brown's life as if they are events in their own lives, etc. What should we say now?

Reprinted by permission of Open University Press, from "Brain Transplants and Personal Identity," in *Philosophy in the Open,* ed. Godfrey Vesey, 1974.

The implications of this case for what we should say about personal identity are considered by Derek Parfit in a paper entitled 'Personal Identity'. Parfit's own view is expressed in terms of a relationship he calls 'psychological continuity'. He analyses this relationship partly in terms of what he calls 'q-memory' ('q' stands for 'quasi'). He sketches a definition of 'q-memory' as follows:

> I am q-remembering an experience if (1) I have a belief about a past experience which seems in itself like a memory belief, (2) someone did have such an experience, and (3) my belief is dependent upon this experience in the same way (whatever that is) in which a memory of an experience is dependent upon it.[3]

The significance of this definition of q-memory is that *two* people can, in theory, q-remember doing what only one person did. So two people can, in theory, be psychologically continuous with one person.

Parfit's thesis is that there is nothing more to personal identity than this 'psychological continuity'. This is *not* to say that whenever there is a sufficient degree of psychological continuity there is personal identity, for psychological continuity could be a one-two, or 'branching', relationship, and we are able to speak of 'identity' only when there is a one-one relationship. It *is* to say that a common belief—in the special nature of personal identity—is mistaken.

In the discussion that follows I began by asking Parfit what he thinks of this common belief.

Personal Identity

VESEY: Derek, can we begin with the belief that you claim most of us have about personal identity? It's this: whatever happens between now and some future time either I shall still exist or I shan't. And any future experience will either be my experience or it won't. In other words, personal identity is an all or nothing matter: either I survive or I don't. Now what do you want to say about that?

PARFIT: It seems to me just false. I think the true view is that we can easily describe and imagine large numbers of cases in which the question, 'Will that future person be me—or someone else?', is both a question which doesn't have any answer at all, and there's no puzzle that there's no answer.

VESEY: Will you describe one such case.

PARFIT: One of them is the case discussed in the correspondence material, the case of division in which we suppose that each half of my brain is to be transplanted into a new body and the two resulting people will both seem to remember the whole of my life, have my character and be psychologically continuous with me in every way. Now in this case of division there were only three possible answers to the question, 'What's going to happen to *me?*' And all three of them seem to me open to very serious objections. So the conclusion to be drawn from the case is that the question of what's going to happen to me, just doesn't have an answer. I think the case also shows that that's not mysterious at all.

VESEY: Right, let's deal with these three possibilities in turn.

PARFIT: Well, the first is that I'm going to be both of the resulting people. What's wrong with that answer is that it leads very quickly to a contradiction.

VESEY: How?

PARFIT: The two resulting people are going to be different people from each other. They're going to live completely different lives. They're going to be as different as any two people are. But if they're different people from each other it can't be the case that I'm going to be both of them. Because if I'm both of them, then one of the resulting people is going to be the same person as the other.

VESEY: Yes. They can't be different people and be the same person, namely me.

PARFIT: Exactly. So the first answer leads to a contradiction.

VESEY: Yes. And the second?

PARFIT: Well, the second possible answer is that I'm not going to be both of them but just one of them. This doesn't lead to a contradiction, it's just wildly implausible. It's implausible because my relation to each of the resulting people is exactly similar.

VESEY: Yes, so there's no reason to say that I'm one rather than the other?

PARFIT: It just seems absurd to suppose that, when you've got exactly the same relation, one of them is identity and the other is nothing at all.

VESEY: It does seem absurd, but there are philosophers who would say that sort of thing. Let's go on to the third.

PARFIT: Well, the only remaining answer, if I'm not going to be both of them or only one of them, is that I'm going to be neither of them. What's wrong with this answer is that it's grossly misleading.

VESEY: Why?

PARFIT: If I'm going to be neither of them, then there's not going to be anyone in the world after the operation who's going to be me. And that implies, given the way we now think, that the operation is as bad as death. Because if there's going to be no one who's going to be me, then I cease to exist. But it's obvious on reflection that the operation isn't as bad as death. It isn't bad in any way at all. That this is obvious can be shown by supposing that when they do the operation only one of the transplants succeeds and only one of the resulting people ever comes to consciousness again.

VESEY: Then I think we would say that this person is me. I mean we'd have no reason to say that he wasn't.

PARFIT: On reflection I'm sure we would all think that I would survive as that one person.

VESEY: Yes.

PARFIT: Yes. Well, if we now go back to the case where both operations succeed . . .

VESEY: Where there's a double success . . .

PARFIT: It's clearly absurd to suppose that a double success is a failure.

VESEY: Yes.

PARFIT: So the conclusion that I would draw from this case is firstly, that to the question, 'What's going to happen to me?', there's no true answer.

VESEY: Yes.

PARFIT: Secondly, that if we decide to say one of the three possible answers, what we say is going to obscure the true nature of the case.

VESEY: Yes.

PARFIT: And, thirdly, the case isn't in any way puzzling. And the reason for that is this. My relation to each of the resulting people is the relation of full psychological continuity. When I'm psychologically continuous with only one person, we call it identity. But if I'm psychologically continuous with two future people, we can't call it identity. It's not puzzling because we know exactly what's going to happen.

VESEY: Yes, could I see if I've got this straight? Where there is psychological continuity in a one-one case, this is the sort of case which we'd ordinarily talk of in terms of a person having survived the operation, or something like that.

PARFIT: Yes.

VESEY: Now what about when there is what you call psychological continuity—that's to say, where the people seem to remember having been me and so on—in a one-two case? Is this survival or not?

PARFIT: Well, I think it's just as good as survival, but the block we have to get over is that we can't say that anyone in the world after the operation is going to be me.

VESEY: No.

PARFIT: Well, we can say it but it's very implausible. And we're inclined to think that if there's not going to be anyone who is me tomorrow, then I don't survive. What we need to realize is that my relation to each of those two people is just as good as survival. Nothing is missing at all in my relation to both of them, as compared with my relation to myself tomorrow.

VESEY: Yes.

PARFIT: So here we've got survival without identity. And that only seems puzzling if we think that identity is a further fact over and above psychological continuity.

VESEY: It is very hard not to think of identity being a further fact, isn't it?

PARFIT: Yes, I think it is. I think that the only way to get rid of our temptation to believe this is to consider many more cases than this one case of division. Perhaps I should give you another one. Suppose that the following is going to happen to me. When I die in a normal way, scientists are going to map the states of all the cells in my brain and body and after a few months they will have constructed a perfect duplicate of me out of organic matter. And this duplicate will wake up fully psychologically continuous with me, seeming to remember my life with my character, etc.

VESEY: Yes.

PARFIT: Now in this case, which is a secular version of the Resurrection, we're very inclined to think that the following question arises and is very real and very important. The question is, 'Will that person who wakes up in three months be me or will he be some quite other person who's merely artifically made to be exactly like me?'

VESEY: It does seem to be a real question. I mean in the one case, if it is going to be me, then I have expectations and so on, and in the other case, where it isn't me, I don't.

PARFIT: I agree, it seems as if there couldn't be a bigger difference between it being me and it being someone else.

VESEY: But you want to say that the two possibilities are in fact the same?

PARFIT: I want to say that those two descriptions, 'It's going to be me' and 'It's going to be someone who is merely exactly like me', don't describe different outcomes, different courses of events, only one of which can happen. They are two ways of describing one and the same course of events. What I mean by that perhaps could be shown if we take an exactly comparable case involving not a person but something about which I think we're not inclined to have a false view.

VESEY: Yes.

PARFIT: Something like a club. Suppose there's some club in the nineteenth century . . .

VESEY: The Sherlock Holmes Club or something like that?

PARFIT: Yes, perhaps. And after several years of meeting it ceases to meet. The club dies.

VESEY: Right.

PARFIT: And then two of its members, let's say, have emigrated to America, and after about fifteen years they get together and they start up a club. It has exactly the same rules, completely new membership except for the first two people, and they give it the same name. Now suppose someone came along and said: 'There's a real mystery here, because the following question is one that must have an answer. But how can we answer it?' The question is, 'Have they started up the very same club—is it the same club as the one they belonged to in England—or is it a completely new club that's just exactly similar?'

VESEY: Yes.

PARFIT: Well, in that case we all think that this man's remark is absurd; there's no difference at all. Now that's my model for the true view about the case where they make a duplicate of me. It seems that there's all the difference in the world between its being me and its being this other person who's exactly like me. But if we think there's no difference at all in the case of the clubs, why do we think there's a difference in the case of personal identity, and how can we defend the view that there's a difference?

VESEY: I can see how some people would defend it. I mean, a dualist would defend it in terms of a soul being a simple thing, but . . .

PARFIT: Let me try another case which I think helps to ease us out of this belief we're very strongly inclined to hold.

VESEY: Go on.

PARFIT: Well, this isn't a single case, this is a whole range of cases. A whole smooth spectrum of different cases which are all very similar to the next one in the range. At the start of this range of cases you suppose that the scientists are going to replace one per cent of the cells in your brain and body with exact duplicates.

VESEY: Yes.

PARFIT: Now if that were to be done, no one has any doubt that you'd survive. I think that's obvious because after all you can *lose* one per cent of the cells and survive. As we get further along the range they replace a larger and larger percentage of cells with exact duplicates, and of course at the far end of this range, where they replace a hundred per cent, then we've got my case where they just make a duplicate out of wholly fresh matter.

VESEY: Yes.

PARFIT: Now on the view that there's all the difference in the world between its being me and its being this other person who is exactly like me, we ought in consistency to think that in some case in the middle of that range, where, say, they're going to replace fifty per cent, the same question arises: it is going to be me or this completely different character? I think that even the most convinced dualist who believes in the soul is going to find this range of cases very embarrassing, because he seems committed to the view that there's some crucial percentage up to which it's going to be him and after which it suddenly ceases to be him. But I find that wholly unbelievable.

VESEY: Yes. He's going to have to invent some sort of theory about the relation of mind and body to get round this one. I'm not quite sure how he would do it. Derek, could we go on to a related question? Suppose that I accepted what you said, that is, that there isn't anything more to identity than what you call psychological continuity in a one-one case. Suppose I accept that, then I would want to go on and ask you, well, what's the philosophical importance of this?

PARFIT: The philosophical importance is, I think, that psychological continuity is obviously, when we think about it, a matter of degree. So long as we think that identity is a further fact, one of the things we're inclined to think is that it's all or nothing, as you said earlier. Well, if we give up that belief and if we realize that what matters in my continued existence is a matter of degree, then this does make a difference in actual cases. All the cases that I've considered so far are of course bizarre science fiction cases. But I think that in actual life it's obvious on reflection that, to give an example, the relations between me now and me next year are much closer in every way than the relations between me now and me in twenty years. And the sorts of relations that I'm thinking of are relations of memory, character, ambition, intention—all of those. Next year I shall remember much more of this year than I will in twenty years. I shall have a much more similar character. I shall be carrying out more of the same plans, ambitions and, if that is so, I think there are various plausible implications for our moral beliefs and various possible effects on our emotions.

VESEY: For our moral beliefs? What do you have in mind?

PARFIT: Let's take one very simple example. On the view which I'm sketching it seems to me much more plausible to claim that people deserve much less punishment, or even perhaps no punishment, for what they did many years ago as compared with what they did very recently. Plausible because the relations between them now and them many years ago when they committed the crime are so much weaker.

VESEY: But they are still the people who are responsible for the crime.

PARFIT: I think you say that because even if they've changed in many ways, after all it was just as much they who committed the crime. I think that's true, but on the view for which I'm arguing, we would come to think that it's a completely trivial truth. It's like the following truth: it's like the truth that all of my relatives are just as much my relatives. Suppose I in my will left more money to my close relatives and less to my distant relatives; a mere pittance to my second cousin twenty-nine times removed. If you said, 'But that's clearly unreasonable because all of your relatives are just as much your relatives', there's a sense in which that's true but it's obviously too trivial to make my will an unreasonable will. And that's because what's involved in kinship is a matter of degree.

VESEY: Yes.

PARFIT: Now, if we think that what's involved in its being the same person now as the person who committed the crime is a matter of degree, then the truth that it was just as much him who committed the crime, will seem to us trivial in the way in which the truth that all my relatives are equally my relatives is trivial.

VESEY: Yes. So you think that I should regard myself in twenty years' time as like a fairly distant relative of myself?

PARFIT: Well, I don't want to exaggerate; I think the connections are much closer.

VESEY: Suppose I said that this point about psychological continuity being a matter of degree—suppose I said that this isn't anything that anybody denies?

PARFIT: I don't think anybody does on reflection deny that psychological continuity is a matter of degree. But I think what they may deny, and I think what may make a difference to their view, if they come over to the view for which I'm arguing—what they may deny is that psychological continuity is all there is to identity. Because what I'm arguing against is this further belief which I think we're all inclined to hold even if we don't realize it. The belief that however much we change, there's a profound sense in which the changed us is going to be just as much us. That even if some magic wand turned me into a completely different sort of person—a prince with totally different character, mental powers—it would be just as much me. That's what I'm denying.

VESEY: Yes. This is the belief which I began by stating, and I think that if we did lose that belief that would be a change indeed.

Notes

1. *Sunday Times,* 9 December, 1973, p. 13.
2. Shoemaker (1963), pp. 23–24.
3. Parfit (1971), p. 15.

Where Am I?

Daniel C. Dennett

Now that I've won my suit under the Freedom of Information Act, I am at liberty to reveal for the first time a curious episode in my life that may be of interest not only to those engaged in research in the philosophy of mind, artificial intelligence, and neuroscience but also to the general public.

Several years ago, I was approached by Pentagon officials who asked me to volunteer for a highly dangerous and secret mission. In collaboration with NASA and Howard Hughes, the Department of Defense was spending billions to develop a Supersonic Tunneling Underground Device, or STUD. It was supposed to tunnel through the earth's core at great speed and deliver a specially designed atomic warhead "right up the Red's missile silos," as one of the Pentagon brass put it.

The problem was that in an early test they had succeeded in lodging a warhead about a mile deep under Tulsa, Oklahoma, and they wanted me to retrieve it for them. "Why me?" I asked. Well, the mission involved some pioneering applications of current brain research, and they had heard of my interest in brains and of course my Faustian curiosity and great courage and so forth. . . . Well, how could I refuse?

The difficulty that brought the Pentagon to my door was that the device I'd been asked to recover was fiercely radioactive, in a new way. According to monitoring instruments, something about the nature of the device and its complex interactions with pockets of material deep in the earth had produced radiation that could cause severe abnormalities in certain tissues of the brain. No way had been found to shield the brain from these deadly rays, which were apparently harmless to other tissues and organs of the body. So it had been decided that the person sent to recover the device should *leave his brain behind.* It would be kept in a safe place where it could execute its normal control functions by elaborate radio links. Would I submit to a surgical procedure that would completely remove my brain, which would then be placed in a life-support system at the Manned Spacecraft Center in Houston? Each input and output pathway, as it was severed, would be restored by a pair of microminiaturized radio transceivers, one attached precisely to the brain, the other to the nerve stumps in the empty cranium. No information would be lost, all the connectivity would be preserved. At first I was a bit reluctant. Would it really work? The Houston brain surgeons encouraged me. "Think of it," they said, "as a mere *stretching* of the nerves. If your brain were just moved over an *inch* in your skull, that would not alter or impair your mind. We're simply going to make the nerves indefinitely elastic by splicing radio links into them."

I was shown around the life-support lab in Houston and saw the sparkling new vat in which my brain would be placed, were I to agree. I met the large and brilliant support team of neurologists, hematologists, biophysicists, and electrical engineers, and after several days of discussions and demonstrations, I agreed to give it a try. I was subjected to an enormous array of blood tests, brain scans, experiments, interviews, and the like. They took down my autobiography at great length, recorded tedious lists of my beliefs, hopes, fears, and tastes. They even listed my favorite stereo recordings and gave me a crash session of psychoanalysis.

The day for surgery arrived at last and of course I was anesthetized and remember nothing of the operation itself. When I came out of anesthesia, I opened my eyes, looked around, and asked the inevitable, the traditional, the lamentably hackneyed postoperative question: "Where am I?" The nurse smiled down at me. "You're in Houston," she said, and I reflected that this still had a good chance of being the truth one way or another. She handed me a mirror. Sure enough, there were the tiny antennae poling up through their titanium ports cemented into my skull.

"I gather the operation was a success," I said. "I want to go see my brain." They led me (I was a bit dizzy and unsteady) down a long corridor and into the life-support lab. A cheer went up from the assembled support team, and I responded with what I hoped was a jaunty salute. Still feeling lightheaded, I was helped over to the life-support vat. I peered through the glass. There, floating in what looked like ginger ale, was undeniably a human brain, though it was almost covered with printed circuit chips, plastic tubules, electrodes, and other paraphernalia. "Is that mine?" I asked. "Hit the output transmitter switch there on the side of the vat and see for yourself," the project director replied. I moved the switch to OFF, and immediately slumped, groggy and nauseated, into the arms of the technicians, one of whom kindly restored the switch to its ON position. While I recovered my equilibrium and composure, I thought to myself: "Well, here I am sitting on a folding chair, staring through a piece of plate glass at my own brain. . . . But wait," I said to myself, "shouldn't I have thought, 'Here I am, suspended in a bubbling fluid, being stared at by my own eyes'?" I tried to think this latter thought. I tried to project into the tank, offering it hopefully to my brain, but I failed to carry off the exercise with any conviction. I tried again. "Here am *I*, Daniel Dennett, suspended in a bubbling fluid, being stared at by my own eyes." No, it just didn't work. Most puzzling and confusing. Being a philosopher of firm physicality conviction, I believed unswervingly that the tokening of my thoughts was occurring somewhere in my brain: yet, when I thought "here I am," where the thought occurred to me was *here,* outside the vat, where I, Dennett, was standing staring at my brain.

I tried and tried to think myself into the vat, but to no avail. I tried to build up to the task by doing mental exercises. I thought to myself, "The sun is shining *over there,*" five times in rapid succession, each time mentally ostending a different place: in order, the sunlit corner of the lab, the visible front lawn of the hospital, Houston, Mars, and Jupiter. I found I had little difficulty in getting my "there"'s to hop all over the celestial map with their proper references. I could loft a "there" in an instant through the farthest reaches of space, and then aim the next "there" with pinpoint accuracy at the upper left quadrant of a freckle on my arm. Why was I having such trouble with "there"? "Here in Houston" worked well enough, and so did "here in the lab," and even "here in this part of the lab," but "here in the vat" always seemed merely an unmeant mental mouthing. I tried closing my eyes while thinking it. This seemed to help, but still I couldn't manage to pull it off, except perhaps for a fleeting instant. I couldn't be sure. The discovery that I couldn't be sure was also unsettling. How did I know *where* I meant by "here" when I thought "here"? Could I *think* I meant one place when in fact I meant another? I didn't see how that could be admitted without untying the few bonds of intimacy between a person and his own mental life that had survived the onslaught of the brain scientists and philosophers, the physicalists and behaviorists. Perhaps I was incorrigible about where I *meant* when I said "here." But in my present circumstances it seemed that either I was doomed by sheer force of mental habit to thinking systematically false indexical thoughts, or where a person is (and hence where his thoughts are tokened for purposes of semantic analysis) is not necessarily where his brain, the physical seat of his soul, resides. Nagged by confusion, I attempted to orient myself by falling back on a favorite philosopher's ploy. I began naming things.

"Yorick," I said aloud to my brain, "you are my brain. The rest of my body, seated in this chair, I dub 'Hamlet.'" So here we all are: Yorick's my brain, Hamlet's my body, and I am Dennett. *Now*, where am I? And when I think "where am I?" where's that thought tokened? Is it tokened in my brain, lounging about in the vat, or right here between my ears where it *seems* to be tokened? Or nowhere? Its *temporal* coordinates give me no trouble; must it not have spatial coordinates as well? I began making a list of the alternatives.

1. *Where Hamlet goes, there goes Dennett.*   This principle was easily refuted by appeal to the familiar brain-transplant thought experiments so enjoyed by philosophers. If Tom and Dick switch brains, Tom is the fellow with Dick's former body—just ask him; he'll claim to be Tom, and tell you the most intimate details of Tom's autobiography. It was clear enough, then, that my current body and I could part company, but not likely that I could be separated from my brain. The rule of thumb that emerged so plainly from the thought experiments was that in a brain-transplant operation, one wanted to be the *donor*, not the recipient. Better to call such an operation a *body* transplant, in fact. So perhaps the truth was,

2. *Where Yorick goes, there goes Dennett.*   This was not at all appealing, however. How could I be in the vat and not about to go anywhere, when I was so obviously outside the vat looking in and beginning to make guilty plans to return to my room for a substantial lunch? This begged the question I realized, but it still seemed to be getting at something important. Casting about for some support for my

intuition, I hit upon a legalistic sort of argument that might have appealed to Locke.

Suppose, I argued to myself, I were now to fly to California, rob a bank, and be apprehended. In which state would I be tried: In California, where the robbery took place, or in Texas, where the brains of the outfit were located? Would I be a California felon with an out-of-state brain, or a Texas felon remotely controlling an accomplice of sorts in California? It seemed possible that I might beat such a rap just on the undecidability of that jurisdictional question, though perhaps it would be deemed an interstate, and hence Federal, offense. In any event, suppose I were convicted. Was it likely that California would be satisfied to throw Hamlet into the brig, knowing that Yorick was living the good life and luxuriously taking the waters in Texas? Would Texas incarcerate Yorick, leaving Hamlet free to take the next boat to Rio? This alternative appealed to me.

Barring capital punishment or other cruel and unusual punishment, the state would be obliged to maintain the life-support system for Yorick though they might move him from Houston to Leavenworth, and aside from the unpleasantness of the opprobrium, I, for one, would not mind at all and would consider myself a free man under those circumstances. If the state has an interest in forcibly relocating persons in institutions, it would fail to relocate *me* in any institution by locating Yorick there. If this were true, it suggested a third alternative.

3. *Dennett is wherever he thinks he is.*   Generalized, the claim was as follows: At any given time a person has a *point of view,* and the location of the point of view (which is determined internally by the content of the point of view) is also the location of the person.

Such a proposition is not without its perplexities, but to me it seemed a step in the right direction. The only trouble was that it seemed to place one in a heads-I-win/tails-you-lose situation of unlikely infallibility as regards location. Hadn't I myself often been wrong about where I was, and at least as often uncertain? Couldn't one get lost? Of course, but getting lost *geographically* is not the only way one might get lost. If one were lost in the woods one could attempt to reassure oneself with the consolation that at least one knew where one was: one was right *here* in the familiar surroundings of one's own body. Perhaps in this case one would not have drawn one's attention to much to be thankful for. Still, there were worse plights imaginable, and I wasn't sure I wasn't in such a plight right now.

Point of view clearly had something to do with personal location, but it was itself an unclear notion. It was obvious that the content of one's point of view was not the same as or determined by the content of one's beliefs or thoughts. For example, what should we say about the point of view of the Cinerama viewer who shrieks and twists in his seat as the roller-coaster footage overcomes his psychic distancing? Has he forgotten that he is safely seated in the theater? Here I was inclined to say that the person is experiencing an illusory shift in point of view. In other cases, my inclination to call such shifts illusory was less strong. The workers in laboratories and plants who handle dangerous materials by operating feedback-controlled mechanical arms and hands undergo a shift in point of view that is crisper and more pronounced than anything Cinerama can provoke. They can feel the heft and slipperiness of the containers they manipulate with their metal fingers. They know perfectly well where they are and are not fooled into false beliefs by the experience, yet it is as if they were inside the isolation chamber they are peering into. With mental effort, they can manage to shift their point of view back and forth, rather like making a transparent Necker cube or an Escher drawing change orientation before one's eyes. It does seem extravagant to suppose that in performing this bit of mental gymnastics, they are transporting *themselves* back and forth.

Still their example gave me hope. If I was in fact in the vat in spite of my intuitions, I might be able to train myself to adopt that point of view even as a matter of habit. I should dwell on images of myself comfortably floating in my vat, beaming volitions to that familiar body *out there*. I reflected that the ease or difficulty of this task was presumably independent of the truth about the location of one's brain. Had I been practicing before the operation, I might now be finding it second nature. You might now yourself try such a *trompe l'oeil*. Imagine you have written an inflammatory letter which has been published in the *Times*, the result of which is that the government has chosen to impound your brain for a probationary period of three years in its Dangerous Brain Clinic in Bethesda, Maryland. Your body of course is allowed freedom to earn a salary and thus continue its function of laying up income to be taxed. At this moment, however, your body is seated in an auditorium listening to a peculiar account by Daniel Dennett of his own similar experience. Try it. Think yourself to Bethesda, and then hark back longingly to your body, far away, and yet *seeming* so near. It is only with long-distance restraint (yours? the government's?) that you can control your impulse to get those hands clapping in polite applause before navigating the old body to the rest room and a well-deserved glass of evening sherry in the lounge.

The task of imagination is certainly difficult, but if you achieve your goal the results might be consoling.

Anyway, there I was in Houston, lost in thought as one might say, but not for long. My speculations were soon interrupted by the Houston doctors, who wished to test out my new prosthetic nervous system before sending me off on my hazardous mission. As I mentioned before, I was a bit dizzy at first, and not surprisingly, although I soon habituated myself to my new circumstances (which were, after all, well nigh indistinguishable from my old circumstances). My accommodation was not perfect, however, and to this day I continue to be plagued by minor coordination difficulties. The speed of light is fast, but finite, and as my brain and body move farther and farther apart, the delicate interaction of my feedback systems is thrown into disarray by the time lags. Just as one is rendered close to speechless by a delayed or echoic hearing of one's speaking voice so, for instance, I am virtually unable to track a moving object with my eyes whenever my brain and my body are more than a few miles apart. In most matters my impairment is scarcely detectable, though I can no longer hit a slow curve ball with the authority of yore. There are some compensations of course. Though liquor tastes as good as ever, and warms my gullet while corroding my liver, I can drink it in any quantity I please, without becoming the slightest bit inebriated, a curiosity some of my close friends may have noticed (though I occasionally have *feigned* inebriation, so as not to draw attention to my unusual circumstances). For similar reasons, I take aspirin orally for a sprained wrist, but if the pain persists I ask Houston to administer codeine to me *in vitro*. In times of illness the phone bill can be staggering.

But to return to my adventure. At length, both the doctors and I were satisfied that I was ready to undertake my subterranean mission. And so I left my brain in Houston and headed by helicopter for Tulsa. Well, in any case, that's the way it seemed to me. That's how I would put it, just off the top of my head as it were. On the trip I reflected further about my earlier anxieties and decided that my first postoperative speculations had been tinged with panic. The matter was not nearly as strange or metaphysical as I had been supposing. Where was I? In two places, clearly: both inside the vat and outside it. Just as one can stand with one foot in Connecticut and the other in Rhode Island, I was in two places at once. I had become one of those scattered individuals we used to hear so much about. The more I considered this answer, the more obviously true it appeared. But, strange to say, the more true it appeared, the less important the question to which it could be the true answer seemed. A sad, but not unprecedented, fate for a philosophical question to suffer. This answer did not completely satisfy me, of course. There lingered some question to which I should have liked an answer, which was neither "Where are all my various and sundry parts?" nor "What is my current point of view?" Or at least there seemed to be such a question. For it did seem undeniable that in some sense *I* and not merely *most of me* was descending into the earth under Tulsa in search of an atomic warhead.

When I found the warhead, I was certainly glad I had left my brain behind, for the pointer on the specially built Geiger counter I had brought with me was off the dial. I called Houston on my ordinary radio and told the operation control center of my position and my progress. In return, they gave me instructions for dismantling the vehicle, based upon my on-site observations. I had set to work with my cutting torch when all of a sudden a terrible thing happened. I went stone deaf. At first I thought it was only my radio earphones that had broken, but when I tapped on my helmet, I heard nothing. Apparently the auditory transceivers had gone on the fritz. I could no longer hear Houston or my own voice, but I could speak, so I started telling them what had happened. In midsentence, I knew something else had gone wrong. My vocal apparatus had become paralyzed. Then my right hand went limp—another transceiver had gone. I was truly in deep trouble. But worse was to follow. After a few more minutes, I went blind. I cursed my luck, and then I cursed the scientists who had led me into this grave peril. There I was, deaf, dumb, and blind, in a radioactive hole more than a mile under Tulsa. Then the last of my cerebral radio links broke, and suddenly I was faced with a new and even more shocking problem: whereas an instant before I had been buried alive in Oklahoma, now I was disembodied in Houston. My recognition of my new status was not immediate. It took me several very anxious minutes before it dawned on me that my poor body lay several hundred miles away, with heart pulsing and lungs respiring, but otherwise as dead as the body of any heart-transplant donor, its skull packed with useless, broken electronic gear. The shift in perspective I had earlier found well nigh impossible now seemed quite natural. Though I could think myself back into my body in the tunnel under Tulsa, it took some effort to sustain the illusion. For surely it was an illusion to suppose I was still in Oklahoma: I had lost all contact with that body.

It occurred to me then, with one of those rushes of revelation of which we should be suspicious, that I had stumbled upon an impressive demonstration of the immateriality of the soul based upon physicalist principles and premises. For as the last radio signal between Tulsa and

Houston died away, had I not changed location from Tulsa to Houston at the speed of light? And had I not accomplished this without any increase in mass? What moved from A to B at such speed was surely myself, or at any rate my soul or mind—the massless center of my being and home of my consciousness. My *point of view* had lagged somewhat behind, but I had already noted the indirect bearing of point of view on personal location. I could not see how a physicalist philosopher could quarrel with this except by taking the dire and counterintuitive route of banishing all talk of persons. Yet the notion of personhood was so well entrenched in everyone's world view, or so it seemed to me, that any denial would be as curiously unconvincing, as systematically disingenuous, as the Cartesian negation, "non sum."

The joy of philosophic discovery thus tided me over some very bad minutes or perhaps hours as the helplessness and hopelessness of my situation became more apparent to me. Waves of panic and even nausea swept over me, made all the more horrible by the absence of their normal body-dependent phenomenology. No adrenaline rush of tingles in the arms, no pounding heart, no premonitory salivation. I did feel a dread sinking feeling in my bowels at one point, and this tricked me momentarily into the false hope that I was undergoing a reversal of the process that landed me in this fix—a gradual undisembodiment. But the isolation and uniqueness of that twinge soon convinced me that it was simply the first of a plague of phantom body hallucinations that I, like any other amputee, would be all too likely to suffer.

My mood then was chaotic. On the one hand, I was fired up with elation of my philosophic discovery and was wracking my brain (one of the few familiar things I could still do), trying to figure out how to communicate my discovery to the journals; while on the other, I was bitter, lonely, and filled with dread and uncertainty. Fortunately, this did not last long, for my technical support team sedated me into a dreamless sleep from which I awoke, hearing with magnificent fidelity the familiar opening strains of my favorite Brahms piano trio. So that was why they had wanted a list of my favorite recordings! It did not take me long to realize that I was hearing the music without ears. The output from the stereo stylus was being fed through some fancy rectification circuitry directly into my auditory nerve. I was mainlining Brahms, an unforgettable experience for any stereo buff. At the end of the record it did not surprise me to hear the reassuring voice of the project director speaking into a microphone that was now my prosthetic ear. He confirmed my analysis of what had gone wrong and assured me that steps were being taken to re-embody me. He did not elaborate, and after a few more recordings, I found myself drifting off to sleep. My sleep lasted, I later learned, for the better part of a year, and when I awoke, it was to find myself fully restored to my senses. When I looked into the mirror, though, I was a bit startled to see an unfamiliar face. Bearded and a bit heavier, bearing no doubt a family resemblance to my former face, and with the same look of spritely intelligence and resolute character, but definitely a new face. Further self-explorations of an intimate nature left me no doubt that this was a new body, and the project director confirmed my conclusions. He did not volunteer any information on the past history of my new body and I decided (wisely, I think in retrospect) not to pry. As many philosophers unfamiliar with my ordeal have more recently speculated, the acquisitions of a new body leaves one's *person* intact. And after a period of adjustment to a new voice, new muscular strengths and weaknesses, and so forth, one's *personality* is by and large also preserved. More dramatic changes in personality have been routinely observed in people who have undergone extensive plastic surgery, to say nothing of sex-change operations, and I think no one contests the survival of the person in such cases. In any event I soon accommodated to my new body, to the point of being unable to recover any of its novelties to my consciousness or even memory. The view in the mirror soon became utterly familiar. That view, by the way, still revealed antennae, and so I was not surprised to learn that my brain had not been moved from its haven in the life-support lab.

I decided that good old Yorick deserved a visit. I and my new body, whom we might as well call Fortinbras, strode into the familiar lab to another round of applause from the technicians, who were of course congratulating themselves, not me. Once more I stood before the vat and contemplated poor Yorick, and on a whim I once again cavalierly flicked off the output transmitter switch. Imagine my surprise when nothing unusual happened. No fainting spell, no nausea, no noticeable change. A technician hurried to restore the switch to ON, but still I felt nothing. I demanded an explanation, which the project director hastened to provide. It seems that before they had even operated on the first occasion, they had constructed a computer duplicate of my brain, reproducing both the complete information-processing structure and the computational speed of my brain in a giant computer program. After the operation, but before they had dared to send me off on my mission to Oklahoma, they had run this computer system and Yorick side by side. The incoming signals from Hamlet were sent simultaneously to Yorick's transceivers and to the computer's array of inputs. And the outputs from

Yorick were not only beamed back to Hamlet, my body; they were recorded and checked against the simultaneous output of the computer program, which was called "Hubert" for reasons obscure to me. Over days and even weeks, the outputs were identical and synchronous, which of course did not *prove* that they had succeeded in copying the brain's functional structure, but the empirical support was greatly encouraging.

Hubert's input, and hence activity, had been kept parallel with Yorick's during my disembodied days. And now, to demonstrate this, they had actually thrown the master switch that put Hubert for the first time in on-line control of my body—not Hamlet, of course, but Fortinbras. (Hamlet, I learned, had never been recovered from its underground tomb and could be assumed by this time to have largely returned to the dust. At the head of my grave still lay the magnificent bulk of the abandoned device, with the word STUD emblazoned on its side in large letters—a circumstance which may provide archeologists of the next century with a curious insight into the burial rites of their ancestors.)

The laboratory technicians now showed me the master switch, which had two positions, labeled B, for Brain (they didn't know my brain's name was Yorick) and H, for Hubert. The switch did indeed point to H, and they explained to me that if I wished, I could switch it back to B. With my heart in my mouth (and my brain in its vat), I did this. Nothing happened. A click, that was all. To test their claim, and with the master switch now set at B, I hit Yorick's output transmitter switch on the vat and sure enough, I began to faint. Once the output switch was turned back on and I had recovered my wits, so to speak, I continued to play with the master switch, flipping it back and forth. I found that with the exception of the transitional click, I could detect no trace of a difference. I could switch in mid-utterance, and the sentence I had begun speaking under the control of Yorick was finished without a pause or hitch of any kind under the control of Hubert. I had a spare brain, a prosthetic device which might some day stand me in very good stead, were some mishap to befall Yorick. Or alternatively, I could keep Yorick as a spare and use Hubert. It didn't seem to make any difference which I chose, for the wear and tear and fatigue on my body did not have any debilitating effect on either brain, whether or not it was actually causing the motions of my body, or merely spilling its output into thin air.

The one truly unsettling aspect of this new development was the prospect, which was not long in dawning on me, of someone detaching the spare—Hubert or Yorick, as the case might be—from Fortinbras and hitching it to yet another body—some Johnny-come-lately

Rosencrantz or Guidenstern. Then (if not before) there would be *two* people, that much was clear. One would be me, and the other would be a sort of super-twin brother. If there were two bodies, one under the control of Hubert and the other being controlled by Yorick, then which would the world recognize as the true Dennett? And whatever the rest of the world decided, which one would be *me*? Would I be the Yorick-brained one, in virtue of Yorick's causal priority and former intimate relationship with the original Dennett body, Hamlet? That seemed a bit legalistic, a bit too redolent of the arbitrariness of consanguinity and legal possession, to be convincing at the metaphysical level. For suppose that before the arrival of the second body on the scene, I had been keeping Yorick as the spare for years, and letting Hubert's output drive my body—that is, Fortinbras—all that time. The Hubert-Fortinbras couple would seem then by squatter's rights (to combat one legal intuition with another) to be the true Dennett and the lawful inheritor of everything that was Dennett's. This was an interesting question, certainly, but not nearly so pressing as another question that bothered me. My strongest intuition was that in such an eventuality *I* would survive so long as *either* brain-body couple remained intact, but I had mixed emotions about whether I should want both to survive.

I discussed my worries with the technicians and the project director. The prospect of two Dennetts was abhorrent to me, I explained, largely for social reasons. I didn't want to be my own rival for the affections of my wife, nor did I like the prospect of the two Dennetts sharing my modest professor's salary. Still more vertiginous and distasteful, though, was the idea of knowing *that much* about another person, while he had the very same goods on me. How could we ever face each other? My colleagues in the lab argued that I was ignoring the bright side of the matter. Weren't there many things I wanted to do but, being only one person, had been unable to do? Now one Dennett could stay at home and be the professor and family man, while the other could strike out on a life of travel and adventure—missing the family of course, but happy in the knowledge that the other Dennett was keeping the home fires burning. I could be faithful and adulterous at the same time. I could even cuckold myself—to say nothing of other more lurid possibilities my colleagues were all too ready to force upon my overtaxed imagination. But my ordeal in Oklahoma (or was it Houston?) had made me less adventurous, and I shrank from this opportunity that was being offered (though of course I was never quite sure it was being offered to *me* in the first place).

There was another prospect even more disagreeable: that the spare, Hubert or Yorick as the case might be, would be detached from any input from Fortinbras and just left detached. Then, as in the other case, there would be two Dennetts, or at least two claimants to my name and possessions, one embodied in Fortinbras, and the other sadly, miserably disembodied. Both selfishness and altruism bade me take steps to prevent this from happening. So I asked that measures be taken to ensure that no one could ever tamper with the transceiver connections or the master switch without my (our? no, *my*) knowledge and consent. Since I had no desire to spend my life guarding the equipment in Houston, it was mutually decided that all the electronic connections in the lab would be carefully locked. Both those that controlled the life-support system for Yorick and those that controlled the power supply for Hubert would be guarded with fail-safe devices, and I would take the only master switch, outfitted for radio remote control, with me wherever I went. I carry it strapped around my waist and—wait a moment—*here it is*. Every few months I reconnoiter the situation by switching channels. I do this only in the presence of friends, of course, for if the other channel were, heaven forbid, either dead or otherwise occupied, there would have to be somebody who had my interests at heart to switch it back, to bring me back from the void. For while I could feel, see, hear, and otherwise sense whatever befell my body, subsequent to such a switch, I'd be unable to control it. By the way, the two positions on the switch are intentionally unmarked, so I never have the faintest idea whether I am switching from Hubert to Yorick or vice versa. (Some of you may think that in this case I really don't know *who* I am, let alone where I am. But such reflections no longer make much of a dent on my essential Dennettness, on my own sense of who I am. If it is true that in one sense I don't know who I am then that's another one of your philosophical truths of underwhelming significance.)

In any case, every time I've flipped the switch so far, nothing has happened. *So let's give it a try. . . .*

"THANK GOD! I THOUGHT YOU'D NEVER FLIP THAT SWITCH! You can't imagine how horrible it's been these last two weeks—but now you know; it's your turn in purgatory. How I've longed for this moment! You see, about two weeks ago—excuse me, ladies and gentlemen, but I've got to explain this to my . . . um, brother, I guess you could say, but he's just told you the facts, so you'll understand—about two weeks ago our two brains drifted just a bit out of synch. I don't know whether *my* brain is now Hubert or Yorick, any more than you do, but in any case, the two brains drifted apart, and of course once the process started, it snowballed, for I was in a slightly different receptive state for the input we both received, a difference that was soon magnified. In no time at all the illusion that I was in control of my body—our body—was completely dissipated. There was nothing I could do—no way to call you. YOU DIDN'T EVEN KNOW I EXISTED! It's been like being carried around in a cage, or better, like being possessed—hearing my own voice say things I didn't mean to say, watching in frustration as my own hands performed deeds I hadn't intended. You'd scratch our itches, but not the way I would have, and you kept me awake, with your tossing and turning. I've been totally exhausted, on the verge of a nervous breakdown, carried around helplessly by your frantic round of activities, sustained only by the knowledge that some day you'd throw the switch.

"Now it's your turn, but at least you'll have the comfort of knowing *I* know you're in there. Like an expectant mother, I'm eating—or at any rate tasting, smelling, seeing—for *two* now, and I'll try to make it easy for you. Don't worry. Just as soon as this colloquium is over, you and I will fly to Houston, and we'll see what can be done to get one of us another body. You can have a female body—your body could be any color you like. But let's think it over. I tell you what—to be fair, if we both want this body, I promise I'll let the project director flip a coin to settle which of us gets to keep it and which then gets to choose a new body. That should guarantee justice, shouldn't it? In any case, I'll take care of you, I promise. These people are my witnesses.

"Ladies and gentlemen, this talk we have just heard is not exactly the talk *I* would have given, but I assure you that everything he said was perfectly true. And now if you'll excuse me, I think I'd—we'd—better sit down."

Feminist Perspectives on the Self

Diana Meyers

The topic of the self has long been salient in feminist philosophy, for it is pivotal to questions about personhood, identity, the body, and agency that feminism must address. In some aspects, Simone de Beauvoir's trenchant observation, "He is the Subject, he is the Absolute—she is the Other," sums up why the self is such an important issue for feminism. To be the Other is to be the non-subject, the non-person, the non-agent—in short, the mere body. In law, in customary practice, and in cultural stereotypes, women's selfhood has been systematically subordinated, diminished, and belittled, when it has not been outright denied. Since women have been cast as lesser forms of the masculine individual, the paradigm of the self that has gained ascendancy in U.S. popular culture and in Western philosophy is derived from the experience of the predominantly white and heterosexual, mostly economically advantaged men who have wielded social, economic, and political power and who have dominated the arts, literature, the media, and scholarship. Responding to this state of affairs, feminist philosophical work on the self has taken three main tacks: (1) critique of established views of the self, (2) reclamation of women's selfhood, and (3) reconceptualization of the self to incorporate women's experience. . . .

1. Critique

Two views of the self have been prominent in contemporary Anglo-American moral and political philosophy—a Kantian ethical subject and homo economicus. Both of these conceptions see the individual as a free and rational chooser and actor—an autonomous agent. Nevertheless, they differ in their emphasis. The Kantian ethical subject uses reason to transcend cultural norms and to discover absolute moral truth, whereas homo economicus uses reason to rank desires in a coherent order and to figure out how to maximize desire satisfaction. Whether the self is identified with pure abstract reason or with the instrumental rationality of the marketplace, though, these conceptions of the self isolate the individual from personal relationships and larger social forces. For the Kantian ethical subject, emotional bonds and social conventions imperil objectivity and undermine commitment to duty. For homo economicus, it makes no difference what social forces shape one's desires provided they do not result from coercion or fraud, and one's ties to other people are to be factored into one's calculations and planning along with the rest of one's desires. Some feminist philosophers modify and defend these conceptions of the self. But their decontextualized individualism and their privileging of reason over other capacities trouble many feminist philosophers.

Twentieth century philosophy's regnant conceptions of the self minimize the personal and moral import of unchosen circumstances and interpersonal relationships. They eclipse family, friendship, passionate love, and community, and they downplay the difficulty of resolving conflicts that arise between these commitments and personal values and aspirations. Since dependency is dismissed as a defective form of selfhood, caregiving responsibilities vanish along with children, the disabled, and the frail elderly. Prevailing conceptions of the self ignore the multiple, sometimes fractious sources of social identity constituted by one's gender, sexual orientation, race, class, age, ethnicity, and so forth. Structural domination and subordination do not penetrate the "inner citadel" of selfhood. Likewise, these conceptions deny the complexity of the intrapsychic world of unconscious fan-tasies, fears, and desires, and they overlook the ways in which such materials intrude upon conscious life. The homogenized—you might say sterilized—rational subject is not prey to ambivalence, anxiety, obsession, prejudice, hatred, or violence. A disembodied mind, the body is peripheral—a source of desires for homo economicus to weigh and a distracting temptation for the Kantian ethical subject. Age, looks, sexuality, and physical competencies are extraneous to the self. As valuable as the capacities for rational analysis and free choice undoubtedly are, it is hard to believe that there is nothing more to the self.

Feminist philosophers have charged that these views are, at best, incomplete and, at worst, fundamentally misleading. Many feminist critiques take the question of who provides the paradigm for these conceptions as their point of departure. Who models this free, rational self? Although represented as genderless, sexless, raceless, ageless, and classless, feminists argue that the Kantian ethical subject and homo economicus mask a white, healthy, youthfully middle-aged, middle-class, heterosexual MAN. He is pictured in two principle roles—as an impartial judge or legislator reflecting on principles and deliberating about policies and as a self-interested bargainer and contractor wheeling and dealing in the marketplace. It is no accident that politics and commerce are both domains from which women have historically been excluded. It is no accident either that the philosophers who originated these views of the self typically endorsed this exclusion. Deeming women emotional and unprincipled, these thinkers advocated confining women to the domestic sphere where their vices could be neutralized, even transformed into virtues, in the role of submissive wife and nurturant mother.

Feminist critics point out, furthermore, that this misogynist heritage cannot be remedied simply by condemning these traditional constraints and advocating equal rights for women, for these conceptions of the self are themselves gendered. In western culture, the mind and reason are coded masculine, whereas the body and emotion are coded feminine (Lloyd 1992). To identify the self with the rational mind is, then, to masculinize the self. If selfhood is not impossible for women, it is only because they resemble men in certain essential respects—they are not altogether devoid of rational will. Yet, feminine selves are necessarily deficient, for they only mimic and approximate the masculine ideal.

Problematic, as well, is the way in which these gendered conceptions of the self contribute to the valorization of the masculine and the stigmatization of the feminine. The masculine realm of rational selfhood is a realm of moral decency—principled respect for others and conscientious fidelity to duty—and of prudent good sense—adherence to shrewd, fulfilling, long-range life plans. However, femininity is associated with emotionally rooted concern for family and friends that spawns favoritism and compromises principles. Likewise, femininity is associated with immersion in unpredictable domestic exigencies that forever jeopardize the best-laid plans and often necessitate resorting to hasty retreats or charting new directions. By comparison, the masculinized self appears to be a sturdy fortress of integrity. How flattering! The self is essentially masculine, and the masculine self is essentially good and wise.

Feminists object that this philosophical consolidation of the preeminence of the masculine over the feminine rests on untenable assumptions about the transparency of the self, the immunity of the self to noxious social influences, and the reliability of reason as a corrective to distorted moral judgment. Today people grow up in social environments in which culturally normative prejudice persists, even in communities where overt forms of bigotry are strictly proscribed (Meyers 1994). Although official cultural norms uphold the values of equality and tolerance, cultures continue to transmit camouflaged messages of the inferiority of historically subordinated social groups through stereotypes and other imagery. These deeply ingrained schemas commonly structure attitudes, perception, and judgment despite the individual's conscious good will (Valian 1998). As a result, people often consider themselves objective and fair, and yet they systematically discriminate against "different" others while favoring members of their own social group (Piper 1990; Young 1990). Fortified by culture and ensconced in the unconscious, such prejudice cannot be dispelled through rational reflection alone (Meyers 1994). In effect, then, the Kantian moral subject countenances "innocent" wrongdoing and occluded reinforcement of the social stratification that privileges the minority of men whom this conception takes as paradigmatic.

These oversights necessitate reconceptualizing the self in two respects. To account for the residual potency of this form of prejudice, feminists urge, the self must be understood as socially situated and murkily heterogeneous. To account for the self's ability to discern and resist culturally normative prejudice, the moral subject must not be reduced to the capacity for reason.

Complementing this line of argument, a number of feminists argue that conceptualizing the self as a seamless whole has invidious social consequences. To realize this ideal, it is necessary to repress inner diversity and conflict and to police the boundaries of the purified self. Alien desires and impulses are consigned to the unconscious, but this unconscious material inevitably intrudes upon conscious life and influences people's attitudes and desires. In particular, the feared and despised Other within is projected onto "other" social groups, and hatred and contempt are redirected at these imagined enemies (Scheman 1993; Kristeva 1991). Misogyny and other forms of bigotry are thus borne of the demand that the self be unitary together with the impossibility of meeting this demand. Worse still, these irrational hatreds cannot be cured unless this demand is repudiated, but to repudiate this demand is to be resigned to a degraded, feminized self. Far from functioning as the guarantor of moral probity, the Kantian moral subject is the condition of the possibility of intractable animosity and injustice.

Another strand of feminist critique targets homo economicus's preoccupation with independence and planning. In an eery suspension of biological reality, selves are conceived as sufficient unto themselves. No one seems to be born and raised, for birth mothers and caregivers are driven offstage (Baier 1987; Code 1987; Held 1987; Benhabib and Cornell 1987; Kittay 1999). The self appears to materialize on its own, endowed with a starter set of basic desires, ready to select additional desires and construct overarching goals, and skilled in performing instrumental rationality tasks. No one's powers ever seem to deteriorate either, for time is suspended along with biology. Since dependency is denied, no morally significant preconsensual or nonconsensual entanglements at the beginning or the end of life need be acknowledged. All affiliations are to be freely chosen, and all transactions are to be freely negotiated. The repudiation of feminine caregiving underwrites the illusion of independence, and the illusion of independence underwrites homo economicus's voluntarism.

To achieve maximal fulfillment, homo economicus must organize his chosen pursuits into a rational life plan. He must decide which desires are most urgent; he must ensure that his desires are co-satisfiable; and he must ascertain the most efficient way to satisfy this set of desires. Madcap spontaneity and seat-of-the-pants improvisation are registered as defeats for "The Man with the Plan." Not only is this vision of a life governed by a self-chosen plan distinctly middleclass, it is gendered (Addelson 1994; Walker 1999). The mother coping with the vagaries of early childhood and the wife accommodating her man's plan are the antitheses of this conception of the self. Uncertain of where they are ultimately headed and seldom sure how to achieve the goals they embrace as they go along, these women violate norms of selfhood. Ironically, middleclass men who grow old also have difficulty measuring up to homo economicus's standards of control. Unable to count on continued health and vigor, unable to anticipate the onset of serious disease or disabling conditions, unable finally to outwit the grim reaper, affluent elderly men violate norms of selfhood along with women and the poor. The price of denying the relationality of the self and idolizing rational self-regulation is that full selfhood eludes all but a lucky, albeit transitory, male elite.

A further problem with this view from a feminist standpoint is that it fails to furnish an adequate account of internalized oppression and the process of overcoming it. It is common for women to comport themselves in a feminine fashion, to scale down their aspirations, and to embrace gender-compliant goals (Bartky 1990; Babbitt 1993). Feminists account for this phenomenon by explaining that women internalize patriarchal values and norms—that is, these pernicious values and norms become integrated in the cognitive, emotional, and conative structure of the self. Once embedded in a woman's psychic economy, internalized oppression conditions her desires. To maximize satisfaction of her desires, then, would be to collaborate in her own oppression. Paradoxically, the more completely she fulfills these desires, the worse off she becomes. Advantaged as he is, homo economicus can safely accept his desires as given and proceed without ado to orchestrate a plan to satisfy them. But women and members of other subordinated groups can ill-afford such complacency, and homo economicus's instrumental reason is too superficial a form of mastery to serve their interests (Babbitt 1993). They need a conception of the self that renders emancipatory transformation of one's values and projects intelligible.

Feminist critique exposes the partiality of the ostensibly universal Kantian ethical subject and homo economicus. These conceptions of the self are: 1) androcentric because they replicate masculine stereotypes and ideals; 2) sexist because they demean anything that smacks of the feminine; and 3) masculinist because they help to perpetuate male dominance. . . .

3. Reconceptualizations

3.1. The Nature of the Self

The primary task of a philosophy of the self is to clarify what makes something a self. Feminist philosophers are acutely aware that this is not a value-free task. To get an analysis of the nature of the self off the ground, one must decide which entities count as selves (or, at least, which entities are noncontroversially counted as selves within one's linguistic community). Since we regard selves as valuable—as members of our moral community and as worthy of respect—these judgments are in part judgments about which entities are valuable. Moreover, values enter into these judgments because we consider selves to be the sorts of things that can achieve (or fail to achieve) ideals of selfhood. Thus, philosophical accounts of the self have implications for conceptions of what it is to lead a good life. As we have seen, many feminist philosophers argue that it is a mistake to hold that rationality alone is essential to the self and that the ideal self is transparent, unified, coherent, and independent, for they discern misogynist subtexts in the atomistic individualism of the Kantian ethical subject and homo economicus (see Section 1). It is incumbent on feminist philosophers, then, to develop more satisfactory accounts of the self—accounts that are compatible with respect for women. Thus, a number of feminist philosophers propose reconstructions of alternative theories of the nature of the self.

Three traditions have been especially influential in recent feminist thought—classic psychoanalysis, objective relations theory, and post-structuralism. Feminist philosophers gravitate toward these approaches to understanding selfhood because they do not share the drawbacks that prompt feminist critique of the Kantian ethical subject and homo economicus. None of these approaches regards the self as homogeneous or transparent; none supposes that a self should be coherent and speak in a single voice; none removes the self from its cultural or interpersonal setting; none sidelines the body. In appropriating these views, feminists bring out their implications in regard to gender, incorporate feminist insights into these theories, and modify the theories to address feminist concerns.

Julia Kristeva transposes the classic Freudian conception of the self and the distinction between consciousness and the unconscious into an explicitly gendered discursive framework (Kristeva 1980). For Kristeva, the self is a subject of enunciation—a speaker who can use the pronoun 'I'. But speakers are not unitary, nor are they fully in control of what they say because discourse is bifurcated. The symbolic dimension of language, which is characterized by referential signs and linear logic, corresponds to consciousness and control. The clear, dry prose of scientific research reports epitomizes symbolic discourse. The semiotic dimension of language, which is characterized by figurative language, cadences, and intonations, corresponds to the unruly, passion-fueled unconscious. The ambiguities and nonstandard usages of poetry epitomize semiotic discourse. These paradigms notwithstanding, Kristeva maintains that all discourse combines elements of both registers. Every intelligible utterance relies on semantic conventions, and every utterance has a tone, even if it is a dull monotone. This contention connects Kristeva's account to feminist concerns about gender and the self. Since the rational orderliness of the symbolic is culturally coded masculine while the affect-laden allure of the semiotic is culturally coded feminine, it follows that no discourse is purely masculine or purely feminine. The masculine symbolic and the feminine semiotic are equally indispensable to the speaking subject, whatever this individual's socially assigned gender may be. It is not possible, then, to be an unsulliedly masculine self or an unsulliedly feminine self. Every subject of enunciation—every self—amalgamates masculine and feminine discursive modalities.

Like the unconscious in classic psychoanalytic theory, the semiotic decenters the self. One may try to express one's thoughts in definite, straightforward language, yet because of the semiotic aspects of one's utterances, what one says carries no single meaning and is amenable to being interpreted in more than one way. In Kristeva's view, this is all to the good, for accessing the semiotic—that which is conveyed, often inadvertently, by the style of an utterance—kindles social critique. The semiotic gives expression to repressed, unconscious material. According to Kristeva, what society systematically represses provides clues to what is oppressive about society and how society needs to be changed. Thus, she discerns a vital ethical potential in the semiotic (Kristeva 1987). Since this ethical potential is explicitly linked to the feminine, moreover, Kristeva's account of the self displaces "masculine" adherence to principle as the prime mode of ethical agency and recognizes the urgent need for a "feminine" ethical approach. Viewing the self as a "questionable-subject-in-process"—a subject who is responsive to the encroachments of semiotic material into conscious life and who is therefore without a fixed or unitary identity—and valorizing the dissident potential of this decentered subjectivity, Kristeva seeks to neutralize the fear of the inchoate feminine that, in her view, underwrites misogyny. In one respect, Nancy Chodorow's appropriation of object relations theory parallels Kristeva's project of reclaiming and revaluing femininity, for Chodorow's account of the relational self reclaims and revalues feminine mothering capacities. But whereas Kristeva focuses on challenging the homogeneous self and the bright line between reason, on the one hand, and emotion and desire, on the other, Chodorow focuses on challenging the self-subsisting self with its sharp self-other boundaries. Chodorow's claim that the self is inextricable from interpersonal relationships calls into question the decontextualized individualism of the Kantian ethical subject and homo economicus.

Chodorow sees the self as relational in several respects (Chodorow 1981). Every child is cared for by an adult or adults, and every individual is shaped for better or worse by this emotionally charged interaction. As a result of feelings of need and moments of frustration, the infant becomes differentiated from its primary caregiver and develops a sense of separate identity. Concomitantly, a distinctive personality emerges. By selectively internalizing and recombining elements of their experience with other people, children develop characteristic traits and dispositions. Moreover, Chodorow attributes the development of a key interpersonal capacity to nurturance. A caregiver who is experienced as warmly solicitous is internalized as a "good internal mother" (Chodorow 1980). Children gain a sense of their worthiness by internalizing the nurturance they receive and directing it toward themselves, and they learn to respect and respond to other people by internalizing their experience of nurturance and projecting it toward others. Whereas Kristeva understands the self as a dynamic interplay between the feminine semiotic and the masculine symbolic, Chodorow understands the self as fundamentally relational and thus linked to cultural norms of feminine interpersonal responsiveness. For Chodorow, the rigidly differentiated, compulsively rational, stubbornly independent self is a masculine defensive formation—a warped form of the rational self—that develops as a result of fathers' negligible involvement in childcare.

Feminist philosophers have noted strengths and weaknesses in both of these views. For example, Kristeva's questionable-subject-in-process seems to enshrine and endorse the very gender dichotomy that causes women so much grief. Yet, Chodorow's rational self seems to glorify weak individuation and scorn the independence and self-assertiveness that many women desperately need. Still, Kristeva's analyses of the psychic, social, and political potency of gender figurations underscore the need for feminist counter-imagery to offset culturally entrenched, patriarchal images of womanhood. And Chodorow's appreciation of the relational self together with her diagnosis of the damage wrought by hyperindividuation advances feminist demands for equitable parenting practices. These contributions notwithstanding, both of these views have come under attack for heterosexist biases as well as for inattention to other forms of difference among women.

Critical race theorists and poststructuralists have been particularly vocal about this failure to come to grips with the diversity of gender, and they have offered accounts of the self designed to accommodate difference. Poststructuralist Judith Butler maintains that personal identity—the sense that there are answers to the questions 'who am I?' and 'what am I like?'—is an illusion (Butler 1990). The self is merely an unstable discursive node—a shifting confluence of multiple discursive currents—and sexed/gendered identity is merely a "corporeal style"—the imitation and repeated enactment of ubiquitous norms. For Butler, psycho-dynamic accounts of the self, including Kristeva's and Chodorow's, camouflage the performative nature of the self and collaborate in the cultural conspiracy that maintains the illusion that one has an emotionally anchored, interior identity that is derived from one's biological nature, which is manifest in one's genitalia. Such accounts are pernicious. In concealing the ways in which normalizing regimes deploy power to enforce the performative routines that construct "natural" sexed/gendered bodies together with debased, "unnatural" bodies, they obscure the arbitrariness of the constraints that are being imposed and deflect resistance to these constraints. The solution, in Butler's view, is to question the categories of biological sex, polarized gender, and determinate sexuality that serve as markers of personal identity, to treat the construction of identity as a site of political contestation, and to embrace the subversive potential of unorthodox performances and parodic identities.

African American feminists are less sanguine than poststructuralists about the felicitous social impact of playful deviations from norms and the laughter they may prompt (Williams 1991; Crenshaw 1993). Nevertheless, some of them have adapted poststructuralist theory to the purposes of critical race theory. Noting that gender, race, and class stratification do not operate in isolation from one another but rather interact to produce compound effects, these theorists conceive of the individual as an intersectional subject—a site where structures of domination and subordination converge (King 1988; Crenshaw 1993). Inter-sectional theory does not purport to offer a comprehensive theory of the self. Its aim is to capture those aspects of selfhood that are conditioned by membership in subordinated or privileged social groups. Accenting the liabilities of belonging to more than one subordinated group, Kimberle Crenshaw likens the position of such individuals to that of a pedestrian hit by several speeding vehicles simultaneously, and Maria Lugones likens their position to that of a stateless border-dweller who is not at home anywhere (Crenshaw 1991; Lugones 1992). Nevertheless, some theorists of mixed ancestry embrace border-dwelling as a model of positive identity (Anzaldua 1987; Alcoff 1995). Moreover, proponents of the intersectional self credit multiply oppressed people with a certain epistemic advantage. In virtue of their suffering and alienation, these individuals are well situated not only to discern which values and practices in their heritage deserve allegiance but also to identify shortcomings in the traditions of the groups to which they belong. Thus, African American women are acutely aware of racism within feminism and sexism within the struggle for racial justice. Their intersectional positioning and subjectivity makes such insight virtually unavoidable.

By and large, recent feminist philosophy of the self reflects skepticism about modernist, unitary accounts of the self. In seeking to remedy the androcentric biases of the latter views, feminist philosophers emphasize features of selfhood that other philosophical schools neglect, including intersubjectivity, heterogeneity, and social construction. Still, some contemporary feminist philosophers express concern that the sorts of conceptions I have sketched are detrimental to feminist aims. Influenced by Jurgen Habermas's communicative ethics, Seyla Benhabib refuses to join poststructuralists in declaring the death of the autonomous, self-reflective individual who is capable of taking responsibility and acting on principle (Benhabib 1995). Although Benhabib is committed to viewing people as socially situated, interpersonally bonded, and embodied, she is also committed to the feasibility of rational philosophical justification of universal moral norms. Moreover, she argues that a narrative conception of the self renders the idea of a core self and coherent identity intelligible without suppressing difference and without insulating the self from social relations (Benhabib 1999). Autobiographical stories can include the many voices within us and the many relationships we have experienced, and these stories are constantly under revision, for they are always being contested by our associates' disparate self-narratives with their divergent versions of events. Nevertheless, these narratives do not collapse into incoherence, and they presuppose a core capacity to describe and reflect on one's experience. For Benhabib, this view of selfhood and reason is indispensable to feminist emancipatory objectives. . . .

4. Conclusion

As this article attests, there is tremendous foment and variety within the field of feminist work on the self. Yet, in reviewing this literature, I have been struck by a recurrent theme—the inextricability of metaphysical issues about the self from moral and political theory. Feminist critiques of regnant philosophical theories of the self expose the normative underpinnings of these theories. Feminist analyses of women's agentic capacities both acknowledge traditional feminine social contributions and provide accounts of how women can overcome oppressive norms and practices. Feminist reconstructions of the nature of the self are interwoven with arguments that draw out the emancipatory benefits of conceiving the self one way rather than another. There is nothing surprising, to be sure, about the salience of normative concerns in feminist philosophizing. Still, I mention it because I believe that feminists' attention to political concerns leads to fresh questions and also that asking novel questions enriches philosophical understanding of the self. Moreover, I would urge that this forthrightness about the political viewpoint that informs philosophy is a virtue, for overlooking the political suppositions and implications of esoteric philosophical view has led to considerable mischief.

References

The following works are cited:

Addelson, Kathryn Pyne. 1994. *Moral Passages:* New York: Routledge.

Alcoff, Linda. 1995. "Mestizo Identity." In *American Mixed Race: The Culture of Microdiversity,* ed., Naomi Zack, 257–278. Lanham, MD and London: Rowman and Littlefield, 1995.

Anzaldua, Gloria. 1987. *Borderlands: The New Mestiza/La Frontera.* San Fransisco: Spinters/Aunt Lute.

Babbitt, Susan E. 1993. "Feminism and Objective Interests? The Role of Transformation Experiences in Rational Deliberation." In *Feminist Epistemologies,* eds., Linda Alcoff and Elizabeth Potter. New York: Routledge, 1993.

Baier, Annette. 1997. "Trust and Anti-Trust." *Ethics* 96 (January 1986): 231–260. ALSO IN: *Feminist Social Thought,* ed., Diana Tietjens Meyers. New York: Routledge, 1997.

Baier, Susan. 1987. "The Need for More than Justice." In *Science, Morality, and Feminist Theory,* eds., Marsha Hanen and Kai Nielsen. Minneapolis: University of Minnesota Press.

Bartky, Sandra Lee. 1990. *Femininity and Domination.* New York: Routledge.

Benhabib, Seyla. 1999. "Sexual Difference and Collective Identities: The New Global Constellation." *Signs* 24: 335–361.

Benhabib, Seyla, and Drucilla Cornell, eds. 1987. *Feminism as Critique.* Minneapolis: University of Minnesota Press.

Benhabib, Seyla, et al. 1995 *Feminist Contentions.* New York: Routledge.

Butler, Judith. 1990. "Gender Trouble, Feminist Theory, and Psychoanalytic Discourse." In *Feminism/Postmodernism,* ed., Linda Nicholson. New York: Routledge.

Chodorow, Nancy. 1980. "Gender, Relation, and Difference in Psychoanalytic Perspective," In *The Future of Difference,* ed., Hester Eisenstein and Alice Jardine. Boston: G.K. Hall.

Chodorow, Nancy. 1981. "On the Reproduction of Mothering: A Methodological Debate." *Signs* 6: 500–514.

Code, Lorraine. 1987. "Second Persons." In *Science, Morality, and Feminist Theory* (Supplement to *Canadian Journal of Philosophy* 13), ed., Marsha Hanen and Kai Nielsen. Calgary: University of Calgary Press.

Crenshaw, Kimberlé. 1991. "Demarginalizing the Intersection of Race and Sex: A Black Feminist Critique of Antidiscrimination Doctrine, Feminist Theory, and Antiracist Politics." In *Feminist Legal Theory,* eds. Katherine T. Bartlett and Rosanne Kennedy. Boulder: Westview Press.

Crenshaw, Kimberlé. 1993. "Beyond Race and Misogyny: Black Feminism and 2 Live Crew." In *Words that Wound,* ed. Mari J. Matsuda, et al. Boulder: Westview Press.

Hartsock, Nancy. 1983. *Money, Sex, Power.* New York: Longman.

Held, Virginia. 1987. "Feminism and Moral Theory." In *Women and Moral Theory,* eds., Eva Feder Kittay and Diana T. Meyers. Totowa: Rowman and Littlefield. ALSO IN: *Feminist Social Thought* (Meyers 1997).

King, Deborah K. 1988. "Multiple Jeopardy, Multiple Consciousness: The Context of a Black Feminist Ideology." *Signs* 14(1): 42–72. ALSO IN: *Feminist Social Thought* (Meyers 1997).

Kittay, Eva Feder. 1999. *Love's Labor.* New York: Routledge.

Kristeva, Julia. 1980. *Desire in Language,* eds., Thomas Gora, Alice Jardine, and Leon Roudiez (Trans). New York: Columbia University Press.

Kristeva, Julia. 1987. *Tales of Love,* Leon Roudiez (Trans). New York: Columbia University Press.

Kristeva, Julia. 1991. *Strangers to Ourselves,* Leon Roudiez (Trans.). New York: Columbia University Press.

Lloyd, Genevieve. 1992. "Maleness, Metaphor, and the 'Crisis' of Reason." In *A Mind of One's Own,* eds., Louise Antony and Charlotte Witt. Boulder: Westview Press.

Lugones, María. 1992. "On 'Borderlands/La Frontera': An Interpretive Essay." *Hypatia* 7:4 (Fall): 31–37.

Piper, Adrian M.S. 1990. "Higher-Order Discrimination." In *Identity, Character and Morality,* eds., Owen Flanagan and Amelie Okensberg Rorty. Cambridge: MIT Press.

Scheman, Naomi. 1993. *Engenderings.* New York: Routledge.

Valian, Virginia. 1998. *Why So Slow? The Advancement of Women.* Cambridge: MIT Press.

Walker, Margaret Urban. 1999. "Getting Out of Line: Alternatives to Life as a Career." In *Mother Time,* ed., Margaret Urban Walker. Lanham, MD: Rowman and Littlefield.

Williams, Patricia J. 1991. *The Alchemy of Race and Rights.* Cambridge: Harvard University Press.

Young, Iris Marion. 1990. *Stretching Out.* Bloomington: Indiana University Press.

WHAT IS THE MIND?

Each of us has a mind. We have thoughts, beliefs, sensations, experiences, hopes, doubts, fears, dreams, and desires. However, it is not clear at all what, exactly, a mind is or what mental states are. Minds seems quite different from the others sorts of things we encounter on a day-to-day basis. Unlike cats, trucks, eggplants, high-rise buildings, or bodies, mental states are not observable, and they do not have shape, size, or texture. Mental states are private—we each have a special access to our own mental states that others do not have. Our mental states are subjective—no one else can have our mental states. Despite what our friends say, they cannot feel our pains. These fundamental differences between the mental and the non-mental give rise to what philosophers call the "mind-body problem," which is the focus of this section of this book. This problem concerns the nature of the mind (and mental states). What kind of thing is the mind? Is it simply part of the body (that is, the brain or central nervous system) or is it something over and above the physical body?

We start our readings with a classical argument for dualism, the position that human beings are made up of two distinct elements (body and mind). In "Alcibiades I," a dialogue that is frequently attributed to Plato, Socrates tries to demonstrate to Alcibiades that body and mind (soul) cannot be identical with each other. The argument might seem outdated, but the general argumentative strategy employed by Socrates—the strategy of distinguishing body and mind by pointing to specific properties that the mind has and the body lacks—is later employed by the modern philosopher René Descartes and all subsequent dualists as well.

In our second reading in this section, "A Critique of Dualism," Paul Churchland argues that neither substance dualism nor what he calls *popular dualism* fairs very well under scrutiny. Even though neuro-science, or "brain" science is far from "complete," given what we do know about the relationship between the mind and the brain, Churchland argues, we have no reason to suppose that there is some non-physical aspect to mental states.

John Foster provides a contemporary defense of substance dualism. In "A Defense of Dualism," he tries to show that dualism can be defended against many standard objections. He argues that a possible causal link between a non-physical mind and a physical brain is metaphysically much less mysterious than most philosophers have made it out to be.

One extreme response to the difficulties faced by dualism is presented by the philosophical behaviorist's account of the mental. According to this version of behaviorism, what it means to be in some mental state or another is simply to behave, or to be disposed to behave, in certain ways in certain circumstances. Behaviorism is a form of physicalism in that it takes mental states or minds to be physical states of a thing. The selection from John Heil, "Philosophical Behaviorism," describes this theory of the mind and the intellectual context in which it arose. While behaviorism may have trouble accounting for many of our Cartesian intuitions about the mind, behaviorists made a significant contribution to philosophy of mind by focusing their examination of the mental on behavior. Consequently, the two main varieties of physicalism that developed subsequent to behaviorism—identity theory and functionalism—include some reference to behavior in their analysis of the mental.

In his essay "The Nature of Mind," David Armstrong questions the behaviorist's analysis of dispositional states. Whereas the behaviorist is committed to the view that mental states can be analyzed in terms of dispositions to behave in certain ways given certain antecedent condi-tions, Armstrong argues that this characterization of dispositions ignores the underlying physical constitution of a thing that disposes it to behave in the way it does. For example, a thing may be described as fragile, having the disposition to break when dropped, and that disposition can be explained in terms of the object's having a certain molecular structure. Similarly, says Armstrong, our dispositions to behave in certain ways in certain conditions can be explained by certain internal states of us—certain neurological states ("brain states" for short). Thus he says

> we can think of perceptions as inner states or events apt for the produc-tion of certain sorts of selective behavior towards the environment. To perceive is like acquiring a key to a door. You do not have to use the key: you can put it in your pocket and never bother about the door. But if you

want to open the door, the key may be essential. The blind man is a man who does not acquire certain keys and, as a result, is not able to operate in his environment in the way that somebody who has sight can operate.

Thus, while mental states ought not be *reduced* to behavior, according to this theory, mental states are identical to those brain or neural states that typically cause certain behaviors. The fact that the identity theory is simple and straightforward and that it is consistent with what we know from science makes it an attractive alternative to dualism. However, as we shall see, it is not without its own set of problems.

Simply put, locks can be picked. That is, if we suppose that one can open a door's lock with something other than its key, then there is something not quite right about the identity theory of the mind. What may be more important than one's having certain keys is what the keys can do. The main idea of our next theory of the mind is *not* that it be made of certain stuff, but rather that the stuff it is made of *functions* in a certain way. According to this theory, we should not define a mind in terms of what it is made of; instead, we should define a mind in terms of what it *does*. In "Madpain and Martian Pain," David Lewis argues that because we can imagine (1) some person who is physiologically just like us and yet mentally quite different from us, and (2) some creature physiologically quite different from us and mentally similar to us, it cannot be the case that what it is to be in some particular mental state is to be in some particular brain state. That is, Lewis raises a serious objection to the identity theory. The theory of the mind he argues for is called *functionalism*. Along with this view comes the idea that mental states are *multiply realizable*—that is, one and the same mental state can be "made up" of different stuff in different creatures. So, perceiving is not like "acquiring a key to open a door," but it is more like *opening* the door. If you and I open the same (or similar) door with quite different keys (or paper clips, hairpins, etc.), we are both perceiving.

Functionalism, however, encounters a problem trying to account for the qualitative character of experience. This problem is motivated by the following thought-experiment called the Inverted Spectrum. It seems possible to imagine two people, Karin and Nirak, who, in the presence of a red tomato, are functionally indistinguishable. That is, they both say things like, "That tomato is red," they can both pick out the red tomato from green tomatoes, and so on. However, while Karin's experience has the qualitative character that "normal" perceivers have when looking at red things, Nirak's experience has the qualitative character that "normal" perceivers have when looking at green things. So, while their mental states are functionally the same, they are phenomenally different. If this is the case, then the phenomenal aspect of experience is not accounted for by a functionalist theory of the mental. Terrance Horgan's essay "Functionalism, Qualia, and the Inverted Spectrum" defends what he calls *partial functionalism* in response to the Inverted Spectrum objection. He argues that while non-phenomenal mental states are best explained in terms that functionalism provides, phenomenal states should be construed as non-relational, neural state types. Thus he favors a theory of the mind that combines some aspects of functionalism with some aspects of identity theory.

In response to the thesis of strong AI—the idea that the appropriately programmed computer literally understands—John Searle argues, in "Minds, Brains, and Programs," that there is more to understanding than fulfilling some functional role. In his Chinese Room thought experiment, he presents a case in which a person who does not understand Chinese is functionally indistinguishable from a native Chinese speaker. If his objection goes through, then there is something wrong with functionalism because there is more to understanding, more to being in a particular mental state, than functionalism would require.

In the final paper in this section, "Epiphenomenal Qualia," Frank Jackson gives his well known objection to physicalism—The Knowledge Argument. In the first version of this argument, we are asked to imagine Fred, a person who can discriminate one more shade of red than other color perceivers. It seems that we could know all the physical facts about Fred's physiology, and yet we could not know facts about *what it is like* for Fred to see this extra color. Therefore, Jackson argues, facts about *what it is like* to see, smell, hear, taste, and so on, are facts that escape a physicalist theory. In the second, and far more influential, version of this argument, we are asked to imagine Mary, a color scientist who has lived her entire life in a black and white laboratory. She observes the world on a black and white monitor. And yet, she knows all of the physical facts about seeing red. The intuition Jackson thinks we should have is that, upon leaving her lab, Mary learns something new about seeing color— she learns *what it is like* to see color. If she does in fact learn something new, and she knew all the *physical* facts, then there is a *non-physical* fact about seeing color. Since seeing is a mental state, if there is something non-physical about seeing, then physicalism is false. The property of experience in virtue of which there is something that it is like to *have* an experience is called a *quale* (or *qualia*, plural). In this paper, Jackson's objection to physicalism is at the same time a defense of what is called *property dualism*—the theory of the mind that says that, for the most part, the mind is a physical thing; however, the mind has certain *non-physical properties*, namely, qualia.

An Argument for Dualism from "Alcibiades I"

Plato   *(Translated by Benjamin Jowett)*

[. . .] **SOCRATES:** And can we ever know what art makes a man better, if we do not know what we are ourselves?

ALCIBIADES: Impossible.

SOCRATES: And is self-knowledge such an easy thing, and was he to be lightly esteemed who inscribed the text on the temple at Delphi? Or is self-knowledge a difficult thing, which few are able to attain?

ALCIBIADES: At times I fancy, Socrates, that anybody can know himself; at other times the task appears to be very difficult.

SOCRATES: But whether easy or difficult, Alcibiades, still there is no other way; knowing what we are, we shall know how to take care of ourselves, and if we are ignorant we shall not know.

ALCIBIADES: That is true.

SOCRATES: Well, then, let us see in what way the self-existent can be discovered by us; that will give us a chance of discovering our own existence, which otherwise we can never know.

ALCIBIADES: You say truly.

SOCRATES: Come, now, I beseech you, tell me with whom you are conversing? with whom but with me?

ALCIBIADES: Yes.

SOCRATES: As I am, with you?

ALCIBIADES: Yes.

SOCRATES: That is to say, I, Socrates, am talking?

ALCIBIADES: Yes.

SOCRATES: And Alcibiades is my hearer?

ALCIBIADES: Yes.

SOCRATES: And I in talking use words?

ALCIBIADES: Certainly.

SOCRATES: And talking and using words have, I suppose, the same meaning?

ALCIBIADES: To be sure.

SOCRATES: And the user is not the same as the thing which he uses?

ALCIBIADES: What do you mean?

SOCRATES: I will explain; the shoemaker, for example, uses a square tool, and a circular tool, and other tools for cutting?

ALCIBIADES: Yes.

SOCRATES: But the tool is not the same as the cutter and user of the tool?

ALCIBIADES: Of course not.

SOCRATES: And in the same way the instrument of the harper is to be distinguished from the harper himself?

ALCIBIADES: It is.

SOCRATES: Now the question which I asked was whether you conceive the user to be always different from that which he uses?

ALCIBIADES: I do.

SOCRATES: Then what shall we say of the shoemaker? Does he cut with his tools only or with his hands?

ALCIBIADES: With his hands as well.

SOCRATES: He uses his hands too?

ALCIBIADES: Yes.

SOCRATES: And does he use his eyes in cutting leather?

ALCIBIADES: He does.

SOCRATES: And we admit that the user is not the same with the things which he uses?

ALCIBIADES: Yes.

SOCRATES: Then the shoemaker and the harper are to be distinguished from the hands and feet which they use?

ALCIBIADES: Clearly.

SOCRATES: And does not a man use the whole body?

ALCIBIADES: Certainly.

SOCRATES: And that which uses is different from that which is used?

ALCIBIADES: True.

SOCRATES: Then a man is not the same as his own body?

ALCIBIADES: That is the inference.

SOCRATES: What is he, then?

ALCIBIADES: I cannot say.

SOCRATES: Nay, you can say that he is the user of the body.

ALCIBIADES: Yes.

SOCRATES: And the user of the body is the soul?

ALCIBIADES: Yes, the soul.

SOCRATES: And the soul rules?

ALCIBIADES: Yes.

SOCRATES: Let me make an assertion which will, I think, be universally admitted.

ALCIBIADES: What is it?

SOCRATES: That man is one of three things.

ALCIBIADES: What are they?

SOCRATES: Soul, body, or both together forming a whole.

ALCIBIADES: Certainly.

SOCRATES: But did we not say that the actual ruling principle of the body is man?

ALCIBIADES: Yes, we did.

SOCRATES: And does the body rule over itself?

ALCIBIADES: Certainly not.

SOCRATES: It is subject, as we were saying?

ALCIBIADES: Yes.

SOCRATES: Then that is not the principle which we are seeking?

ALCIBIADES: It would seem not.

SOCRATES: But may we say that the union of the two rules over the body, and consequently that this is man?

ALCIBIADES: Very likely.

SOCRATES: The most unlikely of all things; for if one of the members is subject, the two united cannot possibly rule.

ALCIBIADES: True.

SOCRATES: But since neither the body, nor the union of the two, is man, either man has no real existence, or the soul is man?

ALCIBIADES: Just so.

SOCRATES: Is anything more required to prove that the soul is man?

ALCIBIADES: Certainly not; the proof is, I think, quite sufficient. [. . .]

A Critique of Dualism
Paul Churchland

. . . The dualistic approach to mind encompasses several quite different theories, but they are all agreed that the essential nature of conscious intelligence resides in something *nonphysical,* in something forever beyond the scope of sciences like physics, neurophysiology, and computer science. Dualism is not the most widely held view in the current philosophical and scientific community, but it is the most common theory of mind in the public at large, it is deeply entrenched in most of the world's popular religions, and it has been the dominant theory of mind for most of Western history. It is thus an appropriate place to begin our discussion.

Substance Dualism

The distinguishing claim of this view is that each mind is a distinct nonphysical thing, an individual "package" of nonphysical substance, a thing whose identity is independent of any physical body to which it may be temporarily "attached." Mental states and activities derive their special character, on this view, from their being states and activities of this unique, nonphysical substance.

This leaves us wanting to ask for more in the way of a *positive* characterization of the proposed mind-stuff. It is a frequent complaint with the substance dualist's approach that his characterization of it is so far almost entirely negative. This need not be a fatal flaw, however, since we no doubt have much to learn about the underlying nature of mind, and perhaps the deficit here can eventually be made good. On this score, the philosopher René Descartes (1596–1650) has done as much as anyone to provide a positive account of the nature of the proposed mind-stuff, and his views are worthy of examination.

Descartes theorized that reality divides into two basic kinds of substance. The first is ordinary matter, and the essential feature of this kind of substance is that it is extended in space: any instance of it has length, breadth, height, and occupies a determinate position in space. Descartes did not attempt to play down the importance of this type of matter. On the contrary, he was one of the most imaginative physicists of his time, and he was an enthusiastic advocate of what was then called "the mechanical philosophy." But there was one isolated corner of reality he thought could not be accounted for in terms of the mechanics of matter: the conscious reason of Man. This was his motive for proposing a second and radically different kind of substance, a substance that has no spatial extension or spatial position whatever, a substance whose essential feature is the activity of *thinking*. This view is known as *Cartesian dualism*.

As Descartes saw it, the real *you* is not your material body, but rather a nonspatial thinking substance, an individual unit of mind-stuff quite distinct from your material body. This nonphysical mind is in systematic causal interaction with your body. The physical state of your body's sense organs, for example, causes visual/auditory/tactile experiences in your mind. And the desires and decisions of your nonphysical mind cause your body to behave in purposeful ways. Its causal connections to your mind are what make your body yours, and not someone else's.

The main reasons offered in support of this view were straightforward enough. First, Descartes thought that he could determine, by direct introspection alone, that he was essentially a thinking substance and nothing else. And second, he could not imagine how a purely physical system could ever use *language* in a relevant way, or engage in mathematical *reasoning,* as any normal human can. Whether these are good reasons, we shall discuss presently. Let us first notice a difficulty that even Descartes regarded as a problem.

If "mind-stuff" is so utterly different from "matter-stuff" in its nature—different to the point that it has no mass whatever, no shape whatever, and no position anywhere in space—then how is it possible for my mind to have any causal influence on my body at all? As Descartes himself was aware (he was one of the first to formulate the law of the conservation of momentum), ordinary matter in space behaves according to rigid laws, and one cannot get bodily movement (= momentum) from nothing. How is this utterly insubstantial "thinking substance" to have any influence on ponderous matter? How can two such different things be in any sort of causal contact? Descartes proposed a very subtle material substance—"animal spirits"—to convey the mind's influence to the body in general. But this does not provide us with a solution, since it leaves us with the same problem with which we started: how something ponderous and spatial (even "animal spirits") can interact with something entirely nonspatial.

In any case, the basic principle of division used by Descartes is no longer as plausible as it was in his day. It is now neither useful nor accurate to characterize ordinary matter as that-which-has-extension-in-space. Electrons, for example, are bits of matter, but our best current theories describe the electron as a point-particle with no extension whatever (it even lacks a determinate spatial position). And according to Einstein's theory of gravity, an entire star can achieve this same status, if it undergoes a complete gravitational collapse. If there truly is a division between mind and body, it appears that Descartes did not put his finger on the dividing line.

Such difficulties with Cartesian dualism provide a motive for considering a less radical form of substance dualism, and that is what we find in a view I shall call *popular dualism.* This is the theory that a person is literally a "ghost in a machine," where the machine is the human body, and the ghost is a spiritual substance, quite unlike physical matter in its internal constitution, but fully possessed of spatial properties even so. In particular, minds are commonly held to be *inside* the bodies they control: inside the head, on most views, in intimate contact with the brain.

This view need not have the difficulties of Descartes'. The mind is right there in contact with the brain, and their interaction can perhaps be understood in terms of their exchanging energy of a form that our science has not yet recognized or understood. Ordinary matter, you may recall, is just a form or manifestation of energy. (You may think of a grain of sand as a great deal of energy condensed or frozen into a small package, according to Einstein's relation, $E = mc^2$.) Perhaps mind-stuff is a well-behaved form or manifestation of energy also, but a different form of it. It is thus *possible* that a dualism of this alternative sort be consistent with familiar laws concerning the conservation of momentum and energy. This is fortunate for dualism, since those particular laws are very well established indeed.

This view will appeal to many for the further reason that it at least holds out the possibility (though it certainly does not guarantee) that the mind might survive the death of the body. It does not guarantee the mind's survival because it remains possible that the peculiar form of energy here supposed to constitute a mind can be produced and sustained only in conjunction with the highly intricate form of matter we call the brain, and must disintegrate when the brain disintegrates. So the prospects for surviving death are quite unclear even on the assumption that popular dualism is true. But even if survival were a clear consequence of the theory, there is a pitfall to be avoided here. Its promise of survival might be a reason for *wishing* dualism to be true, but it does not constitute a reason for *believing* that it *is* true. For that, we would need independent empirical evidence that minds do indeed survive the permanent death of the body. Regrettably, and despite the exploitative blatherings of the supermarket tabloids (**TOP DOCS PROVE LIFE AFTER DEATH!!!**), we possess no such evidence.

As we shall see later in this section, when we turn to evaluation, positive evidence for the existence of this novel, nonmaterial, thinking *substance* is in general on the slim side. This has moved many dualists to articulate still less extreme forms of dualism, in hopes of narrowing further the gap between theory and available evidence.

Property Dualism

The basic idea of the theories under this heading is that while there is no *substance* to be dealt with here beyond the physical brain, the brain has a special set of *properties* possessed by no other kind of physical object. It is these special properties that are nonphysical: hence the term *property dualism.* The properties in question are the ones you would expect: the property of having a pain, of having a sensation of red, of thinking that *P*, of desiring that *Q*, and so forth. These are the properties that are characteristic of conscious intelligence. They are held to be nonphysical in the sense that they cannot ever be reduced to or explained solely in terms of the concepts of the familiar physical sciences. They will require a wholly new and autonomous science— the 'science of mental phenomena'—if they are ever to be adequately understood.

From here, important differences among the positions emerge. Let us begin with what is perhaps the oldest version of property dualism: *epiphenomenalism.* This term is rather a mouthful, but its meaning is simple. The Greek prefix "epi-" means "above," and the position at issue holds that mental phenomena are not a part of the physical phenomena in the brain that ultimately determine our actions and behavior, but rather ride "above the fray." Mental phenomena are thus *epi*phenomena. They are held to just appear or emerge when the growing brain passes a certain level of complexity.

But there is more. The epiphenomenalist holds that while mental phenomena are caused to occur by the various activities of the brain, *they do not have any causal effects in turn.* They are entirely impotent with respect to causal effects on the physical world. They are *mere* epiphenomena. (To fix our ideas, a vague metaphor may be helpful here. Think of our conscious mental states as little sparkles of shimmering light that occur on the wrinkled surface of the brain, sparkles which are caused to occur by physical activity in the brain, but which have no causal effects on the brain in return.) This means that the universal conviction that one's actions are determined by one's desires, decisions, and volitions is false! One's actions are exhaustively determined by physical events in the brain, which events *also* cause the epiphenomena we call desires, decisions, and volitions. There is therefore a constant conjunction between volitions and actions. But according to the epiphenomenalist, it is mere illusion that the former cause the latter.

What could motivate such a strange view? In fact, it is not too difficult to understand why someone might take it seriously. Put yourself in the shoes of a neuroscientist who is concerned to trace the origins of behavior back up the motor nerves to the active cells in the motor cortex of the cerebrum, and to trace in turn their activity into inputs from other parts of the brain, and from the various sensory nerves. She finds a thoroughly physical system of awesome structure and delicacy, and much intricate activity, all of it unambiguously chemical or electrical in nature, and she finds no hint at all of any nonphysical inputs of the kind that substance dualism proposes. What is she to think? From the standpoint of her researches, human behavior is exhaustively a function of the activity of the physical brain. And this opinion is further supported by her confidence that the brain has the behavior-controlling features it does exactly because those features have been ruthlessly selected for during the brain's long evolutionary history. In sum, the seat of human behavior appears entirely physical in its constitution, in its origins, and in its internal activities.

On the other hand, our neuroscientist has the testimony of her own introspection to account for as well. She can hardly deny that she has experiences, beliefs, and desires, nor that they are connected in some way with her behavior. One bargain that can be struck here is to admit the *reality* of mental properties, as nonphysical properties, but demote them to the status of impotent epiphenomena that have nothing to do with the scientific explanation of human and animal behavior. This is the position the epiphenomenalist takes, and the reader can now perceive the rationale behind it. It is a bargain struck between the desire to respect a rigorously scientific approach to the explanation of behavior, and the desire to respect the testimony of introspection.

The epiphenomenalist's "demotion" of mental properties—to causally impotent by-products of brain activity—has seemed too extreme for most property dualists, and a theory closer to the convictions of common sense has enjoyed somewhat greater popularity. This view, which we may call *interactionist property dualism*, differs from the previous view in only one essential respect: the interactionist asserts that mental properties do indeed have causal effects on the brain, and thereby, on behavior. The mental properties of the brain are an integrated part of the general causal fray, in systematic interaction with the brain's physical properties. One's actions, therefore, are held to be caused by one's desires and volitions after all.

As before, mental properties are here said to be *emergent* properties, properties that do not appear at all until ordinary physical matter has managed to organize itself, through the evolutionary process, into a system of sufficient complexity. Examples of properties that are emergent in this sense would be the property of being *solid*, the property of being *colored*, and the property of being *alive*. All of these require matter to be suitably organized before they can be displayed. With this much, any materialist will agree. But any property dualist makes the further claim that mental states and properties are *irreducible,* in the sense that they are not just organizational features of physical matter, as are the examples cited. They are said to be novel properties beyond prediction or explanation by physical science.

This last condition—the irreducibility of mental properties—is an important one, since this is what makes the position a dualist position. But it sits poorly with the joint claim that mental properties emerge from nothing more than the organizational achievements of physical matter. If that is how mental properties are produced, then one would expect a physical account of them to be possible. The simultaneous claim of evolutionary emergence *and* physical irreducibility is prima facie puzzling.

A property dualist is not absolutely bound to insist on both claims. He could let go the thesis of evolutionary emergence, and claim that mental properties are *fundamental* properties of reality, properties that have been here from the universe's inception, properties on a par with length, mass, electric charge, and other fundamental properties. There is even an historical precedent for a position of this kind. At the turn of this century it was still widely believed that electromagnetic phenomena (such as electric charge and magnetic attraction) were just an unusually subtle manifestation of purely *mechanical* phenomena. Some scientists thought that a reduction of electromagnetics to mechanics was more or less in the bag. They thought that radio waves, for example, would turn out to be just travelling oscillations in a very subtle but jellylike aether that fills space everywhere. But the aether turned out not to exist. So electromagnetic properties turned out to be fundamental properties in their own right, and we were forced to add electric charge to the existing list of fundamental properties (mass, length, and duration).

Perhaps mental properties enjoy a status like that of electromagnetic properties: irreducible, but not emergent. Such a view may be called *elemental-property dualism,* and it has the advantage of clarity over the previous view. Unfortunately, the parallel with electromagnetic phenomena has one very obvious failure. Unlike electromagnetic properties, which are displayed at all levels of reality from the subatomic level on up, mental properties are displayed only in large physical systems that have evolved a very complex internal organization. The case for the evolutionary emergence of mental properties through the organization of matter is extremely strong. They do not appear to be basic or elemental at all. This returns us, therefore, to the issue of their irreducibility. Why should we accept this most basic of the dualist's claims? Why be a dualist?

Arguments for Dualism

Here we shall examine some of the main considerations commonly offered in support of dualism. Criticism will be postponed for a moment so that we may appreciate the collective force of these supporting considerations.

A major source of dualistic convictions is the *religious belief* many of us bring to these issues. Each of the major religions is in its way a theory about the cause or purpose of the universe, and Man's place within it, and many of them are committed to the notion of an immortal soul—that is, to some form of substance dualism. Supposing that one is consistent, to consider disbelieving dualism is to consider disbelieving one's religious heritage, and some of us find that difficult to do. Call this the *argument from religion.*

A more universal consideration is the *argument from introspection.* The fact is, when you center your attention on the contents of your consciousness, you do not clearly apprehend a neural network pulsing with electrochemical activity: you apprehend a flux of thoughts, sensations, desires, and emotions. It seems that mental states and properties, as revealed in introspection, could hardly be more different from physical states and properties if they tried. The verdict of introspection, therefore, seems strongly on the side of some form of dualism—on the side of property dualism, at a minimum.

A cluster of important consideration can be collected under the *argument from irreducibility.* Here one points to a variety of mental phenomena where it seems clear that no purely physical explanation could possibly account for what is going on. Descartes has already cited our ability to use language in a way that is relevant to our changing circumstances, and he was impressed also with our faculty of Reason, particularly as it is displayed in our capacity for mathematical reasoning. These abilities, he thought, must surely be beyond the capacity of any physical system. More recently, the introspectible qualities of our sensations (sensory "qualia"), and the meaningful content of our thoughts and beliefs, have also been cited as phenomena that will forever resist reduction to the physical. Consider, for example, seeing the color or smelling the fragrance of a rose. A physicist or chemist might know everything about the molecular structure of the rose, and of the human brain, argues the dualist, but that knowledge would not enable him to predict or anticipate the quality of these inexpressible experiences.

Finally, parapsychological phenomena are occasionally cited in favor of dualism. Telepathy (mind reading), precognition (seeing the future), telekinesis (thought control of material objects), and clairvoyance (knowledge of distant objects) are all awkward to explain within the normal confines of psychology and physics. If these phenomena are real, they might well be reflecting the superphysical nature that the dualist ascribes to the mind. Trivially they are *mental* phenomena, and if they are also forever beyond physical explanation, then at least some mental phenomena must be irreducibly nonphysical.

Collectively, these considerations may seem compelling. But there are serious criticisms of each, and we must examine them as well. Consider first the argument from religion. There is certainly nothing wrong in principle with appealing to a more general theory that bears on the case at issue, which is what the appeal to religions amounts to. But the appeal can only be as good as the scientific credentials of the religions(s) being appealed to, and here the appeals tend to fall down rather badly. In general, attempts to decide scientific questions by appeal to religious orthodoxy have a very sorry history. That the stars are other suns, that the earth is not the center of the universe, that diseases are caused by microorganisms, that the earth is billions of years old, that life is a physicochemical phenomenon; all of these crucial insights were strongly and sometimes viciously resisted, because the dominant religion of the time happened to think otherwise. Giordano Bruno was burned at the stake for urging the first view; Galileo was forced by threat of torture in the Vatican's basement to recant the second view; the firm belief that disease was a punishment visited by the Devil allowed public health practices that brought chronic plagues to most of the cities of Europe; and the age of the earth and the evolution of life were forced to fight an uphill battle against religious prejudice even in an age of supposed enlightenment.

History aside, the almost universal opinion that one's own religious convictions are the reasoned outcome of a dispassionate evaluation of all of the major alternatives is almost demonstrably false for humanity in general. If that really were the genesis of most people's convictions, then one would expect the major faiths to be distributed more or less randomly or evenly over the globe. But in fact they show a very strong tendency to cluster: Christianity is centered in Europe and the Americas, Islam in Africa and the Middle East, Hinduism in India, and Buddhism in the Orient. Which illustrates what we all suspected anyway: that *social forces* are the primary determinants of religious belief for people in general. To decide scientific questions by appeal to religious orthodoxy would therefore be to put social forces in place of empirical evidence. For all of these reasons, professional scientists and philosophers concerned with the nature of mind generally do their best to keep religious appeals out of the discussion entirely.

The argument from introspection is a much more interesting argument, since it tries to appeal to the direct experience of everyman. But the argument is deeply suspect, in that it assumes that our faculty of inner observation or introspection reveals things as they really are in their innermost nature. This assumption is suspect because we already know that our other forms of observation—sight, hearing, touch, and so on—do no such thing. The red surface of an apple does not *look* like a matrix of molecules reflecting photons at certain critical wavelengths, but that is what it is. The sound of a flute does not *sound* like a sinusoidal compression wave train in the atmosphere, but that is what it is. The warmth of the summer air does not *feel* like the mean kinetic energy of millions of tiny molecules, but that is what it is. If one's pains and hopes and beliefs do not *introspectively* seem like electrochemical states in a neural network, that may be only because our faculty of introspection, like our other senses, is not sufficiently penetrating to reveal such hidden details. Which is just what one would expect anyway. The argument from introspection is therefore entirely without force, unless we can somehow argue that the faculty of introspection is quite different from all other forms of observation.

The argument from irreducibility presents a more serious challenge, but here also its force is less than first impression suggests. Consider first our capacity for mathematical reasoning which so impressed Descartes. The last ten years have made available, to anyone with fifty dollars to spend, electronic calculators whose capacity for mathematical reasoning—the calculational part, at least—far surpasses that of any normal human. The fact is, in the centuries since Descartes' writings, philosophers, logicians, mathematicians, and computer scientists have managed to isolate the general principles of mathematical reasoning, and electronics engineers have created machines that compute in accord with those principles. The result is a hand-held object that would have astonished Descartes. This outcome is impressive not just because machines have proved capable of some of the capacities boasted by human reason, but because some of those achievements invade areas of human reason that past dualistic philosophers have held up as forever closed to mere physical devices.

Although debate on the matter remains open, Descartes' argument from language use is equally dubious. The notion of a *computer language* is by now a commonplace: consider BASIC, PASCAL, FORTRAN, APL, LISP, and so on. Granted, these artificial 'languages' are much simpler in structure and content than human natural language, but the differences may be differences only of degree, and not of kind. As well, the theoretical work of Noam Chomsky and the generative grammar approach to linguistics have done a great deal to explain the human capacity for language use in terms that invite simulation by computers. I do not mean to suggest that truly conversational computers are just around the corner. We have a great deal yet to learn, and fundamental problems yet to solve (mostly having to do with our capacity for inductive or theoretical reasoning). But recent progress here does nothing to support the claim that language use must be forever impossible for a purely physical system. On the contrary, such a claim now appears rather arbitrary and dogmatic.

The next issue is also a live problem: How can we possibly hope to explain or to predict the intrinsic qualities of our sensations, or the meaningful content of our beliefs and qualities of our sensations, or the meaningful content of our beliefs and desires, in purely physical terms? This is a major challenge to the materialist. But as we shall see in later sections, active research programs are already under way on both problems, and positive suggestions are being explored. It is in fact not impossible to imagine how such explanations might go, though the materialist cannot yet pretend to have solved either problem. Until he does, the dualist will retain a bargaining chip here, but that is about all. What the dualists need in order to establish their case is the conclusion that a physical reduction is outright impossible, and that is a conclusion they have failed to establish. Rhetorical questions, like the one that opens this paragraph, do not constitute arguments. And it is equally difficult, note, to imagine how the relevant phenomena could be explained or predicted solely in terms of the substance dualist's non-physical mind-stuff. The explanatory problem here is a major challenge to everybody, not just to the materialist. On this issue then, we have a rough standoff.

The final argument in support of dualism urged the existence of parapsychological phenomena such as telepathy and telekinesis, the point being that such mental phenomena are (a) real, and (b) beyond purely physical explanation. This argument is really another instance of the argument from irreducibility discussed above, and as before, it is not entirely clear that such phenomena, even if real, must forever escape a purely physical explanation. The materialist can already suggest a possible mechanism for telepathy, for example. On his view, thinking is an electrical activity within the brain. But according to electromagnetic theory, such changing motions of electric charges must produce electromagnetic waves radiating at the speed of light in all directions, waves that will contain information about the electrical activity that produced them. Such waves can subsequently have effects on the electrical activity of other brains, that is, on their thinking. Call this the 'radio transmitter/receiver' theory of telepathy.

I do not for a moment suggest that this theory is true: the electromagnetic waves emitted by the brain are fantastically weak (billions of imes weaker than the ever present background electromagnetic flux produced by commercial radio stations), and they are almost certain to be hopelessly jumbled together as well. This is one reason why, in the absence of systematic, compelling, and repeatable evidence for the existence of telepathy, one must doubt its possibility. But it is significant that the materialist has the theoretical resources to suggest a detailed possible explanation of telepathy, if it were real, which is more than any dualist has so far done. It is not at all clear, then, that the materialist *must* be at an explanatory disadvantage in these matters. Quite the reverse.

Put the preceding aside, if you wish, for the main difficulty with the argument from parapsychological phenomena is much, much simpler. Despite the endless pronouncements and anecdotes in the popular press, and despite a steady trickle of serious research on such things, there is no significant or trustworthy evidence that such phenomena even exist. The wide gap between popular conviction on this matter, and the actual evidence, is something that itself calls for research. For there is not a single parapsychological effect that can be repeatedly or reliably produced in any laboratory suitably equipped to perform and control the experiment. Not one. Honest researchers have been repeatedly hoodwinked by 'psychic' charlatans with skills derived from the magician's trade, and the history of the subject is largely a history of gullibility, selection of evidence, poor experimental controls, and outright fraud by the occasional researcher as well. If someone really does discover a repeatable parapsychological effect, then we shall have to reevaluate the situation, but as things stand, there is nothing here to support a dualist theory of mind.

Upon critical examination, the arguments in support of dualism lose much of their force. But we are not yet done: there are arguments against dualism, and these also require examination.

Arguments Against Dualism

The first argument against dualism urged by the materialists appeals to the greater *simplicity* of their view. It is a principle of rational methodology that, if all else is equal, the simpler of two competing hypotheses should be preferred. This principle is sometimes called "Ockham's Razor"—after William of Ockham, the medieval philosopher who first enunciated it—and it can also be expressed as follows: "Do not multiply entities beyond what is strictly necessary to explain the phenomena." The materialist postulates only one kind of substance (physical matter), and one class of properties (physical properties), whereas the dualist postulates two kinds of matter and/or two classes of properties. And to no explanatory advantage, charges the materialist.

This is not yet a decisive point against dualism, since neither dualism nor materialism can yet explain all of the phenomena to be explained. But the objection does have some force, especially since there is no doubt at all that physical matter exists, while spiritual matter remains a tenuous hypothesis.

If this latter hypothesis brought us some definite explanatory advantage obtainable in no other way, then we would happily violate the demand for simplicity, and we would be right to do so. But it does not, claims the materialist. In fact, the advantage is just the other way around, he argues, and this brings us to the second objection to dualism: the relative *explanatory impotence* of dualism as compared to materialism.

Consider, very briefly, the explanatory resources already available to the neurosciences. We know that the brain exists and what it is made of. We know much of its microstructure: how the neurons are organized into systems and how distinct systems are connected to one another, to the motor nerves going out to the muscles, and to the sensory nerves coming in from the sense organs. We know much of their microchemistry: how the nerve cells fire tiny electrochemical pulses along their various fibers, and how they make other cells fire also, or cease firing. We know some of how such activity processes sensory information, selecting salient or subtle bits to be sent on to higher systems. And we know some of how such activity initiates and coordinates bodily behavior. Thanks mainly to neurology (the branch of medicine concerned with brain pathology), we know a great deal about the correlations between damage to various parts of the human brain, and various behavioral and cognitive deficits from which the victims suffer. There are a great many isolated deficits—some gross, some subtle—that are familiar to neurologists (inability to speak, or to read, or to understand speech, or to recognize faces, or to add/subtract, or to move a certain limb, or to put information into long-term memory, and so on), and their appearance is closely tied to the occurrence of damage to very specific parts of the brain.

Nor are we limited to cataloguing traumas. The growth and development of the brain's microstructure is also something that neuroscience has explored, and such development appears to be the basis of various kinds of learning by the organism. Learning, that is, involves lasting chemical and physical changes in the brain. In sum, the neuroscientist can tell us a great deal about the brain, about its constitution and the physical laws that govern it; he can already explain much of our behavior in terms of the physical, chemical, and electrical properties of the brain; and he has the theoretical resources available to explain a good deal more as our explorations continue.

Compare now what the neuroscientist can tell us about the brain, and what he can do with that knowledge, with what the dualist can tell us about spiritual substance, and what he can do with those assumptions. Can the dualist tell us anything about the internal constitution of mind-stuff? Of the nonmaterial elements that make it up? Of the laws that govern their behavior? Of the mind's structural connections with the body? Of the manner of its operations? Can he explain human capacities and pathologies in terms of its structures and its defects? The fact is, the dualist can do none of these things, because no detailed theory of mind-stuff has ever been formulated. Compared to the rich resources and explanatory successes of current materialism, dualism is less a theory of mind than it is an empty space waiting for a genuine theory of mind to be put in it.

Thus argues the materialist. But again, this is not a completely decisive point against dualism. The dualist can admit that the brain plays a major role in the administration of both perception and behavior—on his view the brain is the *mediator* between the mind and the body—but he may attempt to argue that the materialist's current successes and future explanatory prospects concern only the mediative functions of the brain, not the *central* capacities of the nonphysical mind, capacities such as reason, emotion, *and* consciousness itself. On these latter topics, he may argue, both dualism and materialism currently draw a blank.

But this reply is not a very good one. So far as the capacity for reasoning is concerned, machines already exist that execute in minutes sophisticated deductive and mathematical calculations that would take a human a lifetime to execute. And so far as the other two mental capacities are concerned, studies of such things as depression, motivation, attention, and sleep have revealed many interesting and puzzling facts about the neurochemical and neurodynamical basis of both emotion and consciousness. The *central* capacities, no less than the peripheral, have been addressed with profit by various materialist research programs.

In any case, the (substance) dualist's attempt to draw a sharp distinction between the unique 'mental' capacities proper to the nonmaterial mind, and the merely mediative capacities of the brain, prompts an argument that comes close to being an outright refutation of (substance) dualism. If there really is a distinct entity in which reasoning, emotion, and consciousness take place, and if that entity is dependent on the brain for nothing more than sensory experiences as input and volitional executions as output, *then one would expect reason, emotion, and consciousness to be relatively invulnerable to direct control or pathology by manipulation or damage to be brain.* But in fact the exact opposite is true. Alcohol, narcotics, or senile degeneration of nerve tissue will impair, cripple, or even destroy one's capacity for rational thought. Psychiatry knows of hundreds of emotion-controlling chemicals (lithium, chlorpromazine, amphetamine, cocaine, and so on) that do their work when vectored into the brain. And the vulnerability of consciousness to the anesthetics, to caffeine, and to something as simple as a sharp blow to the head, shows its very close dependence on neural activity in the brain. All of this makes perfect sense if reason, emotion, and consciousness are activities of the brain itself. But it makes very little sense if they are activities of something else entirely.

We may call this the argument from the *neural dependence* of all known mental phenomena. Property dualism, note, is not threatened by this argument, since, like materialism, property dualism reckons the brain as the seat of all mental activity. We shall conclude this section, however, with an argument that cuts against both varieties of dualism: the argument from *evolutionary history.*

What is the origin of a complex and sophisticated species such as ours? What, for that matter, is the origin of the dolphin, the mouse, or the housefly? Thanks to the fossil record, comparative anatomy, and the biochemistry of proteins and nucleic acids, there is no longer any significant doubt on this matter. Each existing species is a surviving type from a number of variations on an earlier type of organism; each earlier type is in turn a surviving type from a number of variations on a still earlier type of organism; and so on down the branches of the evolutionary tree until, some three billion years ago, we find a trunk of just one or a handful of very simple organisms. These organisms, like their more complex offspring, are just self-repairing, self-replicating, energy-driven molecular structures. (That evolutionary trunk has its own roots in an earlier era of purely chemical evolution, in which the molecular elements of life were themselves pieced together.) The mechanism of development that has structured this tree has two main elements: (1) the occasional blind variation in types of reproducing creature, and (2) the selective survival of some of these types due to the relative reproductive advantage enjoyed by individuals of those types. Over periods of geological time, such a process can produce an enormous variety of organisms, some of them very complex indeed.

For purposes of our discussion, the important point about the standard evolutionary story is that the human species and all of its features are the wholly physical outcome of a purely physical process. Like all but the simplest of organisms, we have a nervous system. And for the same reason: a nervous system permits the discriminative guidance of behavior. But a nervous system is just an active matrix of cells, and a cell is just an active matrix of molecules. We are notable only in that our nervous system is more complex and powerful than those of our fellow creatures. Our inner nature differs from that of simpler creatures in degree, but not in kind.

If this is the correct account of our origins, then there seems neither need, nor room, to fit any nonphysical substances or properties into our theoretical account of ourselves. We are creatures of matter. And we should learn to live with that fact.

Arguments like these have moved most (but not all) of the professional community to embrace some form of materialism. This has not produced much unanimity, however, since the differences between the several materialist positions are even wider than the differences that divide dualism.

A Defense of Dualism

John Foster

By "dualism" I mean the thesis that the mind and its contents are radically nonphysical, that is, that they are neither themselves physical, nor the logical product of anything physical, nor, except causally or nomologically, dependent on anything physical.

It is nowadays generally assumed that dualism has been discredited. Even those who see problems for the alternatives usually are unwilling to countenance dualism as a possible solution. I believe that dualism is correct. . . . I shall consider some of the main objections to dualism and try to show why they are ineffective.

Of course, I do not have space to consider all the objections. Some are nothing more than rhetoric (I would put into this category such objections as "nonphysical entities are queer" and "postulating nonphysical entities is ontologically extravagant" . . .

. . . the . . . objections I consider all concern, in one way or another, the dualist's account of psychophysical causation—his account of the causal relations between body and mind. Dualism itself, of course, does not entail that there are such relations. There is no contradiction in maintaining that the mind, as well as being nonphysical, is causally isolated from the physical world; and with the help of a suitable theism, it may even be possible to explain why things are empirically organized as if there were psychophysical causation, when there is not. But since I do not want my defense of dualism to force me into such an eccentric position, I shall work on the assumption that parallelism, in this extreme form, is untenable and that mind and body are indeed causally related. This still leaves the dualist with a choice between interactionism, which takes the causal relations to run in both directions, and epiphenomenalism, which takes them to run only from body to mind. Here my sympathies, again in line with common sense, are with the interactionist. And consequently, I would feel at least very uncomfortable if there were something which obliged me to choose between abandoning dualism altogether and adopting its epiphenomenalist version. That I do face such a choice is the substance of the [final] objection.

From The Case for Dualism, edited by John R. Smythies and John Beloff (Charlottsville, Va.: University Press of Virginia, 1989).

The Traditional Objection

Perhaps the oldest objection to dualism is that if the mind is nonphysical, the very idea of psychophysical causation—of the body causally affecting the mind or the mind causally affecting the body—is deeply puzzling, if not incoherent. How can such different kinds of thing—the physical and the nonphysical—come into causal contact? How can the material body gain purchase on the immaterial mind, or vice versa? However, put like this, I cannot see what the problem is supposed to be. Obviously, dualistic causation does not operate through physical contact, as when one billiard ball displaces another. But why should it not just be in the nature of things that in certain psychophysical conditions, certain types of neural events cause certain types of mental events, or vice versa? According to Thomas Nagel, we cannot understand how such causation would work. Nagel assumes, I thing correctly, though contrary to Hume's account, that causation involves some kind of objective necessitation. He then argues, in effect, that so long as we think of mental and physical events as radically different in their intrinsic nature, such necessitation is incomprehensible: "what we cannot understand is *how* . . . the brain process necessitates the sensation." But what I cannot understand is how this "how"-question arises. . . . since the causation is direct (the brain event directly causing the mental event, or vice versa), there is no question of an intervening mechanism. Perhaps it is this very directness which Nagel finds puzzling. For in the physical world causal processes are, in general, spatiotemporally continuous, thus providing an intervening mechanism between a cause and any subsequent effect. But there is surely nothing incoherent or problematic about the notion of direct causation. And where causation is direct, I do not see in what sense there could be a question of how it operates, except as a request to specify the causally relevant properties and covering laws. [. . .]

An Objection to Dualistic Interactionism

Some dualists, while accepting that there are psychophysical causal relations, hold that they only run in one direction—from body to mind. They accept, for example, that if I am stung by a wasp, the subsequent pain is caused by the neural response which the sting induces, but they deny that if I decide to smoke my pipe, the subsequent bodily movements involving pipe and matches are caused by my decision. And, quite generally, they accept that a person's mental states are causally affected by the states of his body but deny that his mental states have any causal influence on the states of his body or on anything else in the physical world. This version of dualism is known as "epiphenomenalism," and the version it contrasts with, which accepts psychophysical causation in both directions, is known as "interactionism." I should add that most epiphenomenalists, as well as denying that the mind has any causal influence on the body, also deny that it has a causal influence on anything at all. In particular, they deny that mental states can cause, or contribute to the causation of, other mental states.

Like most other current philosophers, I regard epiphenomenalism as unnatural and implausible. In the first place, it is in radical conflict with our conception of ourselves as agents. If mental states have no causal influence on behavior, then behavior cannot be thought of as intentional in any decent sense, even if the subject happens to have certain intentions which it fulfills. And if behavior is not intentional, it does not qualify as action in a sense which distinguishes it from mere bodily movement. The epiphenomenalist might reply that the general conformity of our behavior to our intentions is not merely accidental; it is ensured by the very structure of our brains and their muscular extensions in the framework of physical and psychophysical law. But even so, the behavior would not be intentional in the requisite sense, since the intentions and the psychophysical laws that control their occurrence would be irrelevant to its production. Second, human behavior exhibits certain complex regularities that call for explanation and that, at present, we explain (at least partly) in psychological terms. These psychological explanations . . . attribute a causal efficacy to the mental; they represent behavior as falling under the control of the subject's beliefs and desires, or under the control of the subject's decisions, which are responsive to (if not determined by) his beliefs and desires. And these explanations gain credence from the fact that, as well as being, in their own terms, successful, they cannot, at present, be replaced by non-psychological explanations that cover the same ground. Third, it is difficult to see how, if epiphenomenalism were true, the mind could form a subject matter for overt discussion. Certainly, if mental states have no causal access to our speech centers, the notion of an introspective report collapses: even if the subject retains an introspective knowledge of his mental states, his utterances would not count as expressing that knowledge if it contributes nothing to their production. But it is not even clear how, on the epiphenomenalistic view, our language, as a medium for our utterances, makes semantic contact with the mind at all. In what sense, for example, could the word "pain," as overtly used, be said to signify a certain type of sensation, if neither the occurrence of the sensations nor our introspective conception of their type affects the overt use . . . ?

None of these points shows that epiphenomenalism is logically untenable, in the sense of being incoherent or self-contradictory . . . Nonetheless, we have, I think, very strong, and perhaps even conclusive, reasons for rejecting it. And, because of this, I should not want my defense of dualism to involve my acceptance of anything but an interactionist position.

It is at this point that the [final] objection arises. For there is an argument which purports to show that dualism of any but an epiphenomenalistic kind is scientifically unacceptable. The argument runs like this:

1. The body is a physical system.
2. As such, the body must be subject to ordinary physical laws.
3. Our theories as to what physical laws obtain are subject to revision. But our current scientific evidence strongly supports the view that at any level of description relevant to a theory of human behavior, these laws are, for all practical purposes, deterministic.
4. So we can reasonably conclude that any bodily event, of a sort which might be cited in a description or explanation of behavior, is causally determined by prior physical events and conditions.
5. But such a conclusion leaves no room for a nonphysical mind to have any causal influence on behavior.
6. Hence, on our present scientific evidence, we face a choice between epiphenomenalism and some kind of identity thesis (if only of the token-token variety).

If it is correct, this argument constitutes an objection to dualistic interactionism. It also, on the face of it, constitutes an objection to dualism as such, if epiphenomenalism is, as I would concede, unacceptable. And, nowadays, it is normally as an objection to dualism, and in support of the identity thesis, that the argument is offered. But here we must be careful. It is true that epiphenomenalism is very implausible and, overtly expressed, may even be self-refuting. And this means that, other things being equal, we should reject it. But it does not mean that we should reject it at all costs. If the only alternative were the identity thesis, then, in my view, epiphenomenalism, despite its implausibility, would be the preferable option. . . . The choice between epiphenomenalism and the identity thesis only counts against dualism on the assumption, which I hold to be false, that epiphenomenalism is not only very implausible but less plausible than its rival. There is also a further point to bear in mind. If the identity thesis is only of a token-token kind, it is not clear how, even if it were coherent, it would avoid the implausibilities of epiphenomenalism. For if mental events have physical effects only by virtue of their physical properties, and if mental properties are not identical with physical properties, or with functional properties of a purely physicalistic kind, then mental properties are causally irrelevant. And if mental properties are causally irrelevant, the identity thesis does not accord the mind the kind of causal efficacy which common sense demands. It does not allow the mental an influence on behavior in any interesting sense. So to provide a genuine alternative to epiphenomenalism, the identity thesis would have to be of a full-blooded materialist form, involving, in addition to token-identity, some physicalistic construal of mental properties. This is something which defenders of token-identity do not always recognize. . . .

However, whether it is an objection to dualism as such or only to interactionism, I have to find some answer to the argument; for I am not willing to concede that epiphenomenalism and the identity thesis are the only empirically acceptable options. In fact, the error in the argument is not hard to identify. We must begin by distinguishing two ways in which science might provide evidence that the functioning of the body is wholly explicable in terms of deterministic physical law. The first way would be by direct research on the body itself—in particular, on the brain, since it is on brain activity, if on anything, that we might expect the mind to exert a direct causal influence. Thus, by monitoring neural activity in various parts of the brain (without disturbing normal functioning), scientists might build up a strong inductive case for the conclusion that the electrochemical state of any neuron at any time is determined by its immediately prior electrochemical state and the states of other neurons directly connected to it. The second way would be by discovering, without reference to the functioning of the human body, that the rest of the physical world seems to be subject to certain physical laws of a sort which, if they applied universally, would make the body a deterministic system. This is the evidence provided by the investigations of physics and chemistry into the properties of matter and energy in general. Now it is predominantly evidence of the second kind to which the argument appeals. The claim is not that a thorough sampling of brain activity reveals a wholly deterministic system, for no such sampling has been conducted. Rather, the claim is that the human body, including the brain, must be physically deterministic if it is to conform to those theories which apply to physical systems in general. But this evidence, just because it bears on the question of the human system only indirectly, is not decisive. It has to be weighed against what we know or have reason to believe, independently, about the relation between body and mind. . . . When everything is taken into account, the most reasonable conclusion to draw is, surely, that through its attachment to a nonphysical mind, the brain is subject to certain influences which do not affect the other physical systems that science investigates and on whose behavior its nomological theories are based. It is conceivable that this conclusion will be called into question by future brain research (if it were, I should have to reconsider my rejection of epiphenomenalism). But as things stand, we are entitled to assume that it will not. [. . .]

Philosophical Behaviorism
John Heil

. . . We began with an examination of Descartes's contention that minds and material bodies are distinct kinds of substance. We then examined a number of related views, views that could be spun out from our Cartesian starting point by rejecting or modifying one or another of its components. In this paper, we shall explore two materialist accounts of the mind.

Materialists deny that the world includes both mental and material substances. Every substance is a material substance. Minds are fashioned somehow from the same materials from which rocks, trees, and stars are made. If we take the fundamental particles that make up inanimate objects and arrange them in the right way, the result is a creature with a mind. The mind is not a separate, non-material entity, but only matter, suitably organized.

Materialism has a long history. Democritus (c. 460–370 BC) described the world as a fleeting arrangement of atoms swirling in the void. Hobbes (1588–1679) and La Mettrie (1707–51) regarded mental phenomena as nothing more than mechanical interactions of material components. Nowadays, materialism of one stripe or another is more often than not taken for granted. The belief that minds are just brains is evidently widespread. Francis Crick's recent description of this as "the astonishing hypothesis" flies in the face of my own experience with undergraduate philosophy students who seem to use "mind" and "brain" interchangeably.

Although many philosophers would, if pressed, describe themselves as materialists, materialism comes in different flavors. Disagreements among materialists tend to overshadow their common rejection of dualism. In recent years, dissatisfaction with materialist assumptions has led to a revival of interest in forms of dualism. Surprisingly, much of this interest has been spawned by work in the neurosciences where difficulties in reconciling characteristics of complex material systems with characteristics of conscious experiences are especially acute.

In this chapter, we shall examine [one] precursor to the contemporary debate: behaviorism. . . . Behaviorism as a philosophical doctrine about the nature of mind differs from behaviorism as a movement in psychology. Philosophical behaviorism is associated with a thesis about the nature of mind and the meanings of mental terms. Psychological behaviorism emerged from a particular conception of scientific method as applied to psychology. This brand of behaviorism dominated experimental work in psychology until the 1960s when it was eclipsed by the information-processing model, a model inspired by the advent of the computing machine.

The relation between philosophy and the empirical sciences, including psychology, is scarcely straightforward. On the one hand, philosophers of mind have had an important part in shaping conceptions of mentality that guide empirical investigators. On the other hand, philosophers have periodically re-evaluated their theories in light of advances in the sciences. One result is that philosophical influences on the sciences find their way back into philosophy. When this happens, a philosophical thesis can gain an undeserved air of empirical respectability in the minds of philosophers eager to embrace the pronouncements of science.

Philosophers, impressed by behaviorism in psychology, sometimes failed to appreciate the extent to which the behaviorist conception of mind was the product of a definite philosophical conception of scientific method. Ironically, the roots of that conception lay in a positivist tradition that many of these same philosophers would have found unappealing. One lesson is that it is a mistake for philosophers of mind to accept uncritically or at face value claims issuing from psychology or the neurosciences.

Behaviorism

Until the twentieth century, the study of the mind was assumed to revolve around the study of conscious states and processes. Subjects in psychological experiments (very often the experimenters themselves or their students) were trained to "introspect," and report on features of their conscious experiences. In this milieu, mental imagery and subtle qualities of sensory episodes had a central place.

At the same time, psychologists were concerned to integrate the study of the mind with the study of the brain. It had long been evident that occurrences in the brain and nervous system were intimately related to mental goings-on. The difficulty was to understand precisely the nature of the relation between minds and brains. It is tempting to think that minds (or selves: I shall continue to use the terms interchangeably, without intending to suggest that they are synonymous) are nothing more than brains. Properties of brains, however, seem to differ importantly from properties of minds. When you undergo a conscious experience, you are vividly aware of characteristics of that experience. When we examine a living brain, the characteristics we observe appear to be utterly different. Think of what it is like to have a headache. Now imagine that you are able to peer at the brain of someone suffering a headache. What you observe, even aided by instruments that reveal the fine structure of the brain, is altogether different from what the headache victim feels. Imagine a neuroscientist, intimately familiar with the physiology of headache, but who has never experienced a headache. There is, it would seem, something the scientist lacks knowledge of, some characteristic the scientist has not encountered and could not encounter simply by inspecting the brain. But then this characteristic would appear not to be a neurological characteristic. When we look at the matter this way, it is hard to avoid concluding that mental characteristics are not brain characteristics, and thus that minds are not brains.

If this were not enough, we would do well to remind ourselves that we evidently enjoy a kind of "access" to our conscious experiences that others could never have. Your experiences are "private." Your awareness of them is direct and authoritative; my awareness of those same experiences is, in contrast, indirect, inferential, and easily overridden. When you have a headache, form an image of your grandmother, or decide to comb your hair, you are in a position to recognize immediately, without the benefit of evidence or observation, that you have a headache, that you are imagining your grandmother, or that you have decided to comb your hair. I can only infer your state of mind by observing your behavior (including your linguistic behavior: I can interrogate you). If mental goings-on are correlated with neurological processes, then I may be able to infer your state of mind by observing your brain. But my access to that state is still indirect. I infer your state of mind by observing a neurological correlate. I do not observe your state of mind.

All this is exactly what we should expect were dualism true. But dualism, or at any rate Cartesian dualism, apparently leads to a bifurcation of the study of intelligent agents. We can study the biology and physiology of such agents, but in so doing we ignore their minds; or we can study their minds, ignoring their material composition.

Now, however, we are faced with a difficulty. Science is limited to the pursuit of objective, "public" states of affairs. An objective state of affairs can be apprehended from more than one perspective, by more than one observer. The contents of your mind, however, are observable (if that is the word) only by you. My route to those contents is through observations of what you say and do. This appears to place minds outside the realm of scientific inquiry. We can study brains, and we may conclude that particular kinds of neurological goings-on are correlated with kinds of mental goings-on. This would enable us reliably to infer states of mind by observing brain activity. But we should not be observing or measuring those states of mind themselves, except in our own case.

Privacy and Its Consequences

Once we start down this road, we may come to doubt that states of mind—as distinct from their physiological correlates—are a fit subject for scientific examination. Eventually, the very idea that we are in a position even to establish correlations between mental occurrences and goings-on in the nervous system can come to be doubted. Imagine that, every time you have a particular kind of experience—every time you see a certain shade of red, for instance, the red of a ripe tomato—your brain goes into a particular state, S. Further, whenever your brain goes into state S, you experience that very shade of red. It looks as though there must be a correlation between experiences of this kind and neurological states of kind S.

Suppose, now, you observe my brain in state S. I announce that I am experiencing a certain shade of red, a shade I describe as the red of a ripe tomato. It might seem that this provides further evidence of the correlation already observed in your own case. But does it? In your own case, you have access both to the mental state and to its neurological correlate. When you observe me, however, you have access only to my neurological condition. What gives you the right to assume that my mental state resembles yours?

True, I describe my experience just as you describe yours. We agree that we are experiencing the color of ripe tomatoes. But of course this is how we have each been taught to characterize our respective experiences. I have a particular kind of visual experience when I view a ripe tomato in bright sunlight. I describe this experience as the kind of experience I have when I view a ripe tomato in bright sunlight. You have a particular kind of experience when you view a ripe tomato under similar observational conditions. And you have learned to describe this experience as the kind of experience you have when you view a ripe tomato in bright sunlight. But what entitles either of us to say that the experiences so described are exactly similar? Perhaps the experience you have is like the experience I would have were I to view a lime in bright sunlight. Our descriptions perfectly coincide, but the state of mind I am describing is qualitatively very different from yours.

It would seem, then, that attempts to correlate kinds of neurological goings-on and kinds of mental occurrences boil down to correlations of neurological goings-on and descriptions of mental occurrences. We learn to describe the qualities of our states of mind by reference to publicly observable objects that typically evoke them. And this leaves open the possibility that, while our descriptions match, the states to which they apply are wildly different.

This may seem an idle worry, a purely philosophical possibility. But ask yourself: what earthly reason do you have for thinking that your states of mind qualitatively resemble the states of mind of others? It is not as though you have observed others' states of mind and discovered they match yours. You lack a single example of such a match. Might you infer inductively from characteristics of your own case to the characteristics of others? (Inductive inference is probabilistic: we reason from the characteristics of a sample of a population to characteristics of the population as a whole.) But canons of inductive reasoning proscribe inferences from a single individual to a whole population unless it is clear that the individual is representative of the population. If you assume that characteristics of your states of mind are representative, however, you are assuming precisely what you set out to establish.

The problem we have been scouting is the old problem of other minds. Granted you can know your own mind, how can you know the minds of others? Indeed, once we put it this way, we can see that the problem is deeper than we might have expected. How can you know that others have minds at all? They behave in ways similar to the ways you behave, and they insist they have pains, images, feelings, and thoughts. But what reason do you have for supposing that they do? You cannot observe others' states of mind. Nor do you have adequate inductive grounds for inferring that they enjoy a mental life from what you can observe about them.

A recent twist on this ancient puzzle introduces the possibility of "zombies," creatures identical to us in every material respect, but altogether lacking conscious experiences. The apparent conceivability of zombies has convinced some philosophers that there is an unbridgeable "explanatory gap" between material qualities and the qualities of conscious experience.

You may be growing impatient with this line of reasoning. Of course we know that others have mental lives similar to ours in many ways—and different as well: it is also possible to know that. Well and good. But it is hard to see how this confidence could be justified so long as we accept the notion that minds and their contents are private affairs, incapable of public scrutiny.

The Beetle in the Box

Perhaps our starting point is what is responsible for our predicament. We have been led down the garden path by a certain conception of mind inherited from Descartes. If we begin to question that conception, we may see our way clear to a solution to our problem, one that better fits our commonsense idea that we can know that others have minds and that their minds resemble ours.

Wittgenstein (1889–1951), in his *Philosophical Investigations* (1953/1968), §293, offers a compelling analogy:

> Suppose everyone had a box with something in it: we call it a "beetle". No one can look into anyone else's box, and everyone says he knows what a beetle is only by looking at his beetle.—Here it would be quite possible for everyone to have something different in his box. One might even imagine such a thing constantly changing.

The picture here resembles the picture of the relation we bear to our own and others' states of mind that we have been taking for granted.

Wittgenstein argues against this picture, not by presenting considerations that imply its falsity, but by showing that our accepting it leads to a paradoxical result: if this is the relation we bear to our own and others' states of mind, then we should have no way of referring to them.

Suppose the word "beetle" had a use in these people's language?—If so it would not be used as the name of a thing. The thing in the box has no place in the language-game at all; not even as a something: for the box might even be empty.—No, one can "divide through" by the thing in the box; it cancels out, whatever it is. That is to say: if we construe the grammar of the expression of sensation on the model of "object and designation" the object drops out of consideration as irrelevant.

What is Wittgenstein's point? You report that your box contains a beetle. Your report is perfectly apt. You have been taught to use the word "beetle" in just this way. Imagine, now, that the object in my box is very different from the object in your box. If we could compare the objects, this would be obvious, although we could never be in a position to compare them. Suppose now that I report that my box contains a beetle. In so doing, I am using the word "beetle" exactly as I have been taught to use it. My utterance, like yours, is perfectly correct.

Suppose, now, we each report, say, that our respective boxes contain a beetle. Is either of us mistaken? No. In the imagined situation, Wittgenstein argues, the word "beetle" is used in such a way that it makes no difference what is inside anyone's box. "Beetle," in our imagined dialect, means, roughly, "whatever is in the box." To wonder whether your beetle resembles my beetle is to misunderstand this use of "beetle." It is to treat "beetle" as though it named or designated a kind of object or entity. But "beetle" is used in such a way that "the object drops out of consideration as irrelevant."

Wittgenstein's point is not merely a linguistic one. Any thoughts we might harbor that we would express using the word "beetle," are similarly constrained. Those thoughts turn out not to concern some particular kind of entity. Differently put: if the word "beetle" does not refer to entities of a particular sort, then neither do thoughts naturally expressible using "beetle."

Philosophical Behaviorism

How might the analogy be extended to states of mind? As a child, you react in various ways to your surroundings. On some occasions, you moan and rub your head. Adults tell you that what you have is called a headache. Others are taught to use "headache" similarly. Does "headache" designate a kind of entity or state?

Perhaps not. Perhaps when you tell me that you have a headache, you are not picking out any definite thing or private condition at all (think of the beetle), but merely evincing your headache. You have been trained in a particular way. When you are moved to moan and rub your head, you are, as a result of this training, moved as well to utter the words "I have a headache." When you ascribe a headache to me, you are saying no more than that I am in a kind of state that leads me to moan, rub my head, or utter "I have a headache." The private character of that state could differ across individuals. It might continually change, or even, in some cases (zombies?), be altogether absent. The function of the word "headache" is not to designate that private character, however. It "drops out of consideration as irrelevant."

Suppose that this account of our use of "headache" applied to our mental vocabulary generally. Then mental terms would not in fact be used to designate kinds of entity or qualitatively similar private episodes as Descartes would have it. Their role is quite different. And in that case, the question whether the state you designate by "experience I have when I view a ripe tomato in bright sunlight" qualitatively matches the state I designate when I use the same expression could not so much as arise. To raise the question is to mischaracterize the use of mental terminology, and thus to utter nonsense.

This line of reasoning supports what is often dubbed philosophical behaviorism. (It is dubbed thus by its opponents. Few philosophers routinely so characterized have applied the label to themselves.) The philosophical behaviorist holds that the Cartesian conception of mind errs in a fundamental way. Minds are not entities (whether Cartesian substances or brains); and mental episodes are not private goings-on inside such entities. We are attracted to the Cartesian picture only because we are misled by what Wittgenstein calls the grammar of our language.

So long as we deploy our language in everyday life we steer clear of philosophical puzzles. Words owe their significance to the "language games" we play with them. An appropriate understanding of any word (hence the concept it expresses) requires a grasp of the part of parts it plays in these language games. When we engage in philosophy, however, we are apt to be misled by the fact that "mind," like "brain," or "baseball," is a substantive noun. We reason that "mind" must designate a kind of entity, and that what we call thoughts, sensations, and feelings refer to qualitatively similar states or modes of this entity. We can avoid confusion only by looking carefully at the way our words are actually deployed in ordinary circumstances.

This prescription is intended by Wittgenstein to apply to philosophy generally. Philosophical problems arise "when language goes on holiday," when we lose touch with the way our words are actually used. In our everyday interactions with one another, we are not puzzled by our capacity to know how others feel or what they are thinking. The philosophical problem of other minds arises when we wrench "mind," "thought," "feeling," and their cognates from the contexts in which they are naturally deployed, put a special interpretation on them, and then boggle at the puzzles that result.

Gilbert Ryle (1900–76) extends Wittgenstein's point. According to Ryle, the supposition that minds are kinds of entity amounts to a "category mistake": "it represents the facts of mental life as if they belonged to one logical type or category . . . when actually they belong to another" (1949, p. 16). Suppose I show you around my university. We stroll through the grounds; I show you various academic and administrative buildings; I take you to the library; I introduce you to students and members of the faculty. When I am done, I ask whether there is anything else you would like to see. You reply: "Yes. You've shown me the grounds, the academic and administrative buildings, the library, students, and faculty; but you haven't shown me the university. I'd like to see that." You have made a category mistake. You have taken the term "university" to designate an entity similar to, but distinct from, those you have seen already.

If you persisted in the belief that "university" designates such an entity despite failing ever to encounter it, you might come to imagine that the entity in question is "non-material." An analogous mistake, says Ryle, encourages Cartesian dualism. We begin with the idea that minds are entities, distinct from, but similar to brains or bodies. When we have trouble locating such entities in the material world, we assume that they must be non-material. We see the mind, to use Ryle's colorful phrase, as the ghost in the machine. But minds are not entities at all, ghostly or otherwise, a fact we should immediately appreciate if only we kept firmly before us the way "mind" functions in ordinary English.

> The theoretically interesting category mistakes are those made by people who are perfectly competent to apply concepts, at least in the situations with which they are familiar, but are still liable in their abstract thinking to allocate those concepts to logical types to which they do not belong.
>
> (1949, P.17)

At the risk of confusing matters by piling analogies on top of analogies, an example of Wittgenstein's may help here. Suppose you look into the cab of a locomotive (or the cockpit of a jetliner). You see levers, knobs, buttons, and switches. Each of these operates in a particular way (some are turned, some slide back and forth, some are pushed or pulled), and each has a particular function in the locomotive's (or jetliner's) operation. We should be misled if we assumed that levers or knobs with similar shapes had similar functions. In the same way, the fact that "mind" is a substantive noun, or that we speak of "states of mind" should not lead us to assume that "mind" functions to designate a particular entity, and that states of mind are states of this entity.

If "mind," like "university," does not function to name a particular kind of material or immaterial ("ghostly") entity, how does it function? Perhaps we ascribe minds to creatures with a capacity to comport themselves, as we should say, "intelligently." A creature possesses a mind, not in virtue of being equipped with a peculiar kind of private ingredient, its mind, but in virtue of being the sort of creature capable of engaging in behavior that exhibits a measure of spontaneity and a relatively complex organization. For their part, states of mind—headaches, intentions, beliefs—are possessed by intelligent creatures in virtue of what they do or would do. Your believing that there is a bear in your path, for instance, is a matter of your taking appropriate evasive measures, your assenting to "There is a bear on the path," and the like. Your intending to attend the World Series is a matter of your being moved to purchase tickets, arranging for transportation, announcing "I'm going to the World Series," and so on.

On a view of this sort, an agent is correctly describable as having states of mind, not only in virtue of what that agent does, but also in virtue of what he would do, what he is "disposed" to do. Thus, if you have a headache, you may be disposed to moan, rub your head, seek out aspirin, and announce "I have a headache." You may do none of these things, however. Imagine, for instance, that you do not want anyone to know that you have a headache. In that case, although you are disposed to behave in particular ways, you do not behave in those ways.

But now we are confronted with a new question. What is it to "be disposed" to behave in a particular way? What are dispositions? A fragile vase possesses a disposition to shatter. In shattering, when struck by a tire iron, for instance, it manifests this disposition. A salt crystal possesses a disposition to dissolve in water. In dissolving upon being placed in water, it manifests its solubility. An object can possess a disposition, however, without manifesting that disposition. A fragile glass need never shatter; a salt crystal need never dissolve.

. . . It is important only to appreciate that any plausible version of philosophical behaviorism requires their introduction. Among other things, dispositions take up the slack between what I do and what I would do. I do, presumably, what I am disposed to do; but I may be disposed to do many things that I never do because the opportunity to do them does not arise or because they are overridden by competing dispositions. You might be disposed to act bravely when faced with danger, but pass your life in tranquil surroundings. This need not detract from your bravery. Of course if you never manifest your bravery, we should have no reason to think you brave—nor, for that matter, need you have any inkling of it. Similarly, we should have no reason to think that a particular unfamiliar substance was water-soluble if its solubility is never manifested. You may be disposed to remain steadfast in a dangerous encounter but nevertheless flee because you are disposed, as well, to spirit away a threatened companion. Similarly, a salt crystal disposed to dissolve in water may fail to dissolve if it is subjected to a powerful electromagnetic field.

In what sense, exactly, does philosophical behaviorism "tie states of mind to behavior"? Behaviorists hold that assertions concerning states of mind can be translated into statements about behavior or dispositions to behave. We have had a taste of this already. If you believe there is a bear in your path, you are disposed to take evasive action, to assent to "There is a bear on the path," to warn your companions, and the like.

The guiding idea is that, if talk about states of mind can be analyzed or paraphrased into talk about behavior (or dispositions to behave), then states of mind will have been "reduced to" (shown to be nothing more than) behavior (or dispositions to behave). Analysis of this sort amounts to the reduction of something to something else. To see the point, think of a parallel case. We sometimes speak of the average family. The income of the average family in rural areas has declined from what it was a decade ago. Is there an average family? Is there an entity (or, for that matter, a collection of entities) designated by the phrase "the average family"? That seems unlikely. In this case, we can see how talk about the average family's income might be reductively analyzed into talk about the income of individual families summed and divided by the number of families. There is nothing more to the average family than this. If we could analyze away claims about minds and mental goings-on, replacing it with claims about behavior and dispositions to behave, then (so the argument goes) we would have succeeded in showing that there is nothing more to an agent's possessing a mind than the agent's behaving or being disposed to behave in appropriately mindful ways.[1]

---

[1]Berkeley defends a reductive analysis of talk about material objects to talk about "ideas" (Berkeley's catch-all term for states of mind). If successful, such an analysis would show that we do not need to suppose that material objects are anything "over and above" ideas. Behaviorists' analyses run in the opposite direction.

What are the prospects for reductive analyses of states of mind? One worry is that behavioral analyses are open-ended. There is no limit on the list of things you might do or be disposed to do if you harbor the belief that there is a bear on the trail, for instance. What you do will depend on the circumstances, and the circumstances can vary in indefinitely many ways. Moreover, it seems clear that among the things you will be disposed to do is to form new beliefs and acquire new desires. Each of these beliefs and desires will need its own behavioral analysis.

This complicates the picture, certainly, but it need not pose an insuperable problem for the philosophical behaviorist. The envisaged analyses need not be finite. We can accept a reductive analysis, provided we can see how it could be extended, even when we are in no position to do so ourselves.

Another difficulty is less easily dismissed. You see a bear on the path and form the belief that there is a bear on the path. But what you do and what you are disposed to do evidently depends on your overall state of mind: what else you believe and want, for instance. And this is so for any state of mind. Suppose you believe that there is a bear on the path, but want to have a closer look, or believe that bears are not dangerous, or suppose you have a yen to live dangerously.

It would seem that your belief is compatible with your behaving or being disposed to behave in any way at all depending on what else you believe and what you want. In that case, however, it looks as though no reductive analysis of states of mind is in the cards. The problem is not just that each of these additional states of mind requires a further behavioral analysis, thus complicating and extending the analytical task. The problem, rather, is that there is apparently no way to avoid mention of further states of mind in any statement of what behavior a given state of mind is likely to produce. It is as though we set out to analyze away talk about the average family only to discover that our analysis reintroduced mention of average families at every turning.

To appreciate the magnitude of the problem, think of your belief that there is a bear on the path. This belief, in concert with the belief that bears are dangerous, and a desire to avoid dangerous animals, may lead you to hurry away. But now imagine that you believe that there is a bear in your path, believe that bears are dangerous, and desire to avoid dangerous animals (your beliefs and desires are as before) but that you believe, in addition, that hurrying away will only attract the attention of bears. In this case, you will be disposed to behave, and behave, very differently.

The example illustrates a general point. Any attempt to say what behavior follows from a given state of mind can be shown false by producing an example in which the state of mind is present but, owing to the addition of new beliefs or desires, the behavior does not follow. Nor will it help to try to rule out such cases by means of a general excluder: if you believe that there is a bear on the path, believe that bears are dangerous, and desire to avoid dangerous animals, then, providing you have no further conflicting beliefs or desires, you will be disposed to turn tail. The problem here is that we have reintroduced mention of states of mind in the exclusion clause. And these are precisely what we were trying to analyze away. The analytical project looks hopeless. . . .

The Legacy of Philosophical Behaviorism

If the attempt to analyze talk of states of mind into talk of behavior is unworkable, what is left of philosophical behaviorism? It is true, certainly, that our grounds for ascribing states of mind to one another are largely behavioral. This is an epistemological point, however, a point about what constitutes evidence for our beliefs about one another's mental lives, and a point a Cartesian could happily accept.

What of Ryle's contention that it is a mistake to regard your possessing a mind as a matter of your body's standing in a particular relation to a distinct entity, your mind? And what of Wittgenstein's suggestion that terms used to ascribe states of mind are not used to designate objects of some definite sort? Both of these ideas are independent of the behaviorist's analytical project, and both survive in accounts of the mind that are self-consciously anti-behaviorist. Thus, one might suppose that to have a mind is just to possess a particular sort of organization, one that issues in what we should call intelligent behavior. And one might imagine that to possess a given state of mind is just to be in some state or other that contributes in a characteristic way to the operation of this organized system.

These themes are central to functionalism, a conception of mind that we [must set aside here]. For the moment, let us simply register behaviorism's lack of concern for the qualitative dimension of states of mind. If your having a headache is solely a matter of your behaving, or being disposed to behave, in a particular way, then the intrinsic qualitative nature of whatever is responsible for your so behaving, or being disposed to behave, is irrelevant. This is explicit in Wittgenstein's beetle in the box analogy. And, as we shall see, this feature of behaviorism is inherited by functionalism.

What could be meant by "intrinsic qualitative nature"? The notion of an intrinsic quality is best understood in contrast to the complementary notion of an extrinsic characteristic. An intrinsic quality is a quality an object has in its own right. Being spherical is an intrinsic quality of a billiard ball. Being near the center of the billiard table is, in contrast, a non-intrinsic, extrinsic feature of the ball.[2] Think of intrinsic qualities as being built into objects, extrinsic characteristics as being possessed by objects only in virtue of relations those objects bear to other objects. In the beetle in the box case, imagine that one person's box contains a marble, and another's contains a sugar cube. Then the intrinsic nature of what is in each box differs. And it is precisely this that "drops out of consideration as irrelevant."

We can distinguish an object's intrinsic qualitative nature from its dispositionalities or causal powers. The billiard ball has the power to roll across the table, the power to shatter a pane of glass, and the power to reflect light in a particular way. But the ball has, as well, a particular qualitative nature: a particular shape, a particular size, a particular temperature. The relation between an object's powers or dispositionalities and its qualitative characteristics is a subtle business, as we shall see later. For the present, we need only recognize that it seems possible to distinguish an object's qualitative aspects from its causal propensities or powers. And, again, behaviorism regards the intrinsic qualitative nature of states of mind as irrelevant.

One way to put this is to say that, according to the behaviorist, states of mind, "*qua* states of mind," lack an intrinsic qualitative nature. Think again of the beetle in the box analogy. Whatever is in the box has some intrinsic qualitative nature. But this nature is irrelevant to its being true that the box contains a beetle: *qua* beetle—considered solely as a beetle—what the box contains lacks intrinsic qualities.

A view of this sort might seem wildly implausible. Surely your headache has an intrinsic qualitative nature, and this is an important part of what makes a headache a headache. These days it is fashionable to put this point by saying that "there is something it is like" to have a headache. What it is like to have a headache differs from what it is like to have other kinds of conscious experience. Part of what makes a given conscious experience a headache is just this "what-it's-likeness."

---

[2]I prefer to contrast intrinsic with extrinsic rather than relational. That two cells bear a certain relation to one another is a relational feature of the cells, but an intrinsic feature of the organism to which they belong.

I have said that the denial of all this might seem implausible. Yet behaviorists do deny it. And, as we shall see, many other philosophers, philosophers dismissive of behaviorism, deny it as well. These philosophers argue that states of mind owe their identity, not to their intrinsic qualitative nature (if indeed they have any such nature at all), but exclusively to their causal powers or, as I prefer, their dispositionalities. We can evaluate such claims only after we have built up an understanding of the underlying metaphysical issues. . . .

References

Crick, Francis (1994). *The Astonishing Hypothesis: The Scientific Search for the Soul,* New York: Scribner.
Ryle, Gilbert (1949). *The Concept of Mind,* London: Hutchinson.
Wittgenstein, Ludwig (1953/1968). *Tractatus Logico-Philosophicus,* trans. D. F. Pears and B. F. McGuinness, London: Routledge and Kegan Paul.

The Nature of Mind

David Armstrong

Men have minds, that is to say, they perceive, they have sensations, emotions, beliefs, thoughts, purposes and desires. What is it to have a mind? What is it to perceive, to feel emotion, to hold a belief or to have a purpose? Many contemporary philosophers think that the best clue we have to the nature of mind is furnished by the discoveries and hypotheses of modern science concerning the nature of man.

What does modern science have to say about the nature of man? There are, of course, all sorts of disagreements and divergencies in the view of individual scientists. But I think it is true to say that one view is steadily gaining ground, so that it bids fair to become established scientific doctrine. This is the view that we can give a complete account of man *in purely physico-chemical terms.* This view has received a tremendous impetus in recent decades from the new subject of molecular biology, a subject that promises to unravel the physical and chemical mechanisms that lie at the basis of life. Before that time, it received great encouragement from pioneering work in neurophysiology pointing to the likelihood of a purely electro-chemical account of the working of the brain. I think it is fair to say that those scientists who still reject the physico-chemical account of man do so primarily for philosophical, or moral or religious reasons, and only secondarily, and half-heartedly, for reasons of scientific detail. This is not to say that in the future new evidence and new problems may not come to light that will force science to reconsider the physico-chemical view of man. But at present the drift of scientific thought is clearly set towards the physico-chemical hypothesis. And we have nothing better to go on than the present.

For me, then, and for many philosophers who think like me, the moral is clear. We must try to work out an account of the nature of mind which is compatible with the view that man is nothing but a physico-chemical mechanism.

And in this paper, I shall be concerned to do just this: to sketch (in barest outline) what may be called a Materialist or Physicalist account of the mind.

The Authority of Science

But before doing this, I should like to go back and consider a criticism of my position that must inevitably occur to some. What reason have I, it may be asked, for taking my stand on science? Even granting that I am right about what is the currently dominant scientific view of man, why should we concede science a special authority to decide questions about the nature of man? What of the authority of philosophy, of religion, of morality, or even of literature and art? Why do I set the authority of science above all these? Why this "scientism"?

It seems to me that the answer to this question is very simple. If we consider the search for truth, in all its fields, we find that it is only in science that men versed in their subject can, after investigation that is more or less prolonged, and which may in some cases extend beyond a single human lifetime, reach substantial agreement about what is the case. It is only as a result of scientific investigation that we ever seem to reach an intellectual consensus about controversial matters.

In the Epistle Dedicatory to *De Corpore*, Hobbes wrote of William Harvey, the discoverer of the circulation of the blood, that he was: "the only man I know, that conquering envy, hath established a new doctrine in his life-time."

Before Copernicus, Galileo and Harvey, Hobbes remarks: "there was nothing certain in natural philosophy." And we might add, with the exception of mathematics, there was nothing certain in any other learned discipline.

These remarks of Hobbes are incredibly revealing. They show us what a watershed in the intellectual history of the human race the seventeenth century was. Before that time, enquiry proceeded, as it were, in the dark. Men could not hope to see their doctrine *established,* that is to say, accepted by the vast majority of those properly versed in the subject under discussion. There was no intellectual consensus. Since that time, it has become a commonplace to see new doctrines, sometimes of the most far-reaching kind, established to the satisfaction of the learned, often within the lifetime of their first proponents. Science has provided us with a method of deciding disputed questions. This is not to say, of course, that the consensus of those who are learned and competent in a subject cannot be mistaken. Of course such a consensus can be mistaken. Sometimes it has been mistaken. But, granting fallibility, what better authority have we than such a consensus?

Now this is of the utmost importance. For in philosophy, in religion, in such disciplines as literary criticism, in moral questions in so far as they are thought to be matters of truth and falsity, there has been a notable failure to achieve an intellectual consensus about disputed questions among the learned. Must we not then attach a peculiar authority to the discipline that can achieve a consensus? And if it presents us with a certain vision of the nature of man, is this not a powerful reason for accepting that vision?

I will not take up here the deeper question *why* it is that the methods of science have enabled us to achieve an intellectual consensus about so many disputed matters. That question, I think, could receive no brief or uncontroversial answer. I am resting my argument on the simple fact that, as a result of scientific investigation, such a consensus has been achieved.

It may be replied—it often is replied—that while science is all very well in its own sphere—the sphere of the physical, perhaps—there are matters of fact on which it is not competent to pronounce. And among such matters, it may be claimed, is the question: what is the whole nature of man? But I cannot see that this reply has much force. Science has provided us with an island of truths, or, perhaps one should say, a raft of truths, to bear us up on the sea of our disputatious ignorance. There may have to be revisions and refinements, new results may set old findings in a new perspective, but what science has given us will not be altogether superseded. Must we not therefore appeal to these relative certainties for guidance when we come to consider uncertainties elsewhere? Perhaps science cannot help us to decide whether or not there is a God, whether or not human beings have immortal souls, or whether or not the will is free. But if science cannot assist us, what can? I conclude that it is the scientific vision of man, and not the philosophical or religious or artistic or moral vision of man, that is the best clue we have to the nature of man. And it is rational to argue from the best evidence we have.[1]

Defining the Mental

Having in this way attempted to justify my procedure, I turn back to my subject: the attempt to work out an account of mind, or, if you prefer, of mental process, within the framework of the physico-chemical, or, as we may call it, the Materialist view of man.

Now there is one account of mental process that is at once attractive to any philosopher sympathetic to a Materialist view of man: this is Behaviourism. Formulated originally by a psychologist, J.B. Watson, it attracted widespread interest and considerable support from scientifically oriented philosophers. Traditional philosophy had tended to think of the mind as a rather mysterious inward arena that lay behind, and was responsible for, the outward or physical behaviour of our bodies. Descartes thought of this inner arena as a *spiritual substance,* and it was this conception of the mind as spiritual object that Gilbert Ryle attacked, apparently in the interest of Behaviourism, in his important book *The Concept of Mind* (1949). He ridiculed the Cartesian view as the dogma of "the ghost in the machine". The mind was not something behind the behaviour of the body, it was simply part of that physical behaviour. My anger with you is not some modification of a spiritual substance that somehow brings about aggressive behaviour; rather it is the aggressive behaviour itself; my addressing strong words to you, striking you, turning my back on you, and so on. Thought is not an inner process that lies behind, and brings about, the words I speak and write: it is my speaking and writing. The mind is not an inner arena, it is an outward act.

It is clear that such a view of mind fits in very well with a completely Materialistic or Physicalist view of man. If there is no need to draw a distinction between mental processes and their expression in physical behaviour, but if instead the mental processes are identified with their

---

[1]The view of science presented here has been challenged in recent years by new Irrationalist philosophies of science. See, in particular, Thomas Kuhn (1962) and Paul Feyerabend (1975). A complete treatment of the problem would involve answering their contentions.

so-called "expressions", then the existence of mind stands in no conflict with the view that man is nothing but a physico-chemical mechanism.

However, the version of Behaviourism that I have just sketched is a very crude version, and its crudity lays it open to obvious objections. One obvious difficulty is that it is our common experience that there can be mental processes going on although there is no behaviour occurring that could possibly be treated as expressions of those processes. A man may be angry, but give no bodily sign; he may think, but say or do nothing at all.

In my view, the most plausible attempt to refine Behaviourism with a view to meeting this objection was made by introducing the notion of a *disposition to behave*. (Dispositions to behave play a particularly important part in Ryle's account of the mind.) Let us consider the general notion of disposition first. Brittleness is a disposition, a disposition possessed by materials like glass. Brittle materials are those that, when subjected to relatively small forces, break or shatter easily. But breaking and shattering easily is not brittleness, rather it is the *manifestation* of brittleness. Brittleness itself is the tendency or liability of the material to break or shatter easily. A piece of glass may never shatter or break throughout its whole history, but it is still the case that it is brittle: it is liable to shatter or break if dropped quite a small way or hit quite lightly. Now a disposition to *behave* is simply a tendency or liability of a person to behave in a certain way under certain circumstances. The brittleness of glass is a disposition that the glass retains throughout its history, but clearly there also could be dispositions that come and go. The dispositions to behave that are of interest to the Behaviourist are, for the most part, of this temporary character.

Now how did Ryle and others use the notion of a disposition to behave to meet the obvious objection to Behaviourism that there can be mental process going on although the subject is engaging in no relevant behaviour? Their strategy was to argue that in such cases, although the subject was not behaving in any relevant way, he or she was disposed to behave in some relevant way. The glass does not shatter, but it is still brittle. The man does not behave, but he does have a disposition to behave. We can say he thinks although he does not speak or act because at that time he was disposed to speak or act in a certain way. *If* he had been asked, perhaps, he would have spoken or acted. We can say he is angry although he does not behave angrily, because he is disposed so to behave. *If* only one more word had been addressed to him, he would have burst out. And so on. In this way it was hoped that Behaviourism could be squared with the obvious facts.

It is very important to see just how these thinkers conceived of dispositions. I quote from Ryle:

> To possess a dispositional property *is not to be in a particular state, or to undergo a particular change*; it is to be bound or liable to be in a particular state, or to undergo a particular change, when a particular condition is realized.[2]

So to explain the breaking of a lightly struck glass on a particular occasion by saying it was brittle is, on this view of dispositions, simply to say that the glass broke because it is the sort of thing that regularly breaks when quite lightly struck. The breaking was the normal behaviour, or not abnormal behaviour, of such a thing. The brittleness is not to be conceived of as a *cause* for the breakage, or even, more vaguely, a *factor* in bringing about the breaking. Brittleness is just the fact that things of that sort break easily.

But although in this way the Behaviourists did something to deal with the objection that mental processes can occur in the absence of behaviour, it seems clear, now that the shouting and the dust have died, that they did not do enough. When I think, but my thoughts do not issue in any action, it seems as obvious as anything is obvious that there is something actually going on in me that constitutes my thought. It is not simply that I would speak or act if some conditions that are unfulfilled were to be fulfilled. Something is currently going on, in the strongest and most literal sense of "going on", and this something is my thought. Rylean Behaviourism denies this, and so it is unsatisfactory as a theory of mind. Yet I know of no version of Behaviourism that is more satisfactory. The moral for those of us who wish to take a purely physicalistic view of man is that we must look for some other account of the nature of mind and of mental processes.

But perhaps we need not grieve too deeply about the failure of Behaviourism to produce a satisfactory theory of mind. Behaviourism is a profoundly unnatural account of mental processes. If somebody speaks and acts in certain ways, it is natural to speak of this speech and action as the *expression* of his thought. It is not at all natural to speak of his speech and action as identical with his thought. We naturally think of the thought as something quite distinct from the speech and action that, under suitable circumstances, brings the speech and action about. Thoughts are not to be identified with behaviour, we think; they

---

[2]Ryle, 1949: 43; emphasis added.

lie behind behaviour. A man's behaviour constitutes the *reason* we have for attributing certain mental processes to him, but the behaviour cannot be identified with the mental processes.

This suggests a very interesting line of thought about the mind. Behaviourism is certainly wrong, but perhaps it is not altogether wrong. Perhaps the Behaviourists are wrong in identifying the mind and mental occurrences with behaviour, but perhaps they are right in thinking that our notion of a mind and of individual mental states is *logically tied to behaviour*. For perhaps what we mean by a mental state is some state of the person that, under suitable circumstances, *brings about* a certain range of behaviour. Perhaps mind can be defined not as behaviour, but rather as the inner cause of certain behaviour. Thought is not speech under suitable circumstances, rather it is something within the person that, in suitable circumstances, brings about speech. And, in fact, I believe that this is the true account, or, at any rate, a true first account, of what we mean by a mental state.

How does this line of thought link up with a purely Physicalist view of man? The position is that while it does not make such a Physicalist view inevitable, it does make it *possible*. It does not entail, but it is compatible with, a purely Physicalist view of man. For if our notion of the mind and of mental states is nothing but that of a cause within the person of certain ranges of behaviour, then it becomes a scientific question, and not a question of logical analysis, what in fact the intrinsic nature of that cause is. The cause might be, as Descartes thought it was, a spiritual substance working through the pineal gland to produce the complex bodily behaviour of which men are capable. It might be breath, or specially smooth and mobile atoms dispersed throughout the body; it might be many other things. But in fact the verdict of modern science seems to be that the sole cause of mind-betokening behaviour in man and the higher animals is the physico-chemical workings of the central nervous system. And so, assuming we have correctly characterized our concept of a mental state as nothing but the cause of certain sorts of behaviour, then we can identify these mental states with purely physical states of the central nervous system.

At this point we may stop and go back to the Behaviourist's dispositions. We saw that, according to him, the brittleness of glass or, to take another example, the elasticity of rubber, is not a state of the glass or the rubber, but is simply the fact that things of that sort behave in the way they do. But now let us consider how a scientist would think about brittleness or elasticity. Faced with the phenomenon of breakage under relatively small impacts, or the phenomenon of stretching when a force is applied followed by contraction when the force is removed, he will assume that there is some current *state* of the glass or the rubber that is responsible for the characteristic behaviour of samples of these two materials. At the beginning, he will not know what this state is, but he will endeavour to find out, and he may succeed in finding out. And when he has found out, he will very likely make remarks of this sort: "We have discovered that the brittleness of glass is in fact a certain sort of pattern in the molecules of the glass." That is to say, he will *identify* brittleness with the state of the glass that is responsible for the liability of the glass to break. For him, a disposition of an object is a state of the object. What makes the state a state of brittleness is the fact that it gives rise to the characteristic manifestations of brittleness. But the disposition itself is distinct from its manifestations: it is the state of the glass that gives rise to these manifestations in suitable circumstances.

This way of looking at dispositions is very different from that of Ryle and the Behaviourists. The great difference is this: If we treat dispositions as actual states, as I have suggested that scientists do, even if states the intrinsic nature of which may yet have to be discovered, then we can say that dispositions are actual causes, or causal factors, which, in suitable circumstances, actually bring about those happenings that are the manifestations of the disposition. A certain molecular constitution of glass that constitutes its brittleness is actually *responsible* for the fact that, when the glass is struck, it breaks.

Now I cannot argue the matter here, because the detail of the argument is technical and difficult, but I believe that the view of dispositions as states, which is the view that is natural to science, is the correct one.[3] I believe it can be shown quite strictly that, to the extent that we admit the notion of dispositions at all, we are committed to the view that they are actual states of the object that has the disposition. I may add that I think that the same holds for the closely connected notions of capacities and powers. Here I will simply have to assume this step in my argument.

But perhaps it will be seen that the rejection of the idea that mind is simply a certain range of man's behaviour in favour of the view that mind is rather the inner *cause* of that range of man's behaviour, is bound up with the rejection of the Rylean view of dispositions in favour of one that treats dispositions as states of objects and so as having actual causal power. The Behaviourists were wrong to identify the mind with behaviour. They were not so far off the mark when they tried to deal with cases where mental happenings occur in the absence of

---

[3]I develop the argument in *Belief, Truth and Knowledge* (1973), ch. 2, sect. 2.

behaviour by saying that these are dispositions to behave. But in order to reach a correct view, I am suggesting, they would have to conceive of these dispositions as actual *states* of the person who has the disposition, states that have actual causal power to bring about behaviour in suitable circumstances. But to do this is to abandon the central inspiration of Behaviourism: that in talking about the mind we do not have to go behind outward behaviour to inner states.

And so two separate but interlocking lines of thought have pushed me in the same direction. The first line of thought is that it goes profoundly against the grain to think of the mind as behaviour. The mind is, rather, that which stands behind and brings about our complex behaviour. The second line of thought is that the Behaviourist's dispositions, properly conceived, are really states that underlie behaviour and, under suitable circumstances, bring about behaviour. Putting these two together, we reach the conception of a mental state *as a state of the person apt for producing certain ranges of behaviour*. This formula: a mental state is a state of the person apt for producing certain ranges of behaviour, I believe to be a very illuminating way of looking at the concept of a mental state. I have found it fruitful in the search for detailed logical analyses of the individual mental concepts.

I do not think that Hegel's Dialectic has much to tell us about the nature of reality. But I think that human thought often moves in a dialectical way, from thesis to antithesis and then to the synthesis. Perhaps thought about the mind is a case in point. I have already said that classical philosophy has tended to think of the mind as an inner arena of some sort. This we may call the Thesis. Behaviourism moves to the opposite extreme: the mind is seen as outward behaviour. This is the Antithesis. My proposed Synthesis is that the mind is properly conceived as an inner principle, but a principle that is identified in terms of the outward behaviour it is apt for bringing about. This way of looking at the mind and mental states does not itself entail a Materialist or Physicalist view of man, for nothing is said in this analysis about the intrinsic nature of these mental states. But if we have, as I have argued that we do have, general scientific grounds for thinking that man is nothing but a physical mechanism, we can go on to argue that the mental states are in fact nothing but physical states of the central nervous system.

The Problem of Consciousness

Along these lines, then, I would look for an account of the mind that is compatible with a purely Materialist theory of man. There are, as may be imagined, all sorts of powerful objections that can be made to my view. But in the rest of this paper, I propose to do only one thing: I will develop one very important objection to my view of the mind—an objection felt by many philosophers—and then try to show how the objection should be met.

The view that our notion of mind is nothing but that of an inner principle apt for bringing about certain sorts of behaviour may be thought to share a certain weakness with Behaviourism. Modern philosophers have put the point about Behaviourism by saying that, although Behaviourism may be a satisfactory account of the mind from *an other-person point of view*, it will not do as a *first-person* account. To explain. In my encounters with other people, all I ever observe is their behaviour: their actions, their speech, and so on. And so, if we simply consider other people, Behaviourism might seem to do full justice to the facts. But the trouble about Behaviourism is that it seems so unsatisfactory as applied to our *own* case. In our own case, we seem to be aware of so much more than mere behaviour.

Suppose that now we conceive of the mind as an inner principle apt for bringing about certain sorts of behaviour. This again fits the other-person cases very well. Bodily behaviour of a very sophisticated sort is observed, quite different from the behaviour that ordinary physical objects display. It is inferred that this behaviour must spring from a very special sort of inner cause in the object that exhibits this behaviour. This inner cause is christened "the mind", and those who take a Physicalist view of man argue that it is simply the central nervous system of the body observed. Compare this with the case of glass. Certain characteristic behaviour is observed: the breaking and shattering of the material when acted upon by relatively small forces. A special inner state of the glass is postulated to explain this behaviour. Those who take a purely Physicalist view of glass then argue that this state is a *material* state of the glass. It is, perhaps, an arrangement of its molecules and not, say, the peculiarly malevolent disposition of the demons that dwell in glass.

But when we turn to our own case, the position may seem less plausible. We are conscious, we have experiences. Now can we say that to be conscious, to have experiences, is simply for something to go on within us apt for the causing of certain sorts of behaviour? Such an account does not seem to do any justice to the phenomena. And so it seems that our account of the mind, like Behaviourism, will fail to do justice to the first-person case.

In order to understand the objection better, it may be helpful to consider a particular case. If you have driven for a very long distance without a break, you may have had experience of a curious state of automatism, which can occur in these conditions. One can suddenly "come to" and realize that one has driven for long distances without being aware of what one was doing, or, indeed, without being aware of anything. One has kept the car on the road, used the brake and the clutch perhaps, yet all without any awareness of what one was doing.

Now if we consider this case, it is obvious that *in some sense* mental processes are still going on when one is in such an automatic state. Unless one's will was still operating in some way, and unless one was still perceiving in some way, the car would not still be on the road. Yet, of course, *something* mental is lacking. Now, I think, when it is alleged that an account of mind as an inner principle apt for the production of certain sorts of behaviour leaves out consciousness or experience, what is alleged to have been left out is just whatever is missing in the automatic driving case. It is conceded that an account of mental processes as states of the person apt for the production of certain sorts of behaviour very possibly may be adequate to deal with such cases as that of automatic driving. It may be adequate to deal with most of the mental processes of animals, which perhaps spend most of their lives in this state of automatism. But, it is contended, it cannot deal with the consciousness that we normally enjoy.

I will now try to sketch an answer to this important and powerful objection. Let us begin in an apparently unlikely place and consider the way that an account of mental processes of the sort I am giving would deal with *sense-perception*.

Now psychologists, in particular, have long realized that there is a very close logical tie between sense-perception and *selective behaviour*. Suppose we want to decide whether an animal can perceive the difference between red and green. We might give the animal a choice between two pathways, over one of which a red light shines and over the other of which a green light shines. If the animal happens by chance to choose the green pathway, we reward it; if it happens to choose the other pathway, we do not reward it. If, after some trials, the animal systematically takes the green-lighted pathway, and if we become assured that the only relevant differences in the two pathways are the differences in the colour of the lights, we are entitled to say that the animal can see this colour difference. Using its eyes, it selects between red-lighted and green-lighted pathways. So we say it can see the difference between red and green.

Now a Behaviourist would be tempted to say that the animal's regular selection of the green-lighted pathway was its perception of the colour difference. But this is unsatisfactory, because we all want to say that perception is something that goes on within the person or animal—within its mind—although, of course, this mental event is normally *caused* by the operation of the environment upon the organism. Suppose, however, that we speak instead of *capacities* for selective behaviour towards the current environment, and suppose we think of these capacities, like dispositions, as actual inner states of the organism. We can then think of the animal's perception as a state within the animal apt, if the animal is so impelled, for selective behaviour between the red- and green-lighted pathways.

In general, we can think of perceptions as inner states or events apt for the production of certain sorts of selective behaviour towards our environment. To perceive is like acquiring a key to a door. You do not have to use the key: you can put it in your pocket and never bother about the door. But if you do want to open the door, the key may be essential. The blind man is a man who does not acquire certain keys and, as a result, is not able to operate in his environment in the way that somebody who has his sight can operate. It seems, then, a very promising view to take of perceptions that they are inner states defined by the sorts of selective behaviour that they enable the perceiver to exhibit, if so impelled.

Now how is this discussion of perception related to the question of consciousness or experience, the sort of thing that the driver who is in a state of automatism has not got, but which we normally do have? Simply this. My proposal is that consciousness, in this sense of the word, is nothing but *perception or awareness of the state of our own mind.* The driver in a state of automatism perceives, or is aware of, the road. If he did not, the car would be in a ditch. But he is not currently aware of his awareness of the road. He perceives the road, but he does not perceive his perceiving, or anything else that is going on in his mind. He is not, as we normally are, conscious of what is going on in his mind.

And so I conceive of consciousness or experience, in this sense of the words, in the way that Locke and Kant conceived it, as like perception. Kant, in a striking phrase, spoke of "inner sense". We cannot directly observe the minds of others, but each of us has the power to observe directly our own minds, and "perceive" what is going on there. The driver in the automatic state is one whose "inner eye" is shut: who is not currently aware of what is going on in his own mind.

Now if this account is along the right lines, why should we not give an account of this inner observation along the same lines as we have already given of perception? Why should we not conceive of it as an inner state, a state in this case directed towards other inner states and not to the environment, which enables us, if we are so impelled, to behave in a selective way *towards our own states of mind*? One who is aware, or conscious, of his thoughts or his emotions is one who has the capacity to make discriminations between his different mental states. His capacity might be exhibited in words. He might say that he was in an angry state of mind, when, and only when, he *was* in an angry state of mind. But such verbal behaviour would be the mere *expression* or *result* of the awareness. The awareness itself would be an inner state: the sort of inner state that gave the man a capacity for such behavioural expressions.

So I have argued that consciousness of our own mental state may be assimilated to *perception* of our own mental state, and that, like other perceptions, it may then be conceived of as an inner state or event giving a capacity for selective behaviour, in this case selective behaviour towards our own mental state. All this is meant to be simply a logical analysis of consciousness, and none of it entails, although it does not rule out, a purely Physicalist account of what these inner states are. But if we are convinced, on general scientific grounds, that a purely physical account of man is likely to be the true one, then there seems to be no bar to our identifying these inner states with purely physical states of the central nervous system. And so consciousness of our own mental state becomes simply the scanning of one part of our central nervous system by another. Consciousness is a self-scanning mechanism in the central nervous system.

As I have emphasized before, I have done no more than sketch a programme for a philosophy of mind. There are all sorts of expansions and elucidations to be made, and all sorts of doubts and difficulties to be stated and overcome. But I hope I have done enough to show that a purely Physicalist theory of the mind is an exciting and plausible intellectual option.

References

Armstrong, D. M. (1973). *Belief, Truth and Knowledge,* Cambridge: Cambridge University Press.

Feyerabend, P. (1963). "Mental Events and the Brain," *Journal of Philosophy* 60: 295–96.

Kuhn, T. (1962). *The Structure of Scientific Revolutions,* Chicago: University of Chicago Press.

Ryle, G. (1949). *The Concept of Mind,* London: Hutchinson.

Mad Pain and Martian Pain

David Lewis

I

There might be a strange man who sometimes feels pain, just as we do, but whose pain differs greatly from ours in its causes and effects. Our pain is typically caused by cuts, burns, pressure, and the like; his is caused by moderate exercise on an empty stomach. Our pain is generally distracting; his turns his mind to mathematics, facilitating concentration on that but distracting him from anything else. Intense pain has no tendency whatever to cause him to groan or writhe, but does cause him to cross his legs and snap his fingers. He is not in the least motivated to prevent pain or to get rid of it. In short, he feels pain but his pain does not at all occupy the typical causal role of pain. He would doubtless seem to us to be some sort of madman, and that is what I shall call him, though of course the sort of madness I have imagined may bear little resemblance to the real thing.

I said there might be such a madman. I don't know how to prove that something is possible, but my opinion that this is a possible case seems pretty firm. If I want a credible theory of mind, I need a theory that does not deny the possibility of mad pain. I needn't mind conceding that perhaps the madman is not in pain in *quite* the same sense that the rest of us are, but there had better be some straightforward sense in which he and we are both in pain.

Also, there might be a Martian, who sometimes feels pain, just as we do, but whose pain differs greatly from ours in its physical realization. His hydraulic mind contains nothing like our neurons. Rather, there are varying amounts of fluid in many inflatable cavities, and the inflation of any one of these cavities opens some valves and closes others. His mental plumbing pervades most of his body—in fact, all but the heat exchanger inside his head. When you pinch his skin you cause no firing of C-fibers—he has none—but, rather, you cause the inflation of many smallish cavities in his feet. When these cavities are inflated, he is in pain. And the effects of his pain are fitting: his thought and activity are disrupted, he groans and writhes, he is strongly motivated to stop you from pinching him and to see to it that you never do again. In short, he feels pain but lacks the bodily states that either are pain or else accompany it in us.

There might be such a Martian; this opinion too seems pretty firm. A credible theory of mind had better not deny the possibility of Martian pain. I needn't mind conceding that perhaps the Martian is not in pain in *quite* the same sense that we Earthlings are, but there had better be some straightforward sense in which he and we are both in pain.

II

A credible theory of mind needs to make a place both for mad pain and for Martian pain. Prima facie, it seems hard for a materialist theory to pass this twofold test. As philosophers, we would like to characterize pain a priori. (We might settle for less, but let's start by asking for all we want.) As materialists, we want to characterize pain as a physical phenomenon. We can speak of the place of pain in the causal network from stimuli to inner states to behavior. And we can speak of the physical processes that go on when there is pain and that take their place in that causal network. We seem to have no other resources but these. But the lesson of mad pain is that pain is associated only contingently with its causal role, while the lesson of Martian pain is that pain is connected only contingently with its physical realization. How can we characterize pain a priori in terms of causal role and physical realization, and yet respect both kinds of contingency?

A simple identity theory straightforwardly solves the problem of mad pain. It goes just as straightforwardly wrong about Martian pain. A simple behaviorism or functionalism goes the other way: right about the Martian, wrong about the madman. The theories that fail our twofold test so decisively are altogether too simple. (Perhaps they are too simple ever to have had adherents.) It seems that a theory that can pass our test will have to be a mixed theory. It will have to be able to tell us that the madman and the Martian are both in pain, but for different reasons: the madman because he is in the right physical state, the Martian because he is in a state rightly situated in the causal network.

Certainly we can cook up a mixed theory. Here's an easy recipe: First, find a theory to take care of the common man and the madman, disregarding the Martian—presumably an identity theory. Second, find a theory to take care of the common man and the Martian, disregarding the madman—presumably some sort of behaviorism or functionalism. Then disjoin the two: say that to be in pain is to be in pain either according to the first theory or according to the second. Alternatively, claim ambiguity: say that to be in pain in one sense is to be in pain according to the first theory, to be in pain in another sense is to be in pain according to the second theory.

This strategy seems desperate. One wonders why we should have a disjunctive or ambiguous concept of pain, if common men who suffer pain are always in pain according to both disjuncts or both disambiguations. It detracts from the credibility of a theory that it posits a useless complexity in our concept of pain—useless in application to the common man, at least, and therefore useless almost always.

I don't object to the strategy of claiming ambiguity. As you'll see, I shall defend a version of it. But it's not plausible to cook up an ambiguity *ad hoc* to account for the compossibility of mad pain and Martian pain. It would be better to find a widespread sort of ambiguity, a sort we would believe in no matter what we thought about pain, and show that it will solve our problem. That is my plan.

III

A dozen years or so ago, D. M. Armstrong and I (independently) proposed a materialist theory of mind that joins claims of type-type psychophysical identity with a behaviorist or functionalist way of characterizing mental states such as pain.[1] I believe our theory passes the twofold test. Positing no ambiguity without independent reason, it provides natural senses in which both madman and Martian are in pain. It wriggles through between Scylla and Charybdis.

Our view is that the concept of pain, or indeed of any other experience or mental state, is the concept of a state that occupies a certain causal role, a state with certain typical causes and effects. It is the concept of a state apt for being caused by certain stimuli and apt for causing certain behavior. Or, better, of a state apt for being caused in certain ways by stimuli plus other mental states and apt for combining with certain other mental states to jointly cause certain behavior. It is the concept of a member of a system of states that together more or less realize the pattern of causal generalizations set forth in commonsense psychology. (That system may be characterized as a whole and its members characterized afterward by reference to their place in it.)

If the concept of pain is the concept of a state that occupies a certain causal role, then whatever state does occupy that role is pain. If the state of having neurons hooked up in a certain way and firing in a certain pattern is the state properly apt for causing and being caused, as we materialists think, then that neural state is pain. But the concept of pain is not the concept of that neural state. ("The concept of . . ." is an intensional functor.) The concept of pain, unlike the concept of that neural state which in fact is pain, would have applied to some different state if the relevant causal relations had been different. Pain might have not been pain. The occupant of the role might have not occupied it. Some other state might have occupied it instead. Something that is not pain might have been pain.

This is not to say, of course, that it might have been that pain was not pain and nonpain was pain; that is, that it might have been that the occupant of the role did not occupy it and some nonoccupant did. Compare: "The winner might have lost" (true) versus "It might have been that the winner lost" (false). No wording is entirely unambiguous, but I trust my meaning is clear.

In short, the concept of pain as Armstrong and I understand it is a *nonrigid* concept. Likewise the word "pain" is a nonrigid designator. It is a contingent matter what state the concept and the word apply to. It depends on what causes what. The same goes for the rest of our concepts and ordinary names of mental states.

Some need hear no more. The notion that mental concepts and names are nonrigid, wherefore what *is* pain might not have been, seems to them just self-evidently false.[2] I cannot tell why they think so. Bracketing my own theoretical commitments, I think I would have no opinion one way or the other. It's not that I don't care about shaping theory to respect naive opinion as well as can be, but in this case I have no naive opinion to respect. If I am not speaking to your condition, so be it.

If pain is identical to a certain neural state, the identity is contingent. Whether it holds is one of the things that varies from one possible world to another. But take care. I do not say that here we have two states, pain and some neural state, that are contingently identical, identical at this world but different at another. Since I'm serious about the identity, we have not two states but one. This one state, this neural state which is pain, is not contingently identical to itself. It does not differ from itself at any world. Nothing does.[3] What's true is, rather, that the concept and name of pain contingently apply to some neural state at this world, but do not apply to it at another. Similarly, it is a contingent truth that Bruce is our cat, but it's wrong to say that Bruce and our cat are contingently identical. Our cat Bruce is necessarily self-identical. What is contingent is that the nonrigid concept of being our cat applies to Bruce rather than to some other cat, or none.

IV

Nonrigidity might begin at home. All actualities are possibilities, so the variety of possibilities includes the variety of actualities. Though some possibilities are thoroughly otherworldly, others may be found on planets within range of our telescopes. One such planet is Mars.

If a nonrigid concept or name applies to different states in different possible cases, it should be no surprise if it also applies to different states in different actual cases. Nonrigidity is to logical space as other relativities are to ordinary space. If the word "pain" designates one state at our actual world and another at a possible world where our counterparts have a different internal structure, then also it may designate one state on Earth and another on Mars. Or, better, since Martians may come here and we may go to Mars, it may designate one state for Earthlings and another for Martians.

We may say that some state *occupies a causal role for a population.* We may say this whether the population is situated entirely at our actual world, or partly at our actual world and partly at other worlds, or entirely at other worlds. If the concept of pain is the concept of a state that occupies that role, then we may say that a state *is pain for a population.* Then we may say that a certain pattern of firing of neurons is pain for the population of actual Earthlings and some but not all of our otherworldly counterparts, whereas the inflation of certain cavities in the feet is pain for the population of actual Martians and some of their otherworldly counterparts. Human pain is the state that occupies the role of pain for humans. Martian pain is the state that occupies the same role for Martians.

A state occupies a causal role for a population, and the concept of occupant of that role applies to it, if and only if, with few exceptions, whenever a member of that population is in that state, his being in that state has the sort of causes and effects given by the role.

The thing to say about Martian pain is that the Martian is in pain because he is in a state that occupies the causal role of pain for Martians, whereas we are in pain because we are in a state that occupies the role of pain for us.

V

Now, what of the madman? He is in pain, but he is not in a state that occupies the causal role of pain for him. He is in a state that occupies that role for most of us, but he is an exception. The causal role of a pattern of firing of neurons depends on one's circuit diagram, and he is hooked up wrong.

His state does not occupy the role of pain for a population comprising himself and his fellow madmen. But it does occupy that role for a more salient population—mankind at large. He is a man, albeit an exceptional one, and a member of that larger population.

We have allowed for exceptions. I spoke of the definitive syndrome of *typical* causes and effects. Armstrong spoke of a state *apt* for having certain causes and effects; that does not mean that it has them invariably. Again, I spoke of a system of states that *comes near to* realizing commonsense psychology. A state may therefore occupy a role for mankind even if it does not at all occupy that role for some mad minority of mankind.

The thing to say about mad pain is that the madman is in pain because he is in the state that occupies the causal role of pain for the population comprising all mankind. He is an exceptional member of that population. The state that occupies the role for the population does not occupy it for him.

VI

We may say that X is in pain *simpliciter* if and only if X is in the state that occupies the causal role of pain for the *appropriate* population. But what is the appropriate population? Perhaps (1) it should be *us;* after all, it's our concept and our word. On the other hand, if it's X we're talking about, perhaps (2) it should be a population that X himself belongs to, and (3) it should preferably be one in which X is not exceptional. Either way, (4) an appropriate population should be a natural kind—a species, perhaps.

If X is you or I—human and unexceptional—all four considerations pull together. The appropriate population consists of mankind as it actually is, extending into other worlds only to an extent that does not make the actual majority exceptional.

Since the four criteria agree in the case of the common man, which is the case we usually have in mind, there is no reason why we should have made up our minds about their relative importance in cases of conflict. It should be no surprise if ambiguity and uncertainty arise in such cases. Still, some cases do seem reasonably clear.

If X is our Martian, we are inclined to say that he is in pain when the cavities in his feet are inflated; and so says the theory, provided that criterion (1) is outweighed by the other three, so that the appropriate population is taken to be the species of Martians to which X belongs.

If X is our madman, we are inclined to say that he is in pain when he is in the state that occupies the role of pain for the rest of us; and so says the theory, provided that criterion (3) is outweighed by the other three, so that the appropriate population is taken to be mankind.

We might also consider the case of a mad Martian, related to other Martians as the madman is to the rest of us. If X is a mad Martian, I would be inclined to say that he is in pain when the cavities in his feet are inflated; and so says our theory, provided that criteria (2) and (4) together outweigh either (1) or (3) by itself.

Other cases are less clear-cut. Since the balance is less definitely in favor of one population or another, we may perceive the relativity to population by feeling genuinely undecided. Suppose the state that plays the role of pain for us plays instead the role of thirst for a certain small subpopulation of mankind, and vice versa. When one of them has the state that is pain for us and thirst for him, there may be genuine and irresolvable indecision about whether to call him pained or thirsty—that is, whether to think of him as a madman or as a Martian. Criterion (1) suggests calling his state pain and regarding him as an exception; criteria (2) and (3) suggest shifting to a subpopulation and calling his state thirst. Criterion (4) could go either way, since mankind and the exceptional subpopulation may both be natural kinds. (Perhaps it is relevant to ask whether membership in the subpopulation is hereditary.)

The interchange of pain and thirst parallels the traditional problem of inverted spectra. I have suggested that there is no determinate fact of the matter about whether the victim of interchange undergoes pain or thirst. I think this conclusion accords well with the fact that there seems to be no persuasive solution one way or the other to the old problem of inverted spectra. I would say that there is a good sense in which the alleged victim of inverted spectra sees red when he looks at grass: he is in a state that occupies the role of seeing red for mankind in general. And there is an equally good sense in which he sees green: he is in a state that occupies the role of seeing green for him, and for a small subpopulation of which he is an unexceptional member and which has some claim to be regarded as a natural kind. You are right to say either, though not in the same breath. Need more be said?

To sum up, Armstrong and I claim to give a schema that, if filled in, would characterize pain and other states a priori. If the causal facts are right, then also we characterize pain as a physical phenomenon. By allowing for exceptional members of a population, we associate pain only contingently with its causal role. Therefore we do not deny the possibility of mad pain, provided there is not too much of it. By allowing for variation from one population to another (actual or merely possible) we associate pain only contingently with its physical realization. Therefore we do not deny the possibility of Martian pain. If different ways of filling in the relativity to population may be said to yield different senses of the word "pain," then we plead ambiguity. The madman is in pain in one sense, or relative to one population. The Martian is in pain in another sense, or relative to another population. (So is the mad Martian.)

But we do not posit ambiguity *ad hoc*. The requisite flexibility is explained simply by supposing that we have not bothered to make up our minds about semantic niceties that would make no difference to any commonplace case. The ambiguity that arises in cases of inverted spectra and the like is simply one instance of a commonplace kind of ambiguity—a kind that may arise whenever we have tacit relativity and criteria of selection that sometimes fail to choose a definite *relatum*. It is the same kind of ambiguity that arises if someone speaks of relevant studies without making clear whether he means relevance to current affairs, to spiritual well-being, to understanding, or what.

VII

We have a place for commonplace pain, mad pain, Martian pain, and even mad Martian pain. But one case remains problematic. What about pain in a being who is mad, alien, and unique? Have we made a place for that? It seems not. Since he is mad, we may suppose that his alleged state of pain does not occupy the proper causal role for him. Since he is alien, we may also suppose that it does not occupy the proper role for us. And since he is unique, it does not occupy the proper role for others of his species. What is left?

(One thing that might be left is the population consisting of him and his un-actualized counterparts at other worlds. If he went mad as a result of some improbable accident, perhaps we can say that he is in pain because he is in the state that occupies the role for most of his alternative possible selves; the state that would have occupied the role for him if he had developed in a more probable way. To make the problem as hard as possible, I must suppose that this solution is unavailable. He did *not* narrowly escape being so constituted that his present state would have occupied the role of pain.)

I think we cannot and need not solve this problem. Our only recourse is to deny that the case is possible. To stipulate that the being in this example is in pain was illegitimate. That seems credible enough. Admittedly, I might have thought offhand that the case was possible. No wonder; it merely combines elements of other cases that are possible. But I am willing to change my mind. Unlike my opinions about the possibility of mad pain and Martian pain, my naive opinions about this case are not firm enough to carry much weight.

VIII

Finally, I would like to try to pre-empt an objection. I can hear it said that I have been strangely silent about the very center of my topic. *What is it like* to be the madman, the Martian, the mad Martian, the victim of interchange of pain and thirst, or the being who is mad, alien, and unique? What is the *phenomenal character* of his state? If it *feels* to him like pain, then it is pain, whatever its causal role or physical nature. If not, it isn't. It's that simple!

Yes. It would indeed be a mistake to consider whether a state is pain while ignoring what it is like to have it. Fortunately, I have not made that mistake. Indeed, it is an impossible mistake to make. It is like the impossible mistake of considering whether a number is composite while ignoring the question of what factors it has.

Pain is a feeling.[4] Surely that is uncontroversial. To have pain and to feel pain are one and the same. For a state to be pain and for it to feel painful are likewise one and the same. A theory of what it is for a state to be pain is inescapably a theory of what it is like to be in that state, of how that state feels, of the phenomenal character of that state. Far from ignoring questions of how states feel in the odd cases we have been considering. I have been discussing nothing else! Only if you believe on independent grounds that considerations of causal role and physical realization have no bearing on whether a state is pain should you say that they have no bearing on how that state feels.

Notes

1. D. M. Armstrong, *A Materialist Theory of the Mind* (London: Routledge, 1968); "The Nature of Mind," in C. V. Borst, ed., *The Mind/Brain Identity Theory* (London: Macmillan, 1970), pp. 67–97; "The Causal Theory of the Mind," *Neue Heft für Philosophie*, no. 11 (Vendenhoek & Ruprecht, 1977), pp. 82–95. David Lewis, "An Argument for the Identity

Theory," *Journal of Philosophy* 63 (1966): 17–25, reprinted with additions in David M. Rosenthal, ed., *Materialism and the Mind-Body Problem* (Englewood Cliffs, N.J.: Prentice-Hall, 1971), pp. 162–171; "Review of *Art, Mind, and Religion*," *Journal of Philosophy* 66 (1969): 22–27, particularly pp. 23–25; "Psychophysical and Theoretical Identifications," *Australasian Journal of Philosophy* 50 (1972): 249–258; "Radical Interpretation," *Synthese* 23 (1974): 331–344.

2. For instance, see Saul A. Kripke, "Naming and Necessity," in Gilbert Harman and Donald Davidson, eds., *Semantics of Natural Language* (Dordrecht: Reidel, 1972), pp. 253–355, 763–769, particularly pp. 335–336. Note that the sort of identity theory that Kripke opposes by argument, rather than by appeal to self-evidence, is not the sort that Armstrong and I propose.

3. The closest we can come is to have something at one world with twin counterparts at another. See my "Counterpart Theory and Quantified Modal Logic," *Journal of Philosophy* 65 (1968): 113–126. That possibility is irrelevant to the present case.

4. Occurrent pain, that is. Maybe a disposition that sometimes but not always causes occurrent pain might also be called "pain."

Functionalism, Qualia, and the Inverted Spectrum

Terrance Horgan

I

Functionalism is the doctrine that every mental state-type may be fully defined by means of its typical causal connections to sensory stimulation, behavior, and other mental state-types similarly defined. Some philosophers, myself included, believe that although functionalism is plausible as regards certain aspects of mentality, nevertheless there is one aspect that is incapable, in principle, of being analyzed functionally: viz., the qualitative, or phenomenal, content of our mental states— i.e., *what it is like* to undergo these states. What we mean by the notion of qualitative content, and why we think that this aspect of mentality cannot be accommodated by functionalism, are nicely summarized by Jerry Fodor:

Try to imagine looking at a blank wall through a red filter. Now change the filter to a green one and leave everything else exactly the way it was. Something about the character of your experience changes when the filter does, and it is this kind of thing that philosophers call qualitative content. . . .

The reason qualitative content is a problem for functionalism is straightforward. Functionalism is committed to defining mental states in terms of their causes and effects. It seems, however, as if two mental states could have all the same causal relations and yet could differ in their qualitative content. Let me illustrate this with the classic puzzle of the inverted spectrum.

It seems possible to imagine two observers who are alike in all relevant psychological respects except that experiences having the qualitative content of red for one observer would have the qualitative content of green for the other. Nothing about their behavior need reveal the difference because both of them see ripe tomatoes and flaming sunsets as being similar in color and both of them call that color "red." Moreover, the causal connection between their (qualitatively distinct) experiences and their other mental states could also be identical. Perhaps they both think of Little Red Riding Hood when they see ripe tomatoes, feel depressed when they see the color green and so on. It seems as if anything that could be packed into the notion of the causal role of their experience could be shared by them, and yet the qualitative content of the experiences could be as different as you like. If this is possible, then the functionalist account does not work for mental states that have qualitative content. If one person is having a green experience while another person is having a red one, then surely they must be in different mental states.

It would seem that if all mental states are fully definable functionally, then the inverted-spectrum thought experiment Fodor describes should be conceptually incoherent. Yet many of us find it remarkably easy to perform such thought experiments, and this makes us very suspicious of claims that they are incoherent. Instead, we find ourselves concluding that functionalism, whatever its virtues in other respects, cannot accommodate qualia. . . .

II

Let us now return to the inverted-spectrum objection to functionalism. To fix our attention on a concrete case, we shall suppose that Jack is a normal color-perceiver, but that Jill has, from the moment of her birth onward, unusual neural "wiring" in the intermediate portions of her visual system—wiring which systematically causes the retinal stimulations induced by light of any given wavelength to generate in her visual cortex the same neural activity that is generated in us by the "spectral inverse" of that wavelength. Thus, if brain state G and brain state R are the state-types induced in John's visual cortex by green objects and red objects respectively, then G is induced in Jill by red objects and R is induced in her by green objects. Nonetheless, since Jill has learned color words in the same ostensive manner John has, she uses those words in the same way he does. Let us further suppose that G plays *completely* the same causal role in Jill that R plays in Jack, and vice versa; thus, if Jack thinks of Little Red Riding Hood when looking at ripe tomatoes then so does Jill, and if Jack becomes depressed when he looks at green objects then so does Jill, and so on.

Thought experiments like this initially seem problematic for functionalism. For when Jack and Jill both look at grass, they surely differ mentally despite being in functionally identical states—a fact that seems to imply that there is more to mentality than what is functionally definable. But now we see how the functionalist can reply to this line of reasoning. He can say that although Jack and Jill are in functionally identical states under one relativization (the one that relativizes Jack's mental states to mankind, and Jill's to her unusual subpopulation), they are in functionally *different* states under another relativization (the one that relativizes both Jack's and Jill's mental states to mankind). Thus, the functionalist can deny that the case of Jack and Jill shows there is more to mentality than is functionally definable. He can say instead that under one relativization, Jack and Jill differ neither functionally nor mentally when they look at grass, whereas under the other relativization they differ *both* functionally and mentally. According to this account, we really commit a subtle form of equivocation if we claim that Jack and Jill differ mentally despite being in functionally identical states: viz., equivocation between two contextually appropriate ways of relativizing mental-state ascriptions.

Should we qualia-lovers concede that this analysis successfully disarms the inverted-spectrum objection to functionalism? I submit that we should not, and for a reason that takes much less time to state than does the analysis itself. For it is just self-evident, I submit, that the qualitative content of Jill's experience when she looks at grass is an absolute, intrinsic feature of her mental life—not a feature that is implicitly population-relative. There is, absolutely and non-relatively, *something it is like* for Jill when she looks at grass. Furthermore, this feature differs from the corresponding intrinsic, non-relative feature of

Jack's mental life when he looks at grass: what it is like for Jill when she looks at grass is the same as what it is like for Jack when he looks at grassy red stuff. Hence their mental states when looking at grass are intrinsically, unqualifiedly different. This difference remains present even if we relativize all *functional* state-ascriptions in such a way that Jack and Jill are in functionally-identical states when looking at grass. Thus, the phenomenal content of color experience does indeed go beyond what is functionally definable. Functionalism cannot accommodate qualia.

As I said, I take the intrinsic, non-relative nature of qualia to be a self-evident fact, a fact which unavoidably impresses itself upon most of us who actually experience these states. The point is virtually impossible to *argue* for, however, because it depends upon an individual's first-person perspective toward his own mental life. Functionalists can, and do, resolutely insist that they are aware of no such features in their own mental life; and since the rest of us lack first-person access to their mental states, we cannot refute them. We can only describe cases like that of Jack and Jill, and ask whether it is not absolutely, undeniably *obvious* that there is an intrinsic, non-population-relative difference between Jack's mental state when looking at grass and Jill's.

Dialectically, we seem to have reached an impasse. Initially it appeared that functionalists were required to take the heroic step of denying the intelligibility of inverted-spectrum stories, and hence that the evident intelligibility of such stories constituted evidence against them. But it turns out that functionalists can make sense of inverted spectra by invoking population-relativization. The qualia-lovers reply that this approach leaves out of account the allegedly self-evident fact that the qualitative content of our mental states is an intrinsic, non-population-relative feature of those states. The functionalists respond by denying that this is a fact at all, let alone a self-evident one. Deadlock.

I shall not try to break this deadlock. Instead, I shall simply direct the subsequent discussion at those who consider it obvious, as I do, that the qualitative aspects of mentality are not definable functionally. I shall propose a theory of mind that makes room for qualia as non-functional mental state-types. If you are not among those to whom the remaining portion of the paper is addressed, and you find yourself wondering what it is about our mental life that is allegedly left out by functional definitions, I can only join with Ned Block in replying with the words once used by Louis Armstrong when he was asked what jazz is: "If you got to ask, you ain't never gonna get to know."

III

I propose a two-part theory. Phenomenal state-types (i.e., qualia) are to be identified with neurophysiological state-types; the identities involved are necessary identities, because the qualia-names involved (as well as the neurophysiological state-names) are rigid designators. Non-phenomenal state-types, on the other hand, are to be construed functionally. . . .

Can we expect all the mental state-types we recognize in everyday mentalese to be neatly separable by means of the phenomenal/non-phenomenal distinction? Not necessarily. It may turn out that many garden-variety mental state-types are really hybrid types, involving both a phenomenal component and a non-phenomenal component. A plausible candidate for such hybrid status, I suggest, is the philosopher's favorite mental state: pain. I think there are really two state-types instantiated in any clear-cut instance of pain: (1) *phenomenal* pain, the "raw feel" of pa in experiences (and the element not definable functionally); and (2) *functional* pain, the state-type which, by definition, has typical causes such as harmful forces impinging upon the creature's surface, and typical effects such as avoidance-behavior. Hybrid types, on the view I am proposing, are instantiated when both the relevant purely-phenomenal type and the relevant purely-functional type are instantiated—even if these latter are not explicitly countenanced in everyday mentalese.

IV

Let us now consider how this theory, which I shall call *partial functionalism*, fares in comparison to full-fledged functionalism. One important advantage of partial functionalism, of course, is that it explicitly accommodates the deeply-felt intuition that the phenomenal aspects of mentality are not definable functionally: the intuition that functionalism leaves out what it is like to undergo mental states like pain, thirst, seeing red, and seeing green.

Another positive feature of partial functionalism is that it not only accommodates this intuition, but it does so while still preserving a fully naturalistic conception of a human being as physico-chemical system whose behavior is completely explainable, in principle, solely in physicochemical terms. For although I am claiming that the qualitative content of our mental life is not definable functionally. I am not thereby rendering it something occult—something apart from the uninterrupted nexus of physico-chemical causation within the human central nervous system. On the contrary, I am claiming that qualia are nothing other than certain neurophysiological state-types. They are not higher-level state-types whose presence and causal efficacy in human beings are mysterious from the perspective of natural science.

One reason for the current wide appeal of functionalism, I think, is that this doctrine seems to mesh so nicely with a naturalistic conception of human beings. Under functionalism it is no more difficult to understand how humans, regarded naturalistically, can undergo mental states than it is to understand how the physical devices we call computers can undergo "computational" states—i.e., states defined abstractly in terms of the computer's program, its "software." Mentality is to physico-chemical activity in humans as computational activity is to physico-chemical activity in computers.

I am claiming that phenomenal state-types are, in Keith Gunderson's happy phrase, "program resistant." That is, the capacity to instantiate them does not arise by virtue of a creature's software, the functional organization of its physico-chemical components. But I espouse naturalism nonetheless, for my contention is that phenomenal state-types are *hardware* state-types rather than software state-types. They are program resistant because they are identical, and necessarily identical, to physico-chemical state-types—not because they are occult state-types that no mere physico-chemical system could instantiate.

But although partial functionalism does seem compatible with the granola conception of human beings, nevertheless one might object that it is theoretically less unified than full-fledged functionalism, and that this fact counts seriously against it.

I deny neither the desirability of theoretical simplicity nor the fact that my theory is somewhat more complex than functionalism. But a theory of mind should not be rendered simple at the cost of failing to accommodate seemingly obvious facts about our mental life—like the fact that in an inverted spectrum situation like that of Jack and Jill, the two persons differ mentally in an absolute, non-population-relative way. Furthermore, since I am not positing qualia as state-types over and above physico-chemical state-types, the greater complexity of my theory concerns only the workings of mental terminology; the ontology of this theory is at least as parsimonious as functionalism's ontology.

Another potential objection to partial functionalism is the charge that it is chauvinistic, in a way that functionalism is not. Surely, the objection goes, a Martian could undergo the same qualia we do even if his neurological hardware were vastly different from our own. Functionalism allows for this possibility, but partial functionalism does not.

Since my theory is partly functionalist, I can grant the plasticity of non-phenomenal mental states, i.e., the realizability of such states in creatures vastly different from ourselves in physico-chemical structure. But is it really plausible to say the same about qualia? I submit that it is not, unless one holds that qualia too are functionally definable. For, if we deny that qualia are functional states, then the most natural way to accommodate them naturalistically is to suppose that they are identical with specific physico-chemical states of the human brain—or at any rate, of brains relevantly similar to human brains. And it then becomes plausible to *deny* the plasticity of qualia, and to contend that a Martian, with his radically different physical makeup, must experience either different qualia than ours or no qualia at all.

The prospect of Martians who are functionally similar to us but who either lack qualia altogether or else have dramatically different qualia, raises with a vengeance the traditional problem of other minds. If partial functionalism is correct, how could we ever tell whether Martians have qualia? Their functional organization would be compatible with both (1) the supposition that their mental lives are qualitatively as rich as our own, and (2) the alternative supposition that they are zombies whose mental lives are qualitatively empty.

Suppose we came to know and like Martians, and to have frequent profound intellectual intercourse with them—including philosophical discussions about minds. At some point, no doubt we would raise the topic of functionalism, the doctrine that all mental state-types are fully definable in terms of typical causal connections to sensory inputs, behavioral outputs, and other similarly-defined mental states. Once we were satisfied that they understood this thesis, we could simply *ask* them whether they find that in their own case, there is more to mental-ity than what is functionally definable. To make the question more specific, we could describe a Martian version of our earlier inverted-spectrum story, involving a Martian Jack and a Martian Jill, and then ask them whether these two individuals would differ mentally in some absolute, non-population-relative way. If they said yes, we would have grounds for inferring that they have qualia; if no, we would have grounds for inferring that they do not.

Admittedly, the matter might be complicated by the existence of some Martian philosophers who really have qualia but still resolutely deny that there is more to theory mentality than what is functionally definable— just as certain human philosophers do. Still, we could obtain evidence for or against Martian qualia by determining whether the issue was *controversial* among philosophically-inclined Martians. If, by and large, they tended to accede to a Lewis-style analysis of inverted-spectrum cases, we could infer that they probably have no qualia. If, on the other hand, many of them insisted that something crucial is left out by such an analysis, and that "If you got to ask" what it is "you ain't never gonna get to know," then we could infer that they probably do have qualia—the stubbornness of the Martian functionalists notwithstanding.

But even if it is possible, under partial functionalism, to know whether or not Martians have qualia, it very well might not be possible to know what these qualia are like. After all, "knowing what a mental state is like" involves being in, or remembering being in, that state yourself—or at any rate, being in, or remembering being in, sufficiently similar states. And since Martian qualia would be physico-chemical state-types instantiatable by creatures with a Martian-like physical composition, we humans might simply lack the neural hardware that is necessary to undergo Martian qualia. And if we could not undergo them, we could not "know what they are like."

Does this show that there is something occult and theoretically mysterious about qualia after all? I think not. For I have been claiming that part of what we mean by "knowing what a mental state is like" is "having undergone that state, or a similar one, one-self." Thus, if we can explain scientifically why humans cannot undergo the physical state-types which are identical to Martian qualia, we will thereby explain *why* humans cannot know what Martian qualia are like. Furthermore, it is still perfectly possible to know *what* they are, even if we cannot know what they are like: they are specific physico-chemical state-types.

Minds, Brains, and Programs

John R. Searle

What psychological and philosophical significance should we attach to recent efforts at computer simulations of human cognitive capacities? In answering this question, I find it useful to distinguish what I will call "strong" AI from "weak" or "cautious" AI (Artificial Intelligence).

According to weak AI, the principal value of the computer in the study of the mind is that it gives us a very powerful tool. For example, it enables us to formulate and test hypotheses in a more rigorous and precise fashion. But according to strong AI, the computer is not merely a tool in the study of the mind; rather, the appropriately programmed computer really is a mind, in the sense that computers given the right programs can be literally said to *understand* and have other cognitive states. In strong AI, because the programmed computer has cognitive states, the programs are not mere tools that enable us to test psychological explanations; rather, the programs are themselves the explanations.

I have no objection to the claims of weak AI, at least as far as this article is concerned. My discussion here will be directed at the claims I have defined as those of strong AI, specifically the claim that the appropriately programmed computer literally has cognitive states and that the programs thereby explain human cognition. When I hereafter refer to AI, I have in mind the strong version, as expressed by these two claims.

I will consider the work of Roger Schank and his colleagues at Yale (Schank & Abelson 1977), because I am more familiar with it than I am with any other similar claims, and because it provides a very clear example of the sort of work I wish to examine. But nothing that follows depends upon the details of Schank's programs. The same arguments would apply to Winograd's SHRDLU (Winograd 1973), Weizenbaum's ELIZA (Weizenbaum 1965), and indeed any Turing machine simulation of human mental phenomena.

Very briefly, and leaving out the various details, one can describe Schank's program as follows: the aim of the program is to simulate the human ability to understand stories. It is characteristic of human beings' story-understanding capacity that they can answer questions about the story even though the information that they give was never explicitly stated in the story. Thus, for example, suppose you are given the following story: "A man went into a restaurant and ordered a hamburger. When the hamburger arrived it was burned to a crisp, and the man stormed out of the restaurant angrily, without paying for the hamburger or leaving a tip." Now, if you are asked "Did the man eat the hamburger?" you will presumably answer, "No, he did not." Similarly, if you are given the following story: "A man went into a restaurant and ordered a hamburger; when the hamburger came he was very pleased with it; and as he left the restaurant he gave the waitress a large tip before paying his bill," and you are asked the question, "Did the man eat the hamburger?," you will presumably answer, "Yes, he ate the hamburger." Now Schank's machines can similarly answer questions about restaurants in this fashion. To do this, they have a "representation" of the sort of information that human beings have about restaurants, which enables them to answer such questions as those above, given these sorts of stories. When the machine is given the story and then asked the question, the machine will print out answers of the sort that we would expect human beings to give if told similar stories. Partisans of strong AI claim that in this question and answer sequence the machine is not only simulating a human ability but also

1. that the machine can literally be said to *understand* the story and provide the answers to questions, and
2. that what the machine and its program do *explains* the human ability to understand the story and answer questions about it.

Both claims seem to me to be totally unsupported by Schank's[1] work, as I will attempt to show in what follows.

One way to test any theory of the mind is to ask oneself what it would be like if my mind actually worked on the principles that the theory says all minds work on. Let us apply this test to the Schank program with the following *Gedankenexperiment*. Suppose that I'm locked in a room and given a large batch of Chinese writing. Suppose furthermore (as is indeed the case) that I know no Chinese, either written or spoken, and that I'm not even confident that I could recognize Chinese writing as Chinese writing distinct from, say, Japanese writing or meaningless squiggles. To me, Chinese writing is just so many meaningless squiggles. Now suppose further that after this first batch of Chinese writing I am given a second batch of Chinese script together with a set of rules for correlating the second batch with the first batch. The rules are in English, and I understand these rules as well as any other native speaker of English. They enable me to correlate one set of formal symbols with another set of formal symbols, and all that "formal" means here is that I can identify the symbols entirely by their shapes. Now suppose also that I am given a third batch of Chinese symbols together with some instructions, again in English, that enable me to correlate elements of this third batch with the first two batches, and these rules instruct me how to give back certain Chinese symbols with certain sorts of shapes in response to certain sorts of shapes given me in the third batch. Unknown to me, the people who are giving me all of these symbols call the first batch "a script," they call the second batch a "story," and they call the third batch "questions." Furthermore, they call the symbols I give them back in response to the third batch "answers to the questions," and the set of rules in English that they gave me, they call "the program." Now just to complicate the story a little, imagine that these people also give me stories in English, which I understand, and they then ask me questions in English about these stories, and I give them back answers in English. Suppose also that after a while I get so good at following the instructions for manipulating the Chinese symbols and the programmers get so good at writing the programs that from the external point of view— that is, from the point of view of somebody outside the room in which I am locked—my answers to the questions are absolutely indistinguishable from those of native Chinese speakers. Nobody just looking at my answers can tell that I don't speak a word of Chinese. Let us also suppose that my answers to the English questions are, as they no doubt would be, indistinguishable from those of other native English speakers, for the simple reason that I am a native English speaker. From the external point of view—from the point of view of someone reading my "answers"—the answers to the Chinese questions and the English questions are equally good. But in the Chinese case, unlike the English case, I produce the answers by manipulating uninterpreted formal symbols. As far as the Chinese is concerned, I simply behave like a computer; I perform computational operations on formally specified elements. For the purposes of the Chinese, I am simply an instantiation of the computer program.

Now the claims made by strong AI are that the programmed computer understands the stories and that the program in some sense explains human understanding. But we are now in a position to examine these claims in light of our thought experiment.

1. As regards the first claim, it seems to me quite obvious in the example that I do not understand a word of the Chinese stories. I have inputs and outputs that are indistinguishable from those of the native Chinese speaker, and I can have any formal program you like, but I still understand nothing. For the same reasons, Schank's computer understands nothing of any stories, whether in Chinese, English, or whatever, since in the Chinese case the computer is me, and in cases where the computer is not me, the computer has nothing more than I have in the case where I understand nothing.

2. As regards the second claim, that the program explains human understanding, we can see that the computer and its program do not provide sufficient conditions of understanding since the computer and

the program are functioning, and there is no understanding. But does it even provide a necessary condition or a significant contribution to understanding? One of the claims made by the supporters of strong AI is that when I understand a story in English, what I am doing is exactly the same—or perhaps more of the same—as what I was doing in manipulating the Chinese symbols. It is simply more formal symbol manipulation that distinguishes the case in English, where I do understand, from the case in Chinese, where I don't. I have not demonstrated that this claim is false, but it would certainly appear an incredible claim in the example. Such plausibility as the claim has derives from the supposition that we can construct a program that will have the same inputs and outputs as native speakers, and in addition we assume that speakers have some level of description where they are also instantiations of a program. On the basis of these two assumptions we assume that even if Schank's program isn't the whole story about understanding, it may be part of the story. Well, I suppose that is an empirical possibility, but not the slightest reason has so far been given to believe that it is true, since what is suggested—though certainly not demonstrated—by the example is that the computer program is simply irrelevant to my understanding of the story. In the Chinese case I have everything that artificial intelligence can put into me by way of a program, and I understand nothing; in the English case I understand everything, and there is so far no reason at all to suppose that my understanding has anything to do with computer programs, that is, with computational operations on purely formally specified elements. As long as the program is defined in terms of computational operations on purely formally defined elements, what the example suggests is that these by themselves have no interesting connection with understanding. They are certainly not sufficient conditions, and not the slightest reason has been given to suppose that they are necessary conditions or even that they make a significant contribution to understanding. Notice that the force of the argument is not simply that different machines can have the same input and output while operating on different formal principles—that is not the point at all. Rather, whatever purely formal principles you put into the computer, they will not be sufficient for understanding, since a human will be able to follow the formal principles without understanding anything. No reason whatever has been offered to suppose that such principles are necessary or even contributory, since no reason has been given to suppose that when I understand English I am operating with any formal program at all.

Well, then, what is it that I have in the case of the English sentences that I do not have in the case of the Chinese sentences? The obvious answer is that I know what the former mean, while I haven't the faintest idea what the latter mean. But in what does this consist and why couldn't we give it to a machine, whatever it is? I will return to this question later, but first I want to continue with the example.

I have had the occasions to present this example to several workers in artificial intelligence, and, interestingly, they do not seem to agree on what the proper reply to it is. I get a surprising variety of replies, and in what follows I will consider the most common of these (specified along with their geographic origins).

But first I want to block some common misunderstandings about "understanding": in many of these discussions one finds a lot of fancy footwork about the word "understanding." My critics point out that there are many different degrees of understanding; that "understanding" is not a simple two-place predicate; that there are even different kinds and levels of understanding, and often the law of excluded middle doesn't even apply in a straightforward way to statements of the form "x understands y"; that in many cases it is a matter for decision and not a simple matter of fact whether x understands y; and so on. To all of these points I want to say: of course, of course. But they have nothing to do with the points at issue. There are clear cases in which "understanding" literally applies and clear cases in which it does not apply; and these two sorts of cases are all I need for this argument.[2] I understand stories in English; to a lesser degree I can understand stories in French; to a still lesser degree, stories in German; and in Chinese, not at all. My car and my adding machine, on the other hand, understanding nothing: they are not in that line of business. We often attribute "understanding" and other cognitive predicates by metaphor and analogy to cars, adding machines, and other artifacts, but nothing is proved by such attributions. We say, "The door *knows* when to open because of its photoelectric cell," "The adding machine *knows how* (*understands how,* is *able*) to do addition and subtraction but not division," and "The thermostat *perceives* changes in the temperature." The reason we make these attributions is quite interesting, and it has to do with the fact that in artifacts we extend our own intentionality;[3] our tools are extensions of our purposes, and so we find it natural to make metaphorical attributions of intentionality to them; but I take it no philosophical ice is cut by such examples. The sense in which an automatic door "understands instructions" from its photoelectric cell is not at all the sense in which I understand English. If the sense in which Schank's programmed computers understand stories is supposed to be the metaphorical sense in which the door understands, and not the sense in which I understand English, the issue would not be worth discussing. But Newell and Simon (1963) write that the kind of cognition they claim for computers is exactly the same as for human beings. I like the straightforwardness of this claim, and it is the sort of claim I will be considering. I will argue that in the literal sense the programmed computer understands what the car and the adding machine understand, namely, exactly nothing. The computer understanding is not just (like my understanding of German) partial or incomplete; it is zero.

Now to the replies:

I. The Systems Reply (Berkeley)

"While it is true that the individual person who is locked in the room does not understand the story, the fact is that he is merely part of a whole system, and the system does understand the story. The person has a large ledger in front of him in which are written the rules, he has a lot of scratch paper and pencils for doing calculations, he has 'data banks' of sets of Chinese symbols. Now, understanding is not being ascribed to the mere individual; rather it is being ascribed to this whole system of which he is a part."

My response to the systems theory is quite simple: let the individual internalize all of these elements of the system. He memorizes the rules in the ledger and the data banks of Chinese symbols, and he does all the calculations in his head. The individual then incorporates the entire system. There isn't anything at all to the system that he does not encompass. We can even get rid of the room and suppose he works outdoors. All the same, he understands nothing of the Chinese, and *a fortiori* neither does the system, because there isn't anything in the system that isn't in him. If he doesn't understand, then there is no way the system could understand because the system is just a part of him.

Actually I feel somewhat embarrassed to give even this answer to the systems theory because the theory seems to me so implausible to start with. The idea is that while a person doesn't understand Chinese, somehow the *conjunction* of that person and bits of paper might understand Chinese. It is not easy for me to imagine how someone who was not in the grip of an ideology would find the idea at all plausible. Still,

I think many people who are committed to the ideology of strong AI will in the end be inclined to say something very much like this; so let us pursue it a bit further. According to one version of this view, while the man in the internalized systems example doesn't understand Chinese in the sense that a native Chinese speaker does (because, for example, he doesn't know that the story refers to restaurants and hamburgers, etc.), still "the man as a formal symbol manipulation system" *really does understand Chinese*. The subsystem of the man that is the formal symbol manipulation system for Chinese should not be confused with the subsystem for English.

So there are really two subsystems in the man; one understands English, the other Chinese, and "it's just that the two systems have little to do with each other." But, I want to reply, not only do they have little to do with each other, they are not even remotely alike. The subsystem that understands English (assuming we allow ourselves to talk in this jargon of "subsystems" for a moment) knows that the stories are about restaurants and eating hamburgers, he knows that he is being asked questions about restaurants and that he is answering questions as best he can by making various inferences from the content of the story, and so on. But the Chinese system knows none of this. Whereas the English subsystem knows that "hamburgers" refers to hamburgers, the Chinese subsystem know only that "squiggle squiggle" is followed by "squoggle squoggle." All he knows is that various formal symbols are being introduced at one end and manipulated according to rules written in English, and other symbols are going out at the other end. The whole point of the original example was to argue that such symbol manipulation by itself couldn't be sufficient for understanding Chinese in any literal sense because the man could write "squoggle squoggle" after "squiggle squiggle" without understanding anything in Chinese. And it doesn't meet that argument to postulate subsystems within the man, because the subsystems are no better off than the man was in the first place; they still don't have anything even remotely like what the English-speaking man (or subsystem) has. Indeed, in the case as described, the Chinese subsystem is simply a part of the English subsystem, a part that engages in meaningless symbol manipulation according to rules in English.

Let us ask ourselves what is supposed to motivate the systems reply in the first place; that is, what *independent* grounds are there supposed to be for saying that the agent must have a subsystem within him that literally understands stories in Chinese? As far as I can tell the only grounds are that in the example I have the same input and output as native Chinese speakers and a program that goes from one to the other. But the whole point of the examples has been to try to show that that couldn't be sufficient for understanding, in the sense in which I understand stories in English, because a person, and hence the set of systems that go to make up a person, could have the right combination of input, output, and program and still not understand anything in the relevant literal sense in which I understand English. The only motivation for saying there *must* be a subsystem in me that understands Chinese is that I have a program and I can pass the Turing test; I can fool native Chinese speakers. But precisely one of the points at issue is the adequacy of the Turing test. The example shows that there could be two "systems," both of which pass the Turing test, but only one of which understands; and it is no argument against this point to say that since they both pass the Turing test they must both understand, since this claim fails to meet the argument that the system in me that understands English has a great deal more than the system that merely processes Chinese. In short, the systems reply simply begs the question by insisting without argument that the system must understand Chinese.

Furthermore, the systems reply would appear to lead to consequences that are independently absurd. If we are to conclude that there must be cognition in me on the grounds that I have a certain sort of input and output and a program in between, then it looks like all sorts of noncognitive subsystems are going to turn out to be cognitive. For example, there is a level of description at which my stomach does information processing, and it instantiates any number of computer programs, but I take it we do not want to say that it has any understanding [cf. Pylyshyn: "Computation and Cognition" *BBS* 3(1) 1980]. But if we accept the systems reply, then it is hard to see how we avoid saying that stomach, heart, liver, and so on, are all understanding subsystems, since there is no principled way to distinguish the motivation for saying the Chinese subsystem understands from saying that the stomach understands. It is, by the way, not an answer to this point to say that the Chinese system has information as input and output and the stomach has food and food products as input and output, since from the point of view of the agent, from my point of view, there is no information in either the food or the Chinese—the Chinese is just so many meaningless squiggles. The information in the Chinese case is solely in the eyes of the programmers and the interpreters, and there is nothing to prevent them from treating the input and output of my digestive organs as information if they so desire.

This last point bears on some independent problems in strong AI, and it is worth digressing for a moment to explain it. If strong AI is to be a branch of psychology, then it must be able to distinguish those systems that are genuinely mental from those that are not. It must be able to distinguish the principles on which the mind works from those on which nonmental systems work; otherwise it will offer us no explanations of what is specifically mental about the mental. And the mental-nonmental distinction cannot be just in the eye of the beholder but it must be intrinsic to the systems; otherwise it would be up to any beholder to treat people as nonmental and, for example, hurricanes as mental if he likes. But quite often in the AI literature the distinction is blurred in ways that would in the long run prove disastrous to the claim that AI is a cognitive inquiry. McCarthy, for example, writes, "Machines as simple as thermostats can be said to have beliefs, and having beliefs seems to be a characteristic of most machines capable of problem solving performance" (McCarthy 1979). Anyone who thinks strong AI has a chance as a theory of the mind ought to ponder the implications of that remark. We are asked to accept it as a discovery of strong AI that the hunk of metal on the wall that we use to regulate the temperature has beliefs in exactly the same sense that we, our spouses, and our children have beliefs, and furthermore that "most" of the other machines in the room—telephone, tape recorder, adding machine, electric light switch,—also have beliefs in this literal sense. It is not the aim of this article to argue against McCarthy's point, so I will simply assert the following without argument. The study of the mind starts with such facts as that humans have beliefs, while thermostats, telephones, and adding machines don't. If you get a theory that denies this point you have produced a counter-example to the theory and the theory is false. One gets the impression that people in AI who write this sort of thing think they can get away with it because they don't really take it seriously, and they don't think anyone else will either. I propose for a moment at least, to take it seriously. Think hard for one minute about what would be necessary to establish that that hunk of metal on the wall over there had real beliefs, beliefs with direction of fit, propositional content, and conditions of satisfaction; beliefs that had the possibility of being strong beliefs or weak beliefs; nervous, anxious, or secure beliefs; dogmatic, rational, or superstitious beliefs; blind faiths or hesitant cogitations; any kind of beliefs. The thermostat is not a candidate. Neither is stomach, liver, adding machine, or telephone. However, since we are taking the idea seriously, notice that its truth would be fatal to strong AI's claim to be a science of the mind. For now the mind is everywhere. What we wanted to know is what distinguishes the mind from thermostats and livers. And if McCarthy were right, strong AI wouldn't have a hope of telling us that.

II. The Robot Reply (Yale)

"Suppose we wrote a different kind of program from Schank's program. Suppose we put a computer inside a robot, and this computer would not just take in formal symbols as input and give out formal symbols as output, but rather would actually operate the robot in such a way that the robot does something very much like perceiving, walking, moving about, hammering nails, eating, drinking—anything you like. The robot would, for example, have a television camera attached to it that enabled it to 'see,' it would have arms and legs that enabled it to 'act,' and all of this would be controlled by its computer 'brain.' Such a robot would, unlike Schank's computer, have genuine understanding and other mental states."

The first thing to notice about the robot reply is that it tacitly concedes that cognition is not solely a matter of formal symbol manipulation, since this reply adds a set of causal relation with the outside world [cf. Fodor: "Methodological Solipsism" *BBS* 3(1) 1980]. But the answer to the robot reply is that the addition of such "perceptual" and "motor" capacities adds nothing by way of understanding, in particular, or intentionality, in general, to Schank's original program. To see this, notice that the same thought experiment applies to the robot case. Suppose that instead of the computer inside the robot, you put me inside the room and, as in the original Chinese case, you give me more Chinese symbols with more instructions in English for matching Chinese symbols to Chinese symbols and feeding back Chinese symbols to the outside. Suppose, unknown to me, some of the Chinese symbols that come to me come from a television camera attached to the robot and other Chinese symbols that I am giving out serve to make the motors inside the robot move the robot's legs or arms. It is important to emphasize that all I am doing is manipulating formal symbols: I know none of these other facts. I am receiving "information" from the robot's "perceptual" apparatus, and I am giving out "instructions" to its motor apparatus without knowing either of these facts. I am the robot's homunculus, but unlike the traditional homunculus, I don't know what's going on. I don't understand anything except the rules for symbol manipulation. Now in this case I want to say that the robot has no intentional states at all; it is simply moving about as a result of its electrical wiring and its program. And furthermore, by instantiating the program I have no intentional states of the relevant type. All I do is follow formal instructions about manipulating formal symbols.

III. The Brain Simulator Reply (Berkeley and M.I.T.)

"Suppose we design a program that doesn't represent information that we have about the world, such as the information in Schank's scripts, but simulates the actual sequence of neuron firings at the synapses of the brain of a native Chinese speaker when he understands stories in Chinese and gives answers to them. The machine takes in Chinese stories and questions about them as input, it simulates the formal structure of actual Chinese brains in processing these stories, and it gives out Chinese answers as outputs. We can even imagine that the machine operates, not with a single serial program, but with a whole set of programs operating in parallel, in the manner that actual human brains presumably operate when they process natural language. Now surely in such a case we would have to say that the machine understood the stories; and if we refuse to say that, wouldn't we also have to deny that native Chinese speakers understood the stories? At the level of the synapses, what would or could be different about the program of the computer and the program of the Chinese brain?"

Before countering this reply I want to digress to note that it is an odd reply for any partisan of artificial intelligence (or functionalism, etc.) to make: I thought the whole idea of strong AI is that we don't need to know how the brain works to know how the mind works. The basic hypothesis, or so I had supposed, was that there is a level of mental operations consisting of computational processes over formal elements that constitute the essence of the mental and can be realized in all sorts of different brain processes, in the same way that any computer program can be realized in different computer hardwares: on the assumptions of strong AI, the mind is to the brain as the program is to the hardware, and thus we can understand the mind without doing neurophysiology. If we had to know how the brain worked to do AI, we wouldn't bother with AI. However, even getting this close to the operation of the brain is still not sufficient to produce understanding. To see this, imagine that instead of a monolingual man in a room shuffling symbols we have the man operate an elaborate set of water pipes with valves connecting them. When the man receives the Chinese symbols, he looks up in the program, written in English, which valves he has to turn on and off. Each water connection corresponds to a synapse in the

Chinese brain, and the whole system is rigged up so that after doing all the right firings, that is after turning on all the right faucets, the Chinese answers pop out at the output end of the series of pipes.

Now where is the understanding in this system? It takes Chinese as input, it simulates the formal structure of the synapses of the Chinese brain, and it gives Chinese as output. But the man certainly doesn't understand Chinese, and neither do the water pipes, and if we are tempted to adopt what I think is the absurd view that somehow the *conjunction* of man *and* water pipes understands, remember that in principle the man can internalize the formal structure of the water pipes and do all the "neuron firings" in his imagination. The problem with the brain simulator is that it is simulating the wrong things about the brain. As long as it simulates only the formal structure of the sequence of neuron firings at the synapses, it won't have simulated what matters about the brain, namely its causal properties, its ability to produce intentional states. And that the formal properties are not sufficient for the causal properties is shown by the water pipe example: we can have all the formal properties carved off from the relevant neurobiological causal properties.

IV. The Combination Reply (Berkeley and Stanford)

"While each of the previous three replies might not be completely convincing by itself as a refutation of the Chinese room counterexample, if you take all three together they are collectively much more convincing and even decisive. Imagine a robot with a brain-shaped computer lodged in its cranial cavity, imagine the computer programmed with all the synapses of a human brain, imagine the whole behavior of the robot is indistinguishable from human behavior, and now think of the whole thing as a unified system and not just as a computer with inputs and outputs. Surely in such a case we would have to ascribe intentionality to the system."

I entirely agree that in such a case we would find it rational and indeed irresistible to accept the hypothesis that the robot had intentionality, as long as we knew nothing more about it. Indeed, besides appearance and behavior, the other elements of the combination are really irrelevant. If we could build a robot whose behavior was indistinguishable over a large range from human behavior, we would attribute intentionality to it, pending some reason not to. We wouldn't need to know in advance that its computer brain was a formal analogue of the human brain.

But I really don't see that this is any help to the claims of strong AI; and here's why: According to strong AI, instantiating a formal program with the right input and output is a sufficient condition of, indeed is constitutive of, intentionality. As Newell (1979) puts it, the essence of the mental is the operation of a physical symbol system. But the attributions of intentionality that we make to the robot in this example have nothing to do with formal programs. They are simply based on the assumption that if the robot looks and behaves sufficiently like us, then we would suppose, until proven otherwise, that it must have mental states like ours that cause and are expressed by its behavior and it must have an inner mechanism capable of producing such mental states. If we knew independently how to account for its behavior without such assumptions we would not attribute intentionality to it, especially if we knew it had a formal program. And this is precisely the point of my earlier reply to objection II.

Suppose we knew that the robot's behavior was entirely accounted for by the fact that a man inside it was receiving uninterpreted formal symbols from the robot's sensory receptors and sending out uninterpreted formal symbols to its motor mechanisms, and the man was doing this symbol manipulation in accordance with a bunch of rules. Furthermore, suppose the man knows none of these facts about the robot, all he knows is which operations to perform on which meaningless symbols. In such a case we would regard the robot as an ingenious mechanical dummy. The hypothesis that the dummy has a mind would now be unwarranted and unnecessary, for there is now no longer any reason to ascribe intentionality to the robot or to the system of which it is a part (except of course for the man's intentionality in manipulating the symbols). The formal symbol manipulations go on, the input and output are correctly matched; but the only real locus of intentionality is the man, and he doesn't know any of the relevant intentional states; he doesn't, for example, *see* what comes into the robot's eyes, he doesn't *intend* to move the robot's arm, and he doesn't *understand* any of the remarks made to or by the robot. Nor, for the reasons stated earlier, does the system of which man and robot are a part.

To see this point, contrast this case with cases in which we find it completely natural to ascribe intentionality to members of certain other primate species such as apes and monkeys and to domestic animals such as dogs. The reasons we find it natural are, roughly, two: we can't make sense of the animal's behavior without the ascription of intentionality, and we can see that the beasts are made of similar stuff to ourselves—that is an eye, that a nose, this is its skin, and so on. Given the coherence of the animal's behavior and the assumption of the same causal stuff underlying it, we assume both that the animal must have mental states underlying its behavior, and that the mental states must be produced by mechanisms made out of the stuff that is like our stuff. We would certainly make similar assumptions about the robot unless we had some reason not to, but as soon as we knew that the behavior was the result of a formal program, and that the actual causal properties of the physical substance were irrelevant we would abandon the assumption of intentionality. [See "Cognition and Consciousness in Nonhuman Species" *BBS* I(4) 1978.]

There are two other responses to my example that come up frequently (and so are worth discussing) but really miss the point.

V. The Other Minds Reply (Yale)

"How do you know that other people understand Chinese or anything else? Only by their behavior. Now the computer can pass the behavioral tests as well as they can (in principle), so if you are going to attribute cognition to other people you must in principle also attribute it to computers."

This objection really is only worth a short reply. The problem in this discussion is not about how I know that other people have cognitive states, but rather what it is that I am attributing to them when I attribute cognitive states to them. The thrust of the argument is that it couldn't be just computational processes and their output because the computational processes and their output can exist without the cognitive state. It is no answer to this argument to feign anesthesia. In "cognitive sciences" one presupposes the reality and knowability of the mental in the same way that in physical sciences one has to presuppose the reality and knowability of physical objects.

VI. The Many Mansions Reply (Berkeley)

"Your whole argument presupposes that AI is only about analogue and digital computers. But that just happens to be the present state of technology. Whatever these causal processes are that you say are essential for intentionality (assuming you are right), eventually we will be able to build devices that have these causal processes, and that will be artificial intelligence. So your arguments are in no way directed at the ability of artificial intelligence to produce and explain cognition."

I really have no objection to this reply save to say that it in effect trivializes the project of strong AI by redefining it as whatever artificially produces and explains cognition. The interest of the original claim made on behalf of artificial intelligence is that it was a precise, well defined thesis: mental processes are computational processes over formally defined elements. I have been concerned to challenge that thesis. If the claim is redefined so that it is no longer that thesis, my objections no longer apply because there is no longer a testable hypothesis for them to apply to.

Let us now return to the question I promised I would try to answer: granted that in my original example I understand the English and I do not understand the Chinese, and granted therefore that the machine doesn't understand either English or Chinese, still there must be something about me that makes it the case that I understand English and a corresponding something lacking in me that makes it the case that I fail to understand Chinese. Now why couldn't we give those somethings, whatever they are, to a machine?

I see no reason in principle why we couldn't give a machine the capacity to understand English or Chinese, since in an important sense our bodies with our brains are precisely such machines. But I do see very strong arguments for saying that we could not give such a thing to a machine where the operation of the machine is defined solely in terms of computational processes over formally defined elements; that is, where the operation of the machine is defined as an instantiation of a computer program. It is not because I am the instantiation of a computer program that I am able to understand English and have other forms of intentionality (I am, I suppose, the instantiation of any number of computer programs), but as far as we know it is because I am a certain sort of organism with a certain biological (i.e., chemical and physical) structure, and this structure, under certain conditions, is causally capable of producing perception, action, understanding, learning, and other intentional phenomena. And part of the point of the present argument is that only something that had those causal powers could have that intentionality. Perhaps other physical and chemical processes could produce exactly these effects; perhaps, for example, Martians also have intentionality but their brains are made of different stuff. That is an empirical question, rather like the question whether photosynthesis can be done by something with a chemistry different from that of chlorophyll.

But the main point of the present argument is that no purely formal model will ever be sufficient by itself for intentionality because the formal properties are not by themselves constitutive of intentionality, and they have by themselves no causal powers except the power, when instantiated, to produce the next stage of the formalism when the machine is running. And any other causal properties that particular realizations of the formal model have, are irrelevant to the formal model because we can always put the same formal model in a different realization where those causal properties are obviously absent. Even if, by some miracle, Chinese speakers exactly realize Schank's program, we can put the same program in English speakers, water pipes, or computers, none of which understand Chinese, the program notwithstanding.

What matters about brain operations is not the formal shadow cast by the sequences of synapses but rather the actual properties of the sequences. All the arguments for the strong version of artificial intelligence that I have seen insist on drawing an outline around the shadows cast by cognition and then claiming that the shadows are the real thing.

By way of concluding I want to try to state some of the general philosophical points implicit in the argument. For clarity I will try to do it in a question and answer fashion, and I begin with that old chestnut of a question:

"Could a machine think?"

The answer is, obviously, yes. We are precisely such machines.

"Yes, but could an artifact, a man-made machine, think?"

Assuming it is possible to produce artificially a machine with a nervous system, neurons with axons and dendrites, and all the rest of it, sufficiently like ours, again the answer to the question seems to be obviously, yes. If you can exactly duplicate the causes, you could duplicate the effects. And indeed it might be possible to produce consciousness, intentionality, and all the rest of it using some other sorts of chemical principles than those that human beings use. It is, as I said, an empirical question.

"OK, but could a digital computer think?"

If by "digital computer" we mean anything at all that has a level of description where it can correctly be described as the instantiation of a computer program, then again the answer is, of course, yes, since we are the instantiations of any number of computer programs, and we can think.

"But could something think, understand, and so on *solely* in virtue of being a computer with the right sort of program? Could instantiating a program, the right program of course, by itself be a sufficient condition of understanding?"

This I think is the right question to ask, though it is usually confused with one or more of the earlier questions, and the answer to it is no.

"Why not?"

Because the formal symbol manipulations by themselves don't have any intentionality; they are quite meaningless; they aren't even *symbol* manipulations, since the symbols don't symbolize anything. In the linguistic jargon, they have only a syntax but no semantics. Such intentionality as computers appear to have is solely in the minds of those who program them and those who use them, those who send in the input and those who interpret the output.

The aim of the Chinese room example was to try to show this by showing that as soon as we put something into the system that really does have intentionality (a man), and we program him with the formal program, you can see that the formal program carries no additional intentionality. It adds nothing, for example, to a man's ability to understand Chinese.

Precisely that feature of AI that seemed so appealing—the distinction between the program and the realization—proves fatal to the claim that simulation could be duplication. The distinction between the program and its realization in the hardware seems to be parallel to the distinction between the level of mental operations and the level of brain operations. And if we could describe the level of mental operations as a formal program, then it seems we could describe what was essential about the mind without doing either introspective psychology or neurophysiology of the brain. But the equation, "mind is to brain as program is to hardware" breaks down at several points, among them the following three:

First, the distinction between program and realization has the consequence that the same program could have all sorts of crazy realizations that had no form of intentionality. Weizenbaum (1976, Ch. 2), for example, shows in detail how to construct a computer using a roll of toilet paper and a pile of small stones. Similarly, the Chinese story understanding program can be programmed into a sequence of water pipes, a set of wind machines, or a monolingual English speaker, none of which thereby acquires an understanding of Chinese. Stones, toilet paper, wind, and water pipes are the wrong kind of stuff to have intentionality in the first place—only something that has the same causal powers as brains can have intentionality—and though the English speaker has the right kind of stuff for intentionality you can easily see that he doesn't get any extra intentionality by memorizing the program, since memorizing it won't teach him Chinese.

Second, the program is purely formal, but the intentional states are not in that way formal. They are defined in terms of their content, not their form. The belief that it is raining, for example, is not defined as a certain formal shape, but as a certain mental content with conditions of satisfaction, a direction of fit (see Searle 1979), and the like. Indeed the belief as such hasn't even got a formal shape in this syntactic sense, since one and the same belief can be given an indefinite number of different syntactic expressions in different linguistic systems.

Third, as I mentioned before, mental states and events are literally a product of the operation of the brain, but the program is not in that way a product of the computer.

"Well if programs are in no way constitutive of mental processes, why have so many people believed the converse? That at least needs some explanation."

I don't really know the answer to that one. The idea that computer simulations could be the real thing ought to have seemed suspicious in the first place because the computer isn't confined to simulating mental operations, by any means. No one supposes that computer simulations of a five-alarm fire will burn the neighborhood down or that a computer simulation of a rainstorm will leave us all drenched. Why on earth would anyone suppose that a computer simulation of understanding actually understood anything? It is sometimes said that it would be frightfully hard to get computers to feel pain or fall in love, but love and pain are neither harder nor easier than cognition or anything else. For simulation, all you need is the right input and output and a program in the middle that transforms the former into the latter. That is all the computer has for anything it does. To confuse simulation with duplication is the same mistake, whether it is pain, love, cognition, fires, or rainstorms.

Still, there are several reasons why AI must have seemed—and to many people perhaps still does seem—in some way to reproduce and thereby explain mental phenomena, and I believe we will not succeed in removing these illusions until we have fully exposed the reasons that give rise to them.

First, and perhaps most important, is a confusion about the notion of "information processing": many people in cognitive science believe that the human brain, with its mind, does something called "information processing," and analogously the computer with its program does information processing; but fires and rainstorms, on the other hand, don't do information processing at all. Thus, though the computer can simulate the formal features of any process whatever, it stands in a special relation to the mind and brain because when the computer is properly programmed, ideally with the same program as the brain, the information processing is identical in the two cases, and this information processing is really the essence of the mental. But the trouble with this argument is that it rests on an ambiguity in the notion of "information." In the sense in which people "process information" when they reflect, say, on problems in arithmetic or when they read and answer questions about stories, the programmed computer does not do "information processing." Rather, what it does is manipulate formal symbols. The fact that the programmer and the interpreter of the computer output use the symbols to stand for objects in the world is totally beyond the scope of the computer. The computer, to repeat, has a syntax but no semantics. Thus, if you type into the computer "2 plus 2 equals?" it will type out "4." But it has no idea that "4" means 4 or that it means anything at all. And the point is not that it lacks some second-order information about the interpretation of its first-order symbols, but rather that its first-order symbols don't have any interpretations as far as the computer is concerned. All the computer has is more symbols. The introduction of the notion of "information processing" therefore produces a dilemma: either we construe the notion of "information processing" in such a way that it implies intentionality as part of the process or we don't. If the former, then the programmed computer does not do information processing, it only manipulates formal symbols. If the latter, then, though the computer does information processing, it is only doing so in the sense in which adding machines, typewriters, stomachs, thermostats, rainstorms, and hurricanes do information processing; namely, they have a level of description at which we can describe them as taking information in at one end, transforming it, and producing information as output. But in this case it is up to outside observers to interpret the input and output as information in the ordinary sense. And no similarity is established between the computer and the brain in terms of any similarity of information processing.

Second, in much of AI there is a residual behaviorism or operationalism. Since appropriately programmed computers can have input-output patterns similar to those of human beings, we are tempted to postulate mental states in the computer similar to human mental states. But once we see that it is both conceptually and empirically possible for a system to have human capacities in some realm without having any intentionality at all, we should be able to overcome this impulse. My desk adding machine has calculating capacities, but no intentionality, and in this paper I have tried to show that a system could have input and output capabilities that duplicated those of a native Chinese speaker and still not understand Chinese, regardless of how it was programmed. The Turing test is typical of the tradition in being unashamedly behavioristic and operationalistic, and I believe that if AI workers totally repudiated behaviorism and operationalism much of the confusion between simulation and duplication would be eliminated.

Third, this residual operationalism is joined to a residual form of dualism; indeed strong AI only makes sense given the dualistic assumption that, where the mind is concerned, the brain doesn't matter. In strong AI (and in functionalism, as well) what matters are programs, and programs are independent of their realization in machines; indeed, as far as AI is concerned, the same program could be realized by an electronic machine, a Cartesian mental substance, or a Hegelian world spirit. The single most surprising discovery that I have made in discussing these issues is that many AI workers are quite shocked by my idea that actual human mental phenomena might be dependent on actual physical chemical properties of actual human brains. But if you think about it a minute you can see that I should not have been surprised; for unless you accept some form of dualism, the strong AI project hasn't got a chance. The project is to reproduce and explain the mental by designing programs, but unless the mind is not only conceptually but empirically independent of the brain you couldn't carry out the project, for the program is completely independent of any realization. Unless you believe that the mind is separable from the brain both conceptually and empirically—dualism in a strong form—you cannot hope to reproduce the mental by writing and running programs since programs must be independent of brains or any other particular forms of instantiation. If mental operations consist in computational operations on formal symbols, then it follows that they have no interesting connection with the brain; the only connection would be that the brain just happens to be one of the indefinitely many types of machines capable of instantiating the program. This form of dualism is not the traditional Cartesian variety that claims there are two sorts of *substances,* but it is Cartesian in the sense that it insists that what is specifically mental about the mind has no intrinsic connection with the actual properties of the brain. This underlying dualism is masked from us by the fact that AI literature contains frequent fulminations against "dualism"; what the authors seem to be unaware of is that their position presupposes a strong version of dualism.

"Could a machine think?" My own view is that *only* a machine could think, and indeed only very special kinds of machines, namely brains and machines that had the same causal powers as brains. And that is the main reason strong AI has had little to tell us about thinking, since it has nothing to tell us about machines. By its own definition, it is about programs, and programs are not machines. Whatever else intentionality is, it is a biological phenomenon, and it is as likely to be as causally dependent on the specific biochemistry of its origins as lactation, photosynthesis, or any other biological phenomena. No one would suppose that we could produce milk and sugar by running a computer simulation of the formal sequences in lactation and photosynthesis, but where the mind is concerned many people are willing to believe in such a miracle because of a deep and abiding dualism: the mind they suppose is a matter of formal processes and is independent of quite specific material causes in the way that milk and sugar are not.

In defense of this dualism the hope is often expressed that the brain is a digital computer (early computers, by the way, were often called "electronic brains"). But that is no help. Of course the brain is a digital computer. Since everything is a digital computer, brains are too. The point is that the brain's causal capacity to produce intentionality cannot consist in its instantiating a computer program, since for any program you like it is possible for something to instantiate that program and still not have any mental states. Whatever it is that the brain does to produce intentionality, it cannot consist in instantiating a program since no program, by itself, is sufficient for intentionality.

Notes

1. I am not, of course, saying that Schank himself is committed to these claims.
2. Also, "understanding" implies both the possession of mental (intentional) states and the truth (validity, success) of these states. For the purposes of this discussion we are concerned only with the possession of the states.
3. Intentionality is by definition that feature of certain mental states by which they are directed at or about objects and states of affairs in the world. Thus, beliefs, desires, and intentions are intentional states; undirected forms of anxiety and depression are not. For further discussion see Searle (1979c).

References

Fodor, J. A. (1968). "The Appeal to Tacit Knowledge in Psychological Explanation." *Journal of Philosophy* 65: 627–40.

Fodor, J. A. (1980). "Methodological Solipsism Considered as a Research Strategy in Cognitive Psychology." *Behavioral and Brain Sciences* 3:1.

McCarthy, J. (1979). "Ascribing Mental Qualities to Machines." In: *Philosophical Perceptives in Artificial Intelligence*, ed. M. Ringle. Atlantic Highlands, NJ: Humanities Press.

Newell, A. (1973). "Physical Symbol Systems." Lecture at the La Jolla Conference on Cognitive Science.

Newell, A., and Simon, H. A. (1963). GPS, a Program That Simulates Human Thought." In: *Computers and Thought.* ed. A. Feigenbaum & V. Feldman, pp. 279–93. New York: McGraw-Hill.

Pylyshyn, Z. W. (1980). "Computation and Cognition: Issues in the Foundations of Cognitive Science." *Behavioral and Brain Sciences* 3.

Schank, R. C., and Abelson, R. P. (1977). *Scripts, Plans, Goals, and Understanding.* Hillsdale, NJ: Lawrence Erlbaum Press.

Searle, J. R. (1979). "The Intentionality of Intention and Action." *Inquiry* 22: 253–80.

Weizenbaum, J. (1965). "Eliza—a Computer Program for the Study of Natural Language Communication Between Man and Machine." *Communication of the Association for Computing Machinery* 9:36–45.

Weizenbaum, J. (1976). *Computer Power and Human Reason.* San Francisco: W. H. Freeman.

Winograd, T. (1973). "A Procedural Model of Language Understanding." In: *Computer Models of Thought and Language,* ed. R. Schank & K. Colby. San Francisco: W. H. Freeman.

Epiphenomenal Qualia
Frank Jackson

It is undeniable that the physical, chemical and biological sciences have provided a great deal of information about the world we live in and about ourselves. I will use the label 'physical information' for this kind of information, and also for information that automatically comes along with it. For example, if a medical scientist tells me enough about the processes that go on in my nervous system, and about how they relate to happenings in the world around me, to what has happened in the past and is likely to happen in the future, to what happens to other similar and dissimilar organisms, and the like, he or she tells me—if I am clever enough to fit it together appropriately—about what is often called the functional role of those states in me (and in organisms in general in similar cases). This information, and its kin, I also label 'physical'.

I do not mean these sketchy remarks to constitute a definition of 'physical information', and of the correlative notions of physical property, process, and so on, but to indicate what I have in mind here. It is well known that there are problems with giving a precise definition of these notions, and so of the thesis of physicalism that all (correct) information is physical information.[1] But—unlike some—I take the question of definition to cut across the central problems I want to discuss in this paper.

I am what is sometimes known as a "qualia freak." I think that there are certain features of the bodily sensations especially, but also of certain perceptual experiences, which no amount of purely physical information includes. Tell me everything physical there is to tell about what is going on in a living brain, the kind of states, their functional role, their relation to what goes on at other times and in other brains, and so on and so forth, and be I as clever as can be in fitting it all together, you won't have told me about the hurtfulness of pains, the itchiness of itches, pangs of jealousy, or about the characteristic experience of tasting a lemon, smelling a rose, hearing a loud noise or seeing the sky.

There are many qualia freaks, and some of them say that their rejection of physicalism is an unargued intuition.[2] I think that they are being unfair to themselves. They have the following argument. Nothing you could tell of a physical sort captures the smell of a rose, for instance. Therefore, physicalism is false. By our lights this is a perfectly good argument. It is obviously not to the point to question its validity, and the premise is intuitively obviously true both to them and to me.

I must, however, admit that it is weak from a polemical point of view. There are, unfortunately for us, many who do not find the premise intuitively obvious. The task then is to present an argument whose premises are obvious to all, or at least to as many as possible. This I try to do in section I with what I will call "the knowledge argument." In section II I contrast the knowledge argument with the modal argument and in section III with the "what is it like to be" argument. In section IV I tackle the question of the causal role of qualia. The major factor in stopping people from admitting qualia is the belief that they would have to be given a causal role with respect to the physical world and especially the brain;[3] and it is hard to do this without sounding like someone who believes in fairies. I seek in section IV to turn this objection by arguing that the view that qualia are epiphenomenal is a perfectly possible one.

I. The Knowledge Argument for Qualia

People vary considerably in their ability to discriminate colors. Suppose that in an experiment to catalog this variation Fred is discovered. Fred has better color vision than anyone else on record; he makes every discrimination that anyone has ever made, and moreover he makes one that we cannot even begin to make. Show him a batch of ripe tomatoes and he sorts them into two roughly equal groups and does so with complete consistency. That is, if you blindfold him, shuffle the tomatoes up, and then remove the blindfold and ask him to sort them out again, he sorts them into exactly the same two groups.

We ask Fred how he does it. He explains that all ripe tomatoes do not look the same color to him, and in fact that this is true of a great many objects that we classify together as red. He sees two colors where we see one, and he has in consequence developed for his own use two words 'red$_1$' and 'red$_2$' to mark the difference. Perhaps he tells us that he has often tried to teach the difference between red$_1$ and red$_2$ to his friends but has got nowhere and has concluded that the rest of the world is red$_1$-red$_2$ color-blind—or perhaps he has had partial success with his children, it doesn't matter. In any case he explains to us that it would be quite wrong to think that because 'red' appears in both 'red$_1$' and 'red$_2$' that the two colors are shades of the one color. He only uses the common term 'red' to fit more easily into our restricted usage. To him red$_1$ and red$_2$ are as different from each other and all the other colors as yellow is from blue. And his discriminatory behavior bears this out: he sorts red$_1$ from red$_2$ tomatoes with the greatest of ease in a wide variety of viewing circumstances. Moreover, an investigation of the physiological basis of Fred's exceptional ability reveals that Fred's optical system is able to separate out two groups of wavelengths in the red spectrum as sharply as we are able to sort out yellow from blue.[4]

I think that we should admit that Fred can see, really see, at least one more color than we can; red$_1$ is a different color from red$_2$. We are to Fred as a totally red–green color-blind person is to us. H. G. Wells' story "The country of the blind" is about a sighted person in a totally blind community.[5] This person never manages to convince them that he can see, that he has an extra sense. They ridicule this sense as quite inconceivable, and treat his capacity to avoid falling into ditches, to win fights and so on as precisely that capacity and nothing more. We would be making their mistake if we refused to allow that Fred can see one more color than we can.

What kind of experience does Fred have when he sees red$_1$ and red$_2$? What is the new color or colors like? We would dearly like to know but do not; and it seems that no amount of physical information about Fred's brain and optical system tells us. We find out perhaps that

Fred's cones respond differentially to certain light waves in the red section of the spectrum that make no difference to ours (or perhaps he has an extra cone) and that this leads in Fred to a wider range of those brain states responsible for visual discriminatory behavior. But none of this tells us what we really want to know about his color experience. There is something about it we don't know. But we know, we may suppose, everything about Fred's body, his behavior and dispositions to behavior and about his internal physiology, and everything about his history and relation to others that can be given in physical accounts of persons. We have all the physical information. Therefore, knowing all this is *not* knowing everything about Fred. It follows that physicalism leaves something out.

To reinforce this conclusion, imagine that as a result of our investigations into the internal workings of Fred we find out how to make everyone's physiology like Fred's in the relevant respects; or perhaps Fred donates his body to science and on his death we are able to transplant his optical system into someone else—again the fine detail doesn't matter. The important point is that such a happening would create enormous interest. People would say "At last we will know what it is like to see the extra color, at last we will know how Fred has differed from us in the way he has struggled to tell us about for so long." Then it cannot be that we knew all along all about Fred. But *ex hypothesi* we did know all along everything about Fred that features in the physicalist scheme; hence the physicalist scheme leaves something out.

Put it this way. *After* the operation, we will know *more* about Fred and especially about his color experiences. But beforehand we had all the physical information we could desire about his body and brain, and indeed everything that has ever featured in physicalist accounts of mind and consciousness. Hence there is more to know than all that. Hence physicalism is incomplete.

Fred and the new color(s) are of course essentially rhetorical devices. The same point can be made with normal people and familiar colors. Mary is a brilliant scientist who is, for whatever reason, forced to investigate the world from a black and white room *via* a black and white television monitor. She specializes in the neurophysiology of vision and acquires, let us suppose, all the physical information there is to obtain about what goes on when we see ripe tomatoes, or the sky, and use terms like 'red,' 'blue,' and so on. She discovers, for example, just which wave-length combinations from the sky stimulate the retina, and exactly how this produces *via* the central nervous system the contraction of the vocal chords and expulsion of air from the lungs that results in the uttering of the sentence 'The sky is blue.' (It can hardly be denied that it is in principle possible to obtain all this physical information from black and white television, otherwise the Open University would of *necessity* need to use color television.)

What will happen when Mary is released from her black and white room or is given a color television monitor? Will she *learn* anything or not? It seems just obvious that she will learn something about the world and our visual experience of it. But then it is inescapable that her previous knowledge was incomplete. But she had *all* the physical information. *Ergo* there is more to have than that, and "physicalism" is false.

Clearly the same style of knowledge argument could be deployed for taste, hearing, the bodily sensations and generally speaking for the various mental states which are said to have (as it is variously put) raw feels, phenomenal features or qualia. The conclusion in each case is that the qualia are left out of the physicalist story. And the polemical strength of the knowledge argument is that it is so hard to deny the central claim that one can have all the physical information without having all the information there is to have.

II. The Modal Argument

By the Modal Argument I mean an argument of the following style.[6] Skeptics about other minds are not making a mistake in deductive logic, whatever else may be wrong with their position. No amount of physical information about another *logically entails* that he or she is conscious or feels anything at all. Consequently there is a possible world with organisms exactly like us in every physical respect (and remember that includes functional states, physical history, et al.) but which differ from us profoundly in that they have no conscious mental life at all. But then what is it that we have and they lack? Not anything physical *ex hypothesi*. In all physical regards we and they are exactly alike. Consequently there is more to us than the purely physical. Thus physicalism is false.[7]

It is sometimes objected that the modal argument misconceives physicalism on the ground that that doctrine is advanced as a *contingent* truth.[8] But to say this is only to say that physicalists restrict their claim to *some* possible worlds, including especially ours; and the modal argument is only directed against this lesser claim. If we in *our* world, let alone beings in any others, have features additional to those of our physical replicas in other possible worlds, then we have non-physical features or qualia.

The trouble rather with the modal argument is that it rests on a disputable modal intuition. Disputable because it is disputed. Some sincerely deny that there can be physical replicas of us in other possible worlds which nevertheless lack consciousness. Moreover, at least one person who once had the intuition now has doubts.[9]

Head-counting may seem a poor approach to a discussion of the modal argument. But frequently we can do no better when modal intuitions are in question, and remember our initial goal was to find the argument with the greatest polemical utility.

Of course, *qua* protagonists of the knowledge argument we may well accept the modal intuition in question; but this will be a *consequence* of our already having an argument to the conclusion that qualia are left out of the physicalist story, not our ground for that conclusion. Moreover, the matter is complicated by the possibility that the connection between matters physical and qualia is like that sometimes held to obtain between aesthetic qualities and natural ones. Two possible worlds which agree in all "natural" respects (including the experiences of sentient creatures) must agree in all aesthetic qualities also, but it is plausibly held that the aesthetic qualities cannot be reduced to the natural.

III. The "What Is It Like to Be" Argument

In "What Is It Like to Be a Bat?" Thomas Nagel argues that no amount of physical information can tell us what it is like to be a bat, and indeed that we, human beings, cannot imagine what it is like to be a bat.[10] His reason is that what this is like can only be understood from a bat's point of view, which is not our point of view and is not something capturable in physical terms which are essentially terms understandable equally from many points of view.

It is important to distinguish this argument from the knowledge argument. When I complained that all the physical knowledge about Fred was not enough to tell us what his special color experience was like. I was not complaining that we weren't finding out what it is like to be Fred. I was complaining that there is something *about* his experience, a property of it, of which we were left ignorant. And if and when we come to know what this property is we still will not know what it is like to *be* Fred, but we will know more *about* him. No amount of knowledge about Fred, be it physical or not, amounts to knowledge "from the inside" considering Fred. We are not Fred. There is thus a whole set of items of knowledge expressed by forms of words like 'that it is *I myself* who is . . .' which Fred has and we simply cannot have because we are not him.[11]

When Fred sees the color he alone can see, one thing he knows is the way his experience of it differs from his experience of seeing red and so on; *another* is that he himself is seeing it. Physicalist and qualia freaks alike should acknowledge that no amount of information of whatever kind that *others* have *about* Fred amounts to knowledge of the second. My complaint though concerned the first and was that the special quality of his experience is certainly a fact about it, and one which physicalism leaves out because no amount of physical information told us what it is.

Nagel speaks as if the problem he is raising is one of extrapolating from knowledge of one experience to another, of imagining what an unfamiliar experience would be like on the basis of familiar ones. In terms of Hume's example, from knowledge of some shades of blue we can work out what it would be like to see other shades of blue. Nagel argues that the trouble with bats et al. is that they are too unlike us. It is hard to see an objection to physicalism here. Physicalism makes no special claims about the imaginative or extrapolative powers of human beings, and it is hard to see why it need do so.[12]

Anyway, our knowledge argument makes no assumptions on this point. If physicalism were true, enough physical information about Fred would obviate any need to extrapolate or to perform special feats of imagination or understanding in order to know all about his special color experience. *The information would already be in our possession.* But it clearly isn't. That was the nub of the argument.

IV. The Bogey of Epiphenomenalism

Is there any really *good* reason for refusing to countenance the idea that qualia are causally impotent with respect to the physical world? I will argue for the answer no, but in doing this I will say nothing about two views associated with the classical epiphenomenalist position. The first is that mental *states* are inefficacious with respect to the physical world. All I will be concerned to defend is that it is possible to hold that certain *properties* of certain mental states, namely those I've called qualia, are such that their possession or absence makes no difference to the physical world. The second is that the mental is *totally* causally inefficacious. For all I will say it may be that you have to hold that the instantiation of *qualia* makes a difference to *other mental states* though not to anything physical. Indeed general considerations to do with how you could come to be aware of the instantiation of qualia suggest such a position.[13]

Three reasons are standardly given for holding that a quale like the hurtfulness of a pain must be causally efficacious in the physical world, and so, for instance, that its instantiation must sometimes make a difference to what happens in the brain. None, I will argue, has any real force. (I am much indebted to Alec Hyslop and John Lucas for convincing me of this.)

(i) It is supposed to be just obvious that the hurtfulness of pain is partly responsible for the subject seeking to avoid pain, saying 'It hurts' and so on. But, to reverse Hume, anything can fail to cause anything. No matter how often *B* follows *A*, and no matter how initially obvious the causality of the connection seems, the hypothesis that *A* causes *B* can be overturned by an over-arching theory which shows the two as distinct effects of a common underlying causal process.

To the untutored the image on the screen of Lee Marvin's fist moving from left to right immediately followed by the image of John Wayne's head moving in the same general direction looks as causal as anything.[14] And of course throughout countless Westerns images similar to the first are followed by images similar to the second. All this counts for precisely nothing when we know the over-arching theory concerning how the relevant images are both effects of an underlying causal process involving the projector and the film. The epiphenomenalist can say exactly the same about the connection between, for example, hurtfulness and behavior. It is simply a consequence of the fact that certain happenings in the brain cause both.

(ii) The second objection relates to Darwin's theory of evolution. According to natural selection the traits that evolve over time are those conducive to physical survival. We may assume that qualia evolved over time—we have them, the earliest forms of life do not—and so we should expect qualia to be conducive to survival. The objection is that they could hardly help us to survive if they do nothing to the physical world.

The appeal of this argument is undeniable, but there is a good reply to it. Polar bears have particularly thick, warm coats. The theory of evolution explains this (we suppose) by pointing out that having a thick, warm coat is conducive to survival in the Arctic. But having a thick coat goes along with having a heavy coat, and having a heavy coat is *not* conducive to survival. It slows the animal down.

Does this mean that we have refuted Darwin because we have found an evolved trait—having a heavy coat—which is not conducive to survival? Clearly not. Having a heavy coat is an unavoidable concomitant of having a warm coat (in the context, modern insulation was not available), and the advantages for survival of having a warm coat outweighed the disadvantages of having a heavy one. The point is that all we can extract from Darwin's theory is that we should expect any evolved characteristic to be *either* conducive to survival *or* a by-product of one that is so conducive. The epiphenomenalist holds that qualia fall into the latter category. They are a by-product of certain brain processes that are highly conducive to survival.

(iii) The third objection is based on a point about how we come to know about other minds. We know about other minds by knowing about other behavior, at least in part. The nature of the inference is a matter of some controversy, but it is not a matter of controversy that it proceeds from behavior. That is why we think that stones do not feel and dogs do feel. But, runs the objection, how can a person's behavior provide any reason for believing he has qualia like mine, or indeed any qualia at all, unless this behavior can be regarded as the *outcome* of the qualia. Man Friday's footprint was evidence of Man Friday because footprints are causal outcomes of feet attached to people. And an epiphenomenalist cannot regard behavior, or indeed anything physical, as an outcome of qualia.

But consider my reading in *The Times* that Spurs won. This provides excellent evidence that the *Telegraph* has also reported that Spurs won, despite the fact that (I trust) the *Telegraph* does not get the results from the *The Times*. They each send their own reporters to the game. the *Telegraph*'s report is in no sense an outcome of *The Times*', but the latter provides good evidence for the former nevertheless.

The reasoning involved can be reconstructed thus. I read in *The Times* that Spurs won. This gives me reason to think that Spurs won because I know that Spurs' winning is the most likely candidate to be what caused the report in *The Times*. But I also know that Spurs' winning would have had many effects, including almost certainly a report in the *Telegraph*.

I am arguing from one effect back to its cause and out again to another effect. The fact that neither effect causes the other is irrelevant. Now the epiphenomenalist allows that qualia are effects of what goes on in the brain. Qualia cause nothing physical but are caused by something physical. Hence the epiphenomenalist can argue from the behavior of others to the qualia of others by arguing from the behavior of others back to its causes in the brains of others and out again to their qualia.

You may well feel for one reason or another that this is a more dubious chain of reasoning than its model in the case of newspaper reports. You are right. The problem of other minds is a major philosophical problem, the problem of other newspaper reports is not. But there is no special problem for epiphenomenalism as opposed to, say, interactionism here.

There is a very understandable response to the three replies I have just made. "All right, there is no knockdown refutation of the existence of epiphenomenal qualia. But the fact remains that they are an excrescence. They *do* nothing, they *explain* nothing, they serve merely to soothe the intuitions of dualists, and it is left a total mystery how they fit into the world view of science. In short we do not and cannot understand the how and why of them."

This is perfectly true; but is no objection to qualia, for it rests on an overly optimistic view of the human animal, and its powers. We are the products of evolution. We understand and sense what we need to understand and sense in order to survive. Epiphenomenal qualia are totally irrelevant to survival. At no stage of our evolution did natural selection favor those who could make sense of how they are caused and the laws governing them, or in fact why they exist at all. And that is why we can't.

It is not sufficiently appreciated that physicalism is an extremely optimistic view of our powers. If it is true, we have, in very broad outline admittedly, a grasp of our place in the scheme of things. Certain matters of sheer complexity defeat us—there are an awful lot of neurons—but in principle we have it all. But consider the antecedent probability that everything in the universe be of a kind that is relevant in some way or other to the survival of *Homo sapiens*. It is very low surely. But then one must admit that it is very likely that there is a part of the whole scheme of things, maybe a big part, which no amount of evolution will ever bring us near to knowledge about or understanding. For the simple reason that such knowledge and understanding is irrelevant to survival.

Physicalists typically emphasise that we are a part of nature on their view, which is fair enough. But if we are a part of nature, we are as nature has left us after however many years of evolution it is, and each step in that evolutionary progression has been a matter of chance constrained just by the need to preserve or increase survival value. The wonder is that we understand as much as we do, and there is no wonder that there should be matters which fall quite outside our comprehension. Perhaps exactly how epiphenomenal qualia fit into the scheme of things is one such.

This may seem an unduly pessimistic view of our capacity to articulate a truly comprehensive picture of our world and our place in it. But suppose we discovered living on the bottom of the deepest oceans a sort of sea slug which manifested intelligence. Perhaps survival in the conditions required rational powers. Despite their intelligence, these sea slugs have only a very restricted conception of the world by comparison with ours, the explanation for this being the nature of their immediate environment. Nevertheless they have developed sciences which work surprisingly well in these restricted terms. They also have philosophers, called slugists. Some call themselves tough-minded slugists, others confess to being soft-minded slugists.

The tough-minded slugists hold that the restricted terms (or ones pretty like them which may be introduced as their sciences progress) suffice in principle to describe everything without remainder. These tough-minded slugists admit in moments of weakness to a feeling that their theory leaves something out. They resist this feeling and their opponents, the softminded slugists, by pointing out—absolutely correctly—that no slugist has ever succeeded in spelling out how this mysterious residue fits into the highly successful view that their sciences have and are developing of how their world works.

Our sea slugs don't exist, but they might. And there might also exist super beings which stand to us as we stand to these slugs. We cannot adopt the perspective of these super beings, because we are not them, but the possibility of such a perspective is, I think, an antidote to excessive optimism.[15]

Addendum: From "What Mary Didn't Know"

I. Three Clarifications

The knowledge argument does not rest on the dubious claim that logically you cannot imagine what sensing red is like unless you have sensed red. Powers of imagination are not to the point. The contention about Mary is not that, despite her fantastic grasp of neurophysiology and everything else physical, she *could not imagine* what it is like to sense red; it is that, as a matter of fact, she *would not know*. But if physicalism is true, she would know; and no great powers of imagination would be called for. Imagination is a faculty that those who *lack* knowledge need to fall back on.

Secondly, the intensionality of knowledge is not to the point. The argument does not rest on assuming falsely that, if S knows that a is F and if $a = b$, then S knows that b is F. It is concerned with the nature of Mary's total body of knowledge before she is released: is it complete, or do some facts escape it? What is to the point is that S may know that a is F and *know* that $a = b$, yet arguably not know that b is F, by virtue of not being sufficiently logically alert to follow the consequences through. If Mary's lack of knowledge were at all like this, there would be no threat to physicalism in it. But it is very hard to believe that her lack of knowledge could be remedied merely by her explicitly following through enough logical consequences of her vast physical knowledge. Endowing her with great logical acumen and persistence is not in itself enough to fill in the gaps in her knowledge. On being let out, she will not say "I could have worked all this out before by making some more purely logical inferences."

Thirdly, the knowledge Mary lacked which is of particular point for the knowledge argument against physicalism is *knowledge about the experiences of others,* not about her own. When she is let out, she has new experiences, color experiences she has never had before. It is not, therefore, an objection to physicalism that she learns *something* on being let out. Before she was let out, she could not have known facts about her experience of red, for there were no such facts to know. That physicalist and nonphysicalist alike can agree on. After she is let out, things change: and physicalism can happily admit that she learns this; after all, some physical things will change, for instance, her brain states and their functional roles. The trouble for physicalism is that, after Mary sees her first ripe tomato, she will realize how impoverished her conception of the mental life of *others* has been *all along*. She will realize that there was, all the time she was carrying out her laborious investigations into the neurophysiologies of others and into the functional roles of their internal states, something about these people she was quite unaware of. All along their experiences (or many of them, those got from tomatoes, the sky, . . .) had a feature conspicuous to them but until now hidden from her (in fact, not in logic). But she knew all the physical facts about them all along; hence, what she did not know until her release is not a physical fact about their experiences. But it is a fact about them. That is the trouble for physicalism.

II. Churchland's Three Objections[16]

(i) Churchland's first objection is that the knowledge argument contains a defect that "is simplicity itself" (23). The argument equivocates on the sense of 'knows about.' How so? Churchland suggests that the following is "a conveniently tightened version" of the knowledge argument:

(1) Mary knows everything there is to know about brain states and their properties.
(2) It is not the case that Mary knows everything there is to know about sensations and their properties.

Therefore, by Leibniz's law.

(3) Sensations and their properties ? brain states and their properties (23).

Churchland observes, plausibly enough, that the type or kind of knowledge involved in premise 1 is distinct from the kind of knowledge involved in premise 2. We might follow his lead and tag the first 'knowledge by description,' and the second 'knowledge by acquaintance'; but, whatever the tags, he is right that the displayed argument involves a highly dubious use of Leibniz's law.

My reply is that the displayed argument may be convenient, but it is not accurate. It is not the knowledge argument. Take, for instance, premise 1. The whole thrust of the knowledge argument is that Mary (before her release) does *not* know everything there is to know about brain states and their properties, because she does not know about certain qualia associated with them. What is complete, according to the argument, is her knowledge of matters physical. A convenient and accurate way of displaying the argument is:

(1)' Mary (before her release) knows everything physical there is to know about other people.
(2)' Mary (before her release) does not know everything there is to know about other people (because she *learns* something about them on her release).

Therefore,

(3)' There are truths about other people (and herself) which escape the physicalist story.

What is immediately to the point is not the kind, manner, or type of knowledge Mary has, but *what* she knows. What she knows beforehand is ex hypothesi everything physical there is to know, but is it everything there is to know? That is the crucial question.

Notes

1. See, e.g., D. H. Mellor, "Materialism and Phenomenal Qualities," *Aristotelian Society Supp. Vol.* 47 (1973), 107–19; and J. W. Cornman, *Materialism and Sensations*, New Haven and London, 1971.
2. Particularly in discussion, but see, e.g., Keith Campbell, *Metaphysics*, Belmont, 1976, p. 67.
3. See, e.g., D. C. Dennett, "Current Issues in the Philosophy of Mind," *American Philosophical Quarterly* 15(1978), 249–61.
4. Put this, and similar simplifications below, in terms of Land's theory if you prefer. See, e.g., Edwin H. Land, "Experiments in Color Vision." *Scientific American* 200 (5 May 1959), 84–99.
5. H. G. Wells, *The Country of the Blind and Other Stories*, London, n.d.
6. See, e.g., Keith Campbell, *Body and Mind*, New York, 1970; and Robert Kirk, "Sentience and Behaviour," *Mind* 83 (1974), 43–60.
7. I have presented the argument in an inter-world rather than the more usual intra-world fashion to avoid inessential complications to do with supervenience, causal anomalies and the like.
8. See, e.g., W. G. Lycan, "A New Lilliputian Argument Against Machine Functionalism," *Philosophical Studies* 35 (1979), 279–87, p. 280; and Don Locke, "Zombies, Schizophrenics and Purely Physical Objects," *Mind* 85 (1976), 97–9.
9. See R. Kirk, "From Physical Explicability to Full-Blooded Materialism," *Philosophical Quarterly* 29 (1979), 229–37. See also the arguments against the modal intuition in, e.g., Sydney Shoemaker, "Functionalism and Qualia," *Philosophical Studies* 27 (1975), 291–315.
10. *Philosophical Review* 83 (1974), 435–50. Two things need to be said about this article. One is that, despite my dissociations to come, I am much indebted to it. The other is that the emphasis changes through the article, and by the end Nagel is objecting not so much to Physicalism as to all extant theories of mind for ignoring points of view, including those that admit (irreducible) qualia.

11. Knowledge *de se* in the terms of David Lewis, "Attitudes de Dicto and de se," *Philosophical Review* 88 (1979), 513–43.
12. See Laurence Nemirow's comments on "What it is . . ." in his review of T. Nagel, *Mortal Questions,* in *Philosophical Review* 89 (1980), 473–7. I am indebted here in particular to a discussion with David Lewis.
13. See my review of K. Campbell, *Body and Mind,* in *Australasian Journal of Philosophy* 50 (1972), 77–80.
14. Cf. Jean Piaget, "The Child's Conception of Physical Causality," reprinted in *The Essential Piaget,* London, 1977.
15. I am indebted to Robert Pargetter for a number of comments and, despite his dissent, to section IV of Paul E. Meehl's "The complete autocerebroscopist's" in Paul Feyerabend and Grover Maxwell (eds), *Mind, Matter and Method,* Minneapolis, 1966.
16. Paul M. Churchland, "Reduction, Qualia, and the Direct Introspection of Brain States." *The Journal of Philosophy* LXXXII, 1 (January 1985): 8–28. Unless otherwise stated, future page references are to this paper.

SECTION SIX

DOES GOD EXIST?

The relationship between faith and reason is of central importance for the history of Western philosophy. For philosophers like Immanuel Kant, René Descartes, or G. W. Hegel, philosophical reflection reaffirmed their religious beliefs. Other thinkers like Bertrand Russell, Karl Marx, or Friedrich Nietzsche found that philosophy led them toward atheism. The readings in this section show how various philosophers have responded to questions about God, faith, and reason.

In our first selection, C. D. Broad analyzes the attempt to establish religious beliefs on the basis of religious experiences. Broad thinks that we should evaluate religious experiences according to the same principles that we use to evaluate ordinary sense perception. This means that we have reasons to take these experiences seriously provided that there are no positive grounds for holding that they are delusional. His overall conclusion tries to stake out a middle ground. Broad writes: " . . . religions known to us are . . . highly confused and are mixed up with a great deal of error and sheer nonsense . . . but the opposite extreme of holding that the whole religious experience of mankind is a gigantic system of pure delusions seems to me almost as far fetched."

Our second selection, "The Five Ways," contains St. Thomas Aquinas' famous five attempts to prove the existence of God. Each argument takes a different starting point. The first argument moves from the existence of change to the existence of an unmoved mover. The second one deduces the existence of a first cause from the existence of causes. The third and fourth way argue from the existence of contingency and excellence to the existence of a necessary and perfect being, whereas the final argument infers the existence of a divine planner from the harmony of nature.

In our third essay, Richard Taylor presents a well-constructed, contemporary version of the cosmological argument. Taylor argues that if we accept the principle of sufficient reason—that is, the principle that for any positive truth there must exist an explanation—then we also must accept that a necessary, self-caused being exists. He argues that it is only in reference to such a being that we can explain the existence of the world.

In 1948, Father F. C. Copleston and Bertrand Russell debated the existence of God on BBC radio. Our selection from this famous debate focuses on Russell's and Copleston's responses to the cosmological argument. Copleston argues that in order to explain the existence of the universe "we must come to a being which contains within itself the reason for its own existence." Russell, on the other hand, finds the idea of something causing the universe as a whole unintelligible. He concludes contra Copleston: " . . . the universe is just there, and that's all."

Although the basic idea of the design argument, the claim that this world is too complex to have evolved without the help of a conscious designer, has been around for a long time, some scientists claim that recent scientific advances provide fresh evidence in support of this argument. In the essay "Molecular Machines: Experimental Support for the Design Inference, " the biochemist Michael Behe argues that biomolecular systems function like tiny, intricate machines and that they exhibit what he calls "irreducible complexity." Behe claims that irreducible complexity proves that such molecules could not have evolved gradually as Darwinism holds, and he concludes that it is more reasonable to believe that they were intelligently designed.

Philip Kitcher responds in his essay "Born Again Creationism" to Behe's arguments. Kitcher argues that neither he nor Behe have any idea how exactly these complex molecular structures have come into existence. However, this does not establish that it is impossible that they have come into being in a manner consistent with a Darwinian account. According to Kitcher, Behe's argument rests on a fallacious appeal to ignorance and his quantitative argument "smacks more of numerology than of science."

In the essay "Pascal's Wager," George Schlesinger defends Pascal's Wager against various objections. He starts out by showing that it is misleading to accuse those who are convinced by Pascal's reasoning to be of a mercenary and selfish nature. He then defends Pascal's Wager against the so called "many-gods objection." Schlesinger argues that the probability that a scrupulously just deity exists is much higher than the existence of a "fancy bred capricious power." This is the reason, according to Schlesinger, that Pascal's Wager plays a crucial role in the contexts of all other theistic arguments as well.

J. L. Mackie presents a clearheaded and straightforward formulation of the logical problem of evil. In his essay "Evil and Omnipotence," Mackie argues that most religious believers are "positively irrational" since they are committed to three logically inconsistent propositions: God is omnipotent; God is wholly good; and evil exists. He goes on to examine theistic attempts to resolve this inconsistency. The result is negative. According to Mackie, the most popular attempts to resolve the inconsistency fail to abandon any of the three inconsistent claims. These theodicies fail, therefore, to provide adequate solutions to the problem of evil.

Richard Swinburne develops a theistic reply to the problem of evil. He tries to show that pain and suffering cannot count as evidence against the existence of God. Swinburne argues that a God who eliminates all pain and suffering is also a God who deprives humans of the ability to make meaningful decisions in their lives. According to Swinburne, genuine freedom requires the existence not only of moral evil but also of natural evil. He writes: ". . . just imagine all the suffering of mind and body caused by disease, earthquake, and accident unpreventable by humans removed at a stroke from our society . . . Many of us would then have such an easy life that we simply would not have much opportunity to show courage, or indeed, manifest much in the way of great goodness at all."

Given that most—if not all—arguments for and against the existence of God fail to establish final conclusions, does it not follow that religious beliefs are simply a matter of faith? In "The Ethics of Belief," William Clifford emphatically denies such a conclusion. He argues that "it is wrong always everywhere, and for anyone, to believe anything upon insufficient evidence." Clifford's position is known as "strong rationalism," since it holds that one cannot be rational in accepting religious beliefs unless they can be shown by convincing reason to be true. Clifford points out that if we act on poorly supported beliefs we are very likely to harm others as well as ourselves.

The direct response to Clifford's positions is provided by William James. In his essay "The Will to Believe," James argues that we cannot settle religious questions on the basis of pure rational analysis of the available evidence. The decision whether or not we want to believe in God is a "genuine option" that we are forced to make and that has a momentous impact on our lives. James considers the example of a man who cannot decide whether or not he should marry because he is not perfectly sure whether his partner is the right person. Pure intellectual analysis cannot settle the question, and to hesitate indefinitely requires that we ignore our passionate nature. According to James, this is also true for our decision regarding whether or not to believe in the existence of God. We need to acknowledge that intellectual analysis alone cannot decide this question. The decision requires a passionate leap. He concludes that "No one of us ought to issue vetoes to the other, nor should we bandy words of abuse. We ought, on the contrary, delicately and profoundly to respect one another's mental freedom . . . "

In the final reading in this section, Deborah Mathieu argues that religion plays a fundamental role in the subjugation of women in society. According to Mathieu, all three major monotheistic religions—Judaism, Christianity, and Islam—are used by men "to brainwash females into accepting the theory of male superiority." The basic argument is simple. Since all three religions hold that God is male, it follows that female humans are more distant from God than male humans, and this is taken as proof that female humans are inferior to males.

The Appeal to Religious Experience

C. D. Broad

I shall confine myself in this article to specifically religious experience and the argument for the existence of God which has been based on it.

This argument differs in the following important respect from the other two empirical types of argument. The Argument from Design and the arguments from ethical premises start from facts which are common to every one. But some people seem to be almost wholly devoid of any specifically religious experience; and among those who have it the differences of kind and degree are enormous. Founders of religions and saints, e.g., often claim to have been in direct contact with God, to have seen and spoken with Him, and so on. An ordinary religious man would certainly not make any such claim, though he might say that he had had experiences which assured him of the existence and presence of God. So the first thing that we have to notice is that capacity for religious experience is in certain respects like an ear for music. There are a few people who are unable to recognize and distinguish the simplest tune. But they are in a minority, like the people who have absolutely no kind of religious experience. Most people have some light appreciation of music. But the differences of degree in this respect are enormous, and those who have not much gift for music have to take the statements of accomplished musicians very largely on trust. Let us, then, compare tone-deaf persons to those who have no recognizable religious experience at all; the ordinary followers of a religion to men who have some taste for music but can neither appreciate the more difficult kinds nor compose; highly religious men and saints to persons with an exceptionally fine ear for music who may yet be unable to compose it; and the founders of religions to great musical composers, such as Bach and Beethoven.

This analogy is, of course, incomplete in certain important respects. Religious experience raises three problems, which are different though closely interconnected. (i) What is the *psychological analysis* of religious experience? Does it contain factors which are present also in certain experiences which are not religious? Does it contain any

Reprinted from C. D. Broad, *Religion, Philosophy and Psychical Research* (London: Routledge & Kegan Paul PLC, 1930), by permission of the publisher.

factor which never occurs in any other kind of experience? If it contains no such factor, but is a blend of elements each of which can occur separately or in non-religious experiences, its psychological peculiarity must consist in the characteristic way in which these elements are blended in it. Can this peculiar structural feature of religious experience be indicated and described? (ii) What are the *genetic and causal conditions* of the existence of religious experience? Can we trace the origin and development of the disposition to have religious experiences (*a*) in the human race, and (*b*) in each individual? Granted that the disposition is present in nearly all individuals at the present time, can we discover and state the variable conditions which call it into activity on certain occasions and leave it in abeyance on others? (iii) Part of the content of religious experience is alleged knowledge or well-founded belief about the nature of reality, e.g., that we are dependent on a being who loves us and whom we ought to worship, that values are somehow conserved in spite of the chances and changes of the material world at the mercy of which they seem *prima facie* to be, and so on. Therefore there is a third problem. Granted that religious experience exists, that it has such-and-such a history and conditions, that it seems vitally important to those who have it, and that it produces all kinds of effects which would not otherwise happen, is it *veridical?* Are the claims to knowledge or well-founded belief about the nature of reality, which are an integral part of the experience, *true or probable?* Now, in the case of musical experience, there are analogies to the psychological problem and to the genetic or causal problem, but there is no analogy to the epistemological problem of validity. For, so far as I am aware, no part of the content of musical experience is alleged knowledge about the nature of reality; and therefore no question of its being veridical or delusive can arise.

Since both musical experience and religious experience certainly exist, any theory of the universe which was incompatible with their existence would be false, and any theory which failed to show the connexion between their existence and the other facts about reality would be inadequate. So far the two kinds of experience are in exactly the same position. But a theory which answers to the condition that it allows of the *existence* of religious experience and indicates the *connexion* between its existence and other facts about reality may leave the question as to its *validity* quite unanswered. Or, alternatively, it may throw grave doubt on its cognitive claims, or else it may tend to support them. Suppose, e.g., that it could be shown that religious experience contains no elements which are not factors in other kinds of experience.

Suppose further it could be shown that this particular combination of factors tends to originate and to be activated only under certain conditions which are known to be very commonly productive of false beliefs held with strong conviction. Then a satisfactory answer to the questions of psychological analysis and causal antecedents would have tended to answer the epistemological question of validity in the negative. On the other hand, it might be that the only theory which would satisfactorily account for the origin of the religious disposition and for the occurrence of actual religious experiences under certain conditions was a theory which allowed some of the cognitive claims made by religious experience to be true or probable. Thus the three problems, though entirely distinct from each other, may be very closely connected; and it is the existence of the third problem in connexion with religious experience which puts it, for the present purpose, in a different category from musical experience.

In spite of this essential difference the analogy is not to be despised, for it brings out at least one important point. If a man who had no ear for music were to give himself airs on that account, and were to talk *de haut en bas* about those who can appreciate music and think it highly important, we should regard him, not as an advanced thinker, but as a self-satisfied Philistine. And, then if he did not do this but only propounded theories about the nature and causation of musical experience, we might think it reasonable to feel very doubtful whether his theories would be adequate or correct. In the same way, when persons without religious experience regard themselves as being *on that ground* superior to those who have it, their attitude must be treated as merely silly and offensive. Similarly, any theories about religious experience constructed by persons who have little or none of their own should be regarded with grave suspicion. (For that reason it would be unwise to attach very much weight to anything that the present writer may say on this subject.)

On the other hand, we must remember that the possession of a great capacity for religious experience, like the possession of a great capacity for musical appreciation and composition, is no guarantee of high general intelligence. A man may be a saint or a magnificent musician and yet have very little common sense, very little power of accurate introspection or of seeing causal connexions, and scarcely any capacity for logical criticism. He may also be almost as ignorant about other aspects of reality as the non-musical or non-religious man is about musical or religious experience. If such a man starts to theorize about music or religion, his theories may be quite as absurd, though in a different way, as those made by persons who are devoid of musical or religious experience. Fortunately it happens that some religious mystics of a high order have been extremely good at introspecting and describing their own experiences. And some highly religious persons have had very great critical and philosophical abilities. St. Teresa is an example of the first, and St. Thomas Aquinas of the second.

Now I think it must be admitted that, if we compare and contrast the statements made by religious mystics of various times, races, and religions, we find a common nucleus combined with very great differences of detail. Of course the interpretations which they have put on their experiences are much more varied than the experiences themselves. It is obvious that the interpretations will depend in a large measure on the traditional religious beliefs in which various mystics have been brought up. I think that such traditions probably act in two different ways.

1. The tradition no doubt affects the theoretical interpretation of experiences which would have taken place even if the mystic had been brought up in a different tradition. A feeling of unity with the rest of the universe will be interpreted very differently by a Christian who has been brought up to believe in a personal God and by a Hindu mystic who has been trained in a quite different metaphysical tradition.
2. The traditional beliefs, on the other hand, probably determine many of the details of the experience itself. A Roman Catholic mystic may have visions of the Virgin and the saints, whilst a Protestant mystic pretty certainly will not.

Thus the relations between the experiences and the traditional beliefs are highly complex. Presumably the outlines of the belief are determined by the experience. Then the details of the belief are fixed for a certain place and period by the special peculiarities of the experiences had by the founder of a certain religion. These beliefs then become traditional in that religion. Thenceforth they in part determine the details of the experiences had by subsequent mystics of that religion, and still more do they determine the interpretations which these mystics will put upon their experiences. Therefore, when a set of religious beliefs has once been established, it no doubt tends to produce experiences which can plausibly be taken as evidence for it. If it is a tradition in a certain religion that one can communicate with saints, mystics of that religion will seem to see and to talk with saints in their mystical visions; and this fact will be taken as further evidence for the belief that one can communicate with saints.

Much the same double process of causation takes place in sense-perception. On the one hand, the beliefs and expectations which we have at any moment largely determine what *interpretation* we shall put on a certain sensation which we should in any case have had then. On the other hand, our beliefs and expectations do to some extent determine and modify some of the sensible characteristics of the *sensa themselves*. When I am thinking only of diagrams a certain visual stimulus may produce a sensation of a sensibly flat sensum; but a precisely similar stimulus may produce a sensation of a sensibly solid sensum when I am thinking of solid objects.

Such explanations, however, plainly do not account for the first origin of religious beliefs, or for the features which are common to the religious experiences of persons of widely different times, races, and traditions.

Now, when we find that there are certain experiences which, though never very frequent in a high degree of intensity, have happened in a high degree among a few men at all times and places; and when we find that, in spite of differences in detail which we can explain, they involve certain fundamental conditions which are common and peculiar to them; two alternatives are open to us. (i) We may suppose that these men are in contact with an aspect of reality which is not revealed to ordinary persons in their everyday experience. And we may suppose that the characteristics which they agree in ascribing to reality on the basis of these experiences probably do belong to it. Or (ii) we may suppose that they are all subject to a delusion from which other men are free. In order to illustrate these alternatives it will be useful to consider three partly analogous cases, two of which are real and the third imaginary.

(*a*) Most of the detailed facts which biologists tells us about the minute structure and changes in cells can be perceived only by persons who have had a long training in the use of the microscope. In this case we believe that the agreement among trained microscopists really does correspond to facts which untrained persons cannot perceive. (*b*) Persons of all races who habitually drink alcohol to excess eventually have perceptual experiences in which they seem to themselves to see snakes or rats crawling about their rooms or beds. In this case we believe that this agreement among drunkards is merely a uniform hallucination. (*c*) Let us now imagine a race of beings who can walk about and touch things but cannot see. Suppose that eventually a few of them developed the power of sight. All that they might tell their still blind friends about colour would be wholly unintelligible to and unverifiable by the latter. But they would also be able to tell their blind friends a great deal about what the latter would feel if they were to walk in certain directions. These statements would be verified. This would not, of course, *prove* to the blind ones that the unintelligible statements about colour correspond to certain aspects of the world which they cannot perceive. But it would show that the seeing persons had a source of additional information about matters which the blind ones could understand and test for themselves. It would not be unreasonable then for the blind ones to believe that probably the seeing ones are also able to perceive other aspects of reality which they are describing correctly when they make their unintelligible statements containing colour-names. The question then is whether it is reasonable to regard the agreement between the experiences of religious mystics as more like the agreement among trained microscopists about the minute structure of cells, or as more like the agreement among habitual drunkards about the infestation of their rooms by pink rats or snakes, or as more like the agreement about colours which the seeing men would express in their statements to the blind men.

Why do we commonly believe that habitual excess of alcohol is a cause of a uniform delusion and not a source of additional information? The main reason is as follows. The things which drunkards claim to perceive are not fundamentally different in kind from the things that other people perceive. We have all seen rats and snakes, though the rats have generally been grey or brown and not pink. Moreover the drunkard claims that the rats and snakes which he sees are literally present in his room and on his bed, in the same sense in which his bed is in his room and his quilt is on his bed. Now we may fairly argue as follows. Since these are the sort of things which we could see if they were there, the fact that we cannot see them makes it highly probable that they are not there. Again, we know what kinds of perceptible effect would generally follow from the presence in a room of such things as rats or snakes. We should expect fox-terriers or mongooses to show traces of excitement, cheese to be nibbled, corn to disappear from bins, and so on. We find that no such effects are observed in the bedrooms of persons suffering from *delirium tremens*. It therefore seems reasonable to conclude that the agreement among drunkards is a sign, not of a revelation, but of a delusion.

Now the assertions in which religious mystics agree are not such that they conflict with what we can perceive with our senses. They are about the structure and organization of the world as a whole and about the relations of men to the rest of it. And they have so little in common with the facts of daily life that there is not much chance of direct collision. I think that there is only one important point on which there is conflict. Nearly all mystics seem to be agreed that time and change and unchanging duration are unreal or extremely superficial, whilst these seem to plain men to be the most fundamental features of the world. But we must admit, on the one hand, that these temporal characteristics present very great philosophical difficulties and puzzles when we reflect upon them. On the other hand, we may well suppose that the mystic finds it impossible to state clearly in ordinary language what it is that he experiences about the facts which underlie the appearance of time and change and duration. Therefore it is not difficult to allow that what we experience as the temporal aspect of reality corresponds in some sense to certain facts, and yet that these facts appear to us in so distorted a form in our ordinary experience that a person who sees them more accurately and directly might refuse to apply temporal names to them.

Let us next consider why we feel fairly certain that the agreement among trained microscopists about the minute structure of cells expresses an objective fact, although we cannot get similar experiences. One reason is that we have learned enough, from simpler cases of visual perception, about the laws of optics to know that the arrangement of lenses in a microscope is such that it will reveal minute structure, which is otherwise invisible, and will not simply create optical delusions. Another reason is that we know of other cases in which trained persons can detect things which untrained people will overlook, and that in many cases the existence of these things can be verified by indirect methods. Probably most of us have experienced such results of training in our own lives.

Now religious experience is not in nearly such a strong position as this. We do not know much about the laws which govern its occurrence and determine its variations. No doubt there are certain standard methods of training and meditation which tend to produce mystical experiences. These have been elaborated to some extent by certain Western mystics and to a very much greater extent by Eastern Yogis. But I do not think that we can see here, as we can in the case of microscopes and the training which is required to make the best use of them, any conclusive reason why these methods should produce veridical rather than delusive experiences. Uniform methods of training and meditation would be likely to produce more or less similar experiences, whether these experiences were largely veridical or wholly delusive.

Is there any analogy between the facts about religious experience and the fable about the blind men some of whom gained the power of sight? It might be said that many ideals of conduct and ways of life, which we can all recognize now to be good and useful, have been introduced into human history by the founders of religions. These persons have made actual ethical discoveries which others can afterwards recognize to be true. It might be said that this is at least roughly analogous to the case of the seeing men telling the still blind men of facts which the latter could and did verify for themselves. And it might be said that this makes it reasonable for us to attach some weight to what founders of religions tell us about things which we cannot understand or verify for ourselves; just as it would have been reasonable for the blind men to attach some weight to the unintelligible statements which the seeing men made to them about colours.

I think that this argument deserves a certain amount of respect, though I should find it hard to estimate how much weight to attach to it. I should be inclined to sum up as follows. When there is a nucleus of agreement between the experiences of men in different places, times, and traditions, and when they all tend to put much the same kind of interpretation on the cognitive content of these experiences, it is reasonable to ascribe this agreement to their all being in contact with a certain objective aspect of reality *unless* there be some positive reason to think otherwise. The practical postulate which we go upon everywhere else is to treat cognitive claims as veridical unless there be some positive reason to think them delusive. This, after all, is our only guarantee for believing that ordinary sense-perception is veridical. We cannot *prove* that what people agree in perceiving really exists independently of them; but we do always assume that ordinary waking sense-perception is veridical unless we can produce some positive ground for thinking that it is delusive in any given case. I think it would be inconsistent to treat the experiences of religious mystics on different principles. So far as they agree they should be provisionally accepted as veridical unless there be some positive ground for thinking that they are not. So the next question is whether there is any positive ground for holding that they are delusive.

There are two circumstances which have been commonly held to cast doubt on the cognitive claims of religious and mystical experience. (i) It is alleged that founders of religions and saints have nearly always had certain neuropathic symptoms or certain bodily weaknesses, and that these would be likely to produce delusions. Even if we accept the premises, I do not think that this is a very strong argument. (*a*) It is equally true that many founders of religions and saints have exhibited great endurance and great power of organization and business capacity which would have made them extremely successful and competent in secular affairs. There are very few offices in the cabinet or in the highest branches of the civil service which St. Thomas Aquinas could not have held with conspicuous success. I do not, of course, regard this as a positive reason *for* accepting the metaphysical doctrines which saints and founders of religions have based on their experiences; but it is relevant as a *rebuttal* of the argument which we are considering. (*b*) Probably very few people of extreme genius in science or art are perfectly normal mentally or physically, and some of them are very crazy and eccentric indeed. Therefore it would be rather surprising if persons of religious genius were completely normal, whether their experiences be veridical or delusive. (*c*) Suppose, for the sake of argument, that there is an aspect of the world which remains altogether outside the ken of ordinary persons in their daily life. Then it seems very likely that some degree of mental and physical abnormality would be a necessary condition for getting sufficiently loosened from the objects of ordinary sense-perception to come into cognitive contact with this aspect of reality. Therefore the fact that those persons who claim to have this peculiar kind of cognition generally exhibit certain mental and physical abnormalities is rather what might be anticipated if their claims were true. One might need to be slightly 'cracked' in order to have some peep-holes into the super-sensible world. (*d*) If mystical experience were veridical, it seems quite likely that it would *produce* abnormalities of behaviour in those who had it strongly. Let us suppose, for the sake of argument, that those who have religious experience are in frequent contact with an aspect of reality of which most men get only rare and faint glimpses. Then such persons are, as it were, living in two worlds, while the ordinary man is living in only one of them. Or, again, they might be compared to a man who has to conduct his life with one ordinary eye and another of a telescopic kind. Their behaviour may be appropriate to the aspect of reality which they alone perceive and think all-important; but, for that very reason, it may be inappropriate to those other aspects of reality which are all that most men perceive or judge to be important and on which all our social institutions and conventions are built.

(ii) A second reason which is commonly alleged for doubt about the claims of religious experience is the following. It is said that such experience always originates from and remains mixed with certain other factors, e.g., sexual emotion, which are such that experiences and beliefs that arise from them are very likely to be delusive. I think that there are a good many confusions on this point, and it will be worthwhile to begin by indicating some of them.

When people say that B 'originated from' A, they are liable to confuse at least three different kinds of connexion between A and B. (i) It might be that A is a necessary but insufficient condition of the existence of B.

(ii) It might be that A is a necessary and sufficient condition of the existence of B. Or (iii) it might be that B simply *is* A in a more complex and disguised form. Now, when there is in fact evidence only for the first kind of connexion, people are very liable to jump to the conclusion that there is the third kind of connexion. It may well be the case, e.g., that no one who was incapable of strong sexual desires and emotions could have anything worth calling religious experience. But it is plain that the possession of a strong capacity for sexual experience is not a *sufficient* condition of having a religious experience; for we know that the former quite often exists in persons who show hardly any trace of the latter. But, even if it could be shown that a strong capacity for sexual desire and emotion is *both* necessary and sufficient to produce religious experience, it would not follow that the latter is just the former in disguise. In the first place, it is not at all easy to discover the exact meaning of this metaphorical phrase when it is applied to psychological topics. And, if we make use of physical analogies, we are not much helped. A mixture of oxygen and hydrogen in presence of a spark is necessary and sufficient to produce water accompanied by an explosion. But water accompanied by an explosion is not a mixture of oxygen and hydrogen and a spark 'in a disguised form', whatever that may mean.

Now I think that the present rather vaguely formulated objection to the validity of the claims of religious experience might be stated somewhat as follows. 'In the individual, religious experience originates from, and always remains mixed with, sexual desires and emotions. The other generative factor of it is the religious tradition of the society in which he lives, the teachings of his parents, nurses, school-masters, etc. In the race religious experience originated from a mixture of false beliefs about nature and man, irrational fears, sexual and other impulses, and so on. Thus the religious tradition arose from beliefs which we now recognize to have been false and from emotions which we now recognize to have been irrelevant and misleading. It is now drilled into children by those who are in authority over them at a time of life when they are intellectually and emotionally at much the same stage as the primitive savages among whom it originated. It is, therefore, readily accepted, and it determines beliefs and emotional dispositions which persist long after the child has grown up and acquired more adequate knowledge of nature and of himself.'

Persons who use this argument might admit that it does not definitely *prove* that religious beliefs are false and groundless. False beliefs and irrational fears in our remote ancestors *might* conceivably be the origin of true beliefs and of an appropriate feeling of awe and reverence in ourselves. And, if sexual desires and emotions be an essential condition and constituent of religious experience, the experience *may* nevertheless be veridical in important respects. We might merely have to rewrite one of the beatitudes and say 'Blessed are the *impure* in heart, for they shall see God'. But, although it is logically possible that such causes should produce such effects, it would be said that they are most unlikely to do so. They seem much more likely to produce false beliefs and misplaced emotions.

It is plain that this argument has considerable plausibility. But it is worth while to remember that modern science has almost as humble an ancestry as contemporary religion. If the primitive witch-smeller is the spiritual progenitor of the Archbishop of Canterbury, the primitive rain-maker is equally the spiritual progenitor of the Cavendish Professor of Physics. There has obviously been a gradual refinement and purification of religious beliefs and concepts in the course of history, just as there has been in the beliefs and concepts of science. Certain persons of religious genius, such as some of the Hebrew prophets and the founders of Christianity and of Buddhism, do seem to have introduced new ethico-religious concepts and beliefs which have won wide acceptance, just as certain men of scientific genius, such as Galileo, Newton, and Einstein, have done in the sphere of science. It seems somewhat arbitrary to count this process as a continual approximation to true knowledge of the material aspect of the world in the case of science, and to refuse to regard it as at all similar in the case of religion. Lastly, we must remember that all of us have accepted the current common-sense and scientific view of the material world on the authority of our parents, nurses, masters, and companions at a time when we had neither the power nor the inclination to criticize it. And most of us accept, without even understanding, the more recondite doctrines of contemporary physics simply on the authority of those whom we have been taught to regard as experts.

On the whole, then, I do not think that what we know of the conditions under which religious beliefs and emotions have arisen in the life of the individual and the race makes it reasonable to think that they are *specially* likely to be delusive or misdirected. At any rate any argument which starts from that basis and claims to reach such a conclusion will need to be very carefully handled if its destructive effects are to be confined within the range contemplated by its users. It is reasonable to think that the concepts and beliefs of even the most perfect religions known to us are extremely inadequate to the facts which they express; that they are highly confused and are mixed up with a great deal of positive error and sheer nonsense; and that, if the human race goes on and continues to have religious experiences and to reflect on them, they will be altered and improved almost out of recognition. But all this could be said, *mutatis mutandis,* of scientific concepts and theories. The claim of any particular religion or sect to have complete or final truth on these subjects seems to me to be too ridiculous to be worth a moment's consideration. But the opposite extreme of holding that the whole religious experience of mankind is a gigantic system of pure delusion seems to me to be almost (though not quite) as far-fetched.

The Five Ways

St. Thomas Aquinas   *(Translated by Laurence Shapcote)*

The First Way: The Argument From Change

The existence of God can be shown in five ways. The first and clearest is taken from the idea of motion. (1) Now it is certain, and our senses corroborate it, that some things in this world are in motion. (2) But everything which is in motion is moved by something else. (3) For nothing is in motion except in so far as it is in potentiality in relation to that towards which it is in motion. (4) Now a thing causes movement in so far as it is in actuality. For to cause movement is nothing else than to bring something from potentiality to actuality; but a thing cannot be brought from potentiality to actuality except by something which exists in actuality, as, for example, that which is hot in actuality, like fire, makes wood, which is only hot in potentiality, to be hot in actuality, and thereby causes movement in it and alters it. (5) But it is not possible that the same thing should be at the same time in actuality and potentiality in relation to the same thing, but only in relation to different things; for what is hot in actuality cannot at the same time be hot in potentiality, though it is at the same time cold in potentiality. (6) It is impossible, therefore, that in relation to the same thing and in the same way anything should both cause movement and be caused, or that it should cause itself to move. (7) Everything therefore that is in motion

Reprinted from Thomas Aquinas, *Summa Theologica,* trans. Laurence Shapcote (London: O. P. Benziger Brothers, 1911).

must be moved by something else. If therefore the thing which causes it to move be in motion, this too must be moved by something else, and so on. (8) But we cannot proceed to infinity in this way, because in that case there would be no first mover, and in consequence, neither would there be any other mover; for secondary movers do not cause movement except they be moved by a first mover, as, for example, a stick cannot cause movement unless it is moved by the hand. Therefore it is necessary to stop at some first mover which is moved by nothing else. And this is what we all understand God to be.

The Second Way: The Argument From Causation

The Second Way is taken from the idea of the Efficient Cause. (1) For we find that there is among material things a regular order of efficient causes. (2) But we do not find, nor indeed is it possible, that anything is the efficient cause of itself, for in that case it would be prior to itself, which is impossible. (3) Now it is not possible to proceed to infinity in efficient causes. (4) For if we arrange in order all efficient causes, the first is the cause of the intermediate, and the intermediate the cause of the last, whether the intermediate be many or only one. (5) But if we remove a cause the effect is removed; therefore, if there is no *first* among efficient causes, neither will there be a last or an intermediate. (6) But if we proceed to infinity in efficient causes there will be no first efficient cause, and thus there will be no ultimate effect, nor any intermediate efficient causes, which is clearly false. Therefore it is necessary to suppose the existence of some first efficient cause, and this men call God.

The Third Way: The Argument From Contingency

The Third Way rests on the idea of the "contingent" and the "necessary" and is as follows: (1) Now we find that there are certain things in the Universe which are capable of existing and of not existing, for we find that some things are brought into existence and then destroyed, and consequently are capable of being or not being. (2) But it is impossible for all things which exist to be of this kind, because anything which is capable of not existing, at some time or other does not exist. (3) If therefore *all* things are capable of not existing, there was a time when nothing existed in the Universe. (4) But if this is true there would also be nothing in existence now; because anything that does not exist cannot begin to exist except by the agency of something which has existence. If therefore there was once nothing which existed, it would have been impossible for anything to begin to exist, and so nothing would exist now. (5) This is clearly false. Therefore all things are not contingent, and there must be something which is necessary in the Universe. (6) But everything which is necessary either has or has not the cause of its necessity from an outside source. Now it is not possible to proceed to infinity in necessary things which have a cause of their necessity, as has been proved in the case of efficient causes. Therefore it is necessary to suppose the existence of something which is necessary in itself, not having the cause of its necessity from any outside source, but which is the cause of necessity in others. And this "something" we call God.

The Fourth Way: The Argument From Degrees Of Excellence

The Fourth Way is taken from the degrees which are found in things. (1) For among different things we find that one is more or less good or true or noble; and likewise in the case of other things of this kind. (2) But the words "more" or "less" are used of different things in proportion as they approximate in their different ways to something which has the particular quality in the highest degree—e.g., we call a thing hotter when it approximates more nearly to that which is hot in the highest degree. There is therefore something which is true in the highest degree, good in the highest degree and noble in the highest degree; (3) and consequently there must be also something which has being in the highest degree. For things which are true in the highest degree also have being in the highest degree (see Aristotle, *Metaphysics,* 2). (4) But anything which has a certain quality of any kind in the highest degree is also the cause of all things of that kind, as, for example, fire which is hot in the highest degree is the cause of all hot things (as is said in the same book). (5) Therefore there exists something which is the cause of being, and goodness, and of every perfection in all existing things; and this we call God.

The Fifth Way: The Argument From Harmony

The Fifth Way is taken from the way in which nature is governed. (1) For we observe that certain things which lack knowledge, such as natural bodies, work for an End. This is obvious, because they always, or at any rate very frequently, operate in the same way so as to attain the best possible result. (2) Hence it is clear that they do not arrive at their goal by chance, but by purpose. (3) But those things which have no knowledge do not move towards a goal unless they are guided by someone or something which does possess knowledge and intelligence—e.g., an arrow by an archer. Therefore, there does exist something which possesses intelligence by which all natural things are directed to their goal; and this we call God.

The Cosmological Argument

Richard Taylor

. . . Suppose you were strolling in the woods and, in addition to the sticks, stones, and other accustomed litter of the forest floor, you one day came upon some quite unaccustomed object, something not quite like what you had ever seen before and would never expect to find in such a place. Suppose, for example, that it is a large ball, about your own height, perfectly smooth and translucent. You would deem this puzzling and mysterious, certainly, but if one considers the matter, it is no more inherently mysterious that such a thing should exist than that anything else should exist. If you were quite accustomed to finding such objects of various sizes around you most of the time, but had never seen an ordinary rock, then upon finding a large rock in the woods one day you would be just as puzzled and mystified. This illustrates the fact that something that is mysterious ceases to seem so simply by its accustomed presence. It is strange indeed, for example, that a world such as ours should exist; yet few people are very often struck by this strangeness but simply take it for granted.

Suppose, then, that you have found this translucent ball and are mystified by it. Now whatever else you might wonder about it, there is one thing you would hardly question; namely, that it did not appear there all by itself, that it owes its existence to something. You might not have the remotest idea whence and how it came to be there, but you would hardly doubt that there was an explanation. The idea that it

Source: Metaphysics, Fourth Edition by R. Taylor, © 1992. Reprinted by permission of Pearson Education, Inc., Upper Saddle River, N.J.

might have come from nothing at all, that it might exist without there being any explanation of its existence, is one that few people would consider worthy of entertaining.

This illustrates a metaphysical belief that seems to be almost a part of reason itself, even though few ever think upon it; the belief, namely, that there is some explanation for the existence of anything whatever, some reason why it should exist rather than not. The sheer nonexistence of anything, which is not to be confused with the passing out of existence of something, never requires a reason; but existence does. That there should never have been any such ball in the forest does not require any explanation or reason, but that there should ever be such a ball does. If one were to look upon a barren plain and ask why there is not and never has been any large translucent ball there, the natural response would be to ask why there should be; but if one finds such a ball, and wonders why it is there, it is not quite so natural to ask why it should *not* be—as though existence should simply be taken for granted. That anything should not exist, then, and that, for instance, no such ball should exist in the forest, or that there should be no forest for it to occupy, or no continent containing a forest, or no Earth, nor any world at all, do not seem to be things for which there needs to be any explanation or reason; but that such things should be *does* seem to require a reason.

The principle involved here has been called the principle of sufficient reason. Actually, it is a very general principle, and it is best expressed by saying that, in the case of any positive truth, there is some sufficient reason for it, something that, in this sense, makes it true—in short, that there is some sort of explanation, known or unknown, for everything.

Now, some truths depend on something else, and are accordingly called *contingent,* while others depend only upon themselves, that is, are true by their very natures and are accordingly called *necessary.* There is, for example, a reason why the stone on my window sill is warm; namely, that the sun is shining upon it. This happens to be true, but not by its very nature. Hence, it is contingent, and depends upon something other than itself. It is also true that all the points of a circle are equidistant from the center, but this truth depends upon nothing but itself. No matter what happens, nothing can make it false. Similarly, it is a truth, and a necessary one, that if the stone on my window sill is a body, as it is, then it has a form, because this fact depends upon nothing but itself for its confirmation. Untruths are also, of course, either contingent or necessary, it being contingently false, for example, that the stone on my window still is cold, and necessarily false that it is both a body and formless, because this is by its very nature impossible.

The principle of sufficient reason can be illustrated in various ways, as we have done, and if one thinks about it, he is apt to find that he presupposes it in his thinking about reality, but it cannot be proved. It does not appear to be itself a necessary truth, and at the same time it would be most odd to say it is contingent. If one were to try proving it, he would sooner or later have to appeal to considerations that are less plausible than the principle itself. Indeed, it is hard to see how one could even make an argument for it without already assuming it. For this reason it might properly be called a presupposition of reason itself. One can deny that it is true, without embarrassment or fear of refutation, but one is then apt to find that what he is denying is not really what the principle asserts. We shall, then, treat it here as a datum—not something that is provably true, but as something that people, whether they ever reflect upon it or not, seem more or less to presuppose.

It happens to be true that something exists, that there is, for example, a world, and although no one ever seriously supposes that this might not be so, that there might exist nothing at all, there still seems to be nothing the least necessary in this, considering it just by itself. That no world should ever exist at all is perfectly comprehensible and seems to express not the slightest absurdity. Considering any particular item in the world it seems not at all necessary that the totality of these things, or any totality of things, should ever exist.

From the principle of sufficient reason it follows, of course, that there must be a reason not only for the existence of everything in the world but for the world itself, meaning by "the world" simply everything that ever does exist, except God, in case there is a god. This principle does not imply that there must be some purpose or goal for everything, or for the totality of all things; for explanations need not be, and in fact seldom are, teleological or purposeful. All the principle requires is that there be some sort of reason for everything. And it would certainly be odd to maintain that everything in the world owes its existence to something, that nothing in the world is either purely accidental, or such that it just bestows its own being upon itself, and then to deny this of the world itself. One can indeed say that the world is in some sense a pure accident, that there simply is no reason at all why this or any world should exist, and one can equally say that the world exists by its very nature, or is an inherently necessary being. But it is at least very odd and arbitrary to deny of this existing world the need for any sufficient reason, whether independent of itself or not, while presupposing that there is a reason for every other thing that ever exists.

Consider again the strange ball that we imagine has been found in the forest. Now, we can hardly doubt that there must be an explanation for the existence of such a thing, though we may have no notion what that explanation is. It is not, moreover, the fact of its having been found in the forest rather than elsewhere that renders an explanation necessary. It matters not in the least where it happens to be, for our question is not how it happens to be *there* but how it happens to be at all. If we in our imagination annihilate the forest, leaving only this ball in an open field, our conviction that it is a contingent thing and owes its existence to something other than itself is not reduced in the least. If we now imagine the field to be annihilated, and in fact everything else as well to vanish into nothingness, leaving only this ball to constitute the entire physical universe, then we cannot for a moment suppose that its existence has thereby been explained, or the need for any explanation eliminated, or that its existence is suddenly rendered self-explanatory. If we now carry this thought one step further and suppose that no other reality ever has existed or ever will exist, that this ball forever constitutes the entire physical universe, then we must still insist on there being some reason independent of itself why it should exist rather than not. If there must be a reason for the existence of any particular thing, then the necessity of such a reason is not eliminated by the mere supposition that certain other things do *not* exist. And again, it matters not at all what the thing in question is, whether it be large and complex, such as the world we actually find ourselves in, or whether it be something small, simple, and insignificant, such as a ball, a bacterium, or the merest grain of sand. We do not avoid the necessity of a reason for the existence of something merely by describing it in this way or that. And it would, in any event, seem quite plainly absurd to say that if the world were composed entirely of a single ball about six feet in diameter, or of a single grain of sand, then it would be contingent and there would have to be some explanation other than itself why such a thing exists, but that, since the actual world is vastly more complex than this, there is no need for an explanation of its existence, independent of itself.

It should now be noted that it is no answer to the question, why a thing exists, to state *how long* it has existed. A geologist does not suppose that she has explained why there should be rivers and mountains merely by pointing out that they are old. Similarly, if one were to ask, concerning the ball of which we have spoken, for some sufficient reason for its being, he would not receive any answer upon being told that it had been there since yesterday. Nor would it be any better answer to say that it had existed since before anyone could remember, or even that it had always existed; for the question was not one concerning its age but its existence. If, to be sure, one were to ask where a given thing came from, or how it came into being, then upon learning that it had always existed he would learn that it never really *came* into being at all; but he could still reasonably wonder why it should exist at all. If, accordingly, the world—that is, the totality of all things excepting God, in case there is a god—had really no beginning at all, but has always existed in some form or other, then there is clearly no answer to the question, where it came from and when; it did not, on this supposition, *come* from anything at all, at any time. But still, it can be asked why there is a world, why indeed there is a beginningless world, why there should have perhaps always been something rather than nothing. And, if the principle of sufficient reason is a good principle, there must be an answer to that question, an answer that is by no means supplied by giving the world an age, or even an infinite age.

This brings out an important point with respect to the concept of creation that is often misunderstood, particularly by those whose thinking has been influenced by Christian ideas. People tend to think that creation—for example, the creation of the world by God—*means* creation *in time*, from which it of course logically follows that if the world had no beginning in time, then it cannot be the creation of God. This, however, is erroneous, for creation means essentially *dependence*, even in Christian theology. If one thing is the creation of another, then it depends for its existence on that other, and this is perfectly consistent with saying that both are eternal, that neither ever came into being, and hence, that neither was ever created at any point of time. Perhaps an analogy will help convey this point. Consider, then, a flame that is casting beams of light. Now, there seems to be a clear sense in which the beams of light are dependent for their existence upon the flame, which is their source, while the flame, on the other hand, is not similarly dependent for its existence upon them. The beams of light arise from the flame, but the flame does not arise from them. In this sense, they are the creation of the flame; they derive their existence from it. And none of this has any reference to time; the relationship of dependence in such a case would not be altered in the slightest if we supposed that the flame, and with it the beams of light, had always existed, that neither had ever *come* into being.

Now if the world is the creation of God, its relationship to God should be thought of in this fashion; namely, that the world depends for its existence upon God, and could not exist independently of God. If God is eternal, as those who believe in God generally assume, then the world may (though it need not) be eternal too, without that altering in the least its dependence upon God for its existence, and hence without altering its being the creation of God. The supposition of God's eternality, on the other hand, does not by itself imply that the world is eternal too; for there is not the least reason why something of finite duration might not depend for its existence upon something of infinite duration—though the reverse is, of course, impossible.

If we think of God as "the creator of heaven and earth," and if we consider heaven and earth to include everything that exists except God, then we appear to have, in the foregoing considerations, fairly strong reasons for asserting that God, as so conceived, exists. Now of course most people have much more in mind than this when they think of God, for religions have ascribed to God ever so many attributes that are not at all implied by describing him merely as the creator of the world; but that is not relevant here. Most religious persons do, in any case, think of God as being at least the creator, as that being upon which everything ultimately depends, no matter what else they may say about Him in addition. It is, in fact, the first item in the creeds of Christianity that God is the "creator of heaven and earth." And, it seems, there are good metaphysical reasons, as distinguished from the persuasions of faith, for thinking that such a creative being exists.

If, as seems clearly implied by the principle of sufficient reason, there must be a reason for the existence of heaven and earth—i.e., for the world—then that reason must be found either in the world itself, or outside it, in something that is literally supranatural, or outside heaven and earth. Now if we suppose that the world—i.e., the totality of all things except God—contains within itself the reason for its existence, we are supposing that it exists by its very nature, that is, that it is a necessary being. In that case there would, of course, be no reason for saying that it must depend upon God or anything else for its existence; for if it exists by its very nature, then it depends upon nothing but itself, much as the sun depends upon nothing but itself for its heat. This, however, is implausible, for we find nothing about the world or anything in it to suggest that it exists by its own nature, and we do find, on the contrary, ever so many things to suggest that it does not. For in the first place, anything that exists by its very nature must necessarily be eternal and indestructible. It would be a self-contradiction to say of anything that it exists by its own nature, or is a necessarily existing thing, and at the same time to say that it comes into being or passes away, or that it ever could come into being or pass away. Nothing about the world seems at all like this, for concerning anything in the world, we can perfectly easily think of it as being annihilated, or as never having existed in the first place, without there being the slightest hint of any absurdity in such a supposition. Some of the things in the universe are, to be sure, very old; the moon, for example, or the stars and the planets. It is even possible to imagine that they have always existed. Yet it seems quite impossible to suppose that they owe their existence to nothing but themselves, that they bestow existence upon themselves by their very natures, or that they are in themselves things of such nature that it would be impossible for them not to exist. Even if we suppose that something, such as the sun, for instance, has existed forever, and will never cease, still we cannot conclude just from this that it exists by its own nature. If, as is of course very doubtful, the sun has existed forever and will never cease, then it is possible that its heat and light have also existed forever and will never cease; but that would not show that the heat and light of the sun exist by their own natures. They are obviously contingent and depend on the sun for their existence, whether they are beginningless and everlasting or not.

There seems to be nothing in the world, then, concerning which it is at all plausible to suppose that it exists by its own nature, or contains within itself the reason for its existence. In fact, everything in the world appears to be quite plainly the opposite, namely, something that not only need not exist, but at some time or other, past or future or both, does not in fact exist. Everything in the world seems to have a finite duration, whether long or short. Most things, such as ourselves, exist only for a short while; they come into being, then soon cease. Other things, like the heavenly bodies, last longer, but they are still corruptible, and from all that we can gather about them, they too seem destined eventually to perish. We arrive at the conclusion, then, that although the world may contain some things that have always existed and are destined never to perish, it is nevertheless doubtful that it contains any such thing, and, in any case, everything in the world is capable of perishing, and nothing in it, however long it may already have existed and however long it may yet remain, exists by its own nature but depends instead upon something else.

Although this might be true of everything in the world, is it necessarily true of the world itself? That is, if we grant, as we seem forced to, that nothing in the world exists by its own nature, that everything in the world is contingent and perishable, must we also say that the world itself, or the totality of all these perishable things, is also contingent and perishable? Logically, we are not forced to, for it is logically possible that the totality of all perishable things might itself be imperishable, and hence, that the world might exist by its own nature, even though it is composed exclusively of things that are contingent. It is not logically necessary that a totality should share the defects of its members. For example, even though every person is mortal, it does not follow from this that the human race, or the totality of all people, is also mortal; for it is possible that there will always be human beings, even though there are no human beings who will always exist. Similarly, it is possible that the world is in itself a necessary thing, even though it is composed entirely of things that are contingent.

This is logically possible, but it is not plausible. For we find nothing whatever about the world, any more than in its parts, to suggest that it exists by its own nature. Concerning anything in the world, we have not the slightest difficulty in supposing that it should perish, or even that it should never have existed in the first place. We have almost as little difficulty in supposing this of the world itself. It might be somewhat hard to think of everything as utterly perishing and leaving no trace whatever of its ever having been, but there seems to be not the slightest difficulty in imagining that the world should never have existed in the first place. We can, for instance, perfectly easily suppose that nothing in the world had ever existed except, let us suppose, a single grain of sand, and we can thus suppose that this grain of sand has forever constituted the whole universe. Now if we consider just this grain of sand, it is quite impossible for us to suppose that it exists by its very nature and could never have failed to exist. It clearly depends for its existence upon something other than itself, if it depends on anything at all. The same will be true if we consider the world to consist not of one grain of sand but of two, or of a million, or, as we in fact find, of a vast number of stars and planets and all their minuter parts.

It would seem, then, that the world, in case it happens to exist at all—and this is quite beyond doubt—is contingent and thus dependent upon something other than itself for its existence, if it depends upon anything at all. And it must depend upon something, for otherwise there could be no reason why it exists in the first place. Now, that upon which the world depends must be something that either exists by its own nature or does not. If it does not exist by its own nature, then it, in turn, depends for its existence upon something else, and so on. Now then, we can say either of two things; namely,

(1) that the world depends for its existence upon something else, which in turn depends on still another thing, this depending upon still another, *ad infinitum*; or (2) that the world derives its existence from something that exists by its own nature and that is accordingly eternal and imperishable, and is the creator of heaven and earth. The first of these alternatives, however, is impossible, for it does not render a sufficient reason why anything should exist in the first place. Instead of supplying a reason why any world should exist, it repeatedly begs off giving a reason. It explains what is dependent and perishable in terms of what is itself dependent and perishable, leaving us still without a reason why perishable things should exist at all, which is what we are seeking. Ultimately, then, it would seem that the world, or the totality of contingent or perishable things, in case it exists at all, must depend upon something that is necessary and imperishable, and that accordingly exists, not in dependence upon something else, but by its own nature.

What has been said thus far gives some intimation of what meaning should be attached to the concept of a self-caused being, a concept that is quite generally misunderstood, sometimes even by scholars. To say that something—God, for example—is self-caused, or is the cause of its own existence, does not mean that this being brings itself into existence, which is a perfectly absurd idea. Nothing can *bring* itself into existence. To say that something is self-caused (*causa sui*) means only that it exists, not contingently or in dependence upon something else but by its own nature, which is only to say that it is a being which is such that it can neither come into being nor perish. Now, whether in fact such a being exists or not, there is in any case no absurdity in the idea. We have found, in fact, that the principle of sufficient reason seems to point to the existence of such a being, as that upon which the world, with everything in it, must ultimately depend for its existence.

A being that depends for its existence upon nothing but itself and is in this sense self-caused, can equally be described as a necessary being; that is to say, a being that is not contingent, and hence not perishable. For in the case of anything that exists by its own nature and is dependent upon nothing else, it is impossible that it should not exist, which is equivalent to saying that it is necessary. Many persons have professed to find the greatest difficulties in this concept, too, but that is partly because it has been confused with other notions. If it makes sense to speak of anything as an *impossible* being, or something that by its very nature does not exist, then it is hard to see why the idea of a necessary being, or something that in its very nature exists, should not be just as comprehensible. And of course, we have not the slightest difficulty in speaking of something, such as a square circle or a formless body, as an impossible being. And if it makes sense to speak of something as being perishable, contingent, and dependent upon something other than itself for its existence, as it surely does, then there seems to be no difficulty in thinking of something as imperishable and dependent upon nothing other than itself for its existence.

From these considerations we can see also what is properly meant by a "first cause," an appellative that has often been applied to God by theologians and that many persons have deemed an absurdity. It is a common criticism of this notion to say that there need not be any first cause, because the series of causes and effects that constitute the history of the universe might be infinite or beginningless and must, in fact, be infinite in case the universe itself had no beginning in time. This criticism, however, reflects a total misconception of what is meant by a first cause. *First* here does not mean first in time, and when God is spoken of as a first cause He is not being described as a being that, at some time in the remote past, *started* everything. To describe God as a first cause is only to say that He is literally a *primary* rather than a secondary cause, an *ultimate* rather than a derived cause, or a being upon which all other things, heaven and earth, ultimately depend for their existence. It is, in short, only to say that God is the creator, in the sense of creation previously explained. Now this, of course, is perfectly consistent with saying that the world is eternal or beginningless. As we have seen, one gives no reason for the existence of a world merely by giving it an age, even if it is supposed to have an infinite age. To use a helpful analogy, we can say that the sun is the first cause of daylight and, for that matter, of the moonlight of the night as well, which means only that daylight and moonlight ultimately depend upon the sun for their existence. The moon, on the other hand, is only a secondary or derivative cause of its light. This light would be no less dependent upon the sun if we affirmed that it had no beginning, for an ageless and beginningless light requires a source no less than an ephemeral one. If we supposed that the sun has always existed, and with it its light, then we would have to say that the sun has always been the first—*i.e.*, the primary or ultimate—cause of its light. Such is precisely the manner in which God should be thought of, and is by theologians often thought of, as the first cause of heaven and earth.

A Debate on the Cosmological Argument

F. C. Copleston and Bertrand Russell

COPLESTON: As we are going to discuss the existence of God, it might perhaps be as well to come to some provisional agreement as to what we understand by the term "God." I presume that we mean a supreme personal being—distinct from the world and creator of the world. Would you agree—provisionally at least—to accept this statement as the meaning of the term "God"?

RUSSELL: Yes, I accept this definition.

COPLESTON: Well, my position is the affirmative position that such a being actually exists, and that His existence can be proved philosophically. Perhaps you would tell me if your position is that of agnosticism or of atheism. I mean, would you say that the non-existence of God can be proved?

RUSSELL: No, I should not say that: my position is agnostic.

COPLESTON: Would you agree with me that the problem of God is a problem of great importance? For example, would you agree that if God does not exist, human beings and human history can have no other purpose than the purpose they choose to give themselves, which—in practice—is likely to mean the purpose which those impose who have the power to impose it?

RUSSELL: Roughly speaking, yes, though I should have to place some limitation on your last clause.

COPLESTON: Would you agree that if there is no God—no absolute Being—there can be no absolute values? I mean, would you agree that if there is no absolute good that the relativity of values results?

RUSSELL: No, I think these questions are logically distinct. Take, for instance, G. E. Moore's *Principia Ethica,* where he maintains that there is a distinction of good and evil, that both of these are definite concepts. But he does not bring the idea of God to support that contention.

COPLESTON: Well, suppose we leave the question of good till later, till we come to the moral argument, and I give first a metaphysical argument. I'd like to put the main weight on the metaphysical argument based on Leibniz's argument from "Contingency" and then later we might discuss the moral argument. Suppose I give a brief statement on the metaphysical argument and that then we go on to discuss it?

RUSSELL: That seems to me to be a very good plan.

COPLESTON: Well, for clarity's sake, I'll divide the argument into distinct stages. First of all, I should say, we know that there are at least some beings in the world which do not contain in themselves the reason for their existence. For example, I depend on my parents, and now on the air, and on food, and so on. Now, secondly, the world is simply the real or imagined totality or aggregate of individual objects, none of which contain in themselves alone the reason for their existence. There isn't any world distinct from the objects which form it, any more than the human race is something apart from the members. Therefore, I should say, since objects or events exist, and since no object of experience contains within itself the reason of its existence, this reason, the totality of objects, must have a reason external to itself. That reason must be an existent being. Well, this being is either itself the reason for its own existence, or it is not. If it is, well and good. If it is not, then we must proceed farther. But if we proceed to infinity in that sense, then there's no explanation of existence at all. So, I should say, in order to explain existence, we must come to a being which contains within itself the reason for its own existence, that is to say, which cannot not exist.

RUSSELL: This raises a great many points and it is not altogether easy to know where to begin, but I think that, perhaps, in answering your argument, the best point at which to begin is the question of necessary being. The word "necessary," I should maintain, can only be applied significantly to propositions. And, in fact, only to such as are analytic—that is to say—such as it is self-contradictory to deny. I could only admit a necessary being if there were a being whose existence it is self-contradictory to deny. I should like to know whether you would accept Leibniz's division of propositions into truths of reason and truths of fact. The former—the truths of reason—being necessary.

COPLESTON: Well, I certainly should not subscribe to what seems to be Leibniz's idea of truths of reason and truths of fact, since it would appear that, for him, there are in the long run only analytic propositions. It would seem that for Leibniz truths of fact are ultimately reducible to truths of reason. That is to say, to analytic propositions, at least for an omniscient mind. Well, I couldn't agree with that. For one thing it would fail to meet the requirements of the experience of freedom. I don't want to uphold the whole philosophy of Leibniz. I have made use of his argument from contingent to necessary being, basing the argument on the principle of sufficient reason, simply because it seems to me a brief and clear formulation of what is, in my opinion, the fundamental metaphysical argument for God's existence.

RUSSELL: But, to my mind, "a necessary proposition" has got to be analytic. I don't see what else it can mean. And analytic propositions are always complex and logically somewhat late. "Irrational animals are animals" is an analytic proposition; but a proposition such as "This is an animal" can never be analytic. In fact, all the propositions that can be analytic are somewhat late in the build-up of propositions.

COPLESTON: Take the proposition "If there is a contingent being then there is a necessary being." I consider that that proposition hypothetically expressed is a necessary proposition. If you are going to call every necessary proposition an analytic proposition, then—in order to avoid a dispute in terminology—I would agree to call it analytic, though I don't consider it a tautological proposition. But the proposition is a necessary proposition only on the supposition that there is a contingent being. That there is a contingent being actually existing has to be discovered by experience, and the proposition that there is a contingent being is certainly not an analytic proposition, though once you know, I should maintain, that there is a contingent being, it follows of necessity that there is a necessary being.

RUSSELL: The difficulty of this argument is that I don't admit the idea of a necessary being and I don't admit that there is any particular meaning in calling other beings "contingent." These phrases don't for me have any significance except within a logic that I reject.

COPLESTON: Do you mean that you reject these terms because they won't fit in with what is called "modern logic"?

RUSSELL: Well, I can't find anything that they could mean. The word "necessary," it seems to me, is a useless word, except as applied to analytic propositions, not to things.

COPLESTON: In the first place, what do you mean by "modern logic"? As far as I know, there are somewhat differing systems. In the second place, not all modern logicians surely would admit the meaninglessness of metaphysics. We both know, at any rate, one very eminent modern thinker whose knowledge of modern logic was profound, but who certainly did not think that metaphysics are meaningless or, in particular, that the problem of God is meaningless. Again, even if all modern logicians held that metaphysical terms are meaningless, it would not follow that they were right. The proposition that metaphysical terms are meaningless seems to me to be a proposition based on an assumed philosophy. The dogmatic position behind it seems to be this: What will not go into my machine is non-existent, or it is meaningless; it is the expression of emotion. I am simply trying to point out that anybody who says that a particular system of modern logic is the sole criterion of meaning is saying something that is over-dogmatic; he is dogmatically insisting that a part of philosophy is the whole of philosophy. After all, a "contingent" being is a being which has not in itself the complete reason for its existence, that's what I mean by a contingent being. You know, as well as I do, that the existence of neither of us can be explained without reference to something or somebody outside us, our parents, for example. A "necessary" being, on the other hand, means a being that must and cannot not exist. You may say that there is no such being, but you will find it hard to convince me that you do not understand the terms I am using. If you do not understand them, then how can you be entitled to say that such a being does not exist, if that is what you do say?

RUSSELL: Well, there are points here that I don't propose to go into at length. I don't maintain the meaninglessness of metaphysics in general at all. I maintain the meaninglessness of certain particular terms—not on any general ground, but simply because I've not been able to see an interpretation of those particular terms. It's not a general dogma—it's a particular thing. But those points I will leave out for a moment. And I will say that what you have been saying brings us back, it seems to me, to the ontological argument that there is a being whose essence involves existence, so that his existence is analytic. That seems to me to be impossible, and it raises, of course, the question what one means by existence, and as to this, I think a subject named can never be significantly said to exist but only a subject described. And that existence, in fact, quite definitely is not a predicate.

COPLESTON: Well, you say, I believe, that it is bad grammar, or rather bad syntax to say for example "T.S.Eliot exists"; one ought to say, for example, "He, the author of *Murder in the Cathedral*, exists." Are you going to say that the proposition, "The cause of the world exists," is without meaning? You may say that the world has no cause; but I fail to see how you can say that the proposition that the "cause of the world exists" is meaningless. Put it in the form of a question: "Has the world a cause?" or "Does a cause of the world exist?" Most people surely would understand the question, even if they don't agree about the answer.

RUSSELL: Well, certainly the question "Does the cause of the world exist?" is a question that has meaning. But if you say, "Yes, God is the cause of the world" you're using God as a proper name; then "God exists" will not be a statement that has meaning; that is the position that I'm maintaining. Because, therefore, it will follow that it cannot be an analytic proposition ever to say that this or that exists. For example, suppose you take as your subject "the existent roundsquare," it would look like an analytic proposition that "the existent round-square exists," but it doesn't exist.

COPLESTON: No, it doesn't, then surely you can't say it doesn't exist unless you have a conception of what existence is. As to the phrase "existent roundsquare," I should say that it has no meaning at all.

RUSSELL: I quite agree. Then I should say the same thing in another context in reference to a "necessary being."

COPLESTON: Well, we seem to have arrived at an impasse. To say that a necessary being is a being that must exist and cannot not exist has for me a definite meaning. For you it has no meaning.

RUSSELL: Well, we can press the point a little, I think. A being that must exist and cannot not exist, would surely, according to you, be a being whose essence involves existence.

COPLESTON: Yes, a being the essence of which is to exist. But I should not be willing to argue the existence of God simply from the idea of His essence because I don't think we have any clear intuition of God's essence as yet. I think we have to argue from the world of experience to God.

RUSSELL: Yes, I quite see the distinction. But, at the same time, for a being with sufficient knowledge, it would be true to say "Here is this being whose essence involves existence!"

COPLESTON: Yes, certainly, if anybody saw God, he would see that God must exist.

RUSSELL: So that I mean there is a being whose essence involves existence although we don't know that essence. We only know there is such a being.

COPLESTON: Yes, I should add we don't know the essence *a priori*. It is only *a posteriori* through our experience of the world that we come to a knowledge of the existence of that being. And then one argues, the essence and existence must be identical. Because if God's essence and God's existence were not identical, then some sufficient reason for this existence would have to be found beyond God.

RUSSELL: So it all turns on this question of sufficient reason, and I must say you haven't defined "sufficient reason" in a way that I can understand—what do you mean by sufficient reason? You don't mean cause?

COPLESTON: Not necessarily. Cause is a kind of sufficient reason. Only contingent being can have a cause. God is His own sufficient reason; and He is not cause of Himself. By sufficient reason in the full sense I mean an explanation adequate for the existence of some particular being.

RUSSELL: But when is an explanation adequate? Suppose I am about to make a flame with a match. You may say that the adequate explanation of that is that I rub in on the box.

COPLESTON: Well, for practical purposes—but theoretically, that is only a partial explanation. An adequate explanation must ultimately be a total explanation, to which nothing further can be added.

RUSSELL: Then I can only say that you're looking for something which can't be got, and which one ought not to expect to get.

COPLESTON: To say that one has not found it is one thing; to say that one should not look for it seems to me rather dogmatic.

RUSSELL: Well, I don't know. I mean, the explanation of one thing is another thing which makes the other thing dependent on yet another, and you have to grasp this sorry scheme of things entire to do what you want, and that we can't do.

COPLESTON: But are you going to say that we can't, or we shouldn't even raise the question of the existence of the whole of this sorry scheme of things—of the whole universe?

RUSSELL: Yes, I don't think there's any meaning in it at all. I think the word "universe" is a handy word in some connections, but I don't think it stands for anything that has a meaning.

COPLESTON: If the word is meaningless, it can't be so very handy. In any case, I don't say that the universe is something different from the objects which compose it (I indicated that in my brief summary of the proof); what I'm doing is to look for the reason, in this case the cause of the objects—the real or imagined totality of which constitute what we call the universe. You say, I think, that the universe—or my existence if you prefer, or any other existence—is unintelligible?

RUSSELL: First may I take up the point that if a word is meaningless it can't be handy. That sounds well but isn't in fact correct. Take, say, such a word as "the" or "than." You can't point to any object that those words mean, but they are very useful words; I should say the same of "universe." But leaving that point, you ask whether I consider that the universe is unintelligible. I shouldn't say unintelligible—I think it is without explanation. Intelligible, to my mind, is a different thing. Intelligible has to do with the thing itself intrinsically and not with its relations.

COPLESTON: Well, my point is that what we call the world is intrinsically unintelligible, apart from the existence of God. You see, I don't believe that the infinity of the series of events—I mean a horizontal series, so to speak—if such an infinity could be proved, would be in the slightest degree relevant to the situation. If you add up chocolates you get chocolates after all and not a sheep. If you add up chocolates to infinity, you presumably get an infinite number of chocolates. So if you add up contingent beings to infinity, you still get contingent beings, not a necessary being. An infinite series of contingent beings will be, to my way of thinking, as unable to cause itself as one contingent being. However, you say, I think, that it is illegitimate to raise the question of what will explain the existence of any particular object?

RUSSELL: It's quite all right if you mean by explaining it, simply finding a cause for it.

COPLESTON: Well, why stop at one particular object? Why shouldn't one raise the question of the cause of the existence of all particular objects?

RUSSELL: Because I see no reason to think there is any. The whole concept of cause is one we derive from our observation of particular things; I see no reason whatsoever to suppose that the total has any cause whatsoever.

COPLESTON: Well, to say that there isn't any cause is not the same thing as saying that we shouldn't look for a cause. The statement that there isn't any cause should come, if it comes at all, at the end of the inquiry, not the beginning. In any case, if the total has no cause, then to my way of thinking it must be its own cause, which seems to me impossible. Moreover, the statement that the world is simply there if in answer to a question, presupposes that the question has meaning.

RUSSELL: No, it doesn't need to be its own cause, what I'm saying is that the concept of cause is not applicable to the total.

COPLESTON: Then you would agree with Sartre that the universe is what he calls "gratuitous"?

RUSSELL: Well, the word "gratuitous" suggests that it might be something else; I should say that the universe is just there, and that's all.

COPLESTON: Well, I can't see how you can rule out the legitimacy of asking the question how the total, or anything at all comes to be there. Why something rather than nothing, that is the question? The fact that we gain our knowledge of causality empirically, from particular causes, does not rule out the possibility of asking what the cause of the series is. If the word "cause" were meaningless or if it could be shown that Kant's view of the matter were correct, the question would be illegitimate I agree; but you don't seem to hold that the word "cause" is meaningless, and I do not suppose you are a Kantian.

RUSSELL: I can illustrate what seems to me your fallacy. Every man who exists has a mother, and it seems to me your argument is that therefore the human race must have a mother, but obviously the human race hasn't a mother—that's a different logical sphere.

COPLESTON: Well, I can't really see any parity. If I were saying "every object has a phenomenal cause, therefore, the whole series has a phenomenal cause," there would be a parity; but I'm not saying that; I'm saying, every object has a phenomenal cause if you insist on the infinity of the series—but the series of phenomenal causes is an insufficient explanation of the series. Therefore, the series has not a phenomenal cause but a transcendent cause.

RUSSELL: That's always assuming that not only every particular thing in the world, but the world as a whole must have a cause. For that assumption I see no ground whatever. If you'll give me a ground I'll listen to it.

COPLESTON: Well, the series of events is either caused or it's not caused. If it is caused, there must obviously be a cause outside the series. If it's not caused then it's sufficient to itself, and if it's sufficient to itself it is what I call necessary. But it can't be necessary since each member is contingent, and we've agreed that the total has no reality apart from its members, therefore, it can't be necessary. Therefore, it can't be (caused)—uncaused—therefore it must have a cause. And I should like to observe in passing that the statement "the world is simply there and is inexplicable" can't be got out of logical analysis.

RUSSELL: I don't want to seem arrogant, but it does seem to me that I can conceive things that you say the human mind can't conceive. As for things not having a cause, the physicists assure us that individual quantum transitions in atoms have no cause.

COPLESTON: Well, I wonder now whether that isn't simply a temporary inference.

RUSSELL: It may be, but it does show that physicists' minds can conceive it.

COPLESTON: Yes, I agree, some scientists—physicists—are willing to allow for indetermination within a restricted field. But very many scientists are not so willing. I think that Professor Dingle, of London University, maintains that the Heisenberg uncertainty principle tells us something about the success (or the lack of it) of the present atomic theory in correlating observations, but not about nature in itself, and many physicists would accept this view. In any case, I don't see how physicists can fail to accept the theory in practice, even if they don't do so in theory. I cannot see how science could be conducted on any other assumption than that of order and intelligibility in nature. The physicist presupposes, at least tacitly, that there is some sense in investigating nature and looking for the causes of events, just as the detective presupposes that there is some sense in looking for the cause of a murder. The metaphysician assumes that there is sense in looking for the reason or cause of phenomena, and, not being a Kantian, I consider that the metaphysician is as justified in his assumption as the physicist. When Sartre, for example, says that the world is gratuitous, I think that he has not sufficiently considered what is implied by "gratuitous."

RUSSELL: I think—there seems to me a certain unwarrantable extension here; a physicist looks for causes; that does not necessarily imply that there are causes everywhere. A man may look for gold without assuming that there is gold everywhere; if he finds gold, well and good, if he doesn't he's had bad luck. The same is true when the physicists look for causes. As for Sartre, I don't profess to know what he means, and I shouldn't like to be thought to interpret him, but for my part, I do think the notion of the world having an explanation is a mistake. I don't see why one should expect it to have, and I think what you say about what the scientist assumes is an over-statement.

COPLESTON: Well, it seems to me that the scientist does make some such assumption. When he experiments to find out some particular truth, behind that experiment lies the assumption that the universe is not simply discontinuous. There is the possibility of finding out a truth by experiment. The experiment may be a bad one, it may lead to no result, or not to the result that he wants, but that at any rate there is the possibility, through experiment, of finding out the truth that he assumes. And that seems to me to assume an ordered and intelligible universe.

RUSSELL: I think you're generalizing more than is necessary. Undoubtedly the scientist assumes that this sort of thing is likely to be found and will often be found. He does not assume that it will be found, and that's a very important matter in modern physics.

COPLESTON: Well I think he does assume or is bound to assume it tacitly in practice. It may be that, to quote Professor Haldane, "when I light the gas under the kettle, some of the water molecules will fly off as vapor, and there is no way of finding out which will do so," but it doesn't follow necessarily that the idea of chance must be introduced except in relation to our knowledge.

RUSSELL: No it doesn't—at least if I may believe what he says. He's finding out quite a lot of things—the scientist is finding out quite a lot of things that are happening in the world, which are, at first, beginnings of causal chains—first causes which haven't in themselves got causes. He does not assume that everything has a cause.

COPLESTON: Surely that's a first cause within a certain selected field. It's a relatively first cause.

RUSSELL: I don't think he'd say so. If there's a world in which most events, but not all, have causes, he will then be able to depict the probabilities and uncertainties by assuming that this particular event you're interested in probably has a cause. And since in any case you won't get more than probability that's good enough.

COPLESTON: It may be that the scientist doesn't hope to obtain more than probability, but in raising the question he assumes that the question of explanation has a meaning. But your general point then, Lord Russell, is that it's illegitimate even to ask the question of the cause of the world?

RUSSELL: Yes, that's my position.

COPLESTON: If it's a question that for you has no meaning, it's of course very difficult to discuss it, isn't it?

RUSSELL: Yes, it is very difficult. What do you say—shall we pass on to some other issue?

COPLESTON: Well, perhaps it's time I summed up my position. I've argued two things. First, that the existence of God can be philosophically proved by a metaphysical argument; secondly, that it is only the existence of God that will make sense of man's moral experience and religious experience. Personally, I think that your way of accounting for man's moral judgments leads inevitably to a contradiction between what your theory demands and your own spontaneous judgments. Moreover, your theory explains moral obligation away, and explaining away is not explanation. As regards the metaphysical argument, we are apparently in agreement that what we call the world consists simply of contingent beings. That is, of beings no one of which can account for its own existence. You say that the series of events needs no explanation: I say that if there were no necessary being, no being which must exist and cannot not exist, nothing would exist. The infinity of the series of contingent beings, even if proved, would be irrelevant. Something does exist; therefore, there must be something which accounts for this fact, a being which is outside the series of contingent beings. If you had admitted this, we could then have discussed whether that being is personal, good, and so on. On the actual point discussed, whether there is or is not a necessary being, I find myself, I think, in agreement with the great majority of classical philosophers.

You maintain, I think, that existing beings are simply there, and that I have no justification for raising the question of the explanation of their existence. But I would like to point that this position cannot be substantiated by logical analysis; it expresses a philosophy which itself stands in need of proof. I think we have reached an impasse because our ideas of philosophy are radically different; it seems to me that what I call a part of philosophy, that you call the whole, in so far at least as philosophy is rational. It seems to me, if you will pardon my saying so, that besides your own logical system—which you call "modern" in opposition to antiquated logic (a tendentious adjective)—you maintain a philosophy which cannot be substantiated by logical analysis. After all, the problem of God's existence is an existential problem whereas logical analysis does not deal to declare that the terms involved in one set of problems are meaningless because they are not required in dealing with another set of problems, is to settle from the beginning the nature and extent of philosophy, and that is itself a philosophical act which stands in need of justification.

RUSSELL: Well, I should like to say just a few words by way of summary on my side. First, as to the metaphysical argument: I don't admit the connotations of such a term as "contingent" or the possibility of explanation in Father Copleston's sense. I think the word "contingent" inevitably suggests the possibility of something that wouldn't have this what you might call accidental character of just being there, and I don't think this is true except in the purely causal sense. You can sometimes give a causal explanation of one thing as being the effect of something else, but that is merely referring one thing to another thing and there's no—to my mind—explanation in Father Copleston's sense of anything at all, nor is there any meaning in calling things "contingent" because there isn't anything else they could be. That's what I should say about that, but I should like to say a few words about Father Copleston's accusation that I regard logic as all philosophy—that is by no means the case. I don't by any means regard logic as all philosophy. I think logic is an essential part of philosophy and logic has to be used in philosophy, and in that I think he and I are at one. When the logic that he uses was new—namely, in the time of Aristotle, there had to be a great deal of fuss made about it; Aristotle made a lot of fuss about that logic. Nowadays it's become old and respectable, and you don't have to make so much fuss about it. The logic that I believe in is comparatively new, and therefore I have to imitate Aristotle in making a fuss about it; but it's not that I think it's all philosophy by any means—I don't think so. I think it's an important part of philosophy, and when I say that, I don't find a meaning for this or that word, that is a position of detail based upon what I've found out about that particular word, from thinking about it. It's not a general position that all words that are used in metaphysics are nonsense, or anything like that which I don't really hold.

As regards the moral argument, I do find that when one studies anthropology or history, there are people who think it their duty to perform acts which I think abominable, and I certainly can't, therefore, attribute Divine origin to the matter of moral obligation, which Father Copleston doesn't ask me to; but I think even the form of moral obligation, when it takes the form of enjoining you to eat your father or what not, doesn't seem to me to be such a very beautiful and noble thing; and, therefore, I cannot attribute a Divine origin to this sense of moral obligation, which I think is quite easily accounted for in quite other ways.

Molecular Machines: Experimental Support for the Design Inference

Michael J. Behe

Darwinism's Prosperity

Within a short time after Charles Darwin published *The Origin of Species* the explanatory power of the theory of evolution was recognized by the great majority of biologists. The hypothesis readily resolved the problems of homologous resemblance, rudimentary organs, species abundance, extinction, and biogeography. The rival theory of the time, which posited creation of species by a supernatural being, appeared to most reasonable minds to be much less plausible, since it would have a putative Creator attending to details that seemed to be beneath His dignity.

As time went on the theory of evolution obliterated the rival theory of creation, and virtually all working scientists studied the biological world from a Darwinian perspective. Most educated people now lived in a world where the wonder and diversity of the biological kingdom were produced by the simple, elegant principle of natural selection.

However, in science a successful theory is not necessarily a correct theory. In the course of history there have also been other theories which achieved the triumph that Darwinism achieved, which brought many experimental and observational facts into a coherent framework, and which appealed to people's intuitions about how the world should work. Those theories also promised to explain much of the universe with a few simple principles. But, by the large, those other theories are now dead.

A good example of this is the replacement of Newton's mechanical view of the universe by Einstein's relativistic universe. Although Newton's model accounted for the results of many experiments in his time, it failed to explain aspects of gravitation. Einstein solved that problem and others by completely rethinking the structure of the universe.

Similarly, Darwin's theory of evolution prospered by explaining much of the data of his time and the first half of the 20th century, but my article will show that Darwinism had been unable to account for phenomena uncovered by the efforts of modern biochemistry during the second half of this century. I will do this by emphasizing the fact that life at its most fundamental level is irreducibly complex and that such complexity is incompatible with undirected evolution.

A Series of Eyes

How do we see?

In the 19th century the anatomy of the eye was known in great detail and the sophisticated mechanisms it employs to deliver an accurate picture of the outside world astounded everyone who was familiar with them. Scientists of the 19th century correctly observed that if a person were so unfortunate as to be missing one of the eye's many integrated features, such as the lens, or iris, or ocular muscles, the inevitable result would be a severe loss of vision or outright blindness. Thus it was concluded that the eye could only function if it were nearly intact.

As Charles Darwin was considering possible objections to his theory of evolution by natural selection in *The Origin of Species* he discussed the problem of the eye in a section of the book appropriately entitled "Organs of extreme perfection and complication." He realized that if in one generation an organ of the complexity of the eye suddenly appeared, the event would be tantamount to a miracle. Somehow, for Darwinian evolution to be believable, the difficulty that the public had in envisioning the gradual formation of complex organs had to be removed.

Darwin succeeded brilliantly, not by actually describing a real pathway that evolution might have used in constructing the eye, but rather by pointing to a variety of animals that were known to have eyes of various constructions, ranging from a simple light sensitive spot to the complex vertebrate camera eye, and suggesting that the evolution of the human eye might have involved similar organs as intermediates.

But the question remains, how do we see? Although Darwin was able to persuade much of the world that a modern eye could be produced gradually from a much simpler structure, he did not even attempt to explain how the simple light sensitive spot that was his starting point actually worked. When discussing the eye Darwin dismissed the question of its ultimate mechanism by stating: "How a nerve comes to be sensitive to light hardly concerns us more than how life itself originated."

He had an excellent reason for declining to answer the question: 19th century science had not progressed to the point where the matter could even be approached. The question of how the eye works—that is, what happens when a photon of light first impinges on the retina—simply could not be answered at that time. As a matter of fact, no question about the underlying mechanism of life could be answered at that time. How do animal muscles cause movement? How does photosynthesis work? How is energy extracted from food? How does the body fight infection? All such questions were unanswerable.

The Calvin and Hobbes Approach

Now, it appears to be a characteristic of the human mind that when it lacks understanding of a process, then it seems easy to imagine simple steps leading from nonfunction to function. A happy example of this is seen in the popular comic strip *Calvin and Hobbes*. Little boy Calvin is always having adventures in the company of his tiger Hobbes by jumping in a box and traveling back in time, or grabbing a toy ray gun and "transmogrifying" himself into various animal shapes, or again using a box as a duplicator and making copies of himself to deal with worldly powers such as his mom and his teachers. A small child such as Calvin finds it easy to imagine that a box just might be able to fly like an airplane (or something), because Calvin doesn't know how airplanes work.

A good example from the biological world of complex changes appearing to be simple is the belief in spontaneous generation. One of the chief proponents of the theory of spontaneous generation during the middle of the 19th century was Ernst Haeckel, a great admirer of Darwin and an eager popularizer of Darwin's theory. From the limited view of cells that 19th century microscopes provided, Haeckel believed that a cell was a "simple little lump of albuminous combination of carbon," not much different from a piece of microscopic Jell-O®. Thus it seemed to Haeckel that such simple life could easily be produced from inanimate material.

In 1859, the year of the publication of *The Origin of Species,* an exploratory vessel, the H.M.S. Cyclops, dredged up some curious-looking mud from the sea bottom. Eventually Haeckel came to observe the mud and thought that it closely resembled some cells he had seen under a microscope. Excitedly he brought this to the attention of no less a personage than Thomas Henry Huxley, Darwin's great friend and defender, who observed the mud for himself. Huxley, too, became convinced that it was Urschleim (that is, protoplasm), the progenitor of life itself, and Huxley named the mud *Bathybius haeckelii* after the eminent proponent of abiogenesis.

The mud failed to grow. In later years, with the development of new biochemical techniques and improved microscopes, the complexity of the cell was revealed. The "simple lumps" were shown to contain thousands of different types of organic molecules, proteins, and nucleic acids, many discrete subcellular structures, specialized compartments for specialized processes, and an extremely complicated architecture. Looking back from the perspective of our time, the episode of *Bathybius haeckelii* seems silly or downright embarrassing, but it shouldn't. Haeckel and Huxley were behaving naturally, like Calvin: since they were unaware of the complexity of cells, they found it easy to believe that cells could originate from simple mud.

Throughout history there have been many other examples, similar to that of Haeckel, Huxley, and the cell, where a key piece of a particular scientific puzzle was beyond the understanding of the age. In science there is even a whimsical term for a machine or structure or process that does something, but the actual mechanism by which it accomplishes its task is unknown: it is called a "black box," In Darwin's time all of biology was a black box: not only the cell, or the eye, or digestion, or immunity, but every biological structure and function because, ultimately, no one could explain how biological processes occurred.

Biology has progressed tremendously due to the model that Darwin put forth. But the black boxes Darwin accepted are now being opened, and our view of the world is again being shaken.

Take our modern understanding of proteins, for example.

Proteins

In order to understand the molecular basis of life it is necessary to understand how things called "proteins" work. Proteins are the machinery of living tissue that build the structures and carry out the chemical reactions necessary for life. For example, the first of many steps necessary for the conversion of sugar to biologically-usable forms of energy is carried out by a protein called hexokinase. Skin is made in large measure of a protein called collagen. When light impinges on your retina it interacts first with a protein called rhodopsin. A typical cell contains thousands and thousands of different types of proteins to perform the many tasks necessary for life, much like a carpenter's workshop might contain many different kinds of tools for various carpentry tasks.

What do these versatile tools look like? The basic structure of proteins is quite simple: they are formed by hooking together in a chain discrete subunits called amino acids. Although the protein chain can consist of anywhere from about 50 to about 1,000 amino acid links, each position can only contain one of 20 different amino acids. In this they are much like words: words can come in various lengths but they are made up from a discrete set of 26 letters.

Now, a protein in a cell does not float around like a floppy chain; rather, it folds up into a very precise structure which can be quite different for different types of proteins. Two different amino acid sequences—two different proteins—can be folded to structures as specific and different from each other as a three-eights inch wrench and a jigsaw. And like the household tools, if the shape of the proteins is significantly warped then they fail to do their jobs.

The Eyesight of Man

In general, biological processes on the molecular level are performed by networks of proteins, each member of which carries out a particular task in a chain.

Let us return to the question, how do we see? Although to Darwin the primary event of vision was a black box, through the efforts of many biochemists an answer to the question of sight is at hand. The answer involves a long chain of steps that begin when light strikes the retina and a photon is absorbed by an organic molecule called 11-cis-retinal, causing it to rearrange itself within picoseconds. This causes a corresponding change to the protein, rhodopsin, which is tightly bound to it, so that it can react with another protein called transducin, which in turn causes a molecule called GDP to be exchanged with a molecule called GTP.

To make a long story short, this exchange begins a long series of further bindings between still more specialized molecular machinery, and scientists now understand a great deal about the system of gateways, pumps, ion channels, critical concentrations, and attenuated signals that result in a current to finally be transmitted down the optic nerve to the brain, interpreted as vision. Biochemists also understand the many chemical reactions involved in restoring all these changed or depleted parts to make a new cycle possible.

To Explain Life

Although space doesn't permit me to give the details of the biochemistry of vision here, I have given the steps in my talks. Biochemists know what it means to "explain" vision. They know the level of explanation that biological science eventually must aim for. In order to say that some function is understood, every relevant step in the process must be elucidated. The relevant steps in biological processes occur ultimately at the molecular level, so a satisfactory explanation of a biological phenomenon such as sight, or digestion, or immunity, must include a molecular explanation.

It is no longer sufficient, now that the black box of vision has been opened, for an "evolutionary explanation" of that power to invoke only the anatomical structures of whole eyes, as Darwin did in the 19th century and as most popularizers of evolution continue to do today. Anatomy is, quite simply, irrelevant. So is the fossil record. It does not matter whether or not the fossil record is consistent with evolutionary theory, any more than it mattered in physics that Newton's theory was consistent with everyday experience. The fossil record has nothing to tell us about, say, whether or how the interactions of 11-cis-retinal with rhodopsin, transducin, and phosphodiesterase could have developed, step by step.

"How a nerve comes to be sensitive to light hardly concerns us more than how life itself originated," said Darwin in the 19th century. But both phenomena have attracted the interest of modern biochemistry in the past few decades. The story of the slow paralysis of research of life's origin is quite interesting, but space precludes its retelling here. Suffice it to say that at present the field of origin-of-life studies has dissolved into a cacophony of conflicting models, each unconvincing, seriously incomplete, and incompatible with competing models. In private even most evolutionary biologists will admit that science has no explanation for the beginning of life.

The same problems which beset origin-of-life research also bedevil efforts to show how virtually any complex biochemical system came about. Biochemistry has revealed a molecular world which stoutly resists explanation by the same theory that has long been applied at the level of the whole organism. Neither of Darwin's black boxes—the origin of life or the origin of vision (or other complex biochemical systems)—has been accounted for by his theory.

Irreducible Complexity

In *The Origin of Species* Darwin stated:

> If it could be demonstrated that any complex organ existed which could not possibly have been formed by numerous, successive, slight modifications, my theory would absolutely break down.

A system which meets Darwin's criterion is one which exhibits irreducible complexity. By irreducible complexity I mean a single system which is composed of several interacting parts that contribute to the basic function, and where the removal of any one of the parts causes the system to effectively cease functioning. An irreducibly complex system cannot be produced directly by slight, successive modification of a precursor system, since any precursor to an irreducibly complex system is by definition nonfunctional.

Since natural selection requires a function to select, an irreducibly complex biological system, if there is such a thing, would have to arise as an integrated unit for natural selection to have anything to act on. It is almost universally conceded that such a sudden event would be irreconciable with the gradualism Darwin envisioned. At this point, however, "irreducibly complex" is just a term, whose power resides mostly in its definition. We must now ask if any real thing is in fact irreducibly complex, and, if so, then are any irreducibly complex things also biological systems?

Consider the humble mousetrap (Figure 1). The mousetraps that my family uses in our home to deal with unwelcome rodents consist of a number of parts. There are: (1) a flat wooden platform to act as a base; (2) a metal hammer, which does the actual job of crushing the little mouse; (3) a wire spring with extended ends to press against the platform and the hammer when the trap is charged; (4) a sensitive catch which

Figure 1
A household mousetrap. The working parts of the trap are labeled. If any of the parts is missing, the trap does not function.

releases when slight pressure is applied; and (5) a metal bar which holds the hammer back when the trap is charged and connects to the catch. There are also assorted staples and screws to hold the system together.

If any one of the components of the mousetrap (the base, hammer, spring, catch, or holding bar) is removed, then the trap does not function. In other words, the simple little mousetrap has no ability to trap a mouse until several separate parts are all assembled.

Because the mousetrap is necessarily composed of several parts, it is irreducibly complex. Thus, irreducibly complex systems exist.

Molecular Machines

Now, are any biochemical systems irreducibly complex? Yes, it turns out that many are.

Earlier we discussed proteins. In many biological structures proteins are simply components of larger molecular machines. Like the picture tube, wires, metal bolts and screws that comprise a television set, many proteins are part of structures that only function when virtually all of the components have been assembled.

A good example of this is a cilium. Cilia are hairlike organelles on the surfaces of many animal and lower plant cells that serve to move fluid over the cell's surface or to "row" single cells through a fluid. In humans, for example, epithelial cells lining the respiratory tract each have about 200 cilia that beat in synchrony to sweep mucus towards the throat for elimination.

A cilium consists of a membrane-coated bundle of fibers called an axoneme. An axoneme contains a ring of 9 double microtubules surrounding two central single microtubules. Each outer doublet consists of a ring of 13 filaments (subfiber A) fused to an assembly of 10 filaments (subfiber B). The filaments of the microtubules are composed of two proteins called alpha and beta tubulin. The 11 microtubules forming an axoneme are held together by three types of connectors: subfibers A are joined to the central microtubules by radial spokes; adjacent outer doublets are joined by linkers that consist of a highly elastic protein called nexin; and the central microtubules are joined by a connecting bridge. Finally, every subfiber A bears two arms, an inner arm and an outer arm, both containing the protein dynein.

But how does a cilium work? Experiments have indicated that ciliary motion results from the chemically-powered "walking" of the dynein arms on one microtubule up the neighboring subfiber B of a second

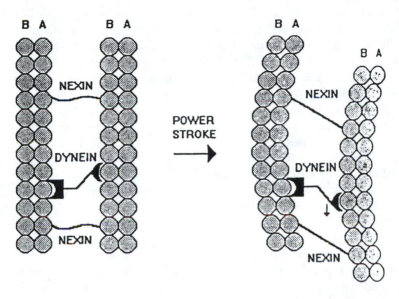

Figure 2
Schematic drawing of part of a cilium. The power stroke of the motor protein
dynein, attached to one microtubule, against subfiber B of a neighboring microtubule causes the fibers to slide past each other. The flexible linker protein,
nexin, converts the sliding motion to a bending motion.

microtubule so that the two microtubules slide past each other (Figure 2).
However, the protein cross-links between microtubules in an intact cilium
prevent neighboring microtubules from sliding past each other by more
than a short distance. These cross-links, therefore, convert the dynein-
induced sliding motion to a bending motion of the entire axoneme.

Now, let us sit back, review the workings of the cilium, and consider
what it implies. Cilia are composed of at least a half dozen proteins:
alpha-tubulin, beta-tubulin, dynein, nexin, spoke protein, and a central
bridge protein. Those combine to perform one task, ciliary motion, and
all of these proteins must be present for the cilium to function. If the
tubulins are absent, then there are no filaments to slide; if the dynein is
missing, then the cilium remains rigid and motionless; if nexin or the
other connecting proteins are missing, then the axoneme falls apart
when the filaments slide.

What we see in the cilium, then, is not just profound complexity,
but it is also irreducible complexity on the molecular scale. Recall that

by "irreducible complexity" we mean an apparatus that requires several distinct components for the whole to work. My mousetrap must have a base, hammer, spring, catch, and holding bar, all working together, in order to function. Similarly, the cilium, as it is constituted, must have the sliding filaments, connecting proteins, and motor proteins for function to occur. In the absence of any one of those components, the apparatus is useless.

The components of cilia are single molecules. This means that there are no more black boxes to invoke; the complexity of the cilium is final, fundamental. And just as scientists, when they began to learn the complexities of the cell, realized how silly it was to think that life arose spontaneously in a single step or a few steps from ocean mud, so too we now realize that the complex cilium can not be reached in a single step or a few steps.

But since the complexity of the cilium is irreducible, then it can not have functional precursors. Since the irreducibly complex cilium can not have functional precursors it can not be produced by natural selection, which requires a continuum of function to work. Natural selection is powerless when there is no function to select. We can go further and say that, if the cilium can not be produced by natural selection, then the cilium was designed.

A Non-Mechanical Example

A non-mechanical example of irreducible complexity can be seen in the system that targets proteins for delivery to subcellular compartments. In order to find their way to the compartments where they are needed to perform specialized tasks, certain proteins contain a special amino acid sequence near the beginning called a "signal sequence."

As the proteins are being synthesized by ribosomes, a complex molecular assemblage called the signal recognition particle or SRP, binds to the signal sequence. This causes synthesis of the protein to halt temporarily. During the pause in protein synthesis the SRP is bound by the transmembrane SRP receptor, which causes protein synthesis to resume and which allows passage of the protein into the interior of the endoplasmic reticulum (ER). As the protein passes into the ER the signal sequence is cut off.

For many proteins the ER is just a way station on their travels to their final destinations (Figure 3). Proteins which will end up in a lysosome are enzymatically "tagged" with a carbohydrate residue called mannose-6-phosphate while still in the ER. An area of the ER

STEP   I   II   III   IV   V

Figure 3

Transport of a protein from the ER to the lysosome. Step 1: Specific enzyme (gray oval) places a marker on the protein (black sphere). This takes place within the ER, which is delimited by a barrier membrane (cross-hatched bar with ends curving to the left). Step II: The marker is specifically recognized by a receptor protein and the clathrin vesicle (hexagonal shape) begins to form. Step III: The clathrin vesicle is completed and buds off from the ER membrane. Step IV: The clathrin vesicle crosses the cytoplasm and attaches through another specific marker to a receptor protein (black box) on the lysosomal membrane and releases its cargo.

membrane then begins to concentrate several proteins; one protein, clathrin, forms a sort of geodesic dome called a coated vesicle which buds off from the ER. In the dome there is also a receptor protein which binds to both the clathrin and to the mannose-6-phosphate group of the protein which is being transported. The coated vesicle then leaves the ER, travels through the cytoplasm, and binds to the lysosome through another specific receptor protein. Finally, in a maneuver involving several more proteins, the vesicle fuses with the lysosome and the protein arrives at its destination.

During its travels our protein interacted with dozens of macromolecules to achieve one purpose: its arrival in the lysosome. Virtually all components of the transport system are necessary for the system to operate, and therefore the system is irreducible. And since all of the components of the system are comprised of single or several molecules, there are no black boxes to invoke. The consequences of even a single gap in the transport chain can be seen in the hereditary defect known as I-cell disease. It results from a deficiency of the enzyme that places the mannose-6-phosphate on proteins to be targeted to the lysosomes. I-cell disease is characterized by progressive retardation, skeletal deformities, and early death.

The Study of "Molecular Evolution"

Other examples of irreducible complexity abound, including aspects of protein transport, blood clotting, closed circular DNA, electron transport, the bacterial flagellum, telomeres, photosynthesis, transcription regulation, and much more. Examples of irreducible complexity can be found on virtually every page of a biochemistry textbook. But if these things cannot be explained by Darwinian evolution, how has the scientific community regarded these phenomena of the past forty years?

A good place to look for an answer to that question is in the *Journal of Molecular Evolution. JME* is a journal that was begun specifically to deal with the topic of how evolution occurs on the molecular level. It has high scientific standards, and is edited by prominent figures in the field. In a recent issue of *JME* there were published eleven articles; of these, all eleven were concerned simply with the analysis of protein or DNA sequences. None of the papers discussed detailed models for intermediates in the development of complex biomolecular structures.

In the past ten years *JME* has published 886 papers. Of these, 95 discussed the chemical synthesis of molecules thought to be necessary for the origin of life, 44 proposed mathematical models to improve sequence analysis, 20 concerned the evolutionary implications of current structures and 719 were analyses of protein or polynucleotide sequences. However, there weren't any papers discussing detailed models for intermediates in the development of complex biomolecular structures. This is not a peculiarity of *JME*. No papers are to be found that discuss detailed models for intermediates in the development of complex biomolecular structures in the *Proceedings of the National Academy of Science, Nature, Science,* the *Journal of Molecular Biology* or, to my knowledge, any journal whatsoever.

Sequence comparisons overwhelmingly dominate the literature of molecular evolution. But sequence comparisons simply can't account for the development of complex biochemical systems any more than Darwin's comparison of simple and complex eyes told him how vision worked. Thus in this area science is mute.

Detection of Design

What's going on? Imagine a room in which a body lies crushed, flat as a pancake. A dozen detectives crawl around, examining the floor with magnifying glasses for any clue to the identity of the perpetrator. In the middle of the room next to the body stands a large, gray elephant. The detectives carefully avoid bumping into the pachyderm's legs as they crawl, and never even glance at it. Over time the detectives get frustrated with their lack of progress but resolutely press on, looking even more closely at the floor. You see, textbooks say detectives must "get their man," so they never consider elephants.

There is an elephant in the roomful of scientists who are trying to explain the development of life. The elephant is labeled "intelligent design." To a person who does not feel obliged to restrict his search to unintelligent causes, the straightforward conclusion is that many biochemical systems were designed. They were designed *not* by the laws of nature, not by chance and necessity. Rather, they were *planned*. The designer knew what the systems would look like when they were completed; the designer took steps to bring the system about. Life on earth at its most fundamental level, in its most critical components, is the product of intelligent activity.

The conclusion of intelligent design flows naturally from the data itself—not from sacred books or sectarian beliefs. Inferring that biochemical systems were designed by an intelligent agent is a humdrum process that requires no new principles of logic or science. It comes simply from the hard work that biochemistry has done over the past forty years, combined with consideration of the way in which we reach conclusions of design every day.

What is "design"? Design is simply the *purposeful arrangement of parts*. The scientific question is how we detect design. This can be done in various ways, but design can most easily be inferred for mechanical objects.

Systems made entirely from natural components can also evince design. For example, suppose you are walking with a friend in the woods. All of a sudden your friend is pulled high in the air and left dangling by his foot from a vine attached to a tree branch.

After cutting him down you reconstruct the trap. You see that the vine was wrapped around the tree branch, and the end pulled tightly down to the ground. It was securely anchored to the ground by a forked branch. The branch was attached to another vine—hidden by leaves—so that, when the trigger-vine was disturbed, it would pull down the forked stick, releasing the spring-vine. The end of the vine formed a loop with a slipknot to grab an appendage and snap it up into the air. Even though the trap was made completely of natural materials you would quickly conclude that it was the product of intelligent design.

Intelligent design is a good explanation for a number of biochemical systems, but I should insert a word of caution. Intelligent design theory has to be seen in context: it does not try to explain everything. We live in a complex world where lots of different things can happen. When deciding how various rocks came to be shaped the way they are a geologist might consider a whole range of factors: rain, wind, the movement of glaciers, the activity of moss and lichens, volcanic action, nuclear explosions, asteroid impact, or the hand of a sculptor. The shape of one rock might have been determined primarily by one mechanism, the shape of another rock by another mechanism.

Similarly, evolutionary biologists have recognized that a number of factors might have affected the development of life: common descent, natural selection, migration, population size, founder effects (effects that may be due to the limited number of organisms that begin a new species), genetic drift (spread of "neutral," nonselective mutations), gene flow (the incorporation of genes into a population from a separate population), linkage (occurrence of two genes on the same chromosome), and much more. The fact that some biochemical systems were designed by an intelligent agent does not mean that any of the other factors are not operative, common, or important.

Conclusion

It is often said that science must avoid any conclusions which smack of the supernatural. But this seems to me to be both bad logic and bad science. Science is not a game in which arbitrary rules are used to decide what explanations are to be permitted. Rather, it is an effort to make true statements about physical reality. It was only about sixty years ago that the expansion of the universe was first observed. This fact immediately suggested a singular event—that at some time in the distant past the universe began expanding from an extremely small size.

To many people this inference was loaded with overtones of a supernatural event—the creation, the beginning of the universe. The prominent physicist A. S. Eddington probably spoke for many physicists in voicing his disgust with such a notion:

> Philosophically, the notion of an abrupt beginning to the present order of Nature is repugnant to me, as I think it must be to most; and even those who would welcome a proof of the intervention of a Creator will probably consider that a single winding-up at some remote epoch is not

really the kind of relation between God and his world that brings satisfaction to the mind.

Nonetheless, the big bang hypothesis was embraced by physics and over the years has proven to be a very fruitful paradigm. The point here is that physics followed the data where it seemed to lead, even though some thought the model gave aid and comfort to religion. In the present day, as biochemistry multiplies examples of fantastically complex molecular systems, systems which discourage even an attempt to explain how they may have arisen, we should take a lesson from physics. The conclusion of design flows naturally from the data; we should not shrink from it; we should embrace it and build on it.

In concluding, it is important to realize that we are not inferring design from what we do not know, but from what we do know. We are not inferring design to account for a black box, but to account for an open box. A man from a primitive culture who sees an automobile might guess that it was powered by the wind or by an antelope hidden under the car, but when he opens up the hood and sees the engine he immediately realizes that it was designed. In the same way biochemistry has opened up the cell to examine what makes it run and we see that it, too, was designed.

It was a shock to the people of the 19th century when they discovered, from observations science had made, that many features of the biological world could be ascribed to the elegant principle of natural selection. It is a shock to us in the twentieth century to discover, from observations science has made, that the fundamental mechanisms of life cannot be ascribed to natural selection, and therefore were designed. But we must deal with our shock as best we can and go on. The theory of undirected evolution is already dead, but the work of science continues.

Born-Again Creationism
Philip Kitcher

The Creationist Reformation

In the beginning, creationists believed that the world was young. But creation "science" was without form and void. A deluge of objections drowned the idea that major kinds of plants and animals had been fashioned a few thousand years ago and been hardly modified since. Then the spirit of piety brooded on the waters and brought forth something new. "Let there be design!" exclaimed the reformers—and lo! there was born-again creationism.

Out in Santee, California, about twenty miles from where I used to live, the old movement, dedicated to the possibility of interpreting *Genesis* literally, continues to ply its wares. Its spokesmen still peddle the familiar fallacies, their misunderstandings of the second law of thermo-dynamics, their curious views about radiometric dating with apparently revolutionary implications for microphysics, the plundering of debates in evolutionary theory for lines that can be usefully separated from their context, and so forth. But the most prominent creationists on the current intellectual scene are a new species, much smoother and more savvy. Not for them the commitment to a literal interpretation of *Genesis* with all the attendant difficulties. Some of them even veer close to accepting the so-called fact of evolution, the claim, adopted by most scientists within a dozen years of the publication of Darwin's *Origin*, that living things are related and that the history of life has been a process of descent with modification. The sticking point for the born-again creationists, as it was for many late-nineteenth-century thinkers, is the mechanism of evolutionary change. They want to argue that natural selection is inadequate, indeed that no natural process could have produced the diversity of organisms, and thus that there must be some designing agent, who didn't just start the process but who has intervened throughout the history of life.

From the viewpoint of religious fundamentalists the creationist Reformation is something of a cop-out. Yet for many believers, the new movement delivers everything they want—particularly the vision of a personal God who supervises the history of life and nudges it to fulfill His purposes—and even militant evangelicals may come to appreciate the virtues of discretion. Moreover the high priests of the Reformation are clad in academic respectability, Professors of Law at University of California-Berkeley and of Biochemistry at Lehigh, and two of the movement's main cheerleaders are highly respected philosophers who teach at Notre Dame. Creationism is no longer hick, but *chic*.

Why Literalism Failed

In understanding the motivations for, and the shortcomings of, born-again creationism, it's helpful to begin by seeing why the movement had to retreat. The early days of the old-style "creation-science" campaign were highly successfully. Duane Gish, debating champion for the original movement, crafted a brilliant strategy. He threw together a smorgasbord of apparent problems for evolutionary biology, displayed them very quickly before his audiences, and challenged his opponents to respond. At first, the biologists who debated him laboriously offered details to show that one or two of the problems Gish had raised could be solved, but then their time would run out and the audience would leave thinking that most of the objections were unanswerable. In the middle 1980s, however, two important changes took place: first, defenders of evolutionary theory began to take the same care in formulating answers as Gish had given to posing the problems, and there were quick, and elegant, ways of responding to the commonly reiterated challenges; second, and more important, debaters began to fight back, asking how the observable features of the distribution and characteristics of plants and organisms, both those alive and those fossilized, could be rendered compatible with a literal interpretation of *Genesis*.

Suppose that the earth really was created about ten thousand years ago, with the major kinds fashioned then, and diversifying only a little since. How are we to account for the distributions of isotopes in the earth's crust? How are we to explain the regular, worldwide, ordering of the fossils? The only creationist response to the latter question has been to invoke the Noachian deluge: the order is as it is because of the relative positions of the organisms at the time the flood struck. Take this suggestion seriously, and you face some obvious puzzles: sharks and dolphins are found at the same depths, but, of course, the sharks occur much, much lower in the fossil record; pine trees, fir trees, and deciduous trees are mixed in forests around the globe, and yet the deciduous trees are latecomers in the worldwide fossil record. Maybe we should suppose that the oaks and beeches saw the waters rising and outran their evergreen rivals?

Far from being a solution to creationism's problems, the Flood is a real disaster. Consider biogeography. The ark lands on Ararat, say eight thousand years ago, and out pop the animals (let's be kind and forget the plants). We now have eight thousand years for the marsupials to find their way to Australia, crossing several large bodies of water in the process. Perhaps you can imagine a few energetic kangaroos making it—but the wombats? Moreover, creationists think that while the animals were sorting themselves out, there was diversification of species within the "basic kinds"; jackals, coyotes, foxes, and dogs descend, so the story goes, from a common "dog kind." Now despite all the sarcasm that they have lavished on orthodox evolutionary theory's allegedly high rates of speciation, a simple calculation shows that the rates of speciation "creation-science" would require to manage the supposed amount of species diversification are truly breathtaking, orders of magnitude greater than any that have been dreamed of in evolutionary theory. Finally, to touch on just one more problem, creationists have to account for the survival of thousands of parasites that are specific to our species. During the days on the ark, these would have had to be carried by less than ten people. One can only speculate about the degree of ill-health that Noah and his crew must have suffered.

A major difficulty for old-style creationism has always been the fact that very similar anatomical structures are co-opted to different ends in species whose ways of life diverge radically. Moles, bats, whales, and dogs have forelimbs based on the same bone architecture that has to be adapted to their methods of locomotion. Not only is it highly implausible that the common blueprint reflects an especially bright idea from a designer who saw the best ways to fashion a burrowing tool, a wing, a flipper, and a leg, but the obvious explanation is that shared bone structure reflects shared ancestry. That explanation has only been deepened as studies of chromosome banding patterns have revealed common patterns among species evolutionists take to be related, as comparisons of proteins have exposed common sequences of amino acids, and, most recently, as genomic sequencing has shown the affinities in the ordering of bases in the DNA of organisms. Two points are especially noteworthy. First, like the anatomical residues of previously functional structures (such as the rudimentary pelvis found in whales), parts of our junk DNA have an uncanny resemblance to truncated, or mutilated, versions of genes found in other mammals, other vertebrates, or other animals. Second, the genetic kinship even among distantly related organisms is so great that a human sequence was identified as implicated in colon cancer by recognizing its similarity to a gene coding for a DNA repair enzyme in yeast. The evidence for common ancestry is so overwhelming that even the born-again creationist, Michael Behe is moved to admit that it is "fairly convincing" and that he has "no particular reason to doubt it" (DBB 5).[1] (Notice that Behe doesn't quite commit himself here—in fact, to use an example from Richard Dawkins that Behe, and others, have discussed, there's an obvious line to describe Behe's phraseology: METHINKS IT IS A WEASEL.)

Imagine creationists becoming aware, at some level, of this little piece of history, and retreating to the bunker in which they plot strategy. What would they come up with? First, the familiar idea that the best defense is a good offense: they need to return to the tried-and-true, give-'em-hell, Duane Gish fire and brimstone attack on evolutionary theory. Second, they need to expose less to counterattack, and that means giving up on the disastrous "creation model" with all the absurdities that *Genesis*-as-literal-truth brings in its train; better to make biology safe for the central tenets of religion by talking about a design model so softly focused that nobody can raise nasty questions about parasites on the ark on the wombats' dash for the Antipodes. Third, they should do something to mute the evolutionists' most successful arguments, those that draw on the vast number of cross-species comparisons at all levels to establish common descent; this last is a matter of some delicacy, since too blatant a commitment to descent with modification might seem incompatible with creative design. So the best tactic here is a carefully choreographed waltz—advance a little toward accepting the "fact of evolution" here, back away there; as we shall see, some protagonists have an exquisite mastery of the steps.

Surprise, surprise. Born-again creationism has arrived at just this strategy. I'm going to look at the two most influential versions.

The Hedgehog and the Fox

Isaiah Berlin's famous division that contrasts hedgehogs (people with one big idea) and foxes (people with lots of little ideas) applies not only to thinkers but to creationists as well. The two most prominent figures on the neo-creo scene are Michael Behe (a hedgehog) and Phillip Johnson (a fox), both of whom receive plaudits from such distinguished philosophers as Alvin Plantinga and Peter van Inwagen. (Since Plantinga and van Inwagen have displayed considerable skill in articulating and analyzing philosophical arguments, the only charitable interpretation of their fulsome blurbs is that a combination of *Schwärmerei* for creationist doctrine and profound ignorance of relevant bits of biology has induced them to put their brains in cold storage.) Johnson, a lawyer by training, is a far more subtle rhetorician than Gish, and he moves from topic to topic smoothly, discreetly making up the rules of evidence to suit his case as he goes. Many of his attack strategies refine those of country-bumpkin creationism, although, like the White Knight in Alice, he has a few masterpieces of his own invention.

Behe, by contrast, mounts his case for born-again creationism by taking one large problem, and posing it again and again. The problem isn't particularly new: it's the old issues of "complex organs" that Darwin tried to confront in the *Origin*. Behe gives it a new twist by drawing on his background as a biochemist, and describing the minute details of mechanisms in organisms so as to make it seem impossible that they could ever have emerged from a stepwise natural process.

Behe's Big Idea

Here's the general form of the problem. Given our increased knowledge of the molecular structures in cells and the chemical reactions that go on within and among cells, it's possible to describe structures and processes in exceptionally fine detail. Many structures have large numbers of constituent molecules and the precise details of their fit together are essential for them to fulfill their functions. Similarly, many biochemical pathways require numerous enzymes to interact with one another, in appropriate relative concentrations, so that some important process can occur. Faced with either of these situations, you can pose an obvious question: how could organisms with the pertinent structures or processes have evolved from organisms that lacked them? That question is an explicit invitation to describe an ancestral sequence of organisms that culminated in one with the structures or processes at the end, where each change in the sequence is supposed to carry some selective advantage. If you now pose the question many times over, canvass various possibilities, and conclude that not only has no evolutionist proposed any satisfactory sequences, but that there are systematic reasons for thinking that the structure or process could not have been built up gradually, you have an attack strategy that appears very convincing.

That, in outline, is Behe's big idea. Here's a typical passage, summarizing his quite lucid and accessible description of the structures of cilia and flagella:

> . . . as biochemists have begun to examine apparently simple structures like cilia and flagella, they have discovered staggering complexity, with dozens or even hundreds of precisely tailored parts. It is very likely that many of the parts we have not considered here are required for any cilium to function in a cell. As the number of required parts increases, the difficulty of gradually putting the system together skyrockets, and the likelihood of indirect scenarios plummets. Darwin looks more and more forlorn. (DBB 73)

This sounds like a completely recalcitrant problem for evolutionists, but it's worth asking just why precisely Darwin should look more and more forlorn.

Notice first that lots of sciences face all sorts of unresolved questions. To take an example close to hand, Behe's own discussions of cilia frankly acknowledge that there's a lot still to learn about molecular structure and its contributions to function. So the fact that evolutionary biologists haven't yet come up with a sequence of organisms culminating in bacteria with flagella or cilia might be regarded as signaling a need for further research on the important open problem of how such bacteria evolved. Not so! declares Behe. We have here "irreducible complexity," and it's just impossible to imagine a sequence of organisms adding component molecules to build the structures up gradually.

What does this mean? Is Behe supposing that his examples point to a failure of natural selection as a mechanism for evolution? If so, then perhaps he believes that there was a sequence of organisms that ended up with a bacterium with a flagellum (say), but that the intermediates in this sequence added molecules to no immediate purpose, presumably being at a selective disadvantage because of this. (Maybe the Good Lord tempers the wind to the shorn bacterium.) Or does he just dispense with intermediates entirely, thinking that the Creator simply introduced all the right molecules *de novo*? In that case, despite his claims, he really does doubt common descent. Behe's actual position is impossible to discern because he has learned Duane Gish's lesson (Always attack! Never explain!). I'll return at the very end to the cloudiness of Behe's account of the history of life.

Clearly, Behe thinks that Darwinian evolutionary theory requires some sequence of precursors for bacteria with flagella and that no appropriate sequence could exist. But why does he believe this? Here's a simple-minded version of the argument. Assume that the flagellum needs 137 proteins. Then Darwinians are required to produce a sequence of 138 organisms, the first having none of the proteins and each one having one more protein than its predecessor. Now, we're supposed to be moved by the plight of organisms numbers 2 to 137, each of which contains proteins that can't serve any function, and is therefore, presumably, a target of selection. Only number 1, the ancestor, and number 138, in which all the protein constituents come together to form the flagellum, have just what it takes to function. The intermediates would wither in the struggle for existence. Hence evolution under natural selection couldn't have brought the bacterium from there to here.[2]

But this story is just plain silly, and Darwinians ought to disavow any commitment to it. After all, it's a common theme of evolutionary biology that constituents of a cell, a tissue, or an organism, are put to new uses because of some modification of the genotype. So maybe the immediate precursor of the proud possessor of the flagellum is a bacterium in which all the protein constituents were already present, but in which some other feature of the cell chemistry interferes with the reaction that builds the flagellum. A genetic change removes the interference (maybe a protein assumes a slightly different configuration, binding to something that would have bound to one of the constituents of the flagellum, preventing the assembly). "But, Professor Kitcher [creos always try to be polite], do you have any evidence for this scenario?" Of course not. That is to shift the question. We were offered a proof of the impossibility of a particular sequence, and when one tries to show that the proof is invalid by inventing possible instances, it's not pertinent to ask for reasons to think that those instances exist. If they genuinely reveal that what was declared to be impossible isn't, then we no longer have a claim that the Darwinian sequence couldn't have occurred, but simply an open problem of the kind that spurs scientists in any field to engage in research.

Behe has made it look as though there's something more here by inviting us to think about the sequence of precursors in a very particular way. He doesn't actually say that proteins have to be added one at a time—he surely knows very well that that would provoke the reaction I've offered—but his defense of the idea that there just couldn't be a sequence of organisms leading up to bacteria with flagella insinuates, again and again, that the problem is that the alleged intermediates would have to have lots of the components lying around like so many monkey-wrenches in the intracellular works. This strategy is hardly unprecedented. Country-bumpkin creos offered a cruder version when they dictated to evolutionists what fossil intermediates would have to be like: the transitional forms on the way to birds would have to have had half-scales and half-feathers, halfway wings—or so we are told.[3] Behe has made up his own ideas about what transitional organisms must have been like, and then argued that such organisms couldn't have existed.

In fact, we don't need to compare my guesswork with his. What Darwinism is committed to (at most) is the idea that modifications of DNA sequence (insertions, deletions, base changes, translocations) could yield a sequence of organisms culminating in a bacterium with a flagellum, with selective advantages for the later member of each adjacent pair. To work out what the members of this sequence of organisms might have been like, our ideas should be educated by the details of how the flagellum is actually assembled and the loci in the bacterial genome that are involved. Until we know these things, it's quite likely that any efforts to describe precursors or intermediates will be whistling in the dark. Behe's examples cunningly exploit our ability to give molecular analysis of the end product and our ignorance of the molecular details of how it is produced.

Throughout his book, Behe repeats the same story. He describes, often charmingly, the complexities of molecular structures and processes. There would be nothing to complain of if he stopped here and said: "Here are some interesting problems for molecularly minded evolutionists to work on, and, in a few decades time, perhaps, in light of increased knowledge of how development works at the molecular level, we may be able to see what the precursors were like." But he doesn't. He tries to argue that the precursors and intermediates required by Darwinian evolutionary theory couldn't have existed. This strategy has to fail because Behe himself is just as ignorant about the molecular basis of development as his Darwinian opponents. Hence he hasn't a clue what kinds of precursors and intermediates the Darwinian account is actually committed to—so it's impossible to demonstrate that the commitment can't be honored. However, again and again, Behe disguises his ignorance by suggesting to the reader that the Darwinian story must take a very particular form—that it has to consist in something like the simple addition of components, for example—and on that basis he can manufacture the illusion of giving an impossibility proof.

Although this is the main rhetorical trick of the book, there are some important subsidiary bits of legerdemain. Like pre-Reformation creationists, Behe loves to flash probability calculations, offering spurious precision to his criticisms. Here's his attack on a scenario for the evolution of a blood-clotting mechanism, tentatively proposed by Russell Doolittle:

> . . . let's do our own quick calculation. Consider that animals with blood-clotting cascades have roughly 10,000 genes, each of which is divided into an average of three pieces. This gives a total of about 30,000 gene pieces. TPA [Tissue Plasminogen Activator] has four different types of domains. By "variously shuffling," the odds of getting those four domains together is 30,000 to the fourth power, which is approximately one-tenth to the eighteenth power. Now, if the Irish

Sweepstakes had odds of winning of one-tenth to the eighteenth power, and if a million people played the lottery each year, it would take an average of about a thousand billion years before *anyone* (not just a particular person) won the lottery. . . . Doolittle apparently needs to shuffle and deal himself a number of perfect bridge hands to win the game. (DBB 94)

This sounds quite powerful, and Behe drives home the point by noting that Doolittle provides no quantitative estimates, adding that "without numbers, there is no science" (DBB 95)—presumably to emphasize that born-again creationists are better scientists than the distinguished figures they attack. But consider a humdrum phenomenon suggested by Behe's analogy to bridge. Imagine that you take a standard deck of cards and deal yourself thirteen. What's the probability that you got exactly those cards in exactly that order? The answer is 1 in 4×10^{21}. Suppose you repeat this process ten times. You'll now have received ten standard bridge hands, ten sets of thirteen cards, each one delivered in a particular order. The chance of getting just those cards in just that order is 1 in $4^{10} \times 10^{210}$. This is approximately 1 in 10^{222}. Notice that the denominator is far larger than that of Behe's trifling 10^{18}. So it must be *really* improbable that you (or anyone else) would ever receive just those cards in just that order in the entire history of the universe. But, whatever the cards were, you did.

What my analogy shows is that, if you describe events that actually occur from a particular perspective, you can make them look improbable. Thus, given a description of the steps in Doolittle's scenario for the evolution of TPA, the fact that you can make the probability look small doesn't mean that that isn't (or couldn't) have been the way things happened. One possibility is that the evolution of blood-clotting was genuinely improbable. But there are others.

Return to your experiment with the deck of cards. Let's suppose that all the hands you were dealt were pretty mundane—fairly evenly distributed among the suits, with a scattering of high cards in each. If you calculated the probability of receiving ten mundane hands in succession, it would of course be much higher than the priority of being dealt those very particular mundane hands with the cards arriving in just that sequence (although it wouldn't be as large as you might expect). There might be an analogue for blood-clotting, depending on how many candidates there are among the 3,000 "gene pieces" to which Behe alludes that would yield a protein product able to play the necessary role. Suppose that there are a hundred acceptable candidates for each position. That means that the chance of success on any particular draw is $(1/30)^4$, which is about 1 in 2.5 million. Now, if there were 10,000 tries per year, it would take, on average, two or three centuries to arrive at the right combination, a flicker of an instant in evolutionary time.

Of course, neither Behe nor I knows how tolerant the blood-clotting system is, how many different molecular ways it allows to get the job done. Thus we can't say if the right way to look at the problem is to think of the situation as the analogue to being dealt a very particular sequence of cards in a very particular order, or whether the right comparison is with cases in which a more general type of sequence occurs. But these two suggestions don't exhaust the relevant cases.

Suppose you knew the exact order of cards in the deck prior to each deal. Then the probability that the particular sequence would occur would be extremely high (barring fumbling or sleight of hand, the probability would be 1). The sequence only *looks* improbable because we don't know the order. Perhaps that's true for the Doolittle shuffling process as well. Given the initial distribution of pieces of DNA, plus the details of the biochemical milieu, principles of chemical recombination might actually make it very probable that the cascade Doolittle hypothesizes would ensue. Once again, nobody knows whether this is so. Behe simply assumes that it isn't.

Let me sum up. There are two questions to pose: What is the probability that the Doolittle sequence would occur? What is the significance of a low value for that probability? The answer to the first question is that we haven't a clue: it might be close to 1, it might be small but significant enough to make it likely that the sequence would occur in a flicker of evolutionary time, or it might be truly tiny (as Behe suggests). The answer to the second question is that genuinely improbable things sometimes happen, and one shouldn't confuse improbability with impossibility. Once these points are recognized, it's clear that, for all its rhetorical force, Behe's appeal to numbers smacks more of numerology than of science. As with his main line of argument, it turns out to be an attempt to parlay ignorance of molecular details into an impossibility proof.

I postpone until the very end another fundamental difficulty with Behe's argument for design, to wit his fuzzy faith that appeal to a creator will make all these "difficulties" evaporate. As we shall see, both he and Johnson try to hide any positive views. With good reason. . . .

Notes

I am extremely grateful to Dan Dennett and Ed Curley for sharing with me their unpublished discussions of the creationist writers I discuss here. I have also learned much from an illuminating essay by Niall Shanks and Karl Joplin, "Redundant Complexity: A Critical Analysis of Intelligent Design in Biochemistry," *Philosophy of Science, 66,* 1999, 268–282. Finally, I'd like to thank Robert Pennock for his editorial encouragement and for the insights of his own excellent treatment of the neo-creos in *Tower of Babel.*

1. I'll be quoting extensively from two creationist works, Michael Behe, *Darwin's Black Box: The Biochemical Challenge to Evolution,* New York: The Free Press, 1996 (cited as DBB) and Phillip Johnson, *Darwin on Trial,* Washington D.C.: Regnery Gateway, 1993 (cited as DOT).
2. I borrow this pithy formulation from Dan Dennett.
3. For further discussion of this issue, see my *Abusing Science: The Case against Creationism,* Cambridge MA: MIT Press, p. 117.

Pascal's Wager
George Schlesinger

Introduction

Pascal's wager is as a rule more easily appreciated than any other argument in support of religious belief. After all, the locution (which represents the essential structure of the wager), "I have nothing to lose and everything to gain by doing such and such," is a common one and readily understood by everybody.

At the same time the wager has been the target of a number of objections. I propose here to deal with three of these; two are widely known, whereas the third is of very recent origin. Finally, I also point out that the gravest objection to the wager requires a reply that is based on an argument indispensable in the context of nearly all other theistic proofs. Hence, that argument may well be regarded as the most central theistic argument.

The first objection has no great logical force but carries considerable psychological weight. It is unique insofar that it contends not so much that the wager violates the rules of sound thinking and is therefore invalid but rather that it is repugnant, and in a religious context, it is especially unseemly. The second objection contends that even if the argument were logically impeccable it would lead nowhere. The last one, surprisingly enough, claims that it is overly effective, so much so that it should not at all matter what an individual does or fails to do, because he or she by virtue of the wager is in a maximally advantageous position anyway with regard to eternal salvation.

The Wager and Greed

It is common knowledge that many well-intentioned individuals reject the wager for reasons that do not require much philosophical sophistication. They find it mercenary. They believe it appeals to the scheming, calculating self and are thus repelled by it. Without delving deep into theological issues, it has seemed to many that applying betting rules, relevant to moneymaking ventures, to a supposedly infinitely more exalted subject to lure skeptics by appealing to their grasping instincts offends religious proprieties.

People have found absurd the very notion that there may be any comparison between the seeker of a transcendent goal in life and a patron of a gambling house. We need not assume that greed as such is held generally in our highly acquisitive society in intense contempt. In the present context, however, it appears to offend the very spirit of what one is supposed to pursue. The essence of religion is generally perceived as the conviction that all profane, self-seeking ambitions are incompatible with the quest for piety. The religious seeker is not one to be mired in self indulgent pursuits but passionately devotes oneself to much nobler and more ultimate concerns.

Now of course Pascal was quite explicit in saying that the skeptic's wagering on God is no more than a first step, and those who take no further steps will have achieved nothing. However, his advice to the wagerer is to start behaving as one would if one actually believed, because Pascal believed that such conduct is likely to lead to a truly dedicated life in the service of God. By starting to observe the rituals of religion, associating with pious persons, and studying the sacred literature, individuals are likely to transform their sentiments and feelings and eventually acquire genuine belief.

Yet Pascal's reply has failed to satisfy many of his critics. If grasping is incompatible with the spirit of religion, then it is not to be used as a vehicle with which to reach any destination. Noble ends are debased when pursued by ignoble means.

Pascal's supporters at this stage are usually inclined to offer distinctions between means that do not and means that do justify their end.

I believe a more important point should be made: we are free to assume that no objective is ever hallowed enough that it should be impermissible to reach it by anything but impeccable means.

First, a relatively simple point about the offensiveness of greed. Suppose there is a person of an extraordinarily high income who gives away almost all his money to charity, retaining only what is necessary for bare existence. Furthermore, this individual does not seek the gratitude of the beneficiaries of these donations nor the admiration of the community. In fact, this person always makes every possible effort to ensure that no one should be charged with selfishness and greed: he is surely aware of his almost unparalleled, heroic, moral accomplishments. Evidently therefore he is a highly greedy individual; what he apparently craves is not material possessions nor the prestige accorded for outstanding philanthropy but the ability to relish the knowledge that he has outdone practically everyone in his contempt for stinginess, in his indifference for fame and praise, and the ability to enjoy the deep satisfaction of having been able to reach the pinnacle of otherdirectedness and the heights of noble magnanimity free of the slightest taint of petty self-regard.

Clearly, if we were to take this line, then we would be forced to conclude that every act which fulfills some wish is greedy and selfish and no freely willed act would ever be free of sin. Thus, the sensible thing to say is that the pursuit of a quest is deplorable when it brings harm either to others or to oneself in the sense that it debases the questing individual (which Pascal calls "poisonous pleasures") who could instead strive for more refined, higher order, life-enhancing pleasures.

Now the pleasure that Pascal holds up before his "calculating clients" is of the most exalted kind, one that is simply inaccessible to an individual who has not spent life passionately serving the Master of the Universe and thereby developing and perfecting one's soul, without which one lacks the capacity to partake in the transmundane bliss available to the select few. Only the suitably goomed soul, when released from its earthly fetters, will bask in the radiance of the Divine presence and delight in the adoring communion with a loving God. If craving for such an end is a manifestation of greed, then it is the manifestation of a noble greed that is to be acclaimed. Therefore, only if one were to assume that the ultimate reward of the righteous is the satisfaction of some cruder yearnings could one charge a follower of Pascal with trying to enkindle our unseemly mercenary motives.

Practice and Belief

However, a more important point needs to be made as well. The essence of true religion is not the intellectual assent to a set of propositions nor is it the verbal profession of certain beliefs. It is a full commitment and devotion, having one's heart and soul virtually consumed by a deep reverence and love of God. Maimonides wrote:

> What is the proper love of God? It is the love of the Lord with a great and very strong love so that one's soul shall be tied to the love of the Lord, and one should be continually enraptured by it, like a lovesick individual. . . . [1]

The immediate question one is bound to ask is, how does one achieve such a state of mind? Belief might be obtained through compelling arguments, or credible evidence, but surely exaltation or love is not an epistemic universal and cannot be planted into one's heart by the methodological rules of knowledge acquisition.

A very brief answer has been hinted at by the sagacious Hillel, who, as the famous story goes, was approached by someone demanding to be taught the whole Law while standing on one foot. Hillel agreed and informed the man that the single sentence, "Whatever is hateful to you do not do it to your fellow-human," contains the essence of all there is to be learned.[2] Hillel's fascinating precis of the Law raises many problems. One of them is in Leviticus 19:18: it says, "You all love your fellow-human as yourself."

Why did he believe it necessary to change the wording of the Scriptures? This particular question may have a simple answer, namely, Hillel realized that one cannot be commanded to have certain sentiments; I could be ordered to act or to refrain from acting in a certain way but not to love someone I happen to dislike. Thus, to reach the stage that the Scripture prescribes where one actually loves other human beings, we have to begin with the kind of behavior that is always associated with such a sentiment, that is, our practical conduct toward our fellow humans should be like that toward our own self: never actually do anything injurious to their interests. Desirable behavior is assumed to generate eventually desirable feelings.

Hillel's insight should be applied in the context of one's relation to God as well. The twelfth-century poet-philosopher Judah Halevi was quite explicit on this point, "Man can reach God only by doing His commands" (*Cuzari*, 2.46). Good thoughts, on their own, are too fleeting and insubstantial, and physical acts are concrete; when one has trained oneself to act in accordance with the dictates of religion and actual behavior closely resembles the behavior of those who posses truly deep religious sentiments, then one has provided oneself with the proper grounds on which fervent love for the Divine may grow. The theory behind this view may be compared with what today is called "behavior modification." This kind of therapy is based on the belief that it is possible to induce feelings of aversion to what is harmful and a natural desire for what is beneficial through adopting certain patterns of behavior. On the more extreme version of this view (as held by Halevi), it is not merely possible but essential to begin one's journey toward authentic theism by looking on the practices mandated by religion as the proper first step toward genuine piety. On this view, the wagerer who starts out satisfying the demands of faith before having acquired actual belief is not merely doing what is calculating and mercenary nor even that which is merely commendable but is engaged in what is absolutely indispensable for reaching the noble objective that is sought.

Are There Infinitely Many Equally Viable Hypotheses?

The second, oft-repeated objection is a relatively powerful, clearly articulated objection, known as the "many-gods objection." Pascal has been charged with making the unwarranted assumption that the problem facing the agnostic is confined to the question of which of two options to choose. In reality, however, in addition to the God of the theist, there are any number of other possible ones as well. How is the wagerer to assess the relative benefits associated with betting on Osiris, Baal, Dagon, Zeus, or Blodenwedd? Pascal provides no argument to guide us to the right deity, worshiping whom one is most likely to secure oneself eternal salvation.

Before attempting to advance any reply, I should point out that though the objection is, as already mentioned, a serious one, we find in the literature several versions, depicting a far more threatening portrayal of the difficulty than it is in reality. Richard Gale, for example, sees the following devastating consequences of the many-gods objection:

> . . . from the fact that it is logically possible that God exists it does not
> follow that the product of the probability of his existence and an infi-
> nite number is infinite. In a fair lottery with a denumerable infinity of

tickets, for each ticket it is true that it is logically possible that it will win, but the probability of its doing so is infinitesimal and the product of an infinitesimal and an infinite number is itself infinitesimal. Thus the expected gain of buying a ticket is not infinite but infinitesimal. There is at least a denumerable infinity of logically possible deities . . . and thus betting on any one of them the expected gain is zero according to this argument.[3]

The opponents of the wager have had the tendency to magnify the gravity of the problem by overcalculating the number of alternatives available for the religious seeker and hence depicting Pascal's counsel as quite hopelessly arbitrary. For example, J. L. Mackie, who lists a number of possible deities that seem to have escaped Pascal's notice, also mentions,

> . . . that there might be a god who looked with more favor on honest doubters or atheists who, in Hume's words, proportioned their belief to the evidence, than on mercenary manipulators of their own understanding. Indeed, this would follow from the ascription to God of moral goodness in any sense we can understand.[4]

Also fairly often heard is the argument that among the infinitely many possible deities, we must not overlook one who grants eternal reward to those who firmly deny the existence of a theistic God and punishes all those who believe in him.

Richard Gale goes even further, suggesting that

> there is the logically possible deity who rewards with infinite felicity all and only those who believe in him and step on only one sidewalk crack in the course of their life, as well as the two-crack deity, the three-crack deity, and so on ad infinitum.[5]

There are several lines one may adopt to meet this kind of objection. One may be based on the realization that Pascal is addressing individuals who, though they may be hardened in their disbelief, do have a notion of what genuine religion is about. In other words, though they deny its truth, they acknowledge its meaningfulness and understand that it is based on a highly optimistic view of human potential and of the sublime possible level of existence it postulates. It is a necessary presupposition of the wager that one understands that the notion of "genuine religion" is conceptually associated with a number of other exalted notions, and those people whom Pascal addresses are to be assumed to have a basic grasp of the sublime concerns of its devout practitioners. Divine worship in an authentic sense (as distinct from a pagan sense, where one is trying to propitiate the supernatural powers on whose whims one's fate depends) is in no way to be likened to a commercial transaction. Whatever the probability of the existence of an afterlife worth seeking with all one's might is, it is certainly not to be viewed as a place to which one may be admitted after one has paid the amount demanded by its Divine Proprietor. "The service of God is not intended for God's perfection; it is intended for our own perfection," says Maimonides. On this view, an individual who has devoted his or her life to Divine service has nurtured and refined his or her soul, rendering it capable of receiving and finding felicity in the celestial radiance available for those prepared to absorb it. In brief, the wagerer is supposed to appreciate that in the context of theism, highly involved systems of theologies have been developed over the centuries, theologies that have an internal coherence and consist of many propositions with an appeal to the intellect as well as to the nobler, human sentiments.

Nothing of this sort exists in the context of, say, the sidewalk deity. It is difficult to conceive a reason why one should come to love such a being or why one should desire to be in its proximity. Of course, one might claim that without any rhyme or reason it capriciously rewards those who obey its arbitrary demands. Still, a Pascalian would insist that because a good portion of theistic belief is in harmony with natural, noble aspirations and is embedded in highly developed theology, it has to be ascribed a considerably higher probability than those with little appeal to the human mind and heart.

Thus, we are permitted to assert the following: if we were to agree that different deities have different probabilities, then even if there are infinitely many candidates for the office of the Master of the Universe, it does not follow that each has zero probability. One may, if one wants to, ascribe a finite value to the probability of the existence of each one of them and yet obtain a sum total of all these (which is the value of the probability of the infinite disjunction of "Zeus exists OR Baal exists OR etc."), an amount that does not exceed one. This should be the case if the various finite probabilities are members of a convergent series, for instance, the sum of the series $1/2 + 1/4 + 1/8 + \ldots$ never actually reaches one. This should be sufficient to lay to rest Gale's fear that if "there is at least a denumerable infinity of logically possible deities . . . [then] betting on any one of them the expected gain is zero."

The Criterion for Betting When the Expected Utilities Are Infinite

I submit a crucial point, one that is contrary to what numerous philosophers hold, namely, that when each possible outcome carries an infinite expected value, it is rational to bet on the outcome most probable to occur. Are there solid grounds for my hypothesis? Let me first point out that grounds are provided for this view by common sense (which in itself would not be sufficient to establish my point). Anyone wishing to verify this experimentally may consider the following two cases, A and B:

> A = Of the billions of people alive at the present moment, one and only one is going to enjoy eternal salvation, whereas the rest vanish into nothingness after completing their lives upon this earth. A truly randomizing device is going to determine the identity of the single lucky individual.
> B = Of the billions of people alive at the present moment, one and only one is going to vanish into nothingness after completing one's existence upon this planet; the rest are going to enjoy eternal salvation. A truly randomizing device is going to determine the identity of the one unlucky individual.

Now, without offering preliminary explanations, ask any number of individuals (and you may include among them some mathematicians) which case they would prefer to obtain? If my experience is reliable to any degree, rarely if ever does anybody argue: although if B is true than I am a billion times more likely to be among the blessed, this is quite irrelevant; the expected utilities are equal and therefore it makes no difference which is true.

Now let us look at a truly compelling argument. In cases where the mathematical expectations are infinite, the criterion for choosing the outcome to bet on is its probability. In all betting situations the sum I am charged to participate I am charged with certainty, whereas the prize I may receive is uncertain. Fairness demands that I be compensated through being charged less than the value of the prize and proportionately so, that is, the lower the probability of winning, the less I should be charged. Thus, it is obvious that the same set of rules cannot apply in case the prize is infinite, as in other cases. Justice cannot demand that the cost for being permitted to bet should equal the expected utilities, because then the fair cost should be infinite. But that is absurd: why should I definitely pay an infinite amount for a less than certain chance of winning back the same amount? It is evident therefore that the situation demands that a different principle must be guiding a wagerer faced with the problem of which of the various outcomes— each associated with infinite utilities—to choose. Because neither expected utilities nor the magnitude of the prize can serve as one's criterion, by elimination it should be reasonable to be guided by the value of the probability: wager on the outcome that is most likely to materialize.

Deities with Different Degrees of Plausibility

Let us consider a number of possible solutions to the many-gods problem. First, it is reasonable that a scrupulously just deity who ensures that each person's celestial reward is in direct proportion to the amount of energy and time invested throughout one's earthly life to the refinement of one's soul so as to increase its susceptibility to that reward, is considerably more probable than a fancy-bred capricious power whose awards are not in any obvious way related to earning, meriting, or the enhanced quality of the receptivity or atonement of the worshipper. Thus, we regard it at least fairly plausible that a deity may exist who does not hand out compensation or reimbursement for the trouble his adherents have gone through in serving him but who is so exalted that it seems reasonable to assume that the highest form of felicity is to center one's life around him. The most important task is to do everything in one's power to adjust and attune one's soul so that it has the capacity of fully resonating with the celestial radiance in which it will be submerged. A mere century or two ago theists did not recoil from using such locutions and were unembarrassed by what today may strike some as inflated grandiloquence. Thus we find the eighteenth-century poet and theologian M. H. Luzatto making (in his widely studied *Mesilat Yesharim*) the brief statement, because he regarded the matter too obvious to require elaboration, "Man came into the world only to achieve nearness to God." Surely such a view is bound to permeate every act and every thought of its adherent; it is part of an inclusive outlook on life and belongs to an extensive system of interconnected propositions.

Furthermore, in the context of the sublime god of the theist, many found it not unreasonable to view life's many trials and tribulations as instruments of soul-making or in any case as means to an end that may surpass our understanding. On the other hand, when referring to deities devoid of the various glorious Divine attributes, it seems more natural to speak like Gloucester: "As flies to wanton boys, are we to the gods. They kill us for their sport."

Thus, the hypothesis is that "a God of faithfulness and without inquity [one who is] just and right . . . " (Deuternomy 31:4), who therefore can be a source of emulation and inspiration and whose attributes altogether resonate with our nobler sentiments, makes a great deal of sense and it is therefore reasonable to ascribe a higher probability to his existence than to an unprincipled, arbitrarily acting, wanton god. And if this is conceded, then it should also seem sensible to hold that the greater those sublime properties, the greater the likelihood the one exemplifying them exists. Hence, the being greater than which is inconceivable, who possesses them to a maximum degree, is to be regarded more probable than any other deity.

Simplicity

The Cambridge statistician H. Jeffreys has shown in the 1920s that whenever we have a finite set of experimental results there are indefinitely many hypotheses that satisfy each result. The only way to select the hypothesis to be adopted is by following the principle of simplicity: of all the equally well-confirmed hypotheses, select the one that is simpler than all the others. It is crucial to realize that Jeffreys does not refer to the simplicity of structure of the systems involved or the simplicity of use and so on; he refers solely to descriptive simplicity and says that among the various expressions that represent the law, we are to adopt the one consisting of the minimal number of terms. It is also worth nothing that Jeffreys' is not a prescriptive but a descriptive principle: scientists have followed it for hundreds of years without explicitly being aware of it, simply because it has never been articulated before that of the indefinitely many alternative hypotheses present in all cases.

Many people willingly concede that the rules of rational reasoning are invariant with subject matter. Consequently, after Pascal has convinced us that we should wager on some supernatural power, we are confronted with the problem of which of the many possible such powers to adopt. In the absence of any facts to assist us, it stands to reason that we should have to use Jeffreys' principle. It is fairly easy to see that the theistic hypothesis is the simplest in the sense specified by Jeffreys.

It is the simplest because it is the only hypothesis that may be expressed with the use of a single predicate: to describe the God of the theist all that is needed is that he is an absolutely perfect being. By contrast, a statement positing the existence of any deity less than absolutely perfect will be relatively complex. For example, though there is a large body of ancient Greek literature concerning Zeus, there are still many aspects of Zeus's character that remain unknown to us. We know for instance that he was sometimes asleep, but we have no idea how many hours of sleep he needed and what effect sleeplessness had on him. We also know that he ate and drank, but not how much or whether he occasionally overgorged himself or how long he could go without any food at all, and so on.

The Principle of Sufficient Reason

Finally, I should advance an argument based on the principle of sufficient reason why the wagerer should go for the being greater than which is not conceivable. Before doing so, I believe it is necessary to defend the principle because many contemporary philosophers deny its validity. J. L. Mackie was speaking for a large number of adherents of empiricism when he said, "There is no sufficient reason to regard the principle of sufficient reason to be valid."[6] Levelheaded empiricists are not supposed to subscribe to *a priori* principles. For this reason, the majority of contemporary writers strongly object to ascribing equal probabilities on the basis of the principle of indifference, which is no more than a variation on the principle of sufficient reason (PSR).

It seems to me that these objections are based on a serious misconception. They are mostly based on the refusal to acknowledge that "experience is mute" and that it is necessary to assume some unconfirmed principles before we are able to surmise what it tells us. As a matter of fact, no empirically confirmed statement can be found anywhere that did not rely on the PSR. The following illustrate the wide range of its application.

1. It is universally held that there is, for instance, overwhelming inductive evidence that the melting point of gold is 1,064 degrees Celsius. It is common knowledge, however, that it is illegitimate to argue inductively from biased sample classes. Thus, the question arises why do physicists feel entitled to maintain that 1,064 degrees Celsius is likely to remain the melting point of gold when all their evidence is based on a biased sample class: all the samples of gold hitherto melted occurred in a universe in which the density of matter (which keeps decreasing) was

higher, the scaling factor (which is constantly increasing) was lower, and the velocity of the universe's expansion (which according to some cosmologists keeps decreasing all the time) was higher than at this crucial moment.

The answer is not that we have no grounds on which to assume that these changes are relevant to the melting point of any metal. In the past, serious biases turned out to be factors we never suspected before of having relevance: all swans were thought to be white, and the fact that the sample class on which this conclusion was based included only non-Australian swans had not occurred to anyone to be of concern. The presumed law that matter cannot be destroyed was based on the failure of every conceivable attempt to do so; you may break, grind, melt, boil and evaporate, or burn to ashes any lump of matter without succeeding to alter the amount in which it continues to exist. The fact that no relevant observations have been made under exceedingly large pressures and temperatures, the kind of which prevail at the center of the sun where matter does diminish through part of it transforming into energy, did not seem to constitute a source of worry. Indeed, at the pre-twentieth century knowledge of what processes take place on the subatomic level, there was no reason why one should suspect that pressure and temperature had relevance to the issue of the conservation of matter. Similarly, our knowledge of physics may be still too deficient for us to be able to see why the scaling factor of the universe should influence the melting point of anything.

The correct answer has to be that we are aware of the possibility of having arrived at our conclusion through the sue of a biased sample class, and consequently there are two lines of action available to us. One is to make no predictions at all. This, of course, would imply the complete paralysis of the scientific enterprise, which we should want to resist if at all possible. The alternative is to make use of the principle of sufficient reason. In the particular context of the melting point of gold, we then proceed in the following manner: in the past the melting point of gold has always been observed to be 1,064 degrees Celsius. In the future it may be different. However, there is no good reason to believe that the melting point will be higher than it will be lower or vice versa. Thus, as long as not proven otherwise, we make the unique prediction that it will be neither higher nor lower but will continue to remain the same as in the past.

2. It was mentioned before that whenever we have a finite set of experimental results there are indefinitely many hypotheses that satisfy each result and that the accepted practice is to select the hypothesis to be adopted by following the principle of simplicity: of all the equally

well-confirmed hypotheses, select the one that is simpler than all the others. What justification is there for this rule? One is the PSR. Should we suggest that some alternative hypothesis be adopted it will immediately be asked: what reason is there to make this particular choice? Why not select a simpler or a more complicated hypothesis? However, the simplest hypothesis has an edge over all others. It is unique. It is the only one in connection with which it is not possible to ask why not choose a simpler hypothesis. We thus justify our selection on the basis of the chosen hypothesis having a significant feature no other hypothesis has. The most complex hypothesis would also have such a feature except that it does not exist (just as the largest integer does not exist).

3. A strong illustration of how compelling the PSR is the fact that even mathematicians have found it useful as a principle of plausible reasoning. L. C. Larson in his highly influential book poses the problem: of all the rectangles which can be inscribed in a given circle, which has greatest area? Larson suggests,

> The principle of insufficient reason leads us to suspect that the rectangle of maximum area that can be inscribed in a circle is a square.

He then goes on to give a rigorous proof of his conjecture without regarding it as necessary to elaborate how precisely the principle led him to it. It is reasonable to assume that what Larson had in mind was that if it were suggested that the sought-after rectangle was one with length x and width $x + n$ then of course the rectangle with length $x + n$ and width x must also have the maximum area. And if there are indeed two rectangles with maximum area, then, of course, there are infinitely many couples that might possibly be the ones we are after. There is, however, one rectangle that is unique in the sense that it has no counterpart: the rectangle with equal length and width. It "stands to reason" that this is the privileged figure we are after.

4. Some 2,400 years ago Democritus argued,

> that there are infinite worlds, hypothesizing that the void is infinite; for why would this part of the void be filled by a world, but that part not? So, if there is a world in one part of the void, then also in all the void. So, since the void is infinite, the worlsds will be infinite too.

Democritus's hypothesis would warrant detailed study; here I can point out only first of all that his "worlds," unlike what we mean when referring to various possible worlds, are not necessarily causally separated from one another and also that he thought of the actual world as having tiny size as compared with what we believe it to be. Yet his hypothesis may be said to have survived to this very day in the form of the far-reaching cosmological principle. It asserts that the universe is the same (i.e., the distribution of galaxies, stars, and planets) everywhere in space (apart from irregularities of a local nature), or that the universe is homogeneous.

The reasoning behind Democritus's hypothesis is once more based on the PSR. Suppose it were suggested that there exist some finite number n worlds. We would be at loss to offer a reason why it was not a number less or greater than n. However, if n is infinite then a unique reason can be given why it is not larger than n.

This last example is of special significance as it shows that the PSR, which is customarily associated with the name of Leibniz, who indeed applied it to numerous issues, was known and made use of two thousand years before him. It provides therefore further evidence of the universal appeal of the PSR and its central role in all our conceptual schemes.

Suppose someone subscribed to a religion that was based on the belief that the deity governing the universe was very benevolent but not absolutely so, possessing merely 95 percent of full benevolence. (It is not important for our purposes to describe how we compute the numerical degree of benevolence.) We might then ask an adherent of this religion: why not ascribe to your deity 96 percent of 94 percent benevolence? No reasonable answer seems available. On the other hand, the theist, when faced with a similar inquiry, might appeal to the PSR. If one settles for any number, like 95 percent, no sufficient reason seems to be available: why not have more or why not have less. However, a reason may be offered for 100 percent benevolence: it is of a unique magnitude, as it is impossible to have more. Suppose someone were to ask: but by the same principle you might as well ascribe 0 percent benevolence and explain your doing so by saying that having less than it is impossible? To this, as mentioned before, the theist reply would be that such a being is not a fit deity to worship, and thus one is to ascribe considerably lower probability to its existence.

Why Wager At All?

We are now in the position to reply to an ingenious objection raised by Antony Duff. Duff points out that the wager works regardless how small the probability, as long as its value is not zero, and that one is going to be the recipient of infinite salvation. If so, he argues, it is quite superfluous that I should follow Pascal's advice and begin acting religiously and make every effort to acquire faith, because,

> . . . suppose I take no steps to make it more likely that I will come to believe in God. There must be some probability, however small, that I will nonetheless come to believe in Him . . . and that probability is enough to generate an infinite expected value for my actions.[7]

Now we have at least two answers to Duff's objection. The briefer answer is to recall the idea advanced previously that it is untenable to maintain that because of the infinitude of the reward it makes no difference how probable is its acquisition. We are instead to assume that it is important to try and increase the probability of obtaining the prospective prize.

The second answer would be based on the principle that a rational wagerer will always want to bet on the outcome associated with the highest expected utilities. But is it possible to gain anything more than infinite salvation? The answer is, in an appropriate sense, yes! An infinitely long string, for example, may be increased in width, or in mass per unit length, and so on. Similarly, eternal life, which of course is infinitely long and cannot be increased in length, may vary in the degree of its depth, intensity, exquisiteness, and so on, during every moment for the eternal duration of that felicitous state. Once we are prepared to entertain the possibility of an afterlife, we are likely to find it reasonable to go along with the traditional view that the magnificence of posthumous reward varies directly with the quality and the portion of the time at one's disposal as well as the magnitude of the exertion invested in acts of piety.

It should also be recalled that as soon as an individual embarks on the road that offers the best chance to lead to the acquisition of genuine religious faith, one is already set on the path of the righteous and is already engaged in the service of God. Clearly, therefore, one who acts upon Pascal's call at once, rather than waiting for the not entirely improbable inspiration to light unassisted upon him at some later time, places oneself in a far more favorable position with respect to the amount of time spent on the purification of one's soul. Thus, even if we conceded that in the context of eternal salvation the value of probability plays no role, the individual following Duff's advice would engage in a conduct associated with a prize of lower quality and thus with lower expected utilities.

A Common Feature to Almost All Theistic Arguments

One of the most commonly cited theistic proofs is the Argument from Design. It is based on the wonders of nature we see around us that are unlikely to be, or perhaps unthinkable that they should be, the results of blind forces. Now even if we regard the argument absolutely compelling, it establishes at most—as we pointed out by Hume—that there exists a creator who is many hundreds times more powerful and intelligent than ourselves. But such a creator's power and intelligence may still fall infinitely short of Omnipotence and Omniscience. About benevolence the argument says even less, and the same goes for Omnipresence or Immutability.

Another famous argument is the Cosmological Argument. It shares all the weaknesses just mentioned in connection with the Argument from Design. Indeed, it should be obvious that all other arguments in support of theism (with the exception of the Ontological Argument, of which only a few would claim to have achieved full clarity) face the many gods objection.

Thus, an individual making use of any of numerous known arguments for the existence of God can get no further than to conclude that there exists some supernatural power and intelligence behind the material universe. That individual is thus facing the need to choose among the various candidates who may fulfill this function.

It seems reasonable to conjecture that whatever is deemed the best justification for the theist's choice in one context is also likely to be so in other contexts as well. Therefore, the most acceptable reply to the many-gods objection may well be regarded as an argument of wide application and thus of central importance in the context of theistic arguments in general.

One of the striking features of Pascal's wager is surely the fact that the most often cited stumbling block it runs into has been the many-gods objection, whereas in the context of theistic arguments, I venture to suggest that this may be read as an indication of the unique strength of the wager. The reason why the many-gods objection has been raised less frequently in the context of the wager was because skeptics felt able to clip the wings of a putative argument at the very initial stages, before it could get off the ground and thus prevent even the conclusion that some supernatural being is to be assumed.

Thus, the Argument from Design is nipped in the bud by insisting that the universe does not exhibit any signs of design; the Cosmological Argument has been cut short because of its alleged, unwarranted, basic assumption that there can be no uncaused contingent particulars. On the other hand, it seems that no serious defect could be discovered in Pascal's wager before it reached the relatively advanced stage of establishing the reasonableness of assuming the existence of some transmundane force.

Notes

1. *Mishneh Torah,* Hilkhot Teshuvah, x.
2. *Shabbat,* 31b.
3. *On the Nature and Existence of God* (Cambridge, 1991), p. 350.
4. *The Miracle of Theism* (Oxford, 1982), p. 203.
5. Gale, op. cit., p. 350.
6. "Three Steps Toward Absolutism," *Space, Time and Causality,* ed. R. Swinburne (Dordrecht, 1981), p. 6.
7. "Pascal's Wager and Infinite Utilities," *Analysis* 46 (1986): 107.

Evil and Omnipotence
J. L. Mackie

The traditional arguments for the existence of God have been fairly thoroughly criticised by philosophers. But the theologian can, if he wishes, accept this criticism. He can admit that no rational proof of God's existence is possible. And he can still retain all that is essential to his position, by holding that God's existence is known in some other, non-rational way. I think, however, that a more telling criticism can be made by way of traditional problem of evil. Here it can be shown, not that religious beliefs lack rational support, but that they are positively irrational, that the several parts of the essential theological doctrine are inconsistent with one another, so that the theologian can maintain his position as a whole only by a much more extreme rejection of reason than in the former case. He must now be prepared to believe, not merely what cannot be proved, but what can be *disproved* from other beliefs that he also holds.

The problem of evil, in the sense in which I shall be using the phrase, is a problem only for someone who believes that there is a God

Source: From J. L. Mackie, *Mind, Vol. 64* (Oxford University Press, 1955): 200–212. Reprinted by permission of Oxford University Press.

who is both omnipotent and wholly good. And it is a logical problem, the problem of clarifying and reconciling a number of beliefs: it is not a scientific problem that might be solved by further observations, or a practical problem that might be solved by a decision or an action. These points are obvious; I mention them only because they are sometimes ignored by theologians, who sometimes parry a statement of the problem with such remarks as "Well, can you solve the problem yourself?" or "This is a mystery which may be revealed to us later" or "Evil is something to be faced and overcome, not to be merely discussed."

In its simplest form the problem is this: God is omnipotent; God is wholly good; and yet evil exists. There seems to be some contradiction between these three propositions, so that if any two of them were true the third would be false. But at the same time all three are essential parts of most theological positions: the theologian, it seems, at once *must* adhere and *cannot consistently* adhere to all three. (The problem does not arise only for theists, but I shall discuss it in the form in which it presents itself for ordinary theism.)

However, the contradiction does not arise immediately; to show it we need some additional premises, or perhaps some quasi-logical rules connecting the terms "good," "evil," and "omnipotent." These additional principles are that good is opposed to evil, in such a way that a good thing always eliminates evil as far as it can, and that there are no limits to what an omnipotent thing can do. From these it follows that a good omnipotent thing eliminates evil completely, and then the propositions that a good omnipotent thing exists, and that evil exists, are incompatible.

Adequate Solutions

Now once the problem is fully stated it is clear that it can be solved, in the sense that the problem will not arise if one gives up at least one of the propositions that constitute it. If you are prepared to say that God is not wholly good, or not quite omnipotent, or that evil does not exist, or that good is not opposed to the kind of evil that exists, or that there are limits to what an omnipotent thing can do, then the problem of evil will not arise for you.

There are, then, quite a number of adequate solutions of the problem of evil, and some of these have been adopted, or almost adopted, by various thinkers. For example, a few have been prepared to deny God's omnipotence, and rather more have been prepared to keep the term "omnipotence" but severely to restrict its meaning, recording quite a number of things that an omnipotent being cannot do. Some have said that evil is an illusion, perhaps because they held that the whole world of temporal, changing things is an illusion, and that what we call evil belongs only to this world, or perhaps because they held that although temporal things *are* much as we see them, those that we call evil are not really evil. Some have said that what we call evil is merely the privation of good, that evil in a positive sense, evil that would really be opposed to good, does not exist. Many have agreed with Pope that disorder is harmony not understood, and that partial evil is universal good. Whether any of these views is *true* is, of course, another question. But each of them gives an adequate solution of the problem of evil in the sense that if you accept it this problem does not arise for you, though you may, of course, have *other* problems to face.

But often enough these adequate solutions are only *almost* adopted. The thinkers who restrict God's power, but keep the term "omnipotence," may reasonably be suspected of thinking, in other contexts, that his power is really unlimited. Those who say that evil is an illusion may also be thinking, inconsistently, that this illusion is itself an evil. Those who say that "evil" is merely privation of good may also be thinking, inconsistently, that privation of good is an evil. (The fallacy here is akin to some forms of the "naturalistic fallacy" in ethics, where some think, for example, that "good" is just what contributes to evolutionary progress, and that evolutionary progress is itself good.) If Pope meant what he said in the first line of his couplet, that "disorder" is only harmony not understood, the "partial evil" of the second line must, for consistency, mean "that which, taken in isolation, falsely appears to be evil," but it would more naturally mean "that which, in isolation, really is evil." The second line, in fact, hesitates between two views, that "partial evil." isn't really evil, since only the universal quality is real, and that "partial evil" is really an evil, but only a little one.

In addition, therefore, to adequate solutions, we must recognise unsatisfactory inconsistent solutions, in which there is only a half-hearted or temporary rejection of one of the propositions which together constitute the problem. In these, one of the constituent propositions is explicitly rejected, but it is covertly re-asserted or assumed elsewhere in the system.

Fallacious Solutions

Besides these half-hearted solutions, which explicitly reject but implicitly assert one of the constituent propositions, there are definitely fallacious solutions which explicitly maintain all the constituent propositions, but implicitly reject at least one of them in the course of the argument that explains away the problem of evil.

There are, in fact, many so-called solutions which purport to remove the contradiction without abandoning any of its constituent propositions. These must be fallacious, as we can see from the very statement of the problem, but it is not so easy to see in each case precisely where the fallacy lies. I suggest that in all cases the fallacy has the general form suggested above: in order to solve the problem one (or perhaps more) of its constituent propositions is given up, but in such a way that it appears to have been retained, and can therefore be asserted without qualification in other contexts. Sometimes there is a further complication: the supposed solution moves to and fro between, say, two of the constituent propositions, at one point asserting the first of these but covertly abandoning the second, at another point asserting the second but covertly abandoning the first. These fallacious solutions often turn upon some equivocation with the words "good" and "evil," or upon some vagueness about the way in which good and evil are opposed to one another, or about how much is meant by "omnipotence." I propose to examine some of these so-called solutions, and to exhibit their fallacies in detail. Incidentally, I shall also be considering whether an adequate solution could be reached by a minor modification of one or more of the constituent propositions, which would, however, still satisfy all the essential requirements of ordinary theism.

"Good Cannot Exist without Evil" or "Evil is Necessary as a Counterpart to Good"

It is sometimes suggested that evil is necessary as a counterpart to good, that if there were no evil there could be no good either, and that this solves the problem of evil. It is true that it points to an answer to the question "Why should there be evil?" But it does so only by qualifying some of the propositions that constitute the problem.

First, it sets a limit to what God can do, saying that God *cannot* create good without simultaneously creating evil, and this means either that God is not omnipotent or that there are *some* limits to what an omnipotent thing can do. It may be replied that these limits are always presupposed, that omnipotence has never meant the power to do what is logically impossible, and on the present view the existence of good without evil would be a logical impossibility. This interpretation of omnipotence may, indeed, be accepted as a modification of our original account which does not reject anything that is essential to theism, and I shall in general assume it in the subsequent discussion. It is, perhaps, the most common theistic view, but I think that some theists at least have maintained that God can do what is logically impossible. Many theists, at any rate, have held that logic itself is created or laid down by God, that logic is the way in which God arbitrarily chooses to think. (This is, of course, parallel to the ethical view that morally right actions are those which God arbitrarily chooses to command, and the two views encounter similar difficulties.) And *this* account of logic is clearly inconsistent with the view that God is bound by logical necessities—unless it is possible for an omnipotent being to bind himself, an issue which we shall consider later, when we come to the Paradox Omnipotence. This solution of the problem of evil cannot, therefore, be consistently adopted along with the view that logic is itself created by God.

But, secondly, this solution denies that evil is opposed to good in our original sense. If good and evil are counterparts, a good thing will not "eliminate evil as far as it can." Indeed, this view suggests that good and evil are not strictly qualities of things at all. Perhaps the suggestion is that good and evil are related in much the same way as great and small. Certainly, when the term "great" is used relatively as a condensation of "greater than so-and-so," and "small" is used correspondingly, greatness and smallness are counterparts and cannot exist without each other. But in this sense greatness is not a quality, not an intrinsic feature of anything; and it would be absurd to think of a movement in favor of greatness and against smallness in this sense. Such a movement would be self-defeating, since relative greatness can be promoted only by a simultaneous promotion of relative smallness. I feel sure that no theists would be content to regard God's goodness as analogous to this—as if what he supports were not the *good* but the *better,* and as if he had the paradoxical aim that all things should be better than other things.

This point is obscured by the fact that "great" and "small" seem to have an absolute as well as a relative sense. I cannot discuss here whether there is absolute magnitude or not, but if there is, there could be an absolute sense for "great," it could mean of at least a certain size, and it would make sense to speak of all things getting bigger, of a universe that was expanding all over, and therefore it would make sense to speak of promoting greatness. But in *this* sense great and small are not logically necessary counterparts: either quality could exist without the other. There would be no logical impossibility in everything's being small or in everything's being great.

Neither in the absolute nor in the relative sense, then, of "great" and "small" do these terms provide an analogy of the sort that would be needed to support this solution of the problem of evil. In neither case are greatness and smallness *both* necessary counterparts *and* mutually opposed forces or possible objects for support and attack.

It may be replied that good and evil are necessary counterparts in the same way as any quality and its logical opposite: redness can occur, it is suggested, only if non-redness also occurs. But unless evil is merely the privation of good, they are not logical opposites, and some further argument would be needed to show that they are counterparts in the same way as genuine logical opposites. Let us assume that this could be given. There is still doubt of the correctness of the metaphysical principle that a quality must have a real opposite: I suggest that it is not really impossible that everything should be, say, red, that the truth is merely that if everything were red we should not notice redness, and so we should have no word "red"; we observe and give names to qualities only if they have real opposites. If so, the principle that a term must have an opposite would belong only to our language or to our thought, and would not be an ontological principle, and, correspondingly, the rule that good cannot exist without evil would not state a logical necessity of a sort that God would just have to put up with. God might have made everything good, though *we* should not have noticed it if he had.

But, finally, even if we concede that this is an ontological principle, it will provide a solution for the problem of evil only if one is prepared to say, "Evil exists, but only just enough evil to serve as the counterpart of good." I doubt whether any theist will accept this. After all, the *ontological* requirement that non-redness should occur would be satisfied even if all the universe, except for a minute speck, were red, and, if there were a corresponding requirement for evil as a counterpart to good, a minute dose of evil would presumably do. But theists are not usually willing to say, in all contexts, that all the evil that occurs is a minute and necessary dose.

"Evil is Necessary as a Means to Good"

It is sometimes suggested that evil is necessary for good not as a counterpart but as a means. In its simple form this has little plausibility as a solution of the problem of evil, since it obviously implies a severe restriction of God's power. It would be a *causal* law that you cannot have a certain end without a certain means, so that if God has to introduce evil as a means to good, he must be subject to at least some causal laws. This certainly conflicts with what a theist normally means by omnipotence. This view of God as limited by causal laws also conflicts with the view that causal laws are themselves made by God, which is more widely held than the corresponding view about the laws of logic. This conflict, would, indeed, be resolved if it were possible for an omnipotent being to bind himself, and this possibility has still to be considered. Unless a favourable answer can be given to this question, the suggestion that evil is necessary as a means to good solves the problem of evil only by denying one of its constituent propositions, either that God is omnipotent or that "omnipotent" means what it says.

"The Universe Is Better with Some Evil in It Than It Could Be If There Were No Evil"

Much more important is a solution which at first seems to be a mere variant of the previous one, that evil may contribute to the goodness of a whole in which it is found, so that the universe as a whole is better as it is, with some evil in it, than it would be if there were no evil. This solution may be developed in either of two ways. It may be supported by an aesthetic analogy by the fact that contrasts heighten beauty, that in a musical work, for example, there may occur discords which somehow add to the beauty of the work as a whole. Alternatively, it may be worked out in connexion with the notion of progress, that the best possible organization of the universe will not be static, but progressive, that the gradual overcoming of evil by good is really a finer thing than would be the eternal unchallenged supremacy of good.

In either case, this solution usually starts from the assumption that the evil whose existence gives rise to the problem of evil is primarily what is called physical evil, that is to say, pain. In Hume's rather half-hearted presentation of the problem of evil, the evils that he stresses are pain and disease, and those who reply to him argue that the existence of pain and disease makes possible the existence of sympathy, benevolence, heroism, and the gradually successful struggle of doctors and reformers to overcome these evils. In fact, theists often seize the opportunity to accuse those who stress the problem of evil of taking a low, materialistic view of good and evil, equating these with pleasure and pain, and of ignoring the more spiritual goods which can arise in the struggle against evils.

But let us see exactly what is being done here. Let us call pain and misery "first order evil" or "evil (1)." What contrasts with this, namely, pleasure and happiness, will be called "first order good" or "good (1)."

Distinct from this is "second order good" or "good (2)" which somehow emerges in a complex situation in which evil (1) is a necessary component—logically, not merely causally, necessary. (Exactly *how* it emerges does not matter: in the crudest version of this solution good (2) is simply the heightening of happiness by the contrast with misery, in other versions it includes sympathy with suffering, heroism in facing danger, and the gradual decrease of first order evil and increase of first order good.) It is also being assumed that second order good is more important than first order good or evil, in particular that it more than outweighs the first order evil it involves.

Now that is a particularly subtle attempt to solve the problem of evil. It defends God's goodness and omnipotence on the ground that (on a sufficiently long view) this is the best of all logically possible worlds, because it includes the important second order goods, and yet it admits that real evils, namely first order evils, exist. But does it still hold that good and evil are opposed? Not, clearly, in the sense that we set out originally: good does not tend to eliminate evil in general. Instead, we have a modified, a more complex pattern. First order good (e.g. happiness) *contrasts with* first order evil (e.g. misery): these two are opposed in a fairly mechanical way; some second order goods (e.g. benevolence) try to maximize first order good and minimize first order evil; but God's goodness is not this, it is rather the will to maximize second order good. We might, therefore, call God's goodness an example of a third order goodness, or good (3). While this account is different from our original one, it might well be held to be an improvement on it, to give a more accurate description of the way in which good is opposed to evil, and to be consistent with the essential theist position.

There might, however, be several objections to this solution.

First, some might argue that such qualities as benevolence—and a fortiori the third order goodness which promotes benevolence—have a merely derivative value, that they are not higher sorts of good, but merely means to good (1), that is, to happiness, so that it would be absurd for God to keep misery in existence in order to make possible the virtues of benevolence, heroism, etc. The theist who adopts the present solution must, of course, deny this, but he can do so with some plausibility, so I should not press this objection.

Secondly, it follows from this solution that God is not in our sense benevolent or sympathetic: he is not concerned to minimise evil (1), but only to promote good (2); and this might be a disturbing conclusion for some theists.

But, thirdly, the fatal objection is this. Our analysis shows clearly the possibility of the existence of a *second* order evil, an evil (2) contrasting with good (2) as evil (1) contrasts with good (1). This would include malevolence, cruelty, callousness, cowardice, and states in which good (1) is decreasing and evil (1) increasing. And just as good (2) is held to be the important kind of good, the kind that God is concerned to promote, so evil (2) will, by analogy, be the important kind of evil, the kind which God, if he were wholly good and omnipotent, would eliminate. And yet evil (2) plainly exists, and indeed most theists (in other contexts) stress its existence more than that of evil (1). We should, therefore, state the problem of evil in terms of second order evil, and against this form of the problem the present solution is useless.

An attempt might be made to use this solution again, at a higher level, to explain the occurrence of evil (2): indeed the next main solution that we shall examine does just this, with the help of some new notions. Without any fresh notions, such a solution would have little plausibility: for example, we could hardly say that the really important good was a good (3), such as the increase of benevolence in proportion to cruelty, which logically required for its occurrence the occurrence of some second order evil. But even if evil (2) could be explained in this way, it is fairly clear that there would be third order evils contrasting with this third order good: and we should be well on the way to an infinite regress, where the solution of a problem of evil, stated in terms of evil (n), indicated the existence of an evil ($n + 1$), and a further problem to be solved.

"Evil Is Due to Human Freewill"

Perhaps the most important proposed solution of the problem of evil is that evil is not to be ascribed to God at all, but to the independent actions of human beings, supposed to have been endowed by God with freedom of the will. This solution may be combined with the preceding one: first order evil (e.g. pain) may be justified as a logically necessary component in second order good (e.g. sympathy) while second order evil (e.g. cruelty) is not *justified*, but is so ascribed to human beings that God cannot be held responsible for it. This combination evades my third criticism of the preceding solution.

The freewill solution also involves the preceding solution at a higher level. To explain why a wholly good God gave men free will although it would lead to some important evils, it must be argued that it is better on the whole that men should act freely, and sometimes err, than that they should be innocent automata, acting rightly in a wholly deter-mined way. Freedom, that is to say, is now treated as a third order good, and as being more valuable than second order goods (such as sympathy and heroism) would be if they were deterministically produced, and it is being assumed that second order evils, such as cru-elty, are logically necessary accompaniments of freedom, just as pain is a logically necessary pre-condition of sympathy.

I think that this solution is unsatisfactory primarily because of the incoherence of the notion of freedom of the will: but I cannot discuss this topic adequately here, although some of my criticisms will touch upon it.

First I should query the assumption that second order evils are logi-cally necessary accompaniments of freedom. I should ask this: if God has made men such that in their free choices they sometimes prefer what is good and sometimes what is evil, why could He not have made men such that they always freely choose the good? If there is no logical impossibility in a man's freely choosing the good on one, or on several, occasions, there cannot be a logical impossibility in his freely choosing the good on every occasion. God was not, then, faced with a choice between making innocent automata and making beings who, in acting freely, would sometimes go wrong: there was open to him the obviously better possibility of making beings who would act freely but always go right. Clearly, his failure to avail himself of this possibility is inconsis-tent with his being both omnipotent and wholly good.

If it is replied that this objection is absurd, that the making of some wrong choices is logically necessary for freedom, it would seem that "freedom" must here mean complete randomness or indeterminacy, including randomness with regard to the alternatives good and evil, in other words that men's choices and consequent action can be "free" only if they are not determined by their characters. Only on this assumption can God escape the responsibility for men's actions; for if he made them as they are, but did not determine their wrong choices, this can only be because the wrong choices are not determined by men as they are. But then if freedom is randomness, how can it be a charac-teristic of *will*? And still more, how can it be the most important good? What value or merit would there be in free choices if these were ran-dom actions which were not determined by the nature of the agent?

I conclude that to make this solution plausible two different senses of "freedom" must be confused, one sense which will justify the view that freedom is third order good, more valuable than other goods would be without it, and another sense, sheer randomness, to prevent us from ascribing to God a decision to make men such that they sometimes go wrong when he might have made them such that they would always freely go right.

This criticism is sufficient to dispose of this solution. But besides this there is a fundamental difficulty in the notion of an omnipotent God creating men with free will, for if men's wills are really free this must mean that even God cannot control them, that is, that God is no longer omnipotent. It may be objected that God's gift of freedom to men does not mean that he *cannot* control their wills, but that he always *refrains* from controlling their wills. But why, we may ask, should God refrain from controlling evil wills? Why should he not leave men free to will rightly, but intervene when he sees them beginning to will wrongly? If God could do this, but does not, and if he is wholly good, the only explanation could be that even a wrong free act of will is not really evil, that its freedom is a value which outweighs its wrongness, so that there would be a loss of value if God took away the wrongness and the freedom together. But this is utterly opposed to what theists say about sin in other contexts. The present solution of the problem of evil, then, can be maintained only in the form that God has made men so free that he *cannot* control their wills.

This leads us to what I call the Paradox of Omnipotence: can an omnipotent being make things which he cannot subsequently control? Or, what is practically equivalent to this, can an omnipotent being make rules which then bind himself? (These are practically equivalent because any such rules could be regarded as setting certain things beyond his control, and vice versa.) The second of these formulations is relevant to the suggestions that we have already met, that an omnipotent God creates the rules of logic or causal laws, and is then bound by them.

It is clear that this is a paradox: the questions cannot be answered satisfactorily either in the affirmative or in the negative. If we answer "Yes," it follows that if God actually makes things which he cannot control, or makes rules which bind himself, he is not omnipotent once he has made them: there are *then* things which he cannot do. But if we answer "No," we are immediately asserting that there are things which he cannot do, that is to say that he is already not omnipotent.

It cannot be replied that the question which sets this paradox is not a proper question. It would make perfectly good sense to say that a human mechanic has made a machine which he cannot control: if there is any difficulty about the question it lies in the notion of omnipotence itself.

This, incidentally, shows that although we have approached this paradox from the freewill theory, it is equally a problem for a theological determinist. No one thinks that machines have free will, yet they may be beyond the control of their makers. The determinist might reply that anyone who makes anything determines its ways of acting, and so determines its subsequent behaviour: even the human mechanic does this by his *choice* of materials and structure for his machine, though he does not know all about either of these: the mechanic thus determines, though he may not foresee, his machine's action. And since God is omniscient, and since his creation of things is total, he both determines and foresees the ways in which his creatures will act. We may grant this, but it is beside the point. The question is not whether God *originally* determined the future actions of his creatures, but whether he can *subsequently* control their actions, or whether he was able in his original creation to put things beyond his subsequent control. Even on determinist principles the answers "Yes" and "No" are equally irreconcilable with God's omnipotence.

Before suggesting a solution of this paradox, I would point out that there is a parallel Paradox of Sovereignty. Can a legal sovereign make a law restricting its own future legislative power? For example, could the British parliament make a law forbidding any future parliament to socialise banking, and also forbidding the future repeal of this law itself? Or could the British parliament, which was legally sovereign in Australia in, say, 1899, pass a valid law, or series of laws, which made it no longer sovereign in 1933? Again, neither the affirmative nor the negative answer is really satisfactory. If we were to answer "Yes," we should be admitting the validity of a law which, if it were actually made, would mean that parliament was no longer sovereign. If we were to answer "No," we should be admitting that there is a law, not logically absurd, which parliament cannot validly make, that is, that parliament is not now a legal sovereign. This paradox can be solved in the following way. We should distinguish between first order laws, that is laws governing the actions of individuals and bodies other than the legislature, and second order laws, that is laws about laws, laws governing the actions of the legislature itself. Correspondingly, we should distinguish two orders of sovereignty, first order sovereignty (sovereignty (1)) which is unlimited authority to make first order laws, and second order sovereignty (sovereignty (2)) which is unlimited authority to make second order laws. If we say that parliament is sovereign we might mean that any parliament at any time has sovereignty (1), or we might mean that parliament has both sovereignty

(1) and sovereignty (2) at present, but we cannot without contradiction mean both that the present parliament has sovereignty (2) and that every parliament at every time has sovereignty (1), for if the present parliament has sovereignty (2) it may use it to take away the sovereignty (1) of later parliaments. What the paradox shows is that we cannot ascribe to any continuing institution legal sovereignty in an inclusive sense.

The analogy between omnipotence and sovereignty shows that the paradox of omnipotence can be solved in a similar way. We must distinguish between first order omnipotence (omnipotence (1)), that is unlimited power to act, and second order omnipotence (omnipotence (2)), that is unlimited power to determine what powers to act things shall have. Then we could consistently say that God all the time has omnipotence (1), but if so no beings at any time have powers to act independently of God. Or we could say that God at one time had omnipotence (2), and used it to assign independent powers to act to certain things, so that God thereafter did not have omnipotence (1). But what the paradox shows is that we cannot consistently ascribe to any continuing being omnipotence in an inclusive sense.

An alternative solution of this paradox would be simply to deny that God is a continuing being, that any times can be assigned to his actions at all. But on this assumption (which also has difficulties of its own) no meaning can be given to the assertion that God made men with wills so free that he could not control them. The paradox of omnipotence can be avoided by putting God outside time, but the freewill solution of the problem of evil cannot be saved in this way, and equally it remains impossible to hold that an omnipotent God *binds himself* by causal or logical laws.

Conclusion

Of the proposed solution of the problem of evil which we have examined, none has stood up to criticism. There may be other solutions which require examination, but this study strongly suggests that there is no valid solution of the problem which does not modify at least one of the constituent propositions in a way which would seriously affect the essential core of the theistic position.

Quite apart from the problem of evil, the paradox of omnipotence has shown that God's omnipotence must in any case be restricted in one way or another, that unqualified omnipotence cannot be ascribed to any being that continues through time. And if God and his actions are not in time, can omnipotence, or power of any sort, be meaningfully ascribed to him?

Why God Allows Evil
Richard Swinburne

The world . . . contains much evil. An omnipotent God could have prevented this evil, and surely a perfectly good and omnipotent God would have done so. So why is there this evil? Is not its existence strong evidence against the existence of God? It would be unless we can construct what is known as a theodicy, an explanation of why God would allow such evil to occur. I believe that that can be done, and I shall outline a theodicy. . . . I emphasize that . . . in writing that God would do this or that, I am not taking for granted the existence of God, but merely claiming that, if there is a God, it is to be expected that he would do certain things, including allowing the occurrence of certain evils; and so, I am claiming, their occurrence is not evidence against his existence.

It is inevitable that any attempt by myself or any one else to construct a theodicy will sound callous, indeed totally insensitive to human suffering. Many theists, as well as atheists, have felt that any attempt to construct a theodicy evinces an immoral approach to suffering. I can only ask the reader to believe that I am not totally insensitive to human suffering, and that I do mind about the agony of poisoning, child abuse, bereavement, solitary imprisonment, and marital infidelity as much as anyone else. True, I would not in most cases recommend that a pastor give this chapter to victims of sudden distress at their worst moment to read for consolation. But this is not because its arguments are unsound; it is simply that most people in deep distress need comfort, not argument. Yet there is a problem about why God allows evil, and, if the theist does not have (in a cool moment) a satisfactory answer to it, then his belief in God is less than rational, and there is no reason why the atheist should share it. To appreciate the argument of this chapter, each of us needs to stand back a bit from the particular situation of his or her own life and that of close relatives and friends (which can so easily seem the only important thing in the world), and ask very generally what good things would a generous and everlasting God give to human beings in the course of a short earthly life. Of course thrills of pleasure and periods of contentment are good things, and—other things being equal—God would certainly seek to provide plenty of those. But a generous God will seek to give deeper good things than these. He will seek to give us great responsibility for ourselves, each other, and the world, and thus a share in his own creative activity of determining what sort of world it is to be. And he will seek to make our lives valuable, of great use to ourselves and each other. The problem is that God cannot give us these goods in full measure without allowing much evil on the way. . . .

[T]here are plenty of evils, positive bad states, which God could if he chose remove. I divide these into moral evils and natural evils. I understand by "natural evil" all evil which is not deliberately produced by human beings and which is not allowed by human beings to occur as a result of their negligence. Natural evil includes both physical suffering and mental suffering, of animals as well as humans; all the trial of suffering which disease, natural disasters, and accidents unpredictable by humans bring in their train. "Moral evil" I understand as including all evil caused deliberately by humans doing what they ought not to do (or allowed to occur by humans negligently failing to do what they ought to do) *and* also the evil constituted by such deliberate actions or negligent failure. It includes the sensory pain of the blow inflicted by the bad parent on his child, the mental pain of the parent depriving the child of love, the starvation allowed to occur in Africa because of negligence by members of foreign governments who could have prevented it, and also the evil of the parent or politician deliberately bringing about the pain or not trying to prevent the starvation.

Moral Evil

The central core of any theodicy must, I believe, be the "free-will defence," which deals—to start with—with moral evil, but can be extended to deal with much natural evil as well. The free-will defence claims that it is a great good that humans have a certain sort of free will which I shall call free and responsible choice, but that, if they do, then necessarily there will be the natural possibility of moral evil. (By the "natural possibility" I mean that it will not be determined in advance whether or not the evil will occur.) A God who gives humans such free will necessarily brings about the possibility, and puts outside his own control whether or not that evil occurs. It is not logically possible—that is, it would be self-contradictory to suppose—that God could give us such free will and yet ensure that we always use it in the right way.

Free and responsible choice is not just free will in the narrow sense of being able to choose between alternative actions, without our choice being causally necessitated by some prior cause. . . . [H]umans could have that kind of free will merely in virtue of being able to choose freely between two equally good and unimportant alternatives. Free and responsible choice is rather free will (of the kind discussed) to make significant choices between good and evil, which make a big difference to the agent, to others, and to the world.

Given that we have free will, we certainly have free and responsible choice. Let us remind ourselves of the difference that humans can make to themselves, others, and the world. Humans have opportunities to give themselves and others pleasurable sensations, and to pursue worthwhile activities—to play tennis or the piano, to acquire knowledge of history and science and philosophy, and to help others to do so, and thereby to build deep personal relations founded upon such sensations and activities. And humans are so made that they can form their characters. Aristotle famously remarked: "we become just by doing just acts, prudent by doing prudent acts, brave by doing brave acts." That is, by doing a just act when it is difficult—when it goes against our natural inclinations (which is what I understand by desires)—we make it easier to do a just act next time. We can gradually change our desires, so that—for example—doing just acts becomes natural. Thereby we can free ourselves from the power of the less good desires to which we are subject. And, by choosing to acquire knowledge and to use it to build machines of various sorts, humans can extend the range of the differences they can make to the world—they can build universities to last for centuries, or save energy for the next generation; and by cooperative effort over many decades they can eliminate poverty. The possibilities for free and responsible choice are enormous.

It is good that the free choices of humans should include *genuine* responsibility for other humans, and that involves the opportunity to benefit *or* harm them. God has the power to benefit or to harm humans. If other agents are to be given a share in his creative work, it is good that they have that power too (although perhaps to a lesser degree). A world in which agents can benefit each other but not do each other harm is one where they have only very limited responsibility for each other. If my responsibility for you is limited to whether or not to give you a camcorder, but I cannot cause you pain, stunt your growth, or limit your education, then I do not have a great deal of responsibility for you. A God who gave agents only such limited responsibilities for their fellows would not have given much. God would have reserved for himself the all-important choice of the kind of world it was to be, while simply allowing humans the minor choice of filling in the details. He would be like a father asking his elder son to look after the younger son, and adding that he would be watching the elder son's every move and would intervene the moment the elder son did a thing wrong. The elder son might justly retort that, while he would be happy to share his father's work, he could really do so only if he were left to make his own judgements as to what to do within a significant range of the options available to the father. A good God, like a good father, will delegate responsibility. In order to allow creatures a share in creation, he will allow them the choice of hurting and maiming, of frustrating the divine plan. Our world is one where creatures have just such deep responsibility for each other. I cannot only benefit my children, but harm them. One way in which I can harm them is that I can inflict physical pain on them. But there are much more damaging things which I can do to them. Above all I can stop them growing into creatures with significant knowledge, power, and freedom; I can determine whether they come to have the kind of free and responsible choice which I have. The possibility of humans bringing about significant evil is a logical consequence of their having this free and responsible choice. Not even God could give us this choice without the possibility of resulting evil.

Now . . . an action would not be intentional unless it was done for a reason—that is, seen as in some way a good thing (either in itself or because of its consequences). And, if reasons alone influence actions, that regarded by the subject as most important will determine what is done; an agent under the influence of reason alone will inevitably do the action which he regards as overall the best. If an agent does not do the action which he regards as overall the best, he must have allowed factors other than reason to exert an influence on him. In other words, he must have allowed desires for what he regards as good only in a certain respect, but not overall, to influence his conduct. So, in order to have a choice between good and evil, agents need already a certain depravity, in the sense of a system of desires for what they correctly believe to be evil. I need to *want* to overeat, get more than my fair share of money or power, indulge my sexual appetites even by deceiving my spouse or partner, want to see you hurt, if I am to have a choice between good and evil. This depravity is itself an evil which is a necessary condition of a greater good. It makes possible a choice made seriously and deliberately, because [it is one] made in the face of a genuine alternative. I stress that, according to the free-will defence, it is the natural possibility of moral evil which is the necessary condition of the great good, not the actual evil itself. Whether that occurs is (through God's choice) outside God's control and up to us.

Note further and crucially that, if I suffer in consequence of your freely chosen bad action, that is not by any means pure loss for me. In a certain respect it is good for *me*. My suffering would be pure loss for me if the only good thing in life was sensory pleasure, and the only bad thing sensory pain; and it is because the modern world tends to think in those terms that the problem of evil seems so acute. If these were the only good and bad things, the occurrence of suffering would indeed be a conclusive objection to the existence of God. But we have already noted the great good of freely choosing and influencing our future, that of our fellows, and that of the world. And now note another great good—the good of our life serving a purpose, of being of use to ourselves and others. Recall the words of Christ, "it is more blessed to give than to receive" (as quoted by St. Paul (Acts 20: 35)). We tend to think, when the beggar appears on our doorstep and we feel obliged to give and do give, that that was lucky for him but not for us who happened to be at home. That is not what Christ's words say. They say that *we* are the lucky ones, not just because we have a lot, out of which we can give a little, but because we are privileged to contribute to the beggar's happiness—and that privilege is worth a lot more than money. And, just as it is a great good freely to choose to do good, so it is also a good to be used by someone else for a worthy purpose (so long, that is, that he or she has the right, the authority, to use us in this way). Being allowed to suffer to make possible a great good is a privilege, even if the privilege is forced upon you. Those who are allowed to die for their country and thereby save their country from foreign oppression are privileged. Cultures less obsessed than our own by the evil of purely physical pain have always recognized that. And they have recognized that it is still a blessing, even if the one who died had been conscripted to fight.

And even twentieth-century man can begin to see that—sometimes—when he seeks to help prisoners, not by giving them more comfortable quarters, but by letting them help the handicapped; or when he pities rather than envies the "poor little rich girl" who has everything and does nothing for anyone else. And one phenomenon prevalent in end-of-century Britain draws this especially to our attention—the evil of unemployment. Because of our system of Social Security, the unemployed on the whole have enough money to live without too much discomfort;

certainly they are a lot better off than are many employed in Africa or Asia or Victorian Britain. What is evil about unemployment is not so much any resulting poverty but the uselessness of the unemployed. They often report feeling unvalued by society, of no use, "on the scrap heap." They rightly think it would be a good for them to contribute; but they cannot. Many of them would welcome a system where they were obliged to do useful work in preference to one where society has no use for them.

It follows from that fact that being of use is a benefit for him who is of use, and that those who suffer at the hands of others, and thereby make possible the good of those others who have free and responsible choice, are themselves benefited in this respect. I am fortunate if the natural possibility of my suffering if you choose to hurt me is the vehicle which makes your choice really matter. My vulnerability, my openness to suffering (which necessarily involves my actually suffering if you make the wrong choice), means that you are not just like a pilot in a simulator, where it does not matter if mistakes are made. That our choices matter tremendously, that we can make great differences to things for good or ill, is one of the greatest gifts a creator can give us. And if my suffering is the means by which he can give you that choice, I too am in this respect fortunate. Though of course suffering is in itself a bad thing, my good fortune is that the suffering is not random, pointless suffering. It is suffering which is a consequence of my vulnerability which makes me of such use.

Someone may object that the only good thing is not *being* of use (dying for one's country or being vulnerable to suffering at your hands), but *believing* that one is of use—believing that one is dying for one's country and that this is of use; the "feel-good" experience. But that cannot be correct. Having comforting beliefs is only a good thing if they are true beliefs. It is not a good thing to believe that things are going well when they are not, or that your life is of use when it is not. Getting pleasure out of a comforting falsehood is a cheat. But if I get pleasure out of a true belief, it must be that I regard the state of things which I believe to hold to be a good thing. If I get pleasure out of the true belief that my daughter is doing well at school, it must be that I regard it as a good thing that my daughter does well at school (whether or not I believe that she is doing well). If I did not think the latter, I would not get any pleasure out of believing that she is doing well. Likewise, the belief that I am vulnerable to suffering at your hands, and that that is a good thing, can only be a good thing if being vulnerable to suffering at your hands is itself a good thing (independently of whether I believe it or not).

Certainly, when my life is of use and that is a good for me, it is even better if I believe it and get comfort therefrom; but it can only be even better if it is already a good for me whether I believe it or not.

But though suffering may in these ways serve good purposes, does God have the right to allow me to suffer for your benefit, without asking my permission? For surely, an objector will say, no one has the right to allow one person A to suffer for the benefit of another one B without A's consent. We judge that doctors who use patients as involuntary objects of experimentation in medical experiments which they hope will produce results which can be used to benefit others are doing something wrong. After all, if my arguments about the utility of suffering are sound, ought we not all to be causing suffering to others in order that those others may have the opportunity to react in the right way?

There are, however, crucial differences between God and the doctors. The first is that God as the author of our being has certain rights, a certain authority over us, which we do not have over our fellow humans. He is the cause of our existence at each moment of our existence and sustains the laws of nature which give us everything we are and have. To allow someone to suffer for his own good or that of others, one has to stand in some kind of parental relationship towards him. I do not have the right to let some stranger suffer for the sake of some good, when I could easily prevent this, but I do have *some* right of this kind in respect of my own children. I may let the younger son suffer *somewhat* for his own good or that of his brother. I have this right because in small part I am responsible for the younger son's existence, his beginning and continuance. If I have begotten him, nourished, and educated him, I have some limited rights over him in return; to a *very limited* extent I can use him for some worthy purpose. If this is correct, then a God who is so much more the author of our being than are our parents has so much more right in this respect. Doctors do have over us even the rights of parents.

But secondly and all-importantly, the doctors *could* have asked the patients for permission; and the patients, being free agents of some power and knowledge, could have made an informed choice of whether or not to allow themselves to be used. By contrast, God's choice is not about how to use already existing agents, but about the sort of agents to make and the sort of world into which to put them. In God's situation there are no agents to be asked. I am arguing that it is good that one agent A should have deep responsibility for another B (who in turn could have deep responsibility for another C). It is not logically possible for God to have asked B if he wanted things thus, for, if A is to be responsible for B's growth in freedom, knowledge, and power, there will not be a B with enough freedom and knowledge to make any choice, before God has to choose whether or not to give A responsibility for him. One cannot ask a baby into which sort of world he or she wishes to be born. The creator has to make the choice independently of his creatures. He will seek on balance to benefit them—all of them. And, in giving them the gift of life—whatever suffering goes with it—that is a substantial benefit. But when one suffers at the hands of another, often perhaps it is not enough of a benefit to outweigh the suffering. Here is the point to recall that it is an additional benefit to the sufferer that his suffering is the means whereby the one who hurt him had the opportunity to make a significant choice between good and evil which otherwise he would not have had.

Although for these reasons, as I have been urging, God has the right to allow humans to cause each other to suffer, there must be a limit to the amount of suffering which he has the right to allow a human being to suffer for the sake of a great good. A parent may allow an elder child to have the power to do some harm to a younger child for the sake of the responsibility given to the elder child; but there are limits. And there are limits even to the moral right of God, our creator and sustainer, to use free sentient beings as pawns in a greater game. Yet, if these limits were too narrow, God would be unable to give humans much real responsibility; he would be able to allow them only to play a toy game. Still, limits there must be to God's rights to allow humans to hurt each other; and limits there are in the world to the extent to which they can hurt each other, provided above all by the short finite life enjoyed by humans and other creatures—one human can hurt another for no more than eighty years or so. And there are a number of other safety-devices in-built into our physiology and psychology, limiting the amount of pain we can suffer. But the primary safety limit is that provided by the shortness of our finite life. Unending, unchosen suffering would indeed to my mind provide a very strong argument against the existence of God. But that is not the human situation.

So then God, without asking humans, has to choose for them between the kinds of world in which they can live—basically either a world in which there is very little opportunity for humans to benefit or harm each other, or a world in which there is considerable opportunity. How shall he choose? There are clearly reasons for both choices. But it seems to me (just, on balance) that his choosing to create the world in which we have considerable opportunity to benefit or harm each other is to bring about a good at least as great as the evil which he thereby allows to occur. *Of course* the suffering he allows is a bad thing; and, other things being equal, to be avoided. But having the natural possibility of causing suffering makes possible a greater good. God, in creating humans who (of logical necessity) cannot choose for themselves the kind of world into which they are to come, plausibly exhibits his goodness in making for them the heroic choice that they come into a risky world where they may have to suffer for the good of others.

Natural Evil

Natural evil is not to be accounted for along the same lines as moral evil. Its main role rather, I suggest, is to make it possible for humans to have the kind of choice which the free-will defence extols, and to make available to humans specially worthwhile kinds of choice.

There are two ways in which natural evil operates to give humans those choices. First, the operation of natural laws producing evils gives humans knowledge (if they choose to seek it) of how to bring about such evils themselves. Observing you catch some disease by the operation of natural processes gives me the power either to use those processes to give that disease to other people, or through negligence to allow others to catch it, or to take measures to prevent others from catching the disease. Study of the mechanisms of nature producing various evils (and goods) opens up for humans a wide range of choice. This is the way in which in fact we learn how to bring about (good and) evil. But could not God give us the requisite knowledge (of how to bring about good or evil) which we need in order to have free and responsible choice by a less costly means? Could he not just whisper in our ears from time to time what are the different consequences of different actions of ours? Yes. But anyone who believed that an action of his would have some effect because he believed that God had told him so would see all his actions as done under the all-watchful eye of God. He would not merely believe strongly that there was a God, but would know it with real certainty. That knowledge would greatly inhibit his freedom of choice, would make it very difficult for him to choose to do evil. This is because we all have a natural inclination to wish to be thought well of by everyone, and above all by an all-good God; that we have such an inclination is a very good feature of humans, without which we would be less than human. Also, if we were directly informed of the consequences of our actions, we would be deprived of the choice whether to seek to discover what the consequences were through experiment and hard cooperative work. Knowledge would be available on tap. Natural processes alone give humans knowledge of the effects of their actions without inhibiting their freedom, and if evil is to be a possibility for them they must know how to allow it to occur.

The other way in which natural evil operates to give humans their freedom is that it makes possible certain kinds of action towards it between which agents can choose. It increases the range of significant choice. A particular natural evil, such as physical pain, gives to the sufferer a choice—whether to endure it with patience, or to bemoan his lot. His friend can choose whether to show compassion towards the sufferer, or to be callous. The pain makes possible these choices, which would not otherwise exist. There is no guarantee that our actions in response to the pain will be good ones, but the pain gives us the opportunity to perform good actions. The good or bad actions which we perform in the face of natural evil themselves provide opportunities for further choice—of good or evil stances towards the former actions. If I am patient with my suffering, you can choose whether to encourage or laugh at my patience; If I bemoan my lot, you can teach me by word and example what a good thing patience is. If you are sympathetic, I have then the opportunity to show gratitude for the sympathy; or to be so self-involved that I ignore it. If you are callous, I can choose whether to ignore this or to resent it for life. And so on. I do not think that there can be much doubt that natural evil, such as physical pain, makes available these sorts of choice. The actions which natural evil makes possible are ones which allow us to perform at our best and interact with our fellows at the deepest level.

It may, however, be suggested that adequate opportunity for these great good actions would be provided by the occurrence of moral evil without any need for suffering to be caused by natural processes. You can show courage when threatened by a gunman, as well as when threatened by cancer; and show sympathy to those likely to be killed by gunmen as well as to those likely to die of cancer. But just imagine all the suffering of mind and body caused by disease, earthquake, and accident unpreventable by humans removed at a stroke from our society. No sickness, no bereavement in consequence of the untimely death of the young. Many of us would then have such an easy life that we simply would not have much opportunity to show courage or, indeed, manifest much in the way of great goodness at all. We need those insidious processes of decay and dissolution which money and strength cannot ward off for long to give us the opportunities, so easy otherwise to avoid, to become heroes.

God has the right to allow natural evils to occur (for the same reason as he has the right to allow moral evils to occur)—up to a limit. It would, of course, be crazy for God to multiply evils more and more in order to give endless opportunity for heroism, but to have *some* significant opportunity for real heroism and consequent character formation is a benefit for the person to whom it is given. Natural evils give to us the knowledge to make a range of choices between good and evil, and the opportunity to perform actions of especially valuable kinds.

There is, however, no reason to suppose that animals have free will. So what about their suffering? Animals had been suffering for a long time before humans appeared on this planet—just how long depends on which animals are conscious beings. The first thing to take into account here is that, while the higher animals, at any rate the vertebrates, suffer, it is most unlikely that they suffer nearly as much as humans do. Given that suffering depends directly on brain events (in turn caused by events in other parts of the body), then, since the lower animals do not suffer at all and humans suffer a lot, animals of intermediate complexity (it is reasonable to suppose) suffer only a moderate amount. So, while one does need a theodicy to account for why God allows animals to suffer, one does not need as powerful a theodicy as one does in respect of humans. One only needs reasons adequate to account for God allowing an amount of suffering much less than that of humans. That said, there is, I believe, available for animals parts of the theodicy which I have outlined above for humans.

The good of animals, like that of humans, does not consist solely in thrills of pleasure. For animals, too, there are more worthwhile things, and in particular intentional actions, and among them serious significant intentional actions. The life of animals involves many serious significant intentional actions. Animals look for a mate, despite being tired and failing to find one. They take great trouble to build nests and feed their young, to decoy predators and explore. But all this inevitably involves pain (going on despite being tired) and danger. An animal cannot intentionally avoid forest fires, or take trouble to rescue its offspring from forest fires, unless there exists a serious danger of getting caught in a forest fire. The action of rescuing despite danger simply cannot be done unless the danger exists—and the danger will not exist unless there is a significant natural probability of being caught in the fire. Animals do not choose freely to do such actions, but the actions are nevertheless worthwhile. It is great that animals feed their young, not just themselves; that animals explore when they know it to be dangerous; that animals save each other from predators, and so on. These are the things that give the lives of animals their value. But they do often involve some suffering to some creature.

To return to the central case of humans—the reader will agree with me to the extent to which he or she values responsibility, free choice, and being of use very much more than thrills of pleasure or absence of pain. There is no other way to get the evils of this world into the right perspective, except to reflect at length on innumerable very detailed thought experiments (in addition to actual experiences of life) in which we postulate very different sorts of worlds from our own, and then ask ourselves whether the perfect goodness of God would require him to create one of these (or no world at all) rather than our own. But I conclude with a very small thought experiment, which may help to begin this process. Suppose that you exist in another world before your birth in this one, and are given a choice as to the sort of life you are to have in this one. You are told that you are to have only a short life, maybe of only a few minutes, although it will be an adult life in the sense that you will have the richness of sensation and belief characteristic of adults. You have a choice as to the sort of life you will have. You can have either a few minutes of very considerable pleasure, of the kind produced by some drug such as heroin, which you will experience by yourself and which will have no effects at all in the world (for example, no one else will know about it); or you can have a few minutes of considerable pain, such as the pain of childbirth, which will have (unknown to you at the time of pain) considerable good effects on others over a few years. You are told that, if you do not make the second choice, those others will never exist—and so you are under no moral obligation to make the second choice. But you seek to make the choice which will make *your* own life the best life for *you* to have led. How will you choose? The choice is, I hope, obvious. You should choose the second alternative.

For someone who remains unconvinced by my claims about the relative strengths of the good and evils involved—holding that, great though the goods are, they do not justify the evils which they involve—there is a fallback position. My arguments may have convinced you of the greatness of the goods involved sufficiently for you to allow that a perfectly good God would be justified in bringing about the evils for the sake of the good which they make possible, if and only if God also provided compensation in the form of happiness after death to the victims whose sufferings make possible the goods. . . . While believing that God does provide at any rate for many humans such life after death, I have expounded a theodicy without relying on this assumption. But I can understand someone thinking that the assumption is needed, especially when we are considering the worst evils. (This compensatory afterlife need not necessarily be the everlasting life of Heaven.)

It remains the case, however, that evil is evil, and there is a substantial price to pay for the goods of our world which it makes possible. God would not be less than perfectly good if he created instead a world without pain and suffering, and so without the particular goods which those evils make possible. Christian, Islamic, and much Jewish tradition claims that God has created worlds of both kinds—our world, and the Heaven of the blessed. The latter is a marvelous world with a vast range of possible deep goods, but it lacks a few goods which our world contains, including the good of being able to reject the good. A generous God might well choose to give some of us the choice of rejecting the good in a world like ours before giving to those who embrace it a wonderful world in which the former possibility no longer exists.

The Ethics of Belief
William Clifford

A shipowner was about to send to sea an emigrant ship. He knew that she was old, and not over-well built at the first; that she had seen many seas and climes, and often had needed repairs. Doubts had been suggested to him that possibly she was not seaworthy. These doubts preyed upon his mind and made him unhappy; he thought that perhaps he ought to have her thoroughly overhauled and refitted, even though this should put him to great expense. Before the ship sailed, however, he succeeded in overcoming these melancholy reflections. He said to himself that she had gone safely through so many voyages and weathered so many storms that it was idle to suppose she would not come safely home from this trip also. He would put his trust in Providence, which could hardly fail to protect all these unhappy families that were leaving their fatherland to seek for better times elsewhere. He would dismiss from his mind all ungenerous suspicions about the honesty of builders and contractors. In such ways he acquired a sincere and comfortable conviction that his vessel was thoroughly safe and seaworthy; he watched her departure with a light heart, and benevolent wishes for the success of the exiles in their strange new home that was to be; and he got his insurance money when she went down in mid-ocean and told no tales.

What shall we say of him? Surely this, that he was verily guilty of the death of those men. It is admitted that he did sincerely believe in the soundness of his ship; but the sincerity of his conviction can in no wise help him, because *he had no right to believe on such evidence as was before him.* He had acquired his belief not by honestly earning it in patient investigation, but by stifling his doubts. And although in the end he may have felt so sure about it that he could not think otherwise, yet inasmuch as he had knowingly and willingly worked himself into that frame of mind, he must be held responsible for it.

Let us alter the case a little, and suppose that the ship was not unsound after all; that she made her voyage safely, and many others after it. Will that diminish the guilt of her owner? Not one jot. When an action is once done, it is right or wrong forever; no accidental failure of its good or evil fruits can possibly alter that. The man would not have been innocent, he would only have been not found out. The question of right or wrong has to do with the origin of his belief, not the matter of it; not what is was, but how he got it; not whether it turned out to be true or false, but whether he had a right to believe on such evidence as was before him.

There was once an island in which some of the inhabitants professed a religion teaching neither the doctrine of original sin nor that of eternal punishment. A suspicion got abroad that the professors of this religion had made use of unfair means to get their doctrines taught to children. They were accused of wresting the laws of their country in such a way as to remove children from the care of their natural and legal guardians; and even of stealing them away and keeping them concealed from their friends and relations. A certain number of men formed themselves into a society for the purpose of agitating the public about this matter. They published grave accusations against individual citizens of the highest position and character, and did all in their power to injure these citizens in the exercise of their professions. So great was the noise they made that a Commission was appointed to investigate the facts; but after the Commission had carefully inquired into all the evidence that could be got, it appeared that the accused were innocent. Not only had they been accused on insufficient evidence, but the evidence of their innocence was such as the agitators might easily have obtained, if they had attempted a fair inquiry. After these disclosures the inhabitants of that country looked upon the members of the agitating society, not only as persons whose judgement was to be distrusted, but also as no longer to be counted honourable men. For although they had sincerely and conscientiously believed in the charges they had made, *yet they had no right to believe on such evidence as was before them.* Their sincere convictions, instead of being honestly earned by patient inquiring, were stolen by listening to the voice of prejudice and passion.

Let us vary this case also, and suppose, other things remaining as before, that a still more accurate investigation proved the accused to have been really guilty. Would this make any difference in the guilt of the accusers? Clearly not; the question is not whether their belief was true or false, but whether they entertained it on wrong grounds. They would no doubt say, 'Now you see that we were right after all; next time perhaps you will believe us.' And they might be believed, but they would not thereby become honourable men. They would not be innocent, they would only be not found out. Every one of them, if he chose to examine himself *in foro conscientiae,* would know that he had acquired and nourished a belief, when he had no right to believe on such evidence as was before him; and therein he would know that he had done a wrong thing.

It may be said, however, that in both of these supposed cases it is not the belief which is judged to be wrong, but the action following upon it. The shipowner might say, 'I am perfectly certain that my ship is sound, but still I feel it my duty to have her examined, before trusting the lives of so many people to her.' And it might be said to the agitator, 'However convinced you were of the justice of your cause and the truth of your convictions, you ought not to have made a public attack upon any man's character until you had examined the evidence on both sides with the utmost patience and care.'

In the first place, let us admit that, so far as it goes, this view of the case is right and necessary; right, because even when a man's belief is so fixed that he cannot think otherwise, he still has a choice in regard to the action suggested by it, and so cannot escape the duty of investigating on the ground of the strength of his convictions; and necessary, because those who are not yet capable of controlling their feelings and thoughts must have a plain rule dealing with overt acts.

But this being premised as necessary, it becomes clear that it is not sufficient, and that our previous judgment is required to supplement it. For it is not possible so to sever the belief from the action it suggests as to condemn the one without condemning the other. No man holding a strong belief on one side of a question, or even wishing to hold a belief on one side, can investigate it with such fairness and completeness as if he were really in doubt and unbiased; so that the existence of a belief not founded on fair inquiry unfits a man for the performance of this necessary duty.

Nor is that truly a belief at all which has not some influence upon the actions of him who holds it. He who truly believes that which prompts him to an action has looked upon that action to lust after it, he has committed it already in his heart. If a belief is not realized immediately in open deeds, it is stored up for the guidance of the future. It goes to make a part of that aggregate of beliefs which is the link between sensation and action at every moment of all our lives, and which is so organized and compacted together that no part of it can be isolated from the rest, but every new addition modifies the structure of the whole. No real belief, however trifling and fragmentary it may seem, is ever truly insignificant; it prepares us to receive more of its like, confirms those which resembled it before, and weakens others; and so gradually it lays a stealthy train in our inmost thoughts, which may some day explode into overt action, and leave its stamp upon our character for ever.

And no one man's belief is in any case a private matter which concerns himself alone. Our lives are guided by that general conception of the course of things which has been created by society for social purposes. Our words, our phrases, our forms and processes and modes of thought, are common property, fashioned and perfected from age to age; an heirloom which every succeeding generation inherits as a precious deposit and a sacred trust to be handed on to the next one, not unchanged but enlarged and purified, with some clear marks of its proper handiwork. Into this, for good or ill, is woven every belief of every man who has speech of his fellows. An awful privilege, and an awful responsibility, that we should help to create the world in which posterity will live.

In the two supposed cases which have been considered, it has been judged wrong to believe on insufficient evidence, or to nourish belief by suppressing doubts and avoiding investigation. The reason of this judgement is not far to seek: it is that in both these cases the belief held by one man was of great importance to other men. But forasmuch as no belief held by one man, however seemingly trivial the belief, and however obscure the believer, is ever actually insignificant or without its effect on the fate of mankind we have no choice but to extend our judgement to all cases of belief whatever. Belief, that sacred faculty which prompts the decisions of our will, and knits into harmonious working all the compacted energies of our being, is ours not for ourselves, but for humanity. It is rightly used on truths which have been established by long experience and waiting toil, and which have stood in the fierce light of free and fearless questioning. Then it helps to bind men together, and to strengthen and direct their common action. It is desecrated when given to unproved and unquestioned statements, for the solace and private pleasure of the believer; to add a tinsel splendour to the plain straight road of our life and display a bright mirage beyond it; or even to drown the common sorrows of our kind by a self-deception which allows them not only to cast down, but also to degrade us. Whoso would deserve well of his fellows in this matter will guard the purity of his belief with a very fanaticism of jealous care, lest at any time it should rest on an unworthy object, and catch a stain which can never be wiped away.

It is not only the leader of men, statesman, philosopher, or poet, that owes this bounden duty to mankind. Every rustic who delivers in the village alehouse his slow, infrequent sentences, may help to kill or keep alive the fatal superstitions which clog his race. Every hard-worked wife of an artisan may transmit to her children beliefs which shall knit society together, or rend it in pieces. No simplicity of mind, no obscurity of station, can escape the universal duty of questioning all that we believe.

It is true that this duty is a hard one, and the doubt which comes out of it is often a very bitter thing. It leaves us bare and powerless where we thought that we were safe and strong. To know all about anything is to know how to deal with it under all circumstances. We feel much happier and more secure when we think we know precisely what to do, no matter what happens, than when we have lost our way and do not know where to turn. And if we have supposed ourselves to know all about anything, and to be capable of doing what is fit in regard to it, we naturally do not like to find that we are really ignorant and powerless, that we have to begin again at the beginning, and try to learn what the thing is and how it is to be dealt with—if indeed anything can be learnt about it. It is the sense of power attached to a sense of knowledge that makes men desirous of believing, and afraid of doubting.

This sense of power is the highest and best of pleasures when the belief on which it is founded is a true belief, and has been fairly earned by investigation. For then we may justly feel that it is common property, and holds good for others as well as for ourselves. Then we may be glad, not that *I* have learned secrets by which I am safer and stronger, but that *we men* have got mastery over more of the world; and we shall be strong, not for ourselves, but in the name of Man and in his strength. But if the belief has been accepted on insufficient evidence, the pleasure is a stolen one. Not only does it deceive ourselves by giving us a sense of power which we do not really possess, but it is sinful, because it is stolen in defiance of our duty to mankind. That duty is to guard ourselves from such beliefs as from a pestilence, which may shortly master our own body and then spread to the rest of the town. What would be thought of one who, for the sake of a sweet fruit, should deliberately run the risk of bringing a plague upon his family and his neighbours?

And, as in other such cases, it is not the risk only which has to be considered; for a bad action is always bad at the time when it is done, no matter what happens afterwards. Every time we let ourselves believe for unworthy reasons, we weaken our powers of self-control, of doubting, of judicially and fairly weighing evidence. We all suffer severely enough from the maintenance and support of false beliefs and the fatally wrong actions which they lead to, and the evil born when one such belief is entertained is great, and wide. But a greater and wider evil arises when the credulous character is maintained and supported, when a habit of believing for unworthy reasons is fostered and made permanent. If I steal money from any person, there may be no harm done by the mere transfer of possession; he may not feel the loss, or it may prevent him from using the money badly. But I cannot help doing this great wrong towards Man, that I make myself dishonest. What hurts society is not that it should lose its property, but that it should become a den of thieves; for then it must cease to be society. This is why we ought not to do evil that good may come; for at any rate this great evil has come, that we have done evil and are made wicked thereby. In like manner, if I let myself believe anything on insufficient evidence, there may be no great harm done by the mere belief; it may be true after all, or I may never have occasion to exhibit it in outward acts. But I cannot help doing this great wrong towards Man, that I make myself credulous. The danger to society is not merely that it should believe wrong things, though that is great enough; but that it should become credulous, and lose the habit of resting things and inquiring into them; for then it must sink back into savagery.

The harm which is done by credulity in a man is not confined to the fostering of a credulous character in others, and consequent support of false beliefs. Habitual want of care about what I believe leads to habitual want of care in others about the truth of what is told to me. Men speak the truth to one another when each reveres the truth in his own mind and in the other's mind; but how shall my friend revere that truth in my mind when I myself am careless about it, when I believe things because I want to believe them, and because they are comforting and pleasant? Will he not learn to cry, 'Peace,' to me, when there is no peace? By such a course I shall surround myself with a thick atmosphere of falsehood and fraud, and in that I must live. It may matter little to me, in my cloud-castle of sweet illusions and darling lies; but it matters such to Man that I have made my neighbours ready to deceive. The credulous man is father to the liar and the cheat; he lives in the bosom of this his family, and it is no marvel if he should become even as they are. So closely are our duties knit together, that whoso shall keep the whole law, and yet offend in one point, he is guilty of all.

To sum up: it is wrong always, everywhere, and for any one, to believe anything upon insufficient evidence.

If a man, holding a belief which he was taught in childhood or persuaded of afterwards, keeps down and pushes away any doubts which arise about it in his mind, purposely avoids the reading of books and the company of men that call in question or discuss it, and regards as impious those questions which cannot easily be asked without disturbing it—the life of that man is one long sin against mankind.

If this judgement seems harsh when applied to those simple souls who have never known better, who have been brought up from the cradle with a horror of doubt, and taught that their eternal welfare depends on *what* they believe, then it leads to the very serious question, *Who hath made Israel to sin?*

It may be permitted me to fortify this judgement with the sentence of Milton:

> A man may be a heretic in the truth; and if he believe things only because his pastor says so, or the assembly so determine, without knowing other reason, though his belief be true, yet the very truth he holds becomes his heresy. (*Areopagitica*)

And with this famous aphorism of Coleridge:

He who begins by loving Christianity better than Truth, will proceed by loving his own sect or Church better than Christianity, and end in loving himself better than all. (*Aids to Reflection*)

Inquiry into the evidence of a doctrine is not to be made once for all, and then taken as finally settled. It is never lawful to stifle a doubt; for either it can be honestly answered by means of the inquiry already made, or else it proves that the inquiry was not complete.

'But,' says one, 'I am a busy man; I have not time for the long course of study which would be necessary to make me in any degree a competent judge of certain question, or even able to understand the nature of the arguments.' Then he should have no time to believe.

The Will to Believe*
William James

[. . .] Let us give the name of hypothesis to anything that may be proposed to our belief; and just as the electricians speak of live and dead wires, let us speak of any hypothesis as either *live* or *dead*. A live hypothesis is one which appeals as a real possibility to him to whom it is proposed. If I ask you to believe in the Mahdi, the notion makes no electric connection with your nature—it refuses to scintillate with any credibility at all. As an hypothesis it is completely dead. To an Arab, however (even if he be not one of the Mahdi's followers), the hypothesis is among the mind's possibilities: It is alive. This shows that deadness and liveness in an hypothesis are not intrinsic properties, but relations to the individual thinker. They are measured by his willingness to act. The maximum of liveness in an hypothesis means willingness to act irrevocably: Practically, that means belief; but there is some believing tendency wherever there is willingness to act at all.

Next, let us call the decision between two hypotheses an *option*. Options may be of several kinds. They may be first, *living* or *dead*; secondly, *forced* or *avoidable*; thirdly, *momentous* or *trivial*; and for

*This essay, originally an address delivered before the Philosophical Clubs of Yale and Brown Universities, was first published in 1896.

our purposes we may call an option a *genuine* option when it is of the forced, living, and momentous kind.

1. A living option is one in which both hypotheses are live ones. If I say to you: "Be a theosophist or be a Mohammedan," it is probably a dead option, because for you neither hypothesis is likely to be alive. But if I say: "Be an agnostic or be a Christian," it is otherwise; trained as you are, each hypothesis makes some appeal, however small, to your belief.

2. Next, if I say to you: "Choose between going out with your umbrella or without it," I do not offer you a genuine option, for it is not forced. You can easily avoid it by not going out at all. Similarly, if I say, "Either love me or hate me," "Either call my theory true or call it false," your option is avoidable. You may remain indifferent to me, neither loving nor hating, and you may decline to offer any judgment as to my theory. But if I say, "Either accept this truth or go without it," I put on you a forced option, for there is no standing place outside of the alternative. Every dilemma based on a complete logical disjunction, with no possibility of not choosing, is an option of this forced kind.

3. Finally, if I were Dr. Nansen and proposed to you to join my North Pole expedition, your option would be momentous; for this would probably be your only similar opportunity, and your choice now would either exclude you from the North Pole sort of immortality altogether or put at least the chance of it into your hands. He who refuses to embrace a unique opportunity loses the prize as surely as if he tried and failed. *Per contra,* the option is trivial when the opportunity is not unique, when the stake is insignificant, or when the decision is reversible if it later prove unwise. Such trivial options abound in the scientific life. A chemist finds an hypothesis live enough to spend a year in its verification: he believes in it to that extent. But if his experiments prove inconclusive either way, he is quit for his loss of time, no vital harm being done.

It will facilitate our discussion if we keep all these distinctions well in mind

[. . .] Evidently, then, our non-intellectual nature does influence our convictions. There are passional tendencies and volitions which run before and others which come after belief, and it is only the latter that are too late for the fair; and they are not too late when the previous passional work has been already in their own direction. [. . .] The state of things is evidently far from simple; and pure insight and logic, whatever they might do ideally, are not the only things that really do produce our creeds.

Our next duty, having recognized this mixed-up state of affairs, is to ask whether it be simply reprehensible and pathological, or whether, on the contrary, we must treat it as a normal element in making up our minds. The thesis I defend is, briefly stated, this: *Our passional nature not only lawfully may, but must, decide an option between propositions, whenever it is a genuine option that cannot by its nature be decided on intellectual grounds; for to say, under such circumstances, "Do not decide, but leave the question open," is itself a passional decision—just like deciding yes or no—and is attended with the same risk of losing the truth. The thesis thus abstractly expressed will, I trust, soon be quite clear* . . .

One more point, small but important, and our preliminaries are done. There are two ways of looking at our duty in the matter of opinion— ways entirely different, and yet ways about whose difference the theory of knowledge seems hitherto to have shown very little concern. *We must know the truth*; and *we must avoid error*—these are our first and great commandments as would-be knowers; but they are not two ways of stating an identical commandment, they are two separable laws. Although it may indeed happen that when we believe the truth A, we escape as an incidental consequence from believing the falsehood B, it hardly ever happens that by merely disbelieving B we necessarily believe A. We may in escaping B fall into believing other falsehoods, C or D, just as bad as B; or we may escape B by not believing anything at all, not even A.

Believe truth! Shun error!—these, we see, are two materially different laws; and by choosing between them we may end by coloring differently our whole intellectual life. We may regard the chase for truth as paramount, and the avoidance of error as secondary; or we may, on the other hand, treat the avoidance of error as more imperative, and let truth take its chance. Clifford, in the instructive passage which I have quoted, exhorts us to the latter course. Believe nothing, he tells us, keep your mind in suspense forever, rather than by closing it on insufficient evidence incur the awful risk of believing lies. You, on the other hand, may think that the risk of being in error is a very small matter when compared with the blessings of real knowledge, and be ready to be duped many times in your investigation rather than postpone indefinitely the chance of guessing true. I myself find it impossible to go with Clifford. We must remember that these feelings of our duty about either truth or error are in any case only expressions of our passional life. Biologically considered, our minds are as ready to grind out falsehood as veracity, and he who says, "Better go without belief forever than believe a lie!" merely shows his own preponderant private horror of becoming a dupe. He may be critical of many of his desires and fears, but this fear he slavishly obeys. He cannot imagine any one questioning its binding force. For my own part, I have also a horror of being duped; but I can believe that worse things than being duped may happen to a man in this world: so Clifford's exhortation has to my ears a thoroughly fantastic sound. It is like a general informing his soldiers that it is better to keep out of battle forever than to risk a single wound. Not so are victories either over enemies or over nature gained. Our errors are surely not such awfully solemn things. In a world where we are so certain to incur them in spite of all our caution, a certain lightness of heart seems healthier than this excessive nervousness on their behalf. At any rate, it seems the fittest thing for the empiricist philosopher.

And now, after all this introduction, let us go straight at our question. I have said, and now repeat it, that not only as a matter of fact do we find our passional nature influencing us in our opinions, but that there are some options between opinions in which this influence must be regarded both as an inevitable and as a lawful determinant of our choice.

I fear here that some of you my hearers will begin to scent danger, and lend an inhospitable ear. Two first steps of passion you have indeed had to admit as necessary—we must think so as to avoid dupery, and we must think so as to gain truth; but the surest path to those ideal consummations, you will probably consider, is from now onwards to take no further passional step.

Well, of course, I agree as far as the facts will allow. Wherever the option between losing truth and gaining it is not momentous, we can throw the chance of *gaining truth* away, and at any rate save ourselves from any chance of *believing falsehood,* by not making up our minds at all till objective evidence has come. In scientific questions, this is almost always the case; and even in human affairs in general, the need of acting is seldom so urgent that a false belief to act on is better than no belief at all. Law courts, indeed, have to decide on the best evidence attainable for the moment, because a judge's duty is to make law as well as to ascertain it, and (as a learned judge once said to me) few cases are worth spending much time over; the great thing is to have them decided on *any* acceptable principle, and got out of the way. But in our dealings with objective nature we obviously are recorders, not makers, of the truth; and decisions for the mere sake of deciding promptly and getting on to the next business would be wholly out of place. Throughout the breadth of physical nature facts are what they are quite independently of us, and seldom is there any such hurry about them that the risks of being duped by believing a premature theory need be faced. The questions here are always trivial options, the hypotheses are hardly living (at any rate not living for us spectators), the choice between believing truth or falsehood is seldom forced. The attitude of sceptical balance is therefore the absolutely wise one if we would escape mistakes. What difference, indeed, does it make to most of us whether we have or have not a theory of the Röntgen rays, whether we believe or not in mind-stuff, or have a conviction about the causality of conscious states? It makes no difference. Such options are not forced on us. On every account it is better not to make them, but still keep weighing reasons *pro et contra* with an indifferent hand.

I speak, of course, here of the purely judging mind. For purposes of discovery such indifference is to be less highly recommended, and science would be far less advanced than she is if the passionate desires of individuals to get their own faiths confirmed had been kept out of the game. See for example the sagacity which Spencer and Weismann now display. On the other hand, if you want an absolute duffer in an investigation, you must, after all, take the man who has no interest whatever in its results: he is the warranted incapable, the positive fool. The most useful investigator, because the most sensitive observer, is always he whose eager interest in one side of the question is balanced by an equally keen nervousness lest he become deceived.[1] Science has organized this nervousness into a regular *technique,* her so-called method of verification; and she has fallen so deeply in love with the method that one may even say she has ceased to care for truth by itself at all. It is only truth as technically verified that interests her. The truth of truths might come in merely affirmative form, and she would decline to touch it. Such truth as that, she might repeat with Clifford, would be stolen in defiance of her duty to mankind. Human passions, however, are stronger than technical rules. "*Le coeur a ses raisons,*" as Pascal says, "*que la raison ne connait pas*";[2] and however indifferent to all but the bare rules of the game the umpire, the abstract intellect, may be, the concrete players who furnish him the materials to judge of are usually, each one of them, in love with some pet "live hypothesis" of his own. Let us agree, however, that wherever there is no forced option, the dispassionately judicial intellect with no pet hypothesis, saving us, as it does, from dupery at any rate, ought to be our ideal.

The question next arises: Are there not somewhere forced options in our speculative questions, and can we (as men who may be interested at least as much in positively gaining truth as in merely escaping dupery) always wait with impunity till the coercive evidence shall have arrived? It seems *a priori* improbable that the truth should be so nicely adjusted to our needs and powers as that. In the great boarding-house of nature, the cakes and the butter and the syrup seldom come out so even and leave the plates so clean. Indeed, we should view them with scientific suspicion if they did.

Moral questions immediately present themselves as questions whose solution cannot wait for sensible proof. A moral question is a question not of what sensibly exists, but of what is good, or would be good if it did exist. Science can tell us what exists; but to compare the *worths,* both of what exists and of what does not exist, we must consult not science, but what Pascal calls our heart. . . .

Turn now from these wide questions of good to a certain class of questions of fact, questions concerning personal relations, states of mind between one man and another. *Do you like me or not?*—for example. Whether you do or not depends, in countless instances, on whether I meet you halfway, am willing to assume that you must like me, and show you trust and expectation. The previous faith on my part in your liking's existence is in such cases what makes your liking come. But if I stand aloof, and refuse to budge an inch until I have objective evidence, until you shall have done something apt, as the absolutists say, *ad extorquendum assensum meum,* ten to one your liking never comes. How many women's hearts are vanquished by the mere sanguine insistence of some man that they *must* love him! He will not consent to the hypothesis that they cannot. The desire for a certain kind of truth here brings about that special truth's existence; and so it is in innumerable cases of other sorts. . . . *And where faith in a fact can help create the fact,* that would be an insane logic which should say that faith running ahead of scientific evidence is the "lowest kind of immorality" into which a thinking being can fall. Yet such is the logic by which our scientific absolutists pretend to regulate our lives!

In truths dependent on our personal action, then, faith based on desire is certainly a lawful and possibly an indispensable thing.

But now, it will be said, these are all childish human cases, and have nothing to do with great cosmical matters, like the question of religious faith. Let us then pass on to that. Religions differ so much in their accidents that in discussing the religious question we must make it very generic and broad. What then do we now mean by the religious hypothesis? Science says things are; morality says some things are better than other things; and religion says essentially two things.

First, she says that the best things are the more eternal things, the overlapping things, the things in the universe that throw the last stone, so to speak, and say the final word. "Perfection is eternal"—this phrase of Charles Secrétan seems a good way of putting this first affirmation of religion, an affirmation which obviously cannot yet be verified scientifically at all.

The second affirmation of religion is that we are better off even now if we believe her first affirmation to be true.

Now, let us consider what the logical elements of this situation are *in case the religious hypothesis in both its branches be really true.* (Of course, we must admit that possibility at the outset. If we are to discuss the question at all, it must involve a living option. If for any of you religion be a hypothesis that cannot, by any living possibility, be true, then you need go no farther. I speak to the "saving remnant" alone.) So proceeding, we see, first, that religion offers itself as a *momentous* option. We are supposed to gain, even now, by our belief, and to lose by our non-belief, a certain vital good. Secondly, religion is a *forced* option, so far as that good goes. We cannot escape the issue by remaining sceptical and waiting for more light, because, although we do avoid error in that way *if religion be untrue,* we lose the good, *if it be true,* just as certainly as if we positively chose to disbelieve. It is as if a man should hesitate indefinitely to ask a certain woman to marry him because he was not perfectly sure that she would prove an angel after he brought her home. Would he not cut himself off from that particular angel-possibility as decisively as if he went and married some one else? Scepticism, then, is not avoidance of option; it is option of a certain particular kind of risk. *Better risk loss of truth than chance of error*—that is your faith-vetoer's exact position. He is actively playing his stake as much as the believer is; he is backing the field against the religious hypothesis, just as the believer is backing the religious hypothesis against the field. To preach scepticism to us as a duty until "sufficient evidence" for religion be found, is tantamount therefore to telling us, when in presence of the religious hypothesis, that to yield to our fear of its being error is wiser and better than to yield to our hope that it may be true. It is not intellect against all passion, then; it is only intellect with one passion laying down its law. And by what, forsooth, is the supreme wisdom of this passion warranted? Dupery for dupery, what proof is there that dupery through hope is so much worse than dupery through fear? I, for one, can see no proof; and I simply refuse obedience to the scientist's command to imitate his kind of option, in a case where my own stake is important enough to give me the right to choose my own form of risk. If religion be true and the evidence for it be still insufficient, I do not wish, by putting your extinguisher upon my nature (which feels to me as if it had after all some business in this matter), to forfeit my sole chance in life of getting upon the winning side—that chance depending, of course, on my willingness to run the risk of acting as if my passional need of taking the world religiously might be prophetic and right.

All this is on the supposition that it really may be prophetic and right, and that, even to us who are discussing the matter, religion is a live hypothesis which may be true. Now, to most of us religion comes in a still further way that makes a veto on our active faith even more illogical. The more perfect and more eternal aspect of the universe is represented in our religions as having personal form. The universe is no longer a mere *It* to us, but a *Thou,* if we are religious; and any relation that may be possible from person to person might be possible here. For instance, although in one sense we are passive portions of the universe, in another we show a curious autonomy, as if we were small active centers on our own account. We feel, too, as if the appeal of religion to us were made to our own active goodwill, as if evidence might be forever withheld from us unless we met the hypothesis halfway to take a trivial illustration: just as a man who in a company of gentlemen made no advances, asked a warrant for every concession, and believed no one's word without proof, would cut himself off by such churlishness from all the social rewards that a more trusting spirit would earn—so here, one who should shut himself up in snarling logicality and try to make the gods extort his recognition willy-nilly, or not get it at all, might cut himself off forever from his only opportunity of making the gods' acquaintance. This feeling, forced on us we know not whence that by obstinately believing that there are gods (although not to do so would be so easy both for our logic and our life) we are doing the universe the deepest service we can, seems part of the living essence of the religious hypothesis. If the hypothesis *were* true in all its parts, including this one, then pure intellectualism, with its veto on our making willing advances, would be an absurdity; and some participation of our sympathetic nature would be logically required. I therefore, for one, cannot see my way to accepting the agnostic rules for truth-seeking, or wilfully agree to keep my willing nature out of the game. I cannot do so for this plain reason, that *a rule of thinking which would absolutely prevent me from acknowledging certain kinds of truth if those kinds of truth were really there, would be an irrational rule.* That for me is the long and short of the formal logic of the situation, no matter what the kinds of truth might materially be.

I confess I do not see how this logic can be escaped. But sad experience makes me fear that some of you may still shrink from radically saying with me, *in abstracto,* that we have the right to believe at our own risk any hypothesis that is live enough to tempt our will. I suspect, however, that if this is so, it is because you have got away from the abstract logical point of view altogether, and are thinking (perhaps without realizing it) of some particular religious hypothesis which for you is dead. The freedom to "believe what we will" you apply to the case of some patent superstition; and the faith you think of is the faith defined by the schoolboy when he said, "Faith is when you believe something that you know ain't true." I can only repeat that this is misapprehension. *In concreto,* the freedom to believe can only cover living options which the intellect of the individual cannot by itself resolve; and living options never seem absurdities to him who has them to consider. When I look at the religious question as it really puts itself to concrete men, and when I think of all the possibilities which both practically and theoretically it involves, then this command that we shall put a stopper on our heart, instincts, and courage, and *wait*—acting of course meanwhile more or less as if religion were *not* true[3]—till doomsday, or till such time as our intellect and senses working together may have raked in evidence enough—this command, I say, seems to me the queerest idol ever manufactured in the philosophic cave. Were we scholastic absolutists, there might be more excuse. If we had an infallible intellect with its objective certitudes, we might feel ourselves disloyal to such a perfect organ of knowledge in not trusting to it exclusively, in not waiting for its releasing word. But if we are empiricists, if we believe that no bell in us tolls to let us know for certain when truth is in our grasp, then it seems a piece of idle fantasticality to preach so solemnly our duty of waiting for the bell. Indeed we *may* wait if we will—I hope you do not think that I am denying that—but if we do so, we do so at our peril as much as if we believed. In either case we *act,* taking our life in our hands. No one of us ought to issue vetoes to the other, nor should we bandy words of abuse. We ought, on the contrary, delicately and profoundly to respect one another's mental freedom: then only shall we bring about the intellectual republic; then only shall we have that spirit of inner tolerance without which all our outer tolerance is soulless, and which is empiricism's glory; then only shall we live and let live, in speculative as well as in practical things.

I began by a reference to Fitz-James Stephen; let me end by a quotation from him. "What do you think of yourself? What do you think of the world? . . . These are questions with which all must deal as it seems good to them. They are riddles of the Sphinx, and in some way or other we must deal with them. . . . In all important transactions of life we have to take a leap in the dark. . . . If we decide to leave the riddles unanswered, that is a choice; if we waver in our answer, that, too, is a choice: but whatever choice we make, we make it at our peril. If a man chooses to turn his back altogether on God and the future, no one can prevent him; no one can show beyond reasonable doubt that he is mistaken. If a man thinks otherwise and acts as he thinks, I do not see that any one can prove that *he* is mistaken. Each must act as he thinks best; and if he is wrong, so much the worse for him. We stand on a mountain pass in the midst of whirling snow and blinding mist, through which we get glimpses now and then of paths which may be deceptive. If we stand still we shall be frozen to death. If we take the wrong road we shall be dashed to pieces. We do not certainly know whether there is any right one. What must we do? 'Be strong and of a good courage.' Act for the best, hope for the best, and take what comes. . . . If death ends all, we cannot meet death better."[4]

Notes

1. Compare Wilfrid Ward's Essay "The Wish to Believe," in his *Witnesses to the Unseen* (Macmillan & Co., 1893).
2. "The heart has its reasons which reason does not know." Editor's Trans.
3. Since belief is measured by action, he who forbids us to believe religion to be true, necessarily also forbids us to act as we should if we did believe it to be true. The whole defence of religious faith hinges upon action. If the action required or inspired by the religious hypothesis is in no way different from that dictated by the naturalistic hypothesis, then religious faith is a pure superfluity, better pruned away, and controversy about its legitimacy is a piece of idle trifling, unworthy of serious minds. I myself believe, of course, that the religious hypothesis gives to the world an expression which specifically determines our reactions, and makes them in a large part unlike what they might be on a purely naturalistic scheme of belief.
4. *Liberty, Equality, Fraternity,* p. 353, 2nd edition (London, 1874).

Male-Chauvinist Religion

Deborah Mathieu

Man for the field and woman for the hearth
Man for the sword and for the needle she
Man with the head and woman with the heart
Man to command and woman to obey
All else confusion.
      ALFRED, LORD TENNYSON[1]

All functioning societies rely on a division of labor: some individuals raise children, some produce food, some construct roads, some adjudicate disputes, and so on. Occasionally these tasks overlap, but often they do not. How do societies decide who does what? How, in other words, are rights and responsibilities allocated?

There is no one universally accepted method of determining which people will perform which roles, and often a given society will employ several methods. One common distributive standard is age: no one over a certain age or under a certain age may perform certain functions. Another distributive standard is ability: an intelligent person with a sense of fairness may adjudicate disputes, for instance, while a brawny person willing to work hard may construct roads. Yet another common standard is gender: males perform one set of tasks while females perform another. There are other allocative standards as well: race, religion, family, class, education, and so on.

The United States has employed all of these (and more) to determine who does what. Most of the criteria are unfair most of the time: your family name, for instance, should be irrelevant to your career (unless you work in the family business), as should your theology (unless you work as a religious official). But I am not concerned with all unfair standards, just with one: gender. If positions are allocated according to gender, then no female—regardless of her talents, her education, her aspirations—may perform those tasks assigned to males.

During the many decades in which the United States used gender as a principle method of distribution, a woman could wash clothes but she could not shine shoes, she could be a barmaid but not a bartender, she could raise children but could not hold public office. Women could not be lawyers, serve on juries, operate elevators, or mine coal. Indeed, it was once illegal in this country for women to perform *most* jobs outside the home.[2] This type of occupational gender segregation, of course, is very common around the world. One result is that work traditionally performed by women—rearing children, cleaning house, teaching grammar school—though necessary and often arduous, is usually undervalued and underpaid.[3]

The separation of tasks according to gender typically means that males act in the public sphere of politics and paid work while females stay in the private sphere of the home. But why would an intelligent woman with a robust sense of fairness concede that she should spend her time cleaning house instead of refereeing disputes? Why would any woman acquiesce to any sort of gender stereotyping, especially when the results are harmful to her?

The answer is simple and somewhat frightening: she believes that only certain narrowly defined roles are appropriate for her. Why would she believe that? Because every facet of her society—the media, her schools, her books, her friends, her parents, even her toys—have conspired to convince her that it is so.

One of the most powerful tools in this respect is religion, for it tells people not only what is proper and good, but what is holy and unholy, natural and unnatural. Having certain activities branded by a sacred text as unholy or unnatural when performed by females certainly helps ensure that females will avoid those activities. Equally inhibiting are declarations from religious leaders. Public declarations by a few Islamic *ulama* that women may not drive automobiles, for instance, surely have more clout than the private remonstrations of a multitude of husbands. In short, when important distinctions are made along gender lines, religious doctrines and practices are valuable instruments of indoctrination.

Of the many male-chauvinist religions, three have been especially successful in relegating females to inferior positions: Christianity, Islam, and Judaism. In addition to the institutionalization of patriarchal, even misogynistic, mores and practices, these familiar religions have much in common: belief in one and only one supreme being, identification of one book as a record of its god's words and deeds, characterization of its god as male, emphasis on compassion, and status as a major world religion. The relationship among these factors is fascinating, especially the roles they have played in the subjugation of females.

Misogyny on High

The practices of Christianity, Islam, and Judaism originated when males and females were assigned different social roles in life: males in the public sphere, females in the private.[4] Because the males' role included designing the rules, they designed the rules to favor themselves. One of the most important rules, of course, was that only males could craft the rules.

This separation of roles extended to religion, so the males designed the rules there as well: they formulated the beliefs and practices, they created the institutions, they controlled the rituals. It should be no surprise, then, that the resulting religions explicitly reinforced the belief that males are superior to females and endorsed a set of social relations in which males controlled females.[5]

Religious practices demonstrated this message constantly. Females could not be religious leaders, and they could be religious participants only from a distance. They were not permitted near the holy sanctuaries, allowed to speak (or sing) in the church/mosque/synagogue, or even allowed to read the holy books. Of course the religious teachings were often harshly judgmental of females. A leader of the early Christian church, for instance, went so far as to blame human sin and suffering on females:

> The sentence of God on this sex of yours lives in this age: the guilt must of necessity live too. You are the Devil's gateway; you are the first deserter of the divine law; you are she who persuaded him whom the devil was not valiant enough to attack. You so carelessly destroyed man, God's image. On account of your desert, even the Son of God had to die.[6]

Indeed, all facets of the religions could be used to dishonor females, even prayer. Every morning, for instance, the Jewish man was expected to thank God: "Blessed art thou, O Lord our God, King of the Universe, who has not made me a woman."

And yet, despite their malice toward the female sex, these three religions flourished. How could this be? How could a theology that demeaned females become a significant religion throughout the world? How could something so blatantly one-sided and unfair gain such legitimacy? It is easy to imagine the existence of a few all-male cults built around the idea (and it is just an idea) of male superiority. But why would millions of sensible women support three worldwide religions based on that idea? How could reasonable women believe in these gods?

Co-opting Females

The first part of the explanation relates to the high value all three religions place on compassion and equality. All virtuous people are equal in the sight of God, the holy books proclaim. To honor each other is to honor God, the books declare, so be kind to each other, show concern for the vulnerable, help those less fortunate, be fair in all your dealings. No doubt females heard these words and believed them, despite the mountains of evidence to the contrary.

The second, and less comforting, reason females accepted these religions is related to the need of those who wield power to justify that status quo to themselves and to others. Men claiming such inordinate power needed to mollify any misgivings the advantaged might have and to gain the acquiescence of the disadvantaged. The benefits of this to those who make and enforce the rules are obvious: if people believe that the status quo is the best system, they will not fight against it, and the privileged can maintain their position (relatively) peacefully.

Therefore males used their religion to brainwash females into accepting the theory of male superiority as fact. The technique has been effective because of its multi-faceted approach: it appeals to the female's intellect as well as her emotions.

The crux of the male's argument for supremacy over females is inherent in all three religions: the contention that the one and only true god is male. Thus the very cores of all three theologies were deployed to subjugate females. The results were devastatingly successful, as well as successfully devastating.

The basic deductive argument is built around two simple syllogisms of the following classic form:

If P, Then Q.
P
_____
Therefore Q.

The first part of the argument goes like this:

If god is male, then human males are more like god than human females are.

God is male.
_____
Therefore human males are more like god than human females are.

The second part of the argument is:

If human males are more like god than human females are, then human males are superior to human females.

Human males are more like god than human females are.
_____
Therefore human males are superior to human females.

The argument is not a sound one. But it still has power, for if you accept the premises, then the conclusions follow inevitably and indisputably.

Those conclusions have led to the disenfranchisement of females, especially within the religions themselves. Why couldn't Christian women be priests? Because a priest impersonates (the male) Christ during Eucharist. Why must Jewish women sit behind a screen in the synagogue, away from the sanctuary? Because they are too flawed to be near the holy objects. Why must Islamic women cover their entire bodies even though Allah commanded only that they dress modestly? Because the (male) *ulama* interpret Allah otherwise, and they know better. Why were women prevented from conducting the religious ceremonies, setting the rules, designing the practices? Because of their inherent inferiority to the men who do. And why is a woman's labor rewarded less than a man's? Need we ask?

It is curious that the deductive arguments noted above could ever be persuasive, for under scrutiny they collapse. Both syllogisms suffer from the same flaw: they rely on premises that are open to dispute. The first shaky premise is the assertion that god is male. It need not be so. Indeed, there are other, equally plausible alternatives: god may be female, or neither male nor female, or both male and female. In short, one may believe in the existence of god and yet deny that god is male.[7] This seems a sound approach for religious females to take, especially as it is to their advantage to do so.

Feminist theologians have staunchly advocated this approach. But this is a very recent development; for thousands of years women agreed that god was male, and many women still do. Why? Because that contention enjoys powerful support: the holy books of the three religions. According to the Jewish *Tenakh,* the Christian *Bible,* and the Islamic *Qur'an,* god is male. Yahweh, Christ, and Allah all have male attributes and male sobriquets: Lord of Hosts, God the Father, God the Son, King of the Universe, He who gives life and death, He who exalts. If you accept any of these books as literally true, then you are likely to view your god as male.

But if females believe that their god is male, and therefore refuse to challenge that part of the argument, they still may challenge another, equally shaky premise: the contention that, if human males are more like god than human females are, then human males are superior to human females. Other plausible options are available here, too. If the god is an inferior one, for instance, then being similar to him may not be an asset; perhaps being similar to god in some way makes one, not better than another, but more vulnerable. Perhaps being different (i.e., female) makes someone more, not less, fit to rule.

Of course the holy books can be used to rebut this challenge as well. God is magnificent, omnipotent, omniscient, wonderful in every way, the three books declare. To be like him, then, is to have positive attributes. And to be unlike him is to have negative attributes. It follows that because males are like god and females are not, males must be superior to females. And surely superior beings should rule inferior ones.

This argument could be broken down into a set of syllogisms, each of which would have at least one shaky premise. But the response would be the same as above: an appeal could be made to any of the three holy books to attest to the inevitability, the undeniability, the universality of female subordinacy. In short, if god is male, then females are in trouble. It is that simple.

This brings us to the second component of religious brainwashing: the appeal to emotions. The religious ceremonies and teachings were designed to make females feel both accepted (if they conform to certain standards) and unacceptable (because of their inherent unworthiness). They were designed, as well, to make the females doubt themselves.

Imagine how a woman might feel as she listened to St. Paul's Letter to the Ephesians read as part of the day's religious ceremony:

> Wives, submit yourselves unto your own husbands, as unto the Lord. For the husband is the head of the wife, even as Christ is the head of the church, and he is the savior of the body. Therefore, as the church is subject unto Christ, so let the wives be to their own husbands in every thing. (Eph 5:22–24)[8]

How would a female feel, seated in the back of the synagogue behind a screen during every religious service of her life? How would she feel when her presence in the synagogue is not even counted toward the quorum needed for a service? How would she feel, covered in black from head to foot in the blazing sun of a desert summer? Would she be angry? Would she be offended? Or might she instead feel inferior, inadequate?

And how might she feel when she realizes that all meaningful choices in life are denied to her? How might she feel when she is told—in school, at home, and in her place of worship—that males are superior to females? Might she come to believe that her want of options, as well as her lack of power, was natural? On what basis might she think otherwise?

And if she believes that everyone else accepts the proposition that she is second-rate, simply because she is female, is she likely to rebel? Is she even likely to question the system? Or is she more apt to question her own feelings, to distrust her ability to understand? If no one else believes that she is intelligent, or even rational, is she likely to presume it? If no one else believes she is capable of performing anything other than the most routine, mundane tasks, will she? Probably not.

So what is the result? Is she likely to be brimming with confidence and self-respect, eager to strike out on her own to make her way in the world? Is she likely to question the foundations of the dominant religion, to argue forcefully against the unfairness of the system? Or is she more likely to be someone who is fearful and insecure, someone who is subservient to others?

The answer is obvious: she behaves as you would expect someone who has been marginalized all her life would behave. She does what she is told, she acquiesces to the system, she accepts her fate. Perhaps she suffers from low self-esteem, perhaps she is passive and dependent and anxious. She behaves, in other words, like an unempowered female. After all, the whole system is designed to make her this way.

In short, males have heavy-handedly used these three religions to advance their own interests and to justify their having the upper hand. It can even be argued that the basic features of the religions—belief in one and only one supreme being, identification of one book as a record of the god's words and deeds, and characterization of its god as male— were designed to augment male domination over female members of his species. Perhaps even the purported emphasis on compassion and equality was merely a smokescreen hiding the truth, a cruel hoax played on females to entice them to acquiesce in their own destruction.

Misogyny and Monotheism

The question is, then, how important is male chauvinism to these religions? Is the misogyny, in other words, as integral a part as the monotheism?

Four responses to this question merit discussion:

1. "anatomy is destiny"[9]
2. god is a male chauvinist
3. the religious images should be taken symbolically
4. sexism has always been superfluous to these religions.

I will explain each in turn and also offer a rebuttal to each.

1. Anatomy Is Destiny

The contention here is that the three religions accurately reflect the fact that males and females are different types of beings. Males are rational while females are emotional; males are rule-oriented while females are relationship-oriented; males are domineering while females are submissive; males are properly heads of households while females are their helpmates; males belong in the public sphere while females belong in the private sphere. It has been this way since time immemorial. It has been this way, not because males have unfairly dominated females, but because it is the natural course of life. This is the way the world was designed, it is the way the world works, and all reasonable people recognize it. To fight this natural order is to invite disaster.

We have heard declarations like these for centuries; but all of them are wrong, terribly, tragically wrong. A female is not by nature someone who stays home to raise children, wash clothes, and bake bread. Nor is she by nature subservient to males. She becomes that type of person by adopting a certain gender role, a view of what is acceptable for her to do/say/think as a female. Gender roles are social constructions that begin at birth, not biological determinates beginning at conception.

There is one question everyone asks when told of a birth: Is it a boy or a girl? We ask because it makes a difference to us; we need to know how to treat this new being. We dress a male differently from a female; we address a male differently from a female; we expect different behaviors from a male than from a female. The children, of course, internalize these differences, and behave accordingly. They tend to repeat behaviors we have rewarded and reinforced, just as they tend to avoid behaviors we have punished and discouraged. They learn gender differences in other ways as well: from observation, for instance, and by generalizing from one type of experience to another.

These patterns continue throughout their lives, as males and females adapt to the dissimilar social expectations and mores imposed on them. The interplay of their behaviors with variations in treatment by others creates different life experiences. And these different life experiences form different sorts of people—people with the characteristics of distinct genders—with different feelings, beliefs, and skills. This, then, is how gender is constructed. And because gender roles are social constructs, they vary from culture to culture, and may even vary within a culture over time.

This is not to say that there are no biological differences between male and female humans; of course there are. The contrasts are sometimes obvious (such as their dramatically dissimilar reproductive organs), sometimes less noticeable (the two X chromosomes of a typical female, versus the one X chromosome and one Y of a typical male). The point is, rather, that these biological differences are less significant than the cultural ones in determining the ways males and females operate in the world. In other words, in the nature/nurture debate, I am arguing that the evidence indicates that more weight should be given to nurture than nature when it comes to gender differences.[10]

It is difficult, though, to convince skeptics of the validity of an ambiguous stance like this: it is true that there are innate differences between males and females *and* that gender is a largely social construct. In contrast, positions on the outside boundaries of the debate offer the comfort of firm absolutes. At one end are the postmodernists, who reject grand explanatory theories in general and theories of innate human traits in particular; all of our options and preferences, they argue, are the result of cultural influences. And at the other end are their archenemies, the sociobiologists, who argue that myriad human traits are genetically based. I am suggesting, instead, that the truth lies somewhere between the two; that, while genes exert a probabalistic influence on human behavior, their influence is muted dramatically by the environment.

This is not the place, however, to engage at length in the contentious nature/nurture debate that has raged across disciplines for years (and which shows no signs of abating). Suffice it to say that it seems clear to me that anatomy is not destiny (at least with regard to most gender differences), that females are not inherently inferior to males, and that cultural conditioning shapes most gender roles.

2. God Is a Male Chauvinist

Nothing about the nature of god follows from my criticisms of these three religions. And I offer no propositions about the true nature of god, or even about the existence of god. Instead, let us assume for the sake of argument that these three religions are correct: god exists and he is a male chauvinist. In this case, it does not matter whether males and females are inherently different because god has designated separate social roles for them. And if we wish to obey god's will, then we will treat males and females as different. If one result is that the members of one gender wield most of the power, then so be it.

This position raises a fundamental question about the response of females to god. Would a male chauvinist god be likely to inspire love in females? Would a biased, unfair god inspire awe? Or devotion? Or would such a being inspire some other reaction in females: something closer to wrath, perhaps, or resentment?

When confronted with a god who consigns you to a drab, dull existence, wouldn't you be angry? When told during religious services that

you are base and inferior, simply because of the design of your genitalia, wouldn't you be indignant? Or perhaps Nelle Morton illustrates
the proper tone for a female to adopt:

> No one is wise enough to know why God made female reproductive
> organs compact and internal so that woman is physically free to move
> about unencumbered and take her natural place of leadership in the
> world of womankind. Or why God made a male's organs external and
> exposed, so that he would demand sheltering and protection from the
> outside in order that he may be kept for reproducing the race.[11]

Surely Morton is correct that the situation calls for at least a little irony.
Maybe even a good dose of sarcasm. But not love, certainly not love.
Fear might be appropriate perhaps, given the unsavory outcomes for
females, but not love. And not awe. After all, there is nothing splendid
about a sexist god. And should we even consider such a limited being to
be a god?

But females did not spurn the gods of these three religions, at least
not generally. Nor were anger, indignation, and irony the typical
responses of females to these gods or their religions. Instead,
Christianity, Islam, and Judaism became powerful in part because of
their female adherents.

That is because attitudes such as irony and indignation are possible
only if you are able to step back from the god, to view the religion
clearly. Females were prevented from doing precisely that. One successful method was to deny them access to education (so they could not
read the holy books themselves) as well as access to any decision-
making processes. Another, equally effective method was to prey on
their emotions, to make them believe they were somehow inadequate,
even irrational.

But today these techniques are not nearly so widespread nor so
effective. And misogyny is no longer so much in vogue. Eventually, as
sexist social systems disappear, so will sexist religions. And as our
mores change, so must our gods.

3. The Religious Images Should Be Taken Symbolically, Not Literally

One way to save these three religions from the charge of unfair sexism is
to deny that the holy books are literally true. The religious images, it is
argued, should be understood as metaphors, as devices for expounding

profound truths too difficult for the average person to describe (or understand) in the abstract. And abstractions are too impersonal and cold to instill the deeply emotional responses that religious faith requires. It seems more natural, for instance, to love and honor the particularized image of Jesus—a god who became a man in order to die for all human sin—than an abstruse concept of forgiveness.

So religious stories use familiar objects to create images we can grasp and to which we are likely to react with reverence and awe. These images are so powerful that we often forget that they are mere symbols. But that is our failing, not the fault of the holy books. We need to remind ourselves that religious discourse was meant to be taken figuratively, that, for instance, Yahweh's promise in Genesis to deliver his chosen people into a "land flowing with milk and honey" is not a contract at all, and certainly not one guaranteeing a future awash in sweetened dairy products; it is, instead, a reassurance of a brighter future, an exhortation to be hopeful.

It should not be surprising, the argument continues, that some of these images are couched in misogynistic language, given the low status of women at the time the religious works were compiled. But this sexism is only a contingent feature of the religions; the religious tenets can be expressed in nonsexist, even nongendered, language. Thus God need not be seen as a male, but understood instead as a perfect nongendered being, "the being than whom a more perfect being cannot be conceived." In short, we should be able to see beyond these time-bound images to appreciate the deeper truths they contain; we should be able to proceed beyond the sexist language of these ancient works to understand the universalist metaphors they express.

As compelling as this argument appears, it is persuasive only if one is willing to deny reality. Among its many weaknesses, three are worth noting here. The first problem is that even the sophisticated have difficulty being abstract. Can you really imagine what it means to be "the being than whom a more perfect being cannot be conceived" or "a ground of all contingency"? Most people cannot. And that is why religious literature continues to maintain a gendered image of god. Even those who seek to expunge sexism from religious practices find it impossible to erase gender altogether. Take, for instance, the Society for the Promotion of Christian Knowledge, Britain's oldest publisher of religious books, which touts its new, nonsexist prayer book. In it, Christianity's most often recited prayer, the Lord's Prayer, has been cleansed of its male chauvinist overtones. Retitled the "Prayer of Jesus," it now appeals not to a male god or an ungendered god but to an androgynous god. Thus where the prayer once began, "Our father, who art in heaven, hallowed be thy name," it now begins: "Beloved, our father and mother, in whom is heaven, hallowed be your name."[12] The new prayer book has met, of course, with considerable resistance. "I think it's heretical," the Archdeacon of York recently said. "I would walk out of a service if that was read."[13] This attitude is reflected in many places, including the Catholic Mass, which still features the centuries-old Nicene Creed:

> We believe in one God, the Father, Almighty, maker of heaven and earth, of all that is seen and unseen. We believe in one Lord, Jesus Christ, the only Son of God, eternally begotten of the Father....

It seems clear that, while change is coming, it is slow and halting, and leaves untouched millions of lives.

A second and related problem is that one may adopt the theoretical principle that religious images are to be taken symbolically yet fail to accept that precept on an emotional level. It often is the case that "images function powerfully long after they have been repudiated intellectually."[14] Thus we find ourselves making declarations on an intellectual level that we simply do not accept on an emotional level. With religious images tending to honor males and dishonor females, we may find ourselves unconsciously doing the same.

Finally, there is the woeful fact that for thousands of years these images were used to subjugate women. Suggesting that the interpretations may have been mistaken, or that we should understand them figuratively, is insufficient; the sexist language is there, and it has caused terrible harm by marginalizing generations of females. And it continues to do so.

4. Male Chauvinism Is and Always Has Been Superfluous to Christianity, Islam, and Judaism

The holy books of all three religions acknowledge the profound value of females: the account of creation in the *Qur'an* describes the common origin of men and women, as does one of the versions of creation in the *Tenakh*, while the Gospels of the *New Testament* indicate that Christ treated females with respect and compassion. Indeed, all of the holy books give the impression that, in ultimate spiritual terms, males and females are equal.[15] Thus the fact that these religions may have been used by males to subjugate females shows only that males will manipulate anything and everything in order to maintain power; it does not show that these religions are necessarily sexist.

This is both the strongest and the weakest of the countervailing considerations. It is the strongest because it is accurate: I have shown only that male chauvinism is a major part of these three religions, I have not demonstrated that it is an essential part. Nor could I. A few Christian sects (such as Christian Scientists and Quakers) have always treated females as the equals of males; the largest Islamic group, Sunni Muslims, believe that females are as competent as males to perform some religious rites; and there have been Jewish female (reform) rabbis since 1972. Surely these are powerful counterexamples to my arguments.

Yes and no. Yes, they demonstrate that these three religions can exist intact minus a certain degree of misogyny. But no, they are not powerful enough to do the job; the examples are too few, and are overwhelmed by the countless instances of raw sexism. Indeed, many religious sects remain robustly male chauvinist, continuing to justify their stance by reference to their sacred texts and customs. The Catholic Church, for instance, declared as recently as 1995 that women may not be priests, not now, not ever.[16] This is to be expected; in the traditional forms of these religions, men continue to keep most of the interesting and influential roles for themselves.

The contention that the male chauvinism of these religions is only contingently a part of them—that they could exist intact without it—is a serious indictment against those who are unwilling to relinquish it. To hold tight to tradition is to embrace patriarchy. And that is not a pretty picture: it conserves an unfair and damaging conception of what it means to be female; it supports a one-sided power grab, allowing males to monopolize key roles; and it may even, as Mary Daly charges, sustain a hoax, "a front for men's plans and a cover for inadequacy, ignorance, and evil."[17]

The traditional forms of these religions are opting, in short, to cast doubt on the nature and value of religion itself. They are opting, as well, to cast doubt on the existence of an infinitely powerful yet benevolent god, for their disgraceful treatment of females raises the same demanding question posed by all great evils: what kind of god would allow this to happen?

Notes

1. Alfred Lord Tennyson, *The Princess: A Medley*. William J. Rolfe, ed., Cambridge, MA: Riverside Press 1884, lines 437–441.

2. See D. M. Stetson, *Women's Rights in the U.S.A.*, Belmont, CA: Wadsworth, 1991; Carol Hymowitz and Michaele Weissman, *A History of Women in America*, N.Y.: Bantam Books, 1978.

3. See Pamela K. Brubaker, *Women Don't Count*, Atlanta: Scholars Press 1994; *The State of the World's Women, 1985*, Oxford: New International Publications, 1985.

4. For a thoughtful history of the evolution of these three religions, see Karen Armstrong, *A History of God*, N.Y.: Ballentine Books, 1993.

5. Rachel Biale, *Women and Jewish Law*, N.Y.: Schocken, 1986; Mary Daly, *Beyond God the Father*, Boston: Beacon Press, 1973; Alice L. Hageman, ed., *Sexist Religion and Women in the Church*, N.Y.: Association Press, 1974; John S. Hawley, *Fundamentalism and Gender*, N.Y.: Oxford University Press, 1994; Jean Holm, ed. *Women in Religion*, N.Y.:Pinter, 1994; Rosemary R. Ruether, ed. *Images of Women in the Jewish and Christian Traditions*, N.Y.: Simon and Schuster, 1973.

6. Tertullian, *On Female Dress*, I, i. Tertullian, a North African theologian, lived about a hundred years after the death of Christ.

    Note as well the male chauvinist writings of other well-known Christian writers: Augustine, Cyprian, Jerome, Aquinas, Karl Barth, Dietrich Bonhoeffer, and Reinhold Niebuhr.

7. You may also dispute the premise by claiming that there is no god, or at least not one that matters much. Two directions are then possible: you can reject all religious belief, or you can choose a system of spirtual thought, that the second alternative contains its own set of sexist elements. Consider, for instance, Buddhism, a non-theistic religion which emphasizes the human roots of suffering. Although the details of Buddhism change with every culture into which it is introduced, a core set of "Noble Truths" is embraced by nearly all Buddhists: suffering is universal, suffering is a result of desire, to eliminate suffering you must eliminate desire, a path can be followed to achieve freedom from desire and suffering. These tenets are gender-neutral and apply to all, without exception. Yet Buddhism is still tainted by misogyny. According to Buddha himself, for instance, the most senior nun must defer to the most junior monk. And in the system of reincarnation, rebirth as a female is generally considered unfortunate compared to rebirth as a male.

8. See also the words ascribed to Paul in 1 Tim. 2: 12: "But I suffer not a woman to teach, nor to usurp authority over the man, but to be in silence." Interestingly, many contemporary scholars agree that Paul never made any of these sexist remarks, that they were appended later to his letters. See e.g., Robin Scroggs, "Paul and the Eschatological Woman," *Journal of the American Academy of Religion* 40: 283–303, 1972.

9. Freud said this, earning the enmity of feminists. Sigmund Freud, *On Sexuality: Three Essays on the Theory of Sexuality and Other Works*, James Strachey, cn., London: Penguin, 1991.

10. For more on gender socialization see: Pierre Bourdieu, *The Logic of Practice,* Stanford, CA: Stanford University Press, 1990; R. W. Connell, *Gender and Power,* Stanford, CA: Stanford University Press, 1987; Michelle H. Garskof, ed. *Roles Women Play,* Belmont, CA: Belmont/Cole, 1971; Eleanor E. Maccoby, ed. *The Development of Sex Differences,* Stanford, CA: Stanford University Press, 1966; Dorothy E. Smith, *The Everyday World as Problematic,* Toronto: University of Toronto Press, 1987.

11. Nelle Morton, "Preaching the Word," in Alice L. Hageman, ed. *Sexist Religion and Women in the Church,* N.Y.: Association Press, 1974, pp. 30–31.

12. *Including Women: A Non-Sexist Prayer Book* is published by the Society for the Promotion of Christian Knowledge, and has been adopted by some Church of England congregations since 1991.

13. "Equal-opportunity Prayers." *Maclean's* August 5, 1991.

14. Morton, *op. cit.*, p. 32.

15. The *Qur'an* even gave women legal rights of inheritance and divorce, rights most Western women would not gain for over a thousand years.

16. Pope John Paul II issued an apostolic letter in 1994 declaring that the Catholic Church may not ordain women; in 1995 the Vatican's Congregation for the Doctrine of the Faith confirmed that this conclusion was infallible and irrevocable.

17. Mary Daly, *op. cit.*, p. 30.

SECTION SEVEN

WHAT OUGHT WE TO DO?

Most people have a good idea of what is and what is not moral. We feel confident saying that we know that it is morally wrong to hurt others, take what is not ours, or be dishonest. Likewise, we know that, as moral agents, we ought to be kind to others, obey the laws, and help others pursue their interests. Still, very few people could say *why* some actions, motives, or character traits are morally good and others are morally bad. We seem to know that we are governed by certain norms or guidelines, and yet, it is no easy task to explicitly state or justify those norms and guidelines. In the essay "The Objective Basis of Morality," Thomas Nagel deals with the question of why morality should matter at all. Would it not be better to ignore moral rules and to follow our own self interest? Nagel argues that anybody who thinks that their own suffering matters to others, must also think that the suffering of others provides them with a reason to care as well. According to Nagel, "the basis of morality is a belief that good and harm to particular people (or animals) is good or bad not just from their point of view, but from a more general point of view, which every thinking person can understand."

An alternative way to explain the objective nature of morality is to think that God has created universal rules for all human beings. This view is often described as the divine command theory. Although the divine command theory of ethics has some attractive features, many philosophers are convinced that there must be more to morality than divine commands. James Rachels' essay "Must God's Commands Conform to Moral Standards?" describes some standard philosophical difficulties that advocates of the divine command theory have to overcome.

Utilitarianism is one of the best-known philosophical theories of ethics. In the selection from his book *Introduction to the Principles of Morals and*

Legislation, Jeremy Bentham gives us a concise description of the basic principles that underlie classical utilitarianism. A person can call herself a utilitarian if she approves or disapproves of any action in proportion to the effect that the action has on the happiness of the community. Happiness in turn is measured by a careful objective analysis of pleasures and pains, that is, classical utilitarianism embraces a form of hedonism. This hedonistic element in classical utilitarianism leads to some famous disagreements between Jeremy Bentham and John Stuart Mill. Bentham believes that all pleasures are commensurable with each other. In the essay "Push-Pin and Poetry" he argues that "prejudice apart, the game of push-pin is of equal value with the arts and science of music and poetry." John Stuart Mill, on the other hand, disagrees with Bentham on this point. In his essay "Higher and Lower Pleasures" he argues that "it is quite compatible with the principle of utility to recognize the fact that some kinds of pleasures are more desirable and more valuable than others."

Utilitarianism urges us to evaluate actions in the light of the consequence the actions bring about. But not all ethical thinkers agree that such a consequentialist analysis is a promising idea. The philosopher Immanuel Kant, for example, rejected consequentialism and developed instead an alternative theory of ethics. In the selection from his *Groundwork of the Metaphysics* of Morals, he argues that it is not the results of one's action that determine the action's moral worth, but it is what motivates one to act in the first place—one's *reasons or intentions*—that determines whether one's actions are moral. Ultimately, Kant thinks that being moral amounts to being rational and that being immoral amounts be being irrational. Kant's deontological approach to ethics has been tremendously influential but it also leads to some famous difficulties. Rae Langton explores some questions about Kantian ethics by analyzing the correspondence between Immanuel Kant and Maria von Herbert.

In recent times, many philosophers have argued that neither consequentialist nor deontological ethical theories are entirely successful. This critique has sparked renewed interest in ancient ethical theories. We therefore include a selection from Aristotle's *Nicomachean Ethics*. Aristotle's moral theory is concerned with an agent's character—the kind of person one is—and how one acquires a virtuous character. The virtuous person is one who uses reason to govern one's emotions with the goal of being a good person and thus living the good life.

Marilyn Friedman, in her essay "The Practice of Partiality," addresses a discrepancy that arises between what we take to be morally permissible, perhaps even morally mandatory, and what is morally justified on either utilitarian or Kantian grounds—namely, the practice of giving special moral consideration to those with whom we have special relationships. The practice of partiality seems to be inconsistent with the utilitarian's requirement that everyone's happiness count equally, as well as with the Kantian requirement that moral maxims be universalizable. Friedman argues that the commonsense moral intuition that we have certain special duties to those close to us can be justified on the basis of the moral value of the very relationships partiality serves. She offers a characterization of the nature of the relationships that ground these special duties but also recognizes an important pragmatic obstacle to the practice of partiality. Specifically, some people are in a better position than others to satisfy their moral obligations of partially.

Since the primary reason for studying normative ethics is to discover how we ought to live, an essential component to ethical theory is its practical application to resolve genuine moral problems. In applied ethics, we examine ethical problems in light of what we understand about ethical theory. The final readings in this section fall under the heading of applied ethics. In these selections, the authors are defending a particular moral position by making appeals, either implicitly or explicitly, to certain fundamental moral principles. We have provided two sets of essays, each of which addresses a moral question from opposing moral positions.

The first essays address the issue of animal rights. In his essay "The Moral Basis of Vegetarianism," Tom Regan examines a number of reasons one might give for denying rights to animals—arguments grounded upon the ability to feel pain, to communicate, or to reason, but argues that none of these arguments are strong. He concludes by saying that the burden of proof falls to those who would deny that animals have rights. Carl Cohen, in "Do Animals have Rights?" argues that, while we may have certain obligations to animals, it does not follow from this that animals have rights. Rights, he argues, are essentially human.

The final essays in this section address the moral controversy surrounding same-sex marriage. In "The Case for Gay Marriage," Michael Nava and Robert Dawidoff argue that exclusionary marriage laws not only violate the rights of gays and lesbians who would marry if they could, but they harm the institution of marriage, contribute to the instability of relationships, reinforce sexual inequality, and are ultimately unfair.

In "The Case Against Gay Marriage," Manuel Lopez argues that the institution of marriage is a fundamental part of our world, providing guidance that helps people live their lives. Marriage as we know it is bound up with natural sexual differentiation and the potential for reproduction. It is an institution that developed over many centuries to meet the needs of heterosexuals. Gay marriage, on the other hand, would inevitably be a kind of imitation. It could not wholly succeed, and would result in a self-conscious parody. Permitting gay marriage would therefore weaken the institution of marriage for everyone.

The Objective Basis of Morality

Thomas Nagel

[. . .] Suppose you work in a library, checking people's books as they leave, and a friend asks you to let him smuggle out a hard-to-find reference work that he wants to own.

You might hesitate to agree for various reasons. You might be afraid that he'll be caught, and that both you and he will then get into trouble. You might want the book to stay in the library so that you can consult it yourself.

But you may also think that what he proposes is wrong—that he shouldn't do it and you shouldn't help him. If you think that, what does it mean, and what, if anything, makes it true?

To say it's wrong is not just to say it's against the rules. There can be bad rules which prohibit what isn't wrong—like a law against criticizing the government. A rule can also be bad because it requires something that *is* wrong—like a law that requires racial segregation in hotels and restaurants. The ideas of wrong and right are different from the ideas of what is and is not against the rules. Otherwise they couldn't be used in the evaluation of rules as well as of actions.

If you think it would be wrong to help your friend steal the book, then you will feel uncomfortable about doing it: in some way you won't want to do it, even if you are also reluctant to refuse help to a friend. Where does the desire not to do it come from; what is its motive, the reason behind it?

There are various ways in which something can be wrong, but in this case, if you had to explain it, you'd probably say that it would be unfair to other users of the library who may be just as interested in the book as your friend is, but who consult it in the reference room, where anyone

[*What Does it All Mean?* (Oxford University Press: New York, 1987), 59–67.]

who needs it can find it. You may also feel that to let him take it would betray your employers, who are paying you precisely to keep this sort of thing from happening.

These thoughts have to do with effects on others—not necessarily effects on their feelings, since they may never find out about it, but some kind of damage nevertheless. In general, the thought that something is wrong depends on its impact not just on the person who does it but on other people. They wouldn't like it, and they'd object if they found out.

But suppose you try to explain all this to your friend, and he says, 'I know the head librarian wouldn't like it if he found out, and probably some of the other users of the library would be unhappy to find the book gone, but who cares? I want the book; why should I care about them?'

The argument that it would be wrong is supposed to give him a reason not to do it. But if someone just doesn't care about other people, what reason does he have to refrain from doing any of the things usually thought to be wrong, if he can get away with it: what reason does he have not to kill, steal, lie, or hurt others? If he can get what he wants by doing such things, why shouldn't he? And if there's no reason why he shouldn't, in what sense is it wrong?

Of course most people do care about others to some extent. But if someone doesn't care, most of us wouldn't conclude that he's exempt from morality. A person who kills someone just to steal his wallet, without caring about the victim, is not automatically excused. The fact that he doesn't care doesn't make it all right: he *should* care. But *why* should he care?

There have been many attempts to answer this question. One type of answer tries to identify something else that the person already cares about, and then connect morality to it.

For example, some people believe that even if you can get away with awful crimes on this earth, and are not punished by the law or your fellow men, such acts are forbidden by God, who will punish you after death (and reward you if you didn't do wrong when you were tempted to). So even when it seems to be in your interest to do such a thing, it really isn't. Some people have even believed that if there is no God to back up moral requirements with the threat of punishment and the promise of reward, morality is an illusion: 'If God does not exist, everything is permitted.'

This is a rather crude version of the religious foundation for morality. A more appealing version might be that the motive for obeying God's commands is not fear but love. He loves you, and you should love Him, and should wish to obey His commands in order not to offend Him.

But however we interpret the religious motivation, there are three objections to this type of answer. First, plenty of people who don't believe in God still make judgments of right and wrong, and think no one should kill another for his wallet even if he can be sure to get away with it. Second, if God exists, and forbids what's wrong, that still isn't what *makes* it wrong. Murder is wrong in itself, and that's *why* God forbids it (if He does). God couldn't make just any old thing wrong—like putting on your left sock before your right—simply by prohibiting it. If God would punish you for doing that it would be inadvisable to do it, but it wouldn't be wrong. Third, fear of punishment and hope of reward, and even love of God, seem not to be the right motives for morality. If you think it's wrong to kill, cheat, or steal, you should want to avoid doing such things because they are bad things to do to the victims, not just because you fear the consequences for yourself, or because you don't want to offend your Creator.

This third objection also applies to other explanations of the force of morality which appeal to the interests of the person who must act. For example, it may be said that you should treat others with consideration so that they'll do the same for you. This may be sound advice, but it is valid only so far as you think what you do will affect how others treat you. It's not a reason for doing the right thing if others won't find out about it, or against doing the wrong thing if you can get away with it (like being a hit and run driver).

There is no substitute for a direct concern for other people as the basis of morality. But morality is supposed to apply to everyone: and can we assume that everyone has such a concern for others? Obviously not: some people are very selfish, and even those who are not selfish may care only about the people they know, and not about everyone. So where will we find a reason that everyone has not to hurt other people, even those they don't know?

Well, there's one general argument against hurting other people which can be given to anybody who understands English (or any other language), and which seems to show that he has *some* reason to care about others, even if in the end his selfish motives are so strong that he persists in treating other people badly anyway. It's an argument that I'm sure you've heard, and it goes like this: 'How would you like it if someone did that to you?'

It's not easy to explain how this argument is supposed to work. Suppose you're about to steal someone else's umbrella as you leave a restaurant in a rainstorm, and a bystander says, 'How would you like it if someone did that to you?' Why is it supposed to make you hesitate, or feel guilty?

Obviously the direct answer to the question is supposed to be, 'I wouldn't like it at all!' But what's the next step? Suppose you were to say, 'I wouldn't like it if someone did that to me. But luckily no one *is* doing it to me. I'm doing it to someone else, and I don't mind that at all!'

This answer misses the point of the question. When you are asked how you would like it if someone did that to you, you are supposed to think about all the feelings you would have if someone stole your umbrella. And that includes more than just 'not liking it'—as you wouldn't 'like it' if you stubbed your toe on a rock. If someone stole your umbrella you'd *resent* it. You'd have feelings about the umbrella thief, not just about the loss of the umbrella. You'd think, 'Where does he get off, taking my umbrella that I bought with my hard-earned money and that I had the foresight to bring after reading the weather report? Why didn't he bring his own umbrella?' and so forth.

When our own interests are threatened by the inconsiderate behavior of others, most of us find it easy to appreciate that those others have a reason to be more considerate. When you are hurt, you probably feel that other people should care about it: you don't think it's no concern of theirs, and that they have no reason to avoid hurting you. That is the feeling that the 'How would you like it?' argument is supposed to arouse.

Because if you admit that you would *resent* it if someone else did to you what you are now doing to him, you are admitting that you think he would have a reason not to do it to you. And if you admit that, you have to consider what that reason is. It couldn't be just that it's *you* that he's hurting, of all the people in the world. There's no special reason for him not to steal *your* umbrella, as opposed to anyone else's. There's nothing so special about you. Whatever the reason is, it's a reason he would have against hurting anyone else in the same way. And it's a reason anyone else would have too, in a similar situation, against hurting you or anyone else.

But if it's a reason anyone would have not to hurt anyone else in this way, then it's a reason *you* have not to hurt someone else in this way (since *anyone* means *everyone*). Therefore it's a reason not to steal the other person's umbrella now.

This is a matter of simple consistency. Once you admit that another person would have a reason not to harm you in similar circumstances, and once you admit that the reason he would have is very general and doesn't apply only to you, or to him, then to be consistent you have to admit that the same reason applies to you now. You shouldn't steal the umbrella, and you ought to feel guilty if you do.

Someone could escape from this argument if, when he was asked, 'How would you like it if someone did that to you?' he answered, 'I wouldn't resent it at all. I wouldn't *like* it if someone stole my umbrella in a rain-storm, but I wouldn't think there was any reason for him to consider my feelings about it.' But how many people could honestly give that answer? I think most people, unless they're crazy, would think that their own interests and harms matter, not only to themselves, but in a way that gives other people a reason to care about them too. We all think that when we suffer it is not just bad *for us*, but *bad, period*.

The basis of morality is a belief that good and harm to particular people (or animals) is good or bad not just from their point of view, but from a more general point of view, which every thinking person can understand. That means that each person has a reason to consider not only his own interests but the interests of others in deciding what to do. And it isn't enough if he is considerate only of some others—his family and friends, those he specially cares about. Of course he will care more about certain people, and also about himself. But he has some reason to consider the effect of what he does on the good or harm of everyone. If he's like most of us, that is what he thinks others should do with regard to him, even if they aren't friends of his. [. . .]

Must God's Commands Conform to Moral Standards?

James Rachels

In both the Jewish and Christian traditions, God is presented as a law-giver who has created us, and the world we live in, for a purpose. That purpose is not completely understood, but much has been revealed through the prophets, the Holy Scriptures, and the church. These sources teach that, to guide us in righteous living, God has promulgated rules that we are to obey. He does not compel us to obey them. We were created as free agents, so we may choose to accept or to reject his commandments. But if we are to live as we *should* live, we must follow God's laws. This, it is said, is the essence of morality.

This line of thought has been elaborated by some theologians into a theory about the nature of right and wrong, known as the *Divine Command Theory*. Essentially, this theory says that "morally right" means "commanded by God," and "morally wrong" means "forbidden by God."

From a theoretical point of view, this conception has a number of pleasing features. It immediately solves the old problem about the subjectivity/objectivity of ethics. According to this theory, ethics is not merely a matter of personal feelings or social custom. Whether something is right or wrong is a perfectly objective matter: it is right if God commands it, wrong if God forbids it. Moreover, the Divine Command Theory suggests an answer to the perennial question of why anyone should bother with morality. Why not just look out for one's own interests? If immorality is the violation of God's commandments, there is an easy answer: on the day of final reckoning, you will be held accountable.

There are, however, serious problems for the theory. Of course, atheists would not accept it, because they do not believe that God exists. But the problems that arise are not merely problems for atheists. There are difficulties even for believers. The main problem was first noted by Plato, the Greek philosopher who lived 400 years before the birth of Jesus.

Plato's writings were in the form of dialogues, usually between Socrates and one or more interlocutors. In one of these dialogues, the *Euthyphro*, there is a discussion concerning whether "right" can be defined as "that which the gods command." Socrates is skeptical and asks: *Is conduct right because the gods command it, or do the gods command it because it is right?* It is one of the most famous questions in the history of philosophy. The contemporary British philosopher Antony Flew suggests that "one good test of a person's aptitude for philosophy is to discover whether he can grasp its force and point."

The point is this. If we accept the theological conception of right and wrong, we are caught in a dilemma. Socrates's question asks us to clarify what we mean. There are two things we might mean, and both options lead to trouble.

1. First, we might mean that conduct is right *because God commands it*. For example, according to Exodus 20:16, God commands us

to be truthful. On this option, the *reason* we should be truthful is simply that God requires it. Apart from the divine command, truth telling is neither good nor bad. It is God's command that *makes* truthfulness right.

But this leads to trouble, for it represents God's commands as arbitrary. It means that God could have given *different* commands just as easily. He could have commanded us to be liars, and then lying and not truthfulness, would be right. (You may be tempted to reply: "But God would never command us to be liars!" But why not? If he did endorse lying, God would not be commanding us to do wrong, because his command would make lying right.) Remember that on this view, honesty was not right *before* God commanded it. Therefore, he could have had no more reason to command it than its opposite; and so, from a moral point of view, his command is perfectly arbitrary.

Moreover, on this view, the doctrine of the goodness of God is reduced to nonsense. It is important to religious believers that God is not only all-powerful and all-knowing, but that he is also *good*; yet if we accept the idea that good and bad are defined by reference to God's will, this notion is deprived of any meaning. What could it mean to say that God's commands are good? If "X is good" simply means "X is commanded by God," then "God's commands are good" would mean only "God's commands are commanded by God"—an empty truism. In his *Discourse on Metaphysics* (1686) Leibniz put the point very clearly:

> So in saying that things are not good by any rule of goodness, but sheerly by the will of God, it seems to me that one destroys, without realizing it, all the love of God and all his glory. For why praise him for what he has done if he would be equally praiseworthy in doing exactly the contrary?

Thus if we choose the first of Socrates's two options, we are stuck with consequences that even the most religious people must find unacceptable.

2. There is a way to avoid these troublesome consequences. We can take the second of Socrates's options. We need not say that right conduct is right because God commands it. Instead, we may say that God commands right conduct *because it is right*. God, who is infinitely wise, realizes that truthfulness is far better than deceitfulness, and so he commands

us to be truthful; he sees that killing is wrong, and so he commands us not to kill; and so on for all the commandments.

If we take this option, we avoid the troublesome consequences that plagued the first alternative. God's commands turn out to be not at all arbitrary; they are the result of his wisdom in knowing what is best. And the doctrine of the goodness of God is preserved: to say that his commands are good means that he commands only what, in perfect wisdom, he sees to be the best. But this option leads to a different problem, which is equally troublesome for the theological conception of right and wrong: indeed, in taking this option, we have virtually *abandoned* the theological conception of right and wrong.

If we say that God commands us to be truthful because truthfulness is right, then we are admitting that there is some standard of right and wrong that is independent of God's will. We are saying that God *sees* or *recognizes* that truthfulness is right: this is very different from his *making* it right. The rightness exists prior to and independent of God's command, and it is the reason for the command. Thus if we want to know why we should be truthful, the reply "Because God commands it" will not take us very far. We may still ask "But why does God command it?" and the answer to *that* question will provide the underlying reasons why truthfulness is a good thing.

All this may be summarized in the following argument:

1. Suppose God commands us to do what is right. Then *either* (a) the right actions are right because he commands them *or* (b) he commands them because they are right.
2. If we take option (a), then God's commands are, from a moral point of view, arbitrary; moreover, the doctrine of the goodness of God is rendered meaningless.
3. If we take option (b), then we have admitted there is a standard of right and wrong that is independent of God's will.
4. Therefore, we must *either* regard God's commands as arbitrary, and give up the doctrine of the goodness of God, *or* admit that there is a standard of right and wrong that is independent of his will, and give up the theological definitions of right and wrong.
5. From a religious point of view, it is undesirable to regard God's commands as arbitrary or to give up the doctrine of the goodness of God.

6. Therefore, even from a religious point of view, a standard of right and wrong that is independent of God's will must be accepted.

Many religious people believe that they should accept a theological conception of right and wrong because it would be impious not to do so. They feel, somehow, that if they believe in God, they *should* think that right and wrong are to be defined ultimately in terms of his will. But this argument suggests otherwise: it suggests that, on the contrary, the Divine Command Theory of right and wrong itself leads to impious results, so that a pious person should *not* accept it. And in fact, some of the greatest theologians, such as St. Thomas Aquinas (ca. 1225–1274), rejected the theory for just this reason.

The Principle of Utility

Jeremy Bentham

I. Nature has placed mankind under the governance of two sovereign masters, *pain* and *pleasure*. It is for them alone to point out what we ought to do, as well as to determine what we shall do. On the one hand the standard of right and wrong, on the other the chain of causes and effects, are fastened to their throne. They govern us in all we do, in all we say, in all we think: every effort we can make to throw off our subjection, will serve but to demonstrate and confirm it. In words a man may pretend to abjure their empire: but in reality he will remain subject to it all the while. The *principle of utility*[1] recognises this subjection,

---

[Introduction to the Principles of Morals and Legislation (Hafner: New York, 1948), 1–7, 29–31. First published in 1789.]

[1]Note by the Author, July 1822: To this denomination has of late been added, or substituted, the *greatest happiness* or *greatest felicity* principle: this for shortness, instead of saying at length *that principle* which states the greatest happiness of all those whose interest is in question, as being the right and proper, and only right and proper and universally desirable, end of human action: of human action in every situation, and in particular in that of a functionary or set of functionaries exercising the powers of Government. The word *utility* does not so clearly point to the ideas of *pleasure* and *pain* as the words *happiness* and *felicity* do: nor does it lead us to the consideration of the *number*, of the interests affected; to the *number*, as being the circumstance, which contributes, in the largest proportion, to the formation of the standard here in question; the *standard of right and wrong*, by which alone the propriety of human conduct, in every situation, can with propriety be tried. This want of a sufficiently manifest connexion between the ideas of *happiness* and *pleasure* on the one hand, and the idea of *utility* on the other, I have every now and then found operating, and with but too much efficiency, as a bar to the acceptance, that might otherwise have been given, to this principle.

and assumes it for the foundation of that system, the object of which is to rear the fabric of felicity by the hands of reason and of law. Systems which attempt to question it, deal in sounds instead of sense, in caprice instead of reason, in darkness instead of light.

But enough of metaphor and declamation: it is not by such means that moral science is to be improved.

II. The principle of utility is the foundation of the present work: it will be proper therefore at the outset to give an explicit and determinate account of what is meant by it. By the principle[2] of utility is meant that principle which approves or disapproves of every action whatsoever, according to the tendency which it appears to have to augment or diminish the happiness of the party whose interest is in question: or, what is the same thing in other words, to promote or to oppose that happiness. I say of every action whatsoever; and therefore not only of every action of a private individual, but of every measure of government.

III. By utility is meant that property in any object, whereby it tends to produce benefit, advantage, pleasure, good, or happiness, (all this in the present case comes to the same thing) or what comes again to the same thing) to prevent the happening of mischief, pain, evil, or unhappiness to the party whose interest is considered: if that party be the community in general, then the happiness of the community: if a particular individual, then the happiness of that individual.

IV. The interest of the community is one of the most general expressions that can occur in the phraseology of morals: no wonder that the meaning of it is often lost. When it has a meaning, it is this. The community is a fictitious *body*, composed of the individual persons who are considered as constituting as it were its *members*. The interest of the community then is, what?—the sum of the interests of the several members who compose it.

V. It is in vain to talk of the interest of the community, without understanding what is the interest of the individual. A thing is said to

---

[2]The word principle is derived from the Latin principium: which seems to be compounded of the two words *primus*, first, or chief, and *cipium*, a termination which seems to be derived from *capio*, to take, as in *mancipium, municipium*; to which are analogous, *auceps, forceps*, and others. It is a term of very vague and very extensive signification: it is applied to any thing which is conceived to serve as a foundation or beginning to any series of operations: in some cases, of physical operations; but of mental operations in the present case.

The principle here in question may be taken for an act of the mind; a sentiment; a sentiment of approbation; a sentiment which, when applied to an action, approves of its utility, as that quality of it by which the measure of approbation or disapprobation or disapprobation bestowed upon it ought to be governed.

promote the interest, or to be *for* the interest, of an individual, when it tends to add to the sum total of his pleasures: or, what comes to the same thing, to diminish the sum total of his pains.

VI. An action then may be said to be conformable to the principle of utility, or, for shortness sake, to utility, (meaning with respect to the community at large) when the tendency it has to augment the happiness of the community is greater than any it has to diminish it.

VII. A measure of government (which is but a particular kind of action, performed by a particular person or persons) may be said to be conformable to or dictated by the principle of utility, when in like manner the tendency which it has to augment the happiness of the community is greater than any which it has to diminish it.

VIII. When an action, or in particular a measure of government, is supposed by a man to be conformable to the principle of utility, it may be convenient, for the purposes of discourse, to imagine a kind of law or dictate, called a law or dictate of utility: and to speak of the action in question, as being conformable to such law or dictate.

IX. A man may be said to be a partizan of the principle of utility, when the approbation or disapprobation he annexes to any action, or to any measure, is determined by and proportioned to the tendency which he conceives it to have to augment or to diminish the happiness of the community: or in other words, to its conformity or unconformity to the laws or dictates of utility.

X. Of an action that is conformable to the principle of utility one may always say either that it is one that ought to be done, or at least that it is not one that ought not to be done. One may say also, that it is right it should be done; at least that it is not wrong it should be done: that it is a right action; at least that it is not a wrong action. When thus interpreted, the words *ought*, and *right* and *wrong*, and others of that stamp, have a meaning: when otherwise, they have none.

XI. Has the rectitude of this principle been ever formally contested? It should seem that it had, by those who have not known what they have been meaning. Is it susceptible of any direct proof? It should seem not: for that which is used to prove every thing else, cannot itself be proved: a chain of proofs must have their commencement somewhere. To give such proof is as impossible as it is needless.

XII. Not that there is or ever has been that human creature breathing, however stupid or perverse, who has not on many, perhaps on most occasions of his life, deferred to it. By the natural constitution of the human frame, on most occasions of their lives men in general embrace this principle, without thinking of it: if not for the ordering of their own actions, yet for the trying of their own actions, as well as of those of other men. There have been, at the same time, not many, perhaps, even of the most intelligent, who have been disposed to embrace it purely and without reserve. There are even few who have not taken some occasion or other to quarrel with it, either on account of their not understanding always how to apply it, or on account of some prejudice or other which they were afraid to examine into, or could not bear to part with. For such is the stuff that man is made of: in principle and in practice, in a right track and in a wrong one, the rarest of all human qualities is consistency.

XIII. When a man attempts to combat the principle of utility, it is with reasons drawn, without his being aware of it, from that very principle itself. His arguments, if they prove any thing, prove not that the principle is *wrong*, but that, according to the applications he supposes to be made of it, it is *misapplied*. Is it possible for a man to move the earth? Yes; but he must first find out another earth to stand upon.

XIV. To disprove the propriety of it by arguments is impossible; but, from the causes that have been mentioned, or from some confused or partial view of it, a man may happen to be disposed not to relish it. Where this is the case, if he thinks the settling of his opinions on such a subject worth the trouble, let him take the following steps, and at length, perhaps, he may come to reconcile himself to it.

1. Let him settle with himself, whether he would wish to discard this principle altogether; if so, let him consider what it is that all his reasonings (in matters of politics especially) can amount to?
2. If he would, let him settle with himself, whether he would judge and act without any principle, or whether there is any other he would judge and act by?
3. If there be, let him examine and satisfy himself whether the principle he thinks he has found is really any separate intelligible principle; or whether it be not a mere principle in words, a kind of phrase, which at bottom expresses neither more nor less than the mere averment of his own unfounded sentiments; that is, what in another person he might be apt to call caprice?
4. If he is inclined to think that his own approbation or disapprobation, annexed to the idea of an act, without any regard to its consequences, is a sufficient foundation for him to judge and act upon, let him ask himself whether his sentiment is to be a standard of right and wrong, with respect to every other man, or whether every man's sentiment has the same privilege of being a standard to itself?

5. In the first case, let him ask himself whether his principle is not despotical, and hostile to all the rest of human race?

6. In the second case, whether it is not anarchical, and whether at this rate there are not as many different standards of right and wrong as there are men? and whether even to the same man, the same thing, which is right to-day, may not (without the least change in its nature) be wrong tomorrow? and whether the same thing is not right and wrong in the same place at the same time? and in either case, whether all argument is not at an end? and whether, when two men have said, 'I like this,' and 'I don't like it,' they can (upon such a principle) have any thing more to say?

7. If he should have said to himself, No: for that the sentiment which he proposes as a standard must be grounded on reflection, let him say on what particulars the reflection is to turn? if on particulars having relation to the utility of the act, then let him say whether this is not deserting his own principle, and borrowing assistance from that very one in opposition to which he sets it up: or if not on those particulars, on what other particulars?

8. If he should be for compounding the matter, and adopting his own principle in part, and the principle of utility in part, let him say how far he will adopt it?

9. When he has settled with himself where he will stop, then let him ask himself how he justifies to himself the adopting it so far? and why he will not adopt it any farther?

10. Admitting any other principle than the principle of utility to be a right principle, a principle that it is right for a man to pursue; admitting (what is not true) that the word *right* can have a meaning without reference to utility, let him say whether there is any such thing as a *motive* that a man can have to pursue the dictates of it: if there is, let him say what that motive is, and how it is to be distinguished from those which enforce the dictates of utility: if not, then lastly let him say what it is this other principle can be good for?

* * *

I. Pleasures then, and the avoidance of pains, are the *ends* which the legislator has in view: it behoves him therefore to understand their *value*. Pleasures and pains are the *instruments* he has to work with: it behoves him therefore to understand their force, which is again, in other words, their value.

II. To a person considered *by himself*, the value of a pleasure or pain considered *by itself*, will be greater or less, according to the four following circumstances[1]:

1. Its *intensity*.
2. Its *duration*.
3. Its *certainty* or *uncertainty*.
4. Its *propinquity* or *remoteness*.

III. These are the circumstances which are to be considered in estimating a pleasure or a pain considered each of them by itself. But when the value of any pleasure or pain is considered for the purpose of estimating the tendency of any *act* by which it is produced, there are two other circumstances to be taken into the account; these are,

5. Its *fecundity*, or the chance it has of being followed by sensations of the *same* kind: that is, pleasures, if it be a pleasure: pains, if it be a pain.
6. Its *purity*, or the chance it has of *not* being followed by sensations of the *opposite* kind: that is, pains, if it be a pleasure: pleasures, if it be a pain.

These two last, however, are in strictness scarcely to be deemed properties of the pleasure or the pain itself; they are not, therefore, in strictness to be taken into the account of the value of that pleasure or that pain. They are in strictness to be deemed properties only of the act, or other event, by which such pleasure or pain has been produced; and accordingly are only to be taken into the account of the tendency of such act or such event.

IV. To a *number* of persons, with reference to each of whom the value of a pleasure or a pain is considered, it will be greater or less, according to seven circumstances: to wit, the six preceding ones; *viz.*

---

[1] These circumstances have since been denominated *elements* or *dimensions* of *value* in a pleasure or a pain. Not long after the publication of the first edition, the following memoriter verses were framed, in the view of lodging more effectually, in the memory, these points, on which the whole fabric of morals and legislation may be seen to rest.

> Intense, long, certain, speedy, fruitful, pure—
> Such marks in *pleasures* and in *pains* endure.
> Such pleasures seek if *private* be thy end:
> If it be *public*, wide let them *extend*.
> Such *pains* avoid, whichever be thy view:
> If pains *must* come, let them *extend* to few.

1. Its *intensity*.
2. Its *duration*.
3. Its *certainty* or *uncertainty*.
4. Its *propinquity* or *remoteness*.
5. Its *fecundity*.
6. Its *purity*.
   And one other; to wit:
7. Its *extent*; that is, the number of persons to whom it *extends*; or (in other words) who are affected by it.

V. To take an exact account then of the general tendency of any act, by which the interests of a community are affected, proceed as follows. Begin with any one person of those whose interests seem most immediately to be affected by it: and take an account,

1. Of the value of each distinguishable *pleasure* which appears to be produced by it in the *first* instance.
2. Of the value of each *pain* which appears to be produced by it in the *first* instance.
3. Of the value of each pleasure which appears to be produced by it *after* the first. This constitutes the *fecundity* of the first *pleasure* and the *impurity* of the first *pain*.
4. Of the value of each *pain* which appears to be produced by it after the first. This constitutes the *fecundity* of the first *pain*, and the *impurity* of the first pleasure.
5. Sum up all the values of all the *pleasures* on the one side, and those of all the pains on the other. The balance, if it be on the side of pleasure, will give the *good* tendency of the act upon the whole, with respect to the interests of that *individual* person; if on the side of pain, the *bad* tendency of it upon the whole.
6. Take an account of the *number* of persons whose interests appear to be concerned; and repeat the above process with respect to each. *Sum up* the numbers expressive of the degrees of *good* tendency, which the act has, with respect to each individual, in regard to whom the tendency of it is *good* upon the whole: do this again with respect to each individual, in regard to whom the tendency of it is *good* upon the whole: do this again with respect to each individual, in regard to whom the tendency of it is *bad* upon the whole. Take the *balance*; which, if on the side of *pleasure*, will give the general *good tendency* of the act, with respect to the total number or community of individuals concerned; if on the side of pain, the general *evil tendency*, with respect to the same community.

VI. It is not to be expected that this process should be strictly pursued previously to every moral judgment, or to every legislative or judicial operation. It may, however, be always kept in view: and as near as the process actually pursued on these occasions approaches to it, so near will such process approach to the character of an exact one. [. . .]

Push-Pin and Poetry
Jeremy Bentham

[. . .] Taken collectively, and considered in their connexion with the happiness of society, the arts and sciences may be arranged in two divisions; viz.—1. Those of amusement and curiosity; 2. Those of utility, immediate and remote. These two branches of human knowledge require different methods of treatment on the part of governments.

By arts and sciences of amusement, I mean those which are ordinarily called the *fine arts*; such as music, poetry, painting, sculpture, architecture, ornamental gardening, &c. &c. Their complete enumeration must be excused: it would lead us too far from our present subject, were we to plunge into the metaphysical discussions necessary for its accomplishment. Amusements of all sorts would be comprised under this head. [. . .]

By arts and sciences of curiosity, I mean those which in truth are pleasing, but not in the same degree as the fine arts, and to which at the first glance we might be tempted to refuse this quality. It is not that these arts and sciences of curiosity do not yield as much pleasure to those who cultivate them as the fine arts; but the number of those who study them is more limited. Of this nature are the sciences of heraldry, of medals, of pure chronology—the knowledge of ancient and barbarous languages, which present only collections of strange words,—and the study of antiquities, inasmuch as they furnish no instruction applicable to morality, or any other branch of useful or agreeable knowledge.

The utility of all these arts and sciences,—I speak both of those of amusement and curiosity,—the value which they possess, is exactly

[*The Rationale of Reward, in The Works of Jeremy Bentham*, ii, ed. John Bowring (Russell and Russell, Inc.: New York, 1962), 253–4. First published in 1825.]

in proportion to the pleasure they yield. Every other species of pre-eminence which may be attempted to be established among them is altogether fanciful. Prejudice apart, the game of push-pin is of equal value with the arts and sciences of music and poetry. If the game of push-pin furnish more pleasure, it is more valuable than either. Everybody can play at push-pin: poetry and music are relished only by a few. The game of push-pin is always innocent: it were well could the same be always asserted of poetry. Indeed, between poetry and truth there is a natural opposition: false morals, fictitious nature. The poet always stands in need of something false. When he pretends to lay his foundations in truth, the ornaments of his superstructure are fictions; his business consists in stimulating our passions, and exciting our prejudices. Truth, exactitude of every kind, is fatal to poetry. The poet must see everything through coloured media, and strive to make every one else to do the same. It is true, there have been noble spirits, to whom poetry and philosophy have been equally indebted; but these exceptions do not counteract the mischiefs which have resulted from this magic art. If poetry and music deserve to be preferred before a game of push-pin, it must be because they are calculated to gratify those individuals who are most difficult to be pleased. [. . .]

Higher and Lower Pleasures

John Stuart Mill

[. . .] The creed which accepts as the foundation of morals, Utility, or the Greatest Happiness Principle, holds that actions are right in proportion as they tend to promote happiness, wrong as they tend to produce the reverse of happiness. By happiness is intended pleasure, and the absence of pain; by unhappiness, pain, and the privation of pleasure. To give a clear view of the moral standard set up by the theory, much more requires to be said; in particular, what things it includes in the ideas of pain and pleasure; and to what extent this is

['Utilitarianism', *Essays on Ethics, Religion and Society*, ed. J. M. Robson, F. E. L. Priestley, and D. P. Dryer (University of Toronto Press: Toronto, 1969), 210–14. First published in 1861.]

left an open question. But these supplementary explanations do not affect the theory of life on which this theory of morality is grounded—namely, that pleasure, and freedom from pain, are the only things desirable as ends; and that all desirable things (which are as numerous in the utilitarian as in any other scheme) are desirable either for the pleasure inherent in themselves, or as means to the promotion of pleasure and the prevention of pain.

Now, such a theory of life excites in many minds, and among them in some of the most estimable in feeling and purpose, inveterate dislike. To suppose that life has (as they express it) no higher end than pleasure—no better and nobler object of desire and pursuit—they designate as utterly mean and grovelling; as a doctrine worthy only of swine, to whom the followers of Epicurus were, at a very early period, contemptuously likened; and modern holders of the doctrine are occasionally made the subject of equally polite comparisons by its German, French, and English assailants.

When thus attacked, the Epicureans have always answered, that it is not they, but their accusers, who represent human nature in a degrading light; since the accusation supposes human beings to be capable of no pleasures except those of which swine are capable. If this supposition were true, the charge could not be gainsaid, but would then be no longer an imputation; for if the sources of pleasure were precisely the same to human beings and to swine, the rule of life which is good enough for the one would be good enough for the other. The comparison of the Epicurean life to that of beasts is felt as degrading, precisely because a beast's pleasures do not satisfy a human being's conceptions of happiness. Human beings have faculties more elevated than the animal appetites, and when once made conscious of them, do not regard anything as happiness which does not include their gratification. I do not, indeed, consider the Epicureans to have been by any means faultless in drawing out their scheme of consequences from the utilitarian principle. To do this in any sufficient manner, many Stoic, as well as Christian elements require to be included. But there is no known Epicurean theory of life which does not assign to the pleasures of the intellect, of the feelings and imagination, and of the moral sentiments, a much higher value as pleasures than to those of mere sensation. It must be admitted, however, that utilitarian writers in general have placed the superiority of mental over bodily pleasures chiefly in the greater permanency, safety, uncostliness, &c., of the former—that is, in their circumstantial advantages rather than in their intrinsic nature. And on all these points utilitarians have fully proved their case; but they might have taken the other, and, as it may be called, higher ground, with entire consistency. It is quite compatible with the principle of utility to recognise the fact, that some *kinds* of pleasure are more desirable and more valuable than others. It would be absurd that while, in estimating all other things, quality is considered as well as quantity, the estimation of pleasures should be supposed to depend on quantity alone.

If I am asked, what I mean by difference of quality in pleasures, or what makes one pleasure more valuable than another, merely as a pleasure, except its being greater in amount, there is but one possible answer. Of two pleasures, if there be one to which all or almost all who have experience of both give a decided preference, irrespective of any feeling of moral obligation to prefer it, that is the more desirable pleasure. If one of the two is, by those who are competently acquainted with both, placed so far above the other that they prefer it, even though knowing it to be attended with a greater amount of discontent, and would not resign it for any quantity of the other pleasure which their nature is capable of, we are justified in ascribing to the preferred enjoyment a superiority in quality, so far outweighing quantity as to render it, in comparison, of small account.

Now it is an unquestionable fact that those who are equally acquainted with, and equally capable of appreciating and enjoying, both, do give a most marked preference to the manner of existence which employs their higher faculties. Few human creatures would consent to be changed into any of the lower animals, for a promise of the fullest allowance of a beast's pleasures; no intelligent human being would consent to be a fool, no instructed person would be an ignoramus, no person of feeling and conscience would be selfish and base, even though they should be persuaded that the fool, the dunce, or the rascal is better satisfied with his lot than they are with theirs. They would not resign what they possess more than he, for the most complete satisfaction of all the desires which they have in common with him. If they ever fancy they would, it is only in cases of unhappiness so extreme, that to escape from it they would exchange their lot for almost any other, however undesirable in their own eyes. A being of higher faculties requires more to make him happy, is capable probably of more acute suffering, and is certainly accessible to it at more points, than one of an inferior type; but in spite of these liabilities, he can never really wish to sink into what he feels to be a lower grade of existence. We may give what explanation we please of this unwillingness; we may attribute it to pride, a name which is given indiscriminately to some of the most and to some of the least estimable feelings of which mankind are capable; we may refer it to the love of liberty and personal independence, an appeal to which was with the Stoics one of the most effective means for the inculcation of it; to the love of power, or to the love of excitement, both of which do really enter into and contribute to it: but its most appropriate appellation is a sense of dignity, which all human beings possess in one form or other, and in some, though by no means in exact, proportion to their higher faculties, and which is so essential a part of the happiness of those in whom it is strong, that nothing which conflicts with it could be, otherwise than momentarily, an object of desire to them. Whoever supposes that this preference takes place at a sacrifice of happiness—that the superior being, in anything like equal circumstances, is not happier than the inferior—confounds the two very different ideas, of happiness, and content. It is indisputable that the being whose capacities of enjoyment are low, has the greatest chance of having them fully satisfied; and a highly-endowed being will always feel that any happiness which he can look for, as the world is constituted, is imperfect. But he can learn to bear its imperfections, if they are at all bearable; and they will not make him envy the being who is indeed unconscious of the imperfections, but only because he feels not at all the good which those imperfections qualify. It is better to be a human being dissatisfied than a pig satisfied; better to be Socrates dissatisfied than a fool satisfied. And if the fool, or the pig, is of a different opinion, it is because they only know their own side of the question. The other party to the comparison knows both sides.

It may be objected, that many who are capable of the higher pleasures, occasionally, under the influence of temptation, postpone them to the lower. But this is quite compatible with a full appreciation of the intrinsic superiority of the higher. Men often, from infirmity of character, make their election for the nearer good, though they know it to be the less valuable; and this no less when the choice is between two bodily pleasures, than when it is between bodily and mental. They pursue sensual indulgences to the injury of health, though perfectly aware that health is the greater good. It may be further objected, that many who begin with youthful enthusiasm for everything noble, as they advance in years sink into indolence and selfishness. But I do not believe that those who undergo this very common change, voluntarily choose the lower description of pleasures in preference to the higher. I believe that before they devote themselves exclusively to the one, they have already become incapable of the other. Capacity for the nobler feelings is in most natures a very tender plant, easily killed, not only by hostile influences, but by mere want of sustenance; and in the majority of young persons it speedily dies away if the occupations to which their position in life has devoted them, and the society into which it has thrown them, are not favourable to keeping that higher capacity in exercise. Men lose their high aspirations as they lose their intellectual tastes, because they have not time or opportunity for indulging them; and they addict themselves to inferior pleasures, not because they deliberately prefer them, but because they are either the only ones to which they have access, or the only ones which they are any longer capable of enjoying. It may be questioned whether any one who has remained equally susceptible to both classes of pleasures, ever knowingly and calmly preferred the lower; though many, in all ages, have broken down in an ineffectual attempt to combine both.

From this verdict of the only competent judges, I apprehend there can be no appeal. On a question which is the best worth having of two pleasures, or which of two modes of existence is the most grateful to the feelings, apart from its moral attributes and from its consequences, the judgment of those who are qualified by knowledge of both, or, if they differ, that of the majority among them, must be admitted as final. And there needs be the less hesitation to accept this judgment respecting the quality of pleasures, since there is no other tribunal to be referred to even on the question of quantity. What means are there of determining which is the acutest of two pains, or the intensest of two pleasurable sensations, except the general suffrage of those who are familiar with both? Neither pains nor pleasures are homogeneous, and pain is always heterogeneous with pleasure. What is there to decide whether a particular pleasure is worth purchasing at the cost of a particular pain, except the feelings and judgment of the experienced? When, therefore, those feelings and judgment declare the pleasures derived from the higher faculties to be preferable *in kind*, apart from the question of intensity, to those of which the animal nature, disjoined from the higher faculties, is susceptible, they are entitled on this subject to the same regard.

I have dwelt on this point, as being a necessary part of a perfectly just conception of Utility or Happiness, considered as the directive rule of human conduct. But it is by no means an indispensable condition to the acceptance of the utilitarian standard; for that standard is not the agent's own greatest happiness, but the greatest amount of happiness altogether; and if it may possibly be doubted whether a noble character is always the happier for its nobleness, there can be no doubt that it makes other people happier, and that the world in general is immensely a gainer by it.

Utilitarianism, therefore, could only attain its end by the general cultivation of nobleness of character, even if each individual were only benefited by the nobleness of others, and his own, so far as happiness is concerned, were a sheer deduction from the benefit. But the bare enunciation of such an absurdity as this last, renders refutation superfluous.

According to the Greatest Happiness Principle, as above explained, the ultimate end, with reference to and for the sake of which all other things are desirable (whether we are considering our own good or that of other people), is an existence exempt as far as possible from pain, and as rich as possible in enjoyments, both in point of quantity and quality; the test of quality, and the rule for measuring it against quantity, being the preference felt by those who, in their opportunities of experience, to which must be added their habits of self-consciousness and self-observation, are best furnished with the means of comparison. This, being, according to the utilitarian opinion, the end of human action, is necessarily also the standard of morality; which may accordingly be defined, the rules and precepts for human conduct, by the observance of which an existence such as has been described might be, to the greatest extent possible, secured to all mankind; and not to them only, but, so far as the nature of things admits, to the whole sentient creation. [. . .]

Groundwork of the Metaphysics of Morals

Immanuel Kant   *(Translated by James Ellington)*

. . . Everything in nature works according to laws. Only a rational being has the power to act according to his conception of laws, i.e., according to principles, and thereby has he a will. Since the derivation of actions from laws requires reason, the will is nothing but practical reason. If reason infallibly determines the will, then in the case of such a being actions which are recognized to be objectively necessary are also subjectively necessary, i.e., the will is a faculty of choosing only that which reason, independently of inclination, recognizes as being practically necessary, i.e., as good. But if reason of itself does not sufficiently determine the will, and if the will submits also to subjective conditions (certain incentives) which do not always agree with objective conditions; in a word, if the will does not in itself completely accord with reason (as is actually the case with men), then actions which are recognized as objectively necessary are subjectively contingent, and the determination of such a will according to objective laws is necessitation. That is to say that the relation of objective laws to a will not thoroughly good is represented as the determination of the will of a rational being by principles of reason which the will does not necessarily follow because of its own nature.

The representation of an objective principle insofar as it necessitates the will is called a command (of reason), and the formula of the command is called an imperative.

All imperatives are expressed by an *ought* and thereby indicate the relation of an objective law of reason to a will that is not necessarily determined by this law because of its subjective constitution (the relation of necessitation). Imperatives say that something would be good to do or to refrain from doing, but they say it to a will that does not always therefore do something simply because it has been represented to the will as something good to do. That is practically good which determines the will by means of representations of reason and hence not by subjective causes, but objectively, i.e., on grounds valid for every rational being as such. It is distinguished from the pleasant as that which influences the will only by means of sensation from merely subjective causes, which hold only for this or that person's senses but do not hold as a principle of reason valid for everyone.[1]

A perfectly good will would thus be quite as much subject to objective laws (of the good), but could not be conceived as thereby necessitated to act in conformity with law, inasmuch as it can of itself, according to its subjective constitution, be determined only by the

---

[1]The dependence of the faculty of desire on sensations is called inclination, which accordingly always indicates a need. The dependence of a contingently determinable will on principles of reason, however, is called interest. Therefore an interest is found only in a dependent will which is not of itself always in accord with reason; in the divine will no interest can be thought. But even the human will can take an interest in something without thereby acting from interest. The former signifies practical interest in the action, while the latter signifies pathological interest in the object of the action. The former indicates only dependence of the will on principles of reason by itself, while the latter indicates the will's dependence on principles of reason for the sake of inclination, i.e., reason merely gives the practical rule for meeting the need of inclination. In the former case the action interests me, while in the latter case what interests me is the object of the action (so far as this subject is pleasant for me).

representation of the good. Therefore no imperatives hold for the divine will, and in general for a holy will; the *ought* is here out of place, because the *would* is already of itself necessarily in agreement with the law. Consequently, imperatives are only formulas for expressing the relation of objective laws of willing in general to the subjective imperfection of the will of this or that rational being, e.g., the human will.

Now all imperatives command either hypothetically or categorically. The former represent the practical necessity of a possible action as a means for attaining something else that one wants (or may possibly want). The categorical imperative would be one which represented an action as objectively necessary in itself, without reference to another end.

Every practical law represents a possible action as good and hence as necessary for a subject who is practically determinable by reason; therefore all imperatives are formulas for determining an action which is necessary according to the principle of a will that is good in some way. Now if the action would be good merely as a means to something else, so is the imperative hypothetical. But if the action is represented as good in itself, and hence as necessary in a will which of itself conforms to reason as the principle of the will, then the imperative is categorical.

An imperative thus says what action possible by me would be good, and it presents the practical rule in relation to a will which does not forthwith perform an action simply because it is good, partly because the subject does not always know that the action is good and partly because (even if he does know it is good) his maxims might yet be opposed to the objective principles of practical reason.

A hypothetical imperative thus says only that an action is good for some purpose, either possible or actual. In the first case it is a problematic practical principle; in the second case an assertoric one. A categorical imperative, which declares an action to be of itself objectively necessary without reference to any purpose, i.e., without any other end, holds as an apodeictic practical principle.

Whatever is possible only through the powers of some rational being can be thought of as a possible purpose of some will. Consequently, there are in fact infinitely many principles of action insofar as they are represented as necessary for attaining a possible purpose achievable by them. All sciences have a practical part consisting of problems saying that some end is possible for us and of imperatives telling us how it can be attained. These can, therefore, be called in general imperatives of skill. Here there is no question at all whether the end is reasonable and good, but there is only a question as to what must be done to attain it. The prescriptions needed by a doctor in order to make his patient thoroughly healthy and by a poisoner in order to make sure of killing his victim are of equal value so far as each serves to bring about its purpose perfectly. Since there cannot be known in early youth what ends may be presented to us in the course of life, parents especially seek to have their children learn many different kinds of things, and they provide for skill in the use of means to all sorts of arbitrary ends, among which they cannot determine whether any one of them could in the future become an actual purpose for their ward, though there is always the possibility that he might adopt it. Their concern is so great that they commonly neglect to form and correct their children's judgment regarding the worth of things which might be chosen as ends.

There is, however, one end that can be presupposed as actual for all rational beings (so far as they are dependent beings to whom imperatives apply); and thus there is one purpose which they not merely can have but which can certainly be assumed to be such that they all do have by a natural necessity, and this is happiness. A hypothetical imperative which represents the practical necessity of an action as means for the promotion of happiness is assertoric. It may be expounded not simply as necessary to an uncertain, merely possible purpose, but as necessary to a purpose which can be presupposed a priori and with certainty as being present in everyone because it belongs to his essence. Now skill in the choice of means to one's own greatest well-being can be called prudence[2] in the narrowest sense. And thus the imperative that refers to the choice of means to one's own happiness, i.e., the precept of prudence, still remains hypothetical; the action is commanded not absolutely but only as a means to a further purpose.

Finally, there is one imperative which immediately commands a certain conduct without having as its condition any other purpose to be attained by it. This imperative is categorical. It is not concerned with the matter of the action and its intended result, but rather with the form of the action and the principle from which it follows; what is essentially

---

[2]The word "prudence" is used in a double sense: firstly, it can mean worldly wisdom, and, secondly, private wisdom. The former is the skill of someone in influencing others so as to use them for his own purposes. The latter is the sagacity to combine all these purposes for his own lasting advantage. The value of the former is properly reduced to the latter, and it might better be said of one who is prudent in the former sense but not in the latter that he is clever and cunning, but on the whole imprudent.

good in the action consists in the mental disposition, let the consequences be what they may. This imperative may be called that of morality.

Willing according to these three kinds of principles is also clearly distinguished by dissimilarity in the necessitation of the will. To make this dissimilarity clear I think that they are most suitably named in their order when they are said to be either *rules of skill, counsels of prudence,* or *commands (laws) of morality.* For law alone involves the concept of a necessity that is unconditioned and indeed objective and hence universally valid, and commands are laws which must be obeyed, i.e., must be followed even in opposition to inclination. Counsel does indeed involve necessity, but involves such necessity as is valid only under a subjectively contingent condition, viz., whether this or that man counts this or that as belonging to his happiness. On the other hand, the categorical imperative is limited by no condition, and can quite properly be called a command since it is absolutely, though practically, necessary. The first kind of imperatives might also be called technical (belonging to art), the second kind pragmatic[3] (belonging to welfare), the third kind moral (belonging to free conduct us such, i.e., to morals).

The question now arises: how are all of these imperatives possible?[4] This question does not seek to know how the fulfillment of the action commanded by the imperative can be conceived, but merely how the necessitation of the will expressed by the imperative in setting a task can be conceived. How an imperative of skill is possible requires no special discussion. Whoever wills the end, wills (so far as reason has decisive influence on his actions) also the means that are indispensably necessary to his actions and that lie in his power. This proposition, as far as willing is concerned, is analytic. For in willing an object as my effect there is already thought the causality of myself as an acting cause, i.e., the use of means. The imperative derives the concept of actions necessary to this end form the concept of willing this end. (Synthetic propositions are indeed required for determining the means to a proposed end; but such propositions are concerned not with the ground, i.e., the act of the will, but only with the way to realize the object of the will.) Mathematics teaches by nothing but synthetic propositions that in order to bisect a line

---

[3]It seems to me that the proper meaning of the word "pragmatic" could be defined most accurately in this way. For those sanctions are called pragmatic which properly flow not from the law of states as necessary enactments but from provision for the general welfare. A history is pragmatically written when it teaches prudence, i.e., instructs the world how it can provide for its interests better than, or at least as well as, has been done in former times.

[4][That is, why should one let his actions be determined at various times by one of the other of these three kinds of imperatives?]

according to a sure principle I must from each of its extremities draw arcs such that they intersect. But when I know that the proposed result can come about only by means of such an action, then the proposition (if I fully will the effect, then I also will the action required for it) is analytic. For it is one and the same thing to conceive of something as an effect that is possible in a certain way through me and to conceive of my self as acting in the same way with regard to the aforesaid effect.

If it were only as easy to give a determinate concept of happiness, then the imperatives of prudence would exactly correspond to those of skill and would be likewise analytic. For there could be said in this case just as in the former that whoever wills the end also wills (necessarily according to reason) the sole means thereto which are in his power. But, unfortunately, the concept of happiness is such an indeterminate one that even though everyone wishes to attain happiness, yet he can never say definitely and consistently what it is that he really wishes and wills. The reason for this is that all the elements belonging to the concept of happiness are unexceptionally empirical, i.e., they must be borrowed from experience, while for the idea of happiness there is required an absolute whole, a maximum of well-being in my present and in every future condition. Now it is impossible for the most insightful and at the same time most powerful, but nonetheless finite, being to frame here a determinate concept of what it is that he really wills. Does he want riches? How much anxiety, envy, and intrigue might he not thereby bring down upon his own head! Or knowledge and insight? Perhaps these might only give him an eye that much sharper for revealing that much more dreadfully evils which are at present hidden but are yet unavoidable, or such an eye might burden him with still further needs for the desires which already concern him enough. Or long life? Who guarantees that it would not be a long misery? Or health at least? How often has infirmity of the body kept one from excesses into which perfect health would have allowed him to fall, and so on? In brief, he is not able on any principle to determine with complete certainty what will make him truly happy, because to do so would require omniscience. Therefore, one cannot act according to determinate principles in order to be happy, but only according to empirical counsels, e.g., of diet, frugality, politeness, reserve, etc., which are shown by experience to contribute on the average the most to well-being. There follows from this that imperatives of prudence, strictly speaking cannot command at all, i.e., present actions objectively as practically necessary. They are to be taken as counsels (*consilia*) rather than as commands (*praecepta*) of reason. The problem of determining certainly and universally what action will promote the happiness of a rational being is completely insoluble. Therefore, regarding such action no imperative that in the strictest sense could command what is to be done to make one happy is possible, inasmuch as happiness is not an ideal of reason but of imagination. Such an ideal rests merely on empirical grounds; in vain can there be expected that such grounds should determine an action whereby the totality of an infinite series of consequences could be attained. This imperative of prudence would, nevertheless, be an analytic practical proposition if one assumes that the means to happiness could with certainty be assigned; for it differs from the imperative of skill only in that for it the end is given while for the latter the end is merely possible. Since both, however, command only the means to what is assumed to be willed as an end, the imperative commanding him who wills the end to will likewise the means thereto is in both cases analytic. Hence there is also no difficulty regarding the possibility of an imperative of prudence.

On the other hand, the question as to how the imperative of morality is possible is undoubtedly the only one requiring a solution. For it is not at all hypothetical; and hence the objective necessity which it presents cannot be based on any presupposition, as was the case with the hypothetical imperatives. Only there must never here be forgotten that no example can show, i.e., empirically, whether there is any such imperative at all. Rather, care must be taken lest all imperatives which are seemingly categorical may nevertheless be covertly hypothetical. For instance, when it is said that you should not make a false promise, the assumption is that the necessity of this avoidance is no mere advice for escaping some other evil, so that is might be said that you should not make a false promise lest you ruin your credit when the falsity comes to light. But when it is asserted that an action of this kind must be regarded as bad in itself, then the imperative of prohibition is therefore categorical. Nevertheless, it cannot with certainty be shown by means of an example that the will is here determined solely by the law without any other incentive, even though such may seem to be the case. For it is always possible that secretly there is fear of disgrace and perhaps also obscure dread of other dangers; such fear and dread may have influenced the will. Who can prove by experience that a cause is not present? Experience only shows that a cause is not perceived. But in such a case the so-called moral imperative, which as such appears to be categorical and unconditioned, would actually be only a pragmatic precept which makes us pay attention to our own advantage and merely teaches us to take such advantage into consideration.

We shall, therefore, have to investigate the possibility of a categorical imperative entirely a priori, inasmuch as we do not here have the advantage of having its reality given in experience and consequently of thus being obligated merely to explain its possibility rather than to establish it. In the meantime so much can be seen for now: the categorical imperative alone purports to be a practical law, while all the others may be called principles of the will but not laws. The reason for this is that whatever is necessary merely in order to attain some arbitrary purpose can be regarded as in itself contingent, and the precept can always be ignored once the purpose is abandoned. Contrariwise, an unconditioned command does not leave the will free to choose the opposite at its own liking. Consequently, only such a command carries with it that necessity which is demanded from a law.

Secondly, in the case of this categorical imperative, or law of morality, the reason for the difficulty (of discerning its possibility) is quite serious. The categorical imperative is an a priori synthetic practical proposition,[5] and since discerning the possibility of propositions of this sort involves so much difficulty in theoretic knowledge, there may readily be gathered that there will be no less difficulty in practical knowledge.

In solving this problem, we want first to inquire whether perhaps the mere concept of a categorical imperative may not also supply us with the formula containing the proposition that can alone be a categorical imperative. For even when we know the purport of such an absolute command, the question as to how it is possible will still require a special and difficult effort, which we postpone to the last section.[6]

If I think of a hypothetical imperative in general, I do not know beforehand what it will contain until its condition is given. But if I think of a categorical imperative, I know immediately what it contains. For since, besides the law, the imperative contains only the necessity that the maxim[7] should accord with this law, while the law

---

[5]I connect a priori, and therefore necessarily, the act with the will without presupposing any condition taken from some inclination (though I make such a connection only objectively, i.e., under the idea of a reason having full power over all subjective motives). Hence this is a practical proposition which does not analytically derive the willing of an action from some other willing already presupposed (for we possess no such perfect will) but which connects the willing of an action immediately with the concept of the will of a rational being as something which is not contained in this concept.

[6][See below Ak. 446–63.]

[7]A maxim is the subjective principle of acting and must be distinguished from the objective principle, viz., the practical law. A maxim contains the practical rule which reason determines in accordance with the conditions of the subject (often his ignorance or his inclinations) and is thus the principle according to which the subject does act. But the law is the objective principle valid for every rational being, and it is the principle according to which he ought to act, i.e., an imperative.

contains no condition to restrict it, there remains nothing but the universality of a law as such with which the maxim of the action should conform. This conformity alone is properly what is represented as necessary by the imperative.

Hence there is only one categorical imperative and it is this: Act only according to that maxim whereby you can at the same time will that it should become a universal law.[8]

Now if all imperatives of duty can be derived from this one imperative as their principle, then there can at least be shown what is understood by the concept of duty and what it means, even though there is left undecided whether what is called duty may not be an empty concept.

The universality of law according to which effects are produced constitutes what is properly called nature in the most general sense (as to form), i.e., the existence of things as far as determined by universal laws. Accordingly, the universal imperative of duty may be expressed thus: Act as if the maxim of your action were to become through your will a universal law of nature.[9]

We shall now enumerate some duties, following the usual division of them into duties to ourselves and to others and into perfect and imperfect duties.[10]

1. A man reduced to despair by a series of misfortunes feels sick of life but is still so far in possession of his reason that he can ask himself whether taking his own life would not be contrary to his duty to himself.[11] Now he asks whether the maxim of his action could become a universal law of nature. But his maxim is this: from self-love I make as my principle to shorten my life when its continued duration threatens more evil than it promises satisfaction. There only remains the question as to whether this principle of self-love can become a universal law of nature. One sees at once a contradiction in a system of nature whose law would destroy life by means of the very same

[8][This formulation of the categorical imperative is often referred to as the formula of universal law.]

[9][This is often called the formula of the law of nature.]

[10]There should be noted here that I reserve the division of duties for a future *Metaphysics of Morals* [in Part II of the *Metaphysics of Morals*, entitled *The Metaphysical Principles of Virtue*, Ak. 417–474]. The division presented here stands as merely an arbitrary one (in order to arrange my examples). For the rest, I understand here by a perfect duty one which permits no exception in the interest of inclination. Accordingly, I have perfect duties which are external [to others], while other ones are internal [to oneself]. This classification runs contrary to the accepted usage of the schools, but I do not intend to justify it here, since there is no difference for my purpose whether this classification is accepted or not.

[11][Not committing suicide is an example of a perfect duty of oneself. See *Metaphysical Principles of Virtue*, Ak. 422–24.]

feeling that acts so as to stimulate the furtherance of life, and hence there could be no existence as a system of nature. Therefore, such a maxim cannot possibly hold as a universal law of nature and is, consequently, wholly opposed to the supreme principle of all duty.

2. Another man in need finds himself forced to borrow money. He knows well that he won't be able to repay it, but he sees also that he will not get any loan unless he firmly promises to repay it within a fixed time. He wants to make such a promise, but he still has conscience enough to ask himself whether it is not permissible and is contrary to duty to get out of difficulty in this way. Suppose, however, that he decides to do so. The maxim of his action would then be expressed as follows: when I believe myself to be in need of money, I will borrow money and promise to pay it back, although I know that I can never do so. Now this principle of self-love or personal advantage may perhaps be quite compatible with one's entire future welfare, but the question is now whether it is right.[12] I then transform the requirement of self-love into a universal law and put the question thus: how would things stand if my maxim were to become a universal law? He then sees at once that such a maxim could never hold as a universal law of nature and be consistent with itself, but must necessarily be self-contradictory. For the universality of a law which says that anyone believing himself to be in difficulty could promise whatever he pleases with the intention of not keeping it would make promising itself and the end to be attained thereby quite impossible, inasmuch as no one would believe what was promised him but would merely laugh at all such utterances as being vain pretenses.

3. A third finds in himself a talent whose cultivation could make him a man useful in many respects. But he finds himself in comfortable circumstances and prefers to indulge in pleasure rather than to bother himself about broadening and improving his fortunate natural aptitudes. But he asks himself further whether his maxim of neglecting his natural gifts, besides agreeing of itself with his propensity to indulgence, might agree also with what is called duty.[13] He then sees that a system of nature could indeed always subsist according to such a universal law, even though every man (like South Sea Islanders) should let his talents rust and resolve to devote his life entirely to idleness, indulgence, propagation, and, in

---

[12][Keeping promises is an example of a perfect duty to others. See *ibid.*, Ak. 423–31.]

[13][Cultivating one's talents is an example of an imperfect duty to oneself. See *ibid.*, Ak. 444–46.]

a word, to enjoyment. But he cannot possibly will that this should become a universal law of nature or be implanted in us as such a law by a natural instinct. For as a rational being he necessarily wills that all his faculties should be developed, inasmuch as they are given him for all sorts of possible purposes.

4. A fourth man finds things going well for himself but sees others (whom he could help) struggling with great hardships; and he thinks: what does it matter to me? Let everybody be as happy as Heaven wills or as he can make himself; I shall take nothing from him nor even envy him; but I have no desire to contribute anything to his well-being or to his assistance when in need. If such a way of thinking were to become a universal law of nature, the human race admittedly could very well subsist and doubtless could subsist even better than when everyone prates about sympathy and benevolence and even on occasion exerts himself to practice them but, on the other hand, also cheats when he can, betrays the rights of man, or otherwise violates them. But even though it is possible that a universal law of nature could subsist in accordance with that maxim, still it is impossible to will that such a principle should hold everywhere as a law of nature.[14] For a will which resolved in this way would contradict itself, inasmuch as cases might often arise in which one would have need of the love and sympathy of others and in which he would deprive himself, by such a law of nature springing from his own will, of all hope of the aid he wants for himself.

These are some of the many actual duties, or at least what are taken to be such, whose derivation from the single principle cited above is clear. We must be able to will that a maxim of our action become a universal law; this is the canon for morally estimating any of our actions. Some actions are so constituted that their maxims cannot without contradiction even be thought as a universal law of nature, much less be willed as what should become one. In the case of others this internal impossibility is indeed not found, but there is still no possibility of willing that their maxim should be raised to the universality of a law of nature, because such a will would contradict itself. There is no difficulty in seeing that the former kind of action conflicts with strict or narrow [perfect] (irremissible) duty, while the second kind conflicts only with broad [imperfect] (meritorious) duty.[15] By means of these examples

---

[14][Benefiting others is an example of an imperfect duty to others. See *ibid.*, Ak. 452–54.]
[15][Compare *ibid.*, Ak. 390–94, 410–11, 421–51.]

there has thus been fully set forth how all duties depend as regards the kind of obligation (not the object of their action) upon the one principle.

If we now attend to ourselves in any transgression of a duty, we find that we actually do not will that our maxim should become a universal law—because this is impossible for us—but rather that the opposite of this maxim should remain a law universally.[16] We only take the liberty of making an exception to the law for ourselves (or just for this one time) to the advantage of our inclination. Consequently, if we weighed up everything from one and the same standpoint, namely, that of reason, we would find a contradiction in our own will, viz., that a certain principle be objectively necessary as a universal law and yet subjectively not hold universally but should admit of exceptions. But since we at one moment regard our action from the standpoint of a will wholly in accord with reason and then at another moment regard the very same action from the standpoint of a will affected by inclination, there is really no contradiction here. Rather, there is an opposition (*antagonismus*) of inclination to the precept of reason, whereby the universality (*universalitas*) of the principle is changed into a mere generality (*generalitas*) so that the practical principle of reason may meet the maxim halfway. Although this procedure cannot be justified in our own impartial judgment, yet it does show that we actually acknowledge the validity of the categorical imperative and (with all respect for it) merely allow ourselves a few exceptions which, as they seem to us, are unimportant and forced upon us.

We have thus at least shown that if duty is a concept which is to have significance and real legislative authority for our actions, then such duty can be expressed only in categorical imperatives but not at all in hypothetical ones. We have also—and this is already a great deal—exhibited clearly and definitely for every application what is the content of the categorical imperative, which must contain the principle of all duty (if there is such a thing at all). But we have not yet advanced far enough to prove a priori that there actually is an imperative of this kind, that there is a practical law which of itself commands absolutely and without any incentives, and that following this law is duty.

---

[16][This is to say, for example, that when you tell a lie, you do so on the condition that others are truthful and believe that what you are saying is true, because otherwise your lie will never work to get you what you want. When you tell a lie, you simply take exception to the general rule that says everyone should always tell the truth.]

Maria von Herbert's Challenge to Kant

Rae Langton

This is a paper about two philosophers who wrote to each other. One is famous; the other is not. It is about two practical standpoints, the strategic and the human, and what the famous philosopher said of them. And it is about friendship and deception, duty and despair. That is enough by way of preamble.[1]

Friendship

In 1791 Kant received a letter from an Austrian lady whom he had never met. She was Maria von Herbert, a keen and able student of Kant's philosophy, and sister to Baron Franz Paul von Herbert, another zealous Kantian disciple. The zeal of her brother the Baron was indeed so great that he had left his lead factory, and his wife, for two years in order to study Kant's philosophy in Weimar and Jena. Upon his return, the von Herbert household had become a centre, a kind of *salon*, where the critical philosophy was intensely debated, against the backdrop of vehement opposition to Kant in Austria as in many German states. The household was, in the words of a student of Fichte's, 'a new Athens', an oasis of Enlightenment spirit, devoted to preaching and propagating the Kantian gospel, reforming religion, and replacing dull unthinking piety with a morality based on reason.[2] Here is the letter.

[1]This paper is a shortened version of 'Duty and Desolation', which appeared in *Philosophy*, 67(1992). As the original version makes evident, my interpretation of Kant owes a great debt to the work of P. F. Strawson ('Freedom and Resentment', in *Freedom and Resentment* (Methuen: London, 1974), 1–25), and Christine Korsgaard, whose views on Kant and lying are developed in 'The Right to Lie: Kant on Dealing with Evil', *Philosophy and Public Affairs*, 15, 4 (1986), 325–49; and, on Kant and friendship, in 'Creating the Kingdom of Ends: Responsibility and Reciprocity in Personal Relations', *Philosophical Perspectives 6: Ethics*, ed. James Tomberlin (The Ridgeview Publishing Company: Atascadero, Calif., 1992). 'Duty and Desolation' was first read at a conference on moral psychology at Monash, Aug. 1991, and has been read at the University of Queensland, the Australian National University, and the University of Delhi. I am indebted to those present on all these occasions for stimulating and searching comments. I am especially grateful to Philip Pettit and Richard Holton for helpful discussion, and to Margaret Wilson and Christine Korsgaard for written comments on an early draft.
[2]According to Arnulf Zweig, in his introduction to *Kant: Philosophical Correspondence, 1759–1799* (University of Chicago Press: Chicago, 1967), 24.

1. To Kant, from Maria von Herbert, August 1791

Great Kant,

As a believer calls to his God, I call to you for help, for comfort, or for counsel to prepare me for death. Your writings prove that there is a future life. But as for this life, I have found nothing, nothing at all that could replace the good I have lost, for I loved someone who, in my eyes, encompassed within himself all that is worth-while, so that I lived only for him, everything else was in comparison just rubbish, cheap trinkets. Well, I have offended this person, because of a long drawn out lie, which I have now disclosed to him, though there was nothing unfavourable to my character in it, I had no vice in my life that needed hiding. The lie was enough though, and his love vanished. As an honourable man, he doesn't refuse me friendship. But that inner feeling that once, unbidden, led us to each other, is no more—oh my heart splinters into a thousand pieces! If I had't read so much of your work I would certainly have put an end to my life. But the conclusion I had to draw from your theory stops me—it is wrong for me to die because my life is tormented, instead I'm supposed to life because of my being. Now put yourself in my place, and either damn me or comfort me. I've read the metaphysic of morals, and the categorical imperative, and it doesn't help a bit. My reason abandons me just when I need it. Answer me, I implore you—or you won't be acting in accordance with your own imperative.

My address is Maria Herbert of Klagenfurt, Carinthia, care of the white lead factory, or perhaps you would rather send it via Reinhold because the mail is more reliable there.

Kant, much impressed by this letter, sought advice from a friend as to what he should do. The friend advised him strongly to relpy, and to do his best to distract his correspondent from 'the object to which she [was] enfettered'.[3] We have the carefully prepared draft of Kant's response.

---

[3]Letter to Kant from Ludwig Ernst Borowski, probably Aug. 1791. The correspondence between Kant and Maria von Herbert, and the related letters, are in volume 11 of the edition of Kant's work published by the Prussian Academy of Sciences (Walter de Gruyter: Berlin, 1922). The English translations given in this paper are closely based on those of Arnulf Zweig, partly revised in the light of the Academy edition, and very much abridged. See Zweig, *Kant: Philosophical Correspondence, 1759–99*, © 1967 by the University of Chicago. All Rights Reserved. (I make use of the translations with the kind permission of Prof. Zweig and the University of Chicago Press. Readers who would like to see fuller versions of the letters should consult the Academy edition, or Zweig translations.)

2. To Maria von Herbert, Spring 1792 (Kant's rough draft)

Your deeply felt letter comes from a heart that must have been created for the sake of virtue and honesty, since it is so receptive to instruction in those qualities. I must do as you ask, namely, put myself in your place, and prescribe for you a pure moral sedative. I do not know whether your relationship is one of marriage or friendship, but it makes no significant difference. For love, be it for one's spouse or for a friend, presupposes the same mutual esteem for the other's character, without which it is no more than perishable, sensual delusion.

A love like that wants to communicate itself completely, and it expects of its respondent a similar sharing of heart, unweakened by distrustful reticence. That is what the ideal of friendship demands. But there is something in us which puts limits on such frankness, some obstacle to this mutual outpouring of the heart, which makes one keep some part of one's thought locked within oneself, even when one is most intimate. The sages of old complained of this secret distrust—'My dear friends, there is no such thing as a friend!'

We can't expect frankness of people, since everyone fears that to reveal himself completely would be to make himself despised others. But this lack of frankness, this reticence, is still very different from dishonesty. What the honest but reticent man says is true, but not the whole truth. What the dishonest man says is something he knows to be false. Such as assertion is called, in the theory of virtue, a lie. It may be harmless, but it is not on that account innocent. It is a serious violation of a duty to oneself; it subverts the dignity of humanity in our own person, and attacks the roots of our thinking. As you see, you have sought counsel from a physician who is no flatterer. I speak for your beloved and present him with arguments that justify his having wavered in his affection for you.

Ask yourself whether you reproach yourself for the imprudence of confessing, or for the immorality intrinsic to the lie. If the former, then you regret having done your duty. And why? Because it has resulted in the loss of your friend's confidence. This regret is not motivated by anything moral, since it is produced by an awareness not of the act itself, but of its consequences. But if your reproach is grounded in a moral judgment of your behaviour, it would be a poor moral physician who would advise you to cast it from your mind.

When your change in attitude has been revealed to your beloved, only time will be needed to quench, little by little, the traces of his justified indignation, and to transform his coldness into a more firmly grounded love. If this doesn't happen, then the earlier warmth of his affection was more physical than moral, and would have disappeared anyway—a misfortune which we often encounter in life, and when we do, must meet with composure. For the value of life, insofar as it consists of the enjoyment we get from people, is vastly overrated.

Here then, my dear friend, you find the customary divisions of a sermon: instruction, penalty and comfort. Devote yourself to the first two; when they have had their effect, comfort will be found by itself.

Kant's letter has an enormously interesting and sensitive discussion of friendship and secrecy, much of which turns up word for word in *The Doctrine of Virtue*, published some six years later.[4] But what Kant's letter fails to say is as at least as interesting as what it says. Herbert writes that she has lost her love, that her heart is shattered, that there is nothing left to make life worth living, and that Kant's moral philosophy hasn't helped a bit. Kant's reply is to suggest that the love is deservedly lost, that misery is an appropriate response to one's own moral failure, and that the really interesting moral question here is the one that hinges on a subtle but necessary scope distinction: the distinction between telling a lie and failing to tell the truth, between *saying 'not-p'*, and *not saying 'p'*. Conspicuously absent is an acknowledgement of Herbert's more than theoretical interest in the question: is suicide compatible with the moral law? And perhaps this is just as well from a practical point of view. The sooner she gives up those morbid thoughts the better; the less said on the morbid subject, the less likely the morbid thoughts will arise. Perhaps it is also just as well, for Kant, from a theoretical point of view. Kant's conviction that suicide is incompatible with the moral law is not nearly as well founded as he liked to think; so here too, the less said, the better. Having posted his moral sedative off to Austria, and receiving no reply from the patient in more than a year, Kant

---

[4]Immanuel Kant, *The Doctrine of Virtue*, (part II of *The Metaphysic of Morals*), trans. Mary Gregor (Harper and Row: London, 1964). One wonders whether these parts of *The Doctrine of Virtue* may have been influenced by Kant's thoughts about Herbert's predicament. An alternative explanation might be that *The Doctrine of Virtue* and Kant's letter to Herbert are both drawing on Kant's lecture notes.

enquired of a mutual friend who often saw her about the effect his letter had had. Herbert then wrote back, with apologies for her delay. This is her second letter.

3. To Kant, from Maria von Herbert, January 1793

Dear and revered sir,

Your kindness, and your exact understanding of the human heart, encourage me to describe to you, unshrinkingly, the further progress of my soul. The lie was no cloaking of a vice, but a sin of keeping something back out of consideration for the friendship (still veiled by love) that existed then. There was a struggle, I was aware of the honesty friendship demands, and at the same time I could foresee the terribly wounding consequences. Finally I had the strength and revealed the truth to my friend, but so late—and when I told him, the stone in my heart was gone, but his love was torn away in exchange. My friend hardened in his coldness, just as you said in your letter. But then afterwards he changed towards me, and offered me again the most intimate friendship. I'm glad enough about it, for his sake—but I'm not really content, because it's just amusement, it doesn't have any point.

My vision is clear now. I feel that a vast emptiness extends inside me, and all around me—so that I almost find my self to be superfluous, unnecessary. Nothing attracts me. I'm tormented by a boredom that makes life intolerable. Don't think me arrogant for saying this, but the demands of morality are too easy for me. I would eagerly do twice as much as they command. They only get their prestige from the attractiveness of sin, and it costs me almost no effort to resist that.

I comfort myself with the thought that, since the practice of morality is so bound up with sensuality, it can only count for this world. I can hope that the afterlife won't be yet another life ruled by these few, easy demands of morality, another empty and vegetating life. Experience wants to take me to task for this bad temper I have against life by showing me that nearly everyone finds his life ending much too soon, everyone is so glad to be alive. So as not to be a queer exception to the rule, I shall tell you of a remote cause of my deviation, namely my chronic poor health, which dates from the time I first wrote to you. I don't study the natural sciences or the arts any more, since I don't feel that I'm genius enough to extend them; and for myself, there's no need to know them. I'm indifferent to everything that doesn't bear on the categorical imperative, and my transcendental consciousness—although I'm all done with those thoughts too.

You can see, perhaps, why I only want one thing, namely to shorten this pointless life, a life which I am convinced will get neither better nor worse. If you consider that I am still young and that each day interests me only to the extent that it brings me closer to death, you can judge what a great benefactor you would be if you were to examine this question closely. I ask you, because my conception of morality is silent here, whereas it speaks decisively on all other matters. And if you cannot give me the answer I seek, I beg you to give me something that will get this intolerable emptiness out of my soul. Then I might become a useful part of nature, and, if my health permits, would make a trip to Königsberg in a few years. I want to ask permission, in advance, to visit you. You must tell me your story then, because I would like to know what kind of life your philosophy has led you to— whether it never seemed to you to be worth the bother to marry, or to give your whole heart to anyone, or to reproduce your likeness. I have an engraved portrait of you by Bause, from Leipzig. I see a profound calm there, and moral depth—but not the astuteness of which the *Critique of Pure Reason* is proof. And I'm dissatisfied not to be able to look you right in the face.

Please fulfill my wish, if it's not too inconvenient. And I need to remind you: if you do me this great favour and take the trouble to answer, please focus on specific details, not on the general points, which I understand, and already understood back when I happily studied your works at the side of my friend. You would like him, I'm sure. He is honest, goodhearted, and intelligent— and besides that, fortunate enough to fit this world.

I am with deepest respect and truth, Maria Herbert.

Herbert's letter speaks for itself. The passion, the turbulence, has vanished. Desolation has taken its place, a 'vast emptiness', a vision of the world and the self that is chilling in its clarity, chilling in its nihilism. Apathy reigns. Desire is dead. Nothing attracts. Bereft of inclination, the self is 'superfluous', as Herbert so starkly puts it. Nothing has any point—except of course the categorical imperative. But morality itself has become a torment, not because it is too difficult, but because it is too easy. Without the counterweight of opposing inclination, what course could there be but to obey? The moral life is the empty, vegetating life, where one sees at a glance what the moral law requires and simply does it, unhampered by the competing attractions of sin. Herbert concludes that morality must be bound up with sensuality, that moral credit depends on the battle of the will with the sensual passions, a battle which, when there are no passions, is won merely, and tediously, by default—and where can be the credit in that? The imperative requires us never to treat persons merely as means to one's own ends. But if one has no ends, if one is simply empty, what could be easier than to obey? Herbert draws hope from her conclusion: if morality is bound to sensuality, with luck the next life will not be thus accursed.

This sounds like heresy. Is it? If so, Kant is blind to it. But perhaps it is not heresy at all. What Kant fails to see—what Herbert herself fails to see—is that her life constitutes a profound challenge to his philosophy, at least construed one way. Consider Kant's views on duty and inclination.

An action has moral worth when it is done for the sake of duty; it is not sufficient that the action conforms with duty.[5] Now, inclinations are often sufficient to make us perform actions that conform with our duty. To preserve one's life is a duty; and most of us have strong inclinations to preserve our lives. To help others where one can is a duty; and most of us are sympathetic enough and amiable enough to be inclined to help others, at least some of the time. But—if we take Kant at his word here—actions thus motivated have no moral worth. The action of moral worth is that of 'the wretched man . . . [for whom] disappointments and hopeless misery have quite taken away the taste for life, who longs for death' but who, notwithstanding, preserves his life. The action that has moral worth is that of the misanthropist, 'the man cold in temperament and indifferent to the sufferings of others' who nonetheless helps others 'not from inclination but from duty'.[6]

This looks as though moral credit depends on both the absence of coinciding inclinations, such as sympathy; and the presence of opposing inclinations, like misanthropy. If so, Herbert is right: morality depends on there being inclinations to defeat. It is important to see though that even here, what Kant says is not motivated by a kind of blind rule worship, but by a sense of the gulf between the two standpoints from which we must view ourselves. We are at once cogs in the grand machine of nature, and free agents in the Kingdom of Ends. We are persons, members of an intelligible world, authors of our actions; and at the same

[5]*The Groundwork of the Metaphysic of Morals*, trans. M.J. Paton (Harper and Row: London, 1964), 397.
[6]Ibid. 398.

time animals, puppets of our genes and hormones, buffeted about by our lusts and loathings. Inclinations are *passions* in the sense that they *just happen* to us. And insofar as we let our actions be driven by them we allow ourselves to be puppets, not persons. We allow ourselves, to use Kant's own metaphors, to become marionettes or automatons, which may appear to be initiators of action, but whose freedom is illusory, 'no better than the freedom of a turnspit, which, when once wound up also carries out its motions by itself'.[7] The inclinations are effects on us, they are *pathe*, and for that reason pathological. If we let them be causes of our behaviour, we abandon our personhood.

Whether they lead us towards the action of duty or away from it, inclinations are among virtue's chief obstacles. When inclination opposes duty, it is an obstacle to duty's performance. When inclination coincides with duty, it is an obstacle at least to knowledge of the action's worth. 'Inclination, be it good-natured or otherwise, is blind and slavish . . . The feeling of sympathy and warmhearted fellow-feeling . . . is burdensome even to right-thinking persons, confusing their considered maxims and creating the wish to be free from them and subject only to law-giving reason.'[8] In the battle against the inclinations we can enlist the aid of that strange thing, respect, or reverence for the moral law. Reverence for the law serves to 'weaken the hindering influence of the inclinations'.[9] Reverence is a kind of feeling, but it is not something we 'passively feel', something inflicted upon us from outside. It is the sensible correlate of our own moral activity, the 'consciousness of the direct constraint of the will through law'.[10] Its function is not to motivate our moral actions, for that would still be motivation by feeling. Rather, its function is to remove the obstacles, to silence inclinations, something we should all look forward to. For inclinations are 'so far from having an absolute value . . . that it must . . . be the universal wish of every rational being to be wholly free from them'.[11]

Kant goes so far as to say we have a *duty of apathy*, a duty he is less than famous for. 'Virtue necessarily presupposes apathy', he says in *The Doctrine of Virtue*. 'The word "apathy" has fallen into disrepute', he continues, 'as if it meant lack of feeling and so subjective indifference regarding objects of choice: it has been taken for weakness. We can

---

[7]Immanuel Kant, *Critique of Practical Reason*, trans. L.W. Beck (Macmillan: London, 1956), 97, 101.
[8]Ibid. 119.
[9]Ibid. 80.
[10]Ibid. 117.
[11]*Groundwork*, 428.

prevent this misunderstanding by giving the name "moral apathy" to that freedom from agitation which is to be distinguished from indifference, for in it the feelings arising from sensuous impressions lose their influence on moral feeling only because reverence for the law prevails over all such feelings'.[12] Something rather similar to apathy is described in the *Critique of Practical Reason*, but this time it is called not apathy, but 'bliss' (*Seligkeit*). Bliss is the state of 'complete independence from inclinations and desires'.[13] While it must be the universal wish of every rational being to achieve bliss, can we in fact achieve it? Apparently not, or not here. Bliss is 'the self-sufficiency which can be ascribed only to the Supreme Being'.[14] The Supreme Being has no passions and inclinations. His intuition is intellectual, and not sensible. He can be affected by nothing, not even our prayers. He can have no *pathe*. God is the being more apathetic than which cannot be conceived.

What of Kant's moral patient? She is well beyond the virtue of apathy that goes with mastery of the inclinations. She has no inclinations left to master. She respects the moral law, and obeys it. But she needn't battle her passions to do so. She has no passions. She is empty—but for the clear vision of the moral law and unshrinking obedience to it. She is well on the way to bliss, lucky woman, and, if Kant is right about bliss, well on the way to Godhead. No wonder she feels that she—unlike her unnamed friend—does not quite 'fit the world'. She obeys the moral law in her day to day dealings with people from the motive of duty alone. She has no other motives. She is no heretic. She is a Kantian saint. Oh brave new world, that has such moral saints in it.[15]

What should Kant have said about inclinations? I have no clear view about this, but some brief remarks may be in order. A saner view is arguably to be found in Kant's own writings. In the *Doctrine of Virtue*[16] Kant apparently advocates the cultivation of natural sentiment to back up the motive of duty. It is hard, though, to reconcile this with his other teachings, which tell us that inclinations, all inclinations, are to be abjured, as 'blind and slavish', in the graphic phrase from the *Critique of Practical Reason*. 'Blind' is the evocative word in the Kantian context, associated as it is with the blind workings of nature, with the sensual as opposed to the intellectual. It calls to mind the

---

[12]*Doctrine of Virtue*, 407.
[13]*Critique of Practical Reason*, 118.
[14]Ibid.
[15]See Susan Wolf, 'Moral Saints', *The Journal of Philosophy*, 79 (1982), 419–39, on the perils of sainthood.
[16]See e.g. *Doctrine of Virtue*, 456.

famous slogan of the first *Critique*: thoughts without content are empty, intuitions without concepts are *blind*. That slogan famously captures the synthesis of rationalism and empiricism Kant thought necessary for knowledge. It acknowledges the twin aspects of human creatures, as Kant sees us: we have a *sensible* intuition, a *passive* intuition, through which we are affected by the world; and an active intellect. We *need both*. If only Kant had effected a similar synthesis in the moral sphere: for if it is true, as he says, that inclinations without reasons are blind, it seems equally true that reasons without inclinations are empty. The moral life without inclinations is a life of 'intolerable emptiness', as Herbert found. We need both.

I said that Herbert has no inclinations: but there are two exceptions. She wants to die. And she wants to visit Kant. She is, it seems, like the would-be suicide Kant describes in *The Groundwork*: her persistence with life has moral worth, because it is so opposed to her inclinations. But is she really like him? Not quite. For she is not even sure that duty points to persistence with life. Notice the change here. In her first letter she believed that self-respect, respect for 'her own being' required her to persist with life. But as her 'being' has begun to contract, as the self has withered, sloughed off, become superfluous—as the emptiness has grown—so too has her doubt. Now her conception of morality is 'silent' on the question of suicide. She wants to die. She has almost no opposing inclinations. And morality is silent. It takes no expert to wonder if she is in danger.

Why does she want to visit Kant? She says (letter 3): 'I would like to know what kind of life your philosophy has led you to'. In the *Critique of Practical Reason* Kant cites approvingly what he took to be the practice of the ancients: no one was justified in calling himself a philosopher—a lover of wisdom—'unless he could show [philosophy's] infallible effect on his own person as an example'.[17] Kant thinks we are justified in inquiring after the effect of philosophy on the philosopher, daunting as the prospect seems today. But what does Herbert have in mind? She wonders, perhaps, whether Kant's life is as empty as her own, and for the same reason. She discovered that love is 'pointless' when inclinations have withered, when you have no passions of your own and therefore no passions to share. And she wonders whether Kant's life reflects this discovery. She wonders whether Kant's philosophy has led him to think that it was simply 'not worth the bother' to marry, or to 'give his whole heart' to anyone. Perhaps she is right to wonder.

---

[17] *Critique of Practical Reason*, 190.

Shipwreck

In reply to an enquiry, Kant received this explanatory letter from a mutual friend, Erhard.

4. To Kant, from J. B. Erhard, January 17, 1793

I can say little of Miss Herbert. She has capsized on the reef of romantic love. In order to realize an idealistic love, she gave herself to a man who misused her trust. And then, trying to achieve such love with another, she told her new lover about the previous one. That is the key to her letter. If my friend Herbert had more delicacy, I think she could still be saved.

Yours, Erhard.

Kant writes again, not to Herbert, but to someone about whom we know little:

5. From Kant, to Elisabeth Motherby, February 11, 1793

I have numbered the letters[18] which I have the honour of passing on to you, my dear mademoiselle, according to the dates I received them. The ecstatical little lady didn't think to date them. The third letter, from another source, provides an explanation of the lady's curious mental derangement. A number of expressions refer to writings of mine that she read, and are difficult to understand without an interpreter.

You have been so fortunate in your upbringing that I do not need to commend these letters to you as an example of warning, to guard you against the wanderings of a sublimated fantasy. But they may serve nonetheless to make your perception of that good fortune all the more lively.

I am, with the greatest respect, my honoured lady's most obedient servant, I. Kant.

Kant is unaware that he has received a letter from a Kantian saint. Indeed, it is hard to believe that he has read her second letter. He relies on the opinion of his friend, whose diagnosis of the patient resorts to that traditional and convenient malady of feminine hysteria. Herbert 'has capsized on the reef of romantic love'. The diagnosis is exactly

---

[18]Letters 1,3, and 4 above. Elisabeth Motherby was the daughter of Kant's friend Robert Motherby, an English merchant in Königsberg.

wrong. Herbert has no passions. Her vision is clear. Her life is empty. But it is easier not to take this in, easier to suppose a simpler illness. She is at the mercy (aren't all women?) of irrational passions. She is evidently beyond the reach of instruction, beyond the reach of his moral sedatives; so Kant abandons her. It is hard to imagine a more dramatic shift from the interactive stance to the objective.[19] In Kant's first letter, Herbert is 'my dear friend', she is the subject for moral instruction, and reprimand. She is responsible for some immoral actions, but she has a 'heart created for the sake of virtue', capable of seeing the good and doing it. Kant is doing his best to communicate, instruct, and console. He is not very good at it, hardly surprising if he believes—as I think he does—that he should master rather than cultivate his moral sentiments. But there is little doubt that the good will is there. He treats her as a human being, as an end, as a person. This is the standpoint of interaction.

But now? Herbert is *die kleine Schwärmerin*, the little dreamer, the ecstatical girl, suffering a 'curious mental derangement', lost in the 'wanderings of a sublimated fantasy', who doesn't think, especially about important things like dating letters. Kant is here forgetting an important aspect of the duty of respect, which requires something like a Davidsonian principle of charity. We have 'a duty of respect for man *even in the logical use of his reason*: a duty not to censure his error by calling it absurdity . . . but rather to suppose that his error must yet contain some truth and to seek this out.'[20] Herbert, now deranged, is no longer guilty. She is merely unfortunate. She is not responsible for what she does. She is the pitiful product of a poor upbringing. She is an item in the natural order, a ship wrecked on a reef. She is a thing.

And, true to Kant's picture, it now becomes appropriate to use her as a means to his own ends. He bundles up her letters, private communications from a 'dear friend', letters that express thoughts, philosophical and personal, some of them profound. He bundles them up and sends them to an acquaintance under the title, 'Example of Warning'. The end is obscure and contradictory: it seems it is to warn somebody who, on Kant's own view, needs no warning. Is it gossip? Ingratiation? But the striking thing is that the letters are no longer seen as human communications. Far from it: Kant's presumption is that they *will not be understood* by their new recipient. For the letters 'refer to writings of mine that she read, that are difficult to understand without an interpreter'.

---

[19]This is Strawson's way of characterizing the two standpoints in Kant's moral philosophy ('Freedom and Resentment').
[20]*Doctrine of Virtue*, 462, my italics.

This is not the speech of persons, to be understood and debated; this is derangement, to be feared and avoided. These are not thoughts, but symptoms. Kant is doing something with her as one does something with a tool: Herbert cannot share the end of the action. She cannot be co-author. Kant's deceiving of her—neatly achieved by reticence—has made sure of that. Her action of pleading for help, asking advice, arguing philosophy, her action of writing to a well-loved philosopher and then to a friend—these have become the action of warning of the perils of romantic love. She did not choose to do *that*. Well may Kant have warned 'My dear friends, there is no such thing as a friend'.

Strategy for the Kingdom's Sake

Enough. This is not a cautionary tale of the inability of philosophers to live by their philosophy. What interests me is what interested Kant at the outset: friendship and deception. What interests me is the very first problem: the 'long drawn out lie, disclosed'. Was it wrong for Herbert to deceive? Is it always wrong to deceive? Apparently, yes from the Kantian perspective. In deceiving we treat our hearers as less than human. We act from the objective standpoint. We force others to perform actions they don't choose to perform. We make them things. If I reply to the murderer, 'No, my friend is not here', I deceive a human being, use his reasoning ability as a tool, do something that has a goal (saving my friend) that I make impossible for him to share, make him do something (abandon his prey) that he did not choose to do. I have made him, in this respect, a thing.

But this is too simple. Recall that Herbert puts her dilemma like this: 'I was aware of the *the honesty friendship demands* and at the same time I could see the terribly wounding consequences . . . The lie . . . was a . . . keeping something back *out of consideration for the friendship.*'[21] She is torn. Friendship demands honesty; and friendship demands dishonesty. Is she confused? Is she in contradiction? Not at all. It is an old dilemma: having an ideal you want to live by, and an ideal you want to seek and preserve. You owe honesty to your friend; but the friendship will vanish if you are honest. Friendship is a very great good: it is the Kingdom of Ends made real and local. Kant says that the man who is without a friend is the man who 'must shut himself up in himself', who must

---

[21]Letter 3, my italics.

remain 'completely alone with his thoughts, as in a prison'.[22] One of the goods of friendship is that it makes possible the kind of relationship where one can unlock the prison of the self, reveal oneself to the compassionate and understanding eye of the other. But Kant sees true friendship to be a very rare thing, rare, he says as a black swan.[23] And what threatens friendship most is asymmetry, inequality with regard to love or respect, which can result in the partial breakdown of the interactive stance. This asymmetry can be brought about by the very act of self revelation: if one person 'reveals his failings while the other person concealed his own, he would lose something of the other's respect by presenting himself so candidly'.[24] What Kant is pointing to is the very problem encountered, far more acutely, by Herbert: in being a friend, in acting in the way that friendship demands, one can sometimes threaten friendship. To act as a member of the Kingdom can make the Kingdom more, and not less, remote. How should we think of Kant's ideal: is the Kingdom an ideal to be lived by, or a goal to be sought? If it is ever the latter, then sometimes—in evil circumstances—it will be permissible, and even required, to act strategically for the Kingdom's sake.[25] There is a question about what evil is. But for Kant it must, above all, be this: the reduction of persons to things. Now consider Herbert's position. There is something we have been leaving out. Herbert is a *woman* in a society in which women start out on an unequal footing and then live out their lives that way, where women—especially women—must perpetually walk a tightrope between being treated as things and treated as persons. She must make her choices against a backdrop of social institutions and habits that strip her of the dignity due to persons, where what she does and what she says will always be interpreted in the light of that backdrop, so that even if she says 'my vision is clear', and speaks in a manner consistent with that claim, her speech will be read as the speech of the deranged, a mere plaything of the passions. Central among the institutions she must encounter in her life is that of the sexual marketplace, where human beings are viewed as having a *price*, and not a dignity, and where the price of women is fixed in a particular way. Women, as things, as items in the sexual marketplace, have a market value that depends in

---

[22]*Doctrine of Virtue*, 471. This is a remarkable metaphor for a philosopher who finds in the autonomous human self, and its self-legislating activity, the only source of intrinsic value.
[23]Ibid. 471. Kant's ignorance of Antipodean bird life is (just) forgivable.
[24]Ibid. 471.
[25]This development of Kant's philosophy is proposed by Korsgaard as a way of addressing the problem of lying to the murderer at the door (Korsgaard, 'The Right to Lie'). I discuss it in more detail in the original version of this paper.

part on whether they have been used. Virgins fetch a higher price than second hand goods. Such are the background circumstances in which Herbert finds herself. They are, I suggest, evil circumstances, evil by Kantian lights (though Kant himself never saw it).

Despite these handicaps, Herbert has achieved a great thing: she has achieved something like a friendship of mutual love and respect, found someone with whom she can share her activities and goals, become a partner in a relationship where ends are chosen in such a way that the ends of both agents coincide (prominent among which was, it seems, the happy study of Kant's works!). She has achieved a relationship where frankness and honesty prevail—with one exception. Her lie is the lie of 'keeping something back for the sake of the friendship'. If she tells the truth, evil circumstance will see to it that her action will not be taken as the honest self-revelation of a person, but the revelation of her thing-hood, her hitherto unrecognised status as used merchandise, as item with a price that is lower than the usual. If she tells the truth, she becomes a thing, and the friendship—that small neighbourhood of the Kingdom—will vanish. Should she lie? Perhaps. If her circumstances are evil, she is permitted to have friendship as her goal, to be sought and preserved, rather than a law to be lived by. So she is permitted to lie. Then other considerations come in. She has a duty to 'humanity in her own person', of which Kant says: 'By virtue of this worth we are not for sale at any price; we possess an inalienable dignity which instils in us reverence for ourselves'. She has a duty of self esteem: she must respect her own person and demand such respect of others, abjuring the vice of servility.[26] I think she may have a duty to lie.

This is strategy, for the Kingdom's sake. Kant would not allow it. He thinks we should act as if the Kingdom of Ends is with us now. He thinks we should rely on God to make it all right in the end. But God will not make it all right in the end. And the Kingdom of Ends is not with us now. Perhaps we should do what we can to bring it about.

Coda

Kant never replied, and his correspondent, as far as I know, did not leave Austria.[27] In 1803 Maria von Herbert killed herself, having worked out at last an answer to that persistent and troubling question—the question

---

[26]*Doctrine of Virtue*, 434, 435.
[27]There is one final letter from her on the record, dated early 1794, in which she expresses again a wish to visit Kant, and reflects upon her own desire for death.

to which Kant, and her own moral sense, had responded with silence. Was that a vicious thing to do? Not entirely. As Kant himself concedes, 'Self murder requires courage, and in this attitude there is always room for reverence for humanity in one's own person.'[28]

Nicomachean Ethics

Aristotle   *(Translated by J. A. K. Thomson and Hugh Tredennick)*

Book I

To understand what moral goodness is we must study the soul of man

. . . Since happiness is an activity of the soul in accordance with perfect virtue, we must examine the nature of virtue; for perhaps in this way we shall be better able to form a view about happiness too. Besides, the true statesman is thought of as a man who has taken special pains to study this subject; for he wants to make his fellow-citizens good and law-abiding people (we have an example of this in the law-givers of Crete and Sparta, and any others who have shown similar qualities). And if this investigation is a part of political science, clearly our inquiry will be in keeping with the plan that we adopted at the outset.

The goodness that we have to consider is human goodness, obviously; for it was the good *for man* or happiness *for man* that we set out to discover. But by human goodness is meant goodness not of the body but of the soul, and happiness also we define as an activity of the soul. This being so, it is evident that the statesman ought to have some acquaintance with psychology, just as, a doctor who intends to treat the eye must have a knowledge of the body as a whole. Indeed the statesman's need is greater than the doctor's, inasmuch as politics is a better and more honourable science than medicine. But the best kind of doctors take a good deal of trouble to acquire a knowledge of the body; so the statesman too must study the soul, but with a view to politics, and only so far as is sufficient for the questions that we are investigating; for

[28]Ibid. 424.

to explore its nature in greater detail would presumably be too laborious for our present purpose.

The several faculties of the soul distinguished

Some aspects of psychology are adequately treated in discourses elsewhere, and we should make use of the results: e.g. that the soul is part rational and part irrational (whether these are separate like the parts of the body or anything else that is physically divisible, or whether like the convex and concave aspects of the circumference of a circle they are distinguishable as two only in definition and thought, and are by nature inseparable, makes no difference for our present purpose). Of the irrational soul one part seems to be common, viz. the vegetative: I mean the cause of nutrition and growth; because one can assume such a faculty of soul in everything that receives nourishment, even in embryos; and this same faculty too in the fully developed creature, because this is more reasonable than to suppose that the latter has a different one. Thus the excellence of this faculty is evidently common and not confined to man; because this part or faculty seems to be most active in sleep, when the good and the bad are least easy to distinguish (hence the saying 'for half their lives the happy are no different from the wretched'). This is a natural consequence, because sleep is a suspension of that function of the soul by which it is distinguished as good and bad—except that to a certain limited extent some of the stimuli reach the soul; this is what makes the dreams of decent people better than those of the ordinary man. But enough of this subject; we may dismiss the nutritive soul, because of its very nature it has no part in human goodness.

But there seems to be another element of the soul which, while irrational, is in a sense receptive of reason. Take the types of man which we call continent and incontinent. They have a principle—a rational element in their souls—which we commend, because it urges them in the right direction and encourages them to take the best course; but there is also observable in them another element, by nature irrational, which struggles and strains against the rational. Just as in the case of the body paralysed limbs, when the subject chooses to move them to the right, swing away in the contrary direction to the left, so exactly the same happens in the case of the soul; for the impulses of the incontinent take them in the contrary direction. 'But in bodies we see what swings away, whereas in the case of the soul we do not.' Probably we should believe nevertheless that the soul too contains an irrational element which opposes and runs counter to reason—in what sense it is a separate element does not matter at all. But this too, as we said seems to be receptive of reason; at any rate in the continent man it is obedient to reason, and is presumably still more amenable in the temperate and in the brave man, because in them it is in complete harmony with the rational principle.

Evidently, then, the irrational part of the soul also consists of two parts. The vegetative has no association at all with reason, but the desiderative and generally appetitive part does in a way participate in reason, in the sense that it is submissive and obedient to it (this is the sense of *logon echein* in which we speak of 'taking account' of one's father or friends, not that in which we speak of 'having an account' of mathematical propositions). That the irrational part is in some way persuaded by reason is indicated by our use of admonition, and of reproof and encouragement of all kinds. If, however, one should speak of the appetitive part of the soul as rational too, it will be the rational part that is divided in two: one rational in the proper sense of the word and in itself, the other in the sense that a child pays attention to its father.

Virtue, too, is divided into classes in accordance with this differentiation of the soul. Some virtues are called intellectual and others moral; Wisdom and Understanding and Prudence are intellectual, Liberality and Temperance are moral virtues. When we are speaking of a man's character we do not describe him as wise or understanding, but as patient or temperate. We do, however, praise a wise man on the ground of his state of mind; and those states that are praiseworthy we call virtues.

Book II

Moral virtues, like crafts, are acquired by practice and habituation

Virtue, then, is of two kinds, intellectual and moral. Intellectual virtue owes both its inception and its growth chiefly to instruction, and for this very reason needs time and experience. Moral goodness, on the other hand, is the result of habit, from which it has actually got its name, being a slight modification of the word *ethos*. This fact makes it obvious that none of the moral virtues is engendered in us by nature, since nothing that is what it is by nature can be made to behave differently by habituation. For instance, a stone, which has a natural tendency downwards, cannot be habituated to rise, however often you try to train it by throwing it into the air; nor can you train fire to burn downwards; nor can anything else that has any other natural tendency be trained to depart from it. The moral virtues, then, are engendered in us neither *by* nor *contrary to* nature; we are constituted by nature to receive them, but their full development in us is due to habit.

Again, of all those faculties with which nature endows us we first acquire the potentialities, and only later effect their actualization. (This is evident in the case of the senses. It was not from repeated acts of seeing or hearing that we acquired the senses but the other way round: we had these senses before we used them; we did not acquire them as the result of using them.) But the virtues we do acquire by first exercising them, just as happens in the arts. Anything that we have to learn to do we learn by the actual doing of it: people become builders by building and instrumentalists by playing instruments. Similarly we become just by performing just acts, temperate by performing temperate ones, brave by performing brave ones. This view is supported by what happens in city-states. Legislators make their citizens good by habituation; this is the intention of every legislator, and those who do not carry it out fail of their object. This is what makes the difference between a good constitution and a bad one.

Again, the causes or means that bring about any form of excellence are the same as those that destroy it, and similarly with art; for it is as a result of playing the harp that people become good and bad harpists. The same principle applies to builders and all other craftsmen. Men will become good builders as a result of building well, and bad ones as a result of building badly. Otherwise there would be no need of anyone to teach them: they would all be *born* either good or bad. Now this holds good also of the virtues. It is the way that we behave in our dealings with other people that makes us just or unjust, and the way that we behave in the face of danger, accustoming ourselves to be timid or confident, that makes us brave or cowardly. Similarly with situations involving desires and angry feelings: some people become temperate and patient from one kind of conduct in such situations, others licentious and choleric from another. In a word, then, like activities produce like dispositions. Hence we must give our activities a certain quality, because it is their characteristics that determine the resulting dispositions. So it is a matter of no little importance what sort of habits we form from the earliest age—it makes a vast difference, or rather all the difference in the world.

In a practical science, so much depends on particular circumstances that only general rules can be given

Since the branch of philosophy on which we are at present engaged is not, like the others, theoretical in its aim—because we are studying not to know what goodness is, but how to become good men, since otherwise it would be useless—we must apply our minds to the problem of how our actions should be performed, because, as we have just said, it is these that actually determine our dispositions.

Now that we should act according to the right principle is common ground and may be assumed as a basis for discussion (the point will be discussed later, both what 'the right principle' is, and how it is related to the other virtues). But we must first agree that any account of conduct must be stated in outline and not in precise detail, just as we said at the beginning that accounts are to be required only in such a form as befits their subject-matter. Now questions of conduct and expedience have as little fixity about them as questions of what is healthful; and if this is true of the general rule, it is still more true that its application to particular problems admits of no precision. For they do not fall under any art or professional tradition, but the agents are compelled at every step to think out for themselves what the circumstances demand, just as happens in the arts of medicine and navigation. However, although our present account is of this kind, we must try to support it.

A cardinal rule: right conduct is incompatible with excess or deficiency in feelings and actions

First, then, we must consider this fact: that it is in the nature of moral qualities that they are destroyed by deficiency and excess, just as we can see (since we have to use the evidence of visible facts to throw light on those that are invisible) in the case of health and strength. For both excessive and insufficient exercise destroy one's strength, and both eating and drinking too much or too little destroy health, whereas the right quantity produces, increases and preserves it. So it is the same with temperance, courage and the other virtues. The man who shuns and fears everything and stands up to nothing becomes a coward; the man who is afraid of nothing at all, but marches up to every danger, becomes foolhardy. Similarly the man who indulges in every pleasure and refrains from none becomes licentious; but if a man behaves like a boor and turns his back on every pleasure, he is a case of insensibility. Thus temperance and courage are destroyed by excess and deficiency and preserved by the mean.

Our virtues are exercised in the same kinds of action as gave rise to them

But besides the fact that the virtues are induced and fostered as a result, and by the agency, of the same sort of actions as cause their destruction, the activities that flow from them will also consist in the same sort of actions. This is so in all the other more observable instances, e.g. in that of strength. This results from taking plenty of nourishment and undergoing severe training, and it is the strong man that will be best able to carry out this programme. So with the virtues. It is by refraining from pleasures that we become temperate, and it is when we have become temperate that we are most able to abstain from pleasures. Similarly with courage; it is by habituating ourselves to make light of alarming situations and to face them that we become brave, and it is when we have become brave that we shall be most able to face an alarming situation.

The pleasure or pain that actions cause the agent may serve as an index of moral progress, since good conduct consists in a proper attitude towards pleasure and pain

The pleasure or pain that accompanies people's acts should be taken as a sign of their dispositions. A man who abstains from bodily pleasures and enjoys the very fact of so doing is temperate; if he finds it irksome he is licentious. Again, the man who faces danger gladly, or at least without distress, is brave; the one who feels distressed is a coward. For it is with pleasures and pains that moral goodness is concerned. Pleasure induces us to behave badly, and pain to shrink from fine actions. Hence the importance (as Plato says) of having been trained in some way from infancy to feel joy and grief at the right things: true education is precisely this. If the virtues are concerned with actions and feelings, and every feeling and every action is always accompanied by pleasure or pain, on this ground too virtue will be concerned with pleasures and pains. The fact that punishments are effected by their means is further evidence, because punishment is a kind of remedial treatment and such treatment is naturally effected by contraries. Again, as we said above, every state of the soul attains its natural development in relation to, and in the sphere of, those conditions by which it is naturally made better or worse. Now when people become bad it is because of pleasures and pains, through seeking (or shunning) the wrong ones, or at the wrong time, or in the wrong way, or in any other manner in which such offences are distinguished by principle. This is why some thinkers actually define the virtues as forms of impassivity or tranquillity. But they are wrong in speaking absolutely instead of adding 'in the right (or wrong) manner and at the right time' and any other due qualifications.

We have decided, then, that this kind of virtue disposes us to act in the best way with regard to pleasures and pains, and contrariwise with the corresponding vice. But we may obtain further light on the same point from the following considerations.

There are three factors that make for choice, and three that make for avoidance: the fine, the advantageous, and the pleasant, and their contraries, the base, the harmful, and the painful. Now with regard to all these the good man tends to go right and the bad man to go wrong, especially about pleasure. This is common to all animals, and accompanies all objects of choice, for clearly the fine and the advantageous are pleasant too. Consciousness of pleasure has grown up with all of us from our infancy, and therefore our life is so deeply imbued with this feeling that it is hard to remove all trace of it. Pleasure and pain are also the standards by which—to a greater or lesser extent—we regulate our actions. Since to feel pleasure and pain rightly or wrongly has no little effect upon conduct, it follows that our whole inquiry must be concerned with these sensations. Heraclitus says that it is hard to fight against emotion, but harder still to fight against pleasure; and the harder course is always the concern of both art and virtue, because success is better in the face of difficulty. Thus on this ground too the whole concern of both morality and political science must be with pleasures and pains, since the man who treats them rightly will be good and the one who treats them wrongly will be bad.

We may take this as a sufficient statement that virtue is concerned with pains and pleasures; that the actions that produce it also increase it, or if differently performed, destroy it; and that the actions that produce it also constitute the sphere of its activity.

Acts that are incidentally virtuous distinguished from those that are done knowingly, of choice, and from a virtuous disposition

A difficulty, however, may be raised as to how we can say that people must perform just actions if they are to become just, and temperate ones if they are to become temperate; because if they do what is just and temperate, they are just and temperate already, in the same way that if they use words or play music correctly they are already literate or musical. But surely this is not true even of the arts. It is possible to put a few words together correctly by accident, or at the prompting of another person; so the agent will only be literate if he does a literate act in a literate way, viz. in virtue of his own literacy. Nor, again, is there an analogy between the arts and the virtues. Works of art have their merit in themselves; so it is enough for them to be turned out with a certain quality of their own. But virtuous acts are not done in a just or temperate way merely because *they* have a certain quality, but only if the agent also acts in a certain state, viz. (1) if he knows what he is doing, (2) if he chooses it, and chooses it for its own sake, and (3) if he does it from a fixed and permanent disposition. Now these—knowledge excepted—are not reckoned as necessary qualifications for the arts as well. For the acquisition of virtues, on the other hand, knowledge has little or no force; but the other requirements are not of little but of supreme importance, granted that it is from the repeated performance of just and temperate acts that we acquire virtues. Acts, to be sure, are called just and temperate when they are such as a just or temperate man would do; but what makes the agent just or temperate is not merely the fact that he does such things, but the fact that he does them in the way that just and temperate men do. It is therefore right to say that a man becomes just by the performance of just, and temperate by the performance of temperate, acts; nor is there the smallest likelihood of any man's becoming good by not doing them. This is not, however, the course that most people follow: they have recourse to their principle, and imagine that they are being philosophical and that in this way they will become serious-minded—behaving rather like invalids who listen carefully to their doctor, but carry out none of his instructions. Just as the bodies of the latter will get no benefit from such treatment, so the souls of the former will get none from such philosophy.

In order to define virtue we must decide to what class or genus it belongs. It is not a feeling or a faculty, but a disposition

We must now consider what virtue is. Since there are three kinds of modification that are found in the soul, viz. feelings, faculties and dispositions, virtue must be one of these three. By feelings I mean desire, anger, fear, daring, envy, joy, friendliness, hatred, longing, jealousy, pity, and in general all conditions that are attended by pleasure or pain. By faculties I mean those susceptibilities in virtue of which we are said to be capable of the feelings in question, e.g. capable of anger or sorrow or pity. By dispositions I mean conditions in virtue of which we are well or ill disposed in respect of the feelings concerned. We have, for instance, a bad disposition towards anger if our tendency is too strong or too weak, and a good one if our tendency is moderate. Similarly with the other feelings.

Now neither the virtues nor the vices are feelings, because we are not called good or bad on the ground of our feelings, but we are so called on the ground of our virtues and vices; nor are we either praised or blamed for our feelings (a man is not praised for being frightened or angry, nor is he blamed just for being angry; it is for being angry in a particular way); but we are praised and blamed for our virtues and vices. Again, when we are angry or frightened it is not by our choice; but our virtues are expressions of our choice, or at any rate imply choice. Besides, we are said to be moved in respect of our feelings, but in respect of our virtues and vices we are said to be not moved but disposed in a particular way. By the same line of reasoning they are not faculties either. We are not called good or bad, nor are we praised or blamed, merely because we are capable of feeling. Again, what faculties we have, we have by nature; but it is not nature that makes us good or bad (we mentioned this point above). So if the virtues are neither feelings nor faculties, it remains that they are dispositions.

We have now stated what virtue is generically.

But what is its differentia? Any excellence enables its possessor to function; therefore this is true of human excellence, i.e. virtue

But we must not only make the simple statement that it is a disposition; we must also say what *kind* of disposition. Let us assert, then, that any kind of excellence renders that of which it is the excellence *good,* and makes it perform its function *well.* For example, the excellence of the eye makes both the eye and its function good (because it is through the excellence of the eye that we see well). Similarly the excellence of a horse makes him both a fine horse and good at running and carrying his rider and facing the enemy. If this rule holds good for all cases, then *human* excellence will be the disposition that makes one a good man and causes him to perform his function well. We have already explained how this will be; but it will also become clear in another way if we consider what is the specific nature of virtue.

This is confirmed by the doctrine of the Mean

In anything continuous and divisible it is possible to take a part which is greater or less than, or equal to, the remainder; and that in relation either to the thing divided or to us. The equal part is a sort of mean between excess and deficiency; and I call mean in relation to the *thing* whatever is equidistant from the extremes, which is one and the same for everybody; but I call mean in relation to us that which is neither excessive nor deficient, and this is *not* one and the same for all. For example, if ten is 'many' and two 'few' of some quantity, six is the mean if one takes it in relation to the thing, because it exceeds the one number and is exceeded by the other by the same amount; and this is the mean by arithmetical reckoning. But the mean in relation to us is not to be obtained in this way. Supposing that ten pounds of food is a large and two pounds a small allowance for an athlete, it does not follow that the trainer will prescribe six pounds; for even this is perhaps too much or too little for the person who is to receive it—too little for Milo but too much for one who is only beginning to train. Similarly in the case of running and wrestling. In this way, then, every knowledgeable person avoids excess and deficiency, but looks for the mean and chooses it—not the mean of the thing, but the mean relative to us.

If, then, every science performs its function well only when it observes the mean and refers its products to it (which is why it is customary to say of well-executed works that nothing can be added to them or taken away, the implication being that excess and deficiency alike destroy perfection, while the mean preserves it)—if good craftsmen, as we hold, work with the mean in view; and if virtue, like nature, is more exact and more efficient than any art, it follows that virtue aims to hit the mean. By virtue I mean moral virtue since it is this that is concerned with feelings and actions, and these involve excess, deficiency and a mean. It is possible, for example, to feel fear, confidence, desire, anger, pity, and pleasure and pain generally, too much or too little; and both of these are wrong. But to have these feelings at the right times on the right grounds towards the right people for the right motive and in the right way is to feel them to an intermediate, that is to the best, degree; and this is the mark of virtue. Similarly there are excess and deficiency and a mean in the case of actions. But it is in the field of actions and feelings that virtue operates; and in them excess and deficiency are failings, whereas the mean is praised and recognized as a success: and these are both marks of virtue. Virtue, then, is a mean condition, inasmuch as it aims at hitting the mean.

Again, failure is possible in many ways (for evil, as the Pythagoreans represented it, is a form of the Unlimited, and good of the Limited), but success is only one. That is why the one is easy and the other difficult; it is easy to miss the target and difficult to hit it. Here, then, is another reason why excess and deficiency fall under evil, and the mean state under good;

For men are bad in countless ways, but good in only one.

A provisional definition of virtue

So virtue is a purposive disposition, lying in a mean that is relative to us and determined by a rational principle, and by that which a prudent man would use to determine it. It is a mean between two kinds of vice, one of excess and the other of deficiency; and also for this reason, that whereas these vices fall short of or exceed the right measure in both feelings and actions, virtue discovers the mean and chooses it. Thus from the point of view of its essence and the definition of its real nature, virtue is a mean; but in respect of what is right and best, it is an extreme.

But the rule of choosing the mean cannot be applied to some actions and feelings, which are essentially evil

But not every action or feeling admits of a mean; because some have names that directly connote depravity, such as malice, shamelessness and envy, and among actions adultery, theft and murder. All these, and more like them, are so called as being evil in themselves; it is not the excess or deficiency of them that is evil. In their case, then, it is impossible to act rightly; one is always wrong. Nor does acting rightly or wrongly in such cases depend upon circumstances—whether a man commits adultery with the right woman or at the right time or in the right way, because to do anything of that kind is simply wrong. One might as well claim that there is a mean and excess and deficiency even in unjust or cowardly or intemperate actions. On that basis there must be a mean of excess, a mean of deficiency, an excess of excess and a deficiency of deficiency. But just as in temperance and courage there can be no mean or excess or deficiency, because the mean is in a sense an extreme, so there can be no mean or excess or deficiency in the vices that we mentioned; however done, they are wrong. For in general neither excess nor deficiency admits of a mean, nor does a mean admit of excess and deficiency.

The doctrine of the mean applied to particular virtues

But a generalization of this kind is not enough; we must apply it to particular cases. When we are discussing actions, although general statements have a wider application, particular statements are closer to

Table of Virtues and Vices

Sphere of Action or Feeling	Excess	Mean	Deficiency
Fear and Confidence	Rashness *thrasutēs*	Courage *andreia*	Cowardice *deilia*
Pleasure and Pain	Licentiousness *akolasia*	Temperance *sōphrosunē*	Insensibility *anaisthēsia*
Getting and Spending (minor)	Prodigality *asōtia*	Liberality *eleutheriotēs*	Illiberality *aneleutheria*
Getting and Spending (major)	Vulgarity *aperiokalia, banausia*	Magnificence *megaloprepeia*	Pettiness *mikroprepeia*
Honour and Dishonour (major)	Vanity *chaunotēs*	Magnanimity *megalopsūchia*	Pusillanimity *mikropsūchia*
Honour and Dishonour (minor)	Ambition *philotīmia*	Proper ambition	Unambitiousness *aphilotīmia*
Anger	Irascibility *orgilotēs*	Patience *prāotēs*	Lack of spirit *aorgēsia*
Self-expression	Boastfulness *alazoneia*	Truthfulness *alētheia*	Understatement *eirōneia*
Conversation	Buffoonery *bōmolochia*	Wittiness *eutrapelia*	Boorishness *agroikia*
Social Conduct	Obsequiousness *areskeia* Flattery *kolakeia*	Friendliness *philia*(?)	Cantankerousness *duskolia* (*duseris*)
Shame	Shyness *kataplēxis*	Modesty *aidōs*	Shamelessness *anaischuntia*
Indignation	Envy *phthonos*	Righteous indignation *nemesis*	Malicious enjoyment *epichairekakia*

the truth. This is because actions are concerned with particular facts, and theories must be brought into harmony with these. Let us, then, take these instances from the diagram.

In the field of Fear and Confidence the mean is Courage; and of those who go to extremes the man who exceeds in fearlessness has no name to describe him (there are many nameless cases), the one who exceeds in confidence is called Rash, and the one who shows an excess of fear and a deficiency of confidence is called Cowardly. In the field of Pleasures and Pains—not in all, especially not in all pains—the mean is Temperance, the excess Licentiousness; cases of defective response to pleasures scarcely occur, and therefore people of this sort too have no name to describe them, but let us class them as Insensible. In the field of Giving and Receiving Money the mean is Liberality, the excess and deficiency are Prodigality and Illiberality; but these show excess and deficiency in contrary ways to one another: the prodigal man goes too far in spending and not far enough in getting, while the illiberal man goes too far in getting money and not far enough in spending it. This present account is in outline and summary, which is all that we need at this stage; we shall give a more accurate analysis later.

But there are other dispositions too that are concerned with money. There is a mean called Magnificence (because the magnificent is not the same as the liberal man: the one deals in large and the other in small outlays); the excess is Tastelessness and Vulgarity, the deficiency Pettiness. These are different from the extremes between which liberality lies; how they differ will be discussed later. In the field of Public Honour and Dishonour the mean is Magnanimity, the excess is called a sort of Vanity, and the deficiency Pusillanimity. And just as liberality differs, as we said, from magnificence in being concerned with small outlays, so there is a state related to Magnanimity in the same way, being concerned with small honours, while magnanimity is concerned with great ones; because it is possible to aspire to honours in the right way, or to a greater or less degree than is right. The man who goes too far in his aspirations is called Ambitious, the one who falls short, Unambitious; the one who is a mean between them has no name. This is true also of the corresponding dispositions, except that the ambitious man's is called Ambitiousness. This is why the extremes lay claim to the intermediate territory. We ourselves sometimes call the intermediate man ambitious and sometimes unambitious; that is, we sometimes commend the ambitious and sometimes the unambitious. Why it is that we do this will be explained in our later remarks. Meanwhile let us continue our discussion of the remaining virtues and vices, following the method already laid down.

In the field of Anger, too, there is excess, deficiency and the mean. They do not really possess names, but we may call the intermediate man Patient and the mean Patience; and of the extremes the one who exceeds can be Irascible and his vice Irascibility, while the one who is deficient can be Spiritless and the deficiency Lack of Spirit.

There are also three other means which, though different, somewhat resemble each other. They are all concerned with what we do and say in social intercourse, but they differ in this respect, that one is concerned with truthfulness in such intercourse, the other two with pleasantness— one with pleasantness in entertainment, the other with pleasantness in every department of life. We must therefore say something about these too, in order that we may better discern that in all things the mean is to be commended, while the extremes are neither commendable nor right, but reprehensible. Most of these too have no names; but, as in the other cases, we must try to coin names for them in the interest of clarity and to make it easy to follow the argument.

Well, then, as regards Truth the intermediate man may be called Truthful and the mean Truthfulness; pretension that goes too far may be Boastfulness and the man who is disposed to it a Boaster, while that which is deficient may be called Irony and its exponent Ironical. As for Pleasantness in Social Entertainment, the intermediate man is Witty, and the disposition Wit; the excess is Buffoonery and the indulger in it a Buffoon; the man who is deficient is a kind of Boor and his disposition Boorishness. In the rest of the sphere of the Pleasant—life in general—the person who is pleasant in the right way is Friendly and the mean is Friendliness; the person who goes too far, if he has no motive, is Obsequious; if his motive is self-interest, he is a Flatterer. The man who is deficient and is unpleasant in all circumstances is Cantankerous and Ill-tempered.

There are mean states also in the sphere of feelings and emotions. Modesty is not a virtue, but the modest man too is praised. Here too one person is called intermediate and another excessive—like the Shy man who is overawed at anything. The man who feels too little shame or none at all is Shameless, and the intermediate man is Modest. Righteous Indignation is a mean between Envy and Spite, and they are all concerned with feelings of pain or pleasure at the experiences of our neighbours. The man who feels righteous indignation is distressed at instances of undeserved good fortune, but the envious man goes further and is distressed at *any* good fortune, while the spiteful man is so far from feeling distress that he actually rejoices.

However, we shall have occasion to continue this discussion elsewhere. After that we shall treat of Justice, distinguishing its two kinds—because the word is used in more senses than one—and explain in what way each of them is a mean. [We shall also treat similarly of the rational virtues.]

The mean is often nearer to one extreme than to the other, or seems nearer because of our natural tendencies

Thus there are three dispositions, two of them vicious (one by way of excess, the other of deficiency), and one good, the mean. They are all in some way opposed to one another: the extremes are contrary both to the mean and to each other, and the mean to the extremes. For just as the equal is greater compared with the less, and less compared with the greater, so the mean states (in both feelings and actions) are excessive compared with the deficient and deficient compared with the excessive. A brave man appears rash compared with a coward, and cowardly compared with a rash man; similarly a temperate man appears licentious compared with an insensible one and insensible compared with a licentious one, and a liberal man prodigal compared with an illiberal one and illiberal compared with a prodigal one. This is the reason why each extreme type tries to push the mean nearer to the other: the coward calls the brave man rash, the rash man calls him a coward; and similarly in all other cases. But while all these dispositions are opposed to one another in this way, the greatest degree of contrariety is that which is found between the two extremes. For they are separated by a greater interval from one another than from the mean, just as the great is further from the small, and the small from the great, than either is from the equal. Again, some extremes seem to bear a resemblance to a mean; e.g. rashness seems like courage, and prodigality like liberality; but between the extremes there is always the maximum dissimilarity. Now contraries are by definition as far distant as possible from one another; hence the further apart things are, the more contrary they will be. In some cases it is the deficiency, in others the excess, that is more opposed to the mean; for instance, the more direct opposite of courage is not the excess, rashness, but the deficiency, cowardice; and that of temperance is not the deficiency, insensibility, but the excess, licentiousness. This result is due to two causes. One lies in the nature of the thing itself. When one extreme has a closer affinity and resemblance to the mean, we tend to oppose to the mean not that extreme but the other. For instance, since rashness is held to be nearer to courage and more like it than cowardice is, it is cowardice that we tend to oppose to courage, because the extremes that are further from the mean are thought to be more opposed to it.

This is one cause, the one that lies in the *thing*. The other lies in ourselves. It is the things towards which we have the stronger natural inclination that seem to us more opposed to the mean. For example, we are naturally more inclined towards pleasures, and this makes us more prone towards licentiousness than towards temperance; so we describe as more contrary to the mean those things towards which we have the stronger tendency. This is why licentiousness, the excess, is more contrary to temperance.

Summing up of the foregoing discussion, together with three practical rules for good conduct

We have now said enough to show that moral virtue is a mean, and in what sense it is so: that it is a mean between two vices, one of excess and the other of deficiency, and that it is such because it aims at hitting the mean point in feelings and actions. For this reason it is a difficult business to be good; because in any given case it is difficult to find the midpoint—for instance, not everyone can find the centre of a circle; only the man who knows how. So too it is easy to get angry—anyone can do that—or to give and spend money; but to feel or act towards the right person to the right extent at the right time for the right reason in the right way—that is not easy, and it is not everyone that can do it. Hence to do these things well is a rare, laudable and fine achievement.

For this reason anyone who is aiming at the mean should (1) keep away from that extreme which is more contrary to the mean, just as Calypso advises:

Far from this surf and surge keep thou thy ship.

For one of the extremes is always more erroneous than the other; and since it is extremely difficult to hit the mean, we must take the next best course, as they say, and choose the lesser of the evils; and this will be most readily done in the way that we are suggesting. (2) We must notice the errors into which we ourselves are liable to fall (because we all have different natural tendencies—we shall find out what ours are from the pleasure and pain that they give us), and we must drag ourselves in the contrary direction; for we shall arrive at the mean by pressing well away from our failing—just like somebody straightening a warped piece of wood. (3) In every situation one must guard especially against pleasure and pleasant things, because we are not impartial judges of pleasure. So we should adopt the same attitude towards it as the Trojan elders did towards Helen, and constantly repeat their pronouncement; because if in this way we relieve ourselves of the attraction, we shall be less likely to go wrong.

To sum up: by following these rules we shall have the best chance of hitting the mean. But this is presumably difficult, especially in particular cases; because it is not easy to determine what is the right way to be angry, and with whom, and on what grounds, and for how long. Indeed we sometimes praise those who show deficiency, and call them patient, and sometimes those who display temper, calling them manly. However, the man who deviates only a little from the right degree, either in excess or in deficiency, is not censured—only the one who goes too far, because he is noticeable. Yet it is not easy to define by rule for how long, and how much, a man may go wrong before he incurs blame; no easier than it is to define any other object of perception. Such questions of degree occur in particular cases, and the decision lies with our perception.

This much, then, is clear: in all our conduct it is the mean that is to be commended. But one should incline sometimes towards excess and sometimes towards deficiency, because in this way we shall most easily hit upon the mean, that is, the right course. . . .

The Practice of Partiality

Marilyn Friedman

Hardly any moral philosopher, these days, would deny that we are each entitled to favor our loved ones. Some would say, even more strongly, that we ought to favor them, that it is not simply a moral option. This notion of partiality toward loved ones is lately gaining wide philosophical acclaim. (Ordinary people, fortunately, have held this view for quite some time.)

It seems indisputable that intimacy and close relationships require partiality, that is, require special attentiveness, responsiveness, and favoritism between or among those who are to be close.[1] Close relationships, in turn, are among what Bernard Williams has called the

---

[1]See Lawrence Blum, *Friendship, Altruism, and Morality* (London: Routledge & Kegan Paul, 1980), chap. 3; and John Kekes, "Morality and Impartiality," *American Philosophical Quarterly* 18 (October 1981): 299.

"ground projects" that are essential for character, integrity, and flour-ishing in a human life.[2] Partiality, accordingly, seems instrumentally essential to integrity and the good life. There seems, in addition, to be sheer intrinsic value in the very benefiting of friends and loved ones.[3]

While the appropriateness of partiality toward loved ones is itself uncontested, its theoretical justification is the subject of a lively con-temporary debate. The hottest question in this debate is whether par-tiality can adequately be justified by any of the dominant theoretical traditions of modern moral philosophy, utilitarian consequentialism, or Kantian deontology. The feature of these theories that seems to threaten the legitimacy of partiality is their requirement of moral impartiality—the requirement to be unbiased and to show equal con-sideration, in some sense, for all persons.[4]

According to critics, impartialist moral theories are not able to account for the moral value of close personal relationships.[5] The impartial standpoint calls for detachment from personal concerns and loyalties, an attitude which Lawrence Blum considers to be inimical to the loving concern and particularized responsiveness that are essential to successful close relationships.[6] The impartial perspective aimed at equal concern for all persons, in John Cottingham's view, radically diminishes or altogether eliminates a person's opportunity to show special attention and concern to her own loved ones.[7]

Each impartialist ethical tradition has its own additional short-comings, from the partialist perspective. Bernard Williams charges utilitarianism with failing to recognize the separateness of persons and, therefore, giving no special moral status to personal integrity or to the

---

[2]"Persons, Character, and Morality," in his *Moral Luck* (Cambridge: Cambridge University Press, 1981), p. 13. On the contribution of partiality to integrity and fulfillment, see also John Cottingham, "Ethics and Impartiality," *Philosophical Studies* 43 (1983): 83–99.

[3]See Blum, *Friendship, Altruism, and Morality*; and Charles Fried, *Right and Wrong* (Cambridge: Harvard University Press, 1978), pp. 170, 179.

[4]Of course, the two traditions define very differently the morally relevant interests of persons that are to be considered. In Chapter 1 of my book *What Are Friends For?* (Cornell University, 1993), I characterized impartiality as an absence of bias. Here I switch to construing it as the equal consideration of all persons. This conceptualization is the one most commonly found in the context of the contemporary debates over partiality. For my purposes, there is no significant difference between the two formulations. The two notions diverge in the areas of animal rights and environmental concerns, but those issues are beyond the scope of this essay.

[5]Some partialists also defend partiality in special relationships other than close personal relationships, for example, relationships among members of the same community, city, or nation. However, there is less agreement about the legitimacy of the partiality shown in these cases. [Here I] concentrate only on partiality in close personal relationships, such as those with parents, children, siblings, friends, and lovers.

[6]See Blum, *Friendship, Altruism, and Morality*, p. 56.

[7]See Cottingham, "Ethics and Impartiality," pp. 89–90.

essential contribution made to personal integrity by relationships and projects which are the agent's own, in some important sense.[8] Kantian deontology, according to Michael Stocker, fails to accord moral value to the motivations, such as loving concern and affectionate inclination, that are necessary ingredients in successful personal relationships, and counts only a depersonalized sense of duty as a genuinely moral motivation.[9]

The recent challenges to impartiality range even more widely. Andrew Oldenquist contends that impartiality calls for equal concern for the whole of humanity, a sentiment which is, in any case, too weak to be effective as moral motivation.[10] Perhaps, the final coup de grace is the claim that genuine impartiality is humanly unachievable, a charge with which I myself concur.[11] In her defense of this view, Iris Young urges, further, that the rhetoric of impartiality[12] be distrusted because it has been used in practice by dominant social groups to disguise their de facto political and cultural hegemony.[13]

Defenders of impartialist moral theories have responded by trying to show that those theories do indeed warrant partiality in special relationships. These rejoinders treat partiality as morally permissible, even obligatory, so long as there is *some* way in which this behavior or the deliberation that justifies it exemplifies an equal consideration of the interests of all. A clarified notion of impartiality has, thus, emerged from these defenses.

Thomas E. Hill, Jr., for example, argues that an impartial perspective is required only when considering basic moral principles, but not when judging the specific moral matters of daily life.[14] Peter Railton draws a distinction between procedures for moral decision making by particular persons in particular situations and the truth conditions of a moral theory: impartiality is part of the latter but need not be part of the former.[15] On Alan Gewirth's view, partiality may be permitted in

---

[8]See Williams, *Moral Luck*, p. 3 and passim.

[9]See Michael Stocker, "The Schizophrenia of Modern Ethical Theories," *Journal of Philosophy* 63 (August 12, 1976): 453–66; and Williams, *Moral Luck*, pp. 3, 15–19.

[10]See Andrew Oldenquist, "Loyalties," *Journal of Philosophy* 79 (April 1982): 181.

[11]See Alasdair MacIntyre, *After Virtue* (Notre Dame, Ind.: University of Notre Dame Press, 1981); and Iris Young, "Impartiality and the Civic Public: Some Implications of Feminist Critiques of Moral and Political Theory," *Praxis International* 5 (January 1986): 384–85.

[12]The rhetorical dimension of uses of the notion of impartiality is insightfully explored by Margaret Walker in "Partial Consideration," *Ethics* 101 (July 1991): 758–74.

[13]Young, "Impartiality and the Civic Public," p. 389.

[14]See Thomas E. Hill, Jr., "The Importance of Autonomy," in Eva Feder Kittay and Diana T. Meyers, eds., *Women and Moral Theory* (Totowa, N.J.: Rowman & Littlefield, 1987), pp. 131–32.

[15]See Peter Railton, "Alienation, Consequentialism, and the Demands of Morality," *Philosophy and Public Affairs* 13 (Spring 1984): 153–55.

individual behavior so long as that behavior is regulated by social institutions which themselves give equal consideration to the interests of all persons.[16] Contemporary Kantians, such as Barbara Herman and Marcia Baron, further contend that a sense of duty is necessary only as a second-order limiting condition on our primary, first-order motivations and that partial sentiments are permissible as first-order motivations so long as they do not violate those second-order constraints.[17]

In nearly all of these discussions, both those that favor and those that oppose impartialist defenses of partiality, controversy centers on the notion of *im*partiality and on whether it supports or repudiates the favoring of loved ones. Partialists have generally been on the offensive and impartialists have been compelled to clarify what impartiality really means and what it actually requires. By contrast, the notion of partiality has not been subjected to vigorous critical investigation, except in a few discussions of its unjustified forms.[18]

In this [reading] I counteract that trend by taking a closer than usual look at the moral complexity of our social practices of partiality. My adoption of this approach does not represent an endorsement of current notions of impartiality. . . . [The] concept of impartiality must be substantially reformulated if it is to survive as a practicable ideal of moral thinking. That the concept of impartiality needs reexamination, however, does not mean that the concept of partiality is transparently defensible. In this discussion, I focus on aspects of partiality that complicate the philosophical defense of it.[19]

In the first section of this [reading], I argue that the moral value of partiality depends partly on the moral value of the relationships that it helps to sustain. It matters to the philosophical issues at stake that personal relationships can be abusive, exploitative, and oppressive. I survey some considerations that are relevant to the critical assessment of personal relationships. In section 2, I consider the vastly unequal social

---

[16]See Alan Gewirth, "Ethical Universalism and Particularism," *Journal of Philosophy* 85, no. 6 (1988): 292–93.

[17]See Barbara Herman, "On the Value of Acting from the Motive of Duty," *Philosophical Review* 67 (July 1981): 233–50; and Marcia Baron, "The Alleged Moral Repugnance of Acting from Duty," *Journal of Philosophy* 81 (April 1984): 197–220.

[18]See Blum, *Friendship, Altruism, and Morality*, pp. 46–47; Marcia Baron, *The Moral Status of Loyalty* (Dubuque, Iowa: Kendall Hunt. 1984): John Cottingham, "Partiality, Favouritism, and Morality," *Philosophical Quarterly* 36, no. 144 (1986): 357–73; and Gewirth, "Ethical Universalism," pp. 295–98.

[19]This focus continues in Chapter 3 [of *What Are Friends For?*] (Cornell University, 1993) where I contrast feminist and nonfeminist defenses of partiality. That chapter begins with its own somewhat varied sketch of the partiality debates.

distribution of the material means for favoring loved ones. Because many people have inadequate resources for caring for their loved ones, our conventional relationship practices of partiality—practices by which we each care only for our "own"—can be disastrous for many people. This observation seriously complicates the defense of partiality.

1. Partiality and the Value of Relationships

Partiality varies widely. It appears in numerous sorts of relationships, is expressed in many forms, and has a correspondingly varied moral status. Devoted attention to one's children is a matter of moral duty; loyalty to a distant relative under criminal indictment is morally permissible but not required; white supremacist cults are morally prohibited. Partiality comprises an area of daily moral life about which most people have deeply held convictions.

When partiality is morally required, this is often (if not always) because of what it contributes to the personal relationships of which it is a part. I favor my children, my friends, and so on because such favoring expresses the love I feel for them, promotes their well-being which is of special concern to me (and which, in some cases, is also my personal responsibility), differentiates my close relationships from relationships to people I do not particularly love, and respects the uniqueness of those I love by the specifically appropriate responsiveness I show to them.[20] To the extent that personal relationships are necessary for integrity and fulfillment in life, then, to that extent partiality is instrumentally required as a means to achieving those morally valuable ends.

Even if integrity and fulfillment require close relationships, however, this does not entail that every close relationship contributes to integrity or fulfillment. It depends on the nature of the relationship in question. Personal relationships vary widely in their moral value. The quality of a particular relationship is profoundly important in determining the moral worth of any partiality which is necessary for sustaining that relationship. To the extent that partiality is a duty in close personal relationships, it is a prima facie duty only, to be fully assessed, among other things, in light of the moral worth of the particular relationships it helps to preserve.

---

[20]On the importance of respect for uniqueness in a caring relationship, see Robin Dillon, "Care and Respect," in Eve Browning Cole and Susan Coultrap-McQuin, eds., *Explorations in Feminist Ethics* (Bloomington, Ind.: Indiana University Press, 1992), pp. 69–81.

Discussions of partiality have, heretofore, largely overlooked the differing moral value of the varied sorts of personal relationships that commonly manifest partiality. Some of these discussions do acknowledge that partiality may be shown in an inappropriate manner, but this is a different issue.[21] Partiality toward loved ones, for example, is wrong on the part of someone who holds a public office that calls for impartial treatment of some large number of persons extending beyond the official's loved ones. Also wrong are partial attitudes toward a particular group which unjustly advantage members of that group over other groups, for example, racism and sexism.[22] When partiality is judged to be wrong in those discussions, its wrongness is linked to circumstances other than the nature of the relationship itself. The issue that concerns me, by contrast, is the partialist's apparent underlying presumption that mere relationship with someone who is, in some sense, "one's own" is, all things considered, always morally worth promoting.

In the most general terms, relationships are morally wrong to the extent that they harm people, especially one or more of the participants in the relationship. The relationship between master and slave is the paradigm of a wrongful relationship, and slavery epitomizes immoral relationship practices. Slavery is an extreme form of harmful relationship but by no means the only such form. Even in intimate, "consensual" relationships, people can be subjected to emotional duress, assault and battery, sexual abuse, and economic exploitation.[23] Anything that sustains relationships such as these, including whatever partiality is shown within them, is prima facie morally improper.

Just how bad these sustaining conditions are in any particular case depends partly on the prospects for ending that relationship. If a battered woman, for instance, cannot leave an abusive relationship because she has no viable economic alternative for herself and her dependent children, then, in that case, it is good for her partner to show the sort of partiality in caring and support that would

---

[21]See the references in note 18.

[22]The key phrase is "unjustly advantage." Sometimes it is just to favor members of certain groups, most especially in attempts to overcome the persistent untoward effects of their history of unjust treatment and the lingering, unjustified biases against them. This, of course, is the familiar notion of "affirmative action," a topic far afield of the present discussion.

[23]Among female homicide victims in the United States, about one-third are slain by a family member or male friend; see Deborah Rhode, *Gender and Justice* (Cambridge: Harvard University Press, 1989), p. 237. See her chapter 7, "Sex and Violence," for a wide-ranging discussion of the abuses to which women in particular are vulnerable in personal relationships.

counterbalance or offset the abuse. To the extent, however, that his partiality diminishes her capacity to recognize her situation for what it is and to pursue any nonoppressive alternatives that are genuinely accessible to her, to the extent that the partiality binds her the more strongly to her still-abusive partner when she could free herself of that tie, then, to that extent, the partiality is insidious and more than simply prima facie bad. In case a troubled relationship can be brought to an end to the betterment of the abused member and her dependents, the morally best option is its dissolution. Sometimes "this marriage" should not be "saved." The current approach to partiality is, thus, incomplete. It fails to take account of the differing moral value of different personal relationships, and it mistakenly presumes that whatever sustains any personal relationship is a moral good without qualification.

Assessing the harm that is done in personal relationships is a complex matter. Intimates and close affiliates can harm each other in a great variety of ways. The harms of a relationship might be a function of its own particularities, or they might be a function of the social conventions for relationships of that sort. A relationship can harm both those who are participants in the relationship and those who are nonparticipants. Nonparticipants can be harmed, for example, if they are unjustifiably excluded from relationship practices which afford some positive value to their participants.[24] My present concern, however, is with the harms to which the participants in a relationship are vulnerable.

Roughly speaking, we may distinguish four levels at which the practice of any particular relationship can be morally evaluated. First, there is the most generic level for defining relationships of a certain sort. The most prominent dictionary definition of "marriage" is wedlock, that is, the relationship between wife and husband; and, by dictionary definition, wives are women while husbands are men. This simple generic meaning covers a variety of actual practices in different cultures, for example, monogamy, polyandry, and polygyny.

Second, relationships can be evaluated at the level of the specific cultural formalization of a relationship practice. Historically, American case law considered husbands to be responsible for the economic support of the marriage household while wives were held responsible for

---

[24]Here I have in mind such examples as the legal and religious bans against lesbian and gay marriage.

child care, domestic work, and the sexual service of their husbands.[25] Any aspect of a relationship on which the law must, at some time or other, pronounce judgment may become a part of its formal social arrangements. Marriage law, in the past, has condoned wife battering by husbands, misconstruing it under a legitimating description: corrective chastisement.[26] Such tolerance made wife battering formally permissible social practice.

Third, there may be informal practices associated with a relationship tradition which are neither formally codified nor legally enforced, yet which are culturally normative. In our culture, a woman who marries a man is still widely expected to drop her own last name and adopt that of her husband and sometimes to submerge herself entirely under his name ("Mrs. John Doe"). Fourth, and finally, any relationship may have its own specific particularities which do not derive from the generic nature of the relationship or from its formal or informal social conventions. The particular emotional abuse heaped upon one spouse by her partner may be quite idiosyncratic to their interaction.

Marital relationships can be evaluated at all of these levels, from particular marriages on up to the most generic level of marriage practice—and similarly for other relationships. A challenge to the generic notion of marriage as a relationship between a woman and a man may well rely on a related, but even more generic, meaning of marriage, namely, that of a close or intimate union. Close and intimate unions may form between women and between men. Some lesbian and gay couples are now seeking, for their own close and intimate unions, the formal imprimatur of legally or religiously sanctioned marriage, an innovation which most religious and legal authorities continue to obstruct. Nevertheless, this example reminds us that evaluation of marriage practice can occur even at its most generic level.

In order to decide which close relationships are morally wrong at any level of assessment, we need to consider more than simply the obvious harms its participants inflict on each other. We need as well some sense of what it is that makes close relationships morally right, what it is that determines the moral worth that they have as relationships.

[25]See Sara Ann Ketchum, "Liberalism and Marriage Law," in Mary Vetterling-Braggin, Frederick A. Elliston, and Jane English, eds., *Feminism and Philosophy* (Totowa, N.J.: Littlefield, Adams, 1977), pp. 264–76.
[26]See Dorie Klein, "The Dark Side of Marriage: Battered Wives and the Domination of Women," in Nicole Hahn Rafter and Elizabeth A. Stanko, eds., *Judge, Lawyer, Victim, Thief: Gender Roles and Criminal Justice* (Boston: Northeastern University Press, 1982), pp. 83–107.

Evaluating the worth of relationships in part requires knowing some-thing about the underlying moral basis of the duties of partiality they generate. Robert Goodin has theorized that partiality is morally required in a relationship to the extent that it contributes to the protec-tion of those who are vulnerable.[27] Social conventions assign responsi-bilities for the care of those who need it to particular others who are (presumed to be) best situated to render care effectively. Such conven-tions are sensible to the extent that they ensure genuine protection for all at dependent stages of their lives and that, in emergencies, there are guidelines which promote effective help to those in danger.[28]

People are typically held responsible for the well-being of those to whom they are connected in some identifiable way, such as by kinship. Our close friends and relations are especially well placed to offer pro-tection to each of us in virtue of the familiarity, concern, and frequency of interaction which are commonly greater in those relationships than in others. Immediate family relationships are among our most impor-tant social relationships for providing care, nurturance, protection, and support. They are keystones in the social arrangements by which children, in particular, are cared for, and are also centrally important for care of the elderly and of infirm persons at any age. In such relationships, the circumstances of being the one uniquely situated to answer to someone's need derives from an ongoing, publicly recog-nized connection with her in virtue of which one is held responsible for her well-being.

Goodin recognizes the need to evaluate social conventions them-selves. Relationship conventions, on his view, are morally justified to the extent that they are genuinely successful in promoting the protec-tion of the vulnerable.[29] For instance, it is because most people care well enough for their own biological offspring that our social arrange-ments should and do hold them accountable, as a rule, for that care.[30] Given arrangements of these sorts, the vulnerability of the one who is cared for is especially a vulnerability with regard to the behavior of

---

[27]*Protecting the Vulnerable* (Chicago: University of Chicago Press, 1985). It is noteworthy that Goodin is particularly concerned to show that the best theoretical account of our responsibilities to loved ones also grounds general duties to strangers, duties that are stronger than is usually allowed by partialists (pp. 9–11). Another perspective on what it is that grounds duties of partiality in personal relationships is offered in Lawrence C. Becker, *Reciprocity* (London: Routledge & Kegan Paul, 1986).
[28]Goodin, *Protecting the Vulnerable*, pp. 109–25.
[29]Ibid., pp. 124–25.
[30]In Chapter 6 [of *What Are Friends for?*] I qualify this view by exploring the gender asymmetry in these practices, particularly the far heavier burden of parental caretaking accountability demanded of women than of men.

those persons who are held responsible for her care. A parent's disregard of the needs of her own young child nearly always constitutes neglect; not so someone else's disregard.

On Goodin's view, once caretaking conventions are in place, even if they are not justifiable as the best arrangements for ensuring care of certain sorts of persons (children, the elderly, etc.), they may still create caretaking obligations, since the existence of conventions almost guarantees that no one else will do the required caretaking in any particular case.[31] Knowing that I am related to someone in a specific and close way alerts me to the fact that other people will not likely attend to her needs. On Goodin's view, my duty to care for someone follows from being the one who is conventionally expected to care for her and, because of that expectation, the only one who is likely to do so.

Following Goodin's account, we may thus view partiality in close personal relationships as prima facie morally required to the extent that it safeguards those who are vulnerable and to the extent that it accords with social conventions that assign responsibilities for the care of vulnerable persons to certain others who are related to them in particular ways. These responsibilities, to emphasize, constitute prima facie duties only. Their overall moral merit depends on the extent to which the relationships in question really do protect those who are vulnerable without exacting too high a price for such care.

One additional qualification merits special emphasis. Goodin contends that one of the deeper factors which determine whether or not the prima facie duties of partiality constitute duties all things considered is the nature of the vulnerability in question and, in particular, its origin. As Goodin recognizes, some vulnerabilities are socially created. Illness, for example, may result from socially created conditions and be exacerbated by societal hindrances to access to health care. Many socially created vulnerabilities can be directly tied to income levels and employment status, themselves substantially a function of market practices.[32] These reflections on the nature of vulnerability extend Goodin's account in crucially important directions.

It is part of Goodin's enriched account of our responsibilities to protect the vulnerable that we should also be striving to change those alterable social arrangements that foster and perpetuate undesirable human

---

[31]Goodin, *Protecting the Vulnerable*, p. 125.
[32]Ibid., pp. 190–91.

vulnerabilities and dependencies.[33] Susan Moller Okin develops this strand of Goodin's thought into a comprehensive critique of marital practices. In Okin's view, "gender-structured marriage *involves women in a cycle of socially caused and distinctly asymmetric vulnerability.*"[34] The social determinants begin early in a woman's life. Okin's findings are worth quoting at length. In her view, women are:

> first set up for vulnerability during their developing years by their personal (and socially reinforced) expectations that they will be the primary caretakers of children, and that in fulfilling this role they will need to try to attract and to keep the economic support of a man, to whose work life they will be expected to give priority. They are rendered vulnerable by the actual division of labor within almost all current marriages. They are disadvantaged at work by the fact that the world of wage work, including the professions, is still largely structured around the assumption that "workers" have wives at home. They are rendered far more vulnerable if they become the primary caretakers of children, and their vulnerability peaks if their marriages dissolve and they become single parents.[35]

The details that support Okin's account are convincing, yet they are not likely to persuade everyone. The moral value of close personal relationships is a hotly contested matter. In our time, the debates over the nature and value of marital and family relationships are often particularly vitriolic. Many of us have a stake in believing that our family relationships are personally fulfilling. We might, otherwise, feel required to change them—often a daunting prospect. Our evaluations of these relationships may, accordingly, take on idealized and mythic dimensions.

To complicate matters further, family relationships, especially under comfortable material circumstances, are culturally invested with the function of providing emotional nurturance as well as material protection for both their more vulnerable and their less vulnerable members. The modern nuclear family is supposed to be a refuge, a "haven in a heartless world."[36] Such norms are widely appealing. How much better it is to love than to hate one's parents, siblings, and so on. Family members who share mutual affection will care, nurture, help, and support

---

[33]Ibid., chapter 7.

[34]Susan Moller Okin, *Justice, Gender, and the Family* (New York: Basic Books, 1989), p. 138.

[35]Ibid., pp. 138–39. See her chapter 7 for the ample data and persuasive arguments that support her conclusions.

[36]The familiar phrase, of course, is the title of Christopher Lasch's book, *Haven in a Heartless World: The Family Besieged* (New York: Basic Books, 1977), a book that bemoans the decline of patriarchal authority in contemporary families.

one another out of spontaneous inclination and enthusiasm and will probably do so more attentively and wisely than if the care is begrudged.

Tangentially, let us recall that some critics of impartiality, with an eye toward the partiality they champion for close relationships, have challenged the Kantian view that the only specifically moral motivation is a sense of duty.[37] Such a motivation, so the criticism goes, excludes the loving concern that is due to our intimates. The critics suppose that it is the impartialist dimension of Kantianism which leads to the motivational emphasis on duty. If a sense of duty is troubling as a moral motive among loved ones, however, this problem is not limited to theories that ground relational duties on impartial considerations. The problem arises for any (deontological) view that holds there to be moral duties of partiality in close personal relationships,[38] whether these duties are accounted for in impartial or in partialist terms.

For certain particular relationships, and for many relationships on occasion, a sense of duty may be the only attitude available to motivate the required caretaking. A sense of duty may well be necessary in relationships based on some permanent tie, such as biological kinship, which endures independently of how the participants feel about each other. If one lacks affection for an elderly and infirm parent, then caring for her out of a sense of duty is surely preferable to neglecting her altogether. The lack of spontaneous compassion of concern does not diminish the caretaking responsibility and may engender additional responsibilities of self-control so that one's behavior does not reveal the lack of affection.[39]

Attitudes of loving concern, thus, are not necessarily owed to all our intimates at all times. A duty to be partial to family members and other intimates is a duty to treat them in certain ways, to favor them with care, protection, and so forth, over other persons whom one could also attend. Duties to favor certain particular persons in certain ways are, in the first instance, duties of behavior; they are not necessarily duties to undertake the required behavior from certain motives. To be sure, (mutual) loving concern shared with those close to us is one of life's greatest joys, an ideal truly worth seeking to the extent that its realization lies within our power. In troubled relationships, however, this

---

[37]See the references in note 9 and the text at that point.

[38]I am inclined to agree with Herman and Baron that the problems can be resolved; see the references in note 17.

[39]For a similar point, see Baron, "The Alleged Moral Repugnance of Acting from Duty," pp. 204–05.

attitude may simply surpass our emotional capacities and lie beyond our abilities to control. It is not uncommon, in daily life, for people to care for those close to them primarily out of a sense of duty, given the vicissitudes of human affections.

Nonmarital family relationships, to return to the question of evaluating close relationships, persist independently of how we feel about the partner—indeed, they persist independently of whether or not the caretaking responsibilities are neglected. (Marital relationships can linger on in a similar manner.) My brother (supposing I had one) will remain my brother whether or not I am partial to him, emotionally or materially. As adults, he and I may choose to avoid each other's company, but our formal relationship continues. Being related in those ways is compatible with feelings of disrespect, spite, jealousy, contempt, hatred, or simple indifference. Partners in such relationships may loathe and mistreat each other, yet remain profoundly involved in each other's lives.

Perhaps it is because family relationships are so permanent that we place such a high premium on the emotional concern family members *could* provide for one another if such relationships functioned at their best. Our relationship conventions and practices, thus, include numerous rituals and occasions that serve, among other things, to promote affection and concern among loved ones: Mother's Day, Father's Day, celebrations of wedding anniversaries, family-oriented religious holiday traditions, and so on. A heavy suffusion of myths, clichés, and cultural idealizations permeate marriage and family relationship practices. In virtue of these myths and idealizations, our feelings about our own family relationships (like many aspects of our emotional lives) are subject to a good deal of social manipulation and dissemblance. Rituals, such as gift giving, may disguise the lack of affection among family members by simulating the manifestation of love. An accompanying set of clichés may blindly assert the existence of love regardless of the facts in a particular case. How often a young child, despondent over a parent's anger or neglect, is told, "of *course*, your father loves you; he simply doesn't know how to show it," by someone who, resorting to a stock cliché, has never even met the father in question.

These myths and idealizations can easily mystify our understandings of how it really is with us in our relationships, and, thereby, further complicate the already monumental task of assessing relationships. Philosophers, it seems, have a special responsibility to assist in the critical assessment of relationships by avoiding further mystification. One way to help penetrate through the mythic and idealized understanding of relationships is to resist arguments that sound like nothing more than appeals to unreflective opinions.[40]

Unreflective opinions about values and practices, however popular those opinions may be, are not decisively authoritative for critical moral reflection or moral theory. Such opinions are, to be sure, important starting points of such reflection. They certainly belong in the cultural dialogue about marital and family relationships, a type of dialogue which, as I urged in the previous chapter, should supplant an abstract, monological ideal of impartiality in the human quest for moral wisdom. Unreflective opinions, however (this is part of my own contribution to the dialogue), cannot constitute conclusive defenses of conventional practices because they simply exhibit (and confirm) the conventionality of those practices. The moral worth of particular relationship practices must be assessed, among other things, in terms of the daily reality of those relationships rather than in terms of the hopes or idealistic aspirations that mystify those practices. Real marriages, for example, usually fall far short of their fairy-tale counterparts, which fade "happily ever after" into the sunset.

Even if unreflective opinions are not decisively authoritative for moral theory, it is nevertheless important to understand those opinions carefully. In this regard, the champions of traditional marriage and family who invoke popular support on behalf of these institutions usually make an additional mistake. A familiar adage tells us that actions speak louder than words. What people, in general, actually think about marriage is probably better revealed by the recent rise in the divorce rate than by idealistic popular pronouncements on the topic of marriage.

Some philosophers and social commentators, seeking a populist defense of traditional marriage and family, try to discount what the divorce rate reveals about popular views of marriage by finding culprits to blame for the "breakdown of the traditional family." Feminists, in particular, are frequent scapegoats for this alleged social disintegration.[41] Such an accusation misses an obvious point. Critics of the institution of marriage do not break into people's homes to serve them with mandatory

---

[40]For an essay that violates this stricture, see Christina Hoff Sommers, "Philosophers against the Family," in George Graham and Hugh LaFollette, eds., *Person to Person* (Philadelphia: Temple University Press, 1989), pp. 82–105. My critical discussion of this and other essays by Sommers appears in my "'They Lived Happily Ever After': Sommers on Women and Marriage," *Journal of Social Philosophy* 21 (Fall/Winter 1990): 57–65. A commentary by Sommers and my rejoinder to her commentary follow in the same journal issue, with a further response by Sommers in the following issue of the journal.

[41]See Sommers, "Philosophers against the Family," pp. 82–83.

divorce decrees. If feminism, for example, has anything to do with the rising divorce rate, it must be in virtue of the increasing plausibility, to more and more people, of feminist critiques of marriage.[42] Feminist criticisms of marriage are not the only analyses of marriage available for public consumption; there is no dearth of published apologetics on behalf of traditional marriage.[43] The inability of such marital defenses to stem the tide of divorces provides invaluable information about what people really think about the daily reality of their married lives.

The declining durability of marriages in general may be due to their frequent inability to provide, without undue personal costs, the protection and care needed by their participants. The context of changing economic circumstances is also significant. As Okin has well shown, when decent economic alternatives to marriage are available to a woman, her economic dependence on her husband diminishes, thus providing her with otherwise unavailable options to leave the relationship should it prove unsatisfactory.[44] Whether the current divorce trends, in themselves, reveal problems with marriage at the generic level, the formal conventional level, the informal conventional level, or merely in a substantially large number of instances is a matter for further investigation.

In the first part of this discussion, I suggested, following Robert Goodin, that duties of partiality in close relationships are based, in part, on the various vulnerabilities of persons in those relationships and, in part, on social conventions that assign responsibilities for the care of the vulnerable to others who stand in certain relationships to them. I cautioned, however, that the duties based on those conventions should be viewed as prima facie duties only, pending a deep evaluation of those conventional practices and the vulnerabilities to which they answer. I then outlined some difficulties in the crucial project of assessing those relationship practices.

In the next section, I turn to a different sort of problem with our practices of partiality in close relationships, namely, that many people lack sufficient resources for favoring their loved ones effectively.

---

[42]A growing divorce rate suggests that many people find their marriages to be unsatisfactory. By shifting responsibility for the rising divorce rate away from the divorcing parties and toward marriage critics, such as feminists (ibid., pp. 82–83, 99, and passim), Sommers, in effect, treats this widespread dissatisfaction as if it were merely the result of the manipulation of popular opinion by marriage critics. Such a low regard for popular opinion is curiously inconsistent with Sommers's insistence that philosophers heed the "opinions of the community" (p. 103). It appears that Sommers herself ignores popular opinion when it inconveniently does not support her views (in this case, about marriage).
[43]George Gilder's defenses of traditional marriage and family were especially prominent during the Reagan presidency; see his *Sexual Suicide* (New York: Quadrangle, 1973).
[44]Okin, *Justice, Gender, and the Family*, pp. 137–38, 167–68.

2. Partiality and Inadequate Resources

Derek Parfit poses an argument that challenges the simple notion that I should help my child rather than a stranger when they each face roughly equivalent dangers and when I cannot help both. Parfit asks and answers the following questions: "When I try to protect my child, what should my aim be? Should it simply be that he is not harmed? Or should it rather be that he is saved from harm *by me*? If you would have a better chance of saving him from harm, I would be wrong to insist that the attempt be made by me. This shows that my aim should take the simpler form."[45] Parfit later extends this point to cover any sort of benefiting of loved ones, not simply the saving of them from harm. Parfit subsequently qualifies his argument, as I note below. First, however, let us consider the position in its original form. Stated in this way, the argument is both right and wrong. Certainly, on a particular occasion when my child is threatened, I should want her to be saved from danger no matter who saves her.

Relationships, however, are long-term interpersonal involvements. Partialists do not generally defend partiality for its own sake. Their defenses always refer to some further value to be served by partiality, for example, the maintenance of close relationships (which might, in turn, derive their value from what they contribute to integrity or the good life). A relationship, as it endures, is at its best if its participants both feel that they derive something special from their partner and have something special to offer their partner.[46] This is part of the sense of uniqueness and irreplaceability that people feel about loved ones and about themselves in relation to their loved ones, when relationships are flourishing. This recognition of, and responsiveness to, uniqueness itself seems to require that people be able to do special things for each other, things which cannot be done by others or for others.[47]

Thus, wanting to have a close personal relationship with someone is more than simply wishing well for her; it also involves wanting to make a distinctive contribution to her well-being, wanting to be an irreplaceably valuable part of her life. Parfit does acknowledge this point. He

[45]Derek Parfit, *Reasons and Persons* (Oxford: Clarendon Press, 1984), p. 96.
[46]This point is made by Williams, "Persons, Character and Morality," p. 15; and by John Hardwig, "In Search of an Ethics of Personal Relationships," in George Graham and Hugh LaFollette, eds., *Person to Person* (Philadelphia: Temple University Press, 1989), p. 67.
[47]Blum extensively discusses this aspect of close relationships in *Friendship, Altruism, and Morality*.

subsequently amends his statement of the argument by noting that there may be some kinds of benefit "that my child should receive *from me*."[48]

Parfit's initial argument, however, is not completely wrong. It remains true that in emergencies one should want loved ones to be saved, no matter by whom. This point can be extended as well to the whole of a relationship. Love for someone over the long haul should include not only a concern to be an irreplaceably valuable part of her life but also the simple concern for her well-being. Because I care for my loved ones, I should want them both to be cared for or benefited by me and to do well, to flourish. Both concerns blend in a loving relationship with someone.

Close personal relationships in any society, as noted earlier, are highly conventionalized by a variety of practices.[49] Those practices organize and normalize partiality, making it legitimate, even required, toward certain persons rather than others, and in certain forms. (If friends do not provide the special care, support, and assistance we think of as appropriate for friendship, then hardly anyone can be expected to do so. After all, what are friends for?) Substantial partiality is expected in close relationships and is normative for them.

The relationship practices by which I justify preferentially saving my child from a danger equally facing several other children (when I can only save one) are the same practices that justify another parent in abandoning my child and saving solely her own when she herself is able to save only one. That is, the practices in question may sometimes be detrimental to my own child, whose welfare is of overriding partial concern to me. Remember that love does (or should) involve not only wanting to benefit one's beloved oneself but also wanting to see the loved one do well. It should matter to the partialist whether or not actual practices of partiality, the conventions determining when and to what extent we should favor loved ones, really do promote overall the well-being of our loved ones. If particular conventions of partiality reduce the wellbeing of some of those we love, then they diminish the extent to which we together find fulfillment and integrity through close relationships.

A partialist might not be troubled by the fact that the same practices which lead me to favor my child will also lead others to disfavor my child. From the partialist's standpoint, some child or other is being favored on each occasion by someone who loves her. The result does not seem to involve a net loss of integrity or fulfillment and so should

[48]Parfit, *Reasons and Persons*, p. 96.
[49]For Parfit's discussion of the role played by social convention in our relationship practices, see ibid., pp. 96–110.

not worry the partialist. To ferret out the worrisome feature of unqualified partiality, we must think about conditions in the "real world" that
are relevant to the partial ways in which we practice close personal
relationships.

It is common among philosophers to think that extant relationship
conventions are operative because people in general benefit from
them.[50] Even if people in general do benefit from certain relationship
conventions, this does not entail that each and every person benefits.
Relationship norms do not take account of the varying social and
economic conditions of people's lives. Whether someone benefits from
certain conventions may have a lot to do with her "social location," her
share in that all-important dispersion, the distribution of the benefits
and burdens of social cooperation. Because of limited resources, some
people, vulnerable children and elderly persons among them, do not
derive from their close personal relationships the values we think those
relationships ought to serve.

An indirect line of thought may best help us to approach this problem. Consider John Cottingham's 1983 attack on what he (in that
essay) presents as a close cousin of the impartiality requirement, the
Christian maxim "love thy neighbor as thyself."[51] Passages in the Bible
indicate that "neighbor" here refers to anyone in need, not simply the
person next door.[52] For the sake of argument, however, let us think
about the meaning of this directive in the narrower sense, an approach
taken also by Cottingham in 1983. Doing so will afford us a vehicle
with which to explore some limits to the partialist's perspective.
Cottingham ridicules the maxim, in its narrow sense, for demanding
that one give the "same importance" to the interests of the person next
door that one gives to one's own interests. Cottingham's attack on the
narrowly interpreted maxim has something to it, but his reasons miss a
key point.

---

[50]R. M. Hare's view, for example, that strong maternal partiality promotes good care for children
seems typical; see *Moral Thinking* (Oxford: Clarendon Press, 1981), p. 137.

[51]Cottingham, *Partiality, Favoritism, and Morality*, p. 87.

[52]According to the New Testament parable of the Good Samaritan (Luke 10:29–37), the "neighbor"
is anyone in need. I am grateful to Cynthia Read for bringing this passage to my (non-Christian)
attention. Cottingham, as well, has recently emphasized that the maxim to love thy neighbor as thyself
applies to any human being; see his "Ethics of Self-Concern," *Ethics* 101 (July 1991): 799, n. 5.
Referring to an earlier draft of this chapter, Cottingham, in his footnote, suggests that my discussion
of the maxim is "off the mark" because I interpret "neighbor" narrowly. Pace Cottingham, my
narrow (mis)interpretation is not a mistake; instead, it is designed to afford a useful vehicle for making
a point about resource differences between neighborhoods. Certainly, Cottingham's own earlier, more
literal reading of "neighbor" also served a rhetorical purpose and was not a distortion of Christian
doctrine.

Whether my neighbor needs any special moral attention from me depends, both literally and metaphorically, on where we live. Until recently, I lived next door to a retired engineering professor from Purdue. He spent every summer at his condominium in Colorado. For his months away, he hired a lawn service to maintain the grounds around his home, including the dozen or so tomato plants that he would install in his garden every spring. Each summer, before leaving for Colorado, he would invite me to help myself to his homegrown, professionally watered tomatoes when they started ripening in August, since he would not return from Colorado until September. My former neighbor deserves my deepest gratitude, but he hardly needs my special moral concern.

The same cannot be said about those people across town who have no condominiums in Colorado, no homes of their own anywhere, no lawn services, no tomato plants, and little else. It is not really the neighbor as such who needs the special concern of others. The one who really needs special attention is the person without resources whose friends and family are equally lacking. She would not be adequately cared for even if all her friends and family were as partial toward her as they could be. There are radical disparities among different "neighborhoods" in the distribution of the resources for caring and protecting others. Those of us who live in comfortable middle-class neighborhoods (or better) need a metaphor other than "love thy neighbor" to express what impartiality really calls for.

Interpreted narrowly, "love thy neighbor as thyself" is itself a statement of one form of partiality: it is *thy* neighbor whom you are exhorted to love, not neighbors in general or neighbors everywhere. Cottingham well knows that it is not the person next door but all inhabitants of the planet who matter to the impartiality thesis.[53] This means that Cottingham's (and my own) attack on the narrow meaning of the injunction to love thy neighbor is actually a criticism of a certain form of partiality and not an attack on the impartiality thesis at all. It is no argument against impartiality that I need not have paid any special moral regard to my engineer neighbor, since he was doing splendidly without me.

Not so for the numerous others who live in dire need. Of course, fulfilling relationships are logically—and empirically—possible under conditions of extreme material need, but they are certainly also severely

---

[53]"Ethics and Impartiality," pp. 90–91.

threatened by such conditions. It is difficult to find fulfillment or integrity, that is, wholeness, in life if those I love are starving. If they continue to starve no matter how much favoritism I show them, because my resources are so meager, then partiality, while it might be necessary for my integrity and fulfillment, is hardly sufficient. In many cases, this insufficiency is profound.

There are, to be sure, some reasons on behalf of favoring the interests of neighbors and acquaintances, even those with resources, over the interests of unknown strangers. When one is acquainted with someone, then one knows something, however minimal, about her. One may be familiar with her needs, wants, situation, or the like. Knowing something about someone's particular circumstances makes it easier to help or care for her effectively than if one knows nothing in particular about her. In such cases of greater familiarity, the risk is lessened that the help or care one renders will be ineffective or, worse yet, detrimental to the recipient.

These considerations modify, but they do not override or even substantially diminish, the moral importance of social and economic conditions in determining how practices of partiality should be organized society-wide. Relationship norms, to reiterate, are silent about those conditions. It matters to the partialist's theoretical stance, however, that large numbers of people do not have adequate resources to favor their loved ones. (This is the point that I have approached indirectly.)[54] As a result, whether or not, and to what extent, someone benefits from certain partialist relationship conventions has a lot to do with her socioeconomic location. It hinges heavily on the sort of luck she had in being born to, adopted by, or linked by marriage to relations with adequate resources for her care, nurturance, and protection.

When many families are substantially impoverished, then practices of partiality further diminish the number of people who can achieve well-being, integrity, and fulfillment through close relationships. If we each tend to our own loved ones only, then some of those loved ones will flourish while others languish. Those who can care for their loved ones well, materially, emotionally, and so on, will enhance the well-being and life prospects of their loved ones and will thereby realize some measure of the sort of personal integrity and fulfillment that is attained through close relationships. Those who cannot take

---

[54]For a related argument, see James Rachels, "Morality, Parents, and Children," in Graham and LaFollette, *Person to Person*, pp. 46–62.

good care of their loved ones will not realize integrity or fulfill-ment through such relationships because they can do little to enhance the well-being of those they love. Partiality, if practiced by all, untempered by any redistribution of wealth or resources, would appear to lead to the integrity and fulfillment of only some persons, but not all.

The implications of this line of thought are particularly relevant to the defenses of partiality that appeal to its role in furthering human integrity and fulfillment, an approach taken by Williams and Cottingham.[55] On such a view, partiality is not intrinsically valuable but derives its value largely from being a necessary ingredient in rela-tionships that themselves realize integrity and fulfillment in someone's life because they are her relationships, connections through which she herself strives to promote the well-being of those she loves. As Cottingham puts it, "to be a person, to have a sense of identity and per-sonal integrity, implies the possession of plans, projects and desires which have a *special status* in your scale of values precisely because they are yours."[56]

Recall the significance of Parfit's argument: in loving my loved ones, my aim is not simply that they be cared for by me, but that they be cared for *well*. If someone cannot care effectively for her loved ones, then her aims remain unrealized, putting her own integrity and fulfill-ment at risk along with the (to her) all-important well-being of her loved ones. Were the unqualified practice of partiality to lead to less integrity or fulfillment than is possible under other social arrangements, then, on this partialist account, there would be something wrong with the unqualified practice of partiality.

If the defense of partiality is predicated on the importance of human integrity and fulfillment in general, then the numbers must count theoretically.[57] It should matter to what I call the "fulfillment defense" of partiality that some people live in circumstances which critically compro-mise the care they can show to loved ones and which, accordingly, dimin-ish their chances of achieving integrity and fulfillment through close

---

[55]Other defenses of partiality, such as Fried's libertarian account, are not so clearly challenged by these considerations, although they might be if we could substitute freedom for integrity and fulfillment, mutatis mutandis.

[56]Cottingham, "Ethics and Impartiality," p. 87.

[57]A similar point is raised by David O. Brink against William's well-known hypothetical counterexample to utilitarianism involving the case of Jim and the nineteen villagers sentenced to death; "Utilitarianism and the Personal Point of View," *Journal of Philosophy* 83 (August 1986): 432.

personal relationships. If partiality is everyone's moral prerogative, and, more so, if it is everyone's responsibility, then, on certain partialist grounds alone, there ought to be a distribution of the resources for protecting, caring for, and otherwise favoring loved ones that permits as many of us as possible to do so in a fulfilling and integrity-conferring manner.

A defense of partiality toward loved ones is incomplete without a defense of the social conventions by which such partiality would be realized in practice and turned into a set of legitimated expectations for a society. Surely Bernard Williams is not merely trying to convince us that it is all right for him to favor members of the Williams clan, John Cottingham is not simply trying to justify his own partiality toward his loved ones, and so on. If partiality, as such, is to be justified, then the defense must be in general terms. If the very practices of partiality are not defensible, then particular instances of it lose one of their primary justifications.

The justification of practices, however, often taken a decidedly different form from the justification of actions that exemplify or fall under those practices.[58] If partiality is to be defended in virtue of the integrity and fulfillment it makes possible for *all* those who practice it, then we must consider the effects of practices of partiality on all who together engage in them, including those who lack the minimum resources for showing partiality effectively. The justification of practices requires us to consider people who are not our friends or relations, for whom we feel no particular affection, and whom we may not even know.

On a fulfillment defense of partiality, social institutions should be structured so that partiality, as practiced in close relationships, contributes to the well-being, integrity, and fulfillment of as many people as possible. I do not pretend to have a blueprint for thus restructuring our institutions. I have no formula for modifying our practices of partiality so as to alleviate the worldwide scarcity of caretaking resources while still preserving the values afforded by partiality itself. The best solution, in my view, will arise out of a sort of public dialogue, a dialogue that its current participants should restructure so as to include in particular the voices of those who lack adequate means for favoring their loved ones effectively.

---

[58]This point has long been recognized. For what is, by now, a classic discussion and application of it, see John Rawls, "Two Concepts of Rules," *Philosophical Review* 64 (1955).

This conclusion, which appears to show consideration for all persons, is derived from certain partialist concerns. Thus, by viewing partiality as morally valuable because of what it ultimately contributes to human well-being, integrity, and fulfillment in life, and by considering the reality of inadequate resources for some, we are led to a notion that sounds suspiciously like my proposed method for promoting a modified, practicable moral impartiality.

In this [reading], I sketched the partiality debate and highlighted features of the practice of partiality that complicate its philosophical defense. First, I proposed that the moral value of partiality depends partly on the moral worth of the particular relationships in which it appears. Second, I suggested that practices of partiality must be tempered by the recognition that many persons lack adequate resources for favoring their loved ones effectively. . . .

The Moral Basis of Vegetarianism

Tom Regan

My initial interest in vegetarianism grew out of my study of the life and writings of Mahatma Gandhi. Gandhi, as is well known, was an advocate of nonviolence (ahimsa⁻), not only in political affairs but in the conduct of one's life generally. The extreme pacifistic position he advocated, from which he derived the obligatoriness of vegetarianism, struck me as inadequate, and I sought a less radical moral basis for vegetarianism, one that those of us in the Western world would find more hospitable. Since the leading theories were (and remain) one or another version of utilitarianism, on the one hand, and, on the other, theories that proclaim basic moral rights, it seemed to me that the moral basis of vegetarianism would have to be found somewhere among these options. That such a basis may be provided by a rights-based theory is what "The Moral Basis of Vegetarianism" attempts to show. Both the moral right not to be caused gratuitous suffering and the right to life, I argue, are possessed by the animals we eat if they are possessed by the humans we do not. To cause animals to suffer cannot be defended merely on the grounds that we like the taste of their flesh, and even if animals were raised so that they led generally pleasant lives and were "humanely" slaughtered that would not insure that their rights, including their right to life, were not violated. Despite the Western custom of supposing that vegetarians must defend their "eccentric" way of life, the essay attempts to shift the burden of proof onto the shoulders of those who should bear it—the nonvegetarians.

Now, there can be no doubt that animals sometimes appear to be in pain. On this point, even Descartes would agree. In order for us to be rationally entitled to abandon the belief that they actually do experience pain, therefore, especially in view of the close physiological resemblances that often exist between them and us, we are in need of some rationally compelling argument that would demonstrate that this belief is erroneous. Descartes's principle argument in this regard fails to present a compelling case for his view. Essentially, it consists in the claim that, since animals cannot speak or use a language, they do not think and since they do not think, they have no minds: lacking in these respects, therefore, they have no consciousness either. Thus, since a necessary condition of a creature's being able to experience pain is that it be a conscious being, it follows, given Descartes's reasoning, that animals do not experience pain. . . .

Imagine a person whose vocal cords have been damaged to such an extent that he no longer has the ability to utter words or even make inarticulate sounds, and whose arms have been paralyzed so that he cannot write, but who, when his tooth abscesses, twists and turns on his bed, grimaces and sobs. We do not say, "Ah, if only he could still speak, we could give him something for his pain. As it is, since he cannot speak, there's nothing we need give him. For he feels no pain." We say he is in pain, despite his loss of the ability to say so.

Whether or not a person is experiencing pain, in short, does not depend on his being able to perform one or another linguistic feat. Why, then, should it be any different in the case of animals? It would seem to be the height of human arrogance, rather than of . . . "superstition," to erect a double standard here, requiring that animals meet a standard not set for humans. If humans can experience pain without being logically required to be able to say so or in any other ways to use a language, then the same standard should apply to animals as well. . . .

Now, an essential part of any enlightened morality is the principle of noninjury. What this principle declares is that we are not to inflict pain on, or otherwise bring about or contribute to the pain in, any being capable of experiencing it. This principle, moreover, is derivable from the more general principle of nonmaleficence, which declares that we are not to do or cause evil, together with the value judgment that pain, considered in itself, is intrinsically evil. . . .

Given the intrinsic evil of pain, and assuming further that pleasure is intrinsically good, it is clear that cases can arise in which the evil (pain) caused to animals is not compensated for by the good (pleasure) caused humans. The classical utilitarians—Bentham, Mill, and Sidgwick—all were aware of this . . .

It has already been pointed out that the pain an animal feels is just as much pain, and just as much an intrinsic evil, as a comparable pain felt by a human being. So, if there is any rational basis for rendering conflicting judgments about the two practices, it must be looked for in some other direction.

The most likely and, on the face of it, the most plausible direction in which to look is in the direction of rights. "Humans," this line of reasoning goes, "have certain natural rights that animals lack, and that is what makes the two practices differ in a morally significant way. For in the case of the practice involving humans, their equal natural right to be spared undeserved pain is being violated, while in the case of the practice involving animals, since animals can have no rights, *their* rights are not being ignored. That is what makes the two cases differ. And that is what makes the practice involving humans an immoral one, while the practice involving animals is not."

Natural though this line of argument is, I do not think it justifies the differential treatment of the animals and humans in question. For on what grounds might it be claimed that the humans, but not the animals have an equal natural right to be spared undeserved pain? Well, it cannot be, as it is sometimes alleged, that all and only human beings have this right because all and only humans reason, make free choices, or have a concept of their identity. These grounds will not justify the ascription of rights to all humans because some humans—infants and the severely mentally defective, for example—do not meet these conditions. Moreover, even if these conditions did form the grounds for the possession of rights; and even if it were true that all human beings met them; it still would not follow that *only* human beings have them. For on what grounds, precisely, might it be claimed that no animals can reason, make free choices, or form a concept of themselves? What one would want here are detailed analyses of these operative concepts together with rationally compelling empirical data and other arguments that support the view that all nonhuman animals are deficient in these respects. It would be the height of prejudice merely to assume that man is unique in being able to reason. To the extent that these beliefs are not examined in the light of what we know about animals and animal intelligence, the supposition that *only* human beings have these capacities is just that—a supposition, and one that could hardly bear the moral weight placed upon it by the differential treatment of animals and humans. . . .

Two objections should be addressed before proceeding. Both involve difficulties that are supposed to attend the attribution of rights to animals. The first declares that animals cannot have rights because they lack the capacity to *claim* them. Now, this objection seems to be a variant of the view that animals cannot have rights because they cannot speak, and, like this more general view, this one too will not withstand a moment's serious reflection. For there are many human beings who cannot speak or claim their rights—tiny infants, for example—and yet who would not be denied the right in question, assuming, as we are, that it is supposed to be a right possessed by *all* human beings. Thus, if a human being can possess this (or any other right) without being able to demand it, it cannot be reasonable to require that animals be able to do so, if they are to possess this (or any other) right. The second objection is different. It declares that the attribution of rights to animals leads to absurdity. For if, say, a lamb has the natural right to be spared undeserved pain, then the wolf, who devours it unmercifully, without the benefit of anesthetic, should be said to violate the lamb's right. This, it is alleged, is absurd, and so, then, is the attribution of rights to animals. Well, absurd it may be to say that the wolf violates the lamb's right. But even supposing that it is, nothing said here implies that such deeds on the part of the wolf violate the lamb's rights. For the lamb can have rights only against those beings who are capable of taking the interests of the lamb into account and [are] trying to determine, on the basis of its interests, as well as other relevant considerations, what, morally speaking, ought to be done. In other words, the only kind of being against which another being can have rights is a being that can be held to be morally responsible for its actions. Thus, the lamb can have rights against, say, most adult human beings. But a wolf, I think it would be agreed, is not capable of making decisions from the moral point of view; nor is a wolf the kind of being that can be held morally responsible; neither, then, can it make sense to say that the lamb has any rights against the wolf. This situation has its counterpart in human affairs. The severely mentally feeble, for example, lack the requisite powers to act morally; thus, *they* cannot be expected to recognize our rights, nor can *they* be said to violate our rights, even if, for example, they should happen to cause us undeserved pain. For as they are not the kind of being that can be held responsible for what they do, neither can they be said to violate anyone's rights by what they do. . . .

Animals who are raised to be eaten by human beings very often are made to suffer. Nor is it simply that they suffer only when they are being shipped to the slaughterhouse or actually being slaughtered. For what is happening is this: The human appetite for meat has become so great that new methods of raising animals have come into being. Called intensive rearing methods, these methods seek to insure that the largest amount of meat can be produced in the shortest amount of time with the least possible expense. In ever increasing numbers, animals are being subjected to the rigors of these methods. Many are being forced to live in incredibly crowded conditions. Moreover, as a result of these methods, the natural desires of many animals often are being frustrated. In short, both in terms of the physical pain these animals must endure, and in terms of the psychological pain that attends the frustration of their natural inclinations, there can be no reasonable doubt that animals who are raised according to intensive rearing methods experience much nontrivial, undeserved pain. Add to this the gruesome realities of "humane" slaughter and we have, I think, an amount and intensity of suffering that can, with propriety, be called "great."

To the extent, therefore, that we eat the flesh of animals that have been raised under such circumstances, we help create the demand for meat that farmers who use intensive rearing methods endeavor to satisfy. Thus, to the extent that it is known that such methods will bring about much undeserved, nontrivial pain on the part of the animals raised according to these methods, anyone who purchases meat that is a product of these methods—and almost everyone who buys meat at a typical supermarket or restaurant does this—is *causally implicated* in a practice that causes pain that is both nontrivial and undeserved for the animals in question. On this point too, I think there can be no doubt. . . .

Now, there are, as I mentioned earlier two further objections that might be raised, both of which, I think, uncover important limitations in the argument of this section. The first is that a meat eater might be able to escape the thrust of my argument by the simple expedient of buying meat from farms where the animals are not raised according to intensive rearing methods a difficult but not impossible task at the present time. For despite the widespread use of these methods, it remains true that there are farms where animals are raised in clean, comfortable quarters, and where the pain they experience is the natural result of the exigencies of animal existence rather than, to use an expression of Hume's, of "human art and contrivance." . . .

The [second] objection that reads thus: "Granted, the amount of pain animals experience in intensive rearing units is deplorable and ought to be eliminated as far as is possible; still, it does not follow that we ought to give up meat altogether or to go to the trouble of hunting or buying it from other farmers. After all, all we need do is get rid of the pain and our moral worries will be over. So, what we should do is this; we should try to figure out how to *desensitize* animals so that they do not feel any pain, even in the most barbarous surroundings. Then, if this could be worked out, there would not be any grounds for worrying about the 'morality' of eating meat. Remove the animals' capacity for feeling pain and you thereby remove the possibility of their experiencing any pain that is gratuitous."

Now, I think it is obvious that nothing that I have said thus far can form a basis for responding to this objection, and though I think there are alternative ways in which one might try to respond to it, the case I try to make against it evolves out of my response to the first objection; I try to show, in other words, that an adequate response to this objection can be based upon the thesis that *it is the killing of animals, and not just their pain, that matters morally.*

Let us begin, then, with the idea that all humans possess an equal natural right to life. And let us notice, once again, that it is an *equal natural* right that we are speaking of, one that we cannot acquire or have granted to us, and one that we all are supposed to have just because we are human beings. On what basis, then, might it be alleged that all and only human beings possess this right to an equal extent? Well, several familiar possibilities come immediately to mind. It might be argued that all and only human beings have an equal right to life because either (*a*) all and only human beings have the capacity to reason, or (*b*) all and only human beings have the capacity to make free choices, or (*c*) all and only human beings have a concept of "self," or (*d*) all and only human beings have all or some combination of the previously mentioned capacities. And it is easy to imagine how someone might argue that, since animals do not have any of these capacities, *they* do not possess a right to life, least of all one that is equal to the one possessed by humans.

I have already touched upon some of the difficulties such views must inevitably encounter. Briefly, it is not clear, first, that no nonhuman animals satisfy any one (or all) of these conditions, and, second, it is reasonably clear that not all human beings satisfy them. The severely mentally feeble, for example, fail to satisfy them. Accordingly, *if* we want to insist that they have a right to life, then we cannot also maintain that they have it because they satisfy one or another of these conditions. Thus, *if* we want to insist that they have an equal right to life, despite their failure to satisfy these conditions, we cannot consistently maintain that animals, because they fail to satisfy these conditions, therefore lack this right.

Another possible ground is that of sentience, by which I understand the capacity to experience pleasure and pain. But this view, too, must encounter a familiar difficulty—namely, that it could not justify restricting the right *only* to human beings. . . .

The onus of justification lies not on the shoulders of those who are vegetarians but on the shoulders of those who are not. If the argument of the present section is sound, it is the nonvegetarian who must show us how he can be justified in eating meat, when he knows that, to do so, an animal has had to be killed. It is the nonvegetarian who must show us how his manner of life does not contribute to practices that systematically ignore the right to life which animals possess, if humans are supposed to possess it on the basis of the most plausible argument considered here. And it is the nonvegetarian who must do all this while being fully cognizant that he cannot defend his way of life merely by summing up the intrinsic goods—the delicious taste of meat, for example—that come into being as a result of the slaughter of animals.

This is not to say that practices that involve taking the lives of animals cannot possibly be justified. . . . For example, perhaps they are satisfied in the case of the Eskimo's killing of animals and in the case of having a restricted hunting season for such animals as deer. But to say that this is (or may be) true of *some* cases is not to say that it is true of all, and it will remain the task of the nonvegetarian to show that what is true in these cases, assuming that it is true, is also true of any practice that involves killing animals which, by his actions, he supports. . . .

Even if it should turn out that there are no natural rights, that would not put an end to many of the problems discussed here. For even if we do not possess natural rights, we would still object to practices that caused nontrivial, undeserved pain for some human beings if their "justification" was that they brought about this or that amount of pleasure or other forms of intrinsic good for this or that number of people; . . . and we would still object to any practice that involved the killing of human beings, even if killed painlessly, if the practice was supposed to be justified in the same way. But this being so, what clearly would be needed, if we cease to invoke the idea of rights, is some explanation of why practices that are not right, when they involve the treatment of people, can be right (or at least permissible) when they involve the treatment of animals. What clearly would be needed, in short, is what we have found to be needed and wanting all along—namely, the specification of some morally relevant feature of being human which is possessed by *all* human beings and *only* by those beings who are human. Unless or until some such feature can be pointed out, I do not see how the differential treatment of humans and animals can be rationally defended, natural rights or no.

Do Animals Have Rights?

Carl Cohen

Whether animals have rights is a question of great importance because if they do, those rights must be respected, even at the cost of great burdens for human beings. A right (unlike an interest) is a valid claim, or potential claim, made by a moral agent, under principles that govern both the claimant and the target of the claim. Rights are precious; they are dispositive; they count.

You have a right to the return of money you lent me; we both understand that. It may be very convenient for me to keep the money, and you may have no need of it whatever; but my convenience and your needs are not to the point. You have a *right* to it, and we have courts of law partly to ensure that such rights will be respected.

If you make me a promise, I have a moral right to its fulfillment—even though there may be no law to enforce my right. It may be very much in your interest to break that promise, but your great interests and the silence of the law cut no mustard when your solemn promise—which we both well understood—had been given. Likewise, those holding power may have a great and benevolent interest in denying my rights to travel or to speak freely—but their interests are overridden by my rights.

A great deal was learned about hypothermia by some Nazi doctors who advanced their learning by soaking Jews in cold water and putting them in refrigerators to learn how hypothermia proceeds. We have no difficulty in seeing that they may not advance medicine in that way; the subjects of those atrocious experiments had rights that demanded respect. For those who ignored their rights we have nothing but moral loathing.

Some persons believe that animals have rights as surely as those Jews had rights, and they therefore look on the uses of animals in medical investigations just as we look at the Nazi use of the Jews, with moral loathing. They are consistent in doing so. If animals have rights they certainly have the right not to be killed, even to advance our important interests.

Some may say, "Well, they have rights, but we have rights too, and our rights override theirs." They may be true in some cases, but it will not solve the problem because, although we may have a weighty *interest* in learning, say, how to vaccinate against polio or other diseases, we do not have a *right* to learn such things. Nor could we honestly claim that we kill research animals in self-defense; they did not attack us. If animals have rights, they certainly have the right not to be killed to advance the interests of others, whatever rights those others may have.

In 1952 there were about 58,000 cases of polio reported in the United States, and 3,000 polio deaths; my parents, parents everywhere, trembled in fear for their children at camp or away from home. Polio vaccination became routine in 1955, and cases dropped to about a dozen a year; today polio has been eradicated completely from the Western Hemisphere. The vaccine that achieved this, party developed and tested only blocks from where I live in Ann Arbor, could have been developed *only* with the substantial use of animals. Polio vaccines had been tried many times earlier, but from those earlier vaccines children had contracted the diseases; investigators had become, understandably, exceedingly cautious.

The killer disease for which a vaccine now is needed most desperately is malaria, which kills about 2 million people each year, most of them children. Many vaccines have been tried—not on children, thank God—and have failed. But very recently, after decades of effort, we learned how to make a vaccine that does, with complete success, inoculate mice against malaria. A safe vaccine for humans we do not yet have—but soon we will have it, thanks to the use of those mice, many of whom will have died in the process. To test that vaccine first on children would be an outrage, as it would have been an outrage to do so with the Salk and Sabin polio vaccines years ago. We use mice or monkeys *because there is no other way.* And there never will be another way because untested vaccines are very dangerous; their use on a living organism is inescapably experimental; there is and will be no way to determine the reliability and safety of new vaccines without repeated tests on live organisms. Therefore, because we certainly may not use human children to test them, we will use mice (or as we develop an AIDS vaccine, primates) *or we will never have such vaccines.*

But if those animals we use in such tests have rights as human children do, what we did and are doing to them is as profoundly wrong as what the Nazis did to those Jews not long ago. Defenders of animal rights need not hold that medical scientists are vicious; they simply believe that what medical investigators are doing with animals is morally wrong. Most biomedical investigations involving animal subjects use rodents; mice and rats. The rat is the animal appropriately considered (and used by the critic) as the exemplar whose moral stature is in dispute here. Tom Regan is a leading defender of the view that rats do have such rights, and may not be used in biomedical investigations. He is an honest man. He sees the consequences of his view and accepts them forthrightly. In *The Case for Animal Rights* (Regan, 1983) he wrote,

> The harms others might face as a result of the dissolution of [some] practice or institution is no defense of allowing it to continue. . . . No one has a right to be protected against being harmed if the protection in question involves violating the rights of others. . . . No one has a right to be protected by the continuation of an unjust practice, one that violates the rights of others. . . . Justice *must* be done, though the . . . heavens fall. (pp. 346–347)

That last line echoes Kant, who borrowed it from an older tradition. Believing that rats have rights as humans do, Regan (1983) was convinced that killing them in medical research was morally intolerable. He wrote,

> On the rights view, [he means, of course, the Regan rights view] we cannot justify harming a single rat *merely* by aggregating "the many human and humane benefits" that flow from doing it. . . . Not even a single rat is to be treated as if that animal's value were reducible to his *possible utility* relative to the interests of others. (p. 384)

If there are some things that we cannot learn because animals have rights, well, as Regan (1983) put it, so be it.

This is the conclusion to which one certainly is driven if one holds that animals have rights. If Regan is correct about the moral standing of rats, we humans can have no right, ever, to kill them—unless perchance a rat attacks a person or a human baby, as rats sometimes do; then our right of self-defense may enter, I suppose. But medical investigations cannot honestly be described as self-defense, and medical investigations commonly require that many mice and rats be killed. Therefore, all medical investigations relying on them, or any other animal subjects—which includes most studies and all the most important studies of certain kinds—will have to stop. Bear in mind that the replacement of animal subjects by computer simulations, or tissue samples, and so on, is in most research a phantasm, a fantasy. Biomedical investigations using animal subjects (and of course all uses of animals as food) will have to stop.

This extraordinary consequence has no argumentative force for Regan and his followers; they are not consequentialists. For Regan the *interests* of humans, their desire to be freed of disease or relieved of pain, simply cannot outweigh the *rights* of a single rat. For him the issue is one of justice, and the use of animals in medical experiments (he believes) is simply not just. But the consequences of his view will give most of us, I submit, good reason to weigh very carefully the arguments he offers to support such far-reaching claims. Do you believe that the work of Drs. Salk and Sabin was morally right? Would you support it now, or support work just like it saving tens of thousands of human children from diphtheria, hepatitis, measles, rabies, rubella, and tetanus (all of which relied essentially on animal subjects)—as well as, now, AIDS, Lyme disease, and malaria? I surely do. If you would join me in this support we must conclude that the defense of animal rights is a gigantic mistake. I next aim to explain why animals *cannot* possess rights.

Why Animals Do Not Have Rights

Many obligations are owed by humans to animals; few will deny that. But it certainly does not follow from this that animals have rights because it is certainly not true that every obligation of ours arises from the rights of another. Not at all. We need to be clear and careful here. Rights entail obligations. If you have a right to the return of the money I borrowed, I have an obligation to repay it. No issue. If we have the right to speak freely on public policy matters, the community has the obligation to respect out right to do so. But the proposition *all rights entail obligations* does not convert simply, as the logicians say. From the true proposition that all trees are plants, it does not follow that all plants are trees. Similarly, not all obligations are entailed by rights. Some obligations, like mine to repay the money I borrowed from you, do arise out of rights. But many obligations are owed to persons or other beings who have no rights whatever in the matter.

Obligations may arise from commitments freely made: As a college professor I accept the obligation to comment at length on the papers my students submit, and I do so; but they have not the right to *demand* that I do so. Civil servants and elected officials surely ought to be courteous to members of the public, but that obligation certainly is not grounded in citizens' rights.

Special relations often give rise to obligations: Hosts have the obligation to be cordial to their guests, but the guest has not the right to demand cordiality. Shepherds have obligations to their dogs, and cowboys to their horses, which do not flow from the rights of those dogs or horses. My son, now 5, may someday wish to study veterinary medicine as my father did; I will then have the obligation to help him as I can, and with pride I shall—but he has not the authority to demand such help as a matter of right. My dog has no right to daily exercise and veterinary care, but I do have the obligation to provide those things for her.

One may be obliged to another for a special act of kindness done; one may be obliged to put an animal out of its misery in view of its condition—but neither the beneficiary of that kindness nor that dying animal may have had a claim of right.

Beauchamp and Childress (1994) addressed what they called the "correlativity of rights and obligations" and wrote that they would defend an "untidy" (pp. 73–75) variety of that principle. It would be very untidy indeed. Some of our most important obligations—to members of our family, to the needy, to neighbors, and to sentient creatures of every sort—have no foundation in rights at all. Correlativity appears critical from the perspective of one who holds a right; your right correlates with my obligation to respect it. But the claim that rights and obligations are *reciprocals,* that *every* obligation flows from another's right, is false, plainly inconsistent with our general understanding of the differences between what we think we ought to do, and what others can justly *demand* that we do.

I emphasize this because, although animals have no rights, it surely does not follow from this that one is free to treat them with callous disregard. Animals are not stones; they feel. A rat may suffer; surely we have the obligation not to torture it gratuitously, even though it be true that the concept of a right could not possibly apply to it. We humans are obliged to act humanely, that is, being aware of their sentence, to apply to animals the moral principles that govern us regarding the gratuitous imposition of pain and suffering; which is not, of course, to treat animals as the possessors of rights.

Animals cannot be the bearers of rights because the concept of rights is essentially *human*; it is rooted in, and has force within, a human moral world. Humans must deal with rats—all too frequently in some part of the world—and must be moral in their dealing with them; but a rat can no more be said to have rights than a table can be said to have ambition.

To say of a rat that it has rights is to confuse categories, to apply to its world a moral category that has content only in the human moral world.

Try this thought experiment. Imagine, on the Serengeti Plain in East Africa, a lioness hunting for her cubs. A baby zebra, momentarily left unattended by its mother, is the prey; the lioness snatches it, rips open its throat, tears out chunks of its flesh, and departs. The mother zebra is driven nearly out of her wits when she cannot locate her baby; finding its carcass she will not even leave the remains for days. The scene my be thought unpleasant, but it is entirely natural, of course, and extremely common. If the zebra has a right to live, if the prey is just but the predator unjust, we ought to intervene, if we can, on behalf of right. But we do not intervene, of course—as we surely would intervene if we saw the lioness about to attack an unprotected human baby or you. What accounts for the moral difference? We justify different responses to humans and to zebras on the ground (implicit or explicit) that their moral stature is very different. The human has a right not to be eaten alive; it is, after all, a human being. Do you believe the baby zebra has the *right* not to be slaughtered by that lioness? That the lioness has the *right* to kill that baby zebra for her cubs? If you are inclined to say, confronted by such natural rapacity—duplicated with untold variety millions of times each day on planet earth—that neither is right or wrong, that neither has a *right* against the other, I am on your side. Rights are of the highest moral consequence, yes; but zebras and lions and rats are totally amoral; there is no morality for them; they do no wrong, ever. In their world there are no rights.

A contemporary philosopher who has thought a good deal about animals, referring to them as "moral patients," put it this way:

> A moral patient lacks the ability to formulate, let alone bring to bear, moral principles in deliberating about which one among a number of possible acts it would be right or proper to perform. Moral patients, in a word, cannot do what is right, nor can they do what is wrong. . . . Even when a moral patient causes significant harm to another, the moral patient has not done what is wrong. Only moral agents can do what is wrong. (Regan, 1983, pp. 152–153)

Just so. The concepts of wrong and right are totally foreign to animals, not conceivably within their ken or applicable to them, as the author of that passage clearly understands.

When using animals in our research, therefore, we ought indeed be humane—but we can never violate the rights of those animals because, to be blunt, they have none. Rights do not *apply* to them.

But humans do have rights. Where do our rights come from? Why are we not crudely natural creatures like rats and zebras? This question philosophers have struggled to answer from earliest times. A definitive account of the human moral condition I cannot here present, of course. But reflect for a moment on the kinds of answers that have been widely given:

- Some think our moral understanding, with its attendant duties, to be a divine gift. So St. Thomas said: The moral law is binding, and humans have the power, given by God, to grasp it binding character, and must therefore respect the rights that other humans possess. God makes us (Saint Augustine said before him) in his own image, and therefore with a will that is free, and gives us the power to recognize that, and therefore, unlike other creatures, we must choose between good and evil, between right and wrong.

- Many philosophers, distrusting theological justifications of rights and duties, sought the ground of human morality in the membership, by all humans, in a moral community. The English idealist, Bradley, called it an organic moral community; the German idealist, Hegel, called it an objective ethical order. These and like accounts commonly center on human interrelations, on a moral fabric within which human agents always act, and within which animals never act and never can possibly act.

- The highly abstract reasoning from which such views emerge has dissatisfied many; you may find more nearly true the convictions of ethical intuitionists and realists who said, as H. A. Prichard, Sir David Ross, and my friend and teacher C. D. Broad, of happy memory, used to say, that there is a direct, underivative, intuitive cognition of rights as possessed by other humans but not by animals.

- Or perhaps in the end we will return to Kant, and say with him that critical reason reveals at the core of human action a uniquely moral will, and the unique ability to grasp and to lay down moral laws for oneself and for others—an ability that is not conceivably within the capacity of any nonhuman animal whatever.

To be a moral agent (on this view) is to be able to grasp the generality of moral restrictions on our will. Humans understand that some things, which may be in our interest, *must not be willed*; we lay down moral laws for ourselves, and thus exhibit, as no other animal can exhibit, moral autonomy. My dog knows that there are certain things she must not do—but she knows this only as the outcome of her learning about her interests, the pains she may suffer if she does what had been taught forbidden. She does not know, cannot know (as Regan agrees) that any conduct is wrong. The proposition *It would be highly advantageous to act in such-and-such a way, but I may not because it would be wrong* is one that no dog or mouse or rabbit, however sweet and endearing; however loyal or attentive to its young, can ever entertain, or intend, or begin to grasp. Right is not in their world. But right and wrong are the very stuff of human moral life, the ever-present awareness of human beings who can do wrong, and who by seeking (often) to avoid wrong conduct prove themselves members of a moral community in which rights may be exercised and must be respected.

Some respond by saying, "This can't be correct, for human infants (and the comatose and senile, etc.) surely have rights, but they make no moral claims or judgments and can make none—and any view entailing that children can have no rights must be absurd." Objections of this kind miss the point badly. It is not individual persons who qualify (or are disqualified) for the possession of rights because of the presence or absence in them of some special capacity, thus resulting in the award or rights to some but not to others. Rights are universally human; they arise in a *human moral world*, in a moral *sphere*. In the human world moral judgments are pervasive; it is the fact that all humans including infants and the senile are members of that moral community—not the fact that as individuals they have or do not have certain special capacities, or merits—that makes humans bearers of rights. Therefore, it is beside the point to insist that animals have remarkable capacities, that they really have a consciousness of self, or of the future, or make plans, and so on. And the tired response that because infants plainly cannot make moral claims they must have no rights at all, or rats must have them too, we ought forever put aside. Responses like these arise out of a misconception of right itself. They mistakenly suppose that rights are tied to some identifiable individual abilities or sensibilities, and they fail to see that rights arise only in a community of moral beings, and that therefore there are spheres in which rights do apply and spheres in which they do not.

Rationality is not at issue; the capacity to communicate is not at issue. My dog can reason, if rather weakly, and she certainly can communicate. Cognitive criteria for the possession of rights, Beauchamp said, are morally perilous. Indeed they are. Nor is the capacity to suffer here at issue. And, if *autonomy* be understood only as the capacity to choose this course rather than that, autonomy is not to the point either. But *moral autonomy*—that is, *moral selflegislation*—is to the point, because moral autonomy is uniquely human and is for animals out of the question, as we have seen, and as Regan and I agree. In talking about autonomy, therefore, we must be careful and precise.

Because humans do have rights, and these rights can be violated by other humans, we say that some humans commit *crimes*. But whether a crime has been committed depends utterly on the moral state of mind of the actor. If I take your coat, or your book, honestly thinking it was mine, I do not steal it. The *actus reus* (the guilty deed) must be accompanied, in a genuine crime, by a guilty mind, a *mens rea*. That recognition, not just of possible punishment for an act, but of moral duties that govern us, no rat or cow ever can posses. In primitive times humans did sometimes bring cows and horses to the bar of human justice. We chuckle at that practice now, realizing that accusing cows of crimes marks the primitive moral view as inane. Animals never can be criminals because they have no moral state of mind.

Mistakes parallel to this in other spheres may be helpful to think about. In the Third Part of *The Critique of Pure Reason*, Immanuel Kant explained with care the metaphysical blunders into which we are led when we misapply concepts of great human import. In our human experience, for example, the concepts of time and space, the relations of cause and effect, of subject and attribute, and others, are essential, fundamental. But, forgetting that these are concepts arising only within the world of our human experience, we sometimes are misled into asking: Was the world caused, or is it uncaused? Did the world have a beginning in time, or did it not? Kant explained—in one of the most brilliant long passages in all philosophical literature—why *it makes no sense to ask such questions*. Cause applies to phenomena we humans encounter *in* the world, it is a category of our experience and cannot apply to the world as a whole. Time is the condition of our experience, not an absolute container in which the world could have begun. The antinomies of pure reason, and after those the paralogisms of pure reason, Kant patiently exhibited as confusions arising from the misapplication of the categories of experience. His lesson is powerful and deep. The misapplication of concepts leads to error and, some time to nonsense. So it is with rights also. To say that rats have rights is to apply to the world of rats a concept that makes good sense when applied to humans, but which makes no sense at all when applied to rats.

Why Animals Are Mistakenly Believed to Have Rights

From the foregoing discussion it follows that, if some philosophers believe that they have proved that animals have rights, they must have erred in the alleged proof. Regan is a leader among those who claim to *argue* in defense of the rights of rats; he contends that the best arguments are on his side. I aim next to show how he and others with like views go astray. Bear in mind that Regan's book is long, its argument tortuous and at times convoluted. In what follows I must compress the report of his views, obviously; but I promise to be fair and to hold Regan responsible for nothing that he does not clearly say. We know—if we are agreed that rats are not the holders of rights—that Regan must have got off the track. Examining *The Case for Animal Rights,* let us see if we can find the faulty switch.

Much of Regan's (1983) book is devoted to a general treatment of the nature of ethical thinking and theory, to discussions of animal consciousness and animal awareness, and to detailed critiques of the views of others whom he thinks in error. Regan sought to show, patiently and laboriously, that the common belief that we do have obligations to animals, although they have no rights, has not been defended satisfactorily. That belief cannot be justified, he contended, by direct duty views of which he finds two categories: those depending on the obligation to be kind or not to be cruel, and those depending on any kind of utilitarian calculation.

None of this counterargument could possibly establish his conclusion that animals do have rights, unless Regan had proved that his listing of all alternative conflicting views was exhaustive, which it was not, and unless he had proved conclusively that every such candidate is untenable, which he did not do. . . .

The case is built entirely on the principle that allegedly *carries over* almost everything earlier claimed about human rights to rats and other animals. What principle is that? It is the principle, put in italics but given no name, that equates moral agents with moral patients:

> *The validity of the claim to respectful treatment, and thus the case for the recognition of the right to such treatment, cannot be any stranger or weaker in the case of moral patients than it is in the case of moral agents.* (Regan, p. 279)

But hold on. Why in the world should anyone think this principle to be true? Back where Regan first recounted his view of moral patients, he allowed that some of them are, although capable of experiencing pleasure and pain, lacking in other capacities. But he is interested, he told us there, in those moral patients—those animals—that are like humans in having *inherent value*. This is the key to the argument for animal rights, the possession of inherent value. How that concept functions in the argument becomes absolutely critical. I will say first briefly what will be shown more carefully later: *Inherent value* is an expression used by Regan (and many like him) with two very different senses—in one of which it is reasonable to conclude that those who have inherent value have rights, and in another sense in which that inference is wholly unwarranted. But the phrase *inherent value* has some plausibility in both contexts, and thus by sliding from one sense of inherent value to the other Regan appears to succeed . . . in making the case for animal rights.

The concept of inherent value first entered the discussion in the seventh chapter of Regan's (1983) book, at which point his principle object is to fault and defeat utilitarian arguments. It is not (he argued there) the pleasures or pains that go "into the cup" of humanity that give value, but the "cups" themselves; humans are equal in value because they are humans, having inherent value. So we are, all of us, equal—equal in being moral agents who have this inherent value. This approach to the moral stature of humans is likely to be found quite plausible. Regan called it the "postulate of inherent value"; all humans, "The lonely, forsaken, unwanted, and unloved are no more nor less inherently valuable then those who enjoy a more hospitable relationship with others" (p. 237). And Regan went on to argue for the proposition that all moral agents are "equal in inherent value." Holding some such views we are likely to say, with Kant, that all humans are beyond price. Their inherent value gives them moral dignity, a unique role in the moral world, as agents having the capacity to act morally and make moral judgments. This is inherent value in Sense 1.

The expression *inherent value* has another sense, however, also common and also plausible. My dog has inherent value, and so does every wild animal, every lion and zebra, which is why the senseless killing of animals is so repugnant. Each animal is unique, not replaceable in itself by another animal or by any rocks or clay. Animals, like humans, are not just things; they live, and as unique living creatures they have inherent value. This is an important point, and again likely to be thought plausible; but here, in Sense 2, the phrase *inherent value* means something quite distinct from what was meant in its earlier uses.

Inherent value in Sense 1, possessed by all humans but not by all animals, which warrants the claim of human rights, is very different from inherent value in Sense 2, which warrants no such claim. The uniqueness of animals, their intrinsic worthiness as individual living things, does not ground the possession of rights, has nothing to do with the moral condition in which rights arise. Regan's argument reached its critical objective with almost magical speed because, having argued that beings with inherent value (Sense 1) have rights that must be respected, he quickly asserted (putting it in italics lest the reader be inclined to express doubt) that rats and rabbits also have rights because they, too, have inherent value (Sense 2).

This is an egregious example of the fallacy of equivocation: the informal fallacy in which two or more meanings of the same word or phrase have been confused in the several premises of an argument (Cohen & Copi, 1994, pp. 143–144). Why is this slippage not seen at once? Partly because we know the phrase *inherent value* often is used loosely, so the reader is not prone to quibble about its introduction; partly because the two uses of the phrase relied on are both common, so neither signals danger; partly because inherent value in Sense 2 is indeed shared by those who have it in Sense 1; and partly because the phrase *inherent value* is woven into accounts of what Regan (1983) elsewhere called the *subject-of-a-life criterion*, a phrase of his own devising for which he can stipulate any meaning he pleases, of course, and which also slides back and forth between the sphere of genuine moral agency and the sphere of animal experience. But perhaps the chief reason the equivocation between these two uses of the phrase *inherent value* is obscured (from the author, I believe, as well as from the reader) is the fact that the assertion that animals have rights appears only indirectly, as the outcome of the application of the principle that moral patients are entitled to the same respect as moral agents—a principle introduced at a point in the book long after the important moral differences between moral patients and moral agents have been recognized, with a good deal of tangled philosophical argument having been injected in between.

I invite readers to trace out this equivocation in detail; my limited space here precludes more extended quotation. But this assurance I will give: there is no argument or set of arguments in *The Case for Animal Rights* that successfully makes the case for animal rights. Indeed, there *could* not be, any more than any book, however long and convoluted, could make the case for the emotions of oak trees, or the criminality of snakes.

Animals do not have rights. Right does not apply in their world. We do have many obligations to animals, of course, and I honor Regan's appreciation of their sensitivities. I also honor his seriousness of purpose, and his always civil and always rational spirit. But he is, I submit, profoundly mistaken. I conclude with the observation that, had his mistaken views about the rights of animals long been accepted, most successful medical therapies recently devised—antibiotics, vaccines, prosthetic devices, and other compounds and instruments on which we now rely for saving and improving human lives and for the protection of our children—could not have been developed; and were his views to become general now (an outcome that is unlikely but possible) the consequences for medical science and for human well-being in the years ahead would be nothing less than catastrophic.

Advances in medicine absolutely require experiments, many of which are dangerous. Dangerous experiments absolutely require living organisms as subjects. Those living organisms (we now agree) certainly may not be human beings. Therefore, most advances in medicine will continue to rely on the use of nonhuman animals, or they will stop. Regan is free to say in response, as he does, "so be it." The rest of us must ask if the argument he presents is so compelling as to force us to accept that dreadful result.

References

Beauchamp, T. L., & Childress, J. F. (1994). *Principles of Biomedical Ethics* (4th ed.), New York: Oxford University Press.

Cohen, C., & Copi, I. M. (1994). *Introduction to Logic* (9th ed.). New York: Macmillan.

Regan, T. (1983). *The Case for Animal Rights*. Berkeley: University of California Press.

The Case for Gay Marriage
Michael Nava and Robert Dawidoff

. . . Marriage is how society recognizes the intimate and lasting bond between two people and, in turn, it has become the cornerstone of the American family. Curiously, the American family as we know it is not "traditional" but innovative. Instead of inherited property or bloodlines or unquestioned patriarchal authority, the American family early on developed the view of marriage as a partnership between two consenting adults, not an agreement on their account by their parents or families. The churches that bless the marriage sacrament took their cue from secular, individualist America and, in general, endorse marriage as something entered into by the participants, if they are of age to contract, because they choose to make that commitment.

In the United States marriage is understood to be the decision of two people to live together and be a partnership, a unit, a family. Neither family nor church participates in the legal ceremony, and the religious wedding acquires legal force by the power vested in the officiant by the civil society, the religious ceremony confirms the civil arrangement. Marriage is not conditioned on the intention or the capacity to have children. Nothing in marriage, except custom, mandates partners of different genders. For example, John Boswell notes that in ancient Rome "marriages between males and between females were legal and familiar among the upper classes."[1] The institution of marriage in our society appears to be one that encourages monogamy as the basis for stable personal lives and as one aspect of the family. If we think about what marriage is for, it becomes clear that it is for people to find ways to live ordered, shared lives; it is intended to be the stablest possible unit of family life and a stable structure of intimacy.

Marriage is part of the formal and informal network of extended family, kinship, and friendship, and it is acknowledged in law as society's preferred way for consenting adults to connect their lives. Society recognizes that people have the right and the desire to have those connections solemnized according to their own beliefs; thus, religious ceremonies of all sorts, established or homemade, are encouraged as adjuncts to the civil bond. But it is the civil bond that the law acknowledges and that society encourages in all sorts of ways. No wonder many gay and lesbian Americans see marriage as their equal right. Marriage is society's way of making things easier and better for people who want to form permanent relationships, share their lives and property, and form families.

Marriage is not mere form. Society recognizes its importance not only rhetorically but with such benefits as preferential tax treatment, spousal Social Security and veteran's benefits, favorable immigration laws, property and support rights upon divorce, and intestate succession. In addition, according to Alissa Friedman, "both state and federal governments allocate a great many rights on the basis of marital status and have created powerful incentives for an individual to marry. Furthermore, private entities like insurance companies often provide special benefits and lower rates for married couples and legally recognized couples. Restrictions on the right to marry, therefore, affect both associational rights and a variety of societal entitlements."[2] . . .

Gays and lesbians want the right to marry for the same reasons other Americans do: to gain the moral, legal, social, and spiritual benefits conferred on the marrying couple and especially on their family unit. The material benefits of marriage are considerable, but it is the moral benefit that is especially attractive to many couples, including gay and lesbian ones. Marriage is, or can be, a moral commitment that two people make to one another. The marriage vow enshrines love, honor, respect, and mutual support and gives people access to resources and community acknowledgment that serve to strengthen their bond. Brought up and socialized as most Americans are, gays and lesbians also regard the prospect of marriage as reverently and respectfully as heterosexuals do. To mock and deny them is ultimately to mock and deny the institution of marriage. The impulse to marry, among gays, is essentially the same as it is among heterosexuals, and the capacity to do it well is probably the same. The only real difference is in the identity of the people who want to get married.

What is drastically different, of course, is that gay and lesbian unions get none of the support, encouragement, and benefits society regularly gives to heterosexual unions, however ill-advised. Instead, gays and lesbians are reviled for their "inability" to form permanent attachments. Of course, relationships between people that have to remain clandestine or have no foundations in law or social convention are just that much harder to maintain. Gay relationships can succeed, but always against heavy odds, odds not of the participants' making; heterosexual marriages fail all too often in spite of every conceivable social, familial, legal, and moral support.

The journal *Demography* recently published the results of a twenty-three-year study of the relationship of cohabitation to marriage; they suggest "the possibility that cohabitation weakens commitment to marriage as an institution." The authors of the study concluded that living together before marriage may not strengthen marriage; on the contrary, living together before marriage commonly produces "attitudes and values which increase the probability of divorce."[3] . . . If, as the *Demography* study indicates, marriage is a key ingredient in the longevity and solidity of intimate relationships, then denial of that most important advantage to one class of citizens on account of sexual orientation is cruelly unfair.

One of the ironies of our situation is that the American marriage that is so celebrated actually borrows from the historical character of gay relationships to describe itself. Far from being unnatural, gay and lesbian ways of living have played important roles in every human society. One almost universal function of those relationships has been to pioneer the more equal relations between the sexes. Long-standing relationships between men and between women are well known to history. Antiquity celebrated the bonds of friendship and loyalty between men, bonds that scholars tell us commonly included the sexual. The relationships among Greek soldiers and philosophers, which have played so critical a role in the traditional Western understanding of noble human relations (including the cohesion of the military unit), were modeled on love between men that regularly included sex.

The lifelong partnerships between middle-class or upper-class women in American history—the famous "Boston marriages"—also influenced decisively the understanding of marriage that American women derived from their colleges and their genteel upbringings. Female friendships played a critical role in the creation of the American institution of marriage as a partnership within which the woman was not owned but respected, not a human beast of burden and procreation but an equal source of authority and values for the family that marriage creates. . . .

The distinctive quality of modern American marriage and family is the equal and respectful, relations between husband and wife as partners, friends, and co-parents, in the place of the economic, procreative, and kinship unit of traditional societies. Men and women are learning to treat one another as they more habitually treat favored members of their own gender—with confidence, trust, equality, respect, and sensitivity. Gays and lesbians are as capable of forming such relationships and making them work as heterosexual men and women are. . . .

Two main obstacles appear to gay marriage: legal definitions of marriage and the claim that marriage is chiefly for procreation or child-rearing. The legal argument boils down to the following: Marriage is a union of man and woman because it's always been that way. The civil law that governs marriage has its roots in ecclesiastical law, which reflects the biblical proscription of homosexuality. The statutes say that marriage is the union of man and woman, so that is what marriage must be. . . .

Even if we accept parenting as one important reason for the institution of marriage, shifting the model of marriage to include common if untraditional parenting units makes sense. Whatever was the case in the past, it is now common for gays and lesbians to be parents, not just to have fathered or borne children in heterosexual unions, but to be raising children as open gays and lesbians. In a survey of gay couples, Mary Mendola looked at gays and lesbians involved in a "gay marriage relationship," as she put it. She found that a quarter of the women and 17 percent of the men reported that they or their partners had children. Nearly 60 percent of the women reported that their children lived with them and their partners most of the time, while 39 percent reported that their children regularly visited. While only 3 percent of the men reported that their children lived with them and their partners, 53 percent reported that their children regularly visited them.[4] Mendola's report is a dozen years old; if anything the numbers have probably increased as more gays and lesbians are producing children by using artificial insemination (the so-called gayby boom) or adopting them or winning custody of them. If society is serious in its claim that marriage produces the best environment for raising children, then marriage must be extended to gays and lesbians who, in increasing numbers, are becoming parents.

Moreover, the studies available on gay parenting demonstrate that gays and lesbians make good parents; the children of gay families appear to do as well as the children of heterosexual ones. If, as it is sometimes argued, these children face difficulties among their peers because of negative attitudes toward homosexuality, the clear solution is to change those attitudes through education. Allowing same-sex marriage would be an important part of that change and would also promote family stability. If, in fact, that kind of stability is one of the reasons that marriage exists, it makes no sense to promote it in some families but not others by restricting marriage to heterosexuals.

Opponents of gay marriage finally arrive at the bedrock of their argument when they assert that allowing gays and lesbians to marry would encourage illegal sexual activity in the face of sodomy laws. . . . [This] implies a moral judgment against that activity (even in places where there are no sodomy laws), then allowing gays and lesbians to marry is contrary to acceptable morality. Of course, the whole point of gay and lesbian activism is to expose the underlying premise of immorality for the bigotry it is. Making an act illegal doesn't mean the act is inherently criminal. . . .

The quarter century of gay and lesbian political activism and openness has not resulted in a dramatic increase in the homosexual population (although it has dramatically increased the awareness of homosexuality and has also increased the numbers of lesbians and gays living openly). This points to the conclusion that this population is relatively stable and will always be a minority. Thus, punitive laws accomplish nothing but to intimidate a class of American citizens and deny them their constitutional rights. Denying gay and lesbian marriage will not eliminate gay and lesbian relationships; it will just make those relationships harder to sustain. If creating unnecessary suffering in the cause of popular prejudice is a permissible goal of legislation, then not only gay Americans are in for a bad time of it. . . .

Far from harming heterosexuals, gay marriage would give family-inclined gay men and lesbians the chance to fulfill this aspiration in conformity with their own natures. The legitimacy of gay marriage would save lives by creating the kind of respect for gays and lesbians that will work as a counterweight to bigotry and bashing. . . .

What We Want

What do gays and lesbians want? What does any person want? Enough to live; basic protections; love, family, freedom. Beyond the basics, in the case of gays and lesbians, would be equal protection of the law, representation along with taxation. And what lies beyond that, it is the individual's place to say. We do not think there is a shared agenda among gays and lesbians that goes much beyond equality and freedom. But there are some other things that we imagine as human counterparts to legal protections.

It would be wonderful if families could see in their children the full range of the affectional possibilities that life in fact holds out. If girlish boys and boyish girls, who do not constitute the full range of homosexuality but who are often the ones targeted, could receive encouragement and praise and the love they deserve instead of derision, intimidation, and disappointment, their lives would be much improved. And it would improve the quality of the culture if these children could grow into adults who, because they were loved and valued, made rich contributions to the culture instead of expending that energy on overcoming the wounds that were inflicted on them.

It would also be wonderful if friends and colleagues of gay people would be as interested in their lives as they are in their company and counsel, if the walls came down and revealed each other's essential humanity. And it would be wonderful to see gay and lesbian judges, mayors, kindergarten teachers, construction workers, actors, fathers, brothers, mothers, sisters, musicians and clerics, all of them acknowledged and honored. In this utopia, little would appear changed, but there would be an addition rather than a diminution of freedom and well-being. . . .

Notes

1. John Boswell, *Christianity, Social Tolerance and Homosexuality*, Chicago: University of Chicago Press, 1980, p. 82.

2. Alissa Friedman, "The Necessity for State Recognition of Same-Sex Marriage: Constitutional Requirements and Evolving Notions of Family," 3 *Berkeley Women's Law Journal* (1988), pp. 134–70.

3. William G. Axinn and Arland Thorton, "The Relationship Between Cohabitation and Divorce: Selectivity or Casual Influence?" *Demography* 29 (August 1992) 3:357, 361.

4. Mary Mendola, *The Mendola Report: A New Look at Gay Couples* (1980), p. 254.

The Case Against Gay Marriage

Manuel A. Lopez

While opinion polls have consistently shown most Americans in favor of maintaining current marriage laws, two-thirds of high school seniors and a majority of those in their twenties favor gay marriage. The reason for this divergence is clear. There has been less public argument against gay marriage than in favor of it. While older people nonetheless tend to retain an older view of marriage, many young people have concluded that opposition to change merely reflects prejudice or squeamishness. Moreover, the case for gay marriage largely boils down to the simple claim that everybody should be treated the same way. This is always a powerful claim in a democracy, especially among the young.

The problem in the debate so far has been the failure to grasp what marriage means in most people's lives. Marriage is so much a part of our world that we have trouble imagining how things would look without it. Some people say marriage is "by definition" between a man and a woman, but that by itself tells us nothing. We have to seriously consider what stands *behind* this definition, and why people are so attached to it.

It seems to me undeniable that the potential for reproduction constitutes something unique about the union of one man and one woman. Science may eventually change that, but sexual reproduction is sure to remain the easiest and manifestly most natural way. Even if some marriages are childless, it surely makes a difference that all marriages are between men and women. Marriages as we know it is bound up with, even a product of, natural sexual differentiation, whose most massive and undeniable feature is the potential for reproduction. This gives rise to a feeling that marriage is part of the natural order, an order bigger than ourselves and our desires. To be sure, widespread divorce has weakened this feeling over the past thirty years; but it remains a powerful force in people's lives, one that we perhaps take for granted precisely because of its ubiquity. Permitting marriage between people of the same sex would make marriage a *different* thing—and not a better one.

More than any other institution, marriage provides guidance that helps people live their lives. One need only think of the times in one's youth when one wondered whom one would eventually marry. (I can attest that even young homosexuals wonder about this—though with a certain ambivalence.) Those youthful daydreams, which are so important in shaping and coloring the rest of one's life, would not be possible in a world without marriage, and would not be easy in a world where marriage was merely one choice among many. Our youthful (and not so youthful) daydreams presuppose marriage as a touchstone, a choice which isn't simply *a* choice but is somehow *the* choice.

Unlike some conservatives, I don't think allowing gays to marry would cause many people to view marriage as "just another contract," similar to buying a car or taking a job. Most people feel that an intimate connection to one other person is an indispensable part of a good life, and I don't think gay marriage would change that. (Legalized polygamy might be another story, at least after several generations.)

However, disconnecting marriage from procreation would make it seem less bound up with a world larger than we are. Marriage would seem more like a commitment we make, an act of the will, and less like an acceptance of or conformity to the fundamental order of things. Perhaps such a change would, to some extent, constitute greater realism. However, I don't think it would produce greater happiness, either in itself or in its consequences, which would include people taking their marriages less seriously, considering alternatives more readily when the going gets rough, and seeking guidance more often in desire, whim, and fashion.

Moreover, true conservatives are wary of fundamental changes in laws and institutions, even when those changes are in themselves improvements. Humans are not so rational that we can dispense with awe or the sense that some things are greater than human enactment. Any major change in marriage laws would weaken people's sense of marriage as something slightly awesome that must be accepted or rejected on its own terms. Any such change would encourage us to pay less attention to the demands of marriage and more attention to ourselves, to consider how we might gratify the desires we feel, even to look within ourselves to see what desires we find.

We humans are ambiguous creatures. We are of course unhappy if our desires are thwarted; but we are also unhappy if we have no guidance apart from desire. Our desires themselves need to be guided or informed by a view of what is good, what constitutes happiness. Some desires can lead to happiness, others cannot; distinguishing between the two is sometimes a delicate task, one at which we all need help, especially when we're young. No institution informs the desires of most human beings in as profound and salutary a manner as marriage.

Of course marriage in its current form fails to provide such guidance for those who are homosexual. Now there are some people who believe homosexuality to be a mere perversion, akin to bestiality or taking drugs, which can in no way lead to a good life. To such people I can only say that this attraction is at the core of what gays are. (The experience of lesbian women seems somewhat different; their sexuality is perhaps more fluid or socially determined.) Whether or not scientists have "proven" that homosexuality has a natural or genetic basis, those who oppose gay marriage are unwise to base their case on an insistence that it doesn't. I suppose it's possible that some subtle observer might understand gay men better than we understand ourselves; but so far this superior understanding has not made itself apparent. Freudian accounts of the emergence of homosexuality offered by self-styled "reparative therapists" are even more convoluted and unconvincing than Freudian accounts of other things.

In my view instituting homosexual marriage would indeed provide guidance to some young homosexuals, and would thereby improve some people's lives. This is a serious argument; however, I don't think marriage could be as crucial to gays as it is to other people. Marriage has developed over many centuries to meet the needs of heterosexuals. Gay marriage would inevitably be a kind of imitation. Like most imitations, it couldn't wholly succeed, and would therefore result in more or less self-conscious parody.

Many gays want the right to marry, without actually wanting to marry. This boils down to a form of "me-too"-ism, a desire to have whatever rights heterosexuals have. Regarding marriage, however, gays already have the rights that heterosexuals have: A gay man can marry a woman, a lesbian woman can marry a man. That such marriages would not be satisfying is unfortunate, but also beside the point. The state can go no further without fundamentally changing marriage. Widening marriage to include people of the same sex means stripping it of much of its meaning and diminishing it for everybody. This would have a relatively small effect on the lives of people who are already married, and whose notion of marriage is already largely settled; but it would have a profound effect on future generations of Americans.

This, it seems to me, is the most important argument against same-sex marriage. However, I must add that there is also legitimate reason for concern on the empirical question of how married gays would behave, with serious consequences for the upbringing of children.

No sensible observer can deny that gay men are, in general, more promiscuous than heterosexual men. (Believe me, I come to this conclusion reluctantly.) If allowed to marry, gay men will, I predict, be more adulterous, and more openly adulterous, than heterosexual couples. Gays will separate and divorce more often. Adultery and divorce will become more common than they already are; and in some subtle way the institution of marriage will be further weakened.

There is already evidence that should give cause for concern. In Sweden for example, demographers Gunnar Andersson and Turid Noack report that male same-sex partnerships have a 50% higher divorce rate than heterosexual marriages. Female same-sex partnerships have a 170% higher divorce rate. This remains true after controlling for age, education, and other factors. Keep in mind that we're looking at those most committed to making it succeed, a very small fraction of gays. At any rate, the damage that gay marriage might do in this respect probably won't occur in the first decade or two. It is precisely once marriage becomes a normal part of gay life that gays will adapt the institution to their own tastes and beliefs. I have nothing against that, except that their example will inevitably influence how marriage is seen by the heterosexual majority.

To be sure, gay marriage wouldn't be as harmful as polygamous or group marriage. While gay marriage should be opposed on its own terms, it's hard to see how polygamy won't eventually follow if gay marriage is established. I realize this suggestion has a ridiculous sound to it (as did gay marriage not long ago); but there are already groups in America supporting polygamy and group marriage, including the American Civil Liberties Union. Believe it or not, since 1991 the position of the ACLU has been quote: "criminal and civil laws prohibiting or penalizing the practice of plural marriage violate constitutional protections." In other words, the state must treat "plural marriage" no differently than marriage as we know it.

Supporters of polygamy or "plural" marriage view their position as the logical conclusion of supporting gay marriage; and there is evidently something to that. If marriage has no intrinsic connection to procreation, but simply means two people who love each other, then why not three, or four? On what principled basis does the state reject a definition of marriage embraced by consenting adult citizens, and deny them what their hearts desire? (Similar arguments might also be made on behalf of incestuous marriages.)

To be sure, there are arguments against polygamy apart from those against gay marriage. Feminists oppose it as tending to exploit women, and people who genuinely care about marriage feel that "plural" marriage is a travesty of the core meaning of the institution. If same-sex marriage becomes the law of the land, however, arguments like the latter one will already have taken a beating. On the other side will be the right of individuals to make their own decisions in life, the importance of consent as the bedrock of our democracy, and above all the illegitimacy of judging or discriminating against people who harm nobody and simply wish to pursue happiness where they believe it lies. One can even imagine proponents of polygamy claiming to hold the true conservative position: Polygamy will mean a lower divorce rate and fewer single-parent homes, since many married people (notably mothers with children) will prefer allowing their spouses an additional spouse to seeking divorce, and so on.

My guess is that if gay marriage comes, polygamy will eventually follow. If it does, American life will take a giant step towards the restless and unhappy hedonism that characterized the Roman Empire. Gay marriage by itself would be a smaller step in the same direction.

Congressman Barney Frank has asked what harm it does if he is allowed to marry his boyfriend. This is a reasonable question; the answer is that it would do little harm to those who are already married, but considerable harm to future generations of Americans.

Credits

Announcing . . .
The Longman Publishers and Penguin Books Partnership in Philosophy

Note to Instructors: Bundle any of the titles listed below with *Ultimate Questions: Thinking About Philosophy*, Second Edition, and your students will receive a significant discount! Contact your local Allyn & Bacon/Longman sales representative for details on how to create a Penguin-Longman Value Package.

The Birds and Other Plays ~ Aristophanes
The Analects ~ Confucius
The Divine Comedy: Inferno ~ Dante Alighieri
The Portable Dante ~ Dante Alighieri
Discourse on Method and Related Writings ~ René Descartes
Meditations and Other Metaphysical Writings ~ René Descartes
Praise of Folly ~ Desiderius Erasmus
The Histories ~ Herodotus
Leviathan ~ Thomas Hobbes
The Iliad ~ Homer
The Odyssey ~ Homer
The Penguin Dictionary of Philosophy ~ Thomas Mautner
Mencius ~ Mencius
On Liberty ~ John Stuart Mill
Utopia ~ Thomas More
A Nietzsche Reader ~ Friedrich Nietzsche
Early Socratic Dialogues ~ Plato
Great Dialogues of Plato ~ Plato
The Last Days of Socrates ~ Plato
The Republic ~ Plato
The Social Contract ~ Jean-Jacques Rousseau
The Three Theban Plays ~ Sophocles
The Confessions of Saint Augustine ~ Saint Augustine
Walden and Civil Disobedience ~ Henry David Thoreau
Tao Te Ching ~ Lao Tzu
Ten Great Works of Philosophy ~ Various
Candide, Zadig, and Selected Stories ~ Francois Voltaire
The Protestant Ethic and the Spirit of Capitalism ~ Max Weber